9th EDITION

The Australian Bed & Breakfast Book

Homes • Farms • Guest Houses

Compiled by J. & J. Thomas

PELICAN PUBLISHING COMPANY
Gretna 1998

Copyright © 1989, 1990, 1991, 1992, 1993, 1994, 1995
By Janete and James Thomas

Copyright © 1996, 1997
By James Thomas
All rights reserved

Published in New Zealand and Australia by Moonshine Press
Published by arrangement in the rest of the world by
   Pelican Publishing Company, Inc.

Pelican editions
   First edition, January 1990
   Second edition, January 1991
   Third edition, January 1992
   Fourth edition, January 1993
   Fifth edition, January 1994
   Sixth edition, January 1995
   Seventh edition, January 1996
   Eighth edition, June 1997
   Ninth edition, January 1998

---

*The word "Pelican" and the depiction of a pelican are trademarks of
Pelican Publishing Company, Inc., and are registered
in the U.S. Patent and Trademark Office.*

ISBN: 1-56554-357-2

Prices in this guide are quoted in Australian dollars.

Drawings by Gerald Bull, Dan Mills, and Rema Naish or provided by hosts

Front-cover illustration: Araluen Lawson Bed & Breakfast, Lawson, New South Wales
Back-cover illustration: Broomelea, Leura, New South Wales

All information in this guidebook has been supplied by the hosts. Information about the homes listed is subject to change without notice. Readers are asked to take this into account when consulting this guide.

Manufactured in the United States of America
Published by Pelican Publishing Company, Inc.
1101 Monroe Street, Gretna, Louisiana 70053

The Australian Bed & Breakfast Book
Schedule of Standards

General:
- Local tourism and transport information available to guests.
- Property appearance neat and tidy, internally and externally.
- Absolute cleanliness of the home in all areas used by the guests.
- Absolute cleanliness of kitchen, refrigerator and food storage areas.
- Roadside identification of property.
- Protective clothing and footwear available for farmstay guests.
- Hosts accept responsibility to comply with local body bylaws.
- Host will be present to welcome and farewell guests.

Bedrooms:
- Each bedroom solely dedicated to guests with –
- bed heating
- heating
- light controlled from the bed
- wardrobe space with variety of hangers
- drawers
- good quality floor covering
- mirror
- power point
- waste paper basket
- drinking glasses
- night light or torch for guidance to w.c. if not adjacent to bedroom
- opaque blinds or curtains on all windows where appropriate
- good quality mattresses in sound condition on a sound base
- clean bedding appropriate to the climate, with extra available
- clean pillows with additional available

Bathroom & toilet facilities:
- At least one bathroom adequately ventilated and equipped with –
  bath or shower
  wash handbasin and mirror
  wastebasket in bathroom
  extra toilet roll
  lock on bathroom and toilet doors
  electric razor point if bedrooms are without a suitable power point
- soap, towels, bathmat, facecloths, fresh for each new guest
- towels changed or dried daily for guests staying more than one night
- Sufficient toilet and bathroom facilities to serve family and guests adequately

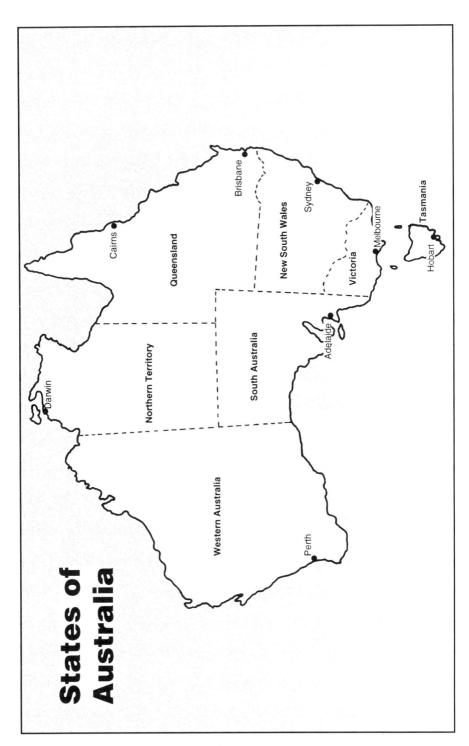

CONTENTS

Schedule of Standards	3
Map–Australian States	4
Tips for Easier Travel	6
Comment Form	7
A Week's Free B&B	9
Introduction	10
Northern Territory	12
New South Wales	16
Australian Capital Territory	233
Victoria	240
Queensland	330
South Australia	390
Western Australia	416
Tasmania	432
Index	449

TIPS FOR EASIER B&B TRAVEL

★ **Ensuite and private bathroom** are for your use exclusively, **Guests share** bathroom means you may be sharing with other guests, **Family share** bathroom means you will be sharing with the family.

★ In the tariff section of each listing **'continental' breakfast** consists of fruit, cereal, toast, tea/coffee; **'full'** breakfast is the same with an additional cooked course; **'special'** breakfast has something special.

★ Do not try to travel too far in one day. Take time to enjoy the company of your hosts and other locals.

★ **Telephone ahead** to enquire about a B&B. It is a nuisance for you if you arrive to find the accommodation has been taken. And besides hosts need a little time to prepare.

★ The most suitable **time to arrive is late afternoon**, and to leave is before 10 in the morning.

★ **If you would like dinner** please give your host sufficient notice to prepare.

★ If you are unsure of anything ask your hosts about it. They will give you a direct answer.

★ Our B&Bs are mostly private homes. **Most do not accept credit cards.**

★ If you have made your reservations from overseas, check that your dates are correct. You might cross the dateline to come to Australia.

★ **Please let your hosts know if you have to cancel**. They will have spent time preparing for you.

★ Australian road signs are getting better, but your best directions come from asking a local.

★ Most listings show hosts accept vouchers. The only **vouchers accepted are Australian Bed & Breakfast Book vouchers.**

★ **Phone numbers throughout Australia are changing** to eight digits. For help to find your hosts' phone number phone Directory Assistance.

Help us to keep our standards high

To help maintain the high reputation of *The Australian B&B Book* we ask for your comments about your stay. Please post the form in the envelope provided. Every comment form you return will go in the draw for **A weeks free B&B**. It will help us if you save your comment forms and return them in one envelope.

Name of Host..

Address..

It was (please circle one):

    Absolutely Perfect,   Excellent,   Good,   Adequate,   Not Satisfactory

- Do you have any comments which could help your host, on such things as breakfast, meals, beds, cleanliness, hospitality, value for money?

Complete this section. It will be detached before we send your comment to the host.

YOUR NAME..

YOUR ADDRESS..

       Please mail this form to Pelican Publishing Company, Inc.,
           P.O. Box 3110, Gretna, LA 70054-3110, USA

A WEEKS FREE B&B

FILL IN A COMMENT FORM AND YOU CAN BE IN THE DRAW FOR A WEEKS FREE B&B FOR TWO

- At each B&B you will find a comment form and an addressed envelope. Simply fill in a comment form and return it to us, and you will be in the draw for **a weeks free B&B**.

- Every comment form you send in will increase your chances of winning the **weeks free B&B**, so complete a form for each place you stay.

- We suggest you save your comment forms in one envelope, and send them in together at the end of your trip.

- If a B&B is temporarily out of comment forms you can complete one at the next one you visit.

- Each person staying can complete a comment form – a couple can complete two separate forms.

- Entries will be drawn on 21 December 1998 and the winner will be notified by mail immediately. Entries to the U.S. address below must be received by 30 October 1998.

The Prize
- The prizewinner will be given vouchers entitling them and a partner to 7 nights B&B at any B&B accepting vouchers in *The Australian Bed and Breakfast Book*.

- The stays can be any time in 1999. They need not be consecutive.

Mail to: Pelican Publishing Company, Inc.
P.O. Box 3110
Gretna, LA 70054-3110
USA

Introduction

Australia has several travel and accommodation guides but *The Australian Bed And Breakfast Book* offers something special. The 640 hosts who are listed here are homeowners who want to share their love of the country with travellers. Each listing has been written by the host, and you will discover the warmth and personality of the host is obvious in their writing. Ours is not simply an accommodation guide but an introduction to a uniquely Australian experience. Any holiday is remembered primarily by the people one meets. How many of us have loved a country simply because of one or two especially memorable individuals encountered there? Bed and Breakfast offers the traveller who wants to experience the feel of the real country and get to know the people to do just that. Bed and Breakfast in Australia means a warm welcome into someone's home. Most of the places listed are homes, with a sprinkling of lodges and guesthouses. Remember that Bed and Breakfast hosts cannot offer hotel facilities so please telephone ahead to book your accommodation and give ample notice if you require dinner. Most of our B&Bs do not have credit card facilities.

Guarantee of standards
Some B&Bs belong to regional associations, which inspect the property, and guarantee a minimum standard of facilities. Hosts belonging to associations display the symbol in their listing. Hosts that display an *AussieHost* logo have taken part in a special workshopo which trains them in communication, customer relations and visitor industry skills.

We expect that all B&Bs in *The Australian Bed and Breakfast Book* will offer excellent hospitality. We ask you to let us know if you stay at one that does not come up to your expectations so that our very high standard can be maintained.

Tariff
Most hosts will charge rates which are fairly consistent throughout the country. Some rates vary because of facilities or location and these are shown in each listing. The prices listed will apply until 31st December 1998 unless stated

otherwise. There will be no extra costs to pay unless you request extra services. Some offer a reduction for children. This usually applies to age 12 and under.

Breakfast is included in the tariff. Some homes offer a continental breakfast which includes fruit, cereal, toast and tea or coffee. Others offer a full breakfast indicated by (full) in the listing, which includes a cooked course as well. Some offer a special breakfast, indicated by (special) which includes some specialties of the house.

Vouchers

Most hosts have indicated in their listings that they will accept vouchers. The vouchers referred to are *The Australian Bed & Breakfast Book* vouchers which can be obtained from your travel agent. *Aust B&B Vouchers accepted* refers only to The Bed & Breakfast Book vouchers.

Self-contained accommodation

Many homes in towns and on farms can offer separate self-contained accommodation. In almost every case linen and food will be provided if required. The tariff will vary depending on your requirements, so check when booking.

Campervans

For those who get to know the country by camping or motor-home, Bed and Breakfast offers wonderful advantages. You will see in many listings the word 'campervans'. These homes have suitable facilities available such as laundry, bathroom, electricity and meals if necessary. The charge, usually for up to four people, is modest and is shown in each listing.

Finding your way around

The homes in each state are listed alphabetically, and each is shown on the state map. The distance between B&Bs is sometimes quite great so we suggest you check the travelling times with your host when you phone ahead to book.
Whether you are from overseas or a fellow Australian please take the opportunity to stay with Aussies in their homes. Chat with your hosts. Enjoy their company. Each host will be your personal travel agent and guide. They want to make everything enjoyable for you.

We wish you an enjoyable holiday and welcome comments from guests. Please write with compliments or suggestions to:

The Australian Bed and Breakfast Book
Moonshine Press
59 Quirk Street
Dee Why
NSW 2099
Australia

Happy travelling

James Thomas

NORTHERN TERRITORY

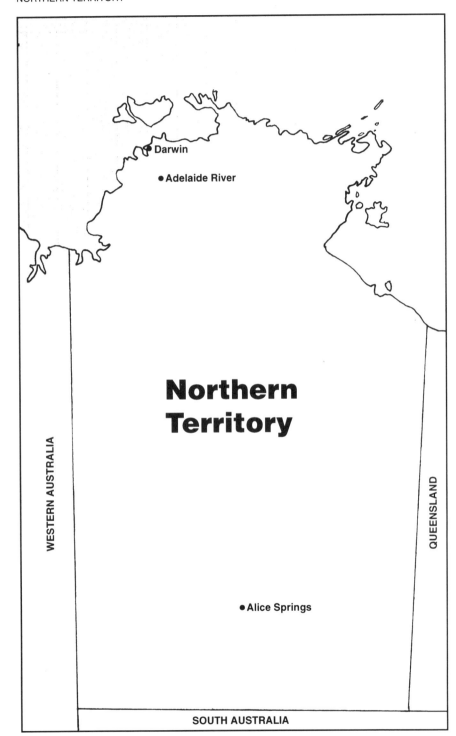

Adelaide River
Homestay/Farmstay/Self-contained Cottage
Address: Mount Bundy Station, Haynes Road
Adelaide River
Northern Territory 0846
Name: Fran and Brian Briggs
Telephone: (08) 8976 7009 **Fax**: (08) 8976 7113
Beds: Homestead: 1 King, 2 Queen, 3 single (3 bedrooms), maximum 8 person..
Cottage: 1 Queen, 1 Twin, 2 Singles (2 bedrooms), maximum 4 persons.
Bathroom: 3 Ensuites
Tariff: Homestead: B&B (full) Double $120, Single $80, Children $50. Cottage: $100 per night (min 2 night stay). 3rd night and thereafter $60 per night. $390 per week. Breakfast available. Credit Cards: Diners Club/American Express/Mastercard/Bankcard.
Nearest Town: Adelaide River - 119 kms South of Darwin

Mount Bundy is a convenient and homely base from which to explore the Top End, enjoy true Territory hospitality and experience the rural life we love. From the large cool homestead set high on a hill the panorama includes buffalo and cattle grazing below. Kangaroos, wallabies, bandicoots and amazing birdlife abound in the acres of green lawns and shady garden setting.

Gourmet breakfasts, sumptuous roast dinners with all the trimmings or something light if you prefer. Maybe your own freshly caught Barramundi. (Adelaide River is 500 metres from homestead).

Choose a campfire, dine with us or enjoy silver service on your balcony under the stars. Close attention is paid to the individual needs of each guest so that you may truly enjoy your stay.

Alice Springs
Traditional B&B   AANT ★★★★☆
Address: Orangewood
9 McMinn Street, Alice Springs, NT 0870
Name: Lynne and Ross Peterkin
Telephone: (08) 8952 4114 **Fax**: (08) 8952 4664
Email: orangewo@ozemail.com.au
Beds: 2 King/Twin, 1 Queen, 1 Double (4 bedrooms)
Bathroom: 3 Ensuite, 1 Private (4 bathrooms)
Tariff: B&B (full) 1 April 1997 - 31 March 1998: King/Twin $160, Queen/Double $140. Credit Cards: Bankcard, Mastercard, Visa.
Nearest Town: Alice Springs - 6 mins walk to town centre

Orangewood offers quality bed and breakfast accommodation in a family home furnished with antiques, special family pieces and original art works. The guest sitting room and library has open fire, piano, music system, television, refrigerator and tea/coffee making facilities. Guest accommodation comprises three bedrooms in the house (one Double, one Queen, one King/Twin) each with ensuite bathroom and a garden cottage (King/Twin). Surrounding the swimming pool in the private rear garden is a grove of citrus trees which gives the house its name. Full breakfast is served in the breakfast room overlooking the rear garden and is supervised by the resident cat, Angus (who can be banished if guests so choose!). We are a non-smoking establishment and, sorry, our accommodation is not suitable for children.

Directions: *Cross Todd River (dry) at Wills Tce causeway, immediate turn left, second turn right into McMinn Street.*
Home Page: http://www.ozemail.com.au/~orangewo/index.html

Darwin
Bed & Breakfast
Address: No. 5 Forest Drive, Humpty Doo
(Corner of Stuart Highway & Forest Drive).
Postal: PO Box 39903, Winnellie NT 0821.
Name: Acacia Homestead Bed & Breakfast
Telephone: (08) 8988 4000 **Fax**: (08) 8988 4450 **Mobile**: (0419) 884 001
Beds: 2 Queen, 2 Single (3 Bedrooms). Cot available.
Bathroom: 3 Ensuites.
Tariff: B&B (Continental - Full by arrangement) Double $85, Single $75, Children $15, Dinner on request. Credit Cards: Amex, Bankcard, Mastercard, Visa
Nearest Town: Darwin 35 km, Palmerston 15 km.

Helen and Phil welcome you to Australia's last frontier, where you can still buy 'crocodile insurance'! Whilst staying with us we can assist you in planning your holiday in the north as we have both grown up in the top end.
Acacia Homestead B&B is a new home situated on 5 acres in a natural bush setting. There is a wide variety of birds, some of which may join you for breakfast. Guest rooms are in an adjoining wing of the house. Each room has private access, ensuite, air-conditioning, ceiling fan, tea / coffee facilities, fridge, colour TV. Guests have shared kitchen facilities, outdoor / undercover BBQ area, large pool. Breakfast is served overlooking pool and gardens.
Conveniently located in the heart of major tourist attractions: Darwin Crocodile Farm, Litchfield National Park, Kakadu National park, Territory Wildlife Park, Howard and Berry Springs Nature / Swimming Reserves, Fogg Dam, golf course to name just a few. Complimentary airport transfers

---

The standard of accommodation in
The Australian Bed and Breakfast Book ranges from homely to luxurious,
but you can always be sure of superior hospitality.

NORTHERN TERRITORY

If you have enjoyed B&B in Australia

How about B&B in New Zealand

To order
The New Zealand B&B Book
send AU$16.95 or the equivalent
in your currency to

Moonshine Press
59 Quirk Street
Dee Why, NSW 2099
Australia

NEW SOUTH WALES

NEW SOUTH WALES

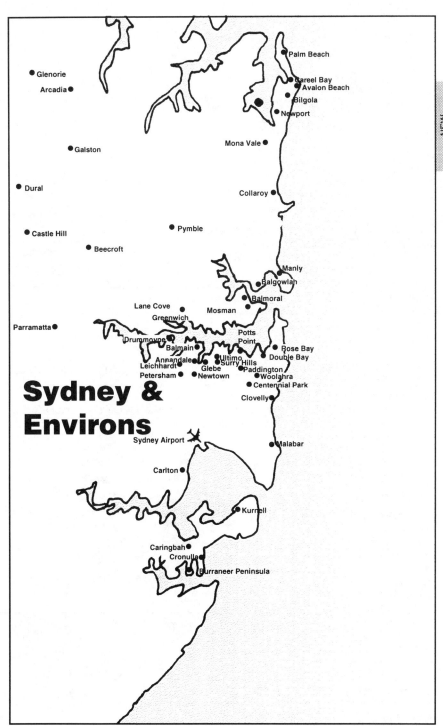

NEW SOUTH WALES

Adaminaby, Snowy Mountains
Homestay+Self-contained Cottage
Address: Happy Valley, Adaminaby 2630
Name: Neville & Kate Locker
Telephone: (02) 6454 2439 **Fax**: (02) 6454 2232
Beds: Homestead: 2 Queen, 2 Single (3 bedrooms)
Cottage: 1 Double, 2 Single (2 bedrooms)
Bathroom: Homestead: 1Private.   Cottage: 1 Private
Tariff: B&B (full) Homestead: Double $110, Single $55. Cottage: Double $110.
Extra single $55. Children U/12 half price. Dinner by prior arrangement $20,
Credit Cards. (Prices firm 1998) Vouchers accepted $20 surcharge
Nearest Town: Adaminaby 3km

Experience the real Australia on our thousand acre sheep and cattle property. Located in the foothills of the Snowy Mountains, close to Kosciusko National Park and only two hours drive from Canberra on the scenic route between Sydney and Melbourne. Happy Valley is a sanctuary for birds and wildlife and Kangaroos are usually to be found at the homestead door. This is Kate's fault, she looks after orphan native animals and treats them so well they refuse to leave. Whatever your interests, we can supply necessary maps, directions, local knowledge and if necessary a packed lunch, to make your visit special.
You can walk to the top of Australia's highest mountains, visit historic sites, swim in a thermal pool, walk through a cave, bush walk in summer, ski in winter. Perhaps explore the farm, play tennis, catch a trout or simply relax.
Happy Valley Homestead is smoke free with comfortable beds, generous cooked breakfast. Dinner available by arrangement. The cottage is close by for those who want added space and privacy. We guarantee a peaceful rural atmosphere, genuine country hospitality and look forward to meeting you.

Adaminaby - Snowy Mountains
SC Accom. + Fly Fishing Lodge
Address: The Outpost,
Yaouk Valley, Adaminaby, 2630
Name: Jill Blackman
Telephone: (02) 6454 2293
Fax: From August 97 (02) 6454 2612
Email: jill@theoutpost.com.au
Beds: 1 Queen, 2 Single (2 bedroom cottage)
Bathroom: 1 Private + extra toilet.
Tariff: B&B (full/cook your own) Double $110. Extra guests $5 per night each.
Not suitable for small children.
Nearest Town: Adaminaby 27km

Hidden away on a beautiful stretch of river at the headwaters of the Murrumbidgee in unspoilt alpine country. The Outpost Fly Fishing Lodge, on 1000 acres of mostly untouched Eucalyptus forest offers many walks where you can see kangaroos, wallabies, wambats, echidnas and many birds, or watch the Platypus feeding at dusk. Enjoy a swim in the river (anglers permitting) or a game of tennis. The recently completed cottage, available on a bed and breakfast basis is fully self contained with two bedrooms, a living room with a wood fire, well equipped kitchen and spacious verandah.
Alternatively you may choose to spoil yourselves and stay fully catered in one of the three bedrooms with private bathrooms in the luxurious lodge, and try your hand at fly fishing while your gourmet meals are being prepared. Then enjoy your meals with wines in the company ot the other guests and your hostess.
Whichever you choose, come and enjoy the serenity and remoteness of this special place.

Adelong
Farmstay in Self-contained Accom.
Address: Yavendale,
Adelong, NSW 2729
Name: Susan & Patrick Roche
Telephone: (069) 464259 (after 5pm)
Fax: (069) 464259
Beds: 1 Double, 2 Single + folding
(2 adjoining bedrooms)
Bathroom: 1 Private
Tariff: B&B (full) Double $80, Single $45,
Children by arrangement. Family rates available.
Dinner by arrangement. Vouchers accepted
Nearest Town: Adelong - approx halfway between Sydney and Melbourne, 15 minutes off the Hume Highway.

We have lived on our working cattle and sheep property for twenty years and have recently restored the garden cottage to offer guests a rural experience. The picturesque district and historic gold-mining township of Adelong provides a range of interests for the visitor. Day trips exploring Tumut, Blowering Dam, Yarrangobilly Caves, Snowy Mountains Scheme and Batlow can be advised by your hosts. On arrival to Yavendale guests are warmly welcomed with tea or coffee and homemade cake. The accommodation is private separated from the main house by a pretty courtyard.
Breakfast is served in the homestead looking out into the garden and creek beyond or guests may choose to be provided with supplies to prepare their own at their leisure. Features include the spacious garden, birdlife, friendly farm animals, gentle walks, tennis court, swimming pool and BBQ, homemade treats and locally produced fruit. Country style dinner by arrangement. **Directions**: *Please phone.*

NEW SOUTH WALES

Adelong
Guest House   NRMA ★★★
Address: 77 Tumut Street, Adelong, NSW 2729
Name: Adelong's Beaufort House Private Historic Hotel
Telephone: (02) 6946 2273 **Fax**: (02) 6946 2273
Beds: 1 Queen, 10 Double, 3 Single, (14 bedrooms)
Bathroom: 5 Ensuite, 3 Guests share
Tariff: B&B (full) Master $85, Double $65, Single $45, Dinner $25. Credit cards.

"Adelong's Beaufort House"
Historic Private Hotel
Motel and Function Centre
offering guest house accommodation

Heritage listed "Adelong's Beaufort House" offers elegant guest house accommodation with personalised care, attention, hospitality, and country-style cuisine.
Situated in the historic Heritage listed town of Adelong NSW, a warm welcome awaits our guests and visitors. Enjoy a night, weekend or longer or pampering by open log fires in winter. Dine at night in style by candle light in our restaurant or in your own private dinning room.
Enjoy home made fare in our coffee shop which is a meeting place for locals who love to regale stories of times gone by to our guest and visitors.
Our function centre specialises in private lunch and dinner parties, theme dinners, weddings, small seminars and conferences and small coach parties.
Stroll along the towns tree lined streets and enjoy the country village lifestyle. Visit the art galleries, antique shops and nurseries explore the unique surrounding area, of the Adelong Falls with its rich gold mining past, go fossicking and find gold as they did a hundred years ago. Pick in season fruit at famous Batlow, or just relax in tranquil surroundings and unwind. Catch up on that good book you promised yourself to read. To complete your stay visit our art gallery and gift emporium, for that special present or souvenir. At Beaufort House we also operate an accommodation booking service and tourist information centre. If we can be of any assistance with your holiday plans please do not hesitate to contact us.
Your host Mike Matthews

NEW SOUTH WALES

Albury
Bed & Breakfast
Address: "Westside", Memorial Drive,
Albury, NSW 2640
Name: Bruce & Dorothy Mitchell
Telephone: (02) 6021 7348
Beds: 1 Double, 2 Single (2 bedrooms)
Bathroom: 2 Private
Tariff: B&B (continental) Double $68, Single $55.
Credit Cards. Vouchers accepted

This large comfortable home is situated on the western side of the Monument Hill in an extensive terraced garden. Breakfast may be served on one of these terraces outside your bedroom.
Albury is a relaxing stop-over between Melbourne and Sydney in the centre of a wonderful region, including the Rutherglen wineries and a number of innovative country restaurants.
Bankcard, VISA, Mastercard, Amex & Diners facilities provided.

Albury
**Rural Retreat Farmstray
and Self-contained Accom.**
Address: "Table Top Mountain
Retreat", Gerogery
Name: Roger & Elizabeth Paterson
Telephone: (02) 6026 0529
Fax: (02) 6026 0653
Mobile: 0412 691 840
Email: tabletopm@albury.net.au
Beds: 3 Queen, 1 Double,
7 Single (6 bedrooms)
Bathroom: 3 Private
Tariff: B&B (full) Double $120-$140,
Single $70, Children half price, Dinner $25.
Nearest Town: Gerogery 30km north of Albury, 7km off the Hume Highway along the Olympic Highway on Bells Road.

We have 1125 hectares of farming country and mountain bushland. Guests have a choice of accommodation in the homestead, or in either of two self contained cottages on the mountain. The cottages are unique, very comfortable and have handmade Euorpean folk art style furniture made by the owners. Meals are optional. A swimming pool and tennis court are available for the guests use in the homestead garden which has been part of the Open Garden Scheme.
Many activities can be enjoyed. Bushwalking or mountain bike riding, 360 degree views on top of Table Top Mountain, 140 species of birds and many different wildflowers are abundant in the Spring. Horseriding, abseiling, 4WD tours and camp oven meals are available by pre-arrangement. Our philosophy is to share this special place with you. It is an ideal retreat to enjoy romance and tranquillity and a place to recharge your batteries. **Home Page**: albury.wodonga.com/tabletop

Albury - Wodonga
Homestay
Address: "Gundowring Bed & Breakfast",
621 Stanley Street, Albury, NSW 2640
Name: Gundowring Bed & Breakfastt"
Telephone: (02) 6041 4437 **Fax**: (02) 6041 4229
Mobile: (019) 312838
Beds: 2 Queen, 2 Double, 2 Single (3 bedrooms)
Bathroom: 3 Ensuite
Tariff: B&B (full) Double $130, Single $110, Credit Cards (BC/MC/VISA).
Vouchers accepted surcharge Double $45, Single $29.
Nearest Town: Albury 2 blocks from Hume Highway

Elegantly restored Gundowring House is situated in a quiet central Albury street at the perimeter of the city's CBD, within easy walking distance of the main shopping centre, a range of fine restaurants, licensed clubs, botanical gardens and convention centre. The house provides well appointed bed and breakfast accommodation, offering two double bedrooms and one twin share, all with ensuite. The cosy guests lounge and graceful dining room presents corporate and touring visitors with a "home away from home" retreat. Off street parking is provided for guests vehicles.
Albury-Wodonga is regarded as the commercial "hub" of the region. Wineries, historic towns, sporting activities, snowfields and summer high country, gourmet foods and a myriad of other attractions are all within easy driving distance. Gundowring provides the ideal accommodation base for visitors to Southern NSW and North-Eastern Victoria.
Due to our location Gundowring is unsuitable for children or pets.

Telephone ahead to enquire about a B&B.
It is a nuisance for you if you simply arrive
to find someone already staying there.
And besides hosts need a litle time to prepare.

Alstonville see Ballina
Anna Bay see Port Stephens

NEW SOUTH WALES

Armidale
Farmstyle Bed & Breakfast   NRMA ★★★
Address: "Poppy's Cottage B&B",
Malvern Hill, Dangarsleigh Rd., Armidale, NSW 2350
Name: Jake & Poppy Abbott
Telephone: (02) 6775 1277 **Fax**: (02) 6772 8290
Mobile: 041 215 3819
Beds: 2 Double, 2 Single + 1 Cot (2 bedrooms)
Bathroom: 1 Ensuite, 1 Private
Tariff: B&B (special) Double $90, Single $65, Children $15-$25, Dinner $25.
Vouchers accepted $10 surcharge
Nearest Town: Armidale - 6km south of Armidale

Poppy's Cottage (only 5 minutes from Armidale) is the perfect stopover on the New England Highway between Sydney and Brisbane/Gold Coast - or the charming and peaceful holiday destination for that much needed "getaway-from-it-all" restful break. An unforgettable, warm and friendly farmstyle Bed & Breakfast experience awaits you in this romantic and cosy atmosphere.

The charming old turn of the century farmhouse on 140 acre farm is home to our 3 children and menagerie of dogs, ducks, hens, geese, pet sheep, cattle and various other farmyard animals - and they are all very friendly! Winnie the pig, who just like Babe thinks she is a dog, provides amusement for everyone. We are hoping her four newly born piglets will inherit her unique personality.

Nestled in an enchanting cottage garden, our guests enjoy the comfort and privacy of their own separate cottage - with ensuite bathroom. Heating, electric blankets, refrigerator, Twinings tea, and plunger coffee are provided along with a barrel of home-made Anzac biscuits. A hearty breakfast includes fresh and poached fruit, yoghurt, freshly squeezed orange, farm eggs and bacon, etc. Delicious 3 course dinners by candlelight (including complimentary bottle of wine) are optional.

Having enjoyed the company and hospitality of B&B's overseas, we now enjoy offering the same experience to our guests in "Poppy's Cottage", (which we have been operating for over six years).

Our location provides a convenient base to explore historic buildings, Cathedrals, University, National Parks and Waterfalls nearby in the New England area.

We do look forward to looking after you.

Armidale, New England
Homestay   NRMA ★★★☆
Address: "Comeytrowe", 184 Marsh St., Armidale 2350
Name: Cris MacDonald
Telephone: (02) 6772 5869 **Fax**: (02) 6772 5869
Beds: 2 Double, 2 Sofa (2 bedrooms)
Bathroom: 1 Ensuite, 1 Private
Tariff: B&B (full) Double $80-$110, Single $55-$80, Children $30. Vouchers accepted $10 surcharge
Nearest Town: Armidale

Come and share with us the pleasures of Comeytrowe (c. 1867, Heritage listed). Situated on one of the hills over looking the town amidst old English Elms, white cedars and a lovely cottage garden with tennis court.
The two double guest rooms are on the ground floor with their own access from either the verandah or the court yard.
Tea and coffee facilities are provided in each guest room. A hearty country breakfast is served in the elegant dining room by an open fire.
  There are many restaurants within walking distance. We are on the "Armidale Heritage Walk". Ten minutes stroll from the centre of town and the Art Museum (home of the Hinton and Coventry Collections). Ten minutes drive to the University of New England and 45 mins to magnificent National Parks.
No smoking.
Directions: *Please phone.*

The standard of accommodation in
The Australian Bed and Breakfast Book ranges from homely to luxurious,
but you can always be sure of superior hospitality.

NEW SOUTH WALES

Armidale
B&B Homestay
Address: 'Glyngaye',
96 Herbert Park Road,
Armidale, NSW 2350
Name: Lloyd & Dorothy Hodges
Telephone: (02) 6775 1689
Beds: 1 Double, 2 Single (2 bedrooms)
Bathroom: 1 Family share
Tariff: B&B (full) Double $60, Single $35,
Children catered for. Campervans facilities available.
Vouchers accepted
Nearest Town: Armidale 7km from town boundary.

'Glyngaye' is situated approximately half way between Sydney and Brisbane, a good overnight stop-over or an ideal base to explore the beautiful New England district including scenic national parks (ideal for bushwalkers) and Armidale's historical buildings, university and churches.
Your hosts Dorothy and Lloyd are a "young at heart" retired couple with many interests. Our comfortable brick home is set on a 40 acre property away from noisy highways, with rural views from all rooms surrounded by a large garden and native arboretum, which encourages many birds.
Only 7km from the town boundary on a quiet sealed country road, we offer friendly hospitality, comfortable accommodation and a hearty country breakfast.
In the winter months our home is heated with in-built wood fires and gas heaters, and the beds are equipped with electric blankets and dooners.
Please phone for brochure with directions.

Armidale
Farmstay-Self-contained Cottage
Address: "Wattleton",
MSF 2003, Armidale 2350
Name: Lea & Allan Waters
Telephone: (02) 6775 3731
Beds: 1 Double, 4 Single
(2 bedrooms)
Bathroom: 1 Private
Tariff: B&B (continental) Double $70,
Single $65, Children $15, Dinner $20,
Credit Cards. Vouchers accepted
Nearest Town: Armidale 35km

Wattleton is a picturesque sheep and cattle property surrounded by rugged New England gorges. with magnificent views. Only half an hour East of Armidale, this holiday destination or overnight stopover appeals to everyone. Couples wanting peace and quiet, active people wanting to bushwalk, bird watch, ride horses, fish, play tennis, spa or swim. Children of all ages can enjoy contact with farm animals, horse ride under supervision in the yards, play with our three boys - Robert (13), James (10), Alexander (7), or just explore and enjoy open space and freedom.
The lovingly restored, spacious, fully self-contained cottage, has all the charm of yesteryear, with its wood fires and timber floors, along with the modern comforts of today. Enjoy day trips to historic Hillgrove, Oxley Wild Rivers National Park, New England National park, Dutton Trout hatchery and our beautiful city of Armidale.

NEW SOUTH WALES

Armidale - Inverell
Farmstay+Self-contained Accom.
Address: "Gwydir Getaway"
'Stony Batter North', Uralla, NSW 2358
Name: Kate & John Dugdale
Telephone: (02) 6723 7234
Fax: (02) 6723 7234
Beds: 2 Double + 1 sofa bed,
4 Single (2 bedroom)
Bathroom: 1 Private, 1 Ensuite
Tariff: B&B (full) Double $80, Single $70, Children welcome $25. Dinner by arrangement $20. S.C. Accom: Double $60, Child $15. Vouchers accepted
Nearest Town: Bundarra 20km, Armidale/Uralla 65km N.E. Highway, Inverell 60km Gwydir Highway.

Relax and enjoy the peace and quiet of your own fully restored historic shearer's cottage nestled beside the Gwydir River on one of the oldest properties in the area. The original cypress lining boards, open fire and sunny verandahs give it special character and make it the perfect place to experience country life at its best.
Unwind and relax in this charming cottage after exploring our 3000 acres and 5kms of Gwydir River - home of the Platypus. Fishing, canoeing, scenic walks, viewing wildlife and tennis are popular pastimes.
Stony Batter North is a working cattle and sheep property so guests are invited to join in farm activities. Children will be made very welcome, especially by the Kelpie dogs. Should you wish to explore the region further we are ideally located for day trips to Uralla, Inverell and Armidale.
We shall look forward to meeting you and sharing our beautiful property with you.

Armidale
Bed & Breakfast
Address: "Monivea", 172 Brown St,
Armidale, NSW 2350
Name: Carrie Conolly
Telephone: (02) 6772 8001
Beds: 1 Double, 2 Single (2 bedrooms)
Bathroom: 1 Ensuite, 1 Family share
Tariff: B&B (full) Double $65, Single $45.
Vouchers accepted
Nearest Town: Armidale

"Monivea" is a post-federation cottage in Armidale, a beautiful city in the New England area. Armidale is nearly 1000ms high, so is a pleasantly cool stop-over between Sydney and Brisbane in summer, is lovely in the cooler months, with autumn colours, spring gardens and an occasional fall of snow in winter.
Whatever the weather, a warm welcome awaits you from your hostess Carrie and a reasonably civilized Siamese cat called Lucy. You can relax and be yourself in a very informal atmosphere, with cosy bedrooms and a small sitting room with a log fire. For a tourist stop-over, uni-residentials, or a pleasant week end away, we would like to welcome you.
Please phone in advance. No smoking.

NEW SOUTH WALES

Armidale
Chalet+B&B   NRMA ★★★★
Address: "Beambolong",
Harry McRae Drive, Armidale 2350
Name: Denni and Alan McKenzie
Telephone: (02) 6771 2019
Fax: (02) 6771 2019
Mobile: (019) 653700
Email: amckenzi@metz.une.edu.au
Beds: 1 King, 1 Double,
14 Single (6 bedrooms)
Bathroom: 2 Ensuites, 1 Guests share
Tariff: B&B (full) Double $60-$155, Single $40,
Children $10, Dinner $30. Credit Cards.
Nearest Town: Armidale

6km from town, Beambolong sits snugly on the side of a hill overlooking a peaceful valley. The stunning views of the Pine Forest and creek will take all your cares away. The Spin-a-fire in the Chalet, or open fire in the Homestead will warm the cockles of your heart. The friendly dogs, the farmyard friends (& horses) will greet you as warmly as your hosts. The Chalet is self-contained and luxurious, including a spa bath with a view, a completely wrap-around verandah and fenced off playground for children. BBQ and full cooking facilities are available. Come and enjoy the many attractions Armidale has to offer, whose motto is: "You can't do it all in one Day!" Both homestead and Chalet have full sound / TV / video systems, games and books.
Please phone for a brochure. No smoking. Pets welcome.
Home Page: http://www.com.au/neiss/armitour

Armidale   NRMA ★★★☆
Self-contained Accommodation
Address: Red Gum Lane,
Armidale, NSW 2350
Name: "Glenhope"
Telephone: (02) 6772 1940
Mobile: 0411 536 638
Beds: 1 Double, 2 Single,1 Double sofa bed (2 bedrooms)
Bathroom: 1 Private + extra toilet.
Tariff: B&B (continental/full) Double $60/$70, Single $50/$55, Speciality breakfast $80. Children $10-$20. (Breakfast provisions provided for cook your own breakfast). Reduced rates for s/c accommodation. Vouchers accepted
Nearest Town: Armidale 4 kms

Nestled in a tranquil valley with rural views of rolling hills and only the sound of bush and birds to distract you. Glenhope has elegant self-contained accommodation attached to the homestead. The cosy interior has all the comforts of home with fine attention to detail and personal touches.
Enjoy your country fresh breakfast at your private outdoor setting, surrounded by the fragrance of the cottage garden.
Take a walk through the paddocks and maybe see the kangaroos grazing with the farm animals and enjoy the many varies of bird life.
Help feed the farm animals or join in the farm activities of the moment. We are only minutes away from restaurants, art gallery, picnic and fishing spots, golf, horse riding, craft and speciality shops and national parks.
No smoking indoors.

NEW SOUTH WALES

Armidale
Self-contained Accommodation
Address: "Creekside", 5 Canambe St,
Armidale, NSW 2350
Name: Ross and Jane Stephens
Telephone: (02) 6772 2018
Beds: 1 Double, 2 Single (divans)
(1 bedroom)
Bathroom: Ensuite
Tariff: B&B (continental/full) Double $80,
Single $60, Children $15 each.
Nearest Town: Within the city of Armidale

"Creekside" is a charming self-contained cottage in the garden of a turn of the century homestead on four acres in the heart of Armidale. Come and enjoy the best of both worlds - country living only minutes from excellent shopping, restaurants, and cultural activities. Comforts include electric blankets, wood fire, TV/video, radio/tape/CD deck and library. A delicious continental breakfast (including bacon and eggs if you wish to cook your own) and linen are provided. Children are very welcome. We have three children, as well as chooks, dogs, pony, a trampoline and plenty of space, including a creek. We have a tennis court with racquets and private coaching available, and are situated on the bikeway which runs through the parkland to the city centre and university. We also now offer "Apple Tree Cottage" at a separate venue for families and groups up to 8 people (details/cost on enquiry)

Armidale
Farmstay+Self-contained Accommodation
Address: "Greenslopes",
1006 Green Hills Rd,
Armidale 2350
Name: Gavin & Narelle Waters
Telephone: (02) 6779 1397
Fax: (02) 6779 1397
Mobile: (015) 298525
Beds: 1 Double, 2 Single
(2 bedrooms)
Bathroom: 1 Private
Tariff: B&B (continental) Double $55, Single $35, Children $15.
Nearest Town: 38km from Armidale, 25km from Guyra on through road.

"Greenslopes" is 900 acres of peace and quiet half way between Sydney and Brisbane. Gavin and Narelle offer a separate modern self contained unit with kitchenette (electric stove, fridge, toaster etc) & bathroom (shower & toilet) exclusively for your use. There are electric blankets and heating. The sunny glassed-in verandah with spectacular views overlooking the Wollomombi Valley is a great place to start the day. Breakfast needs and linen are provided.
Native birds are frequent visitors in our garden.
We are a family farm running Super Fine Merino sheep and stud Simmental cattle. Guests can join in farm activities. We offer on-farm Trout fishing in the Wollomombi River (Oct to June), star gazing, bush walking and clean, clear, fresh air.
Greenslopes is handy to beautiful Ebor Falls, New England National Park, Wollomombi Falls. Overseas visitors welcome. Pickup can be arranged at Armidale or Guyra. Please ring or fax early mornings or evenings for bookings.
No smoking inside. **Directions**: *Please ring.*

NEW SOUTH WALES

Armidale - Uralla
Farmstay/B&B/Self-contained Accom.
Address: "Cruickshank's Cottage",
Tourist Drive 19, Uralla, NSW 2358
Name: Mike & Anne Thackway
Telephone: (02) 6778 2148
Fax: (02) 6778 2148
Mobile: 018 514 428
Beds: 1 Queen, 2 Single (2 bedrooms)
(1 Double sofabed in living room)
plus 2 folding and cot
Bathroom: 1 Private
Tariff: B&B (full) Double $80, Single $55, Children negotiable, Dinner $25 by arrangement, Full board & weekly rates available. Campervans negotiable. Credit Cards Bankcard, Mastercard, Visa, Amex. Vouchers accepted
Nearest Town: 25km south of Armidale, 21km east of Uralla on Tourist Drive 19.

Cruickshanks Cottage awaits you, nestling between low hills beside a winding creek - like a nostalgic symbol of your childhood memories of "Holidays in the Country". Imagine-in-winter-a cosy fire-a wonderful romantic dinner and wine, an early night, then snuggling into a warm bed! Bird song and breakfast in the morning sunshine - good for the soul after a peaceful night. Explore the hills and valleys, walk along the creek, fish for perch and yabbies, cook them on the BBQ. Treat yourselves to long lazy lunches and afternoons of conversation, reading or snoozing on the sunny verandahs. Share this sentimental journey with your children on a working sheep and cattle property - dogs mustering, drenching, tractors, motor bikes, horses + haystacks. Show them where eggs, milk and wool, lambs and calves come from! Something for everyone. Come for a night, most say that's not long enough.

Armidale - Uralla
Farm Style Bed & Breakfast
Address: "Lindon", Lindon Road
via Kingstown Road, Uralla
Name: Barbie & John Beynon
Telephone: (02) 6778 7123
Fax: (02) 6778 7166
Beds: 1 Queen, 1 Double,
1 Twin (3 bedrooms)
Bathroom: 2 Ensuite
Tariff: B&B (full) Double $90,
Single $80, Dinner $30.

Nearest Town: 22km west of Uralla via Kingstown Road, then Lindon Road.

We invite you to enjoy the peace and tranquillity of our sheep and cattle property situated midway between Sydney and Brisbane, just 15 minutes west of Uralla. Our hospitality offers sophistication with a rural flavour - fresh flowers antiques and home produce. The fully equipped cottage c.1900 with wisteria clad verandah and cottage garden overlooks undulating country to spectacular granite hills where Thunderbolt held up many a coach!! For the active there is bushwalking, tennis and croquet, or a leisurely walk in the homestead garden, canoe on the lake or just relax on the terrace with a cappuccino. A perfect way to end the day is a candlelit dinner at the ancient oak table in the stone Greathall, or you may prefer it brought to the cottage. Lindon Cottage is close to Uralla and Armidale, National Parks, craft shops, art galleries, museums, Cathedrals and the UNE.

Armidale
Homestay/Self-contained Accommodation
Address: 15 Garibaldi Street, Armidale (entrance off Allingham Street)
Name: "Turners on the Hill"
Telephone: (02) 6772 9995 **Fax**: (02) 6772 1773 **Mobile**: 0417-262 582
Email: turners@tpgi.com.au
Beds: 1 King, 1 Double (2 Bedrooms)
Bathroom: 2 private
Tariff: B&B (full) King $100, Double $85, Single $65, Children $20. Credit Cards: Bankcard, Mastercard, Visa Vouchers accepted
Nearest Town: In town on the South Hill overlooking the city of Armidale

Turners on the Hill offers the finest accommodation in Armidale.
Spacious bedrooms with superb sofas, pristine bathrooms and private entrances.
The decor is simply splendid, the tableware and linen luxurious and the hospitality open and friendly.
Set amongst hundreds of roses "Turners on the Hill" is surrounded by mature trees with the formal dining room offering a panoramic view of Armidale from the university to the city and its cathedrals.
Complimentary champagne, chocolates, flowers and fruit are the order of the day, and TV, phone, fax and email services available on request.
The distinct four seasons of Armidale are all reflected in this home where open fires with central heating warm Winter, the trees are set ablaze in Autumn, blossoms and icebergs greet Spring and bunches of roses bask in the beauty and warmth of Summer. Armidale is the ideal base camp and stepping stone to the New England National Parks with great gorges, wonderful waterfalls and a European heritage with Anaiwan ancestry. You can wander or white water raft. Ride or fish, see campdrafts and cattle or sheep stations and shearing sheds. This is the four seasons' centre of NSW.

Avoca Beach & Avoca Beach North see Central Coast

NEW SOUTH WALES

Ballina
Homestay+Self-contained Unit
Address: 971 River Drive,
Keith Hall, via Ballina, 2478
Name: John Felsch
Telephone: (02) 6686 2047 **Fax**: (02) 6686 2047
Mobile: (018) 442111
Email: balinfo@om.com.au
Beds: 2 King, 6 Single (4 large bedrooms)
Bathroom: 1 Ensuite, 1 Private, 1 Guest share
Tariff: B&B (continental) Double $50-$90,
Single $30-$45, Children under 3 N/C,3-12yrs half price. Dinner $20. Campervans $20. Credit Cards (BC/MC/VISA), Bartercard accepted. Vouchers accepted
Nearest Town: Ballina: 3km South of Ballina on River Drive off Pacific Highway. 9.71km north of Wardell on River Drive off Pacific Highway

Overlooking the beautiful Richmond River, this two storey brick house has a private, sandy beach with BBQ and cabana, ideal area for waterskiing, jet skis or just relaxing. The area abounds in birds and wildlife. Self-contained unit two bedrooms, pets accommodated outside. I am a sugar cane farmer, my farm extends from the river through to 20km of unspoilt white sand beach. I have travelled extensively and love to meet people.
Stop two nights and receive a complimentary organised trip to a nature park and other places of interest on the north coast.
Come, stop a while in the country and unwind. Free pick-up by Limousine at Ballina Airport, bus and rail terminal. Phone for directions.

Ballina - Alstonville
Bed & Breakfast   NRMA ★★★★☆
Address: "Hume's Hovell", 333 Dalwood Rd., Alstonville
Name: Peter & Suzanne Hume
Telephone: (02) 6629 5371 **Fax**: (02) 6629 5471
Mobile: (014) 663 427 **Email**: aac@nrg.com.au
Beds: 3 King, 2 Single (2 studios, 1 suite)
Bathroom: 2 Ensuite, 1 Private + Spa
Tariff: B&B (full) Double from $115 - $195 (Xmas),
Single $105-$160, Extra person $30 (same area),
Dinner $30pp. Not suitable for children under 5 yrs.
Credit Cards (M/C, B/C,Visa, Amex, Diners Club).
Nearest Town: Alstonville 8km, Ballina 16km and Lismore 18km

"A travellers delight of pure luxury, comfort and hospitality". "Better than a 5 star hotel - We will return" "An amazing place to stay" "A most enjoyable and relaxing visit; great hospitality and a great breakfast." — our guests say it all! —
Situated on a macadamia farm you too can enjoy luxury in the air-conditioned studios, or the two room homestead suite. It's peaceful and relaxing, with complementary juices, fruit, macadamia nuts: and lots more. Luxurious king size beds, TV/Video/ Stereo and library, all for your comfort. On arrival, relax by the pool, enjoy a game of tennis, take a stroll around the farm or explore nearby Victoria Park Rainforest. A special country style breakfast is served by the pool, on the patio or in your suite - it's your choice and our pleasure. Art galleries and handcrafts are nearby, with Byron Bay and beaches only a short scenic drive away. Smoking - outside please.
Wheelchair friendly.
Home Page: ozivacations.com

NEW SOUTH WALES

Ballina
Homestay - Bed & Breakfast
Address: "Landfall",
109 Links Ave., East Ballina
Name: Gaye and Roger Ibbotson
Telephone: (02) 6686 7555
Fax: (02) 6686 7555 **Email**: atadrive@om.com.au
Beds: 1 Double, 2 Single (2 bedrooms) **Bathroom**: 1 Guests share
Tariff: B&B (full) Double $70, Single $45, Dinner $20pp.
Vouchers accepted
Nearest Town: Ballina

Welcome to 'Landfall'. This home was the residence of Captain Tom Martin and his wife Marjorie for some 20 years. Captain Martin named this home 'Landfall' when he retired to Ballina after many years at sea.
'Landfall' is situated in East Ballina overlooking the Ballina Golf Course. Ballina offers Golf, Bowls, Surfing, Fishing, Licenced Clubs, and a variety of Restaurants.
Our home has 1 double bedroom and 1 twin bedroom, with a guest bathroom, and a large lounge with TV and Video. You are welcome to relax in the Atrium with its indoor solar heated salt water swimming pool and spa. Perhaps choose a book from the "Chartroom" library to read in front of the wood fire on a winter's evening. Landfall' is a non smoking home.
A Full Country Style Breakfast with local fruits in season. We have lived in Ballina for 25 years and offer a relaxed stay with warm friendly hospitality. Your hosts Gaye & Roger Ibbotson.

Gift Vouchers

Our B&B vouchers are for a double room for one night's B&B. They cost $89, and if you order one as a gift, we will include a free
Australian Bed & Breakfast Book
worth $16.95

Send your cheque to
Moonshine Press
59 Quirk Street
Dee Why
NSW 2099

Ballina
Homestay
Address: 18 Suvla St, East Ballina, 2478
Name: Shelly Beachouse
Telephone: (02) 6686 8405
Fax: (02) 6686 8405
Beds: 1 Queen, 1 Double (2 bedrooms)
Bathroom: 1 Guests share
Tariff: B&B (full) Double $85, Single $75,
Dinner $20, Credit Cards. Vouchers accepted $10 surcharge
Nearest Town: Ballina 4km south

A casual beachside home overlooking the sparkling surf and sand of beautiful Shelly Beach, and backing on to a nature reserve. A quiet place to relax and unwind. Enjoy a stroll on our beach, collect shells, poke around in the rock pools, wade in the shallows or surf the break, beach fish (rods supplied), climb the headland to the lighthouse and the lookout for expansive views of the district, sail on the river or take a dip in Shaws Bay. The choice is yours.
In the temperate climate we are rarely out of shorts, even in winter, our lounge area is open planned onto a deck where we serve, weather permitting, a full breakfast, including seasonal fruits. You may even spot a migrating whale, or a school of dolphin at play. At night you are only 5 minutes from the town centre with a wide variety of clubs and restaurants. We are a non smoking home....
Your hosts Patricia & Julian Beaver.

Ballina
Beach Homestay
Address: 5 Yabsley Street,
East Ballina, NSW 2478
Name: The Yabsley Bed & Breakfast
Telephone: (02) 66811 505
Fax: (02) 66811 505 **Mobile**: (017) 811 444
Beds: 1 Queen, 1 Double, (2 bedrooms)
Bathroom: 2 Ensuite
Tariff: B&B (full), Double $90. Credit cards accepted.
Nearest Town: Ballina

'The Yabsley' is situated within two minutes walk of Lighthouse Beach, Richmond River and Shaws Bay Lagoon. The house was refurbished in 1996 to provide luxury facilities in each suite.
Guests have a lounge room with a winter fire as well as three private courtyards in which to relax. Full BBQ facilities are available. Leave your car in our private parking at night and visit the dining rooms of the nearby Beach Resort, a BYO Italian Seafood Restaurant, the Shaws Bay Hotel or negotiate a superb meal of your choice cooked by David who specialises in seafood cuisine. At lunch time walk to the headland and enjoy the delights of a cafe meal whilst watching whales and dolphins at play.
Enjoy a leisurely breakfast of local fruits, a variety of hot dishes and cappuccino coffee in a courtyard, the kitchen or the formal dining room.
East Ballina gives access to day trips to the Gold Coast, Border Ranges, all water sports and golf courses.

Bangalow see Byron Hinterland

NEW SOUTH WALES

Batemans Bay - Denhams Beach
Beachfront Homestay
Address: "Edgewood House", 10 Edgewood Place
Denhams Beach via Batemans Bay, NSW 2536
Name: John & Margaret Blunden
Telephone: (044) 713198 **Fax**: (044) 711165
Beds: 3 Queen, 1 Double, 4 Single (5 bedrooms/
One private suite with Queen + 3 Single)
Bathroom: 3 Ensuite (one with spa bath), 1 Private.
Tariff: B&B (full) Double $95-$130, Single $75.
Well behaved children welcome. Credit cards:
Mastercard, Bankcard, Visa.
Vouchers accepted $20 surcharge. *Edgewood House*
Same day restriction Dec to April.
Nearest Town: Batemans Bay 7km north - Canberra 155km

"Edgewood House" is a truly delightful beachside retreat. Absolute ocean frontage and direct access to Denhams Beach where dolphins often outnumber surfers make it an ideal destination for those wishing to escape life's pressures. Two guest areas provide ample room to relax - the cosy winter lounge with its open fire, and the large sunny living room with spectacular views over the azure waters of the bay. Long walks along the beach or the many bushwalking tracks nearby, a round of golf, or puttering up the river in a boat seem to be all that most guests aspire to during the day, but for those who are more energetically inclined, Edgewood House has its own solar heated pool and championship tennis court. Guests are welcome to utilize the BBQ and kitchen facilities, either for tea and coffee making or, for the culinary-minded, to cook their own meals. Owners, John and Margaret Blunden will do everything possible to make your stay a memorable one. **Home Page**: http://www.dawsons.com.au

---

Batemans Bay/Moruya
Guest House/Homestay
Address: 1883 Araluen Rd,
Deua River Valley, Moruya, NSW 2537
Name: Deua River Country Guest House
Telephone: (02) 4474 2205 **Mobile**: (015) 074707
Beds: 2 Double, 2 Single (3 bedrooms)
Bathroom: 1 Ensuite, 1 Guests share, 1 extra toilet
Tariff: B&B (full) Double $80-$85, Single $55,
Children over 12 $30. Dinner $25 pp.
Vouchers accepted
Nearest Town: Moruya

The Deua River Country Guest House is situated in a secluded valley beside the pristine Deua River, just 19 minutes kilometres from Moruya. Our colonial style home is set in 2 acres of beautiful gardens, surrounded by the forest clad hills of the State Forest and Deua National Park.
Our rooms are attractive, sunny and comfortable and open onto the gardens. Guests can relax on the verandahs or by the sitting room open fire, wander by the river, laze on its sandy beaches, or swim in the deep pools, play croquet, discover the birds or simply enjoy the peace.
Guests can walk the fire trails or explore the spectacular nearby scenery or Robin can take you canoeing or by 4WD to start a challenging walk. Guests are welcome to join us for an elegant candle-lit dinner with home-grown produce.
We look forward to welcoming you to our home and the lovely valley.

NEW SOUTH WALES

GUEST HOUSE

Batemans Bay - Nelligen
Historic Guest House/Bed & Breakfast NRMA ★★★★
Address: "Old Nelligen Post Office Guest House",
7 Braidwood Street, Nelligen, NSW 2536
Name: Lillian & Bill Hardie
Telephone: (02) 4478 1179 **Fax**: (02) 4478 1179 **Mobile**: (041) 957 9041
Email: onpogh@bigpond.com
Beds: 1 Queen, 2 Double (3 bedrooms) **Bathroom**: 3 Ensuite
Tariff: B&B (full) Double rooms $95-$105, Queen $105-$115, Single $85-$95, Dinner $30pp, Credit Cards (MC/BC/VISA). Vouchers accepted $15-$25 Surcharge Monday-Thursday, May-September (excluding school & public holidays).
Nearest Town: Batemans Bay - 10 minutes away.

Experience the history of the past as well as the comfort and hospitality of the present. Our Guest House is the original Nelligen Post Office building built in 1900. We offer luxury accommodation at affordable prices. Historic Nelligen, Australia's prettiest town, is situated on the banks of the magnificent Clyde River. Many of the town's buildings have been proposed for heritage listing.

There is much to do in the Nelligen area - a guided historic walking tour of the town, bush walks, tennis, fishing, boating, visit local art and craft galleries, potteries or beaches. Or you can simply take a relaxing stroll along the banks of the scenic Clyde River - you will hardly notice your tensions dropping away as you walk.

The guest house has three luxurious guest rooms each with ensuite. Choose from "The Old Post Office Room" with queen size bed, private entrance and verandah, or the smaller (but spacious) "Front Parlour Room" or the "Children's Room". All rooms have television and tea and coffee-making facilities.

Breakfast at Nelligen is a celebration. There's fresh fruit salad, fresh orange juice, delicious home made muesli or choose from our selection of cereals. The cooked course has a special Scottish addition and we offer home-baked bread and local honeys. For vegetarians we offer special wholemeal pancakes with maple syrup or a mouth watering frittata.

Our four course traditional dinners have become renowned and friends can book the guest house for an indulgent weekend. Vegetarian meals are also available.

Special packages: 'Nelligen, It's Absolutely Fabulous', 'Country Coast & Culture' Weekend courses 'How to Run a Bed & Breakfast' and 'Personal Development'

We can also arrange a Bed and Breakfast 'tour' for you.
We are an adult retreat and have a smoke free environment indoors.
Some comments from our visitors book: 'Absolutely Fabulous!! Thank you'.
'A wonderful Getaway with wonderful people'.
Home Page: www.morning.asn.au/go/onpogh/

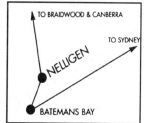

Bathurst

Self-contained Accommodation
Address: "The Waldorf"
Name: Stuart & Susan Loudon
Telephone: (02) 6337 5720
Beds: 1 Double, 2 Single (2 bedrooms)
Bathroom: 1 Private
Tariff: $140 two night double; Discounting for longer stays to $50 per day for 7 nights or longer. $5 night each extra guest. Linen extra. No food provided.
Nearest Town: Bathurst and Oberon (25 km to each)

"The Waldorf" is an early settler's mud cottage on a small farm with superb views of undulating country.
The furnishing is in keeping with yesteryear. Included is modern kitchen and bathroom and washing machine - all in totally private, fully self-contained accommodation.
The climate is cold in winter, but the air is crisp, clear and invigorating. "The Waldorf" is very cosy with an open fire, electric heaters and electric blankets.
The spacious garden is safely fenced for young children and features old fashioned roses and cottage perennials.
We enjoy delightful country walks in the immediate area.
However, the cottage is also within daily touring reach of Jenolan Caves, Abercrombie Caves, Kanangra Walls, and the historic villages of Carcoar, Millthorpe, Hill End and Sofala. There is good trout fishing locally within season. Tennis court.
Directions: Please telephone. (Approximately three hours drive west of Sydney.)

Bathurst

Boutique Accommodation
Address: "Blandford", 214 Lambert St. Bathurst, NSW 2795
Name: Roley & Ruth Little
Telephone: (02) 6331 9995
Fax: (02) 6331 9995
Mobile: (015) 784922
Beds: 3 Queen, (3 bedrooms)
Bathroom: 1 Ensuite, 2 Guests share
Tariff: B&B (full) Double $90-$110, Single $65-$85. Dinner $30pp. Campervans $25 (breakfast $15pp), Credit Cards (BC/MC/VISA, AMEX, DINERS). Vouchers accepted $15 surcharge
Nearest Town: Within the city of Bathurst

NSW TOURISM AWARDS FOR EXCELLENCE
1993 AWARD OF DISTINCTION

NRMA ★★★★ Finalist in the New South Wales Tourism Awards for Excellence 1993.
'Blandford', circa 1870 modernised in Federation style in 1916, is a gracious home set back amongst trees and shrubs, within the city boundary, close to parks, churches, galleries, university, clubs and restaurants. Decor is old style, much of the furniture antique. Bedrooms have comfortable beds, electric blankets, duvets, heaters, fans, bathrobes, clock radios, hairdryers and ironing facilities. Guest lounge and dining rooms have open fires, television, tea and coffee making facilities with homemade biscuits and refrigerator for guests' use. We greet guests with afternoon tea and serve a lavish traditional English breakfast at a time to suit. We have our own chickens, so you can enjoy fresh free-range eggs. Bathurst has many good restaurants, however we serve a gourmet dinner and cater for special diets by prior arrangement. There is a non-smoking rule inside but there are verandahs where those who must may. Off-street parking. Brochure / map available.

Bathurst
B&B or Self-contained Accommodation NRMA ★★★☆
Address: 79 Morrisset Street
Bathurst NSW 2795
Name: "Winter Rose Cottage"
Telephone: (02) 6332 2661
Fax: (02) 6332 2661 **Mobile**: 015 455 540
Email: acraine@csu.edu.au
Beds: 1 Queen, 2 Double, 2 Single (4 bedrooms)
Bathroom: 1 Ensuite, 1 Guest Share
Tariff: B&B (full) Double $70-$95, Single $60, Children $20.
We provide special rates for single women travellers).
Credit Cards Visa, Amex etc. Vouchers accepted
Nearest Town: Bathurst (walking distance CBD)

Better service, better business.

One of my guests wrote in the guest book:
   From Frost & Fog
   From cold enough to harm.....
   a Haven,
   Winter-Rose' cottage full of warmth and charm"
And we are located in a QUIET street within walking distance of the CBD, tennis courts, river walk, fitness centre, hospital, movies, restaurants etc. Choose a cosy cottage style room in the house or the independent garden cottage with queen bed, own bathroom, Sheridan accessories and rustic elegance. The wood fire is in the house. The garden is at its best mid October to November. Bathurst is the oldest inland city with historical treasures, varied architecture, and the GATEWAY to the Central West. We have maps and lots of information for you. We offer country hospitality with that touch of class. Smoking: outside only.

Bathurst
Bed & Breakfast   NRMA ★★★★
Address: "Strathmore Victorian Manor",
202 Russell Street, Bathurst, NSW 2795
Name: Sharon and David Parratt
Telephone: (02) 6332 3252 **Fax**: (02) 6332 3819
Beds: 4 Double, 2 single (5 bedrooms)
Bathroom: 4 Ensuites.
Tariff: B&B (continental) Double $100, Single $85.
Credit Cardsf: Bankcard, mastercard, Visa, Diners, Amex. Corporate and Government rates.
Nearest Town: Bathurst

Strathmore was built as a family home in 1882 by William Mugridge, a Bathurst timber merchant, and has been used for a variety of purposes over the years: An exclusive boarding house, private hospital and apartments.
Extensive restoration and refurbishment has been carried out to return Srathmore to its original beauty. It is tastefully decorated with antique furniture and furnishings in the classic Victorian style.
Strathmore has 5 suites, (one self contained; one twin, three doubles), ensuite bathrooms, TV and ISD/STD telephones.
There is a large lounge, with an open fire, in which guests may relax. Coffee and tea making facilities are always available. Being in the heart of Bathurst, guests can take a leisurely stroll to enjoy the excellent restaurants, cafes, antique and craft shops.
Off street parking is provided. Smoking is not permitted in the rooms, however there are verandahs and a sunny courtyard.

NEW SOUTH WALES

Bathurst
Homestay+Self-contained Accom.
Address: "Elm Tree Cottage",
Cnr Keppel & Mitre Sts, Bathurst 2795.
Postal: P O Box 17, Bathurst 2795
Name: Lyn Boshier
Telephone: (0263) 324920
Fax: (0263) 323132
Mobile: 017 892 844
Email: boshierd@ix.net.au
Beds: 1 King, 1 Queen, 1 Double,
3 Single (5 bedrooms)
Bathroom: 1 Ensuite, 1 Private
Tariff: B&B (full) Double $100-$120, Single $85-$95, Children $30, Dinner $35, Credit Cards (BC/MC/VISA/AMEX). Vouchers accepted $30 surcharge
Nearest Town: Bathurst - 10 minute walk to town centre

Soporific nightcaps and splendid meals await you at Elm Tree Cottage. Experience warm country hospitality in the comfort of your own pretty restored cottage set in a fascinating walled garden. Discover sculptures and murals and a fountain playing peacefully in the background. It is quiet and peaceful yet close to town. Take in the vista through the trees to the hill in the distance whilst enjoying a leisurely breakfast in the sunny family room or courtyard. The self contained cottage is tastefully decorated with a blue and yellow theme with polished floor and cottage furniture. The double bedroom in the main house has an antique brass bed and large bathroom. Freshly brewed coffee and tea are available along with a selection of books and games. To keep the house as fresh as the flowers our guests are requested not to smoke indoors.
Home Page: http://www.ix.net.au/~boshierd

Bathurst - Mount Panorama
Homestay+Self-contained Accom.
Address: "Roseview",
Mountain Straight, Mt. Panorama,
Bathurst, NSW 2795
Name: Zob & Jenny Cieslak
Telephone: (063) 324767
Fax: (063) 324787
Mobile: (018) 643818
Beds: 3 Double, 3 Single (4 bedrooms)
Bathroom: 2 Ensuite, 1 Private
Tariff: B&B (full) Double $90-$100, Single $65, Children over 10yrs. Dinner $20-$25.
Nearest Town: Bathurst 2km to GPO.

"Roseview" is a luxury homestay, with self-contained units also available, situated with magnificent views, beside the Mount Panorama racing circuit. The gardens, the relaxing wildlife and the tennis court are yours while you are here, or you may prefer to laze on the terrace with a drink and later enjoy the barbecue.
We have a large guest lounge room, central heating and all other home comforts for your convenience.
Fax and phone facilities are available to the busy business executive in this modern, convenient, yet extremely relaxing home.
We hope to see you soon.
Children below 12 not catered for.

Bathurst - Rock Forest
Farmstay Guest House
Address: 1125 Ophir Road,
Rock Forest, Bathurst, NSW 2795
Name: 'Jarara'
Telephone: (063) 374 877
Beds: 2 Queen, 2 Double, 1 Single (5 bedrooms)
Bathroom: 2 Ensuite, 1 Guests share
Tariff: B&B (full), Double $95, Single $70,
Dinner $25, Children half price. Vouchers accepted
Nearest Town: Bathurst

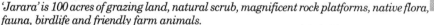

'Jarara' is 100 acres of grazing land, natural scrub, magnificent rock platforms, native flora, fauna, birdlife and friendly farm animals.
The house is solar passive, utilising both the warming winter sun and the summer shade. The huge windows offer expansive views of the surrounding countryside with a backdrop of the Blue Mountains.
Guests have exclusive use of a lounge / dining room, 3 bedrooms (1 with ensuite), bathroom plus separate toilet and self contained suite, all tastefully and comfortably furnished.
Numerous tourist attractions surround historic Bathurst - from gold mining towns to art galleries, craft shops, vineyards, horse riding to car races.
We welcome you.
14 km north west of Bathurst on Ophir Road. Please phone.
Directions: 14 km north west of Bathurst on Ophir Road. Please phone.

Bathurst
Homestay
Address: "Tara", Cherry Lane, Bathurst, NSW 2795
Name: Neil & Colleen Donohue
Telephone: (02) 6332 6029
Mobile: (019) 326233
Email: cmd@writeme.com
Beds: 2 Double, 1 Single (3 bedrooms)
Bathroom: 1 Guests share
Tariff: B&B (full) Double $90, Single $60
Children half price, Dinner $20.
Vouchers accepted $10 surcharge
Nearest Town: Bathurst

"Tara" is an attractive and comfortable country home on the edge of town. Set in a large garden on 7 acres, and furnished with period furniture, it offers affordable boutique accommodation.
Enjoy our warm and friendly hospitality, the peaceful and relaxing atmosphere and pleasant country surroundings. The large guest lounge has open log fire, music, reading material, TV, video, tea & coffee facilities etc. Relish a country breakfast served in the dining room (or in bed if you prefer); afternoon tea - either by the fire or in the garden. Additional services by arrangement include: evening meals, laundry facilities, half and full day 4WD tours to local and district attractions eg. Mt Panorama racetrack, historic homes and villages, wineries, Jenolan caves, horse riding and gold panning facilities.
Just 5 minutes from the Post Office we are close to most amenities: private schools, university, TAFE, Mt Panorama, golf course, antique shops, arts and craft shops, coffee shops and fine restaurants. **Directions**: Please phone.

NEW SOUTH WALES

Bathurst
Homestay+
Self-contained Accom.
Address:
"Stringybark Lodge",
968 Limekilns Road,
Kelso, Bathurst
Name: Margaret & Barry Jones
Telephone: (02) 6337 6529
Beds: 1 Double, 2 Single
(2 bedrooms)
Bathroom: 1 Guests share
Tariff: B&B (full) $55 pp per night. Children POA, Dinner by prior arrangement.
Vouchers accepted
Nearest Town: Bathurst

"Stringybark Lodge" is a 10 minute country drive from Bathurst on a sealed road. So come and visit, share with us our home set in spacious grounds with swimming pool. Enjoy panoramic views, starry skies, bush walks. Delicious country cooking and hospitality awaits you.
"At your own pace for your own peace"
We ask that you don't smoke indoors, please.

Bathurst
Homestay   NRMA ★★★☆
Address: 238 Eglinton Road, Bathurst 2795
Name: "Cherrywood-By-The-River"
Telephone: (0263) 319427
Beds: 1 Queen, 2 Single (2 bedrooms)
Bathroom: 1 Guests share
Tariff: B&B (full) Double $90, Single $50, Children under 12 $25, Dinner $20, Campervans surcharge $10.
Nearest Town: Bathurst

Better service, better business.

"Cherrywood-By-The-River" is a delightful home in a magic rural garden, set on 2 acres. Beyond the garden and ponies paddock, the Macquarie River winds through patchwork fields, with mountains beyond. Stroll to the river or capture this view from our wide verandahs. Gliding enthusiasts notice the Bathurst Gliding Club across the river.
The large lounge and family rooms have cheerful log fires, with TV and tea and coffee making facilities. The dining room has gracious antique where guests enjoy a hot breakfast with homemade bread, jams and marmalades and our own hen eggs. Charming large bedrooms have comfortable beds with electric blankets.
Home of the Cherrywood show ponies, help feed or just admire our mares and foals or ponies being schooled.
A short drive to schools, university, churches, Mount Panorama Race Circuit and craft/cottage industries on local farms.
Please guests, use the verandahs for smoking.
Directions: *Please phone.*

Bathurst
Bed & Breakfast NRMA ★★★☆
Address: "Belle-Vue", 34 Opperman Way, Windradyne Heights, Bathurst, NSW 2795
Name: Belle-Vue
Telephone: (02) 6331 5739
Beds: 1 Queen (1 bedroom)
Bathroom: 1 Private
Tariff: B&B (continental)
Double $80, Single $50.
  Vouchers accepted
Nearest Town: West side of Bathurst City

Located close to the Golf Course in a quiet setting our modern elegant home contains old world charm and has wide rural views with secure undercover parking. Comfortable and airy our home is a stimulating place to stay. A wood fire keeps the whole house warm in winter while in summer it is cool with an outdoor shady deck and barbecue just right for that alfresco breakfast. The garden has plantings of fragrant shrubs to perfume the fresh crisp stimulating country air. Bathurst is Australia's oldest inland city and exhibits many fine old buildings and streetscapes, there's fine eating, lovely antique shops and speciality stores. There are many country and city events to see and do, including the nearby gold villages of Sofala, Hill End, Millthorpe, Carcoar and Rockley. We would be pleased to assist you to have a pleasurable and absorbing stay in Bathurst and sample Australian hospitality.

Bathurst - Mount Panorama
Self-contained B&B
Address: "Lochinvar", Conrod Straight, Mt Panorama, Bathust, NSW 2795
Name: Graham & Maria Ireland
Telephone: (02) 6331 2469
Fax: (02) 6331 2469 **Mobile**: 015 219703
Beds: 2 Queen or 1 Queen/1 Twin (2 bedrooms) **Bathroom**: 2 Ensuite
Tariff: B&B (continental breakfast included first 2 mornings) Cottage hire from: $120 per night, $150 Fri/Sat per night, $500 week (6 nights), Extended stays negotiable. Vouchers accepted $38 surcharge midweek - $65 surcharge Fri/Sat
Nearest Town: Bathurst 4 kms to GPO

You won't be disappointed ! Self-contained luxurious accommodation in your own private cottage. This charming tastefully furnished 2 bedroom cottage is nestled on the famous Mt Panorama racing circuit amidst a beautiful private garden setting commanding spectacular views overlooking Bathurst. Undoubtedly one of the best positions in town and only 5 minutes drive to CBD. Exclusively yours "Lochinvar" boasts the best in luxury accommodation.
- *Two main bedrooms - both with Queen beds (second bedroom can become twin if required), 2 ensuite - all linen provided. Ideally suited for 2 couples to share or family 2 adults, 2 children.*
- *Underfloor heating ensures a cosy stay during winter.*
- *Gourmet kitchen - fully equipped, dishwasher, microwave etc.*
- *Continental breakfast included first two mornings.*
- *Covered verandahs • Barbecue facilities • Lock up garage*

'Lochinvar' is centrally located to local major attractions including Mt Panorama Winery, Motor Racing Hall of Fame, Bathurst Goldfields, & Nature Reserve. Be assured of a warm welcome and memorable stay. **Directions**: *Please phone for details.*

NEW SOUTH WALES

Bathurst - O'Connell
Unique Bed & Breakfast
Address: "The Church and Schoolhouse",
O'Connell Road, O'Connell, NSW 2795
Name: June, Bob & Nicole Jackson
Telephone: (02) 6337 5773
Fax: (02) 6337 5778
Email: church@ix.net.au
Beds: 2 Double, 2 Single (3 bedrooms)
Bathroom: 2 Ensuite
Tariff: B&B (full) Double $125-$145,
Single $85-$105, Children from $20,
Lunch $10-$35, Dinner $20-$45, Credit Cards.
Nearest Town: 20km from Bathurst and Oberon

Experience the peace and tranquillity of the magnificent church of St Francis, one of the oldest buildings in the National Trust listed village of O'Connell.
The location is perfect. Explore historic Bathurst, O'Connell and other nearby villages; the natural wonders of Jenolan and Abercrombie Caves; the vineyards of Bathurst, Mudgee, Orange and Cowra. Try abseiling, canyoning or bushwalking in the National Parks; trout fishing, fossicking and rambling at any of the local rivers and creeks meandering through the region.
Enjoy a truly scrumptious breakfast in the church or gardens. Indulge in a candlelit dinner or perhaps take a gourmet picnic or barbecue to one of the many special attractions in the area.
Family and group bookings are welcome. Please call us to arrange a package.

Bega also see Candelo

Bega
Farmstay
Address: "Bega Country B&B",
Warrigal Range Rd., Brogo
Name: Kym & Gerri
Telephone: (02) 6492 7205
Fax: (02) 6492 7205
Mobile: (018) 277249
Email: kymmog@acr.net.au
Beds: 1 Double, 2 Single (2 bedrooms)
Bathroom: Guest share toilet, 1 Family share
Tariff: B&B (full) Double $60, Single $40,
Children by arrangement,
Dinner $15-$20, Campervans $20. No smoking inside.   Vouchers accepted
Nearest Town: Bega and Cobargo 25kms

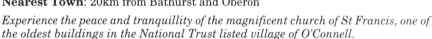

Our home is a hand made mud brick and cedar abode with lots of character, warmth and a relaxing feel about it. We are in a quiet "out of the way" location, with lots of bush to walk in, spectacular views to soak up, and some special secluded spots for solitude. We run a commercial worm farm and are developing an organic herb and native wildflower farm. Organic produce is used and special diets can be catered for. Dinner by arrangement. Attractions within 5km include the Brogo Dam with hire canoes and fishing; and the Wadbilliga National Park (a wilderness park). Beaches are only 40 minutes drive and 20 minutes to Bega Cheese Factory and Grevilla Winery. Guided bushwalks, canoe or vehicle tours by arrangement. **Directions**: *Turn off Princes Hwy (19km north of Bega) to Warrigal Range Road, 6km along and turn right at Worm Farm sign.*

NEW SOUTH WALES

Bega
Bed & Breakfast
Address: "The Pickled Pear"
60-62 Carp Street, Bega NSW 2550
Name: Wendy and Bob Gornall
Telephone: (02) 6492 1393
Beds: 1 King, 1 Queen,
2 Singles (3 bedrooms)
Bathroom: 3 Ensuites (one with Spa)
Tariff: B&B (full) Double $85-$120 (Private Suite $120), Single: $65-$100.
Dinner: $20-$25 (by arrangement). Credit Cards: Bankcard, Mastercard, Visa.
Vouchers accepted Monday - Thursday
Nearest Town: Bega

We have searched for five years for a suitable old home to renovate for bed and breakfast accommodation. "The Pickled Pear" called us back to fulfil our dream. After eight months of the joys of renovation, our 1870's doctor's residence is ready to go!! Special features of "The Pickled Pear" include:

> *scrumptious food *charming ensuites (one with spa)
> * private suite available *candelight dinner by open fire (pre-arranged)
> *weekend markets *old wares
> *secluded beaches nearby *National Parks surround us
> * the aura of history, tranquillity and warmth
> *main street location (walk to shops / clubs / restaurants)
> *read, sleep, walk, fish, paint, golf or whale watch!!

Bega
Self-contained Accom. NRMA ★★★☆
Address: "Girraween", 2 Girraween Crescent, Bega, 2550
Name: "Girraween"
Telephone: (02) 6492 1761 **Fax**: (02) 6492 2877
Beds: 1 Double, 2 Single (2 bedrooms)
Bathroom: 2 Private
Tariff: B&B (full) Double $55, Single $30, Dinner by arrangement.
Nearest Town: Bega

We offer our valued visitors a unique mode of accommodation at realistic prices. A modern self-contained unit overlooking a park with all "Look After Yourself" facilities, or be pampered and allow us to give you a friendly personalised service.
We are situated within easy walking distance of Bega's central business district and R.S.L. Club.
Visiting our famous cheese factory is a must along with museums, winery, golf and bowling clubs.
Only a short drive to pristine beaches, walking tracks and fishing. Laundry facilities are provided along with a BBQ area and garage parking. This unit is true "Value for Money".
We look forward to having you as our guest and the opportunity of providing you with all the comforts of home.

> Some homes share the bathroom,
> others have bathrooms exclusively for guests
> – they are indicated in the listing.

NEW SOUTH WALES

Bega
Self-contained Accommodation
Address: 864 Warrigal Range Road,
Brogo via Bega, NSW 2550
Name: Rock Lily Cottages
Telephone: (02) 6492 7364
Fax: (02) 6492 7364
Beds: 2 Queen, 1 Double (3 bedrooms)
Bathroom: 2 Ensuite
Tariff: B&B (full) Sun to Thur $75 per double per night, Fri & Sat $85 per double per night. Xmas surcharge $10 per night. Credit Cards. Vouchers accepted but not for Fri or Sat nights or at Easter, Christmas or New Years Eve.
Nearest Town: Bega

There are two secluded cottages with leadlight windows and other charming features, nestled into a hillside on the 100 acre property. Each romantic self-contained cottage is surrounded by panoramic views of blue mountains and green rolling hills; contains a kitchen, cosy lounge room, log fire, bathroom, bedroom/s and a barbecue. Generous breakfast provisions are provided. You can bushwalk, swim or hire a canoe at the Brogo Dam, take horse riding lessons on the adjoining property (additional cost) or just soak up the fresh air, magnificent mountain views and country lifestyle. Rock Lily has 2 friendly dogs and 2 horses. Kangaroos, wallabies and wombats come and go, as do wedge-tail eagles, parrots, rosellas, kookaburras and blue wrens. Friendly vaccinated dogs at Manager's discretion. Rock Lily is 27km north of Bega (towards Cobargo). Ring for directions. Non-smokers only. We will try to accommodate special dietary requests. (Opens December 1997)

Bellingen
Self-contained Accommodation
Address: North Bank Road, Bellingen
Name: Maddefords Cottages - Grahame & Glenys
Telephone: (02) 6655 2033
Fax: (02) 6655 2033 **Mobile**: 015 785 774
Email: madfords@midcoast.com.au
Beds: Two cottages: Queen, Double, 2 single (+ Bathroom) in each cottage.
Bathroom: 2 Private
Tariff: B&B (continental - on arrival only) Double $100-$105, Discount for longer stays, Children by arrangement, Dinner N/A, Credit Cards (VISA/BC/MC).
Nearest Town: 2km east of Bellingen on North Bank Road

Situated on the banks of the Bellinger River, about 30 minutes drive from Coffs Harbour, are two beautifully appointed cottages with sweeping views of the river and hills beyond. They provide a tranquil retreat after a day of sightseeing or travelling. Each of the air-conditioned cottages has a separate bedroom with a queen sized bed. The spacious lounge/dining area is furnished with a quality, comfortable period pieces, TV/VCR, a double convertible sofa bed and two single bunk beds. The cottages can sleep six adults if required, and one has disabled access.
The kitchen is fully equipped to produce meals in house, a blessing for those who wish to dine in peace on the verandah overlooking the river. Barbecues, canoes and mountain bikes are available for guests use.
The immediate area provides many attractions including galleries, craft shops, restaurants, national parks, winery, and beaches.

NEW SOUTH WALES

Bellingen
Homestay+Guest House NRMA ★★★☆
Address: 10 Hyde Street,
Bellingen, NSW 2454
Name: Rivendell
Telephone: (02) 6655 0060
Fax: (02) 6655 0060
Beds: 3 Queen, 1 Twin/King (4 bedrooms)
Bathroom: 2 Guests share
Tariff: B&B (full) per room $70-$85. Credit cards. Vouchers accepted Minimum 2 night stays.
Nearest Town: Bellingen

Bellingen lies beside the beautiful Bellinger River in the lush hinterland near Coffs Harbour. In the heart of this heritage village is Rivendell, a beautifully decorated old-style home. Luxurious rooms furnished with antiques, feather and down doonas and fluffy bathrobes, open to shady verandahs and picturesque gardens.
Take a refreshing dip in the saltwater pool, or in winter, relax by the log fire. After dinner settle back with complimentary port and chocolates.
TV, stereo, books, games, magazines and tea/coffee making provided in guest lounge. Mountain bikes for hire.
Local attractions include craft shops and galleries featuring quality local works, swimming holes, picnic spots, golf, whitewater rafting, horse-riding, canoeing, surfing, fresh and saltwater fishing, rainforest walks. Regular events include Craft Market on the 3rd Saturday each month, Jazz on the 1st Friday each month, Jazz Festival in August, Global Carnival September.

Bellingen
Self-contained Accommodation
Address: 1673 Waterfall Way,
Bellingen, NSW 2454
Name: Fernridge Farm Cottage
Telephone: (02) 6655 2142
Fax: (02) 6655 2142
Beds: 1 Queen, 1 Double,
2 Single (2 bedrooms)
Bathroom: 1 Private
Tariff: Double $90, Single $90,
Extra person & children age 3+ $10. Complimentary breakfast basket on arrival.
Nearest Town: 4.5 kms West of Bellingen

Fernridge is a secluded country cottage with sweeping views of the magnificent Bellinger Valley and surrounding mountains. The recently renovated 2 bedroom cottage sleeps 6, and is furnished to provide every home comfort. It has a fully equipped kitchen, a fire for cooler nights and fans for hot ones. There is a TV, VCR, and enough reading matter to keep you relaxing on the sunny verandahs for days!
Only 5 minutes from the township of Bellingen with its arts and crafts and friendly people, Fernridge offers a true rural experience, with alpacas, deer and a variety of wildlife sharing our 120 acres. There are seven national parks, pristine rivers with shady swimming holes, and miles of unspoilt sandy beaches all within a short drive of the cottage.
Come and stay at Fernridge, and you'll understand why so many of our guests return time and time again.

NEW SOUTH WALES

Ben Lomond see Glen Innes
Berambing see Blue Mountains
Berrima see Southern Highlands

Berry
Berry Country Home B&B
Address: 'Tanglewood',
246A Tindalls Lane, Berry, NSW 2535
Name: Sheila & Ray Gall
Telephone: (02) 4464 1826
Fax: (02) 4464 1826 **Mobile**: 041 7208 237
Beds: 1 Double, 2 Single (2 bedrooms)
Bathroom: 1 Guests share
Tariff: B&B (full) Double $90, Single $50.
Dinner (3 course) $25pp. Vouchers accepted
Nearest Town: Berry approximately 6 km

Our country house is built on a hillside near the head of a quiet dairy farming valley in several acres of trees, and we are about six kilometres from the small town of Berry - the "town of trees". Surf and swimming beaches are a few minutes away by car and there are many walks and drives in the areas nearby. Berry has antique shops, craft galleries and restaurants and Kangaroo Valley is "just over the hill".
Your hosts, Sheila and Ray, have travelled in Australia and overseas, using B&B's wherever possible and both have many interests, especially in the practical arts and textiles. You can be met in Berry from bus or train and dinner can be provided by arrangement. We look forward to meeting you at some time in the future.
We do not take pets and we thank you for not smoking indoors.

Berry
Guest House Bed and Breakfast   NRMA ★★★★
Address: "Mananga Homestead B&B"
A 40 Princes Highway, Berry, NSW 2535
Name: Ruth and Steve Logan
Telephone: (02) 4464 1477
Fax: (02) 4464 1477
Mobile: (015) 916 329
Beds: 4 Queen, 1 Double,
1 Single (4 bedrooms)
Bathroom: 4 Ensuite
Tariff: B&B (full), Double $110-$180, Single $90-$135. Credit cards accepted.
Nearest Town: Berry 1/2 km

Mananga is a country classic - a cream coloured weatherboard house, perfectly proportioned and wrapped in verandahs with a complex corrugated iron roof, and a wealth of marvellous details in its joinery (c. 1894). The four guest bedrooms are furnished in an opulent period style. All guest bedrooms have en-suites. Two have restored cast-iron baths and fire places in the bedrooms of two. The guest sitting has an open fire place which leads to the sunny conservative breakfast room. Two hours from Sydney, Mananga is centrally situated, North is Minnamurra Rainforest, West is Kangaroo Valley and Fitzroy Falls. South is Jervis Bay National Park. A five minute drive East takes you to 7 Mile Beach. Beautiful gardens surround Mananga which invites you to just relax on the verandah and watch the cattle graze in the paddocks. Tea making facilities are available. Smokers welcome to use verandahs. We look forward to welcoming you.

NEW SOUTH WALES

Berry - Kangaroo Valley
Homestay
Address: The Yurt at Lothlorien 912a,
Kangaroo Valley Road, Bellawongarah, NSW 2535
Name: Shirley Fenton-Huie
Telephone: (02) 4464 1519 **Fax**: (02) 4464 1023
Beds: Yurt - 1 Double, Homestead - 3 Doubles
Bathroom: Yurt - 1, Homestead - 2
Tariff: B&B (full), Yurt - $125-$140 Double,
Homestead $125-$140 Double. Discount applies midweek.
Nearest Town: Equidistant Berry and Kangaroo Valley

What is a yurt?
A yurt is a round, twelve sided structure, based on the dwellings of wandering Mongolian cattle herders.
The yurt at Lothlorien, unlike its Mongolian counterpart, is made of western red cedar. It is equipped with an ensuite, television, VCR, refrigerator and microwave oven. It is private and secluded - the ideal place to forget about problems and stresses for a while.
The yurt's unique design provides a soothing environment for relaxation. A night in the yurt will leave you invigorated and refreshed.
Massage and aroma therapy available on request.
Lothlorien is an architect designed solar homestead, warm in winter, cool in summer. It is located just 10 minutes from the boutique townships of Berry and Kangaroo valley, and is only 15 minutes from Seven Mile Beach.

Berry - Kangaroo Valley
Bed & Breakfast
Address: 5 Tourist Rd, Beaumont 2577
(via Berry or Kangaroo Valley)
Name: Woorail Country Accommodation
Telephone: (02) 4464 1049 **Fax**: (02) 4464 2654
Beds: 4 Queen, 1 Twin (5 bedrooms)
Bathroom: 3 Ensuite, 1 Private
Tariff: B&B (full) Double $140, Single $70,
Dinner $30, Credit Cards.
Nearest Town: Berry 15km / Kangaroo Valley 10km

*"Woorail" has given "**B**&**B**" a few extra meanings.*
***B**irds & **B**eautiful views. Lyrebirds, rosellas, king parrots, kookaburras, bower birds and others are regular visitors to our feeding station. Uninterrupted views across Kangaroo Valley to Barrengarry Mountain demand your attention as you relax in the acres of garden and bush that are "Woorail".*
***B**erry & **B**ushwalks. Visit Berry, Kangaroo Valley, Fitzroy Falls, Jervis Bay and other nearby attractions.*
Bushwalks to suit all interests are within easy reach.
***B**illiards and **B**ackgammon. Spend time in our games or lounge room with a variety of indoor activities.*
***B**eef and **B**urgundy. Partake of a delicious home style dinner.*
Accompanied by the best wine you care to bring with you. In the morning enjoy an al fresco breakfast, with a view.
***B**urning log fire and **B**ed. Relax in front of the cosy fire and .... "sweet dreams".*

NEW SOUTH WALES

Berry - Shoalhaven
Country Home B&B   NRMA ★★★★☆
Address: "Abbeywood-in-the-Fields", 25 Hillandale Rd, Broughton Vale via Berry, NSW 2535
Name: Roy & Ona Frazier
Telephone: (02) 4464 2148
Beds: 1 Queen, 1 Queen length Double, 3 Single (3 bedrooms)
Bathroom: 2 Ensuite
Tariff: B&B (full) Double $95-$110, Single $65-$70, Children negotiable.
  Vouchers accepted Mon-Thurs only with $15 surcharge
Nearest Town: Berry

In the heart of Arcadian Broughton Vale, nestles "Abbeywood in the Fields", surrounded by rich, productive, picture-book farming land. The country house is surrounded by an 'amphitheatre' formed by the spectacular Barren Grounds escarpment. Seven acres of garden play foreground to the 'borrowed scenery'. Rainforest species have been used as counterpoint to the more formal treatment closer to the house, the focus of which is a Georgian fountain, surrounded by 'boxed' roses and cottage gardens. Climbing roses form a charming tracery around the large verandahs.
A full country cooked breakfast, including fresh muffins, can be enjoyed while viewing the tranquillity of the garden through a conservatory window adorned with jasmine. Cosy log fires, soirees in the music room and garden promenades seem a natural accompaniment to life at 'Abbeywood'. 'Abbeywood' was featured on 'Getaway' in October 1996. On request from the team, Ona was persuaded to sing from her operatic repertoire with Roy accompanying on the 'Grand'. A welcoming afternoon tea with fresh home-baked cakes and slice is offered to our guests.
Historic Berry town, with its inviting antique and craft shops is only 5 minutes away.

Ask your hosts for tourist information.
They are your own personal travel agent and guide.

Berry
Country House
Address: Please phone
Name: Amelia's Country House
Telephone: (02) 4464 2534
Fax: (02) 4464 2534
Beds: 3 Queen, 1 Twin (3 bedrooms)
Bathroom: 3 Ensuite
Tariff: B&B (special) Double $150, Single $100/$150, Dinner from $25pp, Credit Cards (BC/MC/VISA).
Nearest Town: 7km drive north of the township of Berry

Set on four acres atop of Woodhill Mountain, Amelia's is an elegant house with crisp white walls and soaring ceilings resplendent of the Australian Federation period. Each of the guest rooms are individual but the 'Blue Room' tends to receive all the 'oohs and aahs', with its big wrought iron bed and French doors that open onto the verandah. Of course a stay at Amelia's would not be complete without savouring the delights of professional chef, Karen Avery. Breakfast is an event with dishes like Leek & Bacon Tarts or Eggs Florentine. Dinner midweek is a set two courses and $25pp. Whereas dinner on Saturday is $45pp for five courses. Dinner is only available by booking prior to arrival.
The native wildlife and bushwalks are a highlight here also.
Amelia's offers tranquillity and fresh mountain air just ten minutes (7k) from Berry. Bookings are essential, please contact Karen.

Berry
Homestay
Address: 146 Kangaroo Valley Road, Berry, NSW 2535
Name: Christopher's Our Place in Berry
Telephone: (02) 4464 2771 **Fax**: (02) 4464 2771 **Mobile**: (0412) 342771
Beds: 3 King/Queen, 2 Single (3 bedrooms)
Bathroom: 1 Ensuite, 2 Private
Tariff: B&B (full) Double $110-$140, Single $90-$120, Dinner by arrangement $25pp, Credit Cards.
Nearest Town: Berry

We have created a Relaxing Hideaway called CHRISTOPHER'S, Our place in Berry, situated just minutes from the township.
Surrounded by grazing land, mountains and creeks but still only a brisk walk to the shops.
Berry has wonderful restaurants, cafes, antiques and craft shops and, of course, all the Olde Worlde charm of this lovely area.
We will greet you on your arrival with refreshments of your choice, we can do dinner for you by arrangement and breakfast is a country feast.
Our beds are wonderfully comfortable with all guest rooms having private bathrooms and French doors onto patio or verandahs. Guests can enjoy the solar heated pool.
If you feel you need to unwind and relax, then CHRISTOPHER'S is the place where you'll be made most welcome.
Come and see us soon.
If you don't care to drive, Berry also has a train station where we can arrange to meet you.

Berry
Bed and Breakfast
Address: 24 Prince Alfred Street, Berry, NSW 2535
Name: Clunes of Berry
Telephone: (02) 4464 2272
Beds: 4 Double, 2 single (4 bedrooms with private facilities)
Bathroom: 5 Ensuites
Tariff: B&B (continental/country) Double Ensuite $120-$180 per night and $280 per two night weekend.
Nearest Town: Berry, 2 hours south of Sydney

Clunes (from a Gaelic word meaning "a pleasant place" of Berry, a new two-storey cedar cottage which was opened in October, 1991, combines the spirit and traditions of the town with the comforts of today in four bedrooms, each with its own private facilities.

Country-continental breakfast can be taken at the cottage table or on the verandah overlooking the water meadow which is home to ibis, egrets, hawks, yellow cockatoos and swallows.

In the heart of Berry village, with its antique shops, good restaurants and old buildings, Clunes of Berry will be a stepping-off point to explore the beautiful coastline with its sandy beaches, or go walking in the mountains and rain forests with exotic bird life.

The cottage is built on an historic road in Berry on a site previously occupied by the town cattle sale yards, where sales were held monthly.

In earlier years the water meadow was a Chinese market garden. The water meadow was owned by Nobby Jorgensen, who kept his team of eight bullocks, one of which was also called Nobby, on the land. The bullock team was used to bring the hardwood logs from the surrounding mountains to Blows sawmill, four doors along Price Alfred Street. The milled timber was used in many old Berry homes.

NEW SOUTH WALES

Berry
Self-contained Accom. + B&B
Address: 91 Wattamolla Road, Woodhill, Berry, NSW 2535 Postal: PO Box 81, Berry, NSW 2535
Name: "Sundance Park" Perrie Croshaw
Telephone: (02) 4464 2008 **Fax**: (02) 4464 2008
Email: sundance@shoal.net.au
Beds: 2 Queen, 2 Single (3 bedrooms)
Bathroom: 2 Private
Tariff: B&B (full) Double $185, Single $90, Studio $195 per couple, Dinner by arrangement, Credit Cards. Rates apply until September 1998.
Nearest Town: Berry

Take a stress-free break at Sundance Park, nestled at the foot of Broughton Head on 35 acres of lush bushland, less than two hours from Sydney. This modern architect-designed home has sweeping views across to Budderoo National Park, Barren Grounds Nature Reserve and Bird Sanctuary, and the spectacular bluff of the Drawing Room Rocks.
Stay in the self-contained studio for 2, set in a private native planting. A wooden deck surrounds the entrance where sliding glass doors lead to the living area. Upstairs, take in the views while lying in bed. Or choose the double or twin rooms with their private sitting room, solid fuel stove, collection of books and paintings; and pool terrace.
Breakfast by the saltwater pool with a view that disappears into the breathtaking surrounding mountains. The accommodation attracted a five star rating from the Sydney Morning Herald.

Private bathroom is for your use exclusively,
Guests share means you may be sharing with other guests,
Family share means you will be sharing with the family.

NEW SOUTH WALES

Berry - Coolangatta
Homestay+Self-contained Cottage
Address: 1180 Bolong Road
via Berry, NSW 2535
Name: Schoolmasters House
& School House Cottage
Telephone: (02) 4448 7205
AH. (044) 488349 **Fax**: (02) 4448 8305
Beds: Homestay: 1 Queen, 2 Single
Cottage: 1 Double, 4 Single
Bathroom: Homestay: 1 Guests share with spa Cottage: 3-way bathroom
Tariff: B&B (full) Double $85, Single $60, Children over 12yrs, Dinner $20 pp BYO; Cottage $150 per couple & $15 per person thereafter (accommodates 6), Credit Cards. Vouchers accepted $6 surcharge
Nearest Town: Berry

Set on 2 1/2 acres at the foothills of Coolangatta Mtn, surrounded by rural farms on the flats of Shoalhaven River. Schoolmasters House was originally the Schoolmasters residence est.1861 and has been restored to offer a comfortable stay. On arrival enjoy tea or coffee on the verandah watching the cows graze or stroll over the Gallery to see the latest exhibition, you might want to try your hand on the potters wheel in the potters studio, visit the Craft shop in the Old School Building, or visit the restored 1902 Railcar, now a cafe. The B&B offers a full cooked breakfast in the School Masters House or be self-contained in the cottage.
Other activities are: fishing, historic Berry, Kangaroo Valley or a trip to Arthur Boyd's property. Also visit the Naval Aviation Museum at Albatross Air Base, or beautiful Jervis Bay.

Berry - Kangaroo Valley
Bed & Breakfast   NRMA ★★★★
Address: 521 Illaroo Road,
Cambewarra W, NSW 2540
Name: Illaroo Lodge Bed & Breakfast
Telephone: (02) 4446 0443
Fax: (02) 4446 0443
Mobile: (015) 959286
Beds: 2 Queen, 1 Single (2 bedrooms)
Bathroom: 2 Ensuites
Tariff: B&B (full) Double $90-$120, Single $60-$90, Dinner $25, Credit Cards (MC/VISA/BC).
Nearest Town: Equidistant Berry and Kangaroo Valley, 7km NW of Nowra

Illaroo Lodge is a beautifully appointed country home in a park-like setting. The spacious well-treed grounds are a haven for birdlife, and feature a solar heated salt water pool and attractive landscaped gardens. We are situated in a rural area opposite an award winning boutique winery. Accommodation is 4 star, comfortably and attractively furnished, fully air-conditioned and centrally heated, with all modern comforts. Our aim is to spoil guests with a friendly and welcoming environment, quality home style cuisine and caring and attentive personal service. A full country breakfast is provided and dinner is available by arrangement.
Located on the road to Bundanon, the historic home gifted to the nation by artist Arthur Boyd, Illaroo Lodge is centrally located to many of the South Coast's scenic wonders.
Directions: *Proceeding south out of Berry on the Princes Highway, follow signs to Cambewarra Estate Winery; we are opposite.*

Biddon see Gilgandra
Blackheath see Blue Mountains

Blayney - Central West NSW
Guest House/B&B   NRMA ★★★☆
Address: 40 Adelaide St., Blayney, NSW
Name: "Garthmorh"
Telephone: (02) 6368 3312 **Mobile**: (018) 650 078
Beds: 1 Queen, 2 Single (2 bedrooms)
Bathroom: 1 Guests share
Tariff: B&B (continental) Double $65 to $85, Single $45.
Nearest Town: Blayney

Better service, better business.

Garthmorh, built in 1890, is situated within three-quarters of an acre of English style gardens. Garthmorh was built as a doctor's residence and surgery and the first flying doctor Kenyon St. Vincent Welch practised here in 1927-1928. The large rooms, wide hall, tall, original pressed metal ceilings characterise this historic home.
Guests are welcomed with country style hospitality and home made afternoon tea by the open fire or in the leafy garden. Magazines and games are on hand and supper is served or a nightcap is available in front of the fire. Beds are cosy with electric blankets and fluffy doonas.
Blayney is on the Mid Western Highway less than half an hour from both Bathurst and Orange, and ten minutes from the historic villages of Carcoar and Millthorpe.
Day trips to Abercrombie Caves, Carcoar Dam or the many historic villages in Ben Hall Country will make your visit an enjoyable one.

Blue Mountains - Blackheath
Self-contained Garden Suites
Address: "Allendale Cottage", Blackheath (please phone)
Name: "Allendale Cottage"
Telephone: (02) 4787 8270
Beds: 2 Queen (2 bedrooms)
Bathroom: 2 large Ensuite
Tariff: B&B (continental) Weekends (Two nights, per couple) $375. Special rates apply mid week. Please enquire. No smoking inside please. Credit Cards.
Nearest Town: Blackheath 1km, Katoomba 10km, Sydney is 1 1/2 hours drive.

Allendale is a charming mountain cottage set on nine acres of peaceful and historic gardens.
Nestling in these gardens are two cozy self-contained suites, both feature luxurious bathrooms with two-person sunken spas, where floor to ceiling windows give views over the gardens and the many colourful birds that live in the area. Each main room contains a queen-size bed, sofa, dining area and a fireplace to add to the romantic atmosphere, also, private sundecks where you can enjoy breakfast with magical garden views.
Everything you need is provided, including CD and tape player, bubble bath, champagne glass, great coffee, etc. Our suites are for couples only and offer complete privacy. Every window overlooks a rambling garden of rhododendrons and azaleas in spring, the spectacular colours of autumn, the excitement of snow in winter, summer roses and in the lower garden, a natural spring bubbles up creating a pool and valley of coral ferns.
Home Page: www.pnc.com.au./~allendale

Blue Mountains - Berambing
(between Bilpin & Mount Tomah)
Self-contained Cottages
Address: 36 Berambing Crescent, Berambing, NSW 2758
Name: Chapel Hill Retreat
Telephone: (02) 45672156 **Fax**: (02) 45672081
Mobile: (018) 410535
Beds: 1 King, 2 Queen, 3 Double
Bathroom: 3 Ensuite
Tariff: B&B (continental) Double $130-$160, Single $120, Children under 7yrs No charge, 7-12yrs $25, All Credit Cards.
Nearest Town: Richmond or Lithgow

Commanding magnificent views over the Blue Mountains, Chapel Hill is where 'Nature from Nurture'. This 40 acre mountain sanctuary is just 90 minutes drive from Sydney. Accommodation is cottage style. All cottages have queen sized bedrooms, second small bedroom, ensuite bathrooms, fully equipped kitchen, lounge, dining with log fire and sun patio. TV/video library and CD sound system. Incoming guests can arrange to have provisions laid on for self catering or alternatively room service meals are available. A private Chapel set in 5 acres of garden is available for weddings. The historic property is close to Mount Tomah botanical gardens, Mount Wilson and the Zig Zag railway. A registered psychologist is available for stress assessment and management counselling and therapeutic massage if desired. For the more active there is badminton, table tennis, croquet and bush walking through the Blue Mountains National Park.

One of the differences between staying at a hotel and a B&B is that you don't hug the hotel staff when you leave.

Blue Mountains - Blackheath
Homestay
Address: "Amani Cottage",
31 Days Crescent,
Blackheath, NSW 2785
Name: Rosemary & Bill Chapple
Telephone: (02) 4787 8610
Mobile: (041) 11111 391
Beds: 1 Queen, 2 Single (2 bedrooms)
Bathroom: 2 Ensuite
Tariff: B&B (full) Double $90 ($100 weekend),
Single $60, Children by arrangement.
Vouchers accepted Monday to Thursday only.
Nearest Town: Blackheath 2km

Our home is situated in the upper Blue Mountains, near Govetts Leap, overlooking the Grose Valley and the Blue Mountains National Park. Some of the most spectacular walks in the Blue Mountains begin near our home. Convenient to historic gardens at Mt Wilson. We enjoy meeting people and are happy to share this lovely area and the delightful views from the house. We are a newly retired couple with many and varied interests. These include arts, crafts and vintage cars.
Our guest rooms are upstairs, with one double bedroom and one twin bedroom. Each of these rooms has its own en-suite. The guests share a lounge room with TV, gas fire, fridge, microwave oven and facilities for making tea and coffee. Packed lunches by arrangement.
Blackheath is only 2 hours from Sydney by road or rail and we are happy to meet any guests who travel by train, at the station. Non-smokers preferred.
Directions: *Please phone*

Blue Mountains - Blackheath
Homestay
Address: "Kanangra Lodge Blue Mountains", 9 Belvidere Avenue,
Blackheath, NSW 2785
Name: Brian & Anne Lovegrove
Telephone: (02) 4787 8715 **Fax**: (02) 4787 8715
Beds: 3 King, 1 Queen (4 bedrooms)
Bathroom: 3 Ensuite, 1 Private
Tariff: Midweek - 1 night, Sun-Thurs $55 pp,
Weekend - 2 nights, Fri & Sat $130 pp,
5 nights: Sun-Thurs $225 pp
Credit Cards. Vouchers accepted November to February only.
Nearest Town: Katoomba 10km east - Great Western Highway

Kanangra Lodge is an elegant, spacious and luxuriously appointed bed & breakfast catering for adults only in a peaceful, smoke free atmosphere.
It consists of tastefully decorated bedrooms with private facilities, spacious living areas, central heating, open fires and a full breakfast. Friendly, caring owner / hosts and beautiful gardens are part of the many outstanding features available.
* Met at Blackheath Railway Station upon request
* Minutes drive to golf course and world famous scenery on the Upper Blue Mtns
* Sunny northern aspect
* Minutes from a selection of very good restaurants
* Undercover parking
Directions: *Please Phone.*
Home Page: http://www.lisp.com.au/~hideaway/kanangra/

Blue Mountains - Blackheath
Homestay
Address: "Montrose House",
15 Hat Hill Road, Blackheath, NSW 2785
Name: Ron Gamack
Telephone: (02) 4787 7775
Beds: 2 Queen, (2 bedrooms)
Bathroom: 2 Ensuite
Tariff: B&B (full) Sun-Thurs Double $130, Single $75. Fri & Sat Double $150, Single $75.
Credit Cards.
Nearest Town: Blackheath

"Absolutely first class! The best B&B we have experienced in years of world travel". "Delicious food. Excellent company. We enjoyed every minute. Wish we could stay on". "Stimulating and wonderful stay. Superb hospitality". "A lovely relaxing retreat. Breakfasts are wonderful". ....some recent comments from our Guest book.

A warm highland welcome awaits you at "Montrose House", an elegant, century old Blue Mountains home set in extensive grounds and gardens bordered by stands of pines, oaks and rhododendrons.
Each of our two newly decorated suites has a large, beautifully furnished bedroom with cedar panelled en-suite bathroom, a cosy private sitting room and a walk in dressing-room with refrigerator and facilities for coffee and tea making.
The two suites are fully carpeted, centrally heated and decorated in "country" style. Both apartments have a delightful outlook onto gardens and trees.
There's also a heated communal guest lounge, a large comfortable sun-room with views and a tartan lined dining-room where, for much of the year, our renowned breakfasts are served beside a bright and cheery log fire.
"Montrose House" is just five minutes level stroll from shops, train station and good restaurants. Golf, horse-riding and bush walks are all easily accessible by car.
Our gardens and grounds are home to many brilliantly coloured parrots and other native birds. In Spring our visitors delight in spectacular displays of daffodils, tulips and giant rhododendrons.
Let us treat you to the very best of old fashioned country mountain hospitality. We look forward to looking after you.
Directions: Please phone.

NEW SOUTH WALES

Blue Mountains - Blackheath
Self-contained Heritage Accommodation
Address: Stokes House,
39 Inconstant Street,
Blackheath, 2785
Name: Terry & Virginia Land
Telephone: (02) 4787 8289
Beds: 1 Double (1 bedroom)
Bathroom: 1 Private
Tariff: B&B (full) Double $120.
Nearest Town: Blackheath 1km, Katoomba 10km.

Stokes House is a large mountains style house, built at the turn of the century. An acre of English garden was planted at that time and is now a secluded area, populated with abundant birdlife.
The completely private guests suite, which is centrally heated, has its own entrance, spacious sitting room with open fire, TV, CD player, fridge, microwave and tea & coffee making facilities.
The sunny double bedroom has french doors which open onto your own verandah which overlooks the garden.
A country-style breakfast is served in the sitting room or on the verandah.
Stokes House adjoins the Blue Mountains National Park and the famous Blackheath Rhododendron Gardens and is close to a Golf Course, restaurants and all major attractions.
Directions: *Please phone.*

Blue Mountains - Clarence
Country Homestay   NRMA ★★★☆
Address: "Clarence House", Clarence 2790
Name: Erica & Ian de Beuzeville
Telephone: (02) 6355 2643
Fax: (02) 6355 2843
Beds: 3 Double (3 bedrooms)
Bathroom: 1 Ensuite,
1 Guests share
Tariff: B&B Double $90-$110,
Single $60, Dinner $25 pp. Vouchers accepted (not in weekends)
Nearest Town: 10 km east of Lithgow on Bells Line of Road.

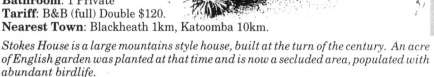

"Clarence House" is a beautiful old country home (c.1880) in a secluded rural setting. We have authentically restored the house and furnished it with our own vast collection of Australiana. Guests enjoy a separate bedroom suite, their own parlour with open fire, and a breakfast room. Dinner is served in the magnificent period dining room. Kangaroos often graze on the lawns, and there is abundant birdlife on the property. We enjoy sharing the history of the house and the area with our guests. We are very close to Zig Zag Railway which offers steam train rides on weekends and school holidays. The gardens at Mt Wilson and Mt Tomah are nearby. Katoomba is a 30 minutes drive. No smoking inside.
Members of the National Trust and Blue Mountains Hideaway Group Inc.

Tell other travellers about your favourite B&Bs

NEW SOUTH WALES

Blue Mountains - Faulconbridge
Heritage Homestay   NRMA ★★★★
Address: 113 Chapman Parade,
Faulconbridge 2776
Name: Annette & Danny Wotherspoon
Telephone: (02) 4751 4273
Beds: 3 Queen, 1 Double, 3 Single (4 bedrooms)
Bathroom: 2 Guests share (also available as private bathrooms). Plumbed vanities in some rooms.
Tariff: B&B (full) Double $130-$160, Single $110-$140. No Pets. Weekend two night minimum. Honeymoon suite available with private bathroom. Vouchers accepted $40 surcharge, midweek, same day restriction.
Nearest Town: Faulconbridge 2km

Part of the original Norman Lindsay estate, our enchanting two storey sandstone cottage is set in wildflower gardens, where you can relax, romance, explore, and have fun. Learning from our travels, we have created a uniquely Australian B&B, luxuriously furnished in a wildflower theme. Enjoy conversation and warm hospitality in our large lounge room around the fire and pianola. Soak in our deep antique claw-foot bath! Help yourself to quality Australian tea and coffee, and fresh home-made biscuits any time. Generous hot breakfasts are served in our sunny dining room or on the garden terrace. Gourmet picnic baskets and special diets by arrangement. Share the romance of the "Sirens" swings in the Terrace Garden. Enjoy local galleries, cycling and bushwalking. Danny is a professional naturalist and guide, providing expert local knowledge. Finalist 1994 / 1995 NSW Tourism Awards. Blue Mountains Hideaways Group Member. No smoking inside; our home is not suitable for children.
Directions: *From Faulconbridge village, follow the signs to Norman Lindsay Gallery. We will collect from Springwood railway station and Richmond RAAF base.*

Blue Mountains - Katoomba
Guest House/Bed & Breakfast   NRMA ★★★★
Address: The McClintock,
15 Abbotsford Rd., Katoomba, NSW
Name: Arthur & Margot Teal
Telephone: (047) 824 240
Fax: (047) 824 858
Beds: 4 Queen/Twin (4 bedrooms)
Bathroom: 4 Ensuite
Tariff: B&B (full) Double $170-$200, Single $85-$100, Dinner by request, Credit Cards (VISA/BC/MC).
Nearest Town: Katoomba

Welcome to the McClintock. Built for the Mayor of the area in the early 1900's, this beautiful house is in a quiet garden setting. Retaining all the original architectural features such as Tasmanian oak panelling and fine stained glass windows, the house provides such comforts as ensuite bathrooms, central heating and open fires.
As your hosts we are well travelled with wide interests from antiques, art and animals to the appreciation of memorable fine food and wine. We enjoy our guests and take pride that we are not just a bed for the night, but a total experience in comfort and good hospitality. The area we live in is of special note as the Blue Mountains offer scenic beauty that is awesome. With plenty to do from bush walking, scenic railways, waterfalls and spectacular lime stone caves to excellent speciality shopping, you will wish your stay was longer. We suggest two nights. Less than two hours from Sydney, drive or complimentary pick up from the train. Write or phone for our brochure.

NEW SOUTH WALES

Blue Mountains - Kurrajong Heights
Self-contained Holiday Cabins
Address: "Madisons Mountain Retreat", 1880 Bells Line of Rd., Kurrajong Heights, NSW 2758
Name: Kath Lockrey
Telephone: (02) 4567 7398 **Fax**: (02) 4567 7862 **Mobile**: (018) 404 643
Beds: 8 holiday cabins - 5 with 1 x King (which can be turned into 2x3ft beds), 3 x Queen, plus double sofa bed and fold out 3/4 bed.
Bathroom: Each 1 bedroom cottage has a private bathroom and three have spas.
Tariff: B&B (Breakfast: ingredients supplied for full or continental breakfast) Double $140-$160, Single $70-$80, Children $20-$30, Credit Cards (Visa/MC/BC).
Nearest Town: North Richmond 18.8km

This peaceful bushland retreat is set on 83 acres with magnificent scenery and bushwalks. We have eight luxury self-contained cabins, each spacious cabin can accommodate up to five people.
Each cabin contains log fire, microwave oven, stove top, fridge and TV to make your stay enjoyable and memorable.
We have three cabins with private spa and one with wheelchair access.
Children are also most welcome.
Other facilities include an 18 metre heated indoor swimming pool, spa, tennis court, gymnasium, BBQ area.
Breakfast is supplied and there are shop facilities.
Relaxing Aromatherapy and Therapeutic Massages are also available.
Hairdresser available by appointment.
You can also visit the sights around Kurrajong Heights, Bilpin, Mt Tomah Botanic Gardens and Mt Wilson with its beautiful gardens, all surrounded by magnificent National Parks. Grass skiing. Visit The Zig Zag Railway or go fishing at the Rainbow Trout Farm near Lithgow.
For further information and bookings please contact Kath or Ken.
PH: (02) 4567 7398 or 018 404 643.

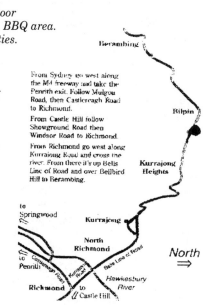

There are some good tips for easier travel on page 7

NEW SOUTH WALES

Blue Mountains - Lawson
Quality Homestay
Address: Araluen Lawson,
59 Wilson Street, Lawson
Name: Gai and George Sprague
Telephone: (02) 4759 1610
Mobile: 0416 220 178
Fax: (02) 4759 2554
Beds: 3 Queen (3 bedrooms)
Bathroom: 3 Ensuites
Tariff: B&B (full) Double $100-$130,
Single $60-$75, Dinner by request, Children by arrangement. Credit Cards accepted. Vouchers accepted
Nearest Town: 1km from Lawson railway station

Overlooking the picturesque fairways of the Central Blue Mountains golf club, Araluen is just 100 metres from the first tee. Greens fees are complimentary to Araluen's guests.
Set in an acre of cottage gardens and native shrubs, this quality home boasts a large sunny living room with an open fire, plus separate reading, games and dining rooms with spacious verandahs.
Ducted heating and cooling including bedrooms. Extensive breakfast selection with home baked breads. Easy bushwalks to five nearby waterfalls - a delight for picnics. Longer and more strenuous walks into valley.
On the Great Western Highway and 730 metres above sea level, Lawson is the site of the original Blue Mountain railway station. Guests travelling by train can be met by your hosts.

Some homes share the bathroom, others have bathrooms
exclusively for guests
– they are indicated in the listing.

Blue Mountains - Leura

Bed & Breakfast
NRMA ★★★★☆
Address: 9 Balmoral Rd., Leura, 2780 NSW
Name: Eastwicke Luxury Bed & Breakfast
Telephone: (02) 4784 1659
Fax: (02) 4784 2962
Mobile: 041 206 5140
Beds: 1 Queen Self-cont. Suite (1 bedroom)
Bathroom: 1 Private
Tariff: B&B (special) Double $150 weekends per night, $120 mid-week per night. Do it yourself special breakfast.
Nearest Town: Walking distance to Leura Village

Here at Eastwicke we offer our guests an exclusive hideaway catering for just one couple in romantic old world surroundings, offering a luxury self-contained suite within our home consisting of a bedroom complete with antique bed and furnishings, sitting room with TV, books and magazines, kitchenette and bathroom. Camembert and chocolates are included on arrival along with fluffy robes and crisp cotton sheets plus all the ingredients for a delicious breakfast are provided by us in the kitchenette so you can rise at your leisure and eat when you feel like it. The suite has its own private entrance so you can come and go as you please.
Our large private garden is surrounded by magnificent mountain pines, and we encourage our guests to enjoy this unique setting.

Blue Mountains - Leura

Bed & Breakfast   NRMA ★★★☆
Address: 1 Tennyson Ave., Leura, 2780 - Please phone first.
Name: Tennyson Bed & Breakfast
Telephone: (02) 4784 1661
Mobile: (019) 663628
Beds: 1 Queen self cont suite (1 bedroom)
Bathroom: 1 Private
Tariff: B&B (continental) Double $130-$145, Single $80-$100, Weekdays Double $115-$125, Do it yourself special breakfast. Non Smoking. Children not catered for. Non Smoking
Nearest Town: Walking distance to Leura Village.

Think of the mountains and images of charming little weatherboard cottages inevitably come to mind. Few fit more comfortably into this genre than Tennyson Cottage. Half the cottage has been given over to guest accommodation. As only one couple can be accommodated this is a retreat designed for total privacy. A private garden entrance leads to a small sitting room where tea, coffee, television and lots of small surprises are to be found. Provisions for a substantial breakfast (cereals, eggs, toast, jam, fruit, yoghurt, juice)
The bedroom is very large and with its polished floors, carefully co-ordinated soft furnishings in shades of pinks and blues is a very romantic space. The suite has its own private bathroom. Situated in the heart of South Leura, Tennyson Cottage is just a short walk to Leura's interesting main street, the Mall and ideally situated for investigating all the surrounding Blue Mountains attractions.
Home Page: http://www.lisp.com.au/hideaway

Blue Mountains - Leura
Guest House
Address: "Broomelea", 273 Leura Mall, Leura, 2780 NSW
Name: Carolyn Reid
Telephone: (02) 4784 2940 **Fax**: (02) 4784 2940
Beds: 4 King/Queen, 1 Double, 2 Single (5 bedrooms)
Bathroom: 3 Ensuite, 2 Private
Tariff: B&B (full) Double $160, Single $120, Credit Cards.
Nearest Town: Leura - 500m north.

A federation home in the grand old style hidden away at the southern end of the Mall and only a short stroll to the restaurants, boutiques and galleries of Leura Village. Elegant rooms, four poster beds, log fires and sun drenched courtyard, evoke memories of yesteryear, while private facilities, central heating, electric blankets, TV and tea and coffee making create the comfort of today.
Relax in the ambience of the heated spa prior to a leisurely stroll to your favourite restaurant.
Set amid an acre of old world garden complete with cascading pond and abundant bird life Broomelea is a little slice of heaven.

Private bathroom is for your use exclusively,
Guests share means you may be
sharing with other guests,
Family share means you will be
sharing with the family.

NEW SOUTH WALES

Blue Mountains - Leura
Bed & Breakfast   NRMA ★★★★
Address: "Woodford of Leura",
48 Woodford Street, Leura, NSW 2780
Name: John & Lesley Kendall
Telephone: (02) 4784 2240
Fax: (02) 4784 2240
Mobile: (015) 410625
Beds: 1 King, 1 Queen, 2 Double,
1 Single (4 bedrooms)
Bathroom: 2 Ensuite, 2 Private
Tariff: B&B (full) Weekend rates: Double $120,
Suites $130/$140; Weekday rates: Double $110,
Suites $120, Extra discounts for multiple day stays, Children by arrangement,
Dinner by arrangement, Credit Cards.
Vouchers accepted Weekdays only - surcharge suites $38, Doubles $29.
Nearest Town: Leura 3/4km, Katoomba 2 1/2km

Fringed by towering pines and set amidst tranquil Sorensen Gardens, this grand old home is just a comfortable stroll from the historic Leura Village. Offering both suites and double rooms, with ensuite or private bathroom, they are complete with TV, electric blankets and tea making facilities.
Promising "country hospitality in an intimate atmosphere" Woodford is famous for its sumptuous breakfasts and traditional 'High-Teas'. It also features central heating, an indoor heated spa, a cosy guest lounge with an open log-fire and there is also a croquet lawn in the spacious grounds. NB. This is a non-smoking house and children by arrangement.   Hosts: John & Lesley Kendall

Blue Mountains - Medlow Bath
Self-contained Accommodation   NRMA ★★★
Address: Medlow Bath
Name: Medlow Cottage"
Telephone: (02) 9546 4719 **Mobile**: (015) 438 608
Beds: 2 Double, 2 Single (3 bedrooms)
Bathroom: 1 Private, 1 Family share
Tariff: B&B (full) Double $130-$140.

Nearest Town: Katoomba 5km E, Blackheath 5km W.

Medlow Bath has a lovely village atmosphere, quiet and peaceful, yet only minutes away from tourist attractions, including restaurants, bushwalking, golf, tennis, scenic drives.
A warm friendly welcome awaits you at our cottage. Set in park-like gardens it is fully self-contained. Features include glowing log fire (gas), electric blankets, feather doonas, TV, video, fresh flowers, separate internal toilet, bath & shower, automatic washing machine, off street parking. Outside in the tree studded garden is a BBQ, gazebo, table and chairs. Generous breakfast provisions are provided and is self-serve. B&B minimum stay 2 nights weekends. Cottage rental is available for longer stay. Tariff per person per night is $35-$50. Weekly $400-$600. Our cottage is ideal for a group of up to 6 friends. Phone bookings essential.
Sorry No Pets - No Smoking in cottage.

NEW SOUTH WALES

Blue Mountains
- Medlow Bath (near Katoomba)
Self-contained Accommodation
Address: "The Garden Cottage",
20 Great Western Highway,
Medlow Bath, NSW 2780
Name: Jenny & Shane Porteous
Telephone: (02) 4788 1075
Fax: (02) 4788 1095 **Mobile**: (041) 997 9794
Beds: 1 Queen, 2 Single (2 bedrooms, plus 2 singles in lounge)
Bathroom: 1 Guests share (plus extra toilet)
Tariff: B&B (special/self-catering) House is let as unit - $300 per weekend, Minimum stay 2 nights, Weekly tariff $500. Vouchers accepted $65/night surcharge on one couple, No surcharge on two couples or family.
Nearest Town: Medlow Bath - Sydney 80 mins by car, 2 hours by train.

Surrounded by tall pines and eucalypts, this brick cottage is set on an acre of land behind our own house and garden. Every thing you expect to find in your own home is provided - cooking equipment, linen, e/blankets, TV, books, games; combustion stove in the lounge room, fuel stove in the kitchen (yes, there is an electric stove, microwave, even a barbecue!). The fridge and pantry are stocked with basics, including full self-catering breakfast - fruit, cereal, bacon, eggs etc.
The house is fenced for your privacy and the safety of your children and dogs, and is wheelchair-friendly. The perfect base for exploring the Mountains - croquet or badminton on the lawn, lovely garden, close to bushwalks and spectacular views. Then curl up in front of the fire with home-made cake and a good book.
Directions: *Please phone or write.*

Blue Mountains - Shipley Plateau
Self-contained Accommodation
Address: "Woodbury", Shipley Road,
Shipley Plateau, NSW 2785
Name: Lisa & Guy
Telephone: (02) 4787 7035
Beds: 2 Double, 1 Single (2 bedrooms)
Bathroom: 1 Private
Tariff: Double $100. Weekly and mid week special rates available.
Nearest Town: Blackheath 4km north, Katoomba 10km east.

A warm country welcome awaits you at "Woodbury", a seven acre property situated on Shipley Plateau.
Enjoy the views to Mount Blackheath from your lounge room or take a short drive down the road to Hargraves Lookout or Mount Blackheath Lookout to admire their spectacular views.
You can take a bush walk right from your door or enjoy a stroll through the gardens where the native birds feed daily. Collect the eggs from the chooks each morning and while you are there, the horses always enjoy an apple or a carrot or two. Better still, just relax, take it easy and enjoy the mountain air.
If escaping the stress of city life, "Woodbury's" modern fully self contained private accommodation features all the comforts you could wish for, including a wood fire, private garden and BBQ area, to assure a peaceful and relaxing stay.
The private accommodation and garden both have wheelchair access.
Directions: *Please phone.*

NEW SOUTH WALES

Blue Mountains - Wentworth Falls
Self-contained Accommodation
Address: Monique Manners,
31 Falls Rd, Wentworth Falls, 2782
Name: Monique's B&B
Telephone: (02) 4757 1646
Fax: (02) 4757 2498
Beds: 1 Queen, 1 Double, 2 Single (3 bedrooms)
Bathroom: 3 Ensuite
Tariff: B&B (full) Per person, per night:
Sunday-Thursday $50, Friday & Saturday $55 to $65,
Children by arrangement. Prices include, at your leisure,
full self-catered breakfast. Credit cards (MC/BC/VISA).
Nearest Town: Wentworth Falls. Katoomba 10km.

* Comfortable 1930's house in charming well established gardens
* Walking distance to village shops, railway station and post office
* Opposite tennis courts, recreation park, bowling club and Charles Darwin Walk * Close to other famous mountain bush walks and "The Falls"
* 3 double rooms with private facilities * Ideal for group of friends, families or small workshops * Cheerful French hospitality * Sunny terrace * Barbecue area * Fully equipped kitchen * Comfortable lounge with enclosed log fire for those colder evenings * Electric blankets * Laundry facilities * Excellent restaurants nearby
*"In house" dinners can also be arranged.
Please note that no smoking is permitted in the house.

Blue Mountains - Wentworth Falls
Country House   NRMA ★★★★
Address: "Whispering Pines",
178-186 Falls Rd.,
Wentworth Falls, NSW 2782
Name: Bill & Maria McCabe
Telephone: (02) 4757 1449
Fax: (02) 4757 1219 **Mobile**: (015) 492534
Email: MCCABE@zeta.org.au

Beds: 3 Queen, 1 Double (4 bedrooms), 1 Self contained studio
Bathroom: 3 Ensuite, 1 Private
Tariff: B&B Double $100-$200, Single $100-$200, Credit Cards (MC/BC/VISA).
Nearest Town: Wentworth Falls 2km, Katoomba 8km west

"Whispering Pines" (c.1898) is a heritage-listed retreat on 4 acres at the head of the most spectacular waterfall in the beautiful Blue Mountains. Our home is perched right on the escarpment and we border the National Park with over 600,000 acres of unspoilt wilderness on our doorstep for you to explore. Birds are abundant - rosellas, king parrots, gang-gangs, and on a quiet night (when the pines aren't whispering) you can hear the falls tumbling into the valley. Our bedrooms are warm and spacious with feather doonas, electric blankets and luxury appointments. They have views down the peaceful Jamison Valley to Mt Solitary and the valleys beyond - a wondrous outlook especially at sunset. Our guests have use of a large lounge with open fire, sunny breakfast room (tea & coffee available at all times) and barbecue facilities. We also have a self-contained accommodation available with all necessities supplied for couples and groups.
Directions: *Please phone first - Complimentary pick up from station available.*
Home Page: www.travelaustralia.com.au/5154191

NEW SOUTH WALES

Blue Mountains - Wentworth Falls
Bed & Breakfast
Address: 30 Bellevue Road,
Wentworth Falls
Name: Blue Mountains "Lakeside Lodge"
Telephone: (02) 4757 3777
Mobile: 0412 77 88 00
Beds: 1 King, 1 Queen, 1 Twin (3 bedrooms)
Bathroom: 2 Ensuite, 1 Private
Tariff: B&B (full) Double from $100,
Single from $75, Dinner $35pp
(prior arrangement essential),
Credit Cards.
Nearest Town: Wentworth Falls approx. 1 km

"Lakeside Lodge" this unique sandstone and cedar lodge style home combines the magic of the mountains plus exclusive lake front location. Minutes to famous mountain attractions such as the spectacular "Valley of the Waters", Wentworth Falls, walks, restaurants and golf course.
There is trout fishing, boating and fascinating birdlife on the lake.
You may care to pamper yourself with one of our special in-house therapeutic Swedish massages or simply luxuriate lakeside.
Open log fires and all the comforts of home. (We are a non-smoking house.) Please phone first. Credit cards.
"THE STAY TO STAY WITH YOU FOREVER"

Blue Mountains - Woodford
Homestay
Address: 97 Bedford Road,
Woodford, NSW 2778
Name: "Braeside" Bed & Breakfast
Telephone: (02) 4758 6279
Fax: (02) 4758 6279
Mobile: (041) 1147486
Beds: 2 King/Queen, 1 Double (3 bedrooms)
Bathroom: 1 Ensuite, 1 Guests share
Tariff: B&B (full) $50-$55 per person,
Dinner $20, Credit Cards.
Vouchers accepted midweek
only + $20 surcharge.
Nearest Town: Springwood 10km, Katoomba 18km

Situated in the heart of the Blue Mountains this comfortable home offers a quiet escape from every day life. Ruth and Don enjoy meeting people and are happy to welcome visitors to their home. Two comfortable guest bedrooms are on the first floor with views towards Sydney and quiet bushland and one on the ground floor overlooking the garden. Rooms have heaters and electric blankets and the comfortable lounge has an open log fire for colder evenings. Breakfast may be enjoyed on the verandah in the morning sun, or in the breakfast room overlooking the garden. Woodford is close to bush walks, antique shops, art galleries etc, and is a central base for exploring the Blue Mountains. There are a variety of restaurants within 15 minutes drive. BBQ facilities are available to guests, or an evening meal may be provided on request. No smoking in the house. Please ring for directions.

Bodalla - Potato Point
Guest House
Address:
Warrian-by-Sea
4 Comerang Place,
Potato Point via Bodalla
Name: BJ Eschmann, WJ Gregory
Telephone: (02) 4473 5274 **Fax**: (02) 4473 5274
Beds: 2 Queen (2 Bedrooms)
Bathroom: 1 Private, 1 Family Share
Tariff: B&B (full) Double $190, Single $150, Dinner $45 pp, Children by arrangement.
Nearest Town: Bodalla

Potato Point is a pretty unspoiled beach 22 kms south of Moruya, 14 kms north of Narooma. It is well situated to explore the Eurodalla Shire. Our cliff top home has complete ocean views and views of the distant mountains are quite spectacular. After visiting Warrian-by-Sea you may realise what Utopia could be like. You may stroll and swim the beach at the bottom of our garden, wander through the virgin bush and sight the kangaroos and exotic birdlife or may be just lounge around our beautiful home basking in the ambience of musical and operatic delights piped through the establishment. Enjoy the indoor Turkish bath (steam room), indoor spa or outdoor inground salt pool. The house is exquisitely furnished with original art, antiques and collectables. We can promise you complete privacy and comfort. Absolute discretion of every stay. Breakfast under glass-roofed skies, on the wide balcony overlooking the ocean or by the palm fringed pool.
Your hosts, both professionally Australian and European trained, are in attendance for your every need. Our home is your home and we trust you will dine with us and sample the finest of French-Mediterranean cuisine.

Bolong see Nowra

Bombala - Nimmitabel
Guest House
Address: "Riverglen Lodge",
Glen Allen Road, Nimmitabel, 2631
Name: Karen Cash
Telephone: (064) 585242
Beds: 2 Queen (2 bedrooms)
Bathroom: 2 Ensuite

Tariff: B&B (full) $110 per person. Children welcome, Dinner $20 Credit Cards.
Vouchers accepted $20 Surcharge
Nearest Town: Cooma/Bombala

Private, stylish 40 acre retreat, abutting Tantawangalo National park and fronting Bombala River. Abounds in mature exotic trees, reminiscent of blue Mountains. Caters mainly to "escapism" in and Australiana flavour with fishing, walking, bird watching, swimming and horseriding readily available.
Accommodation varies from fully catered alpine-styled lodge with very comfortable bedrooms, own ensuites, queen size beds, electric blankets and warm and cosy living areas or to the more rustic self-catering period Australiana cottage, complete with corrugated iron. Unique in its accessibility to the rugged grandeur of the South East Forests and water sports of Eden and Tathra plus the colourful monthly markets of Candelo, Pambula, Cooma and Wyndham, and only 2 hours south of Canberra. Further details supplied on enquiry.
Directions: *Please phone.*

NEW SOUTH WALES

Bombala
Farmstay/B&B/Vineyard
Address: "Kangaroo Camp Retreat", Richardson's Road, Bombala, 2632
Name: Roz & Hans Berekoven
Telephone: (02) 6458 4444
Fax: (02) 6458 4444
Mobile: 018625192
Beds: 2 Queen, 2 Twin (3 bedrooms)
Bathroom: 1 Private, 1 Family share
Tariff: Homestead: B&B (special) Double $80, Single $40, Children half price, Dinner $25.
Nearest Town: Bombala 34km, Cooma 68km, One hour south east of Jindabyne, one hour west of Merimbula

This High Country Getaway, boasts wonderful bush land and panoramic views. Ski the mountains in winter or whale watch at Eden in spring. Discover the beauty of our Australian bush or involve yourself on this 2000 acre property. We have Australia's highest altitude vineyard (980m). Merino sheep and a mixed orchard. Wind and solar energy supply this property with its power wood combustion its warmth. Cook or be catered for. Lounge by the log fire or discover Australia's best kept secret Platypus Country! As a finale enjoy a relaxing massage or facial. Kangaroo Camp is beautifully decorated and well equipped with everything you'll need for a relaxing stay. The Wine Makers Cottage sleeps up to six people, has all the country comforts and privacy one expects. A complimentary breakfast basket is supplied for your first morning. Centrally heated, solar powered, gas or wood cooking. All linen supplied. Double $50, Single $25, Children half price.

Boorowa
Homestay/Farmstay
Address: 'Macclefield', Camberfields Lane, Boorowa, NSW 2586
Name: Anne & Frank Liddle
Telephone: (02) 6385 3762
Beds: 2 Double (2 bedrooms)
Bathroom: 1 Guests share, 1 Family share
Tariff: B&B (full) Double $55, Single $25, Children welcome.
Vouchers accepted
Nearest Town: Boorowa

Macclefield is set in spacious lawns and gardens, with a tennis court for relaxing, lovely sloping hills for a brisk walk.
Boorowa is noted for its fine wool merino sheep breeding, is also a cropping area. Boorowa has a nine hole sand golfing green, and 2 bowling greens, we also have an excellent antique restore and manufacturing company, museum and craft shop.
Our guests at Macclefield are assured of a warm welcome and comfortable stay, home cooked breakfasts of fresh eggs and bacon, an evening meal is available by arrangement.
No smoking in the bedrooms please.
Please ring and we will meet you at the gate.
Macclefield is situated 1 1/2 hours Canberra, 3/4 hour Cowra and Cootamundra, 47km Young and 13km Boorowa.

Boorowa - Young
Self-contained Accommodation & Farmstay
Address: "Kerry's Cottage", Burrowa Flats, Galong, 2585
Name: Kerry-Anne & John Flanery
Telephone: (02) 6386 7226 **Fax**: (02) 6386 7216
Beds: 2 Double (2 bedrooms)
Bathroom: 1 Guests share
Tariff: B&B (full) Double $90, Single $55, Dinner $25pp. Vouchers accepted
Nearest Town: Boorowa 12 miles

"Kerry's Cottage" is the perfect getaway for two couples. It is a authentic 1878 slab cottage restored by John and our three sons and comfortably furnished in a warm country style, with a large living room open fire, large relaxing armchairs and pool table. It is totally self sufficient with all modern conveniences in both the bathroom and kitchen. Twinings teas, Lavazza coffee, homemade jams and biscuits as well as cheese, fruit and a bottle of our local wine are supplied for your pleasure, you will delight in the fresh flowers and fluffy bathrobes and towels which co-ordinate with the décore of each room.

A full breakfast hamper is delivered to you daily. We have some very good local restaurants within a 12 minutes drive, or use the gas BBQ and enjoy alfresco dining by the pool after a vigorous game of night tennis.

We are always very happy to show our guests the numerous farming activities whenever possible and the sheep dogs at work are always very popular, we have a number of farm pets, ducks, guinea fowl, an old English sheep dog, a very old pet sheep and more often than not a orphaned joey being reared by us until ready to go back to the wild.

Activities could include long strolls around the property to watch the superb birdlife, rowing on the dam, golf at one of our local courses, croquet, tennis, swimming, or just curl up with that novel you have been wanting to read.

Phone for directions. Brochures available.

Bowral see Southern Highlands

Braidwood
Homestay
Address: 'The Old Rectory',
62 Wilson St, Braidwood, NSW 2622
Name: Mary Harris
Telephone: (02) 4842 2057
Mobile: (0419) 407 417
Beds: 2 Queen, 1 Double (3 bedrooms)
Bathroom: 2 Ensuite, 1 Private
Tariff: B&B (full) Double $100, Single $60. Dinner $20, Credit Cards.
Vouchers accepted
Nearest Town: Braidwood. 80km east of Canberra and 80km west of Batemans Bay.

The Old Rectory is a beautifully restored home, built by the Anglican Church in 1842. The discovery of gold in the 1850's brought wealth and population to Braidwood. Today it is a little town of great character, with fine buildings and excellent cafes and restaurants. Situated on the Kings Highway between Canberra and Batemans Bay, Braidwood has a population of writers, poets, artists, potters, musicians and woodworkers whose works are seen local galleries, craft and antique shops. It is close to the bushwalking Budawang Mts and trout fishing rivers. Golf and tennis clubs welcome visitors. 'The Old Rectory' has an 'Old English' garden where guests find peace, the adjoining nursery specialises in old-fashioned roses. The rooms are furnished with antiques and there's a fine collection of Australian and British contemporary paintings. The guest rooms are centrally heated, one has a log fire. A splendid breakfast is served in your room. Lunch baskets and dinners by arrangement. Non-smokers only.

Braidwood - Southern Tablelands
Homestay
Address: 'Maybrook', Mongarlowe Rd.
via Braidwood, NSW 2622
Name: Claire and Tony Milner
Telephone: (02) 4842 2190
Beds: 1 Double, 2 Single (2 bedrooms)
Bathroom: 1 Guests share
Tariff: B&B (full) Double $75, Single $60.
Nearest Town: Braidwood, which is
90km east of Canberra on Kings Highway. The property is 9k east of Braidwood.

'Maybrook' is a cattle and sheep property situated 9km from historic Braidwood in the Southern Tablelands. The granite house was built in the early 19th century and is set in a large garden including some original outbuildings and trees. The property combines both open grazing land and attractive timberland country, offering rambling walks, shaded creeks and views to the coastal ranges. Braidwood itself offers a delightful range of cafes, restaurants, craft shops and galleries. The nine-hole golf course is a virtually undiscovered pleasure, with its long fairways and beautiful views. The Budawang and Morton National Parks, and the Monga Rainforest, are only a few miles away, as are the old gold mining areas of Mongarlowe, Major's Creek and Araluen. The area is known for its wildlife including kangaroos, wallabies, wombats, platypus, echidnas, lyre birds and many other birds. A walk through the Maybrook property will almost certainly lead to encounters with this wildlife. Braidwood is not only a lively farming district but has also attracted a surprisingly large number of well known artists, poets and novelists. The township virtually untouched since the 19th century, has been used as a film set in the making of a number of Australian films.

Bungendore
Homestay
Address: "Birchfield", 34 Turallo Tce, Bungendore, NSW 2621
Name: Marcia & Brian Voce
Telephone: (02) 6238 1446
Beds: 1 Double, 1 Single (1 1/2 bedrooms)
Bathroom: 1 Ensuite
Tariff: B&B (full) Double $110, Single $80, Children not catered for. Credit Cards.
Nearest Town: Queanbeyan, NSW 25km and Canberra, ACT

Romantic and peaceful attic accommodation in historic "Birchfield". Double attic bedroom, sitting room, bathroom with spa and private entrance. Breakfast is served in the delightful cottage garden in warm weather.

"Birchfield" is a Victorian Gothic-style house built privately in the 1880s by Father Patrick Birch for his retirement and is now the home of "Birchfield Herbs", garden and nursery, specialising in herbs and old-fashioned plants.

"Birchfield" is located in Bungendore, a friendly, historic rural village, on the Kings Highway, just 30 minutes' drive from Canberra. Bungendore (established in 1837) has many attractions, including Bungendore Woodworks, antique shops, museum, etc. There are a number of buildings in Bungendore of historical interest, including churches, court-house, railway station, school, post office, School of Arts, hotels and shops. Within easy driving distance are cool-climate wineries, Lake George and a renovated old mining village.

Bungendore
Bed & Breakfast
Address: "Elmslea Homestead", Tarago Road, Bungendore, NSW 2621
Name: Toni & Miles Flanagan
Telephone: (02) 6238 1651
Fax: (02) 6238 1988 **Mobile**: (015) 489 459
Beds: 2 Queen, 1 Double, 4 Single (5 bedrooms)
Bathroom: 2 Ensuite, 1 Guests share, 1 Family share
Tariff: B&B (full) Double with ensuite $120, Single with ensuite $90, Double $80, Single $60. Dinner by arrangement. Credit Cards. Vouchers accepted
Nearest Town: Queanbeyan/Canberra 20-30 kms

"Elmslea Homestead" was built in 1910 in classic federation style, featuring high decorative ceilings, French marble fireplaces and art nouveau leadlighting. The original dairy, butchery, laundry, kitchen and dining room have all been converted into guest rooms and are decorated in the original theme of each room. The homestead is situated on the edge of Bungendore Village so it is easy walking distance to the pot-pourri of shops and restaurants. The gardens have many spots to sit and relax under the 150 year old elms. Close by you can visit wineries, go horse-riding, take a picnic by the creek or even have a horse drawn carriage ride around the village. We have many special packages - why not try our "Night of Indulgence"? This grand home provides a general base and easy access to Canberra, the South Coast and the Snow. No smoking please. "Elmslea Homestead" was the 1996 & 1997 winner of 'Hosted Accommodation' in the Capital Country Awards for Excellence as well as winning the 'Unique Accommodation' in the A.C.T. Tourism Awards for 1996 and Hosted Accommodation in 1997.

NEW SOUTH WALES

Burrawang see Southern Highlands

Byron Bay
Bed & Breakfast   NRMA ★★★★
Address: "Rosewood House",
16 Kingsley St, Byron Bay, NSW 2481
Name: Claudia & Peter Kiernan
Telephone: (02) 6685 7657
Fax: (02) 6685 7657
Beds: 1 Twin/King, 3 Double (4 bedrooms)
Bathroom: 3 Ensuite, 1 Private
Tariff: B&B (continental) Double $135,
Single $100 Credit Cards.
* Holiday surcharge applies. From 1 April: Double $140, Single $105.
Nearest Town: Byron Bay

One of very few graceful old homes in the area, Rosewood House circa 1899 in the distinctively Victorian style. Located in a quiet side street in town, and an easy five-minute walk to the beach and shops. Its large 30m palms make a distinguishing statement, and add to the old homes tropical aura. A Victorian colour scheme, Antique furnishings, highly polished floors, four metre ceilings, return verandahs and marble fireplace add to the charm. There are 3 double bedrooms and 1 twin/king room, all with colour matched ensuite bathrooms, ceiling fans - French doors onto verandahs, serviced daily. Original brass beds and carefully chosen soft furnishings create a romantic mood. Breakfast can be taken at the lovely dining table, but most guests choose to soak up the early morning sunshine on the verandah. The house is within easy walking distance of several restaurants.
Afternoon tea on arrival, flowers, complimentary pre dinner drinks and savouries. *

Byron Bay
Boutique Guest House
Address: "Coopers Shoot Guesthouse"
Coopers Shoot Road, Byron Bay, NSW 2481
Name: Jan Sharp
Telephone: (02) 6685 3313
Fax: (02) 6685 3311
Beds: 5 Double
(5 bedrooms/extra single beds available)
Bathroom: 5 Ensuite
Tariff: B&B (special) Double $140,
Single $120, Dinner $35, Credit Cards.
Vouchers accepted $20 surcharge
Nearest Town: Byron Bay (7 mins drive to Byron Centre)

A lovingly restored historic school house set high on the bluff overlooking Byron Bay, 6 mins from the town centre, with a heart stopping view of the coast. The inviting and tranquil atmosphere of the guest house makes it easy to relax. Each guest bedroom is furnished with antiques and has ensuite bathroom and private verandah. Guests are welcomed with simple comforts such as port, fruit, flowers, chocolates, crispy bed linen, cosy quilts and fluffy bathrobes. Accommodation includes a hearty country breakfast which may be served in bed or on a private verandah.
"We left convinced that a weekend was not long enough to enjoy the delights of this hinterland hideaway." Article from S.M. Herald - Good Weekend, 20/11/93.
Internet: *http://www.nrg.com.au.csgh*

Byron Bay
Guest House   NRMA ★★★★
Address: 'Cory's on Cooper',
21 Cooper Street, Byron Bay, NSW 2481
Name: Alison Cory
Telephone: (02) 6685 7834   **Fax**: (02) 6685 7834
Mobile: (019) 155 096
Beds: 1 King or 1 Twin, 2 Queen, (4 bedrooms)
Bathroom: 4 Ensuite
Tariff: B&B (full) Double $185 to $230,
Single $155 to $200.   Credit cards accepted
Nearest Town: 1.5km to centre of Byron Bay

In an acre of lush subtropical garden, this unique 2 storey historic home has been beautifully restored and recently opened as a luxury guest house. The elegant, casual decor and peaceful atmosphere, reminiscent of a bygone era, make it the perfect haven in which to relax. Four spacious, romantic bedrooms, each with enquite (some with baths) overlook the garden and views to the hills. Individually furnished and serviced daily they feature fresh flowers, antiques, televisions, fans, crisp linens, robes, fruit, chocolates and port. Enjoy an early morning swim in the magnificent saltwater pool, a spa, or a stroll along Stunning Tallows beach followed by a leisurely breakfast on the shady verandah. Full breakfasts are served using fresh local produce. On cooler evenings curl up with a book by the open fire in the magnificent lounge room.
Within walking distance of restaurants, galleries, shops and beaches, Cory's is the perfect oasis for those seeking seclusion right in Byron. We are a non smoking household.

Byron Bay
Country Guest House   NRMA ★★★★
Address: "Dunvegan", Pacific Highway,
Byron Bay. Please phone.
Name: Dunvegan
Telephone: (02) 6687 1731
Fax: (02) 6687 1731
Mobile: (0141) 940 4251
Beds: 2 Queen, 1 Double,
1 Twin or 1 King(4 bedrooms)
Bathroom: 4 Ensuite
Tariff: B&B (full) Double $140, Single $100, Dinner $40, Credit Cards.
Vouchers accepted $60 surcharge
Nearest Town: Byron Bay

You will have no problem finding Dunvegan. If you're travelling on the Pacific Highway, you pass our entrance. Located on, but set well back from the Pacific Highway, the comfortable homestead is surrounded by green hills, gardens and bird calls. A private home and not really suited to children, Dunvegan is more an adult retreat, catering to a maximum of eight guests. Accommodation is in one twin or king and three double, spacious and handsomely appointed bedrooms each having its own ensuite and tea-making facilities. An indulgent breakfast is served in your room, on your verandah or in the conservatory, and at a time of your choosing. Your hosts have travelled extensively, enjoy entertaining, and invite you to dine with them: - cooking being a passionate hobby of Barbara's. Complimentary pre-dinner drinks on the terrace, followed by good food, fine music, relaxed conversation and an after-dinner port by the fireside, or alternatively, the TV and a good video from the selection available in the privacy of your own room. Dunvegan is only twelve minutes away from the attractions of Byron Bay.

NEW SOUTH WALES

Byron Bay
Guest House   NRMA ★★★★☆
Address: Top of McGettigans Lane,
Byron Bay, NSW 2481
Name:Victoria & Raemon McEwen
Ewingsdale Country Guest House
Telephone: (02) 6684 7047
Fax: (02) 6684 7047 **Mobile**: 014-936 969
Beds: 2 Queen, 2 Double (4 bedrooms)
Bathroom: 4 Ensuite (1 spa)
Tariff: B&B (full) Double ensuitewith spa $195, Double ensuite $165, Single less $30, Dinner $40pp,Credit Cards (BC/MC/VISA/AMEX/DC).
Nearest Town: Bryon Bay

An elegant country escape featuring magnificent panoramic ocean, mountain and lighthouse views. Built on a hill, this unique architecturally designed homestead is situated only minutes from Byron's famous beach front, shops and restaurants. Enjoy sumptuous breakfasts on the verandah or in the cabana overlooking the pool and tranquil landscape. Stroll through our rain forest garden, enjoy a mountain bike ride along the country lanes or a joy-flight in Ewingsdale's private aircraft. During the evening indulge in a candle-lit dinner, poolside in summer, by the stone fireplace in winter, and be inspired by our quality cuisine. Retire in our well appointed guest rooms where attention to detail is impeccable. All beautiful ensuite rooms feature country Baltic pine, antiques, crisp white linen, fresh flowers, decanters of port and all the finishing touches you would expect form a quintessential country guest house. Internationally renowned for first class hospitality, quality and style, 1977 Tourism Award winner.

Byron Bay
Bed & Breakfast Guesthouse
Address: 11 Carlyle Street
Byron Bay, NSW
Name: Sue & David
Sandals Bed & Breakfast
Telephone: Free call 1800 805 091
(02) 6685 8025 **Fax**: (02) 6685 8599
Mobile: 017 155891
Beds: 1 King, 1 Queen, 2 Twin,
1 Single (5 Bedrooms)
Bathroom: 2 Ensuites, 2 Guests Share
Tariff: B&B (Continental) Double $85, Single $65. (Extra High Season Xmas/Easter). All Credit Cards. Vouchers accepted (excluding high season)
Nearest Town: Byron Bay

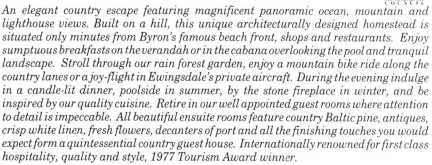

Nestled in a quiet cul-de-sac in the heart of Byron, SANDALS BED & BREAKFAST is a peaceful 4-minute stroll to the main beach. Many unique shops await you in Byron with spectacular ocean and mountain views just a stones throw away. To your hosts, Sue and David, your comfort and relaxation is their only priority. Sandals is your home away from home, a place to unwind, soak up the sunlight and put your feet up. Wake up to a delightful continental breakfast served in our courtyard surrounded by tropical trees and shrubs. We have 5 comfortable rooms with choice of ensuite or shared facilities, and two tastefully appointed lounge areas, of Mediterranean and Classical influence. Tea, coffee and home-made biscuits are served on arrival and available as you desire throughout the day. Why not spoil yourself today at Sandals, you holiday home in the heart of Byron Bay.

NEW SOUTH WALES

Byron Bay
Homestay
Address: Baystay,
30 Marvel Street, Byron Bay
Name: Baystay
Telephone: (02) 6685 7609
Fax: (02) 6685 7509
Mobile: 041 9618401
Email: jwitham@nor.com.au
Beds: 4 Double, 3 Single (5 bedrooms)
Bathroom: 1 Ensuite, 1 Private,
1 Guests share
Tariff: B&B (continental) Double $65, Single $35.
Nearest Town: Byron Bay

A warm welcome awaits you at our house in the heart of beautiful Byron Bay. Only a few minutes walk from clean beaches and from the numerous chic restaurants and boutiques of this eccentric town, our two storey modern house is surrounded by a lush native garden visited by an array of Australian birds.
We have lived in this area for over 15 years and can help you choose from the myriad of activities available in Byron, ranging from local short bush walks, clothing optional beaches to visits to alternative communities or galleries.
The causal ambience of Byron is reflected in our delightful garden unit and our other comfortable guest rooms. A delicious tropical breakfast is usually served in the garden and a BBQ and kitchenette is available for our guests for other meals. Other facilities available for guests include sauna, spa and sporting / beach equipment. We are ideally situated for bus and rail travellers being 400 metres from transit centre.

Byron Hinterland - Bangalow
Homestay Rural Setting B&B
Address: Lot 12 Nashua Road, Fernleigh, NSW 2479
Name: "Osterley"
Telephone: (02) 6687 8554
Beds: 2 Double (2 bedrooms)
Bathroom: 1 Guests share
Tariff: B&B (full) Double $60, Single $35, Dinner $20pp.
Vouchers accepted
Nearest Town: Bangalow 13km north

We are a middle-aged couple, who love giving hospitality to our family and friends in our fully renovated old Queenslander home moved from Brisbane to our five acres in a very pretty rural setting.
Our home is all timber lined and high ceilings. Even though we've done expansive additions we've kept the same comfortable feeling as the existing rooms. From our wide verandahs the views of macadamia orchards and rolling hills are extensive.
Most Sundays there is a local market to explore or activities such as bowls, fishing, surfing at many beaches or just relaxing can be enjoyed.
For folk wishing to stay more than one night you can enjoy the fabulous bush walking and water falls about one hour drive from our home.
Dinner is supplied on request. Special diets catered for.
Directions: *Please phone.*

NEW SOUTH WALES

Byron Hinterland - Bangalow
Homestay
Address: 16 Charlotte Street, Bangalow, 2479
Name: "Hartford House"
Charles & Silvana Dickinson
Telephone: (066) 871810
Mobile: (014) 494212
Beds: 2 Double (2 Bedrooms)
Bathroom: 1 Ensuite, 1 Family share
Tariff: B&B (continental) Double $80 ($100 peak times), Single $50, Children $20, Dinner $15.
Nearest Town: Bangalow

Situated just 10 minutes from Byron Bay this historic home built in 1902 is offering "Homestay Accommodation".
Just walking distance to the village of Bangalow, and 10 minutes drive to the beaches, Hartford House offers tranquillity and comfort in a fully self contained garden apartment or join in with the family and stay in the house in a delightful country style guest room. With this country style accommodation we offer silver service breakfast, colour TV, laundry facilities, swimming pool and all the comforts of this grand home. Over night or weekly bookings for couples or singles welcome.
Home Page: smd@bigpond.com

Byron Hinterland - Clunes
Farmstay+Self-contained Studio
Address: 20 Elliot Road, Clunes, 2480
Name: Suzanne's Farmstay
Telephone: (066) 291228
Fax: (066) 212499 **Mobile**: 014 217 504
Email: mambo@nor.com.au
Beds: 1 Double (1 bedroom)
Bathroom: 1 Ensuite
Tariff: Double $100, Single $90, Children by arrangement. Credit cards, Breakfast hamper available $8pp.
Nearest Town: Lismore

Your own private resort! Farmstay - Self-contained studio. Set on hilltop with vast panorama over the Rainbow region and Byron Bay hinterland of Northern New South Wales. Relax into the beauty of the region in your studio amid our sub-tropical orchards. Walk to our rain forest lined river and swim or fish. Enjoy the use of our floodlit synthetic grass tennis court, salt swimming pool, gym equipment, bicycles and BBQ in the gazebo. BBQ foods can be arranged on reasonable notice. Studio with double bed, ensuite, kitchen, TV and video and is surrounded by verandahs. Breakfast hamper available. We can suggest rain forest trails and secluded rain forest beaches. No smoking indoors. Bankcard accepted.
Licensed general store and butcher nearby.

Ask your hosts for tourist information.
They are your own personal travel agent and guide.

Byron Hinterland
Tropical Bed & Breakfast   NRMA ★★★★
Address: "Green Mango Hideaway",
Lofts Road off Coolamon Scenic Drive, Coorabell
Name: Susie & Mick
Telephone: (02) 6684 7171
Beds: 1 King, 2 Queen (3 bedrooms)
Bathroom: 3 Ensuite
Tariff: B&B (full) King Room: $140-$160,
Double $110-$130, Single $90-$120,
Dinner from $25pp, Credit Cards.
Children not catered for.
Vouchers accepted $30 surcharge Queen room.
Nearest Town: Bangalow 9km, Byron Bay 12km

This secluded Thai-style timber home is nestled in luxuriant gardens amid the rolling hills of Byron's beautiful hinterland. Situated just a short picturesque drive from Byron Bay, and within easy reach of the charming villages and scenic attractions of the area, it is the perfect base from which to explore the region. With a palm-fringed pool, bath house with private spa, wide and shady verandahs, hammocks to lounge in and good food, the emphasis is on informality and relaxation. Accommodation comprises two queen rooms each with ensuite and french doors opening onto the verandah. Upstairs a romantic King room awaits you with a private balcony overlooking the pool. Twin beds are available. The large and comfortable sitting room offers guests TV, video, a library of books and an extensive CD collection. On cooler winter nights you can curl up alongside a roaring log fire. A warm welcome is assured.

Byron Hinterland via Bangalow
Country Guest House & Self Contained Cottage
Address: Possum Creek Lodge Cedarvale Road
Off Possum Creek Rd, Bangalow
Name: Fay and Ian
Telephone: (02) 6687 1188
Fax: (02) 6687 1269
Mobile: 0414 382 320
Beds: Homestead: 3 Queen, 1 Single (3 bedrooms).
Cottage: 1 Queen, 1 (double) Sofa bed, 2 Single (2 bedrooms), sleeps 6.
Bathroom: Homestead: 3 Ensuites. Cottage: 1 Private
Tariff: B&B (Special) Homestead: Queen from $125, Single from $95, Dinner from $30. Children by arrangement. B&B (self catering) Cottage: From $450 per week. From $95 per night. Children welcome. Dinner from $30. Credit Cards. Vouchers accepted (Except Chrismas and Easter). $40 surcharge.
Nearest Town: Byron Bay (12 mins)

Overlooking magnificent scenery and surrounded by peace & tranquillity, Possum Creek Lodge is a proudly restored 100 year old pioneering homestead. The tastefully decorated bedrooms have en suites, queen size beds and two have private verandahs. The gourmet never ending breakfast and optional innovative candlelit dinners are memorable with a choice of menu which is changed daily. Relax by the pool / spa in summer or the open fire in winter. Explore our untouched rainforest, 85 acre of cattle pastures and plantations, the wonders of the surrounding countryside or take a trip into nearby Byron Bay. The "Hilltop Cottage" is reminiscent of Tuscany with its mellow decor and views of rolling hills. Fully self-contained it sleeps up to 6. Whilst complete with its own private garden and barbecue, guests are welcome to all homestead facilities. Fay and Ian provide warm hospitality, a convivial atmosphere and ensure that the needs of the individual are met with unobtrusive attention to detail.

NEW SOUTH WALES

Byron Hinterland
Homestay
Address: 86 Mafeking Rd, Goonengerry via Federal 2480
Name: "Prue's"
Telephone: (02) 6684 9157 best after 6pm **Fax**: (02) 6684 9157
Beds: 2 Double (2 bedrooms)
Bathroom: 1 Guests share
Tariff: B&B (extended) Double $80, Single $60. Dinner by arrangement.
Seniors Card accepted Vouchers accepted
Nearest Town: Byron Bay 25km, Mullumbimby 16km, Lismore 40km

Enjoy a wonderful relaxing stay in a unique Australian mud brick cottage offering every home comfort. Quiet bedrooms and a well lit bathroom, open dining and gallery are decorated in a tasteful oriental style. A breakfast of fresh fruits, variety of breads and cheeses, choice of teas or freshly brewed coffee served inside or on the verandah - both with superb panoramic views. The tropical garden abounds with birdlife and native animals appear at dusk. Take scenic drives to subtropical rainforests, National Parks, beaches, golf courses, visit local markets, art galleries, antique and craft shops. A complimentary refreshing drink awaits you. Please discuss your requirements before arriving to ensure total satisfaction. Smoking on the verandahs only.

Callalla Bay see Nowra
Cambewarra Mtn see Kangaroo Valley
Candelo also see Bega

Candelo - Bega Valley
Self-contained Accommodation NRMA ★★★
Address: "Bumblebrook Farm" Kemps Lane, Candelo, NSW 2550
Name: Rick & Ann Patten
Telephone: (02) 6493 2238 **Fax**: (02) 6493 2299
Beds: 1 Queen, 4 Double, 6 Single (4 bedrooms)
Bathroom: 4 Ensuite
Tariff: B&B (full - cook your own) Double $70-$85, Single $60-$75, Children under 12 free, 12 and over $10. Dinner $30, children under 12 $15. Credit cards (BC/MC/VISA). Vouchers accepted
Nearest Town: Candelo 4km, Merimbula 35km, Bega 20km

Bumblebrook is a 100 acre beef property in the beautiful Bega valley. We are situated on the top of a hill with magnificent views and lovely bush walks, the property has frontage to the Tantawangalo Creek. We have 4 well equipped self-contained units, 2 are double units and 2 family sized units. Breakfast is a "cook-your-own" from ingredients provided by us, including fresh farm eggs and homemade jams. Children are welcome and can often help feed the donkey, chickens, ducks, goats and dogs. With prior notice, guests are very welcome to a friendly, candlelit, family dinner in the homestead. Homegrown and local produce is served where possible. Barbecue facilities are provided by the creek, where swimming holes are abundant, and also in the rustic playground near the units. Golf, tennis, bowls and horse riding are available locally. The Sapphire Coast beaches are only about 25 minutes drive from Bumblebrook. Canberra is about 2 1/2 hours away.

NEW SOUTH WALES

Candelo - Bega Valley
Homestead
Address: Collinswood,
Wolumla Road, Candelo, NSW 2550
Name: Veronica & Robin Owen
Telephone: (02) 6493 2410
Fax: (02) 6493 2407
Mobile: (015) 215237
Email: ppr@acr.net.au
Beds: 2 Queen (2 bedrooms)
Bathroom: 2 Ensuite
Tariff: B&B (full) Double $90 & $100.
Nearest Town: Candelo 3km; Bega 21km; Merimbula 25km

Collinswood is an historic, single storey, rambling Federation homestead, with superb views across the beautiful Bega Valley. Guests can relax in the tranquillity of the home and its fragrant country garden. Rooms are furnished with antiques which add to the peaceful ambience. Candelo is a quaint historical village. Its renowned markets, the largest in the Bega Valley, are held on the first Sunday of each month. Local attractions include forests and national parks, the many outstanding Sapphire Coast beaches, old gold mines and old-fashioned country hospitality at Candelo Hotel.
Leisure pursuits include swimming and surfing, fishing at Tathra and Merimbula, sailing on Lake Wallagoot, water skiing on Bega River, golf on the uncrowded Far South Coast courses (Candelo-Kameruka is the seventh oldest in NSW), tennis, lawn bowls. In winter only a short drive to the Snowy Mountains skifields.
Local delicacies include fresh fish and oysters, Bega Valley cheeses and fruits in season. **Directions**: *By phone.*
Home Page: http://www.acr.net.au/~collinswood/

Candelo
Farmstay+Self-contained Accom.
Address: "Alesstree Cottage",
Kameruka, Candelo, Nr Bega 2550
Name: Francis & Odile Foster
Telephone: (02) 6493 2318 A/H, 6493 2205 B/H
Fax: (02) 6493 2016
Beds: 2 Double, 5 Single (3 bedrooms)
Bathroom: 2 Ensuite, 1 Private
Tariff: $100/night (min. charge), $550/week,
Continental breakfast $6/person/day,
Cheque with ID accepted. Vouchers accepted
$15 surcharge/night accommodation only.
Nearest Town: 4km Candelo, 16km SW Bega off Princes Highway

Alesstree Cottage is situated in the heart of the famous historic Kameruka Estate halfway between Sydney and Melbourne off the Princes Highway and 2 1/2 hours from Canberra off the Snowy Mountains Highway. This brick home built in 1911 can accommodate up to 7 adults and 2 children and is fully furnished and equipped including an open fire etc. Enjoy a walk around the old village, a tennis court and golf links is available or just laze about in the garden, You can stroll to the lake or watch our famous Jersey cows being milked and of course Alesstree Cottage is ideally placed to take advantage of our famous Sapphire Coast Region. Beautiful beaches, great fishing and an abundance of national parks are all within easy reach.
Directions & Bookings *(required). Please phone.*
Home Page: http://www.acr.net.au/~alesstree

Cassilis (Hunter Valley) see Merriwa
Central Coast also see Ourimba
Central Coast - Avoca Beach
Homestay
Address: 113 The Round Drive,
Avoca Beach (Please phone)
Name: Avoca Beach Oasis
Telephone: (02) 4381 1261
Fax: (02) 4381 1261
Beds: 1 Queen (1 bedroom)
Bathroom: 1 Ensuite
Tariff: B&B (full) Double $70.
Vouchers accepted
Nearest Town: Gosford 17kms

Avoca Beach has been a well kept secret on the central coast of NSW. Only two hours drive from Sydney it boasts a surf beach rated in the top ten of NSW, brilliant bird life, almost tropical vegetation, close to the Hunter vineyards, everything for the local and overseas travellers.

Bill and Helen Payne have enjoyed Australian and world travel over many years and have recently acquired a delightful home at Avoca Beach and developed it as a Bed & Breakfast after careful planning and experience of B&Bs throughout the world. We offer a double bedroom with an ensuite, a private sitting room with fridge, microwave, TV, tea making facilities. A swimming pool. A 1km stroll to the beach. A full breakfast. You would be welcome to join us for dinner ($20 each).

Central Coast - Avoca Beach North
Boutique Bed & Breakfast
Address: 31 Surf Rider Ave,
Avoca Beach North, 2260
Name: "Salty Rose Boutique B&B"
Grant & Paula Bradly
Telephone: (02) 4384 6098
Fax: (02) 4385 1244 **Mobile**: (0419) 242613
Beds: 2 Queen (1 with ensuite, 1 with private bathroom)
Bathroom: 1 Ensuite, 1 Private
Tariff: B&B (special) Two adults sharing - $145 per room per night (all year round), Credit Cards.
Nearest Town: Terrigal

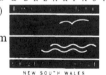

The Salty Rose Bed & Breakfast is a quintessential sea side experience with views overlooking the ocean, beach and headlands. The scent and sound of the surf awakens guests to sea side breakfast delights. The surrounding environs offer bush walking, swimming, diving, fishing, kayaking and sailing. The local lagoon is a haven for local and migratory sea birds while the tall timbered trees offer refuge to native marsupials, parrots and lorikeets. With only two queen sized rooms, one with ensuite the other with a private bathroom, guests are assured of an intimate gateway. Guests also enjoy extensive sun decks, barbecue facilities, air conditioning and an open fireplace. The guest lounge is supplied with plunger coffee, tea, fruit and treats. There is audiovisual and sound equipment as well as an extensive library for guests to use. Grant and Paula share their home with their cat Halfpenny and provide a smoke free environment for their guests. Membership: Boutique Bed & Breakfasts of the Central Coast Inc. Re. No. Y2600936 Registered with Central Coast Tourism Inc. Member Australian Bed & Breakfast Council.
Directions: *Bookings essential*

NEW SOUTH WALES

Central Coast - Erina
Private Suite/Homestay
Address: "Bear Cottage",
26 Kuburra Road, Erina, 2250 NSW
Name: Bear Cottage
Telephone: (02) 4367 7084
Fax: (02) 4367 7084 **Mobile**: (0418) 496546
Beds: 1 Queen (1 suite)
Bathroom: 1 Private
Tariff: B&B (continental) Double $105,
Single $60, Credit Cards.
Nearest Town: Gosford NSW

Bed & Breakfast

Do you enjoy romantic weekends for two or just like to getaway. Bear Cottage on the scenic Central Coast NSW is for you.
Bear Cottage is only minutes to Terrigal Beach, where you can find a large variety of restaurants to tempt any pallet.
If you want adventure the Central Coast has many activities for you to enjoy; swimming, diving, surfing, fishing, parasailing, boating, bushwalking, just to name a few! Or just relax and unwind on one of the many beaches.
Our spacious Queensize suite with private access has all you will need. A delightful decor that looks out to a bushland setting.
We offer our guests champagne on arrival and a breakfast basket each morning. Bear Cottage is only 1 hour drive north of Sydney, 7km from Gosford CBD (just off Terrigal Dr). We would love to have your company. Reservations phone 02 4367 7084.
We are smoke free.

Central Coast - Kulnura
Farmstay+Self-contained Accom. NRMA ★★★☆
Address: "Kiah Retreat", RMB 2248,
Finns Road, Kulnura, NSW 2250
Name: Gail Amos
Telephone: (02) 4376 1348
Fax: (02) 4376 1302
Mobile: (018) 252553
Beds: 1 Double,
2 Single (1 bedroom)
Bathroom: 1 Private
Tariff: B&B (full/self-serve) Double $125,
Single $60, Children $15.
Nearest Town: Kulnura 1km, Gosford 30 mins, Hornsby 40 mins.

The Kiah Retreat is a fully air-conditioned modern country cottage situated on acreage. The cottage features a self-contained kitchen with ingredients supplied for a self-serve breakfast. The comfortable living room has a colour TV, video, radio and record player. The spacious double bedroom has room for 2 bunk beds if required.
The outdoor facilities include BBQ equipment, children's playground and peaceful garden setting. Bring your own horse. There are stables, practice areas and bush trails and horseriding properties nearby. The farm specialises in breeding small acreage cattle. Dexters - the original small breed of cattle.
It is only a short drive to tennis courts, golf and bowling clubs, the Watagan State Forest, wineries, the historic town of Wollombi and taverns for an enjoyable lunch. The Great North Road is nearby for the 4WD and bushwalking enthusiasts.
Kiah Retreat is located 1 1/4 hours drive north of Sydney and is an ideal setting for a relaxing weekend.

NEW SOUTH WALES

Central Coast - Ourimbah
Farmstay, Guest House, Country Retreat
Address: The Ambers Retreat, RMB 4750, Fern Tree Lane, Palmdale, NSW 2258
Name: Ross & Robin Nable & Family
Telephone: (02) 4362 3403
Fax: (02) 4362 3403 **Mobile**: 015 891869
Beds: 3 Queen, 1 Double (4 bedrooms)
Bathroom: 4 Ensuite
Tariff: B&B (full) Double $90/$110, Single $70/$80, Children $25, Dinner $25 pp. Credit cards.
Nearest Town: Ourimbah 3 kms, 80 kms north of Sydney

The Ambers Retreat is an aptly named 22 acre property in a beautiful peaceful valley. Located 1 hour's drive from Sydney and 20 mins to spectacular Central Coast beaches & restaurants.
Surrounded by the beautiful Ourimbah State Forest, nature lovers will enjoy a leisurely stroll through the picturesque walking tracks. Or you may prefer to simply lounge on the front terrace and absorb the beauty and tranquillity of the magnificent valley views and bird life. Our homestead caters for 4 couples at one time. Four guest bedrooms have 3 Queen size, 1 Double bed, all with the privacy of your own ensuite. As evening approaches relax in the large guest room or lounge room both with log fires, which look out onto inground pool & spa.
A sumptuous full breakfast can be enjoyed in guest dining room or on the front terrace. Tea and coffee facilities, plus dinner & lunches on arrangement. We can meet at nearby station.
No smoking inside. Children can be accommodated with a group booking of 3 or 4 rooms.

Central Coast - Ourimbah
Homestay
Address: Lilly Pilly Guest House, Ourimbah Creek Road.
Name: Rosanna Jones
Telephone: (02) 4362 1910
Beds: 2 Double (2 bedrooms)
Bathroom: 1 Ensuite, 1 Family share
Tariff: B&B (full) Double $80, Single $50, Children negotiable. Vouchers accepted $10 surcharge
Nearest Town: Ourimbah - 10km from Gosford and 10km from Wyong

Come and relax at Lilly Pilly Guest House!
Enjoy breakfast on the verandah, with a view of forest and garden trees. Listen to the currawongs and whip-birds.
The main guest room is large with raftered ceilings; it opens onto the garden, deck and verandah and you will usually be the sole guests. Children can be accommodated in a separate room.
There are bush walks and beaches nearby, cycling and sporting facilities, shopping complexes and university; various restaurants and entertainment in the area. Stella the dog, Lizzie the cat and your host will welcome you. There is wheelchair access, and we thank you for not smoking inside. Local oranges, free- range eggs, home-made marmalade, on the menu. Relaxing rural setting, peaceful and private. Good food; varied facilities include beaches, bush-walk, sport, cycling, shopping centre, university.
Directions: *Phone for address and directions.*

Central Coast - Phegans Bay
Separate Guest Cottage   NRMA ★★★
Address: "Minerva's Garden Cottage", Phegans Bay, 2256
Name: Barbara & Brian Goodey
Telephone: (02) 4341 4295
Beds: 2 Single (1 bedroom)
Bathroom: 1 Ensuite
Tariff: B&B (full) Double $70, Single $50.
Vouchers accepted
Nearest Town: Woy Woy - 6km north west of Woy Woy and 8km south of Kariong.

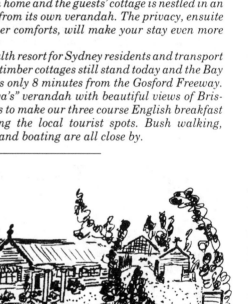

We welcome you to "Minerva's Garden Cottage" in peaceful Phegans Bay on the Central Coast. "Minerva" is our timber federation home and the guests' cottage is nestled in an old world rock garden with water views from its own verandah. The privacy, ensuite bathroom, tea making facilities and other comforts, will make your stay even more enjoyable.
Phegans Bay in the early 1900's was a health resort for Sydney residents and transport was by water from Woy Woy. Some small timber cottages still stand today and the Bay remains a little undiscovered oasis, yet is only 8 minutes from the Gosford Freeway. We normally serve breakfast on "Minerva's" verandah with beautiful views of Brisbane Water. The early morning sun tends to make our three course English breakfast a lazy affair to enjoy before discovering the local tourist spots. Bush walking, aboriginal carvings, ferry rides, fishing and boating are all close by.

Central Coast - Terrigal Beach
Boutique Bed & Breakfast
Address: 28 Serpentine Road, Terrigal 2260
Name: An-Da-Cer House
Telephone: (02) 4367 8368
Fax: (02) 4367 8368
Mobile: (018) 437315
Beds: 3 Queen (3 bedrooms)
Bathroom: 3 Ensuite
Tariff: B&B (full) Double $110-$140, Credit Cards.
Adults retreat.
Nearest Town: Terrigal Beach 3km

An-Da-Cer House blends the romance and charm of yesteryear with the luxurious and comforts of today. Set in a semi-rural area which is picturesque, yet centrally located 3km to beautiful Terrigal Beach. One hour from Sydney.
This rambling old farmhouse style home has three guest suites furnished in an elegant country decor surrounded by lovely old trees. Guests are assured of a relaxing warm atmosphere. There is a large swimming pool, private tennis court available close by at a small cost. Cosy open fires in comfortable living rooms. Video library. Games. Fresh flowers, fruit, tea/coffee, home baked treats. Lavish country breakfast. Non smoking in house. Mid week packages, Fri, Sat bookings Comp. picnic hamper for two night stay.
Member of the Central Coast Boutique Bed & Breakfast inc. Reg# Y2600936

NEW SOUTH WALES

Central Coast - Woy Woy
Bed & Breakfast
Address: 11 Koonora Ave,
Orange Grove, Woy Woy
Name: Blossoms Bed & Breakfast
Telephone: (043) 418732
Fax: (043) 418732 **Mobile**: (015) 786643
Beds: 1 Queen, 2 Single (2 bedrooms)
Bathroom: 1 Private
Tariff: B&B (full) Double $120,
Single $70, Credit Cards.
Nearest Town: 3km south of Woy Woy township, 12km south of Gosford City

Blossoms is a unique 2 bedroom cottage for exclusive use by the guests. Each bedroom has small adjoining sitting room and there is a comfy sunroom leading onto verandah which overlooks garden and magical water views. The cottage features full kitchen facilities, has bath and separate shower, lots of books, lamps and comfy seating. There is a television, video, sound equipment and games. Located in a quiet street backed by a public reserve it is an ideal retreat. Breakfast is provided by way of a gourmet breakfast basket or can be catered for, by arrangement. Complimentary champagne, chocolates and cheese platter greets your arrival. Blossoms is non smoking. Children are generally not catered for.

Central Tilba see Narooma. Cessnock see Hunter Valley. Clarence see Blue Mountains. Clunes see Byron Hinterland

Cobargo
Homestay   NRMA ★★★★
Address: County Boundary Road, Cobargo, 2550
Name: Phill& Rae Smith "Eilan Croft B&B"
Telephone: (02) 6493 7362 **Fax**: (02) 6493 7362
Mobile: (015) 832365
Beds: 2 Queen, 1 Single (2 bedrooms)
Bathroom: 2 Ensuite
Tariff: B&B (full) Double $90-$110, Single $70-$85, Children by arrangement, Dinner $25pp, Credit Cards.
Nearest Town: 8km west of Cobargo, Tilba 25km, Narooma 43km, Bega 45km

Welcome to our lovely 100 year old home, located amidst spectacular mountain scenery, overlooking the historic working village of Cobargo.
Our rooms have comfortable queen beds, electric blankets, doonas, ensuites, TV, heating and private verandahs, where guests can enjoy the views. We have a central lounge / dining room with wood fire, library, tea & coffee making facilities, refrigerator and home baked goodies. We serve delicious dinners by arrangement, and we are a smoke free interior.
Watch the mist roll through the valleys, ramble along country lanes, play petanque, croquet, or just soak up the peace. Nearby, beautiful Bermagui and Narooma beaches, historic Tilba, Foxglove Spires Garden, cheese factories and wineries. Explore wilderness, national parks and walkways, by bushwalking, horse-rides, mountain bike or canoe, play golf, fish, swim, surf, abseil or just relax. We look forward to meeting you, and sharing our love of this beautiful area with you.

NEW SOUTH WALES

Coffs Harbour
Farmstay
Address: "Stone Haven",
111 Bruxner Park Road,
Korora, Coffs Harbour, 2450
Name: Nell & Len Leete
Telephone: (02) 6652 2663
Fax: (02) 6652 2663
Beds: 1 Double, 2 Single (2 bedrooms)
Bathroom: 1 Guests share
Tariff: B&B (full) Double $70, Single $35-$45,
Children half price. Dinner on request when booking $15-$20. Vouchers accepted
Nearest Town: Coffs Harbour on Pacific Highway, 5 km South.

Stone Haven is a banana and tropical fruit plantation in the mountains off the Pacific Highway just outside Coffs Harbour.
The house situated in a idyllic spot within the plantation overlooked by mountains with magnificent ocean views provides comfortable, well presented accommodation. Guests are free to roam in the garden and plantation or relax on the deck to chat, read or just admire the sea views. Coffee, tea available anytime.
The main crop on the plantation is bananas, but avocados, mangos, paw paws are produced as well, with several varieties of more exotic fruit trees.
Adjacent to the plantation are the Bruxner Park Flora Reserve and Orara State Forest which provide excellent walking, driving and picnic opportunities.
Coffs Harbour has all water based activities and every sporting facility. For excitement try white water rafting or 4WD, rainforest and water falls tours. Bookings made. Transfers available. **Directions**: *Please telephone.*

Coffs Harbour
Homestay
Address: "The Nest",
44 Vera Drive, Coffs Harbour, 2450
Name: Wilma & Hans Henriksen
Telephone: (02) 6651 4936
Beds: 4 Single (2 bedrooms)
Bathroom: 1 Ensuite, 1 Private
Tariff: B&B (full) Double $70, Single $45,
Dinner $15-$20. Vouchers accepted
Nearest Town: Coffs Harbour

We are a retired couple who enjoy the company of people from all walks of life, we have travelled extensively and lived in several places in Australia and the Pacific Islands.
Our home "The Nest" (Reiret) is named after the first home we shared in Norway prior to Hans migrating to Australia in 1959. It is modern and comfortable, situated just 3km from the Pacific Highway. Excellent dining venues nearby.
Coffs Harbour is a beautiful place about halfway between Sydney and Brisbane, the only coastal town where the mountains go down to the sea.
Our guest accommodation includes twin bedded rooms, one with ensuite and one with private bathroom, plus a cosy sitting room with books and television.
Coffee and tea available anytime.
Bookings essential. Smoke free house. No credit card facilities.
Directions: *Please telephone ahead.*

Coffs Harbour
Homestay NRMA ★★★☆
Address: "Illoura", 116 Sth. Boambee Rd, Coffs Harbour, NSW 2450
Name: Doris & Bob Cocks
Telephone: (02) 665 31690 (Ring after 5pm if no answer)
Fax: (02) 665 83644

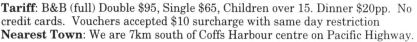

Beds: 1 Queen, 1 Double, 2 King Singles (3 bedrooms)
Bathroom: 1 Guests share
Tariff: B&B (full) Double $95, Single $65, Children over 15. Dinner $20pp. No credit cards. Vouchers accepted $10 surcharge with same day restriction
Nearest Town: We are 7km south of Coffs Harbour centre on Pacific Highway.

Enjoy idyllic living in our little piece of paradise away from the madding crowd, with breathtaking views and only the sounds of the bush and birds to wake you. "Illoura" (Aboriginal for peaceful place) has a million dollar panoramic 360 degree view overlooking banana plantations, beautiful valleys, mountains, the city and ocean. Set high on a ridge with 15 acres of natural bushland that has an abundance of wildlife including koalas, wallabies and goannas that come close to the house and mingle with our cows, goats and chickens. "Illoura" is a place of unique beauty and tranquil seclusion with complete privacy where you can relax and unwind, enjoy good food, magnificent scenery, or congenial company if you so desire, and there is a barbecue by the pool and gazebo for guests use. "Illoura" is ideal as an overnight stay, a weekend retreat, or a peaceful and relaxing holiday destination. Guests have the best of both worlds being conveniently close to the city with many attractions the area has to offer having 3 lovely golf courses (including Bonville International) and beautiful beaches a few minutes away. The quaint historical town of Bellingen with art and craft plus other shops from a by-gone era is within a short distance, with the majestic Dorrigo mountains a little further on. There are rainforest walks, Botanical Gardens, the Zoo, Big Banana, Historical museum, 4WD Tours, pleasure cruises, parasailing and whitewater rafting to pass away your time, as well as art galleries, antique and craft shops.

Our lovely large comfortable informal home has beautiful gardens, rustic olde world charm with elegant antique furnishings, and the guest wing which is at one end of our long and spacious house has its own entrance. The bedrooms are stylishly furnished, have comfortable beds, built-in robes, ceiling fans, doonas, electric blankets, clock radios, fresh flowers and great views having large windows on 2 walls. The large modern guest bathroom is beautifully appointed in cedar panelling and is in 3 sections with a full size bath and shower recess, double wash-basin and separate toilet. You can gaze at spectacular sunsets over the mountains through a wall of glass from the guest lounge / dining room which has a TV, video, stereo, wide range of books, magazines, board games, tea / coffee making facilities and refrigerator, or you are welcomed to join your hosts Doris and Bob in the formal lounge which has a large open stone fireplace. "Illoura" has a high standard of comfort and cleanliness with rooms serviced daily. Breakfast can be taken in the elegant dining room which has sweeping views of the mountains, city and ocean, or on the covered front verandah with the magical million dollar view. A generous Continental or cooked breakfast starting with freshly squeezed orange juice and comport of fresh fruit is served at your convenience. On arrival, guests are given a warm welcome and made to feel at home and are served home baked goodies with freshly brewed tea or coffee. Our interests are golf, other sports, gardening, art and antiques. Smoking outside only, no pets, transfers available if required. Please phone or fax for our brochure.

Coffs Harbour
Homestay
Address: Arusha, 21 Mastons Road, Karangi 2450
Name: Ann and Des Ritchens
Telephone: (066) 538 583
Beds: 2 Queen (2 bedrooms)
Bathroom: 1 Ensuite
Tariff: B&B (full) Double $58, Single $40, Children negotiable, Dinner negotiable. Vouchers accepted
Nearest Town: Coffs Harbour

Enjoy yourselves and be spoilt in quiet comfort (e.g. a cosy fire in your lounge if it is cold) on an acre of 'cottage' garden overlooking pasture to nearby forested hills. You can see cows graze, parrots feed, and choose a breakfast location to suit your mood and the weather.
Ann & Des are welcoming hosts (with afternoon tea on arrival) who have travelled widely and will offer companionship or privacy as you may wish. Guest rooms include tea-making facilities, and are private with undisturbed outlooks.
Arusha is a 10 minute delightful sealed road drive from Coffs Harbour. 200m off the Orara Way route to Grafton. The general store and Post Office are nearby. For evening meals choose from the local restaurants, our BBQ, with us by arrangement, or in the large variety in town.
We have a placid Cavalier spaniel who can share an enclosed garden area with a compatible dog, and a shy Siamese cat.
Welcoming Homestay near town with modern comforts, privacy, lovely rural outlook, and local amenities.

Coffs Harbour - Coramba
Farmstay+Self-contained Accom.
Address: "Ferntree Cottage",
Kingsridge Forest Road, Coramba, NSW 2450
Name: Bob & Margaret Johnson
Telephone: (02) 6654 4112
Fax: (02) 6654 4010

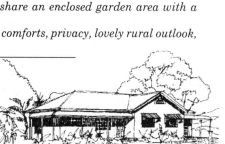

Beds: 1 Queen, 1 Double, 2 Single (3 bedrooms)
Bathroom: 1 Private (with spa), 1 Extra toilet
Tariff: Fully equipped $600 per week or $100 per night. No food provided or B&B (continental) Double $75, Single $40, Children 5-15yrs $15, Dinner by arrangement $20, Credit Cards.
Nearest Town: We are 23km west of Coffs Harbour.

Our newly built cottage is nestled in a peaceful corner on our 125 acre Angus cattle and deer property. It is fully equipped with all the comforts of home, including wood heater, microwave, spa-bath, all laundry facilities and an outdoor BBQ area. All linen and towels provided. There are lots of bush-walking trails where bird-life abound. Kangaroos and wallabies can be seen feeding in the early morning and at dusk. Throw a line in the dam, stroll along the creek, enjoy a game of tennis on our championship court or spend some time at the nearby goldmine.
Coffs Harbour with its beautiful beaches and many holiday activities is only a 20 minute drive.
Maybe you would prefer B&B in our home which is situated 700 metres from the cottage on the hill overlooking the beautiful valley. The house is air-conditioned, the 2 bedrooms and private bathroom (with spa) are upstairs. Our 2 dogs, Charlie and Humphrey are very friendly. Smoking outdoors only. Please phone.

NEW SOUTH WALES

Coffs Harbour - Emerald Beach
Self-contained Seaside Accom.
Address: "Dammerel House",
61 Dammerel Crescent, Emerald Beach, NSW 2456
Name: Jackie Lloyd
Telephone: (066) 561486 **Fax**: (066) 561486
Beds: 1 Double, 1 Twin (2 bedrooms)
Bathroom: 2 Ensuite
Tariff: Self-contained double suite: $65,
with extra ensuite twin bedroom: $80,
Tropical continental breakfast: $15 (double).
Nearest Town: 18km north of
Coffs Harbour on Pacific Highway.

"Dammerel House" at peaceful Emerald Beach, commands sweeping views of Solitary Island Marine Reserve with its islands and headlands. Safe swimming beaches are within a 5 minute walk. The hills of the Great Dividing Range behind Coffs Harbour offer scenic drives, interesting villages to explore, bush walking and National Parks. The holiday resort of Coffs Harbour with its many attractions is 20 minutes drive away.
Your self catering accommodation has a double, a twin bedroom and a lounge and is fully equipped. There are barbeque facilities. A tropical continental breakfast can be provided on request, which you can enjoy on your own private deck overlooking our tranquil garden. The lorikeets will keep you company. Our dog is quiet and friendly. We are a no smoking household.
Please phone in advance. Bookings essential.

Coffs Harbour
Bed & Breakfast NRMA ★★★★☆
Address: 235 The Mountain Way,
Coffs Harbour, NSW 2450
Name: Santa Fe Luxury B&B
Telephone: (02) 6653 7700 **Fax**: (02) 6653 7050
Beds: 1 King, 2 Queen (3 bedrooms)
(1 room - 2 or 3 singles if required)
Bathroom: 3 Ensuite
Tariff: B&B (full) Double $145, Single $100,
Dinner $35, Children N/A, Credit Cards.
Nearest Town: Coffs Harbour

Resort Style Surroundings without the crowds. Santa Fe is 5 acre of 4 1/2 Star total luxury ... adobe walls, commanding colours, pigskin furniture pottery, cactus, flags, waterfalls, ponds, Koi fish, sunflowers, hammocks, gourmet food, and original artworks conjure up images of the American South West - in sub-tropical Coffs Harbour. Only 2 mins to Sapphire Beach. With three ensuite guest rooms each with its own entrance, TV / video and coffee / tea facilities ... privacy is assured. Enjoy the library and sitting room (with log fire). An adobe BBQ area with all facilities is available to guests. No child facilities. Smoking outside.
Coffs Harbour(where the mountains meet the sea) has everything to offer as a holiday destination ... beautiful beaches, almost perfect weather, National Park rainforest walks, arts & crafts, galleries, and for the more adventurous ... white water rafting, tandem sky-diving, jet skiing, Harley bike tours and 4-wheel drive hinterland adventures.

NEW SOUTH WALES

Coffs harbour - Brooklana
Guest House & Self Contained Cottage
Address: 41 Eastern Dorrigo Way, Brooklana 2450 NSW
Name: Pine Crest Horse Treking Resort
Telephone: (02) 6654 5277/6654 5393 **Fax**: (02) 6654 5366
Beds: 2 Double, 4 Single. Cottage: 2 Double, 1 Single. (6 Bedrooms)
Bathroom: Guest House: 2 Share/Cottage: 1 Private
Tariff: B&B (full) Double $65, Single $45, Dinner $20. Cottage $120.
Nearest Town: Coffs harbour 40km East, Dorrigo 30km West

Nestled away in the Coffs Harbour hinterland is Pine Crest, a horse riding and cattle property set on 505 magnificent acres of rolling hills and sub-tropical rainforest.
At Pine Crest you can explore local mountains, rivers and rain forest by foot or on horseback, white water raft down the famous Nymboida River or simply relax and enjoy the scenery on our wide verandas, the choice is yours.
Also on our property is "Brookcottage" a beautiful stone cottage with a loft master bedroom and stunning views down through the Brooklana Valley. Pine Crest guest house is a great place to take a breather from the rat race and enjoy the unspoilt beauty of the Eastern Dorrigo hinterland whether it's horse riding, white water rafting you like, or just for a quiet stay.
Prices for horse riding and white water rafting available on application. Transport Available On Request.

NEW SOUTH WALES

Come-by-Chance
Homestay/Farmstay
Address: "Bungle Gully", Come by Chance, 2832
Name: Bill & Fiona Buchanan
Telephone: (068) 285288 **Fax**: (068) 285266
Beds: 9 Single (5 bedrooms)
Bathroom: 2 Guests share
Tariff: B&B (full) Double $90, Single $55, Children under 12 half price, Dinner $25pp, Campervans $20. Vouchers accepted
Nearest Town: Walgett

Bungle Gully is a beef and farming property with a comfortable air-conditioned homestead surrounded by gauzed verandahs and creeper clad pergolas, ideal for outdoor living. The atmosphere is homely with a typical country kitchen and open fire places.
The garden is large and attractive with a pool and tennis court. There is an airstrip adjacent the house. Bill flies and Fiona is a keen gardener and they both enjoy tennis and golf.
The property is 3km from Come by Chance bordering the Namoi River and 56km SE of Walgett.
Attractions include - Bungle Gully dam, a beautiful water way for boating, fishing, bird watching - abundant wildlife, kangaroos, emus, pigs - scenic picnic and camping spots - Good country cooking in a relaxed, peaceful atmosphere.
Here you can experience a taste of the outback together with farm activities or a day trip to Lightening Ridge. The Warrumbungles are 2 hours away and Dubbo 2 1/2 hours south. Please phone in advance.

Cooma - Monaro District
Farmstay, B&B
Address: "Springwell", Cooma 2630
Name: Patrick & Stephanie Litchfield
Telephone: (02) 6453 5545
Fax: (064) 6453 5539
Beds: 1 Double, 1 Twin, 1 Single (3 bedrooms). 3 Doubles in another wing of house.
Bathroom: 3 Guests share
Tariff: B&B (full) Double $80, Single $40, Children half price; Dinner $20, Campervans welcome. Vouchers accepted
Nearest Town: 15 km south of Cooma on Bobundra Road

We live in a large old homestead on a sheep and cattle grazing property. The property has been worked by this family since the 1860's.
We will happily show guests around the property and join in farm activities when possible.
We have a tennis court which is available to guests and there is ample opportunity to relax by strolling around the garden or just sitting on the large verandahs. For the energetic there is walking on the treeless plains with wonderful views of the Snowy Mountains.
Trips to the unique Snowy Mountain scheme and the snow fields can be reached in just over an hour.
There is trout fishing and horse riding can be arranged.
We will pick up and deliver from public transport.
Directions: *Please phone.*

Cooma - Monaro District
Guest House
Address: Royal Arms, Snowy Mountains Hwy in the centre of Nimmitabel 2631
Name: Royal Arms
Telephone: (02) 6454 6422
Fax: (02) 6454 6433
Beds: 4 Double, 10 Single
Bathroom: 2 Ensuite, 3 Guest share
Tariff: B&B (continental),
Double/Twin $70, Single $37,
Extra person $20, Suites 2 persons $80 to $95. Extra person $20, Dinner $20 (3 course, BYO). Package rate for groups of 10 or more Dinner/Bed/Breakfast $85 per person. Credit cards (B/C, M/C, VISA) accepted. Vouchers accepted
Nearest Town: Nimmitabel between Cooma and Bega/Bombala

The historic Royal Arms in the pioneering village of Nimmitabel has been restored to a Bed & Breakfast Guest House featuring modern facilities whilst retaining its olde world charm with antique furnishings. Delightful facilities, home made treats in your fridge, tea making, fresh flowers, warm and cosy log fires, heaters, electric blankets and doonas.
Since 1989, Jack, Rhondda, family and staff have provided weary travellers with a homely and friendly atmosphere plus hearty country meals, (a tradition that began back in the 1850s when it played host to horse drawn carriages), Morning and Afternoon teas and picnic baskets on request. Bush walks & Historic tours by arrangement. Our delightful building boasts a friendly ghost and was used as the hotel in the 1960s film "The Sundowners", starring Australia's own Peter Finch. The Royal Arms is central to bird watching, swimming, wineries, beaches, ski fields, and only 1 1/2 hours to Canberra. Test your skill trout fishing, and visit other historic features, with in a short walking distance. Come on home to the Royal Arms.

Cooma - Monaro
Farmstay
Address: 'Bulong Homestead', Cooma, NSW - Please phone for directions.
Name: Stephen and Jan Watson
Telephone: (02) 6452 5338 **Fax**: (02) 6452 5338
Mobile: (019) 929532 or (018) 678509
Beds: 1 Double, 2 Single, 1 Cot (2 bedrooms) **Bathroom**: 2 Private
Tariff: B&B (full) Double $95, Single $50, Children under 12yrs half price, Dinner $25. Vouchers accepted
Nearest Town: Cooma 2km, north along Mittagang Road

'Bulong' - built around 1902 - once employed many gardeners and servants. They departed years ago so we invite you to visit our home, stay in the restored servants quarters and be waited upon by us - how times change! 'Bulong' is a working cattle property where you can gain an insight into farm life, go bushwalking, trout fishing, swim in our pool, play croquet or volleyball. Explore our huge rambling gardens, historical ruins, stables, blacksmith shop and shearing shed and view many native animals and birds. Cooma is conveniently situated - just over an hours drive to the snowfields, South Coast or Canberra. Join us for evening meals in the dining room of Bulong Homestead. Here in an atmosphere of Victorian grandeur food and wine can be enjoyed from fine china and silver service whilst listening to Stephen's tales of the High Country. After your busy day you can relax in the deep claw-foot bath or doze by the open fire. All rooms are heated in winter, beds have electric blankets. Our 3 children enjoy having visitors. We first experienced B&B whilst travelling overseas and now hope to return that generous hospitality in a wonderful Australian setting. No smoking inside please.

NEW SOUTH WALES

Cooma
Farmstay
Address: Snowy Mountains Highway, Cooma, NSW 2630
Name: Berry & Liz Carter
Telephone: (02) 6452 4573
Fax: (02) 6452 4692 Mobile: 018 285072
Beds: 1 Queen, 1 Single (1 bedroom)
Bathroom: 1 Ensuite
Tariff: B&B (full) Double $150, Single $75, Children half price, Dinner $25pp,
Credit Cards.
Nearest Town: Cooma

Although only 19km from Cooma Post Office there is a pleasant feeling of isolation at Lama World. Spectacular views across the Monaro plains remind many of the ancestral Andean home of the newest residents of the farm the llamas, alpacas, and guanaco, while the glimpses of wild kangaroo, wombat, echidna, wedge tail eagle etc are quintessentially Australian.
Hosts Berry & Liz Carter pioneered farming lama in Australia and visitors will quickly be infused with their love of the animals and of the land. Visitors often stay to enjoy a MEALLS OF LLEGS picnic with llamas their gentle sherpas! This is not just a place to stay. It is a whole new experience!
Off farm, within an hour, there are many activities available including horse riding, trout fishing, caving, the snowfields (in season), national parks, wineries, and more. The national capital is only ninety minutes easy drive away in one direction and ocean beaches scarcely more in another.

Cooma
Homestay
Address: 8 Sir William Hudson Street, Cooma, NSW 2630
Name: Valley View B&B
Telephone: (02) 6452 1818 **Fax**: (02) 6452 1818
Beds: 1 Queen, 1 Double, 2 Single (3 bedrooms)
Bathroom: 1 Guests share
Tariff: B&B (full) Double $80, Single $50, Children $25.
  Vouchers accepted

Cooma is the gateway to the Snowy Mountains, centrally situated - we are 1 1/2hrs to Canberra, 1 1/2hrs to southern beaches, 1 hour from mountains, where winter means skiing and the rest of the year means wildflowers, walks, spectacular scenery. Over 1 million people visit our area each year.
"Valley View" is a near new 2 storey home with guest accommodation on the ground floor. The bedrooms are a good size, tastefully furnished. A central kitchen/lounge room is shared by guests. Electric blankets and heating, TV and radios provided. Smoking outside only.

Continental breakfast consists of fruit, cereal, toast, tea/coffee,
Full breakfast is the same with a cooked course,
Special breakfast has something special.

NEW SOUTH WALES

Cooma
Homestay
Address: 25 Soho Street, Cooma, 2630
Name: Entwood House
Telephone: (02) 6452 3278
Beds: 1 Double, 1 Single (2 bedrooms)
Bathroom: 1 Private
Tariff: B&B (full) Double $80-$90, Single $40-$45, Credit Cards.
Vouchers accepted $10 surcharge
Nearest Town: Cooma

Relax, unwind and experience the best of south east of Australia. The rural township of Cooma halfway between Melbourne and Sydney is just one hour from the nations capital Canberra, the South Coast beaches and the magnificent Snowy Mountains. Entwood House with its cottage style decor offers you a cosy retreat in a quiet street overlooking the town. A short, leisurely stroll takes you to Cooma heritage main street with its shops, art galleries, cafe and park. Your hosts Bob & Dianne offer you that warm country welcome with room for just three guests. You are assured of their personal service. You can relax and chat on the verandah or sink comfortable into the bay window seat for endless cups of tea or coffee. Imagine a warm cosy fire, comfy beds with fluffy doonas, while occasional snowfalls add the beauty of winter. Pickup from airport or buses can be arranged. We have a very friendly cat and dog.
Directions: *Please phone.*

Coonamble – Outback NSW
Farmstay
Address: "Thurloo", Coonamble, NSW 2829
Name: Simon Ibbott
Telephone: (068) 256208
Beds: 1 Queen, 1 Double, 2 Single (3 bedrooms)
Bathroom: 1 Guests share, 1 Family share
Tariff: B&B (full) Double $60, Single $40, Children half price. Dinner $20.
Campervans welcome. Vouchers accepted
Nearest Town: 31km east of Coonamble on Tooraweenah Road.

Thurloo is a sheep and cattle property of 5500 acres located on the edge of the Australian outback, but still an easy days drive from Sydney.
The lovely mountains and wildlife of the Warrumbungle National Park are only 60 kilometres away or you can visit Lightning Ridge to buy or fossick for the famous black opals.
Then relax by the swimming pool after a game of tennis or perhaps help muster sheep or cattle on the 4 wheel bikes. Visits to see sheep shearing or horse rides on the property can also be arranged. Come to Thurloo via the Blue Mountains and Western Plains Zoo at Dubbo. Enjoy the sights and hospitality and then continue north to the Gold Coast and Brisbane.
Please phone for directions.

Cootamundra - Young
Farmstay+Self-contained Accom.
Address: "Old Nubba Schoolhouse", Wallendbeen, NSW 2588
Name: Fred & Genine Clark
Telephone: (02) 6943 2513 **Fax**: (02) 6943 2590
Email: nubba@geko.net.au
Beds: 1 King, 2 Double, 8 Single (6 bedrooms)
Bathroom: 2 Private, 1 Guests share
Tariff: B&B (full) Double $85, Single $55, Children welcome, Dinner $25. 2 Self-contained cottages + homestead $85. Vouchers accepted
Nearest Town: Cootamundra - Young - Murrumburrah (each 15 mins drive)

Midway between Cootamundra, Young and Harden each 15 minutes drive, 4 hours southwest of Sydney, 1 1/2 hours west of Canberra, midway between Sydney and Melbourne.

"Old Nubba" has been in the family for 3 generations. It is a working mixed farm growing sheep, cattle, oats and triticale. We also have fowls, ducks, geese, dogs, pet lambs and Macey the pig.

"Old Nubba Schoolhouse" has been tastefully converted to guest accommodation and has its own sitting room, bedroom, bathroom, kitchenette and sun verandah. Slow combustion heating, cooling, OH fans, electric blankets and linen are provided. "Killarney Cottage" has recently been renovated. It sleeps 8 people in 3 bedrooms and is fully self contained.

Activities include peace and quiet, bush walks, birdlife, barbecue area on creek, visits to local wineries, historic Lambing Flat goldworkings, 3 golf courses 15 minutes drive and tennis 5 minutes drive in Wallendbeen Village. Fishing, occasional opportunities for guests to be involved in farm activities. 15 minutes drive to several delightful restaurants or have a 3 course country cooked dinner with your hosts.

Please ring for reservations.

Copmanhurst see Grafton
Coramba see Coffs Harbour

NEW SOUTH WALES

Cowra
Farmstay and B&B
Address: "Oakleigh", Cowra, NSW 2794
Name: S. Webster & family
Telephone: (02) 6345 4226 **Fax**: (02) 6342 1430
Beds: 3 Double, 4 Single (4 bedrooms)
Bathroom: 2 Private, 1 Guests share
Tariff: Full Board Double $130, Single $70, Children $40.
Nearest Town: Cowra

"Oakleigh" is a merino sheep property, consisting of 3000 acres over which you can roam at your leisure. It is not a hobby farm but a real piece of Australia where you can help (or watch) muster sheep and cattle, chase a few rabbits or find kangaroos. You will experience home cooked meals and may swim or play tennis with the family. The family all keen sportsmen are grown up but are good hosts and enjoy visitors. Bush barbeques are a specialty. The accommodation is quite extensive and features four beautifully decorated bedrooms. There are log fires in the winter and a swimming pool for summer. The large relaxing garden encloses the tennis court and pool with lawns, shrubs and trees.
Cowra boasts many tourist attractions including: - The famous Japanese Gardens and War Cemetery, the site of the POW camp, a great golf course and Wyangala Dam. Don't miss the opportunity spend some time on this Australian property with all meals provided.

Cowra
Homestay + Self-contained Accommodation
Address: "Riverslea"
Name: Cinda Millard
Telephone: (02) 6345 1835
Fax: (02) 6345 1835
Beds: 2 Double, 6 Single (5 bedrooms)
Bathroom: 2 Private, 1 Guests share, 1 Family share
Tariff: B&B (full) Double $75 - $90, Single $50, Children $25. Dinner $15pp. Campervans $20.
Nearest Town: Cowra 30km, Wyangala Dam on Lachlan River 10km.

Hosts Cinda and Phil Millard are restoring "Riverslea" to its former glory and would love to share with you the grand homestead overlooking the Lachlan River 10km below Wyangala Dam.
There is a guest suite in the home with sunroom by the pool, or cosy cottage with views over the river. At Riverslea you can go fishing, swimming, walking, bird watching or just relax and enjoy the peaceful river flowing by. Riverslea is only a short drive to beautiful Wyangala Dam where boating, bushwalking, fishing, water-slide, golf and the trout farm can be enjoyed.
Only 20 minutes in the car and you're in Cowra with its many attractions - Japanese Gardens, War Cemetery, vineyards, wine tasting, Rose Garden, golf and bowling clubs, good restaurants and coffee shops.
Come and join Cinda and Phil and share a cup of tea or a glass of wine with them, and let them show you their special part of Australia.

NEW SOUTH WALES

Crookwell
Homestay+Farmstay
Address: "Minnamurra",
Crookwell, NSW 2583
Name: Tony & Mary Prell
Telephone: (02) 4848 1226
Fax: (02) 4848 1288
Beds: 1 Double, 2 Twin,
1 Single (4 bedrooms)
Bathroom: 1 Ensuite, 1 Guest share with separate toilet
Tariff: B&B (special) Double $110, Single $55, Children 5-12 half price. Vouchers accepted
Nearest Town: Crookwell 15km, Goulburn 30km.

"Minnamurra" is a 1,080 hectare farm just 3 hours south of Sydney, close to Goulburn and Crookwell. We run sheep and cattle on undulating to hilly country 850 m above sea level.
Our home is warm, friendly and comfortable, with fresh flowers in the bedrooms and tender loving care always on hand. Reading lamps, electric blankets and two pillows on all beds. Special breakfast - other meals by arrangement - good home-style country cooking. Our home is smoke-free and quiet, no children under 5 and no pets in the house. We have our own tennis court and excellent trout fishing is available in the Wollondilly River or on the nearby Pejar Dam. The picturesque countryside is ideal for those who enjoy walking, and at certain times, guests may become involved in farm activities. Fresh air and blue skies. Rest and relaxation. Gracious living.
Winner of a 1995 Regional Award for Excellence in Tourism, finalist in 1996 and Award of Distinction in 1997.

Crookwell
Homestay
Address: "Gundowringa", Crookwell, NSW 2583
Name: Jess & Jeff Prell
Telephone: (048) 481212
Beds: 2 Double, 4 Single (4 bedrooms)
Bathroom: 2 Guests share
Tariff: B&B (full) Double $110, Single $60. Children under 12 half price. Dinner available. Vouchers accepted
Nearest Town: Crookwell and Goulburn

Gundowringa homestead was built in 1905 by Charles Prell OBE. This unique house has been restored to its original gracious style and is now occupied by the third generation of the family.
We have 2 double, 1 twin and 1 single room available for guests, plus 2 beds in a family room. Central heating with individual room control, together with an open fire in the sitting room offset the invigorating outside air of this climate. All beds have electric blankets and bedlights and each room has its own hand basin. Guests share 2 bathrooms.
The autumn and spring colours of our very large garden are spectacular and guests are welcome to wander at will and enjoy the peace and quiet. We have a tennis court and swimming pool which we would be delighted to see used.
Bed and breakfast and dinner available. Children half price.

Delungra see Inverell
Denhams Beach see Batemans Bay

NEW SOUTH WALES

Dorrigo
Bed & Breakfast   NRMA ★★★★
Address: Everinghams Road, Dorrigo
Name: Meriden Heights Retreat
Telephone: (02) 6657 2823
Mobile: 017 914 435
Beds: 1 Double or Twin, 1 Single (2 bedrooms)
Bathroom: 1 Ensuite, 1 Private
Tariff: B&B (full) Double $90, Single $50, Children under 14 years $25, Dinner $20, Credit Cards. Vouchers accepted $11 surcharge for Double
Nearest Town: Dorrigo

Meriden Heights is a small farm of 40 acres and is located just 1500 metres from the World Heritage Dorrigo National Park. Surrounded by lush farmlands the homestead enjoys 360 degrees views from mountain to sea. The accommodation provided is spacious and tastefully furnished and decorated. The beds are comfortable and have electric blankets. Advance bookings will ensure freshly home baked cakes / biscuits for your complimentary morning / afternoon tea. Advance notice is required for evening meals so that only fresh produce is used. Seasonally you can enjoy strawberries or raspberries from the garden. The wide lawns and colourful flower beds make a pleasant surround frequently visited by crimson rosellas and other wild birds. Dorrigo town is close by with fine art and craft galleries. Conveniently situated in relation to beachside towns, national parks and waterfalls Meriden heights is the prime location for your visit to Dorrigo. No smoking indoors preferred.

Dorrigo
Bed & Breakfast   NRMA ★★★☆
Address: "Fernbrook Lodge",
4705 Waterfall Way, Dorrigo, 2453
Name: Ross & Sue Erickson
Telephone: (02) 6657 2573
Fax: (02) 6657 2573
Beds: 2 Queen, 1 Double,
2 Single (4 bedrooms)
Bathroom: All Ensuite
Tariff: B&B (full) Double $75-$85,
Single $55, Children $25. Dinner $17-$30pp.
Nearest Town: Dorrigo 6km, Coffs Harbour 1 hour 10 minutes, Armidale 1 hour 20 min.

We would be delighted to welcome you to our comfortable country home, circa 1920. The peaceful garden, with treeferns, orchids, wonderful birds and butterflies, is backed by four acres of grazing land. View extend to the sea, across woodland and magnificent dairy & beef properties.
Enjoy lots of fresh air, rain and spring water, flowers, herbs, eggs and home grown produce in season, wood & gas fires and electric blankets. Two verandah rooms have independent garden access. As we are 3000ft above sea level it is wise to bring some warm clothing.
By car, we are 10 minutes from Dorrigo National Park Rainforest Centre and within one hour of four other National Parks; the surf beaches of Hungry Head and North Beach; Dangar, Ebor and Wollomombi Falls; cattle studs; white water rafting; trout fishing; wonderful picnic drives and exceptional art and craft.
Afternoon tea and a country breakfast are included and we will cook you dinner by arrangement. Smokers are welcome to enjoy the patios and verandah.

NEW SOUTH WALES

Dubbo
B&B Farmstay
Address: "Immarna", MS 54 Coolbaggie Rd.
PO Box 1743, Dubbo, 2830
Name: Michele Russ
Telephone: (068) 873131 **Mobile**: (0419) 012494
Beds: 2 Queen, 2 Double, 2 Single (4 bedrooms)
Bathroom: 2 Guests share
Tariff: B&B (full) Double/Twin $65, Single $55, Children $15, Cottage: $79, Dinner on request.
Vouchers accepted
Nearest Town: Dubbo and Narromine.
20km north-west Dubbo (accessible from both Newell and Mitchell Hwys)

For a brief overnight stay or a relaxing weekend away, 'Immarna" has to be the near perfect setting for time out from your busy 90's lifestyle to enjoy real hospitality, and fresh country air in tranquil surroundings on a 320 acre working property with bushland and abundant wildlife.

Built in 1908, the renovated "Immarna" homestead accommodates up to 10 guests including a separate cottage all located in expansive gardens.

As if the setting were not enough, we also pamper you with the quality of our food service, prepared by an inhouse chef ... generous breakfasts, bountiful dinners (three menus to select from) and much of the fare home grown. Dinner, morning and afternoon teas and picnic lunches available on request. Children welcome.

Short drives to major attractions like famous Western Plains Zoo, regional art gallery, quality eating houses and cafes. Warren cotton areas and Mudgee wineries are also easily accessible.

Dubbo
Bed & Breakfast
Address: "Sheraton House", 22 Colony Crescent, Dubbo
Name: Sheraton House"
Telephone: (02) 6884 1005
Beds: 1 Queen, 1 Twin, 1 Double, (3 bedrooms)
Bathroom: 1 Private, 2 Guests share
Tariff: B&B (full) Double $90 Single $50, Children $30 each, Dinner $35pp.
Nearest Town: Dubbo

"Sheraton House" has been freshly renovated and is a large home on a 1 acre block in the Sheraton Meadows Estate of Dubbo. All bedrooms have immediate access to bathrooms and a spa bath. All beds have electric blankets and woollen underlays. The entire house is air-conditioned and there is under-floor heating, TV points in all bedrooms, swimming pool and tennis court, off street parking, use of laundry. BBQs and country cooking a speciality. Dubbo is a great holiday destination with our Zoo, old Dubbo Gaol, River Boat, Dundullimal Homestead, Chinchilla Gardens and lots more.

We have pet facilities but do not allow them in the house. No smoking.

We rely on your comments about our B&Bs.
Please send us a comment form supplied by your host.

NEW SOUTH WALES

Dungog
Homestay
Address: Tabbil Creek Homestead, Dungog, NSW 2420
Name: Tabbil Creek Homestead
Telephone: (049) 921870
Fax: (049) 921576
Beds: 4 Single (2 bedrooms)
Bathroom: 1 Ensuite, 1 Private
Tariff: B&B (full) Double $120, Single $60, Children $20, Dinner $25pp.
Vouchers accepted
Nearest Town: Dungog 4km

Enjoy the peace and quiet of country hospitality in the lovely surrounds of a traditional homestead and its extensive garden of lawns and large English trees. Situated at the foot of Barrington Tops, it is ideal as a base to explore the Hunter Valley and the vineyards. 2 1/2 hour drive from Sydney - 1 hour from Newcastle - 1 hour from the vineyards. Dungog Golf Club is within walking distance. There are 2 large twin bedrooms, both with mosquito nets, electric blankets, overhead fans, heaters. Guests have private use of sunroom, with tea and coffee making facilities, homemade biscuits, TV room, patio, tennis court. Full English breakfast served in dining room or verandah. Dinner provided by prior arrangement or light supper. Be assured of a warm welcome with those special luxuries of country living.

Dungog - Barrington Tops Area
Self-contained Accom.
Address: "Villikulla Cottage", Lot 801, Moylans Road, Fosterton Valley via Dungog
Name: Brian Crowley
Telephone: (02) 9810 8906
Fax: (02) 9209 4081 **Mobile**: 0416 170315
Email: brianc@zeta.org.au
Beds: 1 King/Queen, 1 Double, 5 Single (5 bedrooms)
Bathroom: 1 Guests share
Tariff: B&B (continental) Double $70, Single $45, Children $10. Complete cottage can be rented for $70/night without breakfast. Vouchers accepted
Nearest Town: Dungog

Explore the rainforest of Barrington Tops Ranges from Villikulla Cottage.
From the back door you can bushwalk into virtual wilderness. The Williams River is close by for canoeing, fishing, swimming or collecting fresh water mussels. The Barrington Tops area is renowned for its rich native wildlife and flora. Go night-spotting for nocturnal animals in the local forest. The farmhouse is set on the edge of the forest and is the last house before you leave Fosterton Valley for the wild forest. Villikulla Cottage has 5 bedrooms and a spacious living area that leads on to a huge deck with stunning views of the peaceful valley and forests. There're a pot belly stove for winter and BBQ facilities. There are creeks, farm animals, and bush turkeys leave the rainforest to feed at the kitchen door. Wallabies abound close by. Canoe available.
Directions: From Dungog take the Fosterton Road, cross the Williams River, turn left into Moylons Rd and keep to the right for 3kms and you arrive.
Home Page: http://www.zeta.org.au/~johnl/foster.htm

NEW SOUTH WALES

Eden
Homestay
Address: "Bellevue Lodge",
13-15 Bellevue Place, Eden,
NSW 2551 Postal: PO Box 163,
Eden, NSW 2551
Name: Fay & Rudy Speer
Telephone: (02) 649 61575 **Fax**: (02) 6496 1575 **Mobile**: (018) 489575
Beds: 3 Queen, 4 Single (4 bedrooms) **Bathroom**: 2 Ensuite, 1 Guests share
Tariff: B&B (full) Double $85/$95/$115/$125, Single $55-$65, Not suitable for young children. Extra guest $25-$35. Dinner 2 course $20, 3 course $25, Credit Card (VISA/MasterCard/BCard). Vouchers accepted excluding Xmas-New Year + surcharge $10.
Nearest Town: Eden 1km, halfway Sydney-Melbourne on Sapphire Coast

Sea views. Luxury. Personalised service at affordable prices. "Bellevue Lodge" is a 75 SQ mansion set in 1/2 acre of landscaped gardens alive with birds. The unsurpassed views of Two Fold Bay and surrounding mountains are breathtaking. Extensive use of redwood panelling and antiques create a warm and luxurious atmosphere. Separate guests lounge, TV, video, stereo, and billiard rooms. The huge bedrooms have balcony access and are furnished for the comfort of our guests. Eden is a fisherman's paradise, so its natural fresh fish is often requested for dinner. Organic home grown vegetables served in season. Notice appreciated. Country style breakfast includes homemade muesli and jams. Whale watching October-November. Fishing, diving, bush walking, golf, bowls, clubs, unpolluted beaches, boat ramp, all within 3km.
Two night package including dinners $115 pp twin. Located behind Bayview Motel.
Pet: friendly Blue Heeler (outside) Eden's a little paradise we would love to share with you.

Eden - Wonboyn Lake
Bed & Breakfast
Address: "Wonboyn Lake Retreat",
Acacia Avenue, Wonboyn Lake, NSW 2551
Name: Beryl Pedersen
Telephone: (02) 6496 9163
Fax: (02) 6496 9163
Beds: 1 Queen (plus bed couch)
Bathroom: 1 Ensuite
Tariff: B&B (full) Double $60-$80,
Single $30-$40, Children welcome.
Open five months, December to April inclusive.
Vouchers accepted
Nearest Town: Eden

Beryl, much travelled herself, invites you to visit her bush retreat: separate wing, ensuite, private entrance from garden adjoining forest. The environment abounds in natural fauna and flora, a delight for bird-watchers and bush-walkers. Great fishing area - a short step takes you to the lake with private jetty. Closeby is the Wonboyn River, the open beach at Disaster Bay and the beautiful wilderness of the Nadgee Nature Reserve. Bliss! Wonboyn Lake is situated between Eden and NSW/Victorian border, half-way between Sydney/Melbourne and a few hours from Canberra.
Lunch/dinner on request, specialising vegetarian. Local oysters available (extra - order ahead). All meals $55/$110, (4 days $150/$300). Store (licensed) nearby. Children most welcome. Wood or gas BBQ available for own cooking, garden seating or gazebo. Enjoy availability of the book collection and music facilities. A warm welcome awaits you.

NEW SOUTH WALES

Eden
Historic Bed & Breakfast
Address: "Crown And Anchor",
239 Imlay Street, Eden
Name: Judy & Mauro Maurilli
Telephone: (02) 6496 1017
Mobile: (041) 7239346
Beds: 4 Double (4 bedrooms)
Bathroom: 4 Ensuite
Tariff: B&B (full) Double $90-$120, Single $80-$100, Dinner by arrangement, Credit Cards. a 10% discount applies for 3 nights or longer.
Vouchers accepted $10-$29 surcharge
Nearest Town: Eden

The Crown And Anchor was built as a small hotel in the early 1840's and first licensed in 1845. It was the first substantial building in Eden, preceded only by slab and bark huts. As such it commands spectacular views of Twofold Bay and the Ocean as well as a very central and quiet location within five minutes walking distance of restaurants, hotels, the Fishermen's Club, the wharf, the beach, even our favourite snorkelling spot. Watch the whales from the veranda from September to November. Each room has a view of the sea, ensuite bathroom, luxurious bedding, antique furnishing, and some, open fire places.
In fact the whole building is very original and offers an unforgettable and unique experience steeped in early Australian character and charm of long gone whalers and sea faring days.
Complete quiet and privacy is assured, with your hosts occupying semi detached buildings. Service aims to be friendly and first class.
Complementary afternoon tea and evening drinks will be a pleasure.
The generous gourmet breakfast is old fashioned country style with a variety of homemade and fresh market produce complemented by freshly squeezed fruit juices, fine coffee and teas to be enjoyed on the sunny verandah or in front of a warm fire.
Illustrated is one of the original Handbills recently discovered during restorations. Its message is still very true of today ...
Judy and Mauro invite you to share in the on going discovery of arguably the most romantic and authentic building in the area.

Emerald Beach see Coffs Harbour
Emmaville see Glen Innes
Erina see Central Coast

NEW SOUTH WALES

Far North Coast see Wooli
Faulconbridge see Blue Mountains
Figtree see Wollongong

Forbes
Homestay
Address: 12 Battye Street, Forbes, NSW 2871
Name: Sandra Rutledge
Telephone: (02) 6851 2055
Beds: 4 Single (2 bedrooms)
Bathroom: 1 Guests share, 1 Family share plus extra loo
Tariff: B&B (full) Double $140, Single $70, Campervans facilities available, Smokers welcome, BBQ & kitchen available for use. Vouchers accepted
Nearest Town: Forbes

A restored 1850's house with a high front fence, once occupied by the Lord Mayor. Situated two blocks from town where there are a selection of restaurants at reasonable prices. One-day trips from Forbes include the Dubbo Zoo, Japanese gardens at Cowra, Wyangala Dam nearby, the Radio Telescope at Parkes, plus the caves, arboretum and Burrendong Dam at Wellington. In Forbes there are historical points of interest linked to Ben Hall the bushranger, gold mining and vineyards. The attractive railway station has been converted to an Arts & Crafts shop, although wheat trains still stop there. Forbes is on the Newell Highway halfway between Brisbane and Melbourne and five hours from Sydney via the Blue Mountains, Bathurst and Orange, there are also daily flights to and from Sydney, guests can be met at the airport. Forbes has two swimming pools, one heated, a water skiing area, a golf course, tennis courts, a racecourse etc., etc. Farm visits can be arranged.

Forbes
Homestay
Address: Urania House, 4 Bogan Gate Rd., Forbes, NSW 2871
Name: Pam & John Baass
Telephone: (068) 522862 **Fax**: (068) 522862
Beds: 2 Double (2 bedrooms)
Bathroom: 1 Ensuite, Shower, toilet & basin.
Tariff: B&B (continental) Double $60, Single $45. Vouchers accepted
Nearest Town: Forbes

*Urania House stands on a large quiet block surrounded by lawns, trees and gardens. It is 1km from the centre of town. Forbes is a picturesque Town boasting lovely old buildings, parks and lake. An informative and interesting museum is worth a visit. A beautiful 18 hole golf course and Club House with restaurant welcomes all visitors. Guests are accommodated in a separate wing, two double rooms, ensuite and sitting room with TV, A.C and heating. The sitting room opens on to a vine covered pergola where breakfast can be eaten if desired. A private entrance and off street parking. Coffee and tea facilities. A full cooked or continental breakfast. Guests can be picked up from airport or coach stop.
Restaurants and eating out is well catered for. No smoking inside.*

Tell other travellers about your favourite B&Bs

NEW SOUTH WALES

Forbes
Homestay
Address: "Cartref"
Cnr McDonnell & Clematis Sts,
Forbes, NSW 2871
Name: Ken & Esma Smith
Telephone: (068) 522718
Fax: (068) 511686
Beds: 1 Double,
2 Single (2 bedrooms)
Bathroom: 1 Guests share
Tariff: B&B (full) Double $70,
Single $45, Children over 5yrs.
Vouchers accepted
Nearest Town: Forbes

We welcome you to our large comfortable home just 1km from Railway Tourist Information Centre; you will immediately find yourself at home either as one of the family or if you wish in complete privacy. A hot cuppa or ice cold drink awaits you. Enjoy a great night's sleep in brass beds and crisp white linen. Breakfast is hearty country under a vine covered arbour in summer. 3 course dinner by arrangement or you may prefer to try our fine restaurants or clubs.
We have a salt water pool which is a great way to relax after a day on the road in the country where Ben Hall ranged and robbed. Visit his grave in the local cemetery, do a spot of birdwatching in the bird hide, enjoy a game of bowls or a game of golf on the 18 hole golf course.
Forbes, famous for its historic buildings is ideally situated on the Newell H'way.

Forster
Homestay
Address: 52 MacIntosh Street,
Forster, NSW
Name:
Forster Homestyle Bed & Breakfast
Telephone: (02) 6554 7490
Fax: (02) 6554 7490
Mobile: (0412) 656342
Beds: 2 Double, 2 Single (3 bedrooms)
Bathroom: 1 Guests share
Tariff: B&B (continental) Double $60,
Single $45, Children under 10yrs $15 for extra bed in same room as adults.
Nearest Town: Tuncurry/twin town of Forster across the bridge

Neville & Evelyn Jackson and family welcome you to stay at their comfortable home centrally located in Forster. There are fans in all rooms for summer and tile fire for cold snaps in winter in the combined dining / lounge TV room. Help yourself to tea / coffee and fridge facilities.
The guest bathroom features a spa which is available for a small fee. Off street parking is provided and because of close proximity to the Lake, beaches, shops, restaurants, clubs and tourist operators, you may prefer to go walk about and enjoy this lovely area.
Forster has something to offer everyone: surfing and swimming in clean waters, fishing / boating or enjoying the fresh local seafood.
Having lived in Forster for 23 years there is much to tell you ... so come and share the experience with us.
No smoking in Home Please!

Forster - Pacific Palms
Country House B&B   NRMA ★★★★☆
Address: 1788 Coomba Road, Coomba Park, NSW 2428
Name: "Galway Downs" Lakeside Country House
Telephone: (02) 65542019 Reservations Freecall: 1800 644 889 **Fax**: (02) 6554 2019
Beds: 4 King/Queen, 1 Double, 2 Single (5 bedrooms)
Bathroom: 4 Ensuite, 1 Private
Tariff: B&B (full) Double $170, Single $135, Children N/A, Dinner $40-$45pp, Credit Cards.
Nearest Town: We are situated 43km south of Forster near Pacific Palms off the Lakes Way.

This elegant Country House is 3 1/2 hrs. drive north of Sydney near Pacific Palms / Forster on the mid-north coast of NSW.

The ultimate in Fine Lodging Galway Downs has 30 rural acres with 430 metres of absolute waterfront. Three ensuite rooms and two luxurious honeymoon suites open onto wide verandahs with stunning views of lake and meadow with a backdrop of the Wallingat State Forest.

With plump sofas, fragrant flowers, old port and chocolates, open fires, formal billiard room, king or queen size beds, deep bathtubs and afternoon tea each day all expectations are quietly met.

There is a saltwater pool and a private jetty with boats, canoes and surf ski provided. Horse-riding, carriage rides, 4DW tours and a private golf course nearby provide for more active pursuits. There are no facilities for children.

Candlelit Gourmet Dining is optional.

Continental breakfast consists of fruit, cereal, toast, tea/coffee,
Full breakfast is the same with a cooked course,
Special breakfast has something special.

NEW SOUTH WALES

Gilgandra - Biddon
Farmstay
Address: "Biddon Homestead",
Biddon, Newell Highway, NSW 2827
Name: Rob and Moira Hermann
Telephone: (068) 483521
Beds: 'Homestead': 1 Queen.
'Lavender cottage': 2 Queen, 3 Singles
Bathroom: 'Homestead' 1 ensuite. 'Lavender Cottage' own bathroom
Tariff: 'Homestead' B&B (full) Double $80, Single $55. 'Lavender Cottage' B&B (full) Double $100, extra adults $30 p.p. Children $20, under 5's $10 p.c. Weekly rates available. Dinner available. Credit cards. Vouchers accepted
Nearest Town: Gilgandra

Biddon is ideally located between Melbourne & Brisbane on the Newell Highway. The Homestead is on 1100 acres of sheep / wheat country set against the scenic backdrop of the Wurrumbungle Mountain Range. The historic sandstone homestead c1900 offers couples quiet and private accommodation tucked away from the cares of a busy world. No TV - just your choice of music - a large spa bath in the ensuite, evening meals by candlelight. Drinks on the verandahs experiencing our wonderful sunsets and star filled skies.

If however you have a family or are travelling in a group, we have relocated the original Biddon Church (built as part of the property in 1911) and restored it as "'Lavender Cottage'. It offers accommodation (up to 8) providing guests with large and private bedrooms, bathroom with bath and shower, a lovely open lounge with TV, wood fired heater and air conditioner, dining area - where meals can be eaten cooked by Robert at the 'bush Cafe' (which is also operated from the property) or for the more independent there is a fridge, Bar-B-Q, tea / coffee making facilities - everything to make you stay as homelike as we can.

We are sure you will enjoy the pace and tranquillity of the setting with views across the paddocks to our 80 acres of bush, where guests can roam looking for signs of resident families of Wallabies, Echidnas and Kangaroos.

Young children are catered for with a cubby house, sandpit, swing and slippery dip. They may enjoy feeding the chickens and collecting the eggs. (High chair, cot and baby bath are available).

Your breakfast basket, containing delicious home-made bread and jams, can be delivered to your cottage, where you will find everything you need to cook your own breakfast or you may wander across to the Bush Cafe and let Robert spoil you. Morning / afternoon teas, lunches and picnic hampers are available.

There is an inground swimming pool for guests use.

Day trips from Biddon can include visits to Western Plains Zoo, Wellington Caves, Wurrumbungle national park, Siding Springs Observatory, Mudgee Wineries, Warren Cotton Fields, Gilgandra Observatory and Rural Museum.

(No smoking or pets inside please).

NEW SOUTH WALES

Glen Innes - Ben Lomond
Homestay/Farmstay/S.C. Cottage
NRMA ★★☆
Address: "Silent Grove",
Ben Lomond, NSW 2365
Name: John & Dorothy Every
Telephone: (02) 6733 2117 (please use answering machine)
Fax: (02) 6733 2117 **Mobile**: (015) 936799
Beds: 1 Queen, 1 Double, 2 Single (3 bedrooms)
Bathroom: 2 Guests share
Tariff: B&B (full) Double $55, Single $30, Dinner $15, Children welcome – discount, Campervans facilities available.   Vouchers accepted
Nearest Town: Glen Innes 48km north, Guyra 32km south, Ben Lomond Village 8km.

"Silent Grove" (1313 acres) is situated in a peaceful rural setting on the top of the Northern Tablelands, requiring a short detour off the New England Highway on a sealed road. You will be pleased you detoured. Fresh air, fine views. We run shorthorn cattle, merino sheep and prime lambs.
Guests may join in the normal farm activities, take in the panoramic views from the top of Mt Rumby (1503m) and travel through the tranquil Woods's Gorge on a guided tour. Or you may choose a relaxing bush walk - trout fishing, yabbying (in season), tennis court available. August is usually shearing time. In winter time be prepared for an occasional snowfall. Easy access to Armidale, Guyra, Glen Innes (home of the Australian Standing Stones), New England, Gibratar Range, Washpool National Parks.
If you are looking for warm friendly country hospitality then "Silent Grove" is for you. Will pick up from plane, train or bus. Have pet cat.
Self-catering 3 bedroom cottage available.
Directions: *Please telephone, use answering machine or write.*

Glen Innes - New England Tablelands
Bed & Breakfast
Address: 82 Wentworth St.,
Glen Innes, NSW 2370
Name: "Queenswood"
Telephone: (02) 6732 3025
Beds: 1 Queen, 1 King,
2 Single (3 bedrooms)
Bathroom: 1 Ensuite,
1 Guests share
Tariff: B&B (full) King with ensuite $75, Single $45, Children under 14yrs $25, Under 2yrs free, limit of one, Dinner by arrangement BYO.
Nearest Town: Glen Innes (situated in town)

We are very centrally situated, close to parks, clubs, shops and churches. Glen Innes is right at the cross-roads to just about everywhere, plus Australia's only Celtic Standing Stones, National Parks, fossicking areas, bush walking, horse riding, golf and bowls (across the road), wonderful scenery to paint or just to sit and enjoy.
Wilderness Day Tours can be organised to nearby attractions maximum 6 min. 3 people.
"Queenswood" was originally a Girls Grammar School opened in 1899, but has been a family house since 1936.
We have a beautiful climate, invigorating in winter, cool in summer, so if you want to escape the heat, head for the Tablelands of New England.
Discounts available for consecutive nights. Reservations are appreciated. No pets, please. Off-street parking.

NEW SOUTH WALES

Glen Innes - Emmaville
Self-contained Accom. + Bunkhouse
Address: Jimargie Station, Ashford Road, Emmaville, NSW 2371
Name: Jim & Marg Cowin
Telephone: (02) 6733 7277
Fax: (02) 6733 7277
Mobile: (017) 826622
Beds: Units - 4 Double, 4 Single (4 bedrooms), Bunkhouse - 18 Beds
Bathroom: 3 Private
Tariff: B&B (full or basket) Double $70, Single $35, Children $25, Dinner $15pp, Campervans $10pp, No Pets. Vouchers accepted
Nearest Town: 58km north of Glen Innes

An idyllic hideaway which offers a combination of relaxation and exuberance, fresh mountain air, native/feral animals and birds. Peace, tranquillity and stress free with 2000 acres of rugged wilderness and beauty to explore - go bushwalking or bird watching. Jimargie Station has one family and two double units all fully self contained with fridge, gas cooker, microwave, crockery, cutlery, electric blankets and separate bathrooms. We also have a Bunk House to cater for larger groups with electricity, bunks, wood stove, outside toilet and bush shower and numerous camp/campervan sites. A games room is available for all to use and there are numerous bar-b-que areas.
Continental or full breakfasts available or baskets with all the essentials to cook yourself. Dinners can be arranged with prior notice. Extra activities with tuition by a qualified instructor can be tailored to suit your needs including sport fishing, archery, clay pigeon shooting and 4 wheel driving.

Glen Innes
Homestay
Address: Please phone
Name: Lynn & Ian
Telephone: (02) 6732 5701
Fax: (02) 6732 5701
Beds: 2 Queen, 1 Single (3 Bedrooms)
Bathroom: 1 Guests Share
Tariff: B&B (full) Double $90, Single $65. Vouchers accepted
Nearest Town: Glen Innes

Diarmid was a legendary Celtic hero of the 3rd Century AD. Stay at Diarmid's and learn about the Celts in Australia, discover the living history of the Northern Highlands of NSW, see the Australian Standing Stones, travel on guided picnic tours to the historic Ottery Arsenic Mine, Kings Plains Castle, and the most northern meadery in NSW, meet Australia's only horseback postie. Or just relax in the comfort of a beautiful turn of the century Federation home with its elegant guest lounge, fluffy white pillows and delicious home cooked goodies.
Breakfast is eaten in the attractive leafy garden, on the wide verandah, or indoors by the log fire. Free barbecue for guest use.
Diarmid's has safe off street parking and a cuddly "watchdog". We are in a quiet street but close to everything. Special wheat free or diabetic breakfasts by arrangement. Write for our brochure on special packages and guided tours.

NEW SOUTH WALES

Gloucester
Rural Homestay
Address: "Arrowee House",
Barrington Road,
Gloucester, NSW 2422
Name: Kay Wright
Telephone: (02) 6558 2050
Beds: 3 Queen, 2 Single,
3 Double bunks (5 bedrooms)
Bathroom: 4 Ensuite, 1 Guests share
Tariff: B&B (full) Double $70, Single $35,
Children 5-12yrs half price. Dinner $15.
Credit cards. Vouchers accepted
Nearest Town: 1 1/2 hours north Newcastle, 45 mins south Taree.

A delightful rural setting at one of the prettiest spots in the Gt. Lakes region - Gloucester - gateway to Barrington Tops, scenic and picturesque, is where you'll find Arrowee House. A comfortable 5 bedroomed brick home, with a family unit, surrounded by cool verandahs. Accommodating 14 guests all except one room has own ensuite shower / vanity. The main 3 way bathroom has a spa. The spacious lounge / dining area has a cosy wood heater for cool nights and air-conditioning for hot summer days. Table tennis in the rumpus room and piano for the musical. After a day of sightseeing a sumptuous 3 course dinner with a complimentary wine and port optional, followed by a movie pictionary or just relax in the peaceful setting. The large picture windows have uninterupted views of mountains and rolling hills. The delicious cooked English breakfast is accompanied by Kay's home baked bread. What better way to start another enjoyable day.

Gloucester - Barrington Tops
Homestay   NRMA ★★★☆
Address: "Gloucester Cottage Bed & Breakfast",
61 Denison Street, Gloucester, 2422 NSW
Name: Keith & Betty Anido
Telephone: (02) 6558 2658 **Fax**: (02) 6558 2658
Beds: 3 Queen, 1 Double,
6 Single (6 bedrooms)
Bathroom: 2 Guests share, 1 Family share
Tariff: B&B (full) Double $65,
Single $45, Children under 5 $15, 5-13 $25.
Dinner $20. Vouchers accepted
Nearest Town: Gloucester

Better service,
better business.

Comfort and country hospitality - look no further than Gloucester Cottage, the recently restored and extended Federation home a 5 minute stroll from Gloucester Town Centre, scenically situated below the Bucketts Range. Roaring log fires, doonas, electric blankets, breezy verandahs and ceiling fans ensure comfort whatever the weather, and Keith and Betty fill their cosy home with tales from afar, local handcrafted furniture, and rows and rows of books to curl up with. In the kitchen, featuring the old fuel stove and copper, substantial Aussie breakfasts are served while family-style dinners are available by prior arrangement. As Gloucester is only 3 hours from Sydney and Keith can meet the XPT in the courtesy van, Gloucester Cottage is easily accessible for a weekend getaway or a night's stopover. However, its closeness to Barrington and Gloucester Tops, State Forests and sparkling rivers begs a longer stay - bushwalking, cycling, horse riding, white water kayaking, scenic drives and many other activities are all available. (Overseas guests will appreciate Keith's world-famous kookaburra call!)

NEW SOUTH WALES

Gloucester
Rural Homestay NRMA ★★★☆
Address: Burrakay,
17 Gloucester Tops Road,
Gloucester, NSW 2422
Name: Anne & John Cullum
Telephone: (02) 6558 8231
Beds: 1 Queen, 2 Single (2 bedrooms)
Bathroom: 1 Guests share
Tariff: B&B (full) Double $60-$65, single $35-$40,
Children 5-12yrs $20, Not under 5yrs, Dinner $20.
Vouchers accepted
Nearest Town: Gloucester 10km north, Newcastle 1 1/2 hours

Better service, better business.

We invite you to share and enjoy our home on 30 acres with views all round of the beautiful Gloucestershire countryside. We are well situated for touring and walking in the Gloucester and Barrington Tops. There is horse-riding nearby, and canoeing and other activities in the area. In summer, swim or laze by the salt-water pool, or play croquet. Join us in front of a log fire in winter. There is a large air-conditioned lounge / games room with TV for guests use and a sunroom where a delicious breakfast is served which includes home-made bread and jams, and fruit from the garden in season. Dinner is available by prior arrangement, or you can visit a local Gloucester restaurant just ten minutes away. Tea and coffee making facilities are provided. We have a few beef cattle and a small friendly dog. No smoking in the house please. We look forward to welcoming you.
Directions: *Please Phone.*

Goulburn – see Southern Highlands

Grafton
Farmstay, B&B
Address: "Seeview", 440 Rogans Bridge Road,
Seelands, Grafton, 2460 NSW
Name: Mona & Henry Ibbott
Telephone: (066) 449270 **Fax**: (066) 472145
Mobile: (014) 429 872
Beds: 1 Queen, 1 Double 2 Single (3 bedrooms)
Bathroom: 1 Ensuite, 1 Family share
Tariff: B&B (full) Double from $60,
Single from $30, Children half price,
Dinner $15, Children $7.50.
Campervans welcome. Vouchers accepted
Nearest Town: Grafton

Seeview is a pretty 200 acre farm, 10 minutes from Grafton on the banks of the mighty Clarence River. The Big River is noted for its river boats, water skiing and river walks. Grafton is the famous city of the Jacaranda trees and has the markets, craft shops, art galleries, coffee shops, the old Cathedral and other historical buildings of interest. Yamba, our popular beach is just 50 minutes away. Many overseas guests and agricultural students from overseas haved stayed at Seeview and enjoyed the hospitality of the Ibbotts, their friendly dog, Bear. Children, people with disabilities and pets are welcomed - a good stopover on the way to Brisbane or Sydney.

NEW SOUTH WALES

Grafton - Copmanhurst
Farmstay + Self-contained Accom.
Address: "Wave Hill" Station, Copmanhurst, via Grafton, NSW 2460
Name: Steve & Sue Ibbott
Telephone: (02) 6647 2145
Fax: (02) 6647 2145
Email: ibbott@nor.com.au
Beds: 1 Double, 2 Single (2 bedrooms)
Bathroom: 1 Guests share
Tariff: B&B (full) Double $90, Single $50, Children half price. Dinner $20.
Campervans welcome. Vouchers accepted
Nearest Town: Grafton - 70km northwest of Grafton. Phone for directions.

Stephen and Sue and their young family love having guests stay at their 11,000 acre cattle property. It's fun helping with general farm activities such as mustering cattle or just relax on the wide verandahs and watch the abundant birdlife and the cattle grazing. For guests with more energy there's horse riding, tennis, bushwalking and fossicking. Another attraction is a trip to the Clarence River Gorge either on horseback or 4WD vehicle and experience spectacular mountain country with views into Queensland. You can also visit a local ostrich farm or travel to nearby Washpool National Park. For guests wishing to be independent, the original cottage on the property has been renovated. It's rustic but charming and guests have the choice of cooking for themselves, eating at the homestead with the family or having meals delivered to the cottage. We will pick up and deliver from public transport, so come stay with us and experience Australian country life and hospitality.

Grafton
Homestay
Address:
Bracon Ash Country Retreat,
Reilley's Lane via South Grafton
NSW 2460
Name:
Georgina and Richard Corbould-Warren
Telephone: (02) 6643 1847
Fax: (02) 6643 1847
Beds: 1 Queen, 1 Double, 3 Single, (3 bedrooms)
Bathroom: 1 Ensuite, 1 Guest share.
Tariff: B&B (full) Double $70-$75, Single $40, Children $15.
Credit cards accepted. Vouchers accepted
Nearest Town: Grafton

THE PERFECT STOPOVER!
Bracon Ash Country retreat lies only two minutes from Pacific Highway - a day's travel from Sydney or a comfortable half day from Brisbane. The attractions of the Gold Coast are only three hours away.
Your "Home Away From Home" is situated on 23 acres of bushland, close to Grafton City. A retreat where one can find solitude, varied bird life, kangaroos and wallabies. Guests can swim in our large pool or enjoy a walk down our quiet country lane. Whether accommodated in the house or adjacent cottage, guests are invited to join hosts Richard and Georgina for a cooked breakfast in the house or by the pool.
Directions: *10 km South of Grafton city on Pacific Highway. Turn left at Reilley's Lane. 1.5 km down lane on left.*

Grafton
Self-contained Accom.
Address: 244 Prince Street, Grafton, 2460
Name: Mabuhay Accommodation
Telephone: (02) 6643 2555 **Fax**: (02) 6643 2555 **Mobile**: 019 155 260
Beds: 2 Queen & 4 Single or 8 Single (3 bedrooms)
Bathroom: 1 Guests share
Tariff: B&B (continental) Double $50-$60, Single $25-$35, Children under 12yrs $12, Cooked breakfast $5 extra, Dinner $10 (Filipina & Australian cuisine).
Nearest Town: Grafton - 2 mins CBD

"Mabuhay" means welcome in Filipina.
It is a bright spacious self-contained unit, surrounded by beautifully landscaped gardens and barbecue area. Cook your own meals either in the self contained kitchen, or on the barbecue area (all inclusive) or we can cook for you.
We are close to restaurants, clubs and shops.
Grafton has many venues during the year; Easter - Jazz & Blues, April - Grafton Show, July - Horse Raving Carnival, August - Country Music Festival, Oct-Nov Jacaranda Festival.

Grafton
Farmstay
Address: 133 Mylneford Road, Mylneford
Name: Jean & Mac Lindsay
Telephone: (02) 6644 9789
Fax: (02) 6644 9789
Email: macfor@nor.com.au
Beds: 1 Double (1 bedroom)
Bathroom: Guests share
Tariff: B&B (full) Double $70, Single $45, Dinner $15pp, Campervans $20, Credit Cards.
Nearest Town: Grafton

Relax on the banks of the beautiful Clarence River at Riverbank Farm Country Retreat 20 minutes drive from Grafton. Enjoy the peace and tranquillity of the stroll along the riverbank. Laze away some hours on the verandah overlooking the river and cottage gardens. Absorb the wildlife that abounds; take a canoe trip on the river; throw a line in a catch some fish. Rest in the comfort of a colonial style home in a beautifully decorated double private bedroom with its own access to bathroom / and verandah. Home cooked country style breakfast served on the verandah. Morning and afternoon teas and dinner by arrangement.
Your hosts Mac and Jean Lindsay extend to you a warm welcome to enjoy your stay in this truly beautiful place.

Please help us provide the best hospitality in the world.
Fill in a comment form for every place you stay.

NEW SOUTH WALES

Grafton
Farmstay
Address:
965 Old Glen Innes Road,
via Grafton 2460
Name: Tim Treanor
Telephone: (02) 6644 9702
Fax: (02) 6644 9702
Beds: 1 Double, 2 Single (2 bedrooms)
Bathroom: 1 Family share
Tariff: B&B (full) Double $60, Single $40,
Discounted tariff for children, Dinner $20, Credit Cards.
Nearest Town: Grafton 25km

Tims Rest is a secluded 20 hectare retreat on the banks of the Orara River 25km South West of Grafton. The house is hand-crafted from stone and timber with a large fireplace, timber decks and slate floors. Guestrooms are situated in loft-style accommodation 30 metres from the house and offer extra privacy. They are beautifully made from Australian hardwoods with a unique feeling of 'yesteryear'. There are no TVs or microwaves at Tims Rest. The 4km forested bush drive from the main road to the house will let you know you're onto something Special!! Solar power, composting toilet and organic garden ensure the environment is well cared for. Enjoy swimming, fishing, bushwalking and bird watching. World Heritage National Parks and superb white water rafting are 50 minutes away. Abundant wildlife including kangaroos, wallabies and platypus. Tim is well travelled and offers great home-cooked meals with an international flavour. All meals are available. Please phone ahead for bookings and directions. If you need a rest, a recharge and relaxation - come and say hello!!

Grafton
Homestay
Address: 3 Oliver Street,
Grafton, NSW 2460
Name: "Dovedale Bed & Breakfast"
Telephone: (02) 6642 5706
Mobile: (041) 8287041
Beds: 2 Queen, 2 Single (3 bedrooms)
Bathroom: 2 Ensuite
Tariff: B&B (full) Double $82, Single $62,
Children $15, Dinner from $10, Credit Cards.
Vouchers accepted $5 surcharge
Nearest Town: Grafton, 1.6km from P.O.

Built in 1926, this home is a splendid example of architecture in Grafton, blending the aesthetics of the Californian bungalow with the tropical functionalism of the Queenslander. Cool verandahs overlook glimpses of the neighbouring Clarence River through some of the beautiful trees which have made Grafton famous. The guest accommodation provides all facilities and comfort including air-conditioning and you can choose from the garden, verandah or dining area for meals. The 'Garden Room' downstairs has French doors leading to a sunny patio whilst the upstairs 'Bridge Room' has a separate sitting area and an adjoining twin makes it a suite.
George also works as a Whitewater guide on the Nymboida River and a rafting trip can be arranged, or you can take advantage of an intimate knowledge of the wide variety of local national parks including World Heritage listed areas to help enrich your stay. This is a non-smoking establishment.

NEW SOUTH WALES

Grenfell
Farmstay B&B
Address: "Garrawilla",
Grenfell, NSW 2810
Name: Pip & Colin Wood
Telephone:
(063) 433218 (Try any time)
Beds: 4 Single (3 bedrooms)
Bathroom: 1 Ensuite, 1 Private
Tariff: B&B (full) Double $65,
Single $30, Children $1 per year,
Dinner $15. Vouchers accepted
Nearest Town: Grenfell 15km north (near Cowra, Young and Forbes).

Garrawilla is a farming and grazing property with Merino sheep., prime Dorset / Merino cross lambs, a few cattle, and crops of oats, wheat, triticale, canola and lupins. It is within easy reach of Sydney, Canberra and Melbourne.
We have four sheep dogs, a friendly stray called "Poor-Dog", hens, geese, ponies, many native birds, and kangaroos in the bush.
The homestead is modern with older garden, including tennis court. Guests have twin room with ensuite, opening onto outside verandah and garden, shelter for vehicle, TV, electric blankets, heater, fan. two other rooms for children or friends with separate bathroom. Only one set of guests at a time, and a cup of tea and home-made biscuits when you arrive.
Grenfell is a small, friendly country town, a poet's home (henry Lawson), a bushranger's haunt (Ben Hall), Festival of Arts, Guinea Pig Races, Weddin Mountain National park, Canowindra fish fossils, Cowra Japanese Gardens.

Grenfell
Bed & Breakfast (Historic Home)
Address: 7 Weddin St.,
Grenfell, NSW 2810
Name: "Grenfell Hall"
Telephone: (02) 6343 2235
Fax: (02) 6343 2235
Beds: 1 Double, 2 Single (2 bedrooms)
Bathroom: 2 Private
Tariff: B&B (full) Double $100-$110,
Single $50 - $65, Dinner by arrangement.
Vouchers accepted $20 surcharge Mon-Thurs
Nearest Town: Cowra 50km, Young 50km

Grenfell Hall – The past and present meet at Grenfell Hall which is a historic luxury Victorian residence with lots of surprises. Meticulously restored the house has a fascinating history. Once a convent it still has the chapel and original walled garden. Guest's comfort is paramount. Furnished to ensure the romantic past, with luxury rooms, own facilities, superb breakfast and guest bathrobes. Cosy open log fires in winter and shaded verandahs allow guests to view the beauty of the Weddin Mountains. Our superb breakfast makes an excellent start to the day. Tea and coffee always available.
Grenfell is an old gold town and birthplace of Henry Lawson. Ben Hall the bushranger also haunted the area. Explore vineyards and Japanese Garden at Cowra, Weddin Mountains, Young (Cherry Capital of Australia).
Share our historic home with its fine art, unique features and rambling gardens. We look forward to spoiling you. Please book ahead.

Gunning - Southern Tablelands
Guest House B&B Gourmet
Address: Do Duck Inn Guest House
22 Old Hume Highway, Gunning NSW
Name: Maureen and Peter Quinn
Telephone: (02) 4845 1207 **Fax**: (02) 4845 1207
Beds: 1 Queen, 4 Double, 1 Single (5 bedrooms)
Bathroom: 3 Ensuite, 1 Guest Share
Tariff: B&B (special) Double $95-$110, Single $80, Dinner $25-$42.50 (4 course), Children not catered for,   Vouchers accepted Sunday - Thursday $15 Surcharge
Nearest Town: Goulburn 30 mins/Canberra 45 mins/Sydney 2 1/2 hours

The Do Duck Inn is a rare breed of guesthouse, an unexpected place with surprising benefits for travellers and holiday seekers, going to or from almost anywhere. Located in the quiet village of Gunning, just 45 minutes from Canberra, 2 hours from the Snowys, 2 1/2 hours from Sydney, the c. 1890 Do Duck Inn is practically in the middle of nowhere, yet is on the way to almost anywhere.

The Do Duck Inn was recently named as one of the top 10 establishments in NSW yet is as warm and friendly as the country home you'd love to own. Maureen and Peter know that their guests either seek a break with complete relaxation away from their usually hectic lives, or a peaceful nights rest on the way to somewhere else. In both cases, guests are not disappointed. You may enjoy a relaxed drink before a sumptuous dinner and afterwards a quiet port in front of a cosy log fire. After arising from your comfortable cast iron bed next morning, a gourmet breakfast consisting of freshly squeezed orange juice, cereals, fresh fruit platter followed by home baked muffins, croissants or poached eggs served with Maureen's special sauce and afterwards freshly brewed Italian coffee or choice of teas, awaits you.

The Do Duck Inn boasts two sitting rooms with log fires in winter and 3/4 acres of shady gardens in summer and is decorated in linen 'n' lace and antiques.

So why not indulge yourself in this relaxed country atmosphere on the way to almost anywhere.

Children or smokers not catered for. A rare delight!

Can't contact your host? Phone Directory Assistance.

NEW SOUTH WALES

Gunning
Guest House
Address: 1-3 Warrataw Street, Gunning, NSW 2581
Name: Frankfield Guest House – Caxton House Restaurant
Telephone: (02) 4845 1200
Fax: (02) 4845 1490
Beds: 10 Double (10 bedrooms)
Bathroom: 3 Guests share
Tariff: B&B (full) Double $90, Single $55, Children on request, Dinner $25, Credit Cards. Vouchers accepted Mid-week only
Nearest Town: Gunning - 300 metres north of Post Office, 45 km Goulburn, 42km Yass. 64 km Canberra

Built in 1870 as the Frankfield Hotel and now a charming guest house. Each bedroom is fitted out with antique furniture, brass beds and four posters. Weekend Packages available.
Visit Canberra cold climate vineyards, historic Collector, Gundaroo & Bungendore. All within half hours drive. Explore Gunnings' art gallery, historic buildings, tennis courts, golf course and public swimming pool. Or relax in one of the sitting rooms with an open fire, sipping tea or coffee on the verandahs, admiring the extensive garden or enjoying a delicious meal in our period dining room.
2 hours from Sydney, 45 mins from Canberra. Gunning is on the Old Hume Highway with no through traffic but only minutes from the new Highway which gives quick and easy access to and from major centres. This is a true country family home complete with cats, dogs and children.

Guyra
Homestay
+Self-contained Accom.
Address: "Milani", Baldersleigh Road, Guyra, 2365
Name: Wal & Lynne Chapman
Telephone: (067) 755735 **Fax**: (067) 755735
Beds: 1 Double, 1 Twin (2 bedrooms)
Bathroom: 1 Ensuite
Tariff: B&B (full) Double $60, Single $45, Children $45, Dinner $20 per person, Campervans $20 for 4 people.
Nearest Town: 28km west of Guyra

Milani is 8000 acres of natural bush and farmland crossed by one of New England's best trout streams.
Guests can enjoy rugged bushwalking around the hills (see wild-flowers, orchids, birdlife and kangaroos along the way), or more gentle walking along the 6km of streams. You might even spot a platypus. Try trout fishing or discover farm life. At night, gather around the cosy open log fire for a yarn and then join Lynne and Wal for a hearty 3 course country cooked meal. Finish with a relaxing game of pool and a port. In summer have a game of tennis followed by dinner on the verandah with its views across the valley. Guests may prefer to stay in our fully self-contained 3 bedroom cottage. Milani is located in the heart of the tablelands, short drive from spectacular gorges, waterfalls and National Parks, sapphire and gold fossicking, or the heritage of the university and cathedral city of Armidale.

NEW SOUTH WALES

Guyra
Self-contained Accommodation
Address:
Name: Mrs Gwendoline Croft
Telephone: (02) 6779 1205
 – Answering machine
Beds: 1 Double, 3 Single (3 bedrooms)
Bathroom: 1 Private
Tariff: $20 per night per person
& $10 per child per night.
Nearest Town: 5km northof Guyra
along the Old New England Highway

Milparinka Cottage is charming.
A haven of peace on a hillside, away from
the main homestead, with a lake in the distance.
Excellent facilities and old-world furnishings allow for comfort and a wood-burning fire for cooking allows you to experience the past (plus electricity). Also included is a fully tuned Yamaha piano.
The Cottage is one of the original estate buildings, therefore has a "Heritage Charm". The property is a working cattle / sheep station which allows for visitors to see the day-to-day workings of normal life on a station. The nearby village of Guyra lies in the heart of magnificent New England and offers a wide range of facilities and activities eg. coffee shops, antique and old wares, golf, trout fishing, bush walking, horse riding and many more. No meals are provided but excellent shopping is only 5km away, so self reliance is easy.

Hallidays Point
Homestay
Address: "Ozfrens Beach Homestay",
PO Box 89, Hallidays Point NSW 2430
Name: Eric & Wendy Coleman
Telephone: (02) 6559 2846
Beds: 2 Double (2 bedrooms)
Bathroom: 1 Guests share
Tariff: B&B (continental) Double $65,
Single $40, Children under 12 half price.
Dinner by arrangement. Vouchers accepted
Nearest Town: Forster or Taree

Situated on the mid-north coast of NSW between Forster and Taree (3 1/2 hours north of Sydney) our home is close to, and overlooks, the beach at Hallidays Point.
Safe unpolluted swimming (pool and beach); rainforest and beachwalks; and scenic drives are some of the local attractions. Golf and tennis are also available, as are arts and crafts galleries.
Wake up to the sound of the waves and to the birds in our garden. Perhaps a walk and / or a swim before breakfast! Perhaps not! Enjoy breakfast with a view!
Apart from having travelled overseas ourselves, we have hosted many Australian and overseas visitors in our home. We invite you to stay with us in our comfortable home by the sea where a very warm welcome is assured.
Non-smokers preferred. **Directions**: *Please phone.*

Hawks Nest see Tea Gardens

NEW SOUTH WALES

TWO MOONS
——— ARABIANS ———

Howes Valley
**Farmstay/Self-Cont./
Guest House, Self catering.**
Address: Lot 2, Putty Road,
Howes Valley, NSW 2330
Name: Margaret & Arnfred Olsen
Telephone: (02) 6579 4561
Fax: (02) 6579 4556
Beds: 1 Queen, 1 Double,
2 Single, (3 bedrooms)
Bathroom: 1 Private. (We only take one group at a time)
Tariff: B&B (continental), Double $60, Single $50, Dinner by arrangement.
Nearest Town: Singleton 55kms, Windsor 115 kms south.

Two Moons Guest House at Howes Valley in the Lower Hunter, is a two and a half hour drive from Sydney CBD (via Windsor and Colo) on "Two Moons" Arabian stud. It is on 120 acres of rolling grazing land backing to Yengo National Park. Easy to find on tarred road, it sits high on the hill before Oakey Creek Bridge as you drive towards Singleton (40 minutes away) and the vineyards and restaurants at Pokolbin.
The quaint refurbished house is elegantly furnished (3 bedrooms) with its own fully equipped kitchen, living room has TV, video, books and games. With reverse cycle air conditioning, the house is open all year round as a self catering base for exploring Hunter Valley. Putty Road connects directly to New England Higway, a splendid alternative to the crowded Pacific Highway.
Ideal for couples or larger family groups who will enjoy horses, 4 wheel driving in clean air or a short drive to the best wineries. Bushwalking in the adjacent Wollemi National Park is also available. Wollombi historic village is on the other side of Yengo National Park right at our "back door".

Private bathroom is for your use exclusively,
Guests share means you may be sharing with other guests,
Family share means you will be sharing with the family.

Hunter Valley - Cessnock
Guest House/Inn   NRMA ★★★★
Address: "The Cessnock Heritage Inn",
167 Vincent Street, Cessnock, 2325 NSW
Name: "Cessnock Heritage Inn"
Telephone: (02) 4991 2744
Fax: (02) 4991 2720
Beds: 8 Queen, 5 Double, 8 Single
(2 large Family Room with 1 Queen & 2 Single beds) (13 bedrooms)
Bathroom: 13 Ensuite
Tariff: B&B (full) Double $80-$100, Single $60, Children under 12yrs $25, Dinner by arrangement, Credit Cards. Vouchers accepted Sunday to Thursday nights
Nearest Town: Cessnock - centre of town

Situated in the heart of Cessnock only minutes from the Pokolbin Vineyards we offer a new heritage charm and excellent value for money. Beautifully furnished spacious rooms all with queen beds, ensuite bathroom, reverse air conditioning, TV and in-house video, fridge, tea and coffee facilities. A generous country style breakfast awaits in the dining room. Relax in our 'homely' sitting room and share your experiences (or a bottle) of the day. For the romantic we have a Honeymoon Suite with local champagne, chocolates and a late check-out. Close by are shops, pubs, cinema and many award winning restaurants together with winery tours, championship golf courses, horse drawn carriage tours, antique shops, a zoo, and 82 vineyards to tempt the palate. and there's more ...... Whether you want to get away from it all or get together with friends, this is the place to stay!
Directions: *1 1/2 hours north of Sydney. Under an hour is historic Wollombi and Morpeth, National Parks, Mountains, Lakes and Beaches.*
We look forward to welcoming you - please book ahead. Sorry no pets.

Hunter Valley - Mulbring
Farmstay
Address: Vermont Road, Mulbring
Name: The Pecan Farm B&B
Telephone: (02) 4938 0300
Fax: (02) 4938 0444
Beds: 2 Single (1 bedroom)
Bathroom: 1 Ensuite
Tariff: B&B (special) Double $110,
Single $85, Campervans facilities.
Nearest Town: 10 mins off Sydney-Newcastle Freeway, Cessnock turn-off.

The Pecan Farm is located in the famous Hunter Valley (wine country) about 1 1/2 hours drive north of Sydney. It is a 30 acre family run organic farm of fruit and nut trees. We are also establishing the property with native trees as a sanctuary for wildlife in an area where all surrounding properties are cow grazing and pasture land. This is wombat country.
We are situated about 15 minutes drive from Cessnock and the famous Pokolbin Vineyards of Hunter Valley.
Enjoy scenic country walks, a large variety of birdlife, beautiful valley and mountain views, picnic lunches by the creek, participate in farm activities or just relax with home style hospitality and country comforts. The Pecan Farm is home to a variety of farmyard animals and pets.

NEW SOUTH WALES

Hunter Valley - Pokolbin
Motel Style Units   NRMA ★★★
Address: "Elfin Hill",
Marrowbone Road, Pokolbin, 2321
Name: Elfin Hill
Telephone: (02) 4998 7543
Fax: (02) 4998 7817
Beds: 6 Queen, 5 Single (6 bedrooms)
Bathroom: 6 Ensuite
Tariff: B&B (continental) Double $70, Single $68,
Children welcome. $120 (full) weekends (Except
Long Weekends and Xmas.) Credit Cards.
Vouchers accepted Sunday to Thursday nights.
Nearest Town: Cessnock - 4 kms

Elfin Hill's big log cabin is serenely nestled atop, with breathtaking views of the vineyards, Broken Back Range and tall Spotted Gumtrees complete with birdlife. Relax and enjoy the local colour of wine tasting, bushwalking, ballooning, horse riding, cycling and fantastic cuisine! Ideally located amidst the vineyards and only minutes to Cypress Lakes Golf Course and the township of Cessnock. A very quiet secluded spot with covered barbecue area right next to the salt water swimming pool. Janene and Garry are eager to meet you and will genuinely enjoy helping you find your way around the famous Hunter Valley!
Directions: *2 hrs north of Sydney. From Cessnock, follow Mt View Road then right and left into Marrowbone Road and Elfin Hill.*
Home Page: http://www.cyberlink.com.au/bedbreakfast/elfin-hill

Hunter Valley- Pokolbin
Guest House
Address: "Catersfield House"
96 Mistletoe Lane, Pokolbin 2320
Name: Rosemary & Alexander Carter **Telephone**: (02) 4998 7220
Beds: 6 King, 1 Queen, 1 Double   **Bathroom**: 6 ensuites

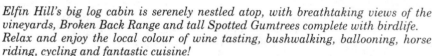

Tariff: B&B: Upstairs King $180 pn weekends (full b/f) $150 pn mid-week (continental b/f). King rooms convertable to twin rooms. Summer House Queen: $210 pn weekends (full b/f), $170 pn mid-week (continental b/f). Terrace Room $130 pn weekends (full b/f), $100 pn mid-week (continental b/f). Minimum 2 nights weekends, unless other arrangement. Singles $20 off price of room. Children under 12 $40, under 5 free if share with parents.
Deposit: 50% on booking. Non-refundable if cancelled within 14 days of arrival date unless rebooked. No refund 3 days prior to arrival. Credit Cards: Bankcard, Mastercard, Visa, American Expirss, Diners. No Campervans.
Nearest Town: Cessnock

Relax and unwind contemplating the beauty of the surrounding vineyards and the ever changing light on the Brokenback Ranges. "Catersfield House" offers unparalleled views from its 6 ensuite bedrooms or total privacy in the self-contained Summer House. Sit in the comfortable lounge room in front of the fire, breakfast in the spacious dining room or simply take in the view from the large terrace. Over the long summer swimming is available in the salt water pool or perhaps you might like to try a game of petanque on the 'top of the hill' terrain. The Valley offers wine tasting, golfing, hot air ballooning, horse and carriage rides, bicycle tours, horse riding and bush walks. Nearby award winning restaurants and the guesthouse's own cafe style food at weekends.

NEW SOUTH WALES

Hunter Valley - Singleton
Guest House
Address: "Fairoak", Raworth St, Singleton, NSW 2330
Name: Jenny & John Macdonald
Telephone: (02) 6571 1586
Mobile: (019) 150120
Beds: 2 Queen, 2 Single (3 bedrooms)
Bathroom: 3 Ensuite
Tariff: B&B (full) Double $75-$95, Single $65-$85. Children $10. Credit Cards. Vouchers accepted $10 surcharge
Nearest Town: Singleton

"Fairoak" is a 1928 country homestead built on 8 acres within the town boundary. We have recently extended our home to provide separate accommodation in the form of 3 large guest bedrooms with ensuites and a guest lounge. All rooms have country furnishings, TVs, air-conditioning, underfloor heating, high ceilings, large bay windows and verandahs with a pleasant outlook over the garden.

Guests can relax in our large sunny lounge and enjoy the cosy fire, small library and a variety of board games. A full breakfast is served in the lounge/dining area.

Singleton is situated in the heart of the Hunter Valley within a 20 minutes drive of many famous vineyards and is only 2 1/2 hours from Sydney and 1 1/4 hours from Newcastle, Port Stephens and Barrington Tops, making it an ideal location for a weekend getaway or a pleasant stop-over for travellers along the New England Highway.

No smokers please. Please phone for directions.

Gift Vouchers

Our B&B vouchers are for a double room for one night's B&B. They cost $89, and if you order one as a gift, we will include a free
Australian Bed & Breakfast Book
worth $16.95

Send your cheque to
Moonshine Press
59 Quirk Street
Dee Why
NSW 2099

NEW SOUTH WALES

Hunter Valley - Wollombi
Self Contained Cottage & Guest House - B&B   NRMA ★★★★
Address: "Capers Cottage & Country House, Wollombi Road, Wollombi, NSW 2325
Name: Anne and John Kelly
Telephone: (02) 4998 3211 **Fax**: (02) 4998 3211 **Mobile**: (018) 465 761
Beds: 6 Queen, 1 Double, 2 Single (8 bedrooms)
Bathroom: 6 Ensuites, 1 Guest Share
Tariff: B&B (full) Double: $110-$150, Single $80-$120. Dinner $30 by arrangement. Children by arrangement. Credit cards.
Nearest Town: Cessnock 30km. Sydney 90mins.

Capers Cottage and Country House are nestled in the Wollombi Valley, an area of tranquil beauty and idyllic surroundings, only minutes from the pleasures of Hunter Valley Wine country, yet only 90 minutes drive from Sydney.

"The Cottage" is extremely cosy, oozing old world charm, with luxury furnishings which will please the most discerning of tastes. It is fully self contained with 3 bedrooms and 2 bathrooms and has an open log fire, gourmet kitchen stocked with all the ingredients for a hearty country breakfast, outside barbecue and eating area with pretty cottage garden & lazy verandahs. The cottage is A/C, all linen is provided, and has TV and video, board games and is ideal for groups or families.

"The Country House" unique 1840's convict hewn sandstone house, recently transferred to Wollombi from Macquarie Street, Sydney. There are 5 luxury bedrooms, each with en-suite, and decorated in Australian Colonial style, some with open log fireplaces, spa baths, and all with French doors opening onto generous country verandahs with views overlooking the Wollombi Valley. Guest lounge & dining room - both with welcoming stone fireplaces, according to the season breakfast & dinners can be enjoyed on the verandahs or in front of the cosy fire. Opening mid 1998.

"Wollombi" explore our heritage village with its rich and colourful past, or indulge and unwind in the blissful tranquillity of our shady verandahs. There is cycling, horse riding, tennis, golf and we are surrounded by national parks. We are close to the renowned Hunter Valley vineyards, and can arrange wine tours and tastings, with delicious picnic lunches, or visit award winning restaurants for that extra special lunch! Transfers from Sydney hotels and airport pick-ups also available.
Non smoking in the house. BYO.

NEW SOUTH WALES

Inverell
Guest House
Address: Warialda Rd, Inverell, 2368
Name: Blair Athol
Telephone: (067) 224912 **Fax**: (067) 224912
Beds: 4 Double, 1 Single (5 bedrooms)
Bathroom: 1 Ensuite, 3 Guests share
Tariff: B&B (continental) Double $45pp, Single $70, Dinner $30pp.
Nearest Town: Inverell

Experience old world charm at a turn of the century country manor. Set amidst 5 acres of botanical type gardens with trees dating back to 1850. 50 acres of peace, tranquillity and spectacular birdlife. Situated 6km west of Inverell on the Warialda Road.
* Delicious homestyle country breakfasts.
* Delightful 4 course dinners, BYO wine.
* Open log fires, invigorating fresh air.
* Tennis court and croquet available.
* Separate self-contained cottage 6 adults max.
* Children not accommodated.

Huskisson see Jervis Bay
Huskisson also see Nowra
Inverell also see Armidale

Inverell - Delungra
Farmstay+Self-contained Accom.
Address: "Myall Downs Farm Holidays"
Delungra, NSW 2403
Name: Ian & Mary Saunders
Telephone: (02) 6723 6421
Fax: (02) 6723 6425
Beds: 1 Double, 4 Single (3 bedrooms)
Bathroom: 1 Guests share
Tariff: B&B (full) Double $70, Single $50,
Children under 12 $25, Dinner $20.
Self-contained Cottage sleeps 6: $100 per night. No pets. Vouchers accepted
Nearest Town: 20 minutes Delungra

Myall Downs has been in the Saunders family since the early 1900's. 3500 acres producing cattle, sheep and grain. Situated 54km west of Inverell, halfway between Sydney / Brisbane and Moree / Glen Innes.
Ian, Mary and adult son John have been hosting for 10 years and welcome you to their traditional country home to be pampered with fine food and home comforts, or self-contained cottage. A spacious garden, wonderful sunsets and starlit nights are special treats for our guests who can enjoy the peace and beauty of the countryside. Farm activities, horse riding, go bushwalking, creek fishing, tennis, family museum, games room. A 4WD tour around the property to see caves, magnificent views from the Pinnacle, kangaroos and many species of trees. All this and more. Families welcome. Other attractions are Inverell - home of the sapphire, Copeton Dam and 1 1/4 hours to Moree's spa baths. Phone Mary for a booking and directions.

Gift Vouchers

Our B&B vouchers are for a double room for one night's B&B. They cost $89, and if you order one as a gift, we will include a free
Australian Bed & Breakfast Book worth $16.95

Send your cheque to
Moonshine Press
59 Quirk Street
Dee Why
NSW 2099

NEW SOUTH WALES

Jamberoo
Homestay
Address: "Burra Glen" Burra Creek Road, Jamberoo. PO Box 28 Jamberoo, NSW 2533
Name: Ken & Gloria Jeffrey
Telephone: (02) 4236 0256 **Fax**: (02) 4236 0699
Beds: 2 Double, 2 Single (2 bedrooms)
Bathroom: 1 Guests share
Tariff: B&B (special) Double $90, Single $60, Children under 12 half price, Dinner $24.
Credit Cards (VISA/BC/MC). Vouchers accepted
Nearest Town: Jamberoo 3km (2 miles)

Between a 1000ft high escarpment and the sea, Jamberoo valley offers some of the greenest and loveliest scenery on the New South Wales Coast. A range of outdoor activities is available in the area, including bushwalking, golf, tennis, bowling and swimming.
A warm welcome awaits you at Burra Glen with picturesque mountain and valley views in quiet peaceful surroundings.
Ken and Gloria have travelled extensively and have appreciated homestay hospitality themselves in other countries. Their lovely home stands in rural surroundings and is beautifully furnished, and has open fireplace. They are very fond of animals and have two dogs, a cat and four sheep all friendly and well behaved.
A hearty breakfast is served in the dining room or in the conservatory. Coddled eggs / smoked salmon. Homemade bread, jams, yoghurt.
*Local attractions include: * Jamberoo Recreation Park * Minnamurra Falls and Rain Forest *Barren Grounds Nature Reserve * Saddleback Mountain Lookout * Kiama Blowhole and surf beaches * Picturesque town of Berry*
Directions: *Please write or phone for directions.*

Jervis Bay - Huskisson
Bed & Breakfast
Address: Paperbark Lodge
605 Woollamia Rd, Woollamia - Please phone.
Name: Jeremy & Irena
Telephone: (02) 4441 6066 **Fax**: (02) 4441 6066
Mobile: (018) 028 462 **Email**: paperbark@shoalhaven.net.au
Beds: 2 Queen, 2 Single (3 bedrooms)
Bathroom: 2 Private

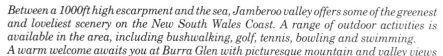

Tariff: B&B (full) Double $150 per room w/e & school hols (min 2 nights). Single $150 w/e (2 nights), Mid-weeks $100 per room, Ask about special rates for children, Credit Cards. Vouchers accepted $30 surcharge and accepted mid-week only.
Nearest Town: Huskisson - Take Jervis Bay Rd, 13km south of Nowra, then 3km down J. B. Road take Woollamia Road - 6km.

"Paperbark" sits on 88 acres only 3km from the bay, with 600 metres frontage onto Currumbene Creek. The creek is the only navigable waterway to Jervis Bay, it is ideal for canoeing, fishing and picnicking. The Lodge is designed to take full advantage of its bush environment, amongst tall stands of trees with verandahs facing the northern sun. Myriads of birds inhabit the dam and wetland close to the Lodge. In winter a wood fire warms the spacious living area. Please ask about pets, we can help. Children are welcome on specific weekends and at school holidays. The area offers cruising on the bay to watch dolphins, seals and penguins. Botanic Gardens in the National Park, bushwalking and bike riding, Arthur Boyd's "Bundanon" is a short drive, and of course swimming and diving in crystal clear water. Two and a half hours from Sydney or Canberra and supper upon arrival on Friday night make us your perfect weekend away.

Jervis Bay - Huskisson
Guest House
Address: 1 Beach Steet, Huskisson, NSW 2540
Name: Jervis Bay Guesthouse
Telephone: (02) 4441 7658 **Fax**: (02) 4441 7659
Email: gdaymate@oztourism.com.au
Beds: 4 Queen (4 bedrooms)
Bathroom: 4 Ensuite
Tariff: B&B (full) Double $150 (spa bath), $135 (Bayview room), $120 (2 rooms), Single $135 (spa bath), $120 (Bayview room), $105 (2 rooms), Credit Cards (AMEX/BC/MC/VISA). Vouchers accepted $65 (spa bath), $50 (Bayview room), $35 (2 rooms) surcharge.
Nearest Town: Huskisson is 22km south of Nowra

The Jervis Bay Guesthouse (planned to open 1/3/98) is in a great position, opposite the white sands of world-renowned Jervis Bay, and within a few minutes walk of Huskisson's shops and restaurants. The house is being purpose-built as a quality "Home-away-from-home" - ideally situated for a weekend's escape from Canberra (3 hrs) or Sydney (2.5 hrs), or as a relaxing stopover on your way south. All bedrooms have ensuites, and either have full or part-views of the bay.
Huskisson's attractions include dolphin-watching cruises, diving, fishing, golf and the Lady Denman Heritage Complex. Further afield you can visit historic Milton (50km), or experience Jervis Bay National Park (15km) with its white beaches, crystal-clear waters, beautiful bushland, and numerous walking tracks and picnic spots.
Bookings can only be taken after 1/2/97. Check progress on the house at:
Home Page: *http://www.oztourism.com.au/~gdaymate/jervis.htm.*
We are smoke-free (except on verandahs), and under 18s free, - though we do have a cat.

Jervis Bay also see Nowra

Jindabyne
Self-contained Apartments   NRMA ★★★
Address: "Arosa Apartmotel", 3 Kosciusko Rd, Jindabyne, NSW 2627
Name: Rita & Walter
Telephone: (064) 562189 **Fax**: (064) 562293 **Mobile**: (041) 233 0834
Beds: 5 Double, 15 Single (10 bedrooms)
Bathroom: 6 Private
Tariff: B&B (continental) Summer: Double $70, Winter: Double $100-$120, Children half price, Credit Cards (VC/MC/BC).
Nearest Town: Jindabyne

Arosa Apartmotel is right in the heart of Jindabyne tucked away in a quiet garden setting opposite shops, restaurants, swimming pool. It's your home away from home. We offer fully self-contained, daily serviced 2 bedroom apartments and motel rooms. We have been in the area for 20 years and can help you with all tourist information. The four seasons of the Snowy Mountains give the greatest range of things to do: skiing, hiking, swimming, water-skiing, horseriding, fishing, canoeing, admire the alpine flora in spring, experience the Kosciusko National Park, its natural landscape, including most of Australia's snow covered areas.
Our summer tariff includes continental breakfast and in the winter we serve a full breakfast. Dinner available on request.

Our B&Bs are mostly private homes.
Most do not accept credit cards.

NEW SOUTH WALES

Jindabyne East
Homestay
Address: "Rimrock",
35 Jerrara Drive,
East Jindabyne, NSW 2627
Name: Michael & Carole Morris
Telephone: (02) 6456 2888
Fax: (02) 6456 2888
Beds: 1 Queen, 4 Single (3 bedrooms)
Bathroom: 1 Ensuite, 1 Guests share
Tariff: B&B (full) Double $80-$160,
Single $40-$80, Children half price, Dinner $20pp.
Vouchers accepted no surcharge
Nearest Town: 8km NE Jindabyne, 55km south of Cooma

"Rimrock" is situated 100 metres from Lake Jindabyne with magnificent views of the lake and the Snowy Mountains. It is a marvellous jumping off spot for the snowfields in winter and in summer you can enjoy the peace and tranquillity of the countryside. For the more energetic there are bushwalks, swimming, sailing, mountain bike riding, horse riding near by and fishing for trout - which your host will be only to pleased to cook for you.
Carole and Michael moved to "Rimrock" having decided to get out of the "Rat Race". They are both keen downhill skiers and enjoy bushwalking in the summer and can advise you on the local area. You are assured of a warm friendly welcome when you stay at "Rimrock" and if you would like to dine with them at night a three course meal will be provided. No smoking or pets.

Kangaroo Valley also see Berry

Kangaroo Valley
Bed & Breakfast   NRMA ★★★★☆
Address: "Tall Trees", 8 Nugents Creek Rd.
Kangaroo Valley, NSW 2577
Name: John & Leonie Hull
Telephone: (02) 4465 1208 **Fax**: (02) 4465 1208
Mobile: (019) 919956
Beds: 2 Queen, 1 Double, 1 Single (3 bedrooms).
1 Private s/c cottage suite 1 Queen.
Bathroom: 3 Ensuite, 1 Private with spa.
Tariff: B&B (full) Double $80-$130, Single $70-$130, Suite $120-$160. Credit Cards (MC/BC/VISA). Vouchers accepted accepted Sunday-Thursday, not Public Holidays
Nearest Town: Kangaroo Valley 1km, Berry 20km

Surrounded by mountain and escarpment views of the Cambewarra and Barrengarry Ranges is Tall Trees 1km from the village of Kangaroo Valley.
We offer our guests privacy and relaxation. Accommodation includes two Queen size bedrooms with air conditioning, one double bedroom with ceiling fan, all with private facilities. Relax and enjoy a cosy log fire in the guest lounge with tea / coffee facilities, a selection of CD's, magazines and books all for your enjoyment.
A full country breakfast is served in our breakfast room which looks out over one acre of gardens and valley views.
Or for that special occasion we have a private cottage suite, with two person spa and woodfire. Breakfast provisions are provided to prepare at your own leisure.
A fine selection of restaurants and gift shops are near by along with canoeing, horse riding, golfing and bush walks.

NEW SOUTH WALES

Kangaroo Valley/Cambewarra Mtn
Luxury Bed & Breakfast   NRMA ★★★★☆
Address: "Barefoot Springs"
Carrington Road,
Cambewarra Mountain (Please phone)
Name: "Barefoot Springs"
Baden & Val Wynn
Telephone: (02) 4446 0509
Fax: (02) 4446 0530 **Mobile**: (019) 915740
Beds: 1 Studio with Queen, spa & fire place, 1 Queen & Ensuite, 1 Suite with 1 Queen, 1 Double bedrooms, private sitting room & 3-way bathroom.
Bathroom:
Tariff: B&B (full) $55-$85pp, Dinner $25pp, Credit Cards.
Nearest Town: Kangaroo Valley - 9.5km SE of Kangaroo Valley off Moss Vale Rd.

"Barefoot Springs" rests high on Cambewarra Mountain (situated between Kangaroo Valley, Berry and the Shoalhaven) where you will relax amongst the rainforest and enjoy the panoramic view of 100km - Shoalhaven River, ocean, Jervis Bay and mountains. Fully cooked breakfast with home baked bread and lovingly picked blackberries is served either in the dining room or on terrace overlooking the coastline and mountains.
The guests lounge has a wood fire and enjoy 260 degree view in the day - a vista of lights at night. Our 40 acre property has a small Angus herd, hens, garlic, cut flowers, waterfalls, creeks and rainforest (listed in the National Estate for preservation). Our new homestead is amongst 5 acres of landscape gardens. Birdlife is prolific, lyrebirds and parrots a feature. Wombats in their hundreds abound.
You'll find this a restful place yet visit many tourist places in 20 minutes.

Katoomba see Blue Mountains

Kempsey
Guest House   NRMA ★★★★
Address: 5 Little Rudder St.
Kempsey, NSW 2440
Name: "Netherby House" Hosts: Robyn & Nick Weare
Telephone: (065) 631777 **Fax**: (065) 631778
Mobile: (014) 461663
Email: netherby@midcoast.com.au
Beds: 4 Queen (1 with a single) (4 bedrooms)
Bathroom: Bathroom: 3 Ensuite, 1 full bathroom
Tariff: B&B (gourmet) Double $130, Single $85, Children $30. Gourmet dinner with port & handmade truffles by arrangement $35pp. **Nearest Town**: Kempsey

"Netherby" is a luxuriously appointed Guest House with gourmet cafe conveniently situated halfway between Sydney and Brisbane on the banks of the MacLeay River in the heart of Kempsey. "Netherby" offers cool fans or air-conditioning in summer, wood fires in winter, period furniture and private facilities. A delightful intimate BYO restaurant and riverfront cafe are provided for guests. Outdoor smoking area provided. Breakfast ranges from continental-style to a special gourmet treat with which will keep you satisfied until dinner - included in your tariff. "Netherby" is the home of "Jacaranda" chocolates. These handmade delicacies include classic French truffles made with fresh local produce - fruits, honeys and macadamia nuts. "Netherby" is the perfect stopover or base to explore the lush Macleay Valley and its coastline, being close to South West Rocks and Crescent Head. We look forward to pampering you.
Home Page: http://www.midcoast.com.au/users/netherby/index.html

NEW SOUTH WALES

Kendall
Homestay/Farmstay
Address: "Beaufort", 468 Lorne Road, Kendall, NSW 2439
Name: Milly & Bob Jones
Telephone: (02) 6559 4364 **Fax**: (02) 6559 4364
Beds: 1 King/Twin (1 bedroom) + 1 double bunk room.
Bathroom: 1 Private
Tariff: B&B (continental) Double $70, Single $35, Children half price. Dinner $22. Vouchers accepted
Nearest Town: Kendall. Halfway between Taree and Port Macquarie - 30 minutes drive. Laurieton 15 minutes east to coast.

"Beaufort" is a thirty acre farm where you can enjoy the views and tranquility of our valley yet still have easy access to the North Coast's most beautiful beaches and waterways. Perfectly situated for a stopover we extend a warm welcome to travellers heading north (or south), as well as holiday-makers planning a longer stay. Our home is casual and comfortable with sunny verandah breakfasts in summer, cosy open fires in winter and delicious country cooking.
Enjoy our animals, feed the birds, explore the farm and bushland, cool off in the pool or relax in the garden. It's an area of scenic beauty and we offer full day trips, with picnic lunch, for people interested in local knowledge and touring the mountains or beaches. We are a dog loving but non-smoking family and Milly has home produce and miniature paintings for sale.
Nearby Kendall is a crafty village (markets 1st and 3rd Sundays) with Laurieton and Port Macquarie just a short drive away for sporting facilities, restaurants and entertainment. **Home Page**: miljones@tpgi.com.au

Kulnura see Central Coast
Kurrajong Heights see Blue Mountains

Lake Cathie
Homestay
Address: 5 Talara Place, Lake Cathie, NSW 2445
Name: Talara House B&B
Telephone: (02) 6585 4186 **Mobile**: (015) 323 379
Beds: 1 Double (1 Bedroom)
Bathroom: 1 Private
Tariff: B&B (Special) Double $80, Single $65, Dinner $20, Children $20. Weekly discount. Vouchers accepted no surcharge
Nearest Town: Port Marquarie, halfway between Brisbane and Sydney

Our modern home is situated in a koala corridor just a short walk from the lake and beach. Our double guest room has off-street parking, private access, tea/coffee making facilities and a porch from which you may enjoy the native birds frolicking in ponds, waterfalls and bird baths.
Your hosts are Robert and Wendy Hirst. We have a ten year old daughter Sophie and a cute Maltese dog, Molly. Wendy's restaurant experience ensures high quality food and her generous breakfast comprises lots of fresh home-made goodies. Optional dinner includes complimentary wine and special diets can be catered for. Smoking OK on all verandahs. Perfect for couples or small families. Children are welcome and can be accommodated with fold up beds. Courtesy pick-up from transport terminals. (some bus companies stop at Lake Cathie). Swim, fish, walk, play the grand piano, indulge!

NEW SOUTH WALES

Lake Macquarie - Morisset
Self-contained Accommodation
Address: Yarrawonga Park, 2264
Name: "Breakaway Bed & Breakfast"
Telephone: (02) 4970 5227
Beds: 1 Double, Single (1 bedroom)
Bathroom: Private
Tariff: B&B (continental) Double $75, Single $50, Children $15, Cooked breakfast $5pp extra.
Nearest Town: Morisset

Just 1 1/2 hours drive from Sydney, our home is situated on the shores of beautiful Lake Macquarie - Australia's largest saltwater lake. This relaxing retreat is nestled in amongst nature with mountain views, lorikeets, possums and beautiful gardens. 20 mins drive to the Watagan Mountains for excellent bushwalking and horseriding. Major shopping complexes and cinemas also 20 mins away. 25 mins to the famous Hunter vineyards, 7 min drive to country club and golf. 20 mins to beaches and restaurants. Boating fishing, sailing and lake cruise facilities close by. Train line nearby, pick up can be arranged. The accommodation is private with reverse cycle air-conditioning, television, lounge, microwave, refrigerator, dining area and electric blankets. BBQ facilities available. We offer a non smoking environment with this accommodation.

Lake Macquarie also see Newcastle

Lake Macquarie - Wangi Wangi
Homestay
Address: 103 Dobell Drive, Wangi Wangi, City of Lake Macquarie, 2267
Name: Pauline & Arthur (Please phone)
Telephone: (02) 4975 1364 **Fax**: (02) 4975 1031
Mobile: (014) 632805
Beds: Rm.1:1 Double + 1 Single fold up,
Rm 2: 2 Single, Rm 3: 1 Double, 1 Single, 1 fold up cot
Bathroom: 1 Ensuite, 1 Guests share
Tariff: B&B (full) Double $90-$100, Single $50, Children under 14yrs half price, Dinner from $20pp.
Vouchers accepted $10 surcharge.
No vouchers Dec/Jan school holiday period.
Nearest Town: Toronto 15 kms

*"Kismet Lodge" Bed & Breakfast, a waterfront reserve, quality brick home, tastefully decorated with interesting art and craft, overlooking beautiful Lake Macquarie on Wangi Peninsula with spectacular views of Pulbah Island, Dobell Park and surrounding bushlands. Central to Shops, Restaurants, Clubs, Dobell House, Hunter Vineyards, Watagan Mountains, Wetlands, Eraring Power Station etc. "Kismet Lodge's" recently renovated rooms have every facility for your comfort and safety, fully carpeted and screened throughout, with secluded Courtyard, Barbecue, Saltwater Pool for your pleasure. Enjoy swimming, golfing, bowling, fishing, boating, bushwalking or just relax with a good book, watch abundant native birds; A Plethora of Delights. Our interests are Tai Chi, Music, Craft, Patchwork Quilting, Art, Boating and our old dog. We are 110km north of Hornsby via F3 Freeway, 40km south of Newcastle - just past Wangi Police Station. There is no INHOUSE smoking and bookings essential.
Phone Pauline or Arthur (02) 4975 1364, Mobile 014 632805, Fax (02) 4975 1031.*
Home Page: http://www.ozmail.com.au/-aprat

Laurieton see South West Rocks
Lawson see Blue Mountains
Lemon Tree Passage see Port Stephens

Lennox Head
"Spendelove" Homestay
Address: 4 Stonehenge Place, Lennox Head, NSW 2478
Name: Dorothy & Joe Torrisi
Telephone: H'stay: (02) 6687 6075 Bus: (02) 6686 9559
Beds: 1 Double, 1 Twin (2 bedrooms)
Bathroom: 1 Guests share
Tariff: B&B (full) Double $90, Single $70.
Nearest Town: Byron Bay 15 mins, Ballina 10 mins, Lismore 30 mins.

Our home overlooks Lennox Head village and Seven Mile Beach to Broken Head. It is a cosy, comfortable house filled with beautiful old furniture, on a large block with lots of trees and privacy. At night from our deck, we see the Byron Bay lighthouse beam. We walk to the beach, Lake Ainsworth and the Bowls Club in just fifteen minutes. We are the proprietors of Summerland Bowls World, a specialised lawn bowls shop at Ballina.
We guarantee excellent hot breakfasts because of our twenty years experience in our own restaurants at Southport, Byron Bay and Ballina.

Leura see Blue Mountains
Lighthouse Beach see Port Maquarrie

Maclean
Guest House Bed & Breakfast   NRMA ★★★☆
Address: 2B Howard St., Maclean, NSW 2463
Name: Martin Trama & Colleen O'Brien
Telephone: (02) 6645 2452
Beds: 4 Queen, 1 Double, 3 Single (6 bedrooms)
Bathroom: 3 Guests share
Tariff: B&B (full) Double $78, Single $57, Children aged 10+ $15.
Credit Cards (MC/VISA/BC).
Weekend packages incl restaurant pick up & return. Also murder mystery weekend package.
Nearest Town: Yamba - 15 mins

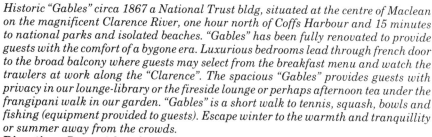

Historic "Gables" circa 1867 a National Trust bldg, situated at the centre of Maclean on the magnificent Clarence River, one hour north of Coffs Harbour and 15 minutes to national parks and isolated beaches. "Gables" has been fully renovated to provide guests with the comfort of a bygone era. Luxurious bedrooms lead through french door to the broad balcony where guests may select from the breakfast menu and watch the trawlers at work along the "Clarence". The spacious "Gables" provides guests with privacy in our lounge-library or the fireside lounge or perhaps afternoon tea under the frangipani walk in our garden. "Gables" is a short walk to tennis, squash, bowls and fishing (equipment provided to guests). Escape winter to the warmth and tranquillity or summer away from the crowds.
Directions:*Buses pick up from all major centres and drop near "Gables". Train, plane to Grafton 30 minutes from Maclean. Ballina airport 1 hr Nth. Byron Bay 1 $^{1/2}$ hrs Nth.*

Medlow Bath see Blue Mountains
Mendooran see Merrygoen
Merewether see Newcastle

Merriwa - Cassilis (Hunter Valley)
Homestay NRMA ★★★☆
Address: "Runnymede", Cassilis via Merriwa
Name: Libby & David Morrow
Telephone: (063) 761183
Fax: (063) 761187
Beds: 2 Double, 2 Single (3 bedrooms)
Bathroom: 2 Ensuite, 1 Family share
Tariff: B&B (full) Double $80-$90, Single $50-$60, Children $30, Dinner $20. Vouchers accepted
Nearest Town: Cassilis 12km, Merriwa 30km

Visitors coming to our property from Sydney will drive up through the Hunter vineyards to a picturesque farming and grazing area - we suggest returning via Mudgee and the spectacular Blue Mountains - a round trip of great variety.
Our old brick homestead is cool in summer, warm in winter with open fire. We can offer 4WD farm tours to see kangaroos in back paddocks, shearing shed etc. Salt water pool, tennis court (lights), verandah for BBQ and relaxing, a large garden with established trees and shrubs.
All the usual country entertainments in Merriwa - races, rodeos, wool festival, art show and facilities for golf, bowls, fossicking and horse riding by arrangement.
Travel times - Sydney 4hrs, Newcastle 2.4, Mudgee / Gulgong 1hr, Dubbo 1.4hr.
We also have for rent a charming house 100 mtrs from Boat Harbour Beach near Pt. Stephens.

Merrygoen - Mendooran
Farmstay
Address: "Kybeyan", Merrygoen, NSW 2831
Name: Denis & Judy Skinner
Telephone: (02) 6886 3554 **Fax**: (2) 06886 3566
Beds: 1 Double, 10 Single (3 bedrooms)
Bathroom: 1 Ensuite, 1 Guests share
Tariff: B&B (continental) Double $75, Single $45, Children 12 & under half price, 16 & under 3/4 price. Dinner $20. Vouchers accepted
Nearest Town: Mendooran (25 km), Dunedoo (44 km). Midway Dubbo–Coonabarabran

Denis and Judy are life time farmers working 3,000 acres enterprise with Santa Gertrudis cattle, Border Leicester sheep stud, Merino ewes, prime lamb, wheat, oats, lucerne and summer forage.
For many years we have conducted farm holidays and have 14 well mannered horses with instruction and supervision all levels. Ours is a genuine "working" and not a "tourist" farm. Guests are welcome to join all activities, mustering with sheep dogs, shearing, lamb ing, harvest ing, milking the cow, drenching and stock sales.
The country is most attractive, rolling, clear and timbered hills which is wonderful for bush walks, photography, painting and wild flowers in spring. Our home is spacious and modern with every comfort for guests and a welcome from our enthusiastic country family. (Full tariff on application.)
We are within easy driving distance of Western Plains Zoo, Dubbo, Siding Springs Observatory and Miniland Coonabarabran, Norfolk Falls, Black Stump, Coolah, Ulungra Springs and crafts.

NEW SOUTH WALES

Millthorpe
Guest House   NRMA ★★★★
Address: "Rosebank Guesthouse"
40 Victoria St.,
Millthorpe, NSW 2798
Name: Virginia De Santis & Gordon Craig
Telephone: (02) 6366 3191
Beds: 5 Queen, 4 Single (6 bedrooms)
Bathroom: 3 Guests share
Tariff: B&B (full) Double$100-$140,
Single $75-$85, Children N/A, Dinner $25-$30, Credit Cards.
Nearest Town: 22km SE of Orange, 40km W of Bathurst.

*Take a step back in time when you visit Rosebank Guesthouse.
This beautifully restored building which is listed in the Register
of the National Estate, is a fine example of Edwardian and Italinate architecture.
Built in 1902 as the Bank of NSW, with manager's residence and servants' quarters, this home has it all - high ceilings, wide verandahs, marble fireplaces, large
gracious rooms, beautiful gardens, central heating, wood fires and an atmosphere
of peace and seclusion. There is even a self-contained garden cottage! The magnificent banking chamber, with 15ft ceiling is now the guests lounge room and houses
a collection of musical instruments, displayed on the original bank counter.
Enjoy the village of Millthorpe, which sprung up in the 1860s and is attracting a
growing number of tourists, with its arts, crafts, furniture and fine food. The entire
village is National Trust classified and is only a "stone throw" away from the wineries
and other attractions of Orange. Mini bus available for group tours.*

Milton
Bed & Breakfast
Address: 131 Princes Highway, Milton
Name: Governors Guest House
Telephone: (02) 4455 1143
Fax: (02) 4455 1143
Beds: 1 Queen, 1 Double,
2 bedrooms
Bathroom: 2 Ensuite
Tariff: B&B (full) Double $95, Single $65,
Credit Cards. Vouchers accepted
Nearest Town: Ulladulla/Mollymook 7kms

*We are situated in the centre of historic Milton on the South Coast, close to beaches,
National Parks and excellent golf courses.
The original house was built in 1873 and the rest of the house has evolved over the
years. Each bedroom has its own theme and ensuite.
Make yourself at home in the relaxed atmosphere of the lounge or TV room which has
tea making and fridge for the use of guests or sit on the leafy terrace. A cooked breakfast
is served and we are within walking distance of good restaurants.
Treat yourself to that weekend away or mid week break. Call Cynthia and make a
booking.*

One of the differences between staying at a hotel and a B&B
is that you don't hug the hotel staff when you leave.

Milton - Yatte Yattah
Guest House/
Self-contained Accommodation
Address: 58A Porters Creek Road,
Yatte Yattah, 2539
Name: The Old Piggery Guest House
Telephone: (02) 4456 4489
Mobile: (018) 603575
Beds: 1 Queen, 1 Double, 3 Single (2 bedrooms)
Bathroom: 1 Guests share, separate toilet
Tariff: B&B (full) Double $90 per couple, Children welcome, Credit Cards.
Nearest Town: Milton

Just three hours from Sydney and nestled at the foot of the Budawang Ranges with spectacular views and only minutes from Lake Conjola beach this 2 bedroom fully self-contained guest house offers a type of peace and tranquillity mostly dreamed of. Set on 5 country acres there is abundant birdlife and farmyard animals. Every modern convenience is available and the house seeps 7. Children welcome. A slow combustion heater adds warmth and cheer in winter. The Budawangs boast some very special bushwalks with well marked trails. A drive of 6 minutes will place you in the quaint and historic village with charming shops and eateries.
In the well appointed kitchen everything necessary to pamper yourselves is available. The country style breakfast ingredients are of course complimentary and replenished daily.
For information and bookings telephone Jenni Meumann (02) 4456 4489.

Monaro District see Cooma

Moree
Bed & Breakfast
Address: "Welcannah"
Name: Peter & Jenny Moses
Telephone: (02) 6754 6533
Fax: (02) 6754 6574
Email: pmoses@mpx.com.au
Beds: 1 Double 2 Twins (3 bedrooms)
Bathroom: 1 Guests share
Tariff: B&B (full) Double $90, Single $55, Dinner $25pp. Vouchers accepted
Nearest Town: Moree

"Welcannah" is 24km from Moree. Moree is in the north west of NSW 647km from Sydney, 488km to Brisbane.
The homestead is a traditional Australian country home built in 1907 with spacious garden featuring a tennis court and swimming pool.
Peter and I both share many interests including golf, tennis, gardening, woodwork, cooking and crafts.
There are many places of interest to visit in Moree. They include the Spa Baths, Trawalla Pecan Nut Farm, Moree Plains Gallery and Cotton Gins.
Children with adults welcome, but pool makes constant supervision necessary.
Directions: *Please phone.*

NEW SOUTH WALES

Morisset see Lake Maquarrie
Moruya also see Batemans Bay
Moruya
Homestay
Address: St Kitt's, 10 Thomas St.
Moruya, NSW 2537
Name: Jean Gordon
Telephone: (02) 4474 4479
Fax: (02) 4474 4479
Mobile: (014) 035 342
Beds: 2 Queen, 1 Double, 1 Single (3 bedrooms)
Bathroom: 3 Ensuite
Tariff: B&B (full) Double from $95, Single $65,
Children on arrangement, Dinner $30pp,
Credit Cards (BC/MC/VISA).
Nearest Town: Moruya

First impressions can be deceptive. Behind a modest frontage St Kitt's has been extended to accommodate spacious living areas and three large, sun-filled bedrooms, each with an ensuite. There are several private sitting areas for guests - inside surrounded by fresh flowers and original artworks, outside on the broad, sheltered verandah. The verandah, which catches the winter morning sun and offers a shady retreat in summer looks out across the classic cottage garden towards the Moruya River. In colder weather there is plenty of room around the pot-bellied heater.
Moruya and the Araluen Valley offer varied terrain and a selection of historic sites to explore. Whatever appetite all that exercise produces will help guests do justice to Jean Gordon's superb home cooking. Then read a book, play a game of scrabble or soak in a long, hot bath before bed.

Moss Vale see Southern Highlands
Mt Warring see Murwillumbah
Mudgee
Guest House
Address: 65 Wallinga Lane, Mudgee, NSW 2850
Name: Old Wallinga Country House
Telephone: (02) 6372 3129 **Fax**: (02) 6372 3129
Beds: 3 King/Queen, 6 Single (4 bedrooms)
Bathroom: 4 Ensuite
Tariff: B&B (full) Double $140, Single $90, Dinner $30pp.
Nearest Town: Mudgee - 3 1/2 hours drive or 40 minutes by air from Sydney

Old Wallinga is 7km south of Mudgee, set in 65 acres and views of gentle rolling hills, grazing cattle and dams which are home to native birds and ducks. We invite you to relax in the guest sitting room with an open fire, library, TV and video. A screened verandah opens onto a courtyard with barbeque facilities, swimming pool and tennis court.
We provide a full breakfast, with dinner by arrangement, and are happy to arrange picnic baskets and tours of the vineyards.
There is much to do and see in and around Mudgee. Its wealth comes from the fertile countryside and Mudgee sheep are still a major producer of superfine wool. Wine has been made in the Mudgee area for more than 150 years, so there are many renowned vineyards in the area. Their winemakers invite you to call and taste the exceptional wines they have produced.
There is a very friendly labrador who loves company.

Mulbring see Hunter Valley

Murwillumbah - Mt Warning
Homestay/Self-contained Accom.
Address: "topSpot", Lot 11,
Toon Close, Uki, NSW 2484
Name: Gloria & Bob
Telephone: (02) 6679 5395
Beds: 1 Queen, 1 Double (2 bedrooms)
SC Studio: 1 Double, 2 Single, 1 Night & Day.
Bathroom: 1 Guests share SC Studio: Private
Tariff: B&B (full) Double $60, Single $40, Extended stay 10% discount, Dinner $20pp (Gourmet). Self-Catering: Huge Studio-type S.C.: Daily Rate $60 per double plus $20 per person. Special Weekly rate applies. Children 13yrs & over welcome.
Nearest Town: Murwillumbah 10km, Uki 2km

Have a lovely stay, sitting, taking in the view direct to Mt Warning, on exploring the many sights and activities of the Tweed Valley, Border Ranges and nearby beaches. You will be staying in a lovely home, on 5 acres, built to take advantage of the views and to enable guests to be part of the day's activities or as private as they like. Breakfasts are a delight. Eat inside, or watching the sun rise on Mt Warning. Meals are prepared, making the most of local produce, and special dietary requirements catered for, if advised at time of booking.
Your hosts having travelled in Australia and overseas themselves, offer the little extras appreciated while away from home.
Enjoy your stay with them. They look forward to meeting you.
Directions: *Easy to find, but please phone.*

Murwillumbah - Uki
Guest House+Self-contained Accom.
Address: Lot 7 Braeside Drive, Uki, NSW 2484
Name: Braeside Homestead
Hosts Janice & Keith Timmer
Telephone: (02) 6679 5289
Beds: 2 Queen, 1 Single (2 bedrooms)
SC. can accommodate 4 persons.
Bathroom: 1 Guests share & self contained
Tariff: B&B (full) Double $65, Single $35. Children half price. Dinner $25 (3 course). SC Unit weekly rate $300. Campervans welcome.
Vouchers accepted
Nearest Town: Murwillumbah 14km, Uki 2km

Braeside Homestead is situated 14km south of Murwillumbah on the Kyogle Road. It is under 2 hours drive south of Brisbane or 40 mins from Coolangatta Airport. It has inspiring views of Mt Warning (only 3km as the crow flies) and surrounding mountains. It is in close proximity to Mt Warning and the Border Park Ranges National Parks. It is a very quiet location and wonderful and peaceful with good old country home comforts.
Smoking is not permitted in house but we have some wonderful verandahs and open areas in which you can relax. We offer B&B $65 double per night or we have separate self-contained unit (can accommodate 4 persons) for a weekly rate of $300.

Myall Lakes see Port Stephens

NEW SOUTH WALES

Nambucca Heads
Bed & Breakfast
Address: Dunaber House
35 Piggott Street
Nambucca Heads, NSW 2448
Name: Brian and Ann Macdonald
Telephone: (02) 6568 9434
Fax: (02) 6568 9434
Beds: 1 Double, 2 Single (2 bedrooms)
Bathroom: 1 Ensuite, 1 Private
Tariff: B&B (full) Double $50-$75,
Single $40-$55. Children by arrangement
Vouchers accepted
Nearest Town: Nambucca Heads (in town)

Ann and Brian Macdonald came from Melbourne to enjoy retirement in the beautiful scenery and kindly climate of the Mid-North Coast. Having stayed in B&B's in many countries they have strong views about what is needed to ensure guests enjoy a relaxed, high-quality and memorable experience and have provided this level of comfort and welcome, along with a flexible attitude to special needs.
Dunaber House is a handsome family home which has been thoughtfully arranged to provide guests with comfort and friendliness as well as privacy and high standards, within walking distance of shops, restaurants, clubs, walks etc. Each suite has TV, fridge, tea-making, a private entrance and access to a verandah looking coastward where you can enjoy the views as you take a relaxed breakfast. Stay overnight or spend a little longer enjoying the variety of activities available in the lovely Nambucca Valley.
Directions: *Leave Pacific Highway by Riverside Drive to Town Centre. 1.1 kms then left into Piggott Street.*

Narooma - Central Tilba
Homestay
Address: Blacksmiths Lane, Central Tilba
Name: "Wirrina"
Telephone: (02) 4473 7279
Fax: (02) 4473 7279 **Mobile**: (017) 919 291
Beds: 2 Double, 2 Single (3 bedrooms)
Bathroom: 1 Ensuite, 1 Guests share
Tariff: B&B (special) Double $85/$95,
Single $60, Dinner $25pp by arrangement.
Credit cards.
Vouchers accepted except January.
Nearest Town: 17km south of Narooma on Princes Highway

Accommodation at Wirrina is in the guest wing of a comfortable, old-style family home. A guest sitting room has tea coffee and homemade biscuits supplied, also cutlery, crockery, wine glasses for those who would like to bring food for supper or dinner. Smoking is permitted on the verandah. Breakfast is a lavish affair at the long table in the kitchen. Dinner is by arrangement. Central Tilba is a National Trust village, still much as it was at the turn of the century. Village shops include a shoemaker, leatherworker, woodturner, and the famous Tilba Cheese Factory. The area is unusually beautiful, with volcanic outcrops in rolling countryside. Pristine beaches and the famous Mount Dromedary are within minutes, and activities such as horseriding, golfing, bushwalking, fishing, are readily available. Look for the pink and green house behind the Cheese Factory. Your hosts are Jon and Kay Esman-Ewin. Peace and beauty at the quiet end of town. Weekly rate available.

Narooma - Tilba Tilba
Bed & Breakfast   NRMA ★★★★
Address: Corkhill Drive, Tilba Tilba, NSW 2546
Name: 'Green Gables' (Gwen Hales)
Telephone: (02) 4473 7435 **Fax**: (02) 4473 7311
Beds: 3 Queen, 1 Single (3 Bedrooms)
Bathroom: 2 Ensuites, 1 Private
Tariff: B&B (full) Double $95-$115, Single $75, Dinner (delivered) $15 each.
Children not catered for. Credit Cards: Visa, Master Card, Bank Card.
Nearest Town: Naroona or Bermagui - 16 kms

Green Gables was built in 1879 as a Temperance Hall for the goldminers of Mount Dromedary.

Tilba Tilba is National Trust village at the base of Mount Dromedary. The mountain rises to a majestic 806 metres and it is a five hour return walk from our front door to the summit.

Our rooms offer every comfort, electric blankets, ducted heating, ceiling fans, your own TV and bathroom, Queen beds and our water supply is pure natural spring water from the mountain. Relax in the lounge-room or the large verandah with the superb country views. Want a hearty hot breakfast, you've got it. Like home-made cake or biscuits with you coffee, its here. Smoking permitted on verandah.

Just over the road is the wonderful four acre garden "Foxglove Spire", which is open to the public.

Narooma and Bermagui are only 10 minutes away with great beaches, fishing, golf etc. The craft villages of Central Tilba and Cobargo are only minutes away. Total relaxation with every comfort.

NEW SOUTH WALES

Narooma - Central Tilba
Bed & Breakfast
Address: Bate Street,
Central Tilba, NSW 2546
Name: Ken & Linda Jamieson
Telephone: (02) 4473 7290
Freecall 1800 355 850
Fax: (02) 4473 7290
Beds: 3 Double,
1 Single (3 bedrooms)
Bathroom: 1 Ensuite, 1 Guests share
Tariff: B&B (full) Double from $70/$75, Single from $55, Dinner by arrangement, Credit Cards. Vouchers accepted
Nearest Town: Narooma or Bermagui

A warm welcome awaits you from hosts Ken and Linda Jamieson and family at the Two Story B&B.
Nestled in foothills of Mt Dromedary situated in National Trust Village of Central Tilba.
Our building is 100 years old built 1894 and was originally the Post Office and residence, it has great character and views overlook a superb valley of rolling hills and lush greenness. Our weather is temperate and beaches are close by, great area for fishing.
Situated 300km south of Sydney.
The Craft Village of Central Tilba is extensive, businesses include: leather shop, tea rooms, alpaca shop, cheese factory, woodturning gallery and more. A short scenic drive takes you to a deer farm and winery also short drives to Bermagui and Cobargo, also bushwalking, fishing and swimming. We offer our guests a choice of continental and full cooked breakfasts also full self-contained kitchen with tea/coffee facilities, off street parking, in a total relaxed atmosphere in pleasant old world charm.

Narooma/Tilba
Farmstay NRMA ★★★☆
Address: Scenic Drive, Narooma, NSW 2546
Postal: PO Box 227, Narooma, NSW 2546
Name: Pub Hill Farm
Telephone: (02) 4476 3177 **Fax**: (02) 4476 3153
Mobile: (015) 502 566
Beds: 1 Double, 2 Single (2 bedrooms)
Bathroom: 2 Ensuite
Tariff: B&B (full) Double $75, Single $60, Children $20 sharing parents room, Under 3 free. Dinner N/A.
Nearest Town: Narooma 8km, Tilba 12km

Pub Hill Farm situated high on a hill, with magnificent water and mountain views, is a working mixed farm. The birdlife is abundant and varied and bushwalks are plentiful on and off the farm. Pub Hill has over 1km of water frontage.

Accommodation consists of one double room within the house (but with it's own entrance) and "The Croft" a garden room with twin beds and private deck. Both rooms are ensuite and have colour TV, microwaves and small fridges. Tea and coffee facilities in each room.

We welcome guests' pets if they are well behaved and the large gardens are fully fenced for their safety. Our garden is also a sanctuary for orphaned wildlife and small eastern grey 'joeys' are usually waiting to be made a fuss of by guests.

Ian & Micki Thomlinson, your hosts, have travelled abroad extensively; have lived in East Africa for many years and enjoy swapping travellers's tales with their guests.
NRMA ★★★☆

Narooma - Tilba Tilba
Country Home
Address: "The Valley Country Home",Tilba Tilba Walking Track, Tilba Tilba, NSW
Name: Catherine McDonough & Lynton Manley
Telephone: (02) 4473 7405 **Fax**: (02) 4473 7300
Beds: 4 King or 8 Single (4 bedrooms)
Bathroom: 4 Ensuite
Tariff: B&B (full) Double $260, Single $130, Dinner $65 per person, Credit Cards.
Nearest Town: Narooma, 15km on Princes Highway

"One of the most unusual and original mansions in the country......something that is part French chateau, part English manor house, but wholly Australian". Sydney Morning Herald, Travel, July 27, 1996.

"The Valley Country Home offers the finest accommodation in the area and the finest food. In fact, it is a showcase for the area's abundant produce". Australian gourmet Traveller, July 1995.

"You can seek out the Valley Country Home for the culinary experience alone. The tranquil luxury of its accommodation is a bonus! Together, the complementary elements of bed and table make this an escape with few equals". Weekends for Two No. 18, November 1996.

Directions: Please phone for directions.

Narooma also see Candelo

NEW SOUTH WALES

Narrabri
Homestay
Address: "Como"
26 Fraser Street,
Narrabri, NSW 2390
Name: Mrs Pam Barrett
Telephone: (067) 923193
Fax: (067) 924570
Beds: 1 Double, 2 Single (2 bedrooms)
Bathroom: 1 Guests share
Tariff: B&B (full) Double $70,
Single $50, Children under 14 years $15, Dinner $20pp.
Nearest Town: Narrabri

"Como" is a comfortable federation style home (circa 1914) located conveniently just two blocks from the Newell Highway and quietly on its own ten acres.
The spacious garden has shady mature trees and an in-ground swimming pool and guests are encouraged to enjoy the grounds during their stay. Pets outside are welcome.
A family atmosphere is a feature of "Como" where guests can enjoy a log fire in winter or the shady verandahs, gazebo and pool in the summer. Country style home cooking is a specialty and children are also welcome.
Narrabri and district offers abundant sights to see and lots to do. The Australian Telescope and Kaputar National Park and cotton picking and ginning in season is a local attraction.
Advance bookings appreciated.

Gift Vouchers

Our B&B vouchers are for a double room for one night's B&B. They cost $89, and if you order one as a gift, we will include a free
Australian Bed & Breakfast Book
worth $16.95

Send your cheque to
Moonshine Press
59 Quirk Street
Dee Why
NSW 2099

NEW SOUTH WALES

Narrandera
Guest House   NRMA ★★★☆
Address: "Historic Star Lodge", Cnr Whitton (Newell Highway) and Arthur St, Narrandera, NSW 2700
Name: John & Margaret Britton
Telephone: (02) 6959 1768 **Fax**: (02) 6959 4164
Email: Historic@ozemail.com.au
Beds: 7 Double, 15 Single (11 bedrooms)
Bathroom: 1 Ensuite, 3 Guests share
Tariff: B&B (continental) Double $60, Single $50, Credit Cards.
Nearest Town: Narrandera - Wagga Wagga 100km, Griffith 90km.

The Historic Star Lodge is a piece of Australia's history, and is classified by the National Trust of NSW. It is a beautiful example of Australian Federation architecture, having wide wrought iron railed verandahs, high pressed metal ceilings, stained glass windows and lots of atmosphere. It was converted to a guest house in 1992 and it is continuing to be restored to its original charm. In winter, our guests relax by an open fire. In summer the bedrooms are air-conditioned. Shops and clubs are within easy walking distance. There are many interesting things to see and do in the district and we are pleased to help you plan your outings. For golfers, the Narrandera Golf Club is rated 4th in country NSW. Visitors are welcome there. We look forward to your company and hope you enjoy our smoke free home.

Nelligen see Batemans Bay
Nelson Bay see Port Stephens

Continental breakfast consists of
fruit, cereal, toast, tea/coffee,
Full breakfast is the same with a cooked course,
Special breakfast has something special.

NEW SOUTH WALES

Newcastle - Lake Macquarie
Homestay NRMA ★★★☆
Address: 57 Cherry Road
Warners Bay, NSW 2282
Name: "Bayside Bed & Breakfast"
Telephone: (02) 4948 9500
Fax: (02) 4947 2057
Beds: 2 Double, 2 Single (3 bedrooms)
Bathroom: 1 Ensuite, 1 Guests share
Tariff: B&B (continental) Double $85,
Single $50, Child concession.
Vouchers accepted
Nearest Town: Newcastle 10km north

Less than two hours north of Sydney on beautiful Lake Macquarie, with boating, fishing and foreshore park, our comfortable home on 2 acres is set in a leafy garden with guest balcony and living areas overlooking the tennis court and pool. It is air conditioned, with sunny breakfast room, and a cosy open fire in winter. Your hosts have travelled extensively abroad and offer you a warm welcome and comfortable stay, in this quiet retreat.

Early morning walks along the Lake are popular, or guests may use the bicycles. We are close to Australian wildlife reserve, Newcastle attractions, golf, beaches, galleries and restaurants or drive to Hunter vineyards, 50 minutes. Picnic hamper and dinner are provided by arrangement, and tea and coffee are always available. We have hosted many international guests in our home and look forward to showing you the real Australian hospitality. Please phone ahead.

Newcastle - Lake Macquarie
Self-contained Accommodation NRMA ★★★
Address: 80 Coal Point Road,
Coal Point, NSW 2283
Name: Treetops
Telephone: (02) 4959 2378
Fax: (02) 4950 6012 **Mobile**: 014 495 851
Beds: 1 Double, 2 single (2 Bedrooms)
Bathroom: 2 Private
Tariff: B&B (continental) Double $75,
Single $45. Vouchers accepted
Nearest Town: Toronto (5 mins from Sydney Freeway).

Just over an hour from Sydney and ten minutes off the expressway, this restful retreat is located overlooking beautiful Lake Macquarie. Nestled in a natural bushland setting on a hillside amid a rambling garden and adjacent to a tree fern gully, this self-contained accommodation offers lake and mountain views, the restful sounds of native birds and fauna, a tranquil retreat for a relaxing stay. The accommodation includes a private entrance and courtyard featuring a terrace eating area overlooking a tree filtered lake view, a private hillside bush walk, views from each window, a spacious bed sitting room and a private bathroom. Lake Macquarie is the largest coastal lake in Australia, it has great fishing spots and excellent sailing and boating facilities, and cruises. Just fifteen minutes from Watagan Mountains, from shopping complexes and the artist William Dobel's house. Only thirty minutes from Hunter vineyards, scenic Newcastle, glorious beaches, historic Morpeth and Maitland.
Non smokers.

NEW SOUTH WALES

Newcastle - Merewether
Bed & Breakfast
Address: "Merewether Beach B&B"
60 Hickson Street, Merewether, NSW 2291
Name: Jane & Alf Scott
Telephone: (02) 4963 3526 **Fax**: (02) 4963 3526
Mobile: (015) 921670
Beds: 1 Double + sofa bed (1 bedroom)
Bathroom: 1 Ensuite
Tariff: B&B (full) Double $95, Single $80.
Vouchers accepted $15 surcharge for double.
Nearest Town: Newcastle - 5km south of the GPO

*Wake up to stunning views. Go to sleep with only the sound of waves breaking on shore. We are perched above the beach with sweeping views of Newcastle city, harbour and coast. There are nature reserves front and back and even a no-through road! Relax in a fully self-contained studio with glassed-in verandah, private entrance and garden on the lower level of our home. Microwave, refrigerator, tea/coffee making facilities, toaster, TV, VCR, clock radio, heater, electric blanket, library, use of laundry etc. Alf's talents as a potter and fine artist are found in the pieces that lovingly adorn the rooms. With Jane's passion for cooking, you can expect a sumptuous country-style breakfast.
A two minutes' stroll from the house takes you to Merewether Beach, ocean baths and restaurants.
We love our town and shall delight in sharing its secrets with you. Let us spoil you!*

Newcastle - East End
Bed & Breakfast
Address: "Ismebury" B&B,
3 Stevenson Place, Newcastle East, 2300
Name: Elizabeth Anne Creevey
Telephone: (02) 4929 5376
Fax: (02) 4927 8404 **Mobile**: (018) 688410
Email: anne.creevey@hunterlink.net.au
Beds: 1 King, 3 Singe, 2 Double (3 bedrooms)
Bathroom: 1 Ensuite, 1 Guests share
Tariff: Friday to Sunday B&B (full) Double from
$98-$156, Single from $84-$136, Suites from
Double $220 to $250 for 4. Prices subject to change,
Weekly & Corporate rates by application, Credit Cards.
Nearest Town: Newcastle city (on edge of CBD area)

Be my special guest in my 1911 Federation Terrace house in the historic East End Village of Newcastle. Restored to the ambience of the Edwardian era and furbished accordingly, with antique furniture, polished boards and rugs all to complement the timber joinery. Relax by the open fire in winter. Watch the clouds drift by from the spa bath, gaze at the ships coming in and out of the Harbour, or hide away in your own suite balcony or verandah. Take a ride on Newcastle's Historic Tram to revel the beauty of our city and a trip on the harbour are also available. Indulge in a horse and buggy ride along the foreshore as early residents would have done, or simply take a heritage walk and savour the harbour and city views and our magnificent beaches. You can also enjoy the many and varied eating establishments from excellent take away to A la Carte, within walking distance. The train and bus are 2 minutes away. We welcome both travellers and business people. Three rooms available.

NEW SOUTH WALES

Newport Island see Port Maquarrie
Nimmitabel see Bombala
Northern Rivers see Grafton

Nowendoc
Self-contained Accommodation   NRMA ★★★
Address: Wingam Rd., Nowendoc 2354
Name: Nowendoc Village Inn
Telephone: (02) 6777 0952 + (02) 6777 0934
Beds: 4 x 1 Bedroom Suites/2 Double & 2 Twin beds. Cottage: 4 Bedroom/4 Twin beds. Cottage: 3 bedroom, 1 Double, 2 Twin beds. Fully eqipped kitchens
Bathroom: Shower rooms and toilets
Tariff: B&B (continental) Double $40, Single $30, Children $10. Credit Cards. Vouchers accepted
Nearest Town: Nowendoc on Gloucester - Armidale Road.

Nowendoc is a small village on the lower Northern Tablelands set in lovely mountain countryside about halfway between Gloucester and Walcha.
Nowendoc is a crossroads - you can travel to Tamworth, Armidale, Taree and Port Macquarie. Walcha 45 minutes away has restaurants, clubs, bowls, golf and on the outskirts the magnificent Apsley Gorge and falls.
The village itself has a 7 day store with liquor license, church, hall and police station.
It is surrounded by eucalypt and pine forests close to trout streams.
We are on the road that is the shortest distance between Sydney and Brisbane.
You are invited to Nowendoc Village Inn.

Nowra - Vincentia, Jervis Bay
Bed & Breakfast
Address: 306 Elizabeth Drive, Vincentia, NSW 2540
Name: Bay View
Telephone: (02) 4441 5805
Beds: 2 Double (2 bedrooms)
Bathroom: 2 Ensuite
Tariff: B&B (continental) Double $75-$85, Single $45-$50.
Nearest Town: Nowra - 3 1/2km south of Huskisson on Water of Jervis Bay

Bay View - Vincentia
We welcome you to enjoy the privacy of our home on beautiful Jervis Bay. As this is a relatively new area our home is only 15 years old of brick construction with large windows to capture the view. Built on two levels the queen size suite is upstairs with a sun-deck and downstairs the double suite has tranquil view through the gum trees of the water which can be reached via our steps. Both areas have their own ensuite, TV lounge and dining alcove with microwave oven, refrigerator and tea and coffee making facilities. Rooms are serviced daily. Ideal area for walking around beaches, National Park and Botanic Gardens with abundance of birds and native animals. Our bay is an aquatic playground for all ages including dolphins and penguins. We are only minutes from golf course, bowling club and tennis courts. Evening entertainment and meals are available at registered clubs and restaurants.
Your hosts, Val and Ian Fielder.

Tell other travellers about your favourite B&Bs

Nowra - Callala Bay, Jervis Bay
Self-contained Accommodation
Address: 26 Fleet Way, Callala Bay
Name: "Pa's Corner"
Telephone: (02) 4446 5640
Beds: 1 Double, 2 Single (1 bedroom)
Bathroom: 1 Private
Tariff: Dec/Jan/Easter: Double $75, Single $55. Low season: Double $55, Single $35. Children under 12 $10, under 5 Free.
Nearest Town: Nowra

Your hosts, Dawn and Greg, invite you to Pa's Corner. Tucked away from the hustle and bustle, Pa's Corner is self-contained and attached to their home. The large front window looks out on flower gardens and the kitchenette/dining area opens on to a screened, outdoor, sitting and BBQ area. A special, hearty breakfast is available for a reasonable charge.
Callala Bay is one of many little villages scattered around beautiful Jervis Bay which is renowned for its sandy, safe, clean beaches and Dolphin pods. Charter a catamaran, fish, sail, wind-surf or swim in the crystal clear water. Play golf, tennis or bowls, bushwalk, visit wineries, historic sites, antique or craft shops. Restaurants and licensed clubs in close proximity. Pa's Corner also offers off-street parking, separate entrance, laundry facilities and room serviced daily.
We will be pleased to pick up from railway. Reasonable rates can be arranged for guided tour of our beautiful area.
Brochure available.

Nowra - Bolong
Farmstay
Address: "Swanlea Farm", RMB 680 Bolong Road, Bolong via Nowra
Name: Jim & Jan Knapp
Telephone: (02) 4421 7872
Fax: (02) 4421 7872
Mobile: (041) 9296828
Beds: 1 King/Queen, 1 Double, 2 Single (3 bedrooms)
Bathroom: 3 Ensuite
Tariff: B&B (special) Double $100-$110, Single $75-$85, Mid-week discount, Credit Cards (BC/MC/VISA).
Nearest Town: Nowra - 8km east of Nowra, 15km from Berry

"Swanlea Farm", 2 hours south of Sydney, is an operational farm with frontages to the Shoalhaven River and Broughton Creek. The original federation homestead has been lovingly restored and is furnished in restful country style. All rooms have ensuites - 2 with their own private verandah. Relax on the wide verandahs or potter in the garden. The guest lounge abounds with books and has a piano, TV, sound system and wood fire for when the weather is chilly. The old farm buildings and surrounds are perfect for the photographer or artist. Berry, Kangaroo Valley and Jervis Bay are close by or visit local wineries, galleries, Arthur Boyd's Bundanon or other local places of interest. Beaches and golf courses are 5 minutes away.
Enjoy our special breakfasts with fresh farm produce. Smoking is OK outdoors. Children are accommodated by arrangement. "Come home to Swanlea".

Nundle
Studio Accommodation
Address: "Oak Cottage", Barry Rd, Hanging Rock via Nundle, NSW 2340
Name: Marcia Schofield
Telephone: (02) 6769 3625
Beds: 1 Double (1 bedroom)
Bathroom: 1 Ensuite
Tariff: B&B (continental) Double $60, Single $40. Dinner $20. Vouchers accepted (includes full breakfast)
Nearest Town: 9km east of Nundle. Nundle is 60km south east of Tamworth.

Enjoy the simplicity and charm of a beautiful and mature New England garden with your own studio accommodation away from the main cottage and situated only 300m from the historic Sheba Dams where you can fish, swim, birdwatch or just read a book. As a working potter I am interested in the visual arts. I make a range of domestic ware and some non functional pots.

Hanging Rock is surrounded by the Nundle State Forest and was once famous for its gold. You can still pan for the precious metal or fossick for gem stones. Nundle is only 9km away and has a P.O., golf course, tennis courts, swimming pool, hotel with a la carte dining and general store. Hanging Rock is half way between Sydney and Brisbane. Tamworth and Quirindi are 45 mins by car. Pets welcome.

Nundle
Guest House
Address: 85 Jenkins Street, Nundle, NSW 2340
Name: Jenkins Street Guest House
Telephone: (2) 6769 3239
Fax: (02) 6769 3239
Beds: 6 Queen, 4 Single, (6 bedrooms)
Bathroom: 2 Ensuite, 2 Private
Tariff: B&B (full), Double $115-$130, Single $80, Dinner $40-$50. Children 12 years and over. Credit cards (M/C, B/C, VISA, Diners).
Dinner, Bed & Breakfast packgages available.
Nearest Town: Tamworth

Jenkins Street Guest House
85 Jenkins Street
Nundle NSW 2340
Tel/Fax 067 693 239

Jenkins Street Guest House offers very elegant accommodation in a fully renovated 1938's National Australian Bank building situated in the historic gold mining town of Nundle. The discovery of gold in 1851 has left Nundle with a wealth of history to be explored - the search for gold continues.

Horse riding, 4 wheel drive tours, gourmet picnics, participation in the farm activity of the day can be organised or maybe a visit to the beautiful gardens and homestead of historic 'Wombramurra' the 16,000 acre property at your doorstep to be enjoyed - play croquet in the extensive Guest House gardens, golf, bowls and tennis nearby, stroll through town and visit antique and craft shops or just relax by the open fires in dining, library and sitting rooms.

Your hosts, Jean-Michel Feray and Leah Hudson, will provide you with the finest of local produce, fresh trout, yabbies, lamb, beef and vegetables from 'Wombramurra's' garden.

Oberon

B&B Guest House   NRMA ★★★★☆
Address: Sydney Road, Oberon 2787
Name: 'Tapio' Guest House in a Garden
Telephone: (02) 6336 2063 **Fax**: (02) 6336 2063
Beds: 1 King, 1 Double, 2 Single (2 bedrooms)
Bathroom: 2 Ensuite
Tariff: B&B (full), on application. Children negotiable. Dogs welcome
Nearest Town: Oberon 2 km from PO.

Sunroom Breakfasts
Trees
Music of your choice
Candlelit dinners
Laughter
Leaves
English teas
Surrounded by Colours
Textures
Tawny Port
Tranquillity.

Dogs in residence: Bobby, Betty, Angelina, Whisper.
Brochure on request. Sapphire sluicing dishes for hire. Dinner by pre-arrangement.
WELL BEHAVED DOGS WELCOME. NRMA rating 4 1/2 stars. Exercise facilities - walking machine or forest.

O'Connell see Bathurst
Olinda see Rylstone

Orange

Homestay   NRMA ★★★☆
Address: "Robin Hill", Neal's Lane,
off Cargo Road, Orange. P O Box 2211, Orange 2800
Name:
"Robin Hill B&B". Hosts: Margaret & Doug Mackay
Telephone: (02) 6365 3336 **Fax**: (02) 6365 3336
Mobile: 0419 653 336
Beds: 1 Double, 1 Twin, 1 Twin/Family
Bathroom: 3 Guests share, vanities in 2 brms
Tariff: B&B (full) Double $90, Single $65,
Children welcome - special mid-week rates. Dinner from $20.
Credit Cards. Cheques by arrangement. Vouchers accepted
Nearest Town: Orange (5km to Post Office).

"Robin Hill" is an interesting architect designed home set in an acre of rambling gardens, where the panoramic views of rolling hills can also be seen from most rooms. Besides Margaret and Doug the other residents are our 18 year old son Phillip, (whose hobby is model railways), one dog and one cat (both available for loan). Bedrooms are warm and cosy (electric blankets) to keep you comfortable in winter. Guests can relax in two comfortable lounges: one with games, TV/Video, and in the other a music centre and piano; books and magazines everywhere!
Just 5 minutes from the centre of Orange, "Robin Hill" is also close to many local attractions such as wineries, scenic spots, restaurants and walking trails.
Country style dinners and picnics prepared by arrangement.
A smoke free home. Member - Orange & District Tourism Inc.

NEW SOUTH WALES

Orange District
Homestay
Address: Campbell's Wyndhover Cottage, "Wyndhover" Cargo Road, Orange, NSW 2800
Name: Norman & Jennifer Campbell
Telephone: TOLL FREE 1800 642 176
Fax: /phone (02) 6365 3397 Mobile: 018 587321
Beds: 1 Queen, 2 Double, 4 Single (5 bedrooms)
Bathroom: 2 Guests share
Tariff: B&B Double $90, Queen/Ensuites $120, Single $65, Children under 15 $30pp, under 5 $15pp. Dinner by arrangement. Credit cards. Vouchers accepted
Nearest Town: 5km/5 mins to Orange CBD. 3 hrs from Sydney or Canberra.

Be a house guest at Orange, Australia's Colour City in the beautiful Central Tablelands of the Great Dividing Range in NSW. Come to our comfortable chalet style stone cottage and its warm and friendly atmosphere. Wyndhover Cottage with its cosy log fires and sunny decks, nestled on the slopes of Mount Canobolas. Imagine waking up to unrivalled panoramas few see, enjoying a great breakfast and looking to a day exploring the many pleasures our district has to offer.

"Wyndhover", a 25 acre boutique vineyard and Christmas tree grove, is only minutes away from parks and gardens, heritage villages, wineries, golf and bowls, galleries, antique shops, restaurants, lakes, streams and the bustling Orange city and shopping centre..

Enjoy your day and maybe have a generous home cooked dinner with us at "Wyndhover". Our low humidity summers seldom exceed 28 degrees C.

Morning and afternoon tea provided on arrival and departure. Same day bookings welcome but reservations recommended. No smoking inside our cottage please.

Let us welcome and spoil you soon at Wyndhover Cottage.

Orange
Homestay

MEMBER
INN·HOUSE
bed • and • breakfast
VICTORIA, AUSTRALIA

Address: "Killarney Homestead" Darley Road, Nashdale, NSW (via Orange)
Name: Beth Magick
Telephone: (02) 6365 3419
Beds: 2 Double, 2 Single (3 bedrooms)
Bathroom: 1 Ensuite, 1 Guests share
Tariff: B&B (full) Double $70, Single $40, Dinner $15pp by arrangement.
Nearest Town: Orange NSW (Nashdale is 10km west)

Killarney Homestead is a country retreat set amongst the orchards of Nashdale just west of Orange. The perfect location to relax and enjoy friendly home-style hospitality in the comfort of a restored Federation home. Nashdale is on the slopes of Mt Canobolas. Only minutes from Orange's parks, historic buildings, galleries, gardens and golf courses.

This is an ideal spot to use as a base when visiting the many sights of the Central West. Historic Bathurst, Cowra's Japanese Gardens and War Cemetery, the heritage listed village of Carcoar, Parkes' radio telescope, Wellington caves, Burrendong dam, and Dubbo's Western Plains zoo.

Excellent bushwalking is available in the Mt Canobolas National Park (just up the road from Killarney Homestead) and the Australian National Field Days site is nearby at Borenore.

NEW SOUTH WALES

Orange - Central Western N.S.W.
Homestay
Address: "Koombalah",
Cargo Road, Orange 2800, NSW
Name: Margot Niven
Telephone: (02) 6361 4509
Beds: 2 Queen, 1 Kingsize single (3 bedrooms)
Bathroom: 1 Ensuite, 1 Private
Tariff: B&B (full) Queen $120, Single $60,
Children negotiable. Dinner $30pp. Credit cards.
Tariff: Subject to increase during 1997.
Nearest Town: Orange NSW

Situated 4km west of Orange P.O. in a rural setting, on 1.5 acres of gardens featuring tulips and daffodils, magnolias, cherry and apple blossom in spring. Summer is temperate, with no humidity and a range of temperature 20 - 28 degrees. Autumn is a kaleidoscope of colour with the exotic ornamental trees. Winter is bracing with snow settling occasionally. The house is centrally heated plus an open fire and combustion heater. All beds have electric blankets and doonas. Breakfast may be taken in the sunny family room, overlooking the solar heated pool. In view of Wentworth and Duntry league golf courses. Enjoy relaxing, swimming, playing golf, sight seeing, go trout fishing, horse riding, tennis, tenpin bowling, lawn bowls or croquet. Investigate our craft and specialty shops, excellent restaurants, regional art gallery, scenic drives and local wineries. There are always home cooked biscuits, fresh flowers, organically grown vegetables seasonal) and large fluffy towels.

Orange
B&B Historic Guest House NRMA ★★★★☆
Address: "Cotehele House"
177 Anson St., Orange, NSW 2800
Name: John & Robyn Sainsbury
Telephone: (02) 6361 2520
Fax: (02) 6361 8635
Mobile: (0417) 274 020
Email: cotehele.house@cww.octec.org.au
Beds: 5 Queen,
1 Double (6 bedrooms)
Bathroom: 4 Ensuite, 2 Guests share
Tariff: B&B (full) Double $100-$140, Single $80-$90.
Dinner on request, Credit Cards. Vouchers accepted $20-$56 surcharge
Nearest Town: Orange (CBD 0.5km)

The Magistrate's House - Cotehele - is a mid-Victorian residence built in 1878 for the first magistrate located west of the Blue Mountains in the historic central New South Wales' city of Orange. Cotehele has been meticulously restored and decorated in true English country style. Original touches include the maid's and tradesmen's bells, gas lamp, tiled entry foyer, slab-built stables and carriage room. Paramount at Cotehele is our guests' comfort, with the six bedrooms decorated and furnished to ensure a quiet, restful night. All beds are queen-sized with guest bathrobes supplied. The guest lounge and dining areas together with the bedrooms are served by ducted reverse cycle air-conditioning for comfort throughout the year. Our superb breakfast makes an excellent start to the day. Complimentary afternoon tea is served and picnic hampers are available by arrangement. Golf, tennis, day-tours, vineyards, parklands, orchards and unsurpassed scenery abound in the region. The perfect place to enjoy elegant and luxurious hospitality.

NEW SOUTH WALES

Orange
Homestay NRMA ★★★
Address: 9 Crinoline St.,
Orange, NSW 2800
Name: Sue & Neil Skinner
Telephone: (02) 6362 5729
Fax: (02) 6361 2679
Mobile: 0414 306 349
Beds: 1 Queen/2 singles, 1 Double,
1 Single (3 bedrooms)
Bathroom: 2 Ensuites, 1 Guests share
Tariff: B&B (full or continental) Double $80, Single $55, Children by arrangement, Dinner $15pp. Student rates available. Vouchers accepted
Nearest Town: Orange

NRMA Rating 3 1/2 Stars. Cleveland is a new brick / veneer house in north Orange at the end of a cul-de-sac. It is a very quiet house as there are no very close neighbours. The house is on a flat block of land and the guests have off street parking. All the beds have electric blankets and the house is gas heated for the winter and evaporate cooled for summer. The house is non smoking and we have one spoilt cat. We welcome children but do not allow pets. Tourist interests include Mt Canoblas, Lake Canoblas, apple orchards, wineries, Gem Museum, Borenore Caves, art gallery, Banjo Patteron's birthplace, historical homes, old gold mines, beautiful parks, tree lined street plus beautiful scenery. **Directions**: *Travelling west on Summer Street (the main street), turn right into Anson Street. Travelling east on Summer Street (the main street), turn left into Anson Street, Crinoline St is the first street on the right after the Phillip St round-a-bout. Look for number 9 on the mailbox or gutter in drive way or sign above garage doors.*

Orange
Farmstay, Self-contained Accommodation, B&B
Address: "Koolabah Farm"
Cargo Rd, Lidster via Orange, NSW 2800
Name: Dian Barber
Telephone: (02) 6365 6118 **Fax**: (02) 6365 6120
Mobile: 0417-275 150
Beds: Homestead: 1 Double, 3 Single (2 Bedrooms).
Self-contained Cottage: 1 Queen, 2 Singles (2 Bedrooms)
Bathroom: Homestead: 1 Guests Share.
Self-contained Cottage: 1 Guests Share
Tariff: Homestead: B&B (full) Double $100, Single $80,
Children $20. Self-contained Cottage: Double $110, Single $90. Dinner $25. Credit Cards. Vouchers accepted $20 surcharge Homestead, $29 Cottage.
Nearest Town: Orange - 20 kms.

Rolling hills and magnificent sunsets is the setting for Koolabah Farm, Bed & Breakfast and Farmstay, set on 223 hectares near Orange in the NSW Central Tablelands. This is a working sheep and cattle property, so guests are encouraged to join in the farm activities. Guests can choose between the turn of the century homestead, with cosy log fires in winter, or wide shady verandahs in summer and the restored manager's cottage offering today's facilities with yesterday's memories set in a cottage garden with magnificent views. Koolabah Farm is 3 1/2 hours drive from Sydney and 19 kms from Orange with its theatre, gardens and a sip away from award winning wineries. Nearby are the historic towns of Millthorpe and Molong to browse for something special, or Canowindra, home of the fish fossil museum and hot air ballooning. All this makes Koolabah Farm the perfect country getaway. **Directions**: *20kms Southwest of Orange on the Cargo Road.*

Orange
Homestay and Self-contained Accommodation
Address: "BED OF ROSES", Forbes Road, Orange, NSW 2800
Name: Dee & Rob Napier
Telephone: (02) 6362 6946 **Fax**: (02) 6361 7492 **Mobile**: (015) 784684
Main Homestead:
Beds: 1 Queen, 2 Double (3 bedrooms).
Bathroom: 1 Ensuite, 1 Guest Share.
Tariff: B&B (full) Double $90-$110, Single $70-$90.
Wild Rose Cottage:
Beds: 1 Queen, 2 Single (2 bedrooms)
Bathroom: 1 Private
Tariff: S.C (Breakfast provisions)   Double $120, Single $100, extra person $20.
Perfect for two to four guests, Wild Rose Cottage is available to one party only.
Credit Cards (VISA/MC/BC). Checkout 12 noon.
Nearest Town: 5 minutes west of Orange on the Forbes Road

Capture the quiet relaxation and elegance of our country home. Settle into luxurious comfort with down quilts, family antiques and flower filled rooms. BED OF ROSES is set in 3 hectares of beautifully maintained gardens overlooking a lake. The garden is open for the Australian Open Garden Scheme.
Dee is a garden designer, and Rob is an Associate Professor in Farm Management. They have both travelled extensively and stayed in B&B's around the world so know what a traveller, business person or holiday maker expects - heaps of luxury, peace, tranquillity and friendly hosts - so they have supplied all this in abundance!
Directions: *Please phone, fax or write for directions and brochure.*
We look forward to seeing you soon at BED OF ROSES

Ourimbah see Central Coast

Pacific Palms see Forster

NEW SOUTH WALES

Pambula
Homestay
Address: McKell's, 47 Toalla Street, Pambula, NSW 2549
Name: Amanda and Ernst Kemmerer
Telephone: (02) 6495 6310
Beds: 1 Queen, 1 Double, 2 Single (3 bedrooms)
Bathroom: 1 Guests share
Tariff: B&B (special) Double $95, Single $68 Vouchers accepted
Nearest Town: Merimbula 5 km, Eden 15 km

McKell Cottage c.1840 Heritage listed and is the birthplace of Governor General Sir William McKell. The cottage is set on a hill overlooking the roof tops of historic Pambula Village and surrounding countryside. The wood slab cottage has been fully renovated, but retains the olde worlde charm of yesteryear.
The bedrooms have open fire places for those cooler months, country decorations, and floral doonas. All rooms open onto the shady verandah which overlooks a secluded cottage garden. Breakfast is served on the verandah on warm summer mornings, or in the family dining area. Dinner can be served by arrangement only.
There are national parks, beautiful beaches, golf courses, bowls, fishing, oyster and mussel barns, and seasonal whale watching trips can be arranged. Your hosts Amanda and Ernst enjoy gardening, sport, reading, crafts, and meeting people. McKells is a smoke free environment, close to airport and has off street parking.

Parkville see Scone
Phegans Bay see Central Coast
Pokolbin see Hunter Valley

Port Macquarie
Homestay
Address: 5 Grandview Parade, Port Macquarie, NSW 2444
Name: Doris and John Gill
Telephone: (02) 6583 3865
Beds: 1 Queen, 2 Single, (2 bedrooms) **Bathroom**: 1 Guests share
Tariff: B&B (full), Double $60, Single $35.
Children welcome. Vouchers accepted
Nearest Town: Port Macquarie halfway Sydney to Brisbane

Port Macquarie has many attractions for both adults and children. The beaches are all a little different and the area abounds in fine eating places and night life. There are excellent scenic walking routes from level paths to gently undulating and traversing areas ranging from wetlands to beach fronts. Sea breezes keep the summers at a pleasant temperature and winters are amazingly mild. We are situated two and a half kilometres from the town centre, and a ten minute walk from the famous Flynns Beach or a quick two minutes in the car. A bus service passes the door for those who wish to use this facility. Our spacious first floor self contained accommodation consists of two bedrooms (one queen, one twin), lounge/ dining with TV, a half bathroom and kitchen facilities which include a refrigerator and microwave. It also features a verandah offering sea views and balmy evenings. Visitors are assured of a warm welcome and we can also meet travellers arriving by train or coach.

NEW SOUTH WALES

Port Macquarie
Homestay   NRMA ★★★☆
Address: 31 Timber Ridge,
Pacific Drive, Port Macquarie,
NSW 2444
Name: Timber Ridge B & B
Telephone: (02) 658 20099
Beds: 1 Queen, 2 Single (2 bedrooms)
Bathroom: 1 Private
Tariff: B&B (full) Double $75, Single $60.
Vouchers accepted
Nearest Town: Port Macquarie

Timber Ridge B & B just 4.5km from the centre of Port Macquarie is an ideal stopover for travellers or those seeking active recreational pursuits. Guests are accommodated in separate wing which has private access. Two bedrooms are reserved for guests (1 double, 1 twin), sitting room (TV/video) and tea making facilities including small fridge.
Hosts Noreen and Warren have an intimate knowledge of the surrounding area and if requested will assist in planning sightseeing trips or recreational activities.
"Timber Ridge" nestles on a hillside amongst gum trees overlooking the Pacific Ocean. The house is cooled by sea breezes in summer and warmed by combustion wood fire in winter. Golf courses and bowling clubs are within a short drive with unspoiled beaches and rainforest reserves a short walk from the house.
Guests enjoy a smoke free atmosphere - children over 15 yrs welcome. Transfers from bus, train or plane arranged.
Brochure available.   NRMA Rating   ★★★★

Port Macquarie - Newport Island
Homestay   NRMA ★★★☆
Address: 29 Laguna Place, Newport Island, Port Macquarie, 2444
Name: Joy's Doo Drop Inn
Telephone: (02) 6583 3405 **Fax**: (02) 6582 5910
Beds: 2 Double, 1 Twin (3 bedrooms)
Bathroom: 1 Ensuite, 1 Private, 1 Guests share with spa
Tariff: B&B (full) Double $70-$80, Twin $70-$80, Ensuite $80-$90.   Vouchers accepted
Nearest Town: Wauchope - Taree - Kempsey

Joy's Doo Drop Inn, where a good night's sleep counts, is situated approx. 2km from Port Macquarie Post Office and within level walking distance to large shopping centre R.S.L. and bowling clubs.
Relax in a modern and friendly home, located on the tranquil canal waters.
Guests are offered a high standard of service e.g.-
Solar heated salt pool
BBQ facilities
Fish from your own private jetty
Family room with TV, video and C.D. player
Unlimited tea coffee and biscuits
Fans in all rooms
Elec. hair drier and electric blankets
Port Macquarie is close to wineries, good sporting facilities (bowls, tennis, golf and surf), River cruises, river and deep sea fishing, visit historical museums, convict built St Thomas Church and convict cemetery.
Directions are simple, but please ask when booking. Courtesy pick up from airport, train and coach. Brochures available.   NRMA rating   ★★★☆

NEW SOUTH WALES

Port Macquarie - Lighthouse Beach
Homestay+Self-contained Accommodation   NRMA ★★★★
Address: 91 Matthew Flinders Dr., Port Macquarie, 2444
Name: Lighthouse Beach B&B Homestay
Telephone: (02) 6582 5149
Beds: 2 Queen, 2 Single/King (3 bedrooms)
Bathroom: 2 Ensuite, 1 Private
Tariff: B&B (special) Double $85-$120, Single $70-$95, Children over 16, Dinner by arrangement. Moderate weekly rates.   Vouchers accepted $6.50-$30 surcharge
Nearest Town: Port Macquarie 10 minutes south of Post Office.

Located at the very northern end of the magnificent, forest fringed 16km Long Lighthouse Beach we are perfectly placed to offer you a high quality elegant haven in a quiet and natural environment, featuring the famous Koala Hospital and sanctuary, dolphins in the rivers, and beaches, and Sea Acres - Elevated board walk in a coastal rainforest.

Barry and Mary Jean warmly welcome you to enjoy the comforts of our beachside home and to relax in a 4 star accommodation in the Rainforest or Reef ensuite rooms, both luxuriously appointed together with TV, Fridge, M/W oven and Dining setting, beside the solar heated pool and spa (a magic blue lagoon by night!). Our larger ground floor Hibiscus Suite, ideal for that longer stay or special occasion (Honeymoon, Romantic Weekend etc) offers queen bedroom, bathroom, kitchen, Dining in open plan with a large comfortable lounge with front and rear garden and ocean views. All rooms are self contained with private access and security garage parking with remote control opening doors. Enjoy our home made jams and juices and a selection of seasonal fruits with a freshly prepared breakfast whilst observing the birdlife and bushland of the seaside, and perhaps in the evening a barbecue on the terrace? Five minutes walk to full local shopping including restaurants and liquor shop, home-style dinner by arrangement.

We are proud to offer you a clean, comfortable and a warmly hospitable stay in a smoke free environment. Lighthouse Beach Bed and Breakfast "the home to resort to".

Pick up from transport terminals by arrangement. Local Bus at door.

Directions: *From South: via Kew and Laurieton turn right at roundabout 1km North of Port Macquarie Golf Club. From Port Macquarie: follow beaches to Lighthouse Beach.*

NEW SOUTH WALES

Port Macquarie - Lighthouse Beach
Bed & Breakfast/Homestay
Address: 53 Matthew Flinders Drive,
Port Macquarie, NSW 2444
Name: Dolphin View Bed & Breakfast
Telephone: (02) 6582 3561
Beds: 1 Queen, 1 Double (2 bedrooms)
Bathroom: 2 Ensuite
Tariff: B&B (full) Double $75-$95,
Single $60-$85, Dinner by arrangement,Credit Cards. Vouchers accepted $6 surcharge (Queen)excluding Christmas/Easter holidays
Nearest Town: 7km south of Port Macquarie

Dolphin View enjoys an absolute beachfront position on beautiful Lighthouse Beach. As the name suggests it is often an ideal spot to watch the dolphins surfing the waves. Both bedrooms and the spacious guests' TV/video lounge (with log fire) offer panoramic ocean views and are tastefully furnished with all the comforts of home. Guests are welcome to swim in the salt water pool or just relax on the sun loungers. Hosts John and Margaret have 20 years experience in B&Bs and in the hospitality industry and look forward to sharing their home with you where a warm, friendly welcome is assured. Situated close to beach, camel rides, rainforests, local shopping centre, restaurants, golf courses. Bus service at door to and from town centre. Pick up from bus terminal/airport by arrangement. Sorry we have no facilities for children or pets and are a smoke free establishment.

Port Macquarie also see Newcastle and Lake Cathie

Port Stephens - Anna Bay
Bed and Breakfast NRMA ★★★☆
Address: 23 Port Stephens Drive
Annay Bay, Port Stephens Shire
Name: The Bays Bed & Breakfast
Telephone: (02) 4982 1438.
Toll free: 1800 674 465
Fax: (02) 4982 1438
Beds: 3 Queen, 2 Single (4 bedrooms)
Bathroom: 4 Ensuite (Guest/family share)
Tariff: B&B (full) Double $75-$100,
Single $45-$60. Dinner $15-$20.
Children welcome. Credit Cards.
Vouchers accepted $10 surcharge
Nearest Town: Nelson Bay. North of Newcastle

An elegant country escape, our recently renovated home set on ten acres has so much to offer the weary traveller. Awaken to the serenade of the kookaburras and other bird calls. Enjoy the sumptuous country style breakfast on our enclosed verandah overlooking bushland and gardens. Take a stroll on our property and perhaps catch a glimpse of a koala or two, or partake in the abundant local attractions, e.g. 4WD coastal tours, winery, tobogganing and magnificent beaches etc. The dolphin cruise is a must as Port Stephens is "The Dolphin Capital"! In the evening you could savour the various restaurants just a short drive away. Retire for the evening in our well appointed guestrooms, all have large TV's, tables and cane seating, coffee/tea making facilities and private ensuites. Come and try the wonderful experience of the Bays Bed & Breakfast and you will want to return again and again.

NEW SOUTH WALES

Port Stephens - Lemon Tree Passage
Homestay/Bed & Breakfast   NRMA ★★★★
Address: "Larkwood of Lemon Tree",
1 Oyster Farm Road, Lemon Tree Passage
Name: Tony & Vivien
Telephone: (02) 4982 4656
Fax: (02) 4982 4656 **Mobile**: 0417 254 791
Beds: 3 Queen, 1 Single (3 bedrooms)
Bathroom: 3 Ensuite
Tariff: B&B (full) Queen $90, Single $65,
Dinner by pre-arrangement $20pp.
Credit Cards: Mastercard, Bankcard, Visa.
Nearest Town: Lemon Tree Passage

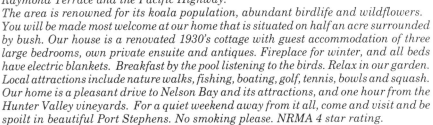

Lemon Tree Passage is located on the shores of beautiful Port Stephens. It is just two and a half hours north of Sydney or twenty minutes drive from Raymond Terrace and the Pacific Highway.
The area is renowned for its koala population, abundant birdlife and wildflowers. You will be made most welcome at our home that is situated on half an acre surrounded by bush. Our house is a renovated 1930's cottage with guest accommodation of three large bedrooms, own private ensuite and antiques. Fireplace for winter, and all beds have electric blankets. Breakfast by the pool listening to the birds. Relax in our garden. Local attractions include nature walks, fishing, boating, golf, tennis, bowls and squash. Our home is a pleasant drive to Nelson Bay and its attractions, and one hour from the Hunter Valley vineyards. For a quiet weekend away from it all, come and visit and be spoilt in beautiful Port Stephens. No smoking please. NRMA 4 star rating.

Port Stephens/Myall Lakes
Homestay
Address: 38 Moira Pde, Hawks Nest
Name: Gleniss & Bob Pyers
Telephone: (02) 4997 0943 **Fax**: (02) 4997 0943
Beds: 1 Queen, 2 Single (2 bedrooms)
Bathroom: 1 Private
Tariff: B&B (full) Double $75, Single $55.
Nearest Town: Tea Gardens

Our 2 storey modern home is situated on the waterfront at Hawks Nest close to the boat ramp and just 2 1/2 hours from Sydney.
Your self-contained ground floor accommodation consists of 2 bedrooms, lounge / dining / kitchen, private bathroom and toilet and a large covered patio overlooking the waterfront.
Cross the road for a fish in the river, stroll to either of our 2 magnificent beaches, Hawks Nest Surf Beach and Jimmy's Beach on Port Stephens, explore the wonders of the pristine Myall Lakes National Park, a dolphin watch cruise on Port Stephens, a game of golf or bowls, a 1 hour drive to the vineyards or just relax on the patio and enjoy the boats and the bird life.
Disabled access.

There are some good tips for easier travel on page 7

Port Stephens - Nelson Bay
Homestay   NRMA ★★★☆
Address: "Croft Haven Bed & Breakfast"
202 Salamander Way,
Nelson Bay, NSW 2317
Name: Glenis & John Goodwin
Telephone: (02) 4984 1799
Fax: (02) 4984 1799
Mobile: (015) 864 139
Beds: 1 Queen, 2 Double (3 bedrooms)
Bathroom: 1 Guests share,
1 Disabled bathroom/toilet
Tariff: B&B (full) Double $85-$95, Single $75-$85
Dinner by request.
Nearest Town: Nelson Bay - 4km southwest of P.O.

Croft Haven is the ideal resting place for you in beautiful Port Stephens. Only 2 1/2 hours north of Sydney, relax and unwind in our bushland retreat, amongst an abundance of bird life. Start the day with our hearty, country style breakfast including home baked bread. Wood fires in both casual and formal lounge areas, where you can enjoy our home library or perhaps a game of Backgammon! Play the pianola or sit back and enjoy music from our varied collection. The decor of the romantic bedrooms with luxury bathrobes will charm you and all the beds have luxurious doonas and electric blankets for your comfort. Smoke free zone indoors. Close to all activities from bushwalking, boating, and golfing to the local winery. Bicycle tracks wind around the bay foreshore. The Sydney - Newcastle bus stops opposite Croft Haven and Newcastle airport is 20 minutes. 'Ruff' our friendly old Border Collie welcomes you to our bushland 'HAVEN'.

Port Stephens - Nelson Bay
Guest House/Bed & Breakfast
Address: "Nelson Bay Bed & Breakfast",
81 Stockton Street, Nelson Bay, 2315
Name: Steve & Sonia
Telephone: (02) 4984 3655
Fax: (02) 4984 3655 **Mobile:** (019) 459830
Beds: 3 Queen (3 bedrooms)
Bathroom: 3 Ensuite
Tariff: B&B (full) Double $90-$140, Single $70-$120, Children by arrangement,
Dinner by arrangement, Credit Cards.
Nearest Town: Nelson Bay 500 metres, Newcastle 50km.

A unique Bed & Breakfast in a unique area. We are 2 1/2 hours north of Sydney, 30 mins from Williamtown Airport (pick up available). Our architect designed, purpose built B&B offers 3 Queen rooms all with ensuites (one with spa). Each room has a TV, private entry and deck. Separate guest facilities and living area, BBQ and pushbikes are provided. A bushland setting just off the Main Road. 5 minute walk to town with marina, restaurants, cinema, clubs and beautiful beaches. Close proximity to the Hunter Vineyards and Barrington Tops makes Port Stephens an ideal base for longer stays. Play golf with the kangaroos and koalas, cruise with the dolphins and whales, 4WD on the largest sandhills in the Southern Hemisphere. A delicious breakfast beckons you and a peaceful environment encourages bird and wildlife. Ask about our gift certificates and package deals.
After travelling extensively come and see why we call Nelson Bay home.

NEW SOUTH WALES

Port Stephens - Nelson Bay
Homestay
Address: "Pillinda Lodge", 32 Ullora Road, PO Box 484, Nelson Bay, NSW 2315
Name: Colin & Jeanne Harrison
Telephone: (02) 4981 4499
Fax: (02) 4981 4499
Beds: 1 Queen (1 bedroom)
Bathroom: 1 Ensuite
Tariff: B&B (full) Double $120,
Credit Cards (VISA/MC/BC). Vouchers accepted $20 surcharge Mon-Thurs.
Nearest Town: Nelson Bay CBD 1km

Pillinda Lodge is a modern timber lodge style residence set in the treetops above Nelson Bay, combining the peaceful solitude of Australia bush surroundings, including guest lorikeets and rosellas, with panoramic views of Port Stephens. Your room is a queen bedroom with ensuite and private balcony with water views.
Only 2 1/2 hours north of Sydney you can swim with dolphins; golf with kangaroos; cuddle a koala; travel the massive coastal sand dunes by camel or 4-wheel drive; begin a wine tasting tour; hike; bike; fish; swim, surf, snorkel or scuba dive in pristine turquoise waters; or read by the fireside at Pillinda Lodge.
After sailing around the world on our own yacht, this is where we decided to relax and enjoy life ... and we welcome you to do the same.

Port Stephens - Salamander Bay, Wanda Beach
Self-contained Accommodation and Homestay.   NRMA ★★★☆
Address: "The Beach House", 171 Soldiers Pt Rd., Salamander Bay, NSW 2317
Name: C.E. & D.W. Warner
Telephone: (02) 4982 7100
Fax: (02) 4982 7123
Mobile: (019) 327 429
Email: cwarner@mail.newcastle.edu.au
Beds: 1 Queen, 1 Double, 2 Bunks (2 bedrooms)
Bathroom: 1 Private
Tariff: B&B (full) Double $80-$140, Single $60-$100, Children welcome, Credit Cards.
Nearest Town: Nelson Bay 7km, Newcastle 50km

On the beach at Port Stephens (2 1/2 hours drive north of Sydney), 1 double bedroom, 1 family bedroom, private bathroom, private lounge with colour TV and pot belly stove for winter, private kitchen/dining. Credit card, fax, phone available.
Walk out your front door onto Wanda Beach with extensive water views to the heads of Port Stephens, safe swimming and use of kayaks, sailboards, and dinghy at no extra cost. There are gas BBQs for your use and an 8 seat beach setting with "Enviroshade". We are close to local golf, bowling and sailing clubs, restaurants, hotel and regional shopping centre and a short drive to local winery, national park and famous Stockton Beach sand-dunes. We can arrange dolphin cruises and fishing trips at your request. Start your stay with a complimentary bottle of champagne and then relax by the sea.
Home Page: http://www.jcu.edu.au/dept/Tourism/Aussie-BnB/109.htm

NEW SOUTH WALES

Port Stephens - Salamander Bay
Homestay/B & B
Address: "Breakwater House", 82 Salamander Way, Salamander Bay, NSW 2317
Name: Pat & Neil Warburton
Telephone: (02) 4982 0790 **Fax**: (02) 4982 0794 **Mobile**: 0418 443432
Email: warburt@hunterlink.net.au
Beds: 2 Queen, 1 Twin (3 bedrooms)
Bathroom: 2 Ensuite, 1 Private
Tariff: B&B (full) Double $95-$120, Single $70-$90, Dinner by arrangement, Credit Cards.
Nearest Town: Salamander - 1km west of Salamander shopping centre

Exploring Port Stephens, you will find Breakwater House within easy walking distance of Salamander Bay, 2 1/2 hours drive north of Sydney. Set on half an acre, overlooking bushland and local golf course, the house has three elegantly furnished rooms, two with private facilities. Guests can relax on shady verandahs or in the cosy lounges, enjoy a book from the library, listen to music, watch television, play billiards or be amused by the resident beagles' playful antics. Newcastle Airport is 20 minutes drive or the Sydney-Newcastle buses stop at the end of our driveway.
Activities include walking, bike riding, fishing, dolphin watching, sailing or relaxing on the beach - tour booking service available. Your hosts have travelled extensively and enjoy entertaining, and invite you to dine with them - dinner or packed lunch baskets by arrangement. Full BBQ facilities available and ample off-street parking. Non smoking establishment.

Phone numbers throughout Australia are changing to 8 digits.
For help contact Directory Assistance.

NEW SOUTH WALES

Port Stephens - Salamander Bay
Luxury Homestay   NRMA ★★★★
Address: Please phone ahead.
Name: Beachgarden
Telephone: (02) 4982 0788 **Fax**: (02) 4982 0788
Mobile: (015) 250255
Email: waites@ozemail.com.au
Beds: 1 Queen (1 bedroom)
Bathroom: 1 Ensuite
Tariff: B&B (continental) Double $160,
Single $110, Credit Cards (MC/BC/VISA). Smoke Free property.
Nearest Town: Salamander Bay

Position - Peace -Privacy
Beachgarden on Wanda Beach at Salamander Bay (2 hours north of Sydney) is as the name implies, a delightful spot on the beach with a restful garden and courtyard adjoining the guest suite. The north-east facing beach is but a short stroll through the garden to the front of the house where you can sit atop of the boathouse and watch for dolphins and pelicans or wander up the beach to the local tavern and mingle with the lucky folk of this gentle corner of Port Stephens. Our area holds much of interest for the tourist and sports minded - a championship golf course - tennis complex - boat cruises - selection of water based activities -bushwalks. Local shops / restaurants 50 metres. Facilities: • *Refrigerator / small kitchen*
   • *Tea & coffee making facilities*   • *TV & reverse cycle air-conditioning*
   • *BBQ* • *Level ground floor access*   • *Off street parking*
Home Page: http://www.ozemail.com.au/~waites

Port Stephens - Lower Hunter Valley
Bed & Breakfast
Address: 6 Michael Drive,
Salt Ash, NSW 2318
Name: Koala Country"
Telephone: (049) 826432
Beds: 1 Double,
1 Single (2 bedrooms)
Bathroom: 1 Guests share
Tariff: B&B (full) Double $80,
Single $65. Vouchers accepted
Nearest Town: Approx 10km from
Tanilba Bay off Lemon Tree Passage Road

We want you to feel welcomed and special
at our rural retreat - home baked specialties with tea and coffee are always 'on'.
Whether your interests draw you to the pristine ocean beaches and beautiful enclosed waterways of Port Stephens, or the Barrington Tops and Gloucester Mountains, or the Vineyards of the Lower Hunter, or the koala habitats of the Tilligerry Peninsula, or the array of restaurants and coffee nooks around Nelson Bay - "Koala Country" is right at the heart of this holiday paradise.
Just for two - your bedroom is quiet, secluded sunny and comfortable.
You'll enjoy a delightful breakfast - served in our garden beside the inground pool or in the sunroom around a cosy log fire.
Your hosts, Craig and Noni our dog Char and our 'girls' - the ducks, look forward to showing you some genuine country hospitality. Unfortunately children are not catered for. For brochure and directions please phone us.

Potato Point see Bodalla. Queanbean see Canberra ACT

Quirindi
Farmstay
Address: "4D" Station, Quirindi, NSW 2343
Name: Mary Jean & Steve Willis
Telephone: (02) 6747 4712 or
Alternative phone (02) 6747 4768
Fax: (02) 6747 4712
Beds: 1 Double, 7 Single (5 bedrooms)
Bathroom: 1 Guest share, 1 Family share
Tariff: B&B (full) Double $80, Single $45, Children under 3 free, under 12 half price. Dinner $15. Full board POA. Vouchers accepted
Nearest Town: Quirindi 42 km west

Live with a family on a working farm of approximately 4,000 acres, part of an original holding held by the family for 5 generations. Crops - wheat, oats, barley, chickpeas and sorghum. Cattle and sheep. Flat plains and timbered hills where kangaroos and wildlife abound. Tennis court, table tennis, cray fishing in summer, bush walks. Log fires and fuel stove in winter. Barbeques. Two sons, one married, help with management of farm. The house was built in 1939 and we have been entertaining overseas guests for the last 18 years and have made many friends. We will meet people at the Quirindi railway station, bus terminal or Quirindi Airport. We are available to entertain you. Maybe a drive to see local feedlot operation. Hostess interested in cooking, crafts, history, aboriginal artifacts and antiques. **Directions**: *Please phone or fax for map. A good half way house between Brisbane and Sydney. 1 hour drive from Gunnedah and Tamworth. 1 1/2 hours drive from Warrumbungle Mountains. Picnic baskets available.*

Rock Forest see Bathurst

Rylstone - Olinda
Self Contained Accommodation Farmstay
Address: "Frank's Breakaway" Narrango road, Olinda, Via Rylstone 2849
Name: Reg and Jenny Franks
Telephone: (063) 796 236 **Fax**: (063) 796 235
Beds: 3 Queen, 1 Double, 3 Single (3 bedrooms)
Bathroom: 2 Private
Tariff: B&B (full, special on request) Double $65, Single $33, Dinner $15, Children negotiable. Vouchers accepted
Nearest Town: Rylstone (25km)

"Frank's Breakaway" allows you to relax or explore a beautiful 609 acre property surrounded by spectacular sandstone outcrops typical of the Wallemi National Park which it joins. Drive or walk along the Cudgegong River to Dunn Swamp (seen on GETAWAY). Fish if you wish - Kangaroos, wombats, platypus, lyrebirds live here. Enjoy aboriginal paintings in the area. Return to the comfort of a recently renovated spacious house with dishwasher, mircrowave, electric stove, two open fires, covered gas barbecue area, comfortable beds (all bed linen provided). House is tastefully decorated.
Ask to see sheep shorn, collect fresh eggs, harvest fruit and vegetables, check the cattle, see wildflowers, bushwalk, climb rocks, enjoy local craft, smell the fresh air, enjoy clear starlit nights - but most of all enjoy genuine Australian hospitality and service from your hosts, Reg and Jenny Franks. We aim to make your stay happy and memorable. Catering on request.

Rye Park - Yass
Country Retreat NRMA ★★★
Address: "Old School"
Yass Street, Rye Park,
NSW 2586
Name:
Margaret & John Emery
Telephone: (02) 4845 1230
& (02) 6227-2243
Fax: (02) 48451260
Mobile: (0418) 483613
Beds: 3 King/Queen,
1 Double, 1 Twin
(5 bedrooms)
Bathroom: 1 Ensuite,
1 Private, 1 Guests share,
1 Family share
Tariff: B&B (full)
Double $100, Single $70,
Children $30, Dinner $40,
Credit Cards (BC/MC/VISA)
Vouchers accepted
$11 Surcharge
Nearest Town: 21km SE
of Boorowa, 42km N of Yass

The Old School was built in 1876 and used as a school until 1974. One can still find ink on the floorboards, but the schoolroom has lost its school house chill. The school now resembles a rambling country house, where guests relax on down sofas and are warmed by generous fires. A piano, and an antique church organ displaying mouse proof pedals wait for those who play. Surrounded by three and a half acres of lawns, and gardens with masses of climbing roses, the house has quiet corners, courtyards and sunny areas that create an atmosphere that encourages relaxation.
Emphasis is placed on fine fresh food with influences from Asia, Italy, Belgium and India. Tour local wineries, Peter Crisp's Artglass Studio, play golf and catch trout. The school is a retreat from city life for those who wish to unwind, walk in the country, relax and indulge in creative food.
Telephone for a brochure, and menu to whet the appetite.
The School is also available for couples and groups, on a self-contained basis.

Salamander Bay see Port Stephens
Salt Ash see Port Stephens

NEW SOUTH WALES

Scone
Homestay
Address: Russley Bed & Breakfast
Segenhoe Road, Scone, NSW 2337
Name: Vivienne McIntosh and Ian Moses
Telephone: (02) 6543 7230 **Fax**: (02) 6543 8143
Beds: 2 Queen, 2 Double, 1 Single (4 bedrooms)
Bathroom: 2 Guest Share
Tariff: B&B (full) Double $125 and $105, Single $100 and $90, Credit Cards.
Vouchers accepted $25 surcharge (not accepted in May)
Nearest Town: Between Muswellbrook and Scone, off NEH on Segenhoe Rd.

Located in the historic Hunter Valley, only 3 hours from Sydney, Russley is the perfect place to get away from the city rush. Between Aberdeen and Scone (the Horse capital of Australia) Russley is only 2 kms off New England Highway, close to wineries and horse studs.
Built in 1894 for the first manager of the famous Segenhoe Stud, Russley has old world charm and is furnished in an eclectic style mixing old with new. Guests rooms are large and open onto wide verandahs overlooking the gardens. Continental or full cooked breakfasts are served. Picnic baskets available by arrangement at prevailing prices. BYO. Reservations necessary. Tennis court and salt chlorinated pool. Children not catered for.

Telephone ahead to enquire about a B&B.
It is a nuisance for you if you simply
arrive to find someone already staying there.
And besides hosts need a litle time to prepare.

NEW SOUTH WALES

Scone - Wingen
Bed & Breakfast
Address: "Abbotsford"
The Old Coach House,
New England Highway, Wingen, 2337
Name: Peter & Robyn Pash
Telephone: (02) 6545 0406
Fax: (02) 6545 0406
Beds: 1 Queen, 1 Double, 1 Twin,
5 Single (3 bedrooms)
Bathroom: 1 Ensuite, 1 Family share downstairs
Tariff: B&B (full) Double $75 - $95, Single $40,
Children $15, Dinner $18. Campervans welcome, Credit Cards. Vouchers accepted
Nearest Town: Scone 22km, Murrurundi 18km

We live in an old two storey coach house situated in the upper Hunter Valley 22km north of Scone on the New England Highway. Our home was built in 1840 and used as a coaching inn until the turn of the century. It is nestled in the foothills of the Liverpool Ranges, with lovely views of surrounding hills and farmland. We have 100 acres with cattle, sheep, goats, horses, geese and chooks. Our home is very comfortable with log fires and fuel stove in winter and swimming pool and cool gardens in summer, full of antiques and old world charm. We offer tea and coffee facilities, guest lounge with TV and open fire, Devonshire teas. Luncheon and dinner in our restaurant. Scone is the Horse Capital of Australia - featuring Horse Week Festival in May, other local interests include Hunter Valley vineyards, Burning Mountain, Glenbourne Dam and bushwalking. We will meet guests at Scone. Facilities also available for animals. A paradise for artists.

Scone - Parkville
Quality Self-contained Accommodation NRMA ★★★☆
Address: "Jacaranda Lodge",
Dry Creek Road, Parkville via Scone, NSW 2337
Name: Jill Dyson
Telephone: (02) 6747 1334
Plse. leave message on answerphone if necessary
Fax: (02) 6747 1242 **Mobile**: (015) 005013
Email: dysonj@mpx.com.au
Beds: 2 Queen, 1 Double sofabed, 1 Single (3 bedrooms)
Bathroom: 1 Private

Tariff: B&B (continental) Double $120 (without bkfst $110), Single $90, Extra adult $20, Children $10, Mon-Fri from $380 double, from $480 per week double. Vouchers accepted Sunday to Thursday only, surcharge $20.
Nearest Town: Scone 12km

Take a break from the hectic pace of the city and come to the beautiful Upper Hunter Valley. Only 3 1/2 hours from Sydney, "Jacaranda Lodge" is close enough for a weekend away. Nestled under the rocky outcrop of the Wingen Maid, on forty acres of natural bushland, have this beautiful environment all to yourself. Relax with the cosy fires in winter or large shady pergola in summer. Enjoy the birdlife and the resident kangaroos who visit from time to time. Or enjoy the many local attractions ranging from bushwalking at the Burning Mountain, to historic Murrurundi, local caves, horse studs, wineries etc. "Jacaranda Lodge" has all the facilities you need for your total comfort - dishwasher, microwave, barbeque, air-conditioning, TV, video, music (CDs and tapes), electric blankets, games and books. All linen is provided. Owner lives nearby. Well behaved pets allowed - including horses. Most people return to "Jacaranda Lodge" again and again.
Directions: *Please phone. Map available*

NEW SOUTH WALES

Scone - Aberdeen
Bed & Breakfast
Address: "Segenhoe Inn",
56 Main Road, Aberdeen, 2336
Name: Bette & Stan Rogers
Telephone: (02) 6543 7382
Fax: (02) 6543 7382
Mobile: (041) 7251381
Beds: 2 Queen, 2 Double, 1 Twin (5 bedrooms)
Bathroom: 2 Guests share
Tariff: B&B (full) Double $75-$95, Single $50-$70, Credit Cards.
Nearest Town: Scone 12km, Muswellbrook 12km

The Segenhoe Inn invites you to share with them in the beautiful Hunter Valley just three hours from Sydney. Built circa 1834 this lovely old sandstone building has a charm and history to delight guests.
Our upstairs bedrooms are decorated in delightful old world charm. The guests dining/lounge room warms guests with a cosy open fire in winter. Or enjoy breakfast outside under the sparkling jacaranda trees in summer. Spacious gardens and lawns provide a peaceful and colourful background for visitors to enjoy.
Tea and coffee making facilities and television, VCR and CD available.
Scone, the Horse Capital of Australia boasts many studs.
Local attractions include Lake Glenbawn for boating, fishing, skiing, picnic. Award wining wineries are nearby, also golf, tennis and bowls. Restaurants are within easy distance.
Incorporated in the building is a delightful gift and craft shop including cottage furniture. No smoking inside please. Bookings preferable.

Shipley Plateau see Blue Mountains
Shoalhaven see Berry
Snowy Mountains see Adaminaby, Cooma, Bombala, Jindabyne, Nimmitabel

South West Rocks
Homestay
Address: 5 Kevin Hogan Place,
New Entrance, South West Rocks, NSW 2431
Name: Thorpeleigh Homestay
Telephone: (02) 6566 7146 or if unavailable (02) 6566 6946
Beds: 2 Queen, 2 Single (3 bedrooms) **Bathroom**: 1 Ensuite, 2 Guests share
Tariff: B&B (full) Double $110, Single $55, Children under 12 half price, Dinner $20. Weekly rates available. Vouchers accepted no surcharge
Nearest Town: South West Rocks 38km east of Kempsey (Pacific Highway), midway Sydney-Brisbane. Transfers to and from plane, train, bus arranged.

THORPELEIGH HOMESTAY is situated in South West Rocks on beautiful Trial Bay. Average temperature ... winter 21 C - summer 28 C. Surrounded by national parks, rainforest and pristine beaches. Excellent local recreational facilities, fine dining opportunities as well as internationally acclaimed diving, fishing and bushwalking. Thorpeleigh Homestay is designed for your relaxation and enjoyment, whether lounging beside the fire enjoying a good book, listening to music or having a quiet drink on the secluded deck beside the pool. An airy light filled fully equipped art studio is situated on the second floor with a 180 degree view, a beautiful spot for quiet contemplation or creative activities. By prior arrangement, an evening meal can be provided using fresh local ingredients. For old fashioned country hospitality in a quiet relaxing atmosphere, please phone Jenny (02) 6566 7146 or if unavailable June (02) 6566 6946.

NEW SOUTH WALES

South West Rocks
Self-catering Cottage
Address:
2074 South West Rocks Road,
South West Rocks, 2431
Name: Crockford Cottage
Telephone: (02) 6559 4433
Beds: 1 Queen, 2 Single
Bathroom: Private
Tariff: B&B (full) Double $90 + $10 extra person per night, or $500 per week.
Adults preferred. Vouchers accepted $11 surcharge
Nearest Town: South West Rocks

Unique 2 bedroom, self-catering farm cottage, circa 1920 charmingly restored. Stands on 14 acres beside the Macleay River. All modern conveniences including wood burning slow combustion fire, microwave, electric blankets and TV.
One queen size bed and 2 singles with all linen supplied and ingredients for a full cooked breakfast. 8 mins from tourist seaside resort of S.W. Rocks and 10 mins from Hat Head and Kempsey. Situated on a loop road between Kempsey and Macksville, it is accessible from both North and South. Trial Bay Gaol, Arts & Crafts Centres, antique shops and restaurants all within easy reach. Fishing, swimming and national parks and walking all close by.
Modelled on colonial accommodation of Tasmania. The cottage is exclusively yours to relax and enjoy.

Southern Highlands - Berrima District
Farmstay
Address: Merrioola,
High Range, Mittagong, 2575
Name: Noel & Elizabeth Symonds
Telephone: (02) 4878 5119
Beds: 1 Twin (1 bedroom)
Bathroom: 1 Ensuite
Tariff: B&B (full) Double $100,
Single $50. Dinner on request $20.
Nearest Town: Berrima 18 km.

Merrioola is a comfortable homestead, surrounded by an inviting leafy country garden.
Magnificent views to Sydney, the Blue Mountains and over the Southern Highlands are seen from High Range - a basalt outcrop 830 metres high. We run a commercial cattle herd on our 213 hectare property, where wildlife and bird life abound.
There are many local attractions suitable for walking or driving, including the Wombeyan Caves, Joadja Vineyard, Fitzroy and Belmore Falls, and the adjacent Nattai National Park. Berrima village is nearby, as is Sturt Craft Centre at Mittagong. Many local gardens open in both Spring and Autumn.
Our comfortable guest room has twin beds with ensuite, electric blankets, heating, bedside lamps and an electric jug. We offer you our country hospitality with continental or cooked breakfast. Dinner is available on request.

Australia is known as the friendliest country in the world
and our hosts will live up to that reputation.

NEW SOUTH WALES

Southern Highlands - Bowral
B&B/Farmstay /S.C. Cottage
Address: "Glendale", Cnr. Kangaloon
and Sheepwash Roads, Bowral, 2576
Name: Ian & Jennifer Jackson
Telephone: (02) 4887 1350
Fax: (02) 4887 1350 **Mobile**: (019) 150779
Email: glendale@acenet.com.au
Beds: 2 Queen (2 bedrooms)
Bathroom: 1 Guests share
Tariff: B&B (full) $130-$300. Sun-Thurs special package.
Dinner by arrangement. Campervans welcome.
No young children, no smoking and no pets allowed.
Credit Cards (VISA/BC/MC). Vouchers accepted Mon to Thurs only, $60 surcharge
Nearest Town: Bowral - 10km SE along Kangaloon Road to Sheepwash Road.

Glendale B&B is a romantic country escape for visitors wishing to experience the atmosphere of the Southern Highlands. A charming self-contained cottage set on 40 acres fronting the Wingecarribee River. Glendale B&B began life over 100 years ago as a dairy farm and later became the Glenquarry PO. The Cottage has been meticulously restored to operate as a cosy and private retreat for one or two couples wanting to get away and offers two lounges with open fireplaces, TV, VCR and CD. "Babe" country in the Southern Highlands is one of NSW's most interesting regions. Rich in early colonial history, the nearby towns of Berrima, Moss Vale and Mittagong have many attractions including antique and craft shops, local markets, national parks and Bradman Museum. Guests can also accommodate their horses in our stable complex and your hosts, as qualified pilots, can take you on a sightseeing flight over Sydney Harbour Bridge and city skyline.

Southern Highlands - Bowral and Surrounding Area
Accommodation Bowral and the Southern Highlands
Address: C/- Southern Highlands
Accommodation Association Inc.
PO Box 791
Bowral, NSW 2576
Name: Accommodation Enquiry and Booking Service
Telephone: (02) 4861 4997 **Fax**: (02) 4861 6576
Beds: Various
Bathroom: Various
Tariff: Various according to style and standard of accommodation
Nearest Town: Mittagong to Bundanoon; Berrima to Robertson

We provide a free accommodation enquiry and booking service in the Southern Highlands. We offer a choice of 20 B&B's and 20 other accommodation establishments such as hotels, motels, guest houses and camping throughout the Highlands. Your hosts are committed to providing excellent service, comfort and value for money. The Southern Highlands is well under two hours from Sydney or Canberra and is renowned for its beautiful countryside, historic towns and quiet villages nestling among the rich, green hills. National parks and glorious scenery abound. Bicycle and horse riding, golf and bush walking are popular activities but many people come to the area to simply relax and enjoy the brisk, clean air or potter among antique shops and museums, galleries and open gardens or to enjoy some of the gourmet restaurants and friendly inns and bistros.
We will happily advise you on the various types of accommodation, prices, and availability without obligation and make bookings for you without charge.

NEW SOUTH WALES

Southern Highlands - Burrawang
Bed & Breakfast
Address: Church Street, Burrawang, NSW 2577
Name: The Keep
Telephone: (02) 4886 4558 **Fax**: (02) 4886 4558
Mobile: 041 222 8601
Beds: 2 King/Queen, 2 Double, 2 Single (4 bedrooms)
Bathroom: 2 Ensuite, 2 Private
Tariff: B&B (full) Double $130-$170,
Single $90-$150, Dinner $30-$50, Credit Cards.
Nearest Town: Bowral

THE KEEP (1870) is an elegant, country house situated in the historic village of Burrawang. The property is an ideal haven from which to explore the Southern Highlands. The tranquillity of the setting complements the luxury found within the rooms. The house is centrally heated with large open fires in the dining room and sitting room. Some bedrooms have four poster beds and open fireplaces. THE KEEP is renowned for its culinary flare, the cuisine is French inspired, innovative and delicious.
Transport: Car - 120km south of Sydney (1 1/2 hours) - 150k north Canberra (2 hours)
Bus - regular services from Sydney, Wollongong and Canberra
Train - regular services from Sydney and Canberra

Southern Highlands - Goulburn
Farmstay+Self-contained Accommodation
Address: 'Yuruga", Greenwich Park Rd,
via Goulburn, NSW 2580
Name: Joan & Kevin Tye
Telephone: 0248 415166
Beds: 1 Double, 2 Bunks (Large bed-sitting room, Cot available)
Bathroom: 1 Private
Tariff: B&B (full) Double $70, Single $40, Children $15, Under 5 yrs Free. Dinner $15pp. Vouchers accepted
Nearest Town: Marulan/Goulburn

'Yuruga' is an aboriginal word meaning 'expansive view'. We are ideally situated 20 minutes off the National Highway 31 and adjacent to Tarlo River National Park. The historic areas of Berrima, Goulburn and Canberra are all within easy reach.
Our property is 1000 acres with grazing sheep and many native trees and animals in clear, pure air at an elevation of nearly 3000 ft with glorious views. It is an ideal peaceful retreat for bird-watchers, photographers, star-gazers or walkers. Snack or lunch packs available.
You may choose a continental or country style full breakfast brought to your suite, adjacent to the house, or we will provide breakfast facilities to enable you to eat at your leisure. An evening meal can also be provided.
You can be assured of genuine Australian hospitality during your stay with us. Please phone for booking and directions.

NEW SOUTH WALES

Southern Highlands - Goulburn
Self-contained Accommodation or B&B   NRMA ★★★
Address: "South Hill"
Garroorigang Road
Goulburn NSW 2580
Name: Elizabeth and Ian Lipscomb
Telephone: (0248) 219 591
Fax: (0248) 219 591
Beds: 6 Double, 6 Single (7 bedrooms)
Bathroom: 2 Ensuite, 2 Guest share
Tariff: B&B (continental) Double $80-$100, Single $50-$80, Children $20. Credit Cards. Vouchers accepted
Nearest Town: Goulburn

If you enjoy open space, heritage buildings and convivial company at breakfast, South Hill is the place to stay. Set on a blustery hill in Goulburn, South Hill is a two storey farm mansion which grew like Topsy from 1850 to 1995.
With its three staircases, ballroom and convent verandahs it wears its heritage with pride and enjoys the attention received as a B&B.
Its accompanying farm buildings also carry over 100 years of wear. From South Hill's verandahs you can watch the trains or the highway that carry you to Sydney - 2 hours away or Canberra - 1 hour away.
Goulburn (3km away) has many fine restaurants; golf courses, you can skydive or parachute at the airport, and national Parks are nearby. The extensive library will give you pleasure as you search for a book to enjoy by a wood fire in a homely and comfortable atmosphere surrounded by family collections and antiques.

Southern Highlands - Moss Vale
Homestay/Self-contained Accommodation
Address: 'Lynton', 618 Argyle Street, Moss Vale, NSW 2577
Name: Lynton Bed & Breakfast & Loft
Telephone: (02) 4868 2552
Fax: (02) 4868 2552   **Email**: johnmaud@hinet.net.au
Beds: 1 King, 2 Double, 2 Single (3 bedrooms)
Bathroom: 2 Ensuite, 1 Private
Tariff: B&B (full) Friday & Saturday $250 per room. Friday or Saturday $150 per room. Sunday to Thursday $95 per room (Except Public Holidays when weekend rates apply). Children negotiable, Dinner $40pp. Loft (self-contained & self catering) from $65 Sunday - Thursday, $190 Friday & Saturday or $95 Friday or Saturday. Children welcome. Credit Cards (BC/MC/VISA). Vouchers accepted Sunday to Thursday only.
Nearest Town: Moss Vale - which is halfway between Sydney and Canberra

Our delightful Victorian home, circa 1860 is surrounded by 3 acres of tranquil gardens. Less than 2 hours drive from Sydney or Canberra, Lynton offers the perfect 'getaway' for those who want to relax by an open fire in winter in the comfortable guests' sitting room and enjoy a gourmet breakfast in the elegantly appointed dining room or those who wish for complete privacy in the self contained "Loft". The "Loft" can accommodate up to 4 people and is self-catering. An ideal place for school holidays. Enquire about our school holiday and summer package rates. The Southern Highlands is famous for its beautiful gardens in Autumn and Spring and historic Berrima, only 8 kms away is one of NSW's best known tourist areas. Bowral is a 10 minute drive. There is a wide selection of antique shops, local crafts and restaurants, also golf, horse riding and bush walking in nearby Morton National Park adjacent to Fitzroy, Belmore and Carrington Falls. Our aim is to ensure that your stay at "Lynton" is as comfortable and relaxed as possible.

NEW SOUTH WALES

Southern Highlands - Moss Vale
Luxury Homestay
Address: "Heronswood House",
165 Argyle Street, Moss Vale
Name: Brian & Tina Davis
Telephone: (02) 4869 1477
Fax: (02) 4869 4079
Mobile: 018445326
Beds: 3 Queen, 1 Double, 1 Single (4 bedrooms)
Bathroom: 2 Ensuite, 1 Guests share
Tariff: B&B (full) Double $90/$120, Single $55/$65,
Dinner N/A, Credit Cards. Vouchers accepted Mid-week only
Nearest Town: 1km N Moss Vale - 200m north of intersection with Illawarra Highway

Homestyle
ACCOMMODATION
(B&B)

Situated in the heart of the Southern Highlands of NSW this turn of the century home offers you friendly and comfortable accommodation. Four tastefully decorated bedrooms, two with ensuites, one with ramp access and an ensuite adapted for the physically disabled. The spacious lounge, dining room, sun room kitchenette and barbecue are available to guests. For comfort all rooms are fully centrally heated. Smoking is permitted in the sun room only. This beautiful old brick home is situated on the north side of Moss Vale and close to the Illawarra Highway. The wide verandahs and one acre of gardens encourage you to relax and enjoy the delights of the Southern Highlands with its abundance of antique and craft shops, historical attractions and the Bradman Museum. The area abounds in beautiful scenery with Moreton National Park, Fitzroy Falls and Kangaroo Valley in close proximity. Golf courses, horse riding and bush walking trails are all close by.

Southern Highlands - Sutton Forest
Homestay/B & B   SMH ★☆★★★
Address: "Sutton Downs",
Golden Vale Road,
Sutton Forest, NSW 2577
Name: Jeni & Charles Scourfield
Telephone: (02) 4868 3126
Fax: (02) 4868 3126
Beds: 2 King/Queen, 2 Single (2 bedrooms)
Bathroom: 2 Private
Tariff: B&B (full) (Per room or per couple): Mon-Thurs: $100 per night, Weekend: $150 per night, $250 per two nights or $350 per three nights. (December to March: 10% discount), Dinner by arrangement, No children, unless by arrangement, No pets, Credit Cards (Visa/MC/BC). Vouchers accepted $20 surcharge Mon - Thurs only.
Nearest Town: Moss Vale 6km

Peace, views, comfort and hospitality are the ingredients we invite you to enjoy in our large country home. Although there are no other houses in sight, and the warbles of magpies are the loudest noise to distract you, we are only a few minutes from the Southern Highlands towns of Moss Vale, Bowral, Berrima and well under two hours drive from Sydney or Canberra. Two large guest bedrooms, each with its own luxury bathroom, are privately situated at the end of separate wings of the house. The guest lounge, filled with antique furniture and warmed by log fire, is where you'll enjoy complimentary Devonshire tea in the afternoon. You are welcome to stroll around the farm or simply relax. Most of our guests like to try some of the local gourmet restaurants but we are happy to provide a superb dinner by arrangement. Jeni and Charles aim to ensure your enjoyment exceeds your expectations. We were awarded a 5 star rating by the Sydney Morning Herald in June 1997. Please phone or fax for directions.

Southern Tablelands see Braidwood, Gunning, Taralga

Sunny Corner
Homestay + Self-contained Accommodation
Address: Sunny Corner, NSW 2795
Name: 'Honeysuckle Cottage',
Telephone: (063) 595 244
Beds: 2 Double, 2 Single (3 bedrooms)
Bathroom: 2 Private
Tariff: B&B (full) Double $80, Single $50. Special rates for longer stays. Vouchers accepted
Nearest Town: Bathurst 35km and Lithgow 33km.

We live in an old silvermining village, 4000ft above sea level, surrounded by state pine forest, nature reserves, the purest air imaginable and almost daily sunshine. 'Honeysuckle Cottage' was built in the late 1960s by a family in search of an alternative lifestyle away from city pressures. We love the relaxed atmosphere and have spent our seven years here improving the house and garden. Our interests include walking, birdwatching, art and craft, travelling, gardening. Local walks are up hill, down dale, through the forest and around the disused mine. Within easy driving distance are the Blue Mountains, Sofala / Hill End, Jenolan Caves, Bathurst, Mudgee / Gulgong and national parks.
The large double bedroom overlooks the garden; breakfast is served in our country kitchen. Our fully self-contained cottage, 'The Mudlark', sleeps up to 4. Double bedroom with ensuite overlooks the herb garden, attic has 2 single beds, cosy living / kitchen room.
Please telephone for more details and directions. Non smokers preferred.

Sutton Forest – see Southern Highlands

Sydney - Annandale
Homestay
Address: 234 Johnston Street, Annandale, Sydney 2038
Name: Annandale Bed & Breakfastt"
Telephone: (02) 9660 1640
Fax: (02) 9660 1640
Mobile: (017) 114277
Beds: 1 Queen, 2 Single (2 bedrooms)
Bathroom: 2 Ensuite

Tariff: B&B (special) Double $110-$120, Single $75-$80, Dinner by arrangement, Credit Cards (BC/MC/VISA). Vouchers accepted $29 surcharge. Same day restriction.
Nearest Town: Sydney

Annandale is an inner city suburb, noted for its wide streets and variety of early architecture. Our home, a beautifully restored Victorian villa, air-conditioned and very comfortable is 4km from the city centre and 500 metres to public transport and a harbourside park. We offer superior accommodation and meals. There is a guest lounge and tea and coffee are available at any time. Complimentary drinks are served in the evening and dinner is by arrangement. A superb full breakfast is served in the conservatory overlooking our attractive garden and large heated swimming pool. Laundry facilities can be used at any time. Kevin and Diana welcome both travellers and business people and can advise on tours and places of interest in our beautiful city. Maps, brochures and transport details are available. Our pets, Sunday (cat) and Lucy (dog) are well behaved and friendly. No smoking indoors.
Home Page: annanbb@ozemail.com.au

NEW SOUTH WALES

Sydney - Arcadia
Self-contained Cottage
Address: 2 Marrakesh Place,
Arcadia, NSW 2159
Name: Willow Glen Cottage
Telephone: (02) 9653 2038
Fax: (02) 9653 2874 **Mobile**: (015) 664204
Beds: 1 Queen, 1 Single (2 bedrooms)
Bathroom: 1 Private
Tariff: B&B (continental) Double $120,
Single $100, Children on application.
Nearest Town: Hornsby or Dural

Willow Glen Cottage is set in picturesque bushland adjoining the Colah Creek Valley near Dural and Berowra Waters and only 45 mins from Sydney. Accommodation is a spacious colonial style cottage with loft bedroom, large living area with wood fire place and cathedral ceilings. A large verandah overlooks the jetty and tranquil waters of lagoon. Accommodation facilities include: colour television, VCR with movie library, sound system, kitchen, in-rooms snacks / drinks, tea & coffee making facilities, iron with board and hair dryer.

Activities and local attractions include: horse and buggy rides, possum feeding, bird watching, bushwalking, famous horse studs, art, antique and craft galleries, Swanes and Hargraves nurseries, Riverside Oaks PGA golf course, Dural Country Club, Berowra Waters boat charters, Restaurants and BBQ area, many historical sites or simply relax and enjoy the abundant bird and native animal life.

There are many fine restaurants in the area including: Seafood, Italian, Asian, Indian, Steakhouse and A-La-Carte. The Dural Country Club offers various dining experiences plus weekly shows with local and international artists.

Sydney - Avalon Beach
Homestay+Self-contained
Address: "Crookaburra Lodge", Ruskin Rowe, Avalon, 2107
Name: Patricia Crook
Telephone: (02) 9918 8316 **Fax**: (02) 9918 8316
Beds: 1 Queen, 2 Single (2 bedrooms) Self-contained: 1 Double bedroom with ensuite bathroom.
Bathroom: 1 Private, 1 Guests share
Tariff: B&B (full) Double $95, Single $65, Children on application.
Self-contained: $120.
Nearest Town: Avalon Village, City Sydney

Charming Tudor style home with old world character set on 1 acre of heritage listed grounds, tropical bushland, native flora and fauna, BBQ and swimming pool. Avalon Village shops, beaches and pool are within level walking distance.

The area offers surfing or calm water beaches, fishing, bush walking, ferry cruises, shopping, yacht hire, scenic drive, excellent restaurants.

Bus and taxi transport to Sydney.

Tariff is $95 Double, $65 Single, $120 Self-contained flat with 1 bedroom. Full breakfast included.

Bookings of 3 nights or more, include airport pick up. Should you have any special dietary needs we will be happy to oblige. Please note we are a non-smoking establishment. Please phone for directions.

NEW SOUTH WALES

Sydney - Avalon Beach (Northern Beaches)
Homestay
Address: 51 Riviera Ave.,
Avalon Beach
Name: Helga & Gordon
Telephone: (02) 9918 7002
Fax: (02) 9918 7002
Beds: 1 Double,
2 Single (2 bedrooms)
Bathroom: 1 Guests share
Tariff: B&B (full) Double $110,
\Single $90.
Nearest Town: City of Sydney 36km

Avalon Beach Bed & Breakfast is situated on Sydney's famous Northern Beaches Peninsula, between the magnificent sailing waterways of Pittwater and the beautiful beaches of the Pacific Ocean. This large comfortable home sits atop Avalon Hill with spectacular panoramic views over Pittwater, the surrounding district and out to sea. We have luxury guest accommodation for four adults, one double room and one twin with guest share bathroom facilities. With magnificent views and balconies from all rooms, this spacious home also contains a billiard room and bar where many a happy social evening has been spent with the friendly Aussie hosts.
Incredible sailing, surfing beaches, bush walking, golf courses, tennis, lawn bowls, cinema, laundromat, busses, ferry, interesting cafes, restaurants and shopping are all a part of and within easy reach of Avalon Village.
Your hosts, Helga and Gordon have travelled extensively, enjoy entertaining and welcome you to their friendly home.

Sydney - Balgowlah
Homestay
Address: 2/3 West Lake Place,
Balgowlah, Sydney, NSW 2093
Name: Mrs Isobel Lawrence
Telephone: (02) 9949 1392
Beds: 1 Double, 1 Single (2 bedrooms)
Bathroom: 1 Guests share
Tariff: B&B (full) Double $85, Single $60.
  Vouchers accepted
Nearest Town: Manly

"Twin Peaks"
A tastefully renovated modern home 5 minutes away from world famous Manly Beach. Two guest bedrooms (one double, one single) both overlooking Balgowlah Golf Course, giving the feeling of being in the country with all the amenities of the city a short stroll away. New bathroom with spa, 2 separate toilets, guests share. Very quiet, private and sunny location, 20 minutes by bus to city centre or take the ferry (30 minutes), Jet Cat (15 minutes) from Manly across our wonderful harbour past the Opera House to Circular Quay, the Rocks and all the city attractions. Restaurants abound both in Balgowlah Village and Manly.
Bush walks, golf, tennis, surfing and swimming at your fingertips. Reverse cycle heating / air-conditioning and use of lounge and Cable TV for your comfort. Relax and enjoy our hospitality with full English breakfast provided. Weekly rates negotiated. Telephone (02) 9949-1392. We look forward to your company.

NEW SOUTH WALES

Sydney - Balmain
Homestay   NRMA ★★★★
Address: 27 Lawson St., Balmain, NSW 2041
Name: "Balmain Bed & Breakfast"
Telephone: (02) 9810 4108 **Fax**: (02) 9818 4918
Mobile: (018) 709873
Email: rnmorgan@ozemail.com.au
Beds: 1 Queen, 2 (long) Single (2 bedrooms)
Bathroom: 2 Ensuite
Tariff: B&B (continental) Double $120, Single $90, Credit Card (VISA/BC/MC).
Nearest Town: 3kms west Sydney CBD

On the historic Balmain Peninsula, 10 minutes from the city centre by bus or ferry, this century-old worker's cottage, is located in a quiet one-way street in lively Balmain Village. The cottage has been architect-renovated specifically for B&B.
Two guest bedrooms each with private facilities, are separated from the main house by a leafy courtyard with its own street entrance. Large windows, a northerly aspect, air conditioning and underfloor heating ensure a high level of creature comforts. We serve an extended Continental breakfast using our home preserves. Good restaurants and pubs are plentiful within walking distance.
French, Swahili spoken. SMOKING: outdoors only.
Directions: Buses: City 432, 433 - alight at "Cat & Fiddle"; 441, 442 - at "Exchange Hotel" Ferry: Circular Quay Wharf No. 5 or Darling Harbour Wharf - to Balmain East Wharf then bus to 'Cat & Fiddle' or 'Exchange'.
Home Page: http://www.ozemail.comau~rnmorgan/html

Sydney - Balmain
Homestay
Address: "The Old Keg House"
88 Church Street,
corner of Cameron Street, Balmain 2041
Name: The Old Keg House
Telephone: (02) 9555 8642 **Fax**: (02) 9555 2609
Mobile: 041 901 2410
Email: rescon@ozemail.com.au
Beds: 1 Double (1 bedroom).
Plus double sofa bed in music room
Bathroom: 1 Private
Tariff: B&B (Continental) Double $100.
Children on application Vouchers accepted $10 surcharge
Nearest Town: Sydney CBD 3km

The Old Keg House was built in 1870 originally as full board and lodging for shipwrights and sea captains. Today this lovely heritage home, tastefully decorated with antique pieces, is ideal for the tourist or business traveller. We are in the centre of historic Balmain with its pubs, cafes and restaurants, and a 3 minute walk away from the ferry (a stunning harbour trip) and bus, just 10 minutes to the city and Darling Harbour. We are an outgoing family with 3 friendly young children, who love Sydney. Guests breakfast in the large music room, with its baby grand, looking out across the park to the harbour bridge. Our home office is fully equipped for the business traveller, and of course we keep you up to date with what is happening, ideas and information you need to explore Sydney. No smoking please. **Directions**: *Bus: 441 or 442 from QVB to Church St. Balmain Ferry: Circular Quay to Thames St.*

Sydney - Balmoral
Homestay
Address: 6 Kahibah Road, Mosman, NSW 2088
Name: Balmoral Bed and Breakfast
Telephone: (02) 9969 6415
Fax: (02) 9969 6415
Beds: 1 Double, 1 Single, (2 bedrooms)
Bathroom: 1 Ensuite, 1 Family share
Tariff: B&B (full), Double $80, Single $50 Vouchers accepted $5 surcharge
Nearest Town: Sydney 5km

Situated in the harbourside suburb of Mosman, Balmoral Bed & Breakfast is ideally located for visitors to Sydney. Five minutes walk to Balmoral Beach and 25 minutes by ferry and / or bus to the city.
Recommended is a visit to nearby Taronga Zoo. Allow a few hours there to enjoy koalas, wombats, kangaroos, echidnas and platypuses and to soak up the glorious harbour views.
Guests are eligible for discounts on entrance to Taronga Zoo, Sydney Aquarium and the Imax Theatre.
Jan shares her Federation home with her two teenage children and 3 alley cats. All rooms have electric blankets, central heating and ceiling fans.
The guests' lounge has a TV/VCR. Heated pool, iron, hairdryer, tea/coffee are available for guests' use. Mosman is famous for its shops. There is also a wide variety of excellent cafes and reataurants, from haute-cuisine to take-away.

Sydney - Beecroft
Homestay
Address: 22 The Crescent, Beecroft, NSW 2119
Name: "Fiddlewood". Host: Beverley
Telephone: (02) 9876 8970
Beds: 1 Double, 2 Single (3 bedrooms)
Bathroom: 1 Ensuite, 1 Family share
Tariff: B&B (full) Double $75, Single $50
Children by arrangement. Dinner $20.
Campervans $20. Vouchers accepted
Nearest Town: City of Sydney

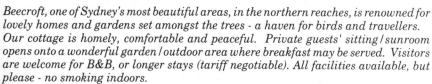

Beecroft, one of Sydney's most beautiful areas, in the northern reaches, is renowned for lovely homes and gardens set amongst the trees - a haven for birds and travellers. Our cottage is homely, comfortable and peaceful. Private guests' sitting / sunroom opens onto a wonderful garden / outdoor area where breakfast may be served. Visitors are welcome for B&B, or longer stays (tariff negotiable). All facilities available, but please - no smoking indoors.
We enjoy sharing conversation over a meal with guests, or by the fire (but note - winters are very mild). Interests include - travel, theatre, music, cooking, bush walking, art and gardening.
Good restaurants are nearby; the area is wonderful for walks and Koala Park is 8 minutes drive. City and North Coast trains are 3 minutes walk. We would be happy to share our knowledge of Sydney and environs, drive travellers on tours to the City, Blue Mountains, North / South Coasts etc. (by arrangement). Transport to and from airport available.
Please phone or write - we look forward to seeing you.

NEW SOUTH WALES

Sydney - Bilgola Plateau (Northern Beaches)

Homestay   AAA ★★★★☆
Address: 15 Farview Road, Bilgola Plateau, 2107
Name: Colette Campbell
Telephone: (02) 9918 6932
Fax: (02) 9918 6485 **Mobile**: 0418 407 228
Email: Pittwater@intercoast.com.au
Beds: 1 Queen, 2 Double (3 bedrooms)
Bathroom: 1 Ensuite, 1 Private
Tariff: B&B (full) Double $120-$150, Dinner $35pp.
Nearest Town: Avalon Beach

"Arrive as Guests, depart as Friends"
No longer secret. Sydney's famous Northern Beaches Peninsula between Pittwater and the Pacific Ocean. A comfortable family home situated on high plateau with fabulous views of surrounding bush, beaches and coastline through to the city lights. Extensively renovated and furnished to a luxury standard, guest accommodation is one Queen size room with ensuite and double bedded two room suite with large spa bathroom. There is a solar heated pool and reverse cycle air conditioning for your comfort. James and Colette are charming hosts who will make every effort to ensure your stay is memorable. Colette is an enthusiastic cook and all meals are prepared using the best of Australian produce, without preservatives of course. Gourmet Evening Meals, City or Airport transfers, Special Hoenymoon Package, Picnic / Boating baskets All by prior arrangement Thank You. We are a non smoking household and would appreciate you to phone ahead. Bilgola is 45 minutes from CBD. Unfortunately not suitable for young children.
Internet Home Page: http://www.atn.com.au/nsw/syd/accom/pittwat.htm

Gift Vouchers

Our B&B vouchers are for a double room for one night's B&B. They cost $89, and if you order one as a gift, we will include a free
Australian Bed & Breakfast Book
worth $16.95

Send your cheque to
Moonshine Press
59 Quirk Street
Dee Why
NSW 2099

NEW SOUTH WALES

Sydney - Burraneer Peninsula
Homestay
Address: 3 Hazel Place, Burraneer, (Cronulla), NSW 2230
Name: Beverley & Alan
Telephone: (02) 9523 4540
Fax: (02) 9523 4540
Mobile: (0414) 991 187
Email: bviewbb@ozemail.com.au
Beds: 2 Double (2 bedrooms)
Bathroom: 1 Guests share
Tariff: B&B (full) Double $90, Single $60. Vouchers accepted $10 surcharge
Nearest Town: Cronulla, 20km south Sydney centre.

Our home with 180 degree views, overlooks Gunnamatta Bay and The Royal National Park. Our guests have use of the middle level of our large home. Lounge and guest breakfast room have beautiful water views. Tea/coffee making facilities, refrigerator, electric blankets. Heated swimming pool, therapeutic spa, and outdoor area are fully enclosed. Afternoon tea and Chocolates on arrival. We are 15 mins from Sydney Airport, will gladly arrange transport, shuttle bus to our door. Four mins from Local and Interstate Rail and Bus Services, Cronulla beaches, shops, Cinemas, excellent restaurants, golf, bowls, surfing and nice walks. Five mins to Miranda Fair Shopping Complex. Train to Sydney Centre. Take a Ferry trip to The Royal National Park. We can arrange visits to restaurants and/or scenic flights north or south of the city, in a float plane departing our bay. Tours of Sydney and environs. Local Koala Park, the Blue Mountains, Bush walking or Local tours. Beverley is an eggshell artist and her gallery will delight. Experience warm hospitality in tranquil surroundings. A comfortable, cosy retreat for those who like luxury and charm.
Home Page: http//www.cyberlink.com.au/bedbreakfast/bayview

Sydney - Careel Bay/Avalon (Northern Beaches)
Homestay
Address: 90 George St., Careel Bay
Name: Careel Bay Retreat
Telephone: (02) 9918 2873
Beds: 1 Queen (1 bedroom)
Bathroom: 1 Ensuite
Tariff: B&B (full) Double $150, Single $100.
Nearest Town: Sydney

This luxury waterfront home offers the ultimate in supreme outlook and quality relaxation. There are a number of interesting activities at the doorstep to cater for the adventurous such as:
* Scenic flights on the Palm Beach Sea Plane
* Ferry cruises up the Hawkesbury River
* A water taxi to take you anywhere on Pittwater.
However we doubt you will be tempted to go anywhere once you sit back, relax and enjoy the wonderful water outlook - your room provides an exclusive view of Careel Bay with all the trimmings to exceed your expectations of ambience, elegance and serenity with private access to the swimming pool.
A comfortable nights rest should give you the energy to make some decisions about the menu for your home cooked breakfast after that we will leave you to relax again.
We are a non-smoking home.
The hardest part about staying here will be leaving!

NEW SOUTH WALES

Sydney - Caringbah
Homestay
Address: "Bush Haven"
31 Flide Street, Caringbah, Sydney 2229
Name: Ron & Faye Jarvis
Telephone: (02) 9525 4801
Beds: 2 Singles (1 Bedroom)
Bathroom: 1 Family Share
Tariff: B&B (full) Double $70, Single $40, Campervans welcome.
Vouchers accepted
Nearest Town: Caringbah

It has been said "when God holidays in Sydney he stays in The Sutherland Shire". Caringbah is centrally located in the Shire, a 45 minute train trip south of Sydney Centre. Only two stations from Cronulla with surfing beaches, one station from Miranda Westfield Shopping Centre, with 350 shops and eight cinemas. We are neighbours of "The Royal National Park".
Bush Haven is a flat, six minute walk from Caringbah with the convenience of rail station, shops and many restaurants. We provide quality hosts accommodation, consisting of a bright 2 single bed bedroom and bathroom. The lounge is left for the use of our visitors, with great TV viewing, video and wood fire.
Breakfast is what you would expect a good old fashioned full cooked breakfast to be. Diets will be happily catered for. We have comfort, security and convenience. Unfortunately we do not have amenities for children or pets.

Sydney - Caringbah
Homestay
Address: Please phone or fax
Name: Homestay at Caringbah
Telephone: (02) 9544 0126 **Fax**: (02) 9544 0126 **Mobile**: (018) 297 586
Email: homestay@ar.com.au
Beds: 2 Double, 4 Single (6 bedrooms)
Bathroom: 2 Ensuite, 2 Family share
Tariff: B&B (full) Double $80, Single $45, Children under 12yrs half price in room. Dinner $20. Credit cards.
Nearest Town: Miranda or Cronulla

Our family home and Caringbah
Our home is in the quiet, residential suburb of Caringbah, which has many parks and trees, and is located south of Sydney, near the Royal National Park.
Family Information
John and Clotilda are both university graduates. John, with an Economics degree from Sydney University, now runs a Karaoke business. He is also a successful Australian entertainer who writes and produces music.
Clotilda, with a bachelor of arts degree and been a secretary for the Australian Stock Exchange, is now a successful wife, mother and home manager. The family includes five children, providing a warm friendly atmosphere. We have 2 dogs and are non smokers. (OK outside)
Close to: Tram Museum, Cronulla Surfing Beach, Largest Shopping Centre in Australia (Miranda), Cinemas, Golf Courses, Tennis & Squash Centres, Ferry Ride to Bundeena, Pub & Restaurants. Leisurely Visit: Captain Cook's historic landing point at Kurnell, Camellia Gardens, Symbio Koala Park, Bush Walking in National Park, Horse Riding, Sky-diving, Hang Gliding.
Home Page: http;//www.homestay.com.au

Sydney - Carlton
Self Contained Accommodation
Address: Please telephone
Name: Les & Merril
Telephone: (02) 9546 2642
Beds: 1 Queen (1 bedroom)
Bathroom: 1 Private
Tariff: B&B (full) Double $80 1 night only, $70 extra nights, Single $60.
Dinner $20. Vouchers accepted
Nearest Town: Hurstville, 15 kms south of Sydney

We are a family of four, with two grown-up daughters, no longer living at home. We are situated south of Sydney Harbour on a hill overlooking Botany and Kogarah Bays. The view from our home is panoramic.
The city of Sydney is 20 minutes away by train and the International Airport is only 15 minutes away by car.
If you drive for 20 minutes south you are out of the city and not far from beautiful scenic spots of the New South Wales south coast.
You would be very welcome to join us for a meal or we would be happy to suggest one of the excellent restaurants in our area.
Our accommodation is fully self-contained and includes a queensize bed, fully equipped kitchen, bathroom, private living room and TV. It also has a separate entrance. Non smokers preferred.
Directions: Please telephone.

Sydney - Castle Hill
Homestay   NRMA ★★★★
Address: "Hathersage",
10 Glenhaven Road, Glenhaven, NSW 2156
Name: Leigh & Elizabeth Mawhood
Telephone: (02) 9634 4598
Fax: (02) 9634 4598
Mobile: (0418) 679799
Beds: 1 King, 2 Queen (3 bedrooms)
Bathroom: 2 Ensuite, 1 Private
Tariff: B&B (full) Double $95, Single $55.
Dinner $20pp. Credit Cards (MC/BC/VISA).
Vouchers accepted $15 surcharge
Nearest Town: Castle Hill -35 minutes journey north west Sydney CBD.

"Hathersage" is an authentic two storey English manor built approximately 50 years ago for an English gentleman. Set on 1 1/2 acres and set in well established trees and an award winning garden.
Our first guest room has a kingsize four poster bed with large balcony and ensuite. Second room; with its own bathroom also has a lounge area plus a Tudor touch of a single room attached. Our third room with queensize bed is downstairs and has its own ensuite. All rooms have TV, tea/coffee and home made biscuits and guests can enjoy the use of our tennis court or relax in the summerhouse.
We are close to the Koala Park, Hawkesbury River and one step to the Blue Mountains. The area is serviced by public transport to Parramatta, Hornsby and the City. We enjoy providing luxury homestay accommodation and look forward to welcoming you.
FINALIST IN THE HAWKESBURY TOURISM AWARDS.
Directions:

NEW SOUTH WALES

Sydney - Centennial Park
Homestay
Address: GPO Box 185, Paddington, NSW 2021
Name: Bed and Breakfast On The Park
Telephone: (02) 9361 5310 **Fax**: (02) 9360 5717 **Mobile**: 0419 202 779
Beds: 2 King or 2 Twin, 1 Double, 1 Single. 4 Bedrooms, 2 with vanity units, all with colour TV.
Bathroom: 1 Guests Share, separate WC with hand basin.
Tariff: B&B (full) Double $110, Single $65-$100. Airport to Residence: KST bus will bring guests to and from their residence $10 return.
Day Tours: Your host will arange with Clipper
Nearest Town: Sydney 3km

Gracious, Edwardian Duplex home with luxury furnishings and a generous balcony overlooks the country environs of magnificent Centennial Park - one of the most desirable addresses in Sydney. Entrance door 2 on front verandah. The house appeared in the movie 'Phar Lap', about the world famous racehorse.
Stained glass windows, high ornate ceilings and marble fireplace, offer an ambience of style and tranquillity in the drawing room. Breakfast is served in the sunny, spacious dining room.
Located only 15 minutes from Sydney airport, a quick bus trip brings you to the city centre, Opera House, Circular Quay, historic Rocks District, Darling Harbour, Universities or Sydney's famous beaches.
A short stroll to the famous Paddington markets and Oxford Street. Woollahra antique shops, art galleries, cinemas and boutiques, where bistros, coffee shops, local hotels and restaurants buzz with cosmopolitan activity every day of the week; on to Double Bay, a unique village with European style, "the place to see and be seen!"
Business executives and travellers may care to enjoy the local amenities of tennis, golf, Randwick Racecourse and The Sydney Cricket Ground / Football Stadium. Major events at the Sydney Showground include The Royal Easter Show and the bi-annual National Antique Fair.
Directly opposite their Sydney residence is the 220 hectares Centennial Park, styled on an English country park. Attractions are architecture, historical monuments, horse riding, cycling, jogging, turf cricket wickets and football fields. Find peace and tranquillity in the enchanting Pine Grove or Rose Garden and view the magnificent Avenue of Palms. Experience the magical quality of the marshland in the centre of the park, prolific with birdlife. Picnic on the green banks of the lakes or reed-fringed ponds alternatively, dine at the popular Centennial Park Cafe.
On your arrival you will be greeted graciously and made very welcome by your charming hostess, whose international and local expertise ensures you of a comfortable and memorable stay.
The resident cats are Edwina and Mountbatten, who roam and grace the lawns and gardens.
Non Smoking.

NEW SOUTH WALES

Sydney - Clovelly
B&B Guest House   NRMA ★★★★
Address: "Peartree Cottage", 36 Winchester Road, Clovelly, 2031
Name: Christine & Patrick Turner
Telephone: (02) 9665 1911 **Fax**: (02) 9315 7879 **Mobile**: (014) 417117
Email: peartree@ozemail.com.au
Beds: 1 Double, 2 Single (2 bedrooms)
Bathroom: 1 Guests share
Tariff: B&B (full) Double $105-$120, Twin $90-$110, Single $75-$85, Child concession. Credit Cards: Bankcard/Mastercard/Visa. Vouchers accepted $20 surcharge
Nearest Town: Sydney 8km to Opera House, Rocks, Darling Harbour: Bondi Beach 3km.

*Winner of the Randwick City Council Awards for Business Excellence 1996 & 1997, Hospitality / Entertainment Division for Best Presentation / Promotion / Service.
English Country Style Hospitality By the Sea.*
"I warmly welcome you to a bed and breakfast with a difference! Peartree Cottage is a delightful Federation home full of traditional English charm.
Each room has tea / coffee making facilities and access to all modern amenities. At the end of a hectic day, enjoy breezes on the balcony with Clovelly ocean views, relax in the scented cottage garden or refresh yourself in the inground saltwater swimming pool, while you experience genuine hospitality.
Pamper yourself with a choice of delicious breakfasts (champagne breakfast also available), personalized picnic baskets, beach barbecues, gourmet snacks and evening meals.
Peartree Cottage is just minutes from Sydney's famous attractions, eastern suburbs beaches including Coogee and Bondi, cosmopolitan Paddington, multi-cultural restaurants, Sydney Cricket Ground, Football Stadium, Showground, Randwick Racecourse, scuba diving and snorkelling in Clovelly Bay.
We offer personalised sightseeing tours, a pick-up and drop-off service with public transport only 200 metres away. It is 15 minutes to the airport.
Having travelled widely myself, I know what makes a bed and breakfast memorable. It's my pleasure to offer the same special experience to you".
Christine
Home Page: http://www.ozemail.com.au/~peartree

NEW SOUTH WALES

Sydney - Collaroy Beach (Northern Beaches)
Homestay   NRMA ★★★
Address: Scotter's Bed & Breakfast.
Name: Valerie & Richard
Telephone: (02) 9982 6394 **Mobile**: (018) 647998
Beds: 2 Double, (2 bedrooms)
Bathroom: 2 Ensuite, 2 Private
Tariff: B&B (full) Double $95 for one night, $85 for two nights or more. Discount for a week. Singles by arrangment, $65 for one night, $55 for two or more. Not suitable for children.
Nearest Town: City of Sydney 20km, Manly 10km

Gracious, north facing beach house, stately rooms, ornate ceilings, ocean and coastal views. Quiet location only metres to restaurants, cinema, shops, beach, services club, short walk to tennis courts, golf course, coastal walks.
Sydney and Manly transport, airport bus door to door. Valerie and Richard have travelled extensively and are well known for their generous hospitality. They have many interests including tennis, bowls, theatre, singing, music, bonsai, food, wine books, meeting people from other countries. There are two double rooms, one with antique furniture, private ensuites, one with a bath. Guest lounge with tea making and colour TV. Library with books and magazines. Large formal dining room with antique furniture, where breakfast is served, full or continental. In summer you may like to have breakfast on a sun drenched deck with views of the ocean and local golf course. We are a non smoking household.
Directions: *Please phone for directions.*

Sydney - Cronulla
Homestay
Address: 10 Rose Street,
Cronulla, Sydney, NSW 2230
Name: Gifford & Betsy Eardley
Telephone: (02) 9523 1577
Fax: (02) 9523 1577
Beds: 1 Double, 2 Single (2 bedrooms)
Bathroom: 1 Private
Tariff: B&B (full) Double $75, Single $50,
Children $15. Discounts for extended stays and families.
Nearest Town: Sydney City

Our quiet seaside home on beautiful Cronulla peninsula is convenient to the Airport - ideal for first and last Homestays. Guests transferred to / from airport, coach or train. Sydney's Tourist attractions are readily accessible by excellent Train service.
Brochure / maps / information forwarded. Off-street parking. Enjoy delightful seaside walks, cycling, swimming, etc, or just relax in the fresh air. Ferries to Royal National Park. Close to Camellia Gardens, historic Kurnell (Australia's birthplace), Koala Park, Miranda Shopping Mall. Personalised tours arranged - Blue Mountains, Southern Highlands, etc. Our comfortable private guest rooms are ground floor with TV, refrigerator, tea / coffee making facilities, microwave etc. Laundry available. Corner store nearby. Cronulla's Mall offers restaurants, fast-food, clubs, banks, post office, cinema etc.
Gifford was a schoolmaster. Our interests include steam trains, music, art, theatre, rotary and travel, and our lovely home incorporates gratifying features of places we have visited. We enjoy sharing a welcoming "cuppa and cakes" with guests.
Please, no smoking indoors.

NEW SOUTH WALES

Sydney - Cronulla
Self Contained Unit
Address: Please phone, fax or email
Name: "Bayview Apartments", Beverley and Alan
Telephone: (02) 9523 4540 **Fax**: (02) 9523 4540 **Mobile**: 0414 991 187
Email: bviewbb@ozemail.com.au
Beds: 2 Queen or 2 Single (2 Bedrooms).
Bathroom: 1 Private
Tariff: B&B (self contained) Unit $160 per double, extra person $10 (sleeps 4-5). Weekly and extended stay discounts available June - October. Vouchers accepted two per night
Nearest Town: Cronulla - Sydney CBD 0 20km.

We have a delightful, 2 bedroom, self-contained ground floor unit. Spacious open plan lounge, dining, kitchen, with view of Gunamatta Bay. Internal laundry. Large balcony where you can relax after a busy day. Lock-up garage.
Excellent position. Short walking distance to all amenities. Local and Interstate Rail and Bus Service - 7 mins; ferry - 5 mins; shops and beaches all within 10 mins. Gunamatta Bay 150 metres or take a stroll in Gunamatta Park.
Sydney airport 20 mins. We will gladly arrange pick-up and delivery, bookings necessary. Take a ferry trip to the Royal National Park. Stroll around the ocean front to Gunamatta Bay. Close to cinemas, Cronulla Mall, surf and swimming beaches, tram museum, Camellia Gardens, Symbio Koala Park.
Fast train to Sydney centre. Excellent restaurants. Tours of Sydney and environs, The Blue Mountains. Excellent waterways and activities. Fully equipped kitchen, microwave, washing machine, TV. We also operate Bayview Bed & Breakfast on the Burraneer Peninsula. See previous adverts. Also self-contained 2 bed unit at Cronulla, see advert following. **Home Page**: http//www.cyberlink.com.au/bedbreakfast/bayview

Sydney - Double Bay
Bed & Breakfast   NRMA ★★★☆
Address: Double Bay Bed & Breakfast
63 Cross St, Double Bay 2028
Name: Bill & Margaret Cox
Telephone: (02) 9363 4776
Fax: (02) 9363 1992 **Mobile**: (014) 492691
Email: doubaybb@ozemail.com.au
Beds: 1 King/Queen, 1Queen/Twin, 1 Double (3 bedrooms)
Bathroom: 1 1/2 Guests share
Tariff: B&B (special) Double $100-$148,
Single $85-$130, Children $35, Credit cards.
Accommodation Levy. Vouchers accepted $15.50 - $42.50 surcharge
Nearest Town: Sydney C.B.D. 4 km.

Double Bay Bed and Breakfast is in the heart of Double Bay village. Stroll amongst tree-lined streets; experience elegant shopping; eat at excellent restaurants and cafes and all just 150 metres from Sydney's beautiful harbour. This 1901 large Victorian terrace is an elegant and restful base to explore Sydney, be it with family and friends or at a conference/business activity. Bedrooms are large, comfortable, king/twin, queen double or single beds. Pretty bathrooms. The guest lounge/dining rooms have an electic mix of antiques, marble fire place, music and TV. Delicious full breakfast, pretty courtyard, tea/coffee making facilities, ceiling fans, room heaters, guest refrigerator, laundry, maps, brochures, timetables, phone, fax, email assist in our guests comfort. Ferry, bus and train are nearby. CBD 10 minutes, Bondi Beach and airport are just 20 minutes. Bill and Margaret take pleasure in sharing their love of Sydney and warmly welcome guests.

NEW SOUTH WALES

Sydney - Double Bay
Bed & Breakfast
Address: Unit 3, No. 6 Ocean Avenue, Double Bay, 2028
Name: Denise Austin's Bed & Breakfast
Telephone: (02) 9328 1945 **Fax**: (02) 9328 1609
Beds: 3 Double, 2 Single (3 bedrooms/1 bedroom with Double bed + ensuite, 2 bedrooms with Double beds plus 1 Single, share bathroom)
Bathroom: 1 Ensuite, 1 Guests share
Tariff: B&B (full) Double ensuite $140, Double $120, Single $95-$115, Children 12yrs, Dinner $25, Credit Cards. Non-smoking. Vouchers accepted $38-$56 surcharge Double room
Nearest Town: Sydney CBD 4km

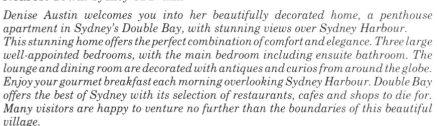

Denise Austin welcomes you into her beautifully decorated home, a penthouse apartment in Sydney's Double Bay, with stunning views over Sydney Harbour.
This stunning home offers the perfect combination of comfort and elegance. Three large well-appointed bedrooms, with the main bedroom including ensuite bathroom. The lounge and dining room are decorated with antiques and curios from around the globe. Enjoy your gourmet breakfast each morning overlooking Sydney Harbour. Double Bay offers the best of Sydney with its selection of restaurants, cafes and shops to die for. Many visitors are happy to venture no further than the boundaries of this beautiful village.
Conveniently located, Denise's bed and breakfast has public transport almost at the door and is a short walk from harbour ferries. Sydney CBD, Bondi Beach, Paddington and Kings Cross are only minutes away.
Denise welcomes you to stay for a night or longer at one of Sydney's best kept secrets.

Sydney - Drummoyne, Inner City West
Homestay
Address: Drummoyne - Please phone for address and directions.
Name: Tricia Gray
Telephone: (02) 9181 3715
Beds: 1 Single (1 bedroom)
Bathroom: 1 Private
Tariff: B&B (continental) Single $55.
Nearest Town: Sydney City

Drummoyne is a beautiful suburb nearly surrounded by water just 4km from city by either Rivercat ferry or bus - 15 mins. Your accommodation is in a delightful luxury waterfront apartment with views to Harbour Bridge, and breakfast on balcony. Pool and fishing facilities available. Visitors are welcome to local Sailing and Rugby clubs also good choice of local restaurants.
I am well travelled lady with many interests and would be delighted to show guests our beautiful city. Privately escorted day tours to Blue Mountains etc. can be arranged. No smoking in apartment. Thank you.

Phone numbers throughout Australia are changing to 8 digits.
For help contact Directory Assistance.

Sydney - Galston
Guest House NRMA ★★★★☆
Address: 16 Calderwood Road, Galston, NSW 2159
Name: Anne Hayes
Telephone: (02) 653 2498 & (02) 653 2282 **Fax**: (02) 653 2282
Beds: 1 Queen, 2 Twin, 1 Single (4 bedrooms)
Bathroom: 2 Ensuite, 1 Private, 1 Guests share
Tariff: B&B (full) Queen $43-$50pp, Twin $35-$40pp, Single $35-$45pp. Dinner $7.50-$25pp. Treasured pets welcome.
Nearest Town: Dural - 35 minute journey North West Sydney CBD

"CalderWood" is conveniently located half way between NSW's Central Coast and Sydney Central Business District.

The Guest House is built on five acres of beautiful garden and natural bushland situated in Galston, one of the most picturesque areas in New South Wales. Private bushwalking facilities, amid a splendid semi rain-forest environment, are available to interested visitors.

Recently Calderwood has attracted a Four and a Half Star Rating by the Australian Automobile Association. Tariffs remain unchanged with an emphasis on value for money. Guests are offered a high standard of service - e.g.

- private tea and coffee making facilities;
- television & video;
- mini fridge, microwave, electric frying pan and toaster, hair dryer, electric blankets;
- private telephone & fax;
- reverse-cycle airconditioning;
- outdoor heated spa

Meals: Breakfast - Au gratis
Lunch - Negotiable
Dinner (3 course) - $7.50 – $25 per person

AAA Rating: ★★★★☆

Directions: *Refer brochure, available on request.* **Transfers:** *Available by prior arrangement (e.g. Hornsby Interchange and Sydney Airport)*

Sydney - Dural - Hills Rural District
Self-contained Cottage
Address: 16 Bangor Road, Middle Dural, 2158
Name: Hilltop Cottage"
Telephone: (02) 9652 1482
Mobile: (018) 258754
Beds: 1 Double (1 bedroom)
Bathroom: 1 Private
Tariff: B&B (full) Double $90, Dinner $25pp by arrangement, Campervans facilities.
Vouchers accepted Sun-Thurs only.
Nearest Town: Hornsby/Castle Hill (15 mins)

"Hilltop Cottage" is situated north west of Sydney on 5 acres of private seclusion (suburb free) at Middle Dural (approx. 45 mins from CBD) and only a short distance from the best garden nurseries and antique shops in the district. Wisemans Ferry or Windsor are within an easy hour drive.

If staying at the "Cottage" is more your style - a good book or a swim in our pool is an option - for our more energetic guests the use of our tennis court is available. On arrival, we welcome you with a "Hilltop Cottage" style afternoon tea. Your hosts, who enjoy entertaining, welcome you to dine with them.

For our interstate and overseas guests, transport to and from the airport can be arranged.

Please telephone us to discuss your time away from the every day.

No smoking indoors, thank you.

Sydney - Glebe
Homestay
Address: 18 Boyce Street, Glebe, NSW 2037
Name: Cathie Lesslie
Telephone: (02) 9692 0548
Beds: 3 Double, 1 Single (3 bedrooms)
Bathroom: 1 Guests share, 1 Family share
Tariff: B&B (full) Double $75, Single $50, Children welcome. Vouchers accepted
Nearest Town: Sydney

This quiet, leafy terrace house is in Glebe, an old, beautiful suburb close to Sydney University. Boyce Street runs off Glebe Point Road where there is an interesting variety of cafes, restaurants, shops and a cinema. You can walk to Darling Harbour from here, and the middle of the city is twenty minutes away by bus.

The rooms are large, comfortable and airy, all of them furnished with television, a desk, a fridge and tea and coffee facilities. One of the rooms has an extra bed as well. Breakfast is served downstairs, where you choose from a menu including fresh juice, fresh fruit, bacon and eggs and home-made croissants. The aim here is for you to feel comfortable and at ease.

It is necessary to phone first for bookings.

Sydney - Glebe
Homestay
Address: "Bellevue Terrace",
19 Bellevue Street, Glebe, NSW 2037
Name: Lisa Manchur
Telephone: (02) 9660 6096
Fax: (02) 9660 6096
Beds: 1 Queen, 1 Double, 2 Single (3 bedrooms)
Bathroom: 1 1/2 Guests share, 1 Family share
Tariff: B&B (full) Double $80, Single $60,
Children $30, Dinner $20.
Vouchers accepted
Nearest Town: Sydney

You are invited to stay in my spacious, elegant terrace house situated in the lovely old inner city suburb of Glebe, which is the home of Sydney University, as well as a myriad of restaurants, boutiques, galleries and a number of excellent pubs. Walking distance to Darling Harbour, Chinatown, Paddy's Market and the Powerhouse Museum or take the bus to the city centre which is only 3kms away.
I have travelled extensively and lived in Europe, Canada and East Africa. I am happy to supply you with maps, brochures and lots of ideas for things to see and do in Sydney. Guests are welcome to tea and coffee whenever they wish. Delicious home cooked evening meals available by arrangement.

Sydney - Glebe
Homestay
Address: Please phone
Name: "Harolden"
Telephone: (02) 9660 5881
Mobile: 041 7254345
Beds: 1 Double, 1 Single (2 bedrooms)
Bathroom: 1 Guests share
Tariff: B&B (full) Double $80, Single $55.
Dinner $20.
Nearest Town: Sydney City (CBD)

Explore Sydney from the comfort of a gracious Victorian inner city home. Convenient to public transport, a mere 15 minutes from Darling Harbour, Sydney Harbour, The Rocks, Botanic Gardens, Art Gallery, and Museums. "Harolden" situated in the heart of historic Glebe is within easy walking distance to the diverse restaurants of Glebe Point road, the University of Sydney main campus and local hospitals.
Your host a descendant from the First Fleet to arrive at Sydney Cove in 1788, is knowledgeable about Sydney, well travelled within Australia, and only too pleased to discuss Sydney's points of interest.
You can unwind in the warmth of log fires or enjoy breakfast in the delightful garden. Lunch can be provided at a favorite picnic spot if required and dinner by arrangement. Tea and coffee is available at all times.
You are always assured of a warm welcome.

Sydney - Glebe
B&B Guest House
Address: 270 Glebe Point Road, Glebe, NSW 2037
Name: Liz Trickett
Telephone: (02) 9552 1141 **Fax**: (02) 9692 9462
Beds: 1 King, 5 Queen, 2 Single (7 bedrooms)
Bathroom: 7 Ensuite
Tariff: B&B (continental) Double $140, Single $110. Vouchers accepted Surcharge $50 double, $25 single. Vouchers not accepted weekends
Nearest Town: Sydney

Trickett's is a lovely Victorian mansion whose magnificent ballroom was once used as the Children's Court. Today this historic building has been fully restored to its original splendour. Large bedrooms with high ceilings, all beautifully decorated, all with ensuite, have top range Sealy beds. Breakfast is served in the conservatory and in summer out on the secluded deck overlooking the garden with bottle brush trees providing a wonderful splash of colour. The tranquillity makes one forget the city is a short 431 bus ride away and Darling Harbour, Fish Markets, Power House Museum, the Chinese Temple and Sydney University are close by.

Glebe is an historic suburb full of interesting old homes that have been lovingly restored; and old fashioned gardens giving strong overtones of a bygone era. We are at the quieter "waterend" of Glebe Point Road, and a little further up lies the restaurant heart of Glebe, well known all over Sydney. Off street parking is available. We enjoy providing a luxury homestay for travellers and business people.

There are some good tips for easier travel on page 7

Sydney - Glenorie, Hills District
Self-contained Accommodation   NRMA ★★★★
Address: 1395 Old Northern Road, Glenorie, 2157 (on scenic drive No. 15)
Name: Roger & Margaret Nancarrow
Telephone: (02) 9652 1507
Fax: (02) 9652 1507
Beds: 1 Queen (1 bedroom)
Bathroom: 1 Ensuite
Tariff: B&B Sun-Thurs: Double $100, Single $70, Fri/Sat: Double $120, Single $80. Vouchers accepted $15 surcharge
Nearest Town: Hornsby/Castle Hill 15km.

We are located in the Hills District 40km north west of Sydney. The area is renowned for its orchards, plant nurseries and scenic bushland. The northern beaches, central coast, Wiseman's Ferry and Blue Mountains are all within one hours drive.
Situated on 5 secluded acres of natural bushland, Camellia Haven offers a well appointed, self-contained cottage in the modern country style. The adjoining terraces and surrounding garden ensure an ideal atmosphere for relaxation.
We offer • generous breakfast provisions with fresh fruit • modern, fully equipped kitchen with refrigerator/freezer, microwave, stove • spacious living room with wood heater and TV • spacious bedroom with top quality Queen size bed • contemporary bathroom with laundry facilities • air conditioning and heating • close proximity to local shops, restaurants and Country Club • strictly no smoking • transfers from Sydney Airport/City can be arranged. • reduced tariff for stays more than 3 days.

Sydney - Greenwich Heights
B&B Homestyle Specialists
Address: "Leafy Glen", 15 Hinkler St, Greenwich, NSW 2065
Name: Jeanette & David Lloyd
Telephone: (02) 9438 1204
Fax: (02) 9438 1484
Beds: 1 Queen, 1 Double, 3 Single (3 bedrooms)
Bathroom: 1 Guests Private, 1 Family share
Tariff: B&B (special) Double $80, Single $55, Children welcome, Dinner by arrangement. Vouchers accepted
Nearest Town: Sydney

Situated in a tranquil bushland setting this large delightfully renovated Federation home has kept all the charm of a bygone period. There is ample off street parking. The two double bedrooms are well appointed with adjoining sunny courtyard/verandah which offers privacy for guests. A hearty breakfast of your choice is our speciality. Tea and coffee available at all times.
David and Jeanette are well travelled and have an excellent knowledge of Sydney and Environs to assist guests with any sightseeing.
Their interests are Theatre, Tennis, Cycling, Golf and Sailing.
The nearest station is St Leonard's. Pick up and delivery can be arranged. We are two minutes drive from Crows Nest one of Sydney's main Restaurant areas, 10 minutes to the City centre and a short distance to Lane Cove golf course.
Come and enjoy the experience of our warm and friendly hospitality.

NEW SOUTH WALES

Sydney - Greenwich
Bed & Breakfast
Address: "Riverview", 16 Wallace St., Greenwich Point 2065
Name: Roger & Carol Najor
Telephone: (02) 9906-7550 **Fax**: (02) 9906-7617
Mobile: (019) 912192
Beds: 1 King, 1 Double, 1 Twin or Single (3 bedrooms)
Bathroom: 2 Guests share
Tariff: B&B (full) Double/Twin $85, Single $55, Weekly discounts available. Vouchers accepted
Nearest Town: 13 minutes by ferry to Circular Quay, Opera House and the Rocks, (Greenwich Wharf 2 minutes walk from house) - 3km by car to city.

The rambling Federation style house was the actor Peter Finch's boyhood home. It is situated in a quiet area, surrounded by Sydney Harbour - an idyllic oasis close to the city. The sweet fragrance of their frangipani and honey suckle fills the air. Imagine, gazing at sunsets over rippled water, taking in the sounds of the native birds, kookaburras and rainbow lorikeets - an especially romantic setting for couples. There is a park with tennis courts for hire across the road. Swimmers enjoy the enclosed harbourside pool and relaxing on the sandy beach (200 metres away).
They enjoy helping guests with sightseeing advice and sharing their knowledge of Australian culture and customs. They never tire of escorting guests on local scenic bushwalks and drives to stunning harbour look-outs all at no charge, of course.
Each room is decorated in a different Australian wildflower design. Baskets of fruit and fresh flowers, fluffy bathrobes and special soaps all help to make people feel at home. Tea and coffee making facilities are available in the guest kitchen anytime. Carol always keeps the cookie jar full of homemade wattleseed Anzac biscuits.
A generous and stylish breakfast is served including the best fruit frappés in town, freshly squeezed orange juice, steaming hot muffins with "Riverview" jams (home grown citrus and quinces), freshly ground Lavazza coffee and Twinings teas are offered.
Tantalizing specialities of the house are:-
Creamy scrambled eggs with bagels, smoked salmon and herbs from the garden - wafer thin crepes with fresh ricotta and tropical fruit - seasonal fruit platter with yoghurt - the famous homemade Aussie damper bread with lashings of Leatherwood honey. Be awakened by the aroma of home baked yeast breads wafting through the house.

CLOSE TO ALL CITY SIGHTSEEING ATTRACTIONS!
NO WONDER THIS PLACE IS A FAVOURITE WITH WORLD TRAVELLERS!

Sydney - Kurnell (Birthplace of Australia)
Bed & Breakfast
Address: 224 Prince Charles Pde.
Kurnell, 2231 NSW
Name: "Silversands B&B"
Suzanne Molloy
Telephone: (02) 9668 9352
Fax: (02) 9668 9352
Beds: 1 Double, 1 Single (2 bedrooms)
Bathroom: 1 Guests share with spa
Tariff: B&B (full) Double $85,
Single $50, Children over 12yrs.
Nearest Town: Cronulla - 28km south Sydney, 35 mins airport.

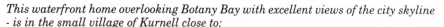

This waterfront home overlooking Botany Bay with excellent views of the city skyline - is in the small village of Kurnell close to:
- Botany Bay National Park - 1 min
- Bushwalking tracks
- Cape Solander scenic drive / walk / cycle
- Swimming enclosure, fishing, windsurfing, sailing, skiing on Botany Bay
- Boat harbour - 4 wheel drive park - 2 mins
- Golf driving range / golf course - 7 mins
- Cronulla Plaza, Cronulla Leagues Club - 7 mins

Guests with own / hire vehicle would have greater access to surrounding attractions, however public transport is available.

Sydney - Lane Cove
Homestay
Address: Lane Cove
Name: Osborne park
Telephone: (02) 9427 6992
Beds: 1 Queen (1 bedroom)
Bathroom: 1 Ensuite
Tariff: B&B (full) Double $100,
Dinner by arrangement.
Nearest Town: Lane Cove,
10 minutes to Sydney centre.

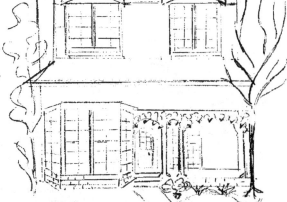

Our traditional 2 storey home is situated in the garden suburb of Lane Cove on Sydney's lower North Shore, surrounded by quiet bushland and golf course. We offer our guests comfortable upstairs accommodation with views to the city. Gourmet breakfast is served in elegant dining room adjoining garden.
Convenient public transport, 10 minutes by car to CBD, and off street parking. Car pick up can be arranged.
Our interests include travel, art and gardening and love to escort our guests on local scenic bush and Harbour walks.

One of the differences between staying at a hotel and a B&B is that you don't hug the hotel staff when you leave.

NEW SOUTH WALES

Sydney - Leichhardt
Homestay   NRMA ★★
Address: 5 Day Street, Leichhardt, NSW 2040
Name: Pension Albergo
Telephone: (02) 9560 0179 or (02) 9810 8906 **Fax**: (02) 9209 4081
Mobile: 0416 170 315 **Email**: brianc@zeta.org.au
Beds: 1 Double, 4 Single (3 bedrooms)
Bathroom: 1 Guest share, 1 Family share
Tariff: B&B (continental) Double $70, Single $45, Children $10.   Vouchers accepted
Nearest Town: Leichhardt - inner Sydney suburb.

Pension Albergo is a Victorian home offering three guest rooms in a peaceful part of Leichhardt located between the city and the Olympic games venue yet close to restaurants, coffee bars and delicatessens. City centre transport is at its doorstep and shopping abounds close by. At Pension Albergo guests have a large bedroom where they have space, peace and privacy. The Irish-Australian hosts create a friendly, helpful atmosphere where guests are introduced to a distinct Sydney experience reflecting its multicultural character with restaurants, clubs and cafes for the Italian, South American, Thai and Vietnamese communities. Guests have a dining room which turns into a lounge / TV area after break fast and a sunny garden to sit and take all in or swap travel stories with other guests. Breakfast is served at flexible times and consists of cereal and fruit juice followed by Albergo's famous "Jungle Juice" – fresh in-season fruit salad chosen from the local Italian fruit markets and chopped daily – and fresh croissants from the local French patisserie, hot Italian rolls, tea and percolated coffee.   Also, take advantage of our magnificent Central Coast beach house or farm house set on the edge of Barrinton Tops rainforest. Buses 440 and 438 from the city to Leichhardt Town Hall take you to 1 minute from the Pension Albergo.
Home Page: http://www.zeta.org.au/~johnl/albergo.htm

Sydney - Leichhardt
Guest House + SC Accom.
Address: 73 Renwick Street, Leichhardt
Name: Pensione Italia (Alfio & Maria)
Telephone: (02) 9560 2249 **Fax**: (02) 9560 2249 **Mobile**: (019) 367954
Beds: 2+4 Double (2+4 bedrooms)
Bathroom: 2 Private, 1 Guests share
Tariff: B&B (continental) Double $70, Single $45. SC Flat: Flat 1 (double bedroom, own facilities, kitchen, TV) $80; Flat 2 (double bedroom, own facilities, kitchen, lounge, TV) Up to 2 people $90, 3 people $100.   Vouchers accepted
Nearest Town: Sydney CBD

Pensione Italia is located in Leichhardt, the original "Little Italy of Sydney".
To this day the area keeps its Italian flavour with its village atmosphere.
The Pensione is situated within 3 minutes walk of restaurants, cafes, shops, clubs and transport, 5km to the city.
We are perfectly located in the Olympic corridor, halfway between the City and the main Olympic venues.
A generous breakfast is provided and included in the tariff. For dinner you may choose to try the authentic Italian restaurant next door.
To experience and enjoy your visit to one of the world's most attractive cities you need a convenient and comfortable base and that is what Pensione Italia will provide you with.
Booking preferred. No cheques or credit cards. One night stays are welcome. Ask for special weekly rates. Pay on arrival.
We look forward to seeing you.

Sydney - Malabar Heights
Homestay
Address: 131 Bilga Cres., Malabar Heights, NSW 2036
Name: Marlies Woolford
Telephone: (02) 9661 5595 **Fax**: (02) 9661 5595 **Mobile**: 0418968402
Beds: 4 Single (3 bedrooms)
Bathroom: 1 Ensuite, 2 Family share
Tariff: B&B (full) Double $85, Single $65, Dinner on request.
 Vouchers accepted $6 surcharge
Nearest Town: Sydney 12km

Our chalet style home is situated in a quiet location, only 20 min from the heart of Sydney, overlooking 2 golf courses, a charming beach and the Pacific Ocean, all within walking distance.
Nearby Botany Bay National Park offers very scenic walking tracks, partly bush, partly coastal, with spectacular views.
Historic La Perouse, 5 min away, has various attractions, ie snakeshows, Aboriginal Art, Bare Island Fortification, Museum, - very popular also for diving, fishing and windsurfing.
We have regular bus service to the City adjacent to our entrance.
The Airport is only 10 min away.
Our neighbouring suburb is Maroubra, proudly hosting Sydney's major clothing discount centres.
There are many clubs and restaurants to choose from.
The bavarian style atmosphere of our home offers warmth and friendliness.
We look forward to pampering you with a full home cooked breakfast which, on a fine day, is served on the terrace, overlooking the golf courses and our tranquil little beach.

Sydney - Manly (Northern Beaches)
Guest House
Address: "Periwinkle Manly Cove Guest House",
18-19 East Esplanade, Manly
Name: Rhonda Roth
Telephone: (02) 9977 4668 **Fax**: (02) 9977 6308
Beds: 2 Queen, 15 Double, 17 Single (17 bedrooms)
Bathroom: 10 Ensuite, 4 Guests share
Tariff: B&B (continental) Double with ensuite $115*, Single with ensuite $95*. Shared bathroom $95 Double, $75 Single. $5 extra for water view). Credit Cards (Visa/BC/MC).
Nearest Town: Sydney

A Guest House By The Sea

Just 12 minutes to city centre by high speed Jet Cat, the Periwinkle was built in 1895 on an original land grant and offers charm with traditional bed & breakfast hospitality. Newly restored, it features stylish rooms, high ceilings and "Sydney lacework" verandahs overlooking a delightful courtyard. With a superb harbour beachfront location, Periwinkle is within a short stroll of new Manly Wharf speciality shopping and entertainment complex, the Corso restaurants, Oceanarium, art gallery, cinema and, of course, Manly's famous ocean beach.

- Victorian era lounge / open fire
- Guests' kitchen, BBQ and laundromat
- Harbour beachfront and views
- 6 bedrooms with water views
- 7 bedrooms (share facilities)
- Refrigerators and ceiling fans
- Heaters and electric blankets
- Some off street parking

Sydney - Manly
Self-contained Accommodation
Address: "Tara Cottage",
70 Birkley Rd., Manly, 2095
Name: Anne & Harry Sprintz
Telephone: (02) 9976 3235
Fax: (02) 9977 1522
Mobile: 0416 329 580
Beds: 1 Double, 1 Single
(plus folding bed and cot)
Bathroom:
Tariff: B&B (full "continental") Double $85, Single $65, $15 per child under 15 and $20 per young adult over 15. Cooked breakfast $5 extra pp. No credit cards.
Nearest Town: Sydney (CBD) 15 mins by Jetcat, 30 mins by Ferry and 35 mins by Car or Bus.

Our 100 year old "Settlers Cottage" is only 5 mins walk to Manly ferry, beaches, cosmopolitan restaurants and shops plus many tourist attractions. Accommodation is a 2 level self-contained cottage "Sophie's Place", providing; lounge/dining area, separate w.c., basin and shr, sleeping loft with glimpses of ocean views, colour TV, microwave oven, refrig. elec blankets, heater and storage space and is separated from the main house by a landscaped courtyard, available for BBQs and outside dining.

Anne, a former nurse and Harry, a practising architect, welcome you to share the delights of Manly's "Village" atmosphere, their company and the privacy and peace a separate cottage provides

We have travelled extensively worldwide and enjoy company, music, history, art, travel, sport, books, craftwork (quilting), military history and our part of the world. Within 5 mins drive are golf courses, cinemas, major shopping centre, licensed clubs and 15 mins drive to National Parks, Pittwater sailing and ocean beaches.

On street & rear lane car parking is available. Guests pets can be accompanied by prior arrangement, we also provide a no smoking environment..

Sydney - Manly
Bed & Breakfast
Address: 14 Cliff Street, Manly
Name: Cliff House
Telephone: (02) 9977 6681 **Mobile**: (018) 520 482
Beds: 1 Queen, 2 Double, 2 Single (3 bedrooms)
Bathroom: 1 Private, 1 Guests share
Tariff: B&B (continental) Double/Twin Private bathroom $150, Double share bathroom $105, Twin share bathroom $95/$105, Single $75-$85, $20 per extra bed, Low season rates available (June-August) Shoulder season rates (Sept - Nov, April - May) and discounts for three or more nights. Children 12yrs & over by arrangement, Credit Cards. Non-smoking establishment. Vouchers accepted $15 surcharge
Nearest Town: Manly 5 mins walk, Sydney 15 mins by Jetcat, 30 mins by ferry, 30 mins by car

Cliff House is set in a quiet tree-lined street, five minutes walk from the surf and trendy ocean-front restaurants at South Steyne.
A fine example of Federation architecture, Cliff House features large, well-appointed rooms characteristic of the period, and guests' lounge with access to sweeping verandah and garden. It is close to the ferry, beaches, Manly shopping village, Ocean-World Aquarium, and 15 minutes to city attractions.
One of the first areas in Sydney to be settled, Manly has a very interesting history. The main centre of Manly is a mall known as the Corso. A lively pedestrian scene by day and night the Corso offers numerous shops and outdoor cafés.
Cliff House is within easy walking distance of all the attractions but is at the same time in a very quiet location. Your hosts Marie, Joy and friendly cat will make you most welcome.
Cliff House is available to new arrivals after 5pm unless by prior arrangement.

Sydney - Mona Vale (Northern Beaches)
Self-contained Accommodation
Address: "Pindara",
47 Rednal St., Mona Vale, 2103
Name: Phillip & Robyn Muller
Telephone: (02) 9997 6483
Beds: 1 Queen
Bathroom: 1 Private
Tariff: B&B (continental hamper) Double $90. Vouchers accepted plus $10
Nearest Town: Sydney

Our home is situated in a quiet waterfront st overlooking Winji Jimmi Bay at the southern end of Pittwater. Mona Vale is one of the most spectacular areas of the northern beaches and is approximately 40 minutes travelling time from Sydney. It is renowned for its proximity to Pittwater and its abundance of recreational facilities. It is a haven for native birds and ideal environment from which to explore Kuringai National Park.
We are close to a variety of excellent restaurants, cinemas. Golf courses, bowling clubs and Mona Vale has a comprehensive shopping centre. A short ferry ride will take you to Scotland Island and Pittwater's western foreshores. A ferry from Palm Beach enables you to explore the magnificent Hawksbury River.
Accommodation is fully self contained and consists of a double bedroom, lounge/dining room, bathroom and kitchen. A continental breakfast hamper is supplied which you can enjoy in the sitting room, on the verandah or by the pool.

NEW SOUTH WALES

Sydney - Mossman
Homestay
Address: 73 Cabramatta Rd, Mosman, Sydney, NSW 2088
Name: Mrs S. Manthey
Telephone: (02) 9908-3630
Fax: (02) 9908-3630
Email: Lethe@onaustralia.com.au
Beds: 1 Queen, 2 Single (2 bedrooms)
Bathroom: 1 Guests share
Tariff: B&B (full) Double $85, Single $60. Vouchers accepted
Nearest Town: Sydney

Lethé
Beautifully restored federation home offering friendly spacious B&B accommodation in prestigious leafy Mosman on Sydney's Lower North Shore. Features include one large Queen-size bedroom and one large Twin (2 singles) bedroom with separate guest bathroom and toilet. Working open fireplaces in dining room and lounge with TV and video available. Close to cinemas, restaurants, 5 mins. to Taronga Zoo or Balmoral beach and only 4 bus stops from city across the bridge or a more leisurely bus and ferry ride across the harbour to Circular Quay, the Rocks and all the city attractions. Our home is ideally situated for seeing all the many delights which Sydney has to offer. Full English breakfast with fresh fruit and cereals provided.
Phone (02) 9908 3630 for a pleasurable and memorable stay.

Sydney - Newport (Northern Beaches)
Homestay + Self-Contained Accommodation
Address: Please telephone or fax
Name: "Blue Waters". Valerie and John
Telephone: (02) 9999 1245 **Fax**: (02) 9999 4530
Beds: 1 Queen, 1 Double, 2 Single (3 bedrooms)
Bathroom: 2 Private
Tariff: B&B (continental) Double $120., single $110. Self contained unit $120 Double plus $30 for each extra person. $10 discount given for additional nights stay. Children by arrangement. Vouchers accepted Mon-Thurs (2 nights minimum) + $30 surcharge
Nearest Town: Sydney CBD 45mins drive. Airport bus to door.

"Blue Waters" is a modern two-storey residence overlooking Pittwater. There is a choice of accommodation; a self contained unit with extensive water views, or a luxury garden suite with private courtyard. Both have private separate entrances, tea making facilities, TV, radio, ceiling fans and heating. The two bedroom unit has a fully equipped kitchen, laundry facilities, balcony and telephone. The suite has a private sitting room and courtyard adjacent to orchid garden.
"Blue Waters" gardens are shaded by numerous Kentia Palms. A variety of native birds, including Kookaburras visit us regularly. Our neighbour, the Royal Motor Yacht Club offers famous dining and recreational facilities.
Ethnic restaurants, art shops, galleries and boutiques nearby. The scenic quality of Pittwater area is world famous, offering all water activities, delights of Kurring-gai National park and surfing beaches. Our guests invariably depart with happy memories of our warm-hearted hospitality and the splendour of Pittwater. Distant places often offer no more. **Directions**: *Please telephone*

NEW SOUTH WALES

Sydney - Newtown
Guest House
Address: Sydney Federation House
46 Station Street
Newtown 2042
Name: Maureen Bailey
Telephone: (02) 9519 2208
Beds: 2 Double, 2 Twin (4 Bedrooms)
Bathroom: 2 Guests Share
Tariff: B&B (full) Double $105-$120,
Single $90-$100, Dinner $25 pp.
Vouchers accepted $25-$38 surcharge
Nearest Town: Sydney Centre, downtown 5 km.

A large beautifully restored Victorian residence retaining all its original features, including polished timber floors, high ceilings, ornate ceiling Roses, superb marble fire places. Accommodation over three levels includes four large bedrooms, two bathrooms, enormous lounge and dining room, well appointed large pine country kitchen. With its vast proportions and light filled interiors, this is a delightful Terrace filled with antique furnishings and situated on a direct bus and train route only minutes to Sydney centre and a one minute stroll to Newton's famous King Street cafe strip. Three course home cooked meals are available on request. The hostess Maureen has just returned to Sydney, her home city, after creating a four star B&B in Perth which was a finalist in 1994 Tourism Awards. Come and enjoy the warm friendly atmosphere at Sydney Federation House with Maureen who has widely travelled both overseas and interstate and can offer many travel and touring tips.

Sydney - Paddington
Homestay
Address: "Rose Ash", 11 Queen Road,
Paddington, NSW 2021
Name: Sally Southcombe
Telephone: (02) 9331 4970 **Fax**: (02) 9331 4970
Beds: 1 Double, 2 Single (3 bedrooms)
Bathroom: 1 Guest share
Tariff: B&B (continental) Double $80,
Single $60, Children over 12 years only
(no reduction). Vouchers accepted
Nearest Town: 3km from centre of Sydney

My hundred year old terrace house is very close to Oxford Street where you will find boutiques, coffee shops and a market which is held every Saturday. The local pubs have restaurants and there are many small cheap cafes and take away food outlets.
The buses to Circular Quay, the shops in the city centre, Bondi and Central Railway are on Oxford Street. Nearby Queen Street Woollahra has many antique shops.
I am originally from New Zealand but have lived in Sydney for many years. I was an Australian Airlines flight attendant and I worked for 20 years at the New Zealand Consulate General. I am interested in travel, opera, dining out, gardening, going to the theatre and calligraphy.
I have one double room with a wrought iron lace balcony, and air conditioning. There are 2 single bedrooms. All bedrooms have tea/coffee making facilities and TVs. No smoking. **Directions**: *Queen Road runs from Paddington Street to Underwood Street.*

NEW SOUTH WALES

Sydney - Paddington
Homestay
Address: Paddington Terrace, 76 Elizabeth St., Paddington, Syndey, NSW 2021
Name: Diane & Ron Johnson
Telephone: (02) 9363 0903 **Fax**: (02) 9327 1476
Beds: 1 Queen, 2 Single (2 bedrooms)
Bathroom: Guests share
Tariff: B&B (continental) Double $95, Single $75.
Nearest Town: Sydney - City 3km, Bondi 4km

Our terrace house in the heritage suburb of Paddington is 100 years old and overlooks a quiet reserve. It offers relaxing surroundings in a picturesque area among the now famous rows of Victorian Terrace and their lace balconies. Breakfast is served in a leafy conservatory. Close to the CBD, Opera House, Bondi Beach.
There is excellent transport (buses and trains) and Rushcutters Bay and King's Cross are a 10 minute walk away. Stroll among the galleries and pubs, cafes and restaurants of Paddington. Oxford St with its boutiques, eateries and Saturday Market is close by. Diane, a school librarian and Ron, a retired history teacher have travelled extensively in Australia and overseas, and have lived in their home for over 20 years. They enjoy meeting fellow travellers, walking, theatre, music and football. Ron has written a history of Paddington and Diane is a keen photographer.
Please phone for directions.
Home Page: http://www.cyberlink.com.au/bedbreakfast/paddington

Sydney - Palm Beach
Self-contained Accom.
Address:
"The Ferry House" - Please phone
Name: Patricia Thomson
Telephone: (02) 9974 4342
Beds: 1 Queen, 1 Double, 1 Single (2bedrooms)
Bathroom: 1 Private
Tariff: Double $115, Single $90, $25 per extra adult, $10 per child. Continental breakfast $15 per couple, if required. Seasonal mid-weekly/weekly rates available.
Vouchers accepted $10 surcharge
Nearest Town: Sydney 40km.

The Ferry House is a Mediterranean style villa situated across the road from Snapperman's Beach and the Palm Beach ferry. There are good views of Pittwater from almost every room. The attractive and comfortable accommodation comprises two bedrooms (sleeping 5). The front bedroom has a four poster queen size bed with views. There is a large living / dining room with French doors opening onto a garden of palms, hibiscus and flowering creepers. The kitchenette is new and has a microwave, dishwasher and stove. There are polished floors throughout.
Good restaurants, cafes and shops nearby. Also boat-hire, golf course and sea-plane. Children welcome. Dogs by arrangement.
Tariff: $90 Single, Double $115, $25 per extra adult, $10 per child. Continental breakfast $15 per couple, if required. Seasonal weekly and mid weekly rates available.

Sydney - Palm Beach (Northern Beaches)
Self-contained Accommodation
Address: Please telephone
Name: "Darwinia"
Telephone: (02) 9974 5604
Beds: 1 Queen (1 bedroom) **Bathroom**: 1 Ensuite
Tariff: B&B (continental) Double $130, Single $120.
Children not catered for. Vouchers accepted $40
surcharge two night min. Feb to Nov.
Nearest Town: 40km north of Sydney, 50 minutes by car,
90 minutes by L90 bus, 15 minutes by seaplane.

Palm Beach is Sydney's premier beach suburb, set at the northern end of a peninsula, bounded by the Pacific Ocean and Pittwater, a yachting paradise. "Darwinia's" guests are warmly welcomed and can choose to relax in privacy or have our company whenever the mood takes them. Own entry to large parquet-floored living-room including kitchenette (frig. M/W etc), CTV/CD, pool table, well-stocked bookshelves and pianola. Superb view over tranquil Pittwater to Mackerel and Resolute beaches with occasional pelicans cruising overhead and watch beautiful sunsets beyond the rugged bushland hills of Ku-Ring-Gai Chase National Park. The spacious bedroom is charmingly furnished with attention to detail: underfloor heating, writing desk, ceiling fan, hairdrier, electric blanket, lounge chair and ironing facilities and through the glass wall of the shower cubicle can be viewed myriad birdlife. Both rooms open to a 24' patio with gas BBQ, blessed by maximum winter sun. Just minutes walk to surfing beach and pool, bus, ferry, golf, cafes and restaurants. Laundromat, cinema, tennis nearby. No smoking.

Sydney - Petersham
Bed & Breakfast
Address: 25 Railway St, Petersham, NSW 2049
Name: "Brooklyn" Bed & Breakfast
Telephone: (02) 9564 2312
Beds: 1 King, 3 Double, 4 Single (5 bedrooms)
Bathroom: 2 Private plus separate toilet.
Tariff: B&B (continental) Double $70,
Single $50-$60. Children welcome. Campervans.
Credit Cards. Vouchers accepted
Nearest Town: Sydney

"Brooklyn" is a grand Victorian House used as the setting for the ABC Television series "G.P" and is furnished with beautiful antiques. It has featured on the "Getaway" programme and the "Getaway" book. Most rooms have large balconies with garden furniture, one has large private courtyard. The rooms are large and can be used as twin, double or triple rooms and although the location is central it is very quiet. Parking is also available. Beds have feather quilts, electric blankets and are very comfortable. You can be in the city in 10 mins by public transport which is fast and efficient. There are many excellent affordable Australian, European and Asian restaurants within a three minute walk. The University of Sydney is 10 mins away and 20 mins to the airport and there are Victorian homes of architectural interest in the area. The tariff includes breakfast (as much as you can eat) of fruit, cereals, croissants, toast, brewed coffee / tea and complimentary tea and coffee throughout the day. There is a guest dining and television / lounge room with open fire and many guests have enjoyed playing the beautiful antique upright grand piano. Hosts are well travelled and friendly and enjoy getting to know their guests and enjoy trips to the local cafes with guests, where they serve "great coffee".

NEW SOUTH WALES

Sydney - Parramatta
B&B Guest House
Address: 21 Boundary Street, Parramatta, NSW 2150
Name: Harborne B&B
Telephone: (02) 9687 8988 **Fax**: (02) 9687 8912
Email: harborne@wesleylodge.com.au
Beds: 7 Queen, 1 Single, (8 bedrooms)
Bathroom: 4 Ensuites, 1 Guests Share
Tariff: B&B (full), Double $90-$130, Single $80-120. Credit cards accepted.
Nearest Town: Parramatta 2km, Sydney City 25km or 1 hour by rivercat or train.

Harborne is a magnificent Georgian sandstone mansion, which was originally built in 1858 and recently restored as a charming 8 room bed and breakfast Guest House. The home is surrounded by lush gardens with an inground swimming pool and is situated only five minutes from the Parramatta CBD. The home and gardens have been classified by the National Trust.
Harborne now boasts a feast of modern amenities mixed with olde-world charm including colour television in all rooms, telephone and fax service and private ensuite in four rooms. There is a glazed breakfast atrium overlooking the beautiful garden, and kitchenette with tea and coffee making facilities available to guests.
Harborne is the ideal alternative to the large impersonal hotels. We invite you to experience our warm and friendly hospitality and magnificent heritage home.
To place your reservation or make an enquiry please call us now on (02) 9687 8988.

NEW SOUTH WALES

Sydney - Potts Point
Guest House
Address: 8 Challis Ave.,
Potts Point 2011
Name: Simpsons of Potts Point
Telephone: (02) 9356 2199
Fax: (02) 9356 4476
Beds: 14 Queen,
3 Single (14 bedrooms)
Bathroom: 14 Ensuite
Tariff: B&B (continental)
Double $160, Single $140, All Credit Cards accepted.

Word of mouth built the reputation of Simpsons of Potts Point after it opened in 1988. In many ways it's still an insiders' hotel in a matchless location. The 1892 building is classified by the National Trust - its 14 bedrooms have private bathrooms, air-conditioning and heritage furnishings, and the building has high ceilings, spacious rooms, stained glass windows and grand hallways.
Simpsons is regarded as Sydney's finest bed and breakfast and has won State Awards for accommodation. It is located in quiet exclusive Potts Point and is only one mile from the heart of Sydney, within walking distance of some of the city's finest restaurants.

Sydney - Potts Point
Historic Boutique Hotel   NRMA ★★★★
Address: 122 Victoria Street,
Sydney-Potts Point, NSW 2011
Name: Victoria Court Sydney
Telephone: (02) 9357 3200
Fax: (02) 9357 7606
Email: vicsyd@ozemail.com.au(bb)
Beds: 22 King/Queen, 3 Single (25 bedrooms)
Bathroom: All with Ensuite
Tariff: B&B (continental) Double $99-$240,
Single $60-$240. Credit Cards.
Vouchers accepted May, June
Nearest Town: within Sydney

Victoria Court, whose charming terrace house dates from 1881, is centrally located on quiet, leafy Victoria Street in elegant Potts Point; the ideal base from which to explore Sydney. It is within minutes of the Opera House, the Central Business District and Beaches.
Friendly and personalised service is offered in an informal atmosphere and amidst Victorian charm. No two rooms are alike; most have marble fireplaces, some have four poster beds and others feature balconies with views over National Trust classified Victoria Street. All rooms have en-suite bathrooms, hairdryers, air-conditioning, colour television, radio-clock, coffee / tea making facilities and direct dial telephones. In the immediate vicinity are some of Sydney's most renowned restaurants and countless cafes with menus priced to suit all pockets. Public transport, car rental, travel agencies and banks are nearby. An airport bus operates to and from Victoria Court and security parking is available.
Home Page: http://www.VictoriaCourt.com.au

NEW SOUTH WALES

Sydney - Pymble
Self-contained Accommodation
Address: Please telephone
Name: "Pymble Cottage"
Telephone: (02) 9144 1256
Beds: 1 Double
(1 bedroom/spa bathroom/sitting room)
Bathroom: 1 Private
Tariff: B&B (continental) Double $105
Single $95. Children not catered for.
Nearest Town: Sydney - 30 minutes by rail

Surrounded by historic homes on Sydney's leafy North Shore, Pymble Cottage is nestled in cottage gardens up a tree-lined driveway. Secluded and peaceful, yet within easy walking distance of Pymble Station, the cottage is close to Ku-Ring-Gai National Park and a 1/2 hour drive to the Northern Beaches. St. Ives Shopping Centre and a variety of restaurants are also close by.
Guests have their own entry to a sitting room which includes a colour TV, fridge and microwave. Breakfast provisions, including fresh fruit in season are supplied.
The double bed has an electric blanket, and the private bathroom includes a spa bath. Linen is provided and guests may use the laundry, but are asked not to smoke in the house.

Sydney - Surry Hills
Homestay
Address: 249 Riley Street,
Surry Hills, NSW 2010
Name: The Cottage
Telephone: (02) 9212 7384
Fax: (02) 9211 0810 **Mobile**: (019) 336123
Beds: 2 Double, 1 Single (2 Bedrooms)
Bathroom: 1 Private, 1 Guests share
Tariff: B&B (continental) Double $80, Single $60.

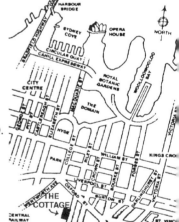

The Cottage is a charming 2 level cottage situated in Sydney's inner city area, with public transport at hand. It is ideally located for easy access to the many Sydney attractions. Walking distance to: City 15 minutes through beautiful Hyde Park. Capitol Theatre, Chinatown, Entertainment Centre, Darling Harbour, Art Gallery of New South Wales and Botanical Gardens 10 to 20 minutes. 2.5km to the Opera House, Circular Quay and the Rocks, 1.5km to the Sydney Stadium, Cricket Ground and Showground. Restaurants and cafes are 5-10 minutes walk away. The Airporter Shuttle Bus picks up and sets down at the door. My main interest is art. Part of the cottage is actually an Art Gallery, providing a unique environment in which to enjoy breakfast.
Non-smokers preferred.

Always have a phone card with you.
Most public phones do not take coins.

NEW SOUTH WALES

Sydney - Rose Bay
Superior Homestay   NRMA ★★★
Address: "Syl's Sydney Homestay", 75 Beresford Rd, Rose Bay
Name: Sylvia & Paul Ure
Telephone: (02) 9327 7079 **Fax**: (02) 9362 9292 **Mobile**: (0411) 350010
Email: homestay@infolearn.com.au
Beds: 3 Double, 4 Single (3 bedrooms)
Bathroom: 1 Ensuite, 1 Private, 1 Guest share
Tariff: B&B (continental) Double $90, $95 and $100. Single $60, $65 and $70. Children under 12 years $15. Extra person in room or flat $20 (aftr the first two people). Weekly and extended stay discounts available Feb-Nov. Self-contained Apartment $120 Dble. Credit Cards (BC/MC/VISA/AMEX). Vouchers accepted $10-$30 surcharge
Nearest Town: Sydney 6km: Bondi Beach 3 kms

Our Homestay was featured on the British TV series "Wish You were Here" which went to air in Dec 1991.

Rose Bay is one of Sydney's most beautiful inner city harbourside suburbs, close to Downtown Sydney, the Opera House and famous Bondi Beach. It is an excellent area for golf, tennis, windsurfing and sailing with several excellent restaurants within walking distance.

Sylvia and Paul have travelled extensively, love sport and were brought up in the area which is well serviced by bus, train and ferry. We have 3 outgoing children and two dogs.

Guests may enjoy all the facilities of our new home with extensive harbour views and we are delighted to share our hospitality in a relaxed informal setting with information about tours, sightseeing and transport. Guests may borrow tennis racquets etc or leave luggage while travelling further afield. All rooms have TVs.

Our self contained garden apartment is ideal for families (accommodates up to 6) and children are welcome. We provide tours of Sydney and surrounding areas. Babysitting by arrangement.

Bookings may be made by phone, fax or mail or e-mail.

NEW SOUTH WALES

Sydney - Ultimo
Homestay
Address: Please telephone
Name: Simone
Telephone: (02) 9552 6807 **Fax**: (02) 9552 6807
Beds: 2 Single (1 bedroom)
Bathroom: 1 Family share
Tariff: B&B (full) Per person: $50 per night, Children 12yrs & over at adult price, Dinner by arrangement $25pp. Vouchers accepted
Nearest Town: City of Sydney 1km

My modern, comfortable fly-screened 1st floor unit home has the perfect northerly aspect, overlooking a quiet leafy park, with native and other birds in abundance. It is not beneath any flight paths. Special visitor parking available. Convenient to all forms of transport: bus, train, airport, sea-plane, ferry, hydrofoil, Jet-Cat, water taxi, harbour cruises, monorail, and Light-Rail.
Close to the Sydney Opera House, Sydney Entertainment Centre, picture theatres, live theatres, restaurants, China Town, the Casino and Darling Harbour, venue for some Olympic Games events..
Tea/coffee making facilities always available with home-made biscuits/cake. I am happy to prepare meals to meet special dietary needs.
Laundry facilities/iron available. Lounge room and TV shared with host.
My home is a non-smoking area, but my verandah welcomes everyone.
Directions: *Please phone or fax.*

Gift Vouchers

Our B&B vouchers are for a double room for one night's B&B. They cost $89, and if you order one as a gift, we will include a free
Australian Bed & Breakfast Book
worth $16.95

Send your cheque to
Moonshine Press
59 Quirk Street
Dee Why
NSW 2099

NEW SOUTH WALES

Sydney - Woollahra
Homestay
Address: "Mayfield" 7 Magney Street, Woollahra, NSW 2025. Please phone to book.
Name: John-Ernest & Selma Maynard
Telephone: (02) 9369 2611 **Fax**: (02) 9369 2611
Beds: 1 Double, 2 Single (3 bedrooms)
Bathroom: 1 Ensuite, 1 Family share
Tariff: B&B (full) Double $80, Single $60, Children according to age. Vouchers accepted
Nearest Town: Sydney city centre 4km, Bondi Beach 3km.

Our cottage, circa 1906, is in a quiet leafy heritage listed cul-de-sac, ideally located for the visitor to easily explore and enjoy Sydney's varied attractions.
The 400 bus runs direct from the Airport to Bondi Junction Rail / Bus centre, only 3 minutes walk away.
Here is fast, frequent Rail / Bus transport in all directions: 5 minutes to Paddington's famous Saturday market, smart shops and vibrant atmosphere; 10 minutes city centre, 20 minutes to the Opera House and Darling Harbour; Bondi's surfing beach and cliff walks.
Elegant Woollahra impresses visitors with its charming old buildings. It contains many art galleries and antique shops. Our home is close to spacious 110 year old Centennial Park, with its lakes, bicycle and horseriding tracks.
Randwick Racecourse, Sydney Cricket Ground and Football Stadium are all a brief busride away. Excellent transport to University of NSW, University of Technology and Sydney University.
Widely travelled, we have featured in the Qantas booklet and have welcomed homestay guests for 16 years.
John, design engineer, speaks German and French and is interested in computers, world affairs and politics. Selma lectured on nutrition and enjoys cooking, reading, walking, art galleries and museums.
Hearty varied breakfasts our specialty. Complimentary variety of teas, coffee and homemade biscuits whenever you wish.
One Abyssinian cat. Please enjoy your smoking in the garden and verandahs.
We take pleasure in using our wide knowledge of Sydney to help our guests enjoy their stay and look forward to welcoming you.

Tell other travellers about your favourite B&Bs

NEW SOUTH WALES

Tamworth - Wallabadah
Farmstay+B&B
Address: "Warrawoona",
Wallabadah, NSW 2343
Name: Phillip & Margaret Carter
Telephone: (02) 6746 5663
Beds: 2 Twin, 1 Single (3 bedrooms)
Bathroom: 1 Guest share
Tariff: B&B (full) Double $65, Single $30,
Children negotiable; Dinner $17. Vouchers accepted
Nearest Town: Just 7km north of Wallabadah, 46km south of Tamworth

Wallabadah is approximately 4 1/2 hours drive from Sydney and Warrawoona is situated just north of Wallabadah on the New England Highway. A perfect place to stop overnight on your way north to Queensland or south to Sydney.
Our brick veneer home overlooks a valley and hills to the north and is set in a large garden.
We prepare stud cattle for shows and sales and often have several breeds of cattle being looked after at any one time. Often these cattle are some of the best in Australia. We also have fine wool Merino sheep.
A good Australian breakfast is offered to our guests and dinner is served in our large living room, in winter in front of an open fire. Guests have the use of their own bathroom.
5 minute drive Tourist Drive 23 Nundle & Hills of Gold & Hanging Rock.
Directions: *Please phone.*

Tamworth
Homestay+B&B   NRMA ★★★☆
Address: "Lalla Rookh Country House",
Werris Creek Road, Duri, NSW 2344
Name: Bob & Sue Moore
Telephone: (02) 6768 0216
Fax: (02) 6768 0330   **Mobile**: (015) 293938
Email: powderkg@zip.com.au
Beds: 2 Queen, 1 Double, 2 Single (4 bedrooms)
Bathroom: 2 Ensuite, 1 Guests share
Tariff: B&B (full) Double $86, Single $65; Dinner $26, No facilities for children.
No pets. Credit Cards (BC/MC/VISA/JCB). Vouchers accepted
Nearest Town: Tamworth - 20 km south on Werris Creek Road (Tourist Route 25)

You are assured of a warm and friendly welcome to Lalla Rookh where Sue and Bob have been entertaining guests for many years.
The home abounds with antiques, old furniture, a pottery collection, old books and a multitude of "Treasures" collected in Australia and overseas. Sue and Bob enjoy interesting and beautiful things and delight in sharing them with others. They also enjoy sharing good country cooking, Australian wines and interesting conversation - so dinner is a leisurely affair often lasting all evening!
Enjoy relaxing on the terrace, drinks in front of the fire, hearty breakfasts, fresh flowers, comfortable beds, large fluffy towels, wandering in the garden, watching the birds and admiring the view.
The area abounds with craft galleries and workshops, old towns and villages and has a gold mining history.
Only minutes from the New England Highway (Route 15) - an ideal stopping place between Sydney and Brisbane.
Home Page: http://www.atn.com.au/nsw/north/accom/lalla.htm.

Tamworth

Homestay/Farmstay or S.C. Garden Lodge
Address: "Laramee", Limbri Rd.
Kootingal, NSW 2352
Name: Laramee Country Home
Telephone: (02) 6764 4246
Fax: (02) 6764 4209
Mobile: (019) 915568
Beds: 2 Double, 6 Single (5 bedrooms)
Bathroom: 1 Private, 1 Guests share
Tariff: B&B (full) Double $88, Single $44, Children under 12yrs $22. Dinner $22 each. Self-contained garden lodge (sleeps 4) $70 night or $350 week. Vouchers accepted $9 surcharge
Nearest Town: Tamworth

Laramee is a traditional country home with vine-shaded verandahs, overlooking a large rambling garden with a first class tennis court. Inside, the atmosphere is warm and welcoming, with antiques and country furniture, fresh flowers, good books and every comfort. Julien serves delicious meals, from intimate dinners by the fire to sumptuous family meals in the dining room and memorable breakfasts in the sunny timber-lined kitchen. Julien gardens and enjoys drawing and watercolours and various handcrafts. She and Ross share a love of music, travel and their busy life on the 3600 acre property of beautiful hills and valleys. They have given pleasure to exhausted business people, outdoor adventurers, romantic honeymooners, frustrated city horse-lovers who want to ride or muster all day, dreamers, (who just like to be pampered and fed) overseas visitors who find the "real Australia" and families with young children who keep coming back.
Only 8 minutes from New England Highway - please telephone for directions.

Tamworth

B&B, Self-contained Accom.
Address: "Fresa Granja",
RMB 516F, Tamworth, 2340
Name: Helen & John
Telephone: (02) 6765 6766 or 6766 7114
Fax: (02) 6766 7285 **Mobile**: (014) 975392
Beds: 1 Queen, 1 Double, 2 Single (2 bedrooms)
Bathroom: 1 Guests share
Tariff: B&B (continental) Double $80, \Single $45, Children $20. Dinner $25.
Full breakfast on request. Vouchers accepted
Nearest Town: 10km south of Tamworth city.

Our modern, comfortable Spanish style home nestles in a grove of Pecan Trees on 33 acres. Our spacious self-contained guests accommodation adjoins the homestead and has views over the city and Goonoo Goonoo River. Facilities include its own modern bathroom and fully equipped kitchen for guests use only, where you may prepare your own meals or enjoy gourmet style meals prepared by your hosts. Suitable for overnight or longer stays.
We offer undercover parking and room for trailers and boats. You are minutes away from dining, entertaining and sporting facilities in the Country Music Capital of 40,000 people. John, a Stockbroker and Helen a Banker have travelled extensively overseas and within Australia with our family who have grown up and now living interstate. Children and pets by negotiation. Smoke free environment.
Prefer you to book before arrival.

NEW SOUTH WALES

Tamworth
Rural Homestay
Address: Stirling Rd.
Moore Creek, NSW 2340
Name: "Comlongon"
Telephone: (02) 6767 1100
Fax: (02) 67671046
Mobile: (041) 960 7308
Email: comlongon@rocketmail.com
Beds: 1 Double (1 bedroom)
Bathroom: 1 Family share
Tariff: B&B (full) Double $65,Single $40, Dinner $15-$20,
Credit Cards. Vouchers accepted
Nearest Town: 12km NW of Tamworth.

Comlongon is a modern brick home on 5 acres of natural bushland outside Tamworth. Be greeted with afternoon tea and enjoy the picturesque valley views from the verandahs. Air conditioning, a log fire, ceiling fans and electric blankets add to your comfort. Please order your choice of a 2-3 course meal or typical Aussie style BBQ when booking. Dine in the formal dining room or with the family. BYO. Breakfast can be full English style or the "house special" pancakes.
Tony and Susan are well-travelled and welcome individual travellers or couples into their home. Visitors will share a bathroom with their two young daughters. Your desire for solitude or companionship will be respected. Smokers are welcome to use the verandah. No pets please - two border collies and a cat!
Tamworth is an excellent half-way stopover between Sydney and Brisbane on the New England highway. Please phone for directions.

Taralga - Southern Tablelands
Homestay
Address: 35 Orchard Street
Taralga, 2580
Name: Walton-Green
Telephone: (02) 4840 2268
Beds: 2 Double, 1 Single
(3 bedrooms)
Bathroom: 1 Guests share
Tariff: B&B (full) Double $80,
Single $50.
Nearest Town:
45km north of Goulburn

This is a charming double storey, double brick residence built in 1938. Furnishings are simple yet elegant and reflect the charm reminiscent of yesteryear. Woodfires burn in winter and provide a warm and cosy atmosphere. Sweets, homemade cake and biscuits, tea or coffee are served on arrival. Enjoy delicious home cooked country style breakfast served in the family dining room overlooking the tranquil countryside.
Stroll around our village and admire the beautiful stone buildings, wonder through the craft shop or visit the Historical Museum and Settlers Cottage. The spectacular rugged mountain scenery, the Abercrombie River and the beautiful Wombeyan Caves Reserve are close by and a pleasant days outing.

Can't contact your host? Phone Directory Assistance.

Taree
Homestay and Self Contained Accommodation
Address: "Deans Creek Lodge"
Cnr. Deans Creek Rd. &
Bucketts Way, Tinonee, NSW 2430
Name: Brian & Pauline Carney
Telephone: (02) 6553 1257
Fax: (02) 6553 1187
Email: deansck@midcoast.com.au
Beds: 4 Double, 2 Single (5 bedrooms)
Bathroom: 2 Guests share
Tariff: B&B (full) Double $75-$85, Single $45-$55, Children P.O.A. Dinner on request. Credit Cards. Cottage Tariff on application. Vouchers accepted
Nearest Town: Tinonee 1km, Taree 8km

Be yourself, de-stress and try something different - is the theme of Deans Creek Lodge. This ten acre property is home and hobby farm for Brian and Pauline, who as "ex City Slickers" are dabbling at raising crops and calves. The contemporary style, environmentally friendly farm house is set amidst well established gardens which attract a wide variety of birdlife and overlooks Kiwarrak State Forest. Stay in our "Kingfisher Cottage", fully self-contained with everything you might expect in a stay at a country hideaway, from the wide, shady verandah to the well-appointed kitchen, to the welcoming, comfortable beds and of course the peaceful, rural views. Come and spend some time in the hassle free Manning Valley which is rich in history, dotted with hidden rainforest, flanked by numerous beaches and surrounded by miles of superb waterways. We provide in-house or fully self-contained stays in a peaceful, rural setting with country cooking and hospitality. This remarkable area deserves a visit and for those wishing to de-stress it is "just perfect".

Taree/Wingham
Farmstay/Self-contained Accom.
Address: "Tallowood Ridge"
79 Mooral Creek Road,
Cedar Party via Wingham, NSW 2429
Name: Ron & Shirley Smith
Telephone: (02) 6557 0438
Fax: (02) 6557 0438
Mobile: (014) 077228
Beds: 2 Double, 4 Single (3 bedrooms)
Bathroom: 1 Ensuite, 1 Private
Tariff: B&B (full) Double $55-$65,
Single $35-$40, Discount available for extra days. Children $20, Dinner $20pp by arrangement, Campervans $20. Vouchers accepted
Nearest Town: Wingham 8km, Taree 20km

Nestled in the heart of the picturesque Manning Valley "Tallowood Ridge" offers you the peace and quite of our country lifestyle. Our spacious modern home is set on 85 acres of indurating hills, forest trees and many colourful birds. The completely private guest suite has its own entrance into the spacious bed sitting room with ensuite, lounge, TV, games and books. The fully equipped breakfast room overlooks the salt water pool and magnificent views. We also have a fully equipped self-contained cabin which accommodates 4. We farm beef cattle and grow organic vegetables and herbs. Home made jams and farm eggs. Local attractions are only minutes away, giant Moreton Bay Figs in Wingham Bush, Historic Buildings, Museum, Golf Club, Bowling Club, Restaurants. 40 minutes drive to picturesque Ellenborough Falls and picnic area. No smoking inside please.

NEW SOUTH WALES

Tathra
Guest House
Address: 27 Bega Street, Tathra, NSW 2550
Name: Karen Jackson & Terry O'Leary
Telephone: (02) 6494 4084 (BH) & (02) 6494 1844 (AH) **Fax**: (02) 6494 5010
Beds: 3 Queen, 2 Single (4 bedrooms)
Bathroom: 1 Guests share
Tariff: B&B (full) Double $95, Single $65.
Nearest Town: Bega

Tathra Lodge Guesthouse is situated in the lovely seaside town of Tathra just 17 kilometres from Bega. The house is an early 1900 Federation style home, featuring lovely large rooms and pressed metal ceilings.
Marble fireplaces and polished floors are a main feature of the house as well as the expansive gardens.
It's just 5 minutes walk to the Beach and close to all public facilities.
A full breakfast is provided in the sunroom overlooking Tathra township and guests may also enjoy the comfort of the sitting room and outdoor sundeck, where native birdlife abound.
The other great advantage of Tathra Lodge Guesthouse is the incorporation of a Beauty Salon which adjoins the guesthouse. Full Beauty Therapy, Aromatherapy, Electrolysis and Solarium treatments are available to guests who may wish to indulge.
Bookings are essential and we feel sure that your stay at Tathra Lodge will be a rewarding and enjoyable experience.
Hosts Karen and Terry.

Tathra/Bermagui
Homestay,
Self-contained Accommodation
Address: Lot 42, Barrabookas Rd. Nth. Tanja, NSW 2550
Name: "Tanja Thyme"
Telephone: (02) 6494 0268
Beds: 2 Queen.
Bathroom: Homestay: 1 Family Share. Cabin: 1 Private
Tariff: B&B (full) Double $85, Single $70. Vouchers accepted $10 surcharge
Nearest Town: Bega, NSW 2550

A beguiling comfortable limestone residence with semi detached timber cabin. Suit couples for bed and breakfast or self contained holiday accommodation. Breakfast in private or together on verandah, overlooking tranquil valley with mountain vista.
Relax with a book or explore and enjoy our National Park, a wonderful combination of lagoons, sea caves, ocean beaches and outstanding bush walks.
Directions: *Tanja borders Mimosa Rocks National Park which is located 420 kms south of Sydney, 220 km south east of Canberra and 22 km north east of Bega. Access to Tanja Thyme Bed and Breakfast is via the Bermagui/Tathra Coast Rd. A warm Welcome is assured by Evelyn and her gregarious pets.*

There are some good tips for easier travel on page 7

NEW SOUTH WALES

Tea Gardens/Hawks Nest
Homestay/Farmstay
Address: Lot 9 Viney Creek Road,
Viney Creek via Hawks Nest
Name: Lavender Grove Farm
Telephone: (02) 4997 1411
Fax: (02) 4997 1411
Beds: 1 Queen, 1 Double,
2 Single (3 bedrooms)
Bathroom: 1 Private, 1 Family share
Tariff: B&B (full) Double $110-$130, Single $65-$90,
Children $20-$30, Campervans facilities, Credit Cards. Vouchers accepted surcharge.
Nearest Town: Hawks Nest/Tea Gardens

Lavender Grove Farm is 30 acres nestled amongst grazing land and pine forests just 10 minutes from Hawks Nest only 2 hours north of Sydney.
Our home is beautifully appointed and very comfortable, affording total privacy taking only one family (or couple) at a time, although very suitable for friends travelling together. Guests have full use of huge lounge with open log fire and bar area, own bathroom with spa bath, TV, video, sound system and baby grand piano. Bar fridge, tea/coffee making facilities with home baked goodies.
Beautiful solar heated, salt water pool. Laze on the large balcony, watch magical sunsets while kangaroos emerge. Spoil cows, chooks, ducks and Ben the horse. Close to sparkling clean beaches, Port Stephens, Myall river and lakes. Excellent golf course/club facilities, wonderful bush walks down original dirt roads. Full country breakfasts, free range eggs, delicious country cuisine. We aim to pamper our guests.

Tea Gardens/Hawks Nest
Bed & Breakfast Studios   NRMA ★★★★☆
Address: "The Bell Buoy Bed & Breakfast Studios on The Waterfront",
117 Marine Drive, Tea Gardens, NSW 2324
Name: Marion & Geoff Weymouth
Telephone: (02) 4997 1688 **Fax**: (02) 4997 1679
Beds: 2 Queen, 1 Single (2 suites/3 bedrooms)
Bathroom: 2 Ensuite
Tariff: B&B (full) Double $100-$130, Single $75-$95,
Children $25, Credit Cards (AMEX/BC/MC/VISA).
Vouchers accepted $30 surcharge

THE BELL BUOY
BED & BREAKFAST
STUDIOS
Australia's Holiday Coast
117 Marine Drive
(on the Waterfront)
Tea Gardens NSW 2324
Phone: 049 971688
Fax: 049 971679
Your Hosts
Marion & Geoff Weymouth

A scene of absolute serenity awaits you at Tea Gardens, a small slice of real Australia; gateway to the Myall Lakes N.P., Myall Coast and the blue water wonderland of Port Stephens. The Bell Buoy offers you the niceties of the traditional Bed & Breakfast with the luxury of 4 star waterfront, individual, ensuite studios for your comfort and privacy. Pamper yourselves at the Bell Buoy with comfy Queen beds, fluffy towels, snuggly robes, private champagne or a hearty country breakfast overlooking the river. The Bell Buoy is a short waterfront stroll to superb restaurants serving local gourmet seafood, shops, clubs and the famous Dolphin Watch, port and river cruises. See koalas, kangaroos, dolphins and dingoes in the wild; hire a boat or bike, enjoy 18 holes of golf, a rainforest or bush walk along the world famous Mungo Track or 41km of magnificent white sand beaches - all just 2 1/2 hours north of Sydney by expressway. "Go on! Pamper yourselves!"

NEW SOUTH WALES

Tenterfield
Self-contained Accommodation
Address: "Spring Valley",
Mt Lindesay Rd., Tenterfield
Name: Mike Rudge
Telephone: (02) 6736 1798
Beds: 1 Double, 2 Single (2 bedrooms)
Bathroom: 1 Private
Tariff: B&B (full) Double $70,
Single $50, Children $20, Dinner $20,
Credit Cards. Vouchers accepted
Nearest Town: Tenterfield

Spring Valley Cottage used to stable draft horses in the early 1900's. It is now renovated and furnished in warm Australiana style, set in its own garden.
The cottage is only a few metres from the homestead so our family is very pleased to help you feel at home and tell you about the unique Bald Rock and Boonoo Boonoo National Parks that are only 25 minutes drive from the property. The Granite Belt wineries are 15 minutes away.
Guests can enjoy farm walks where they are met by friendly horses, goats and cattle. Spring Valley is an Alpaca stud so we are always happy to tell people more about these beautiful animals. There are plenty of animals only a short walk from the cottage. For a quiet night on your way North / South or a weekend of country relaxation, bushwalking or wine tasting, Spring Valley is a superb base.

Gift Vouchers

Our B&B vouchers are for a double room for one night's B&B. They cost $89, and if you order one as a gift, we will include a free
Australian Bed & Breakfast Book
worth $16.95

Send your cheque to
Moonshine Press
59 Quirk Street
Dee Why
NSW 2099

NEW SOUTH WALES

Termeil
Guest House   NRMA ★★★★☆
Address: Old Princes Highway, Termeil, NSW 2539
Name: William & Michele Barry
Telephone: (02) 4457 1188 **Fax**: (02) 4457 1498
Beds: 6 Double, 3 Family (9 bedrooms)
Bathroom: All ensuite
Tariff: B&B (full) Double $144-$188, Single $100-$125, Children half price. Dinner $40. Credit Cards.
Nearest Town: Ulladulla, 22km north. Batemans Bay 30km south. Both on the Princes Highway.

You know there is something special about Barry's when you come down the steep drive and wind your way through the trees to discover the Guest House hidden amongst 14 hectares of semi-tropical rainforest and bushland.
Set on beautifully manicured lawns and gardens, the Guest House interweaves traditional turn of the century design with the finest standards of comfort.
This private hideaway has nine individually furnished bedrooms each with aspects of unspoilt countryside. The wide verandahs let you watch the abundant birdlife; or you can settle in the reading room and enjoy complimentary afternoon tea.
The majestic windows, gabled ceiling and antique style furniture in the Dining Room provide an idyllic setting for your evening meal. Dinner is an important part of every guest's stay. The menu changes nightly offering fresh local produce prepared to the highest standard.
A leisurely game of tennis, an invigorating swim, a jog on the Forest Fitness Trail or a game of croquet will help you unwind.
The Guest House's location is framed between the ocean and the mountains. Secluded beaches are only ten minutes away in the car at Bawley Point and the Budawang Ranges are adjacent, offering thousands of hectares of natural beauty ready to be explored!
The winner of the NSW Tourism Awards for Excellence' "Award of Distinction"-1994 and 1995 and 'finalist' in 1996.

Terrigal see Central Coast
Tilba Tilba see Narooma

NEW SOUTH WALES

Tumut
Homestay   NRMA ★★★★
Address: "Cramarric",
East Street, Tumut, NSW 2720
Name: Marianne & Peter Read
Telephone: (02) 6947 2122
Beds: 1 Queen, 1 Double,
 3 Single (4 bedrooms)
Bathroom: 1 Ensuite,
1 Guests share, 1 Family share
Tariff: B&B (full) Double $55-$75, Single $30-$40,Dinner $25. Vouchers accepted
Nearest Town: Tumut (2 km South from PO)

Winner of the Tumut Shire 1993 Major Award for Best Contribution to Tourism and featured on TV's "Healthy, Wealthy and Wise". "Cramarric" offers quality accommodation at modest tariff. Set in two acres, the hand-crafted home is a smorgasboard of medieval features including inglenook log fires, panelled rooms and a variety of ceiling styles. Fish ponds, two lakes and a 'snug' add to the cottage garden.
Tumut is noted for its scenery, autumn colours, excellent trout fishing and the Hume and Hovell walking track with sections to suit all levels. Horse riding, white water rafting, the Snowy Hydro-Electric Scheme, Yarrangobilly Caves. Adelong Falls Gold Battery, Batlow Orchards and Mount Selwyn Snowfields - all less than one hours drive provide plenty of diversity for the curious traveller.
Complimentary drinks, homemade jams and marmalades and biscuits, add a touch of class.
Directions: *From PO follow Cooma signs to 60/100 Km delimit then left into East Street.*

Tumut
Homestay
Address: "Lombardi Lodge"
Lacmalac Road, Tumut, NSW
Name: Catherine Chittick
Telephone: (02) 6947 3905
or answer machine: (069) 473925
Fax: (02) 6947 3925
Beds: 2 Double, 1 Single (3 bedrooms)
Bathroom: 1 Private, Guests share
Tariff: B&B (full) Double $80, Single $45,
Children P.O.A. Vouchers accepted
Nearest Town: Tumut 1km from town centre,
Wynyard St. over old bridge 1st turn right up Lacmalac Road.

Lombardi Lodge is a comfortable modern homestead with bullnosed verandahs set in 20 acres of parkland only 1km from the Tumut town centre - peace and tranquillity is assured. We have owned a peach orchard and beef cattle stud in the area for many years and are pleased to assist visitors with advice about the many local attractions. Enjoy genuine country hospitality with open fires or air conditioned comfort as the season dictates. A full country breakfast is served on the sunny outside courtyard with stunning views of the Snowy Mountain Ranges, bird life abounds and there are many varied walks available through the avenues of elm and poplar trees for which Tumut is famous. A true all season holiday destination with a great diversity of outdoor activity and sport, unequalled anywhere in inland Australia. Great walking country, trout fishing in lakes and rivers. Mt Selwyn snowfields and clean crisp air that gets your appetite going. Please phone for bookings.

NEW SOUTH WALES

Tumut
Farmstay
Address: "Yurunga", PO Box 79, Tumut, 2720
Name: Olive & John Knox
Telephone: (069) 472306
Beds: 1 Double, 5 Single (3 bedrooms)
Bathroom: 1 Ensuite, 1 Guests share
Tariff: B&B (continental) Ensuite $70, Double $60, Single $40, Children by arrangement.
Vouchers accepted
Nearest Town: Tumut

Set in a beautiful garden, 3km (the outskirts) of Tumut on the main Gundagai / Tumut Road, 'Yurunga' is a sheep and cattle property extending to the Tumut River. This friendly comfortable home is set in a beautiful award winning all seasons country garden with wonderful accompanying bird life. Whether your prefer quiet anonymity or personalised hospitality, John and Olive welcome you to enjoy sharing the delights of their treasured home.
Golf, bowls, water sports, walking tracks, snow skiing, 'Festival of the Falling Leaves', scenic air flights, day trips, restaurants, all abound. The engineering feats of the Snowy Mountain Scheme and timber industry are very interesting.
Be assured your needs will be met for a relaxed and pleasant stay from our picturesque Tumut location.

Tumut
Homestay+Self-contained Accom.
NRMA ★★★☆
Address: "Willowbank"
8 Sydney Street, Tumut, NSW 2720
Name: Leo & Janet Sturman
Telephone: (02) 6947 2678 (Ans. machine)
Fax: (02) 6947 2678
Beds: 2 Queen, 2 King Singles (3 bedrooms)
Bathroom: 1 Ensuite, 1 Family share
Tariff: B&B (full) Double $55, Single $35.
Dinner 2 course $15, 3 course $20: One self-

contained accommodation which has queensize bed, ensuite, full kitchen, microwave, R/C air conditioning, colour TV and all linen provided, is $60 double and doesn't include breakfast. We can serve a full breakfast either in the unit or the home for an extra $9.50 per person or continental breakfast for $5 per person.
Credit cards (BC/MC/VISA). Vouchers accepted
Nearest Town: Tumut 1km (max).

What makes "Willowbank" an ideal place to stay? Just about everything worth seeing and doing. Fishing, bushwalking and skiing are 'just around the corner'. We offer very comfortable beds, great food and good company. Your hosts have had interesting lifestyles. Janet is an ex-stewardess with an international airline and Leo, retired early from academia, has been / is artist playwright, actor, poet among other things, so there is no shortage of good conversation.
The house and facilities are modern but with a collection of objet d'art and old furniture collected over the years which makes for a decor both comfortable and interesting. Tumut is one of the friendliest towns on earth and well worth a browse. An indication of the lifestyle is that it doesn't have one traffic light - see for yourself! Our non smoking family of four includes two cats. We tailor breakfasts to any taste, just ask! We would love to make you welcome! - (But it pays to book!)

NEW SOUTH WALES

Tumut
Homestay
Address: "Crawley House"
55 Carey Street,
Tumut, NSW 2720
Name: Ron & Pat Morrison
Telephone: (02) 6947 1246
Mobile: (014) 965336
Beds: 1 Double,
2 Single (2 bedrooms)
Bathroom: Family share
Tariff: B&B (full) Double $55,
Single $30, Credit Cards.
Nearest Town: Tumut

Crawley House is a Victorian home set in the rich Tumut Valley 5 minutes walk from the central business area and 10 minutes to the river and parks. The property was first acquired by Christopher William Crawley of Junee by Crown Grant. The house with large verandahs and open fireplaces is furnished with antique furniture. Bedrooms have ceiling fans, electric blankets, lambs wool underlays and gowns are provided. Tumut is famous for its avenues of elm and poplar trees, river walks and trout fishing. Mt Selwyn snowfields, Kosciusko National Park and Yarrango Billy Caves are less than one hours drive.

Tweed Heads Hinterland
Homestay
Address: Lot 6 Thoroughbred Place, Terranora, NSW
Name: Nanga Mai Lodge". Hosts: Graeme & Dale Sambrook
Telephone: (07) 5590 4699
Beds: 1 Queen, 1 Double (2 bedrooms) - We only take one party at a time.
Bathroom: 1 Private
Tariff: B&B (full) Double $70, Single $45, Sorry children not catered for.
  Vouchers accepted
Nearest Town: Tweed Heads/Coolangatta 10km north

Our home is situated on a hill with a panoramic view over a rural valley all the way to the sea.
Features include 1 double, 1 queen bedroom with a private bathroom and separate sitting room allowing guests their own space and privacy. A full breakfast can be enjoyed in our dining area or on the verandah overlooking the swimming pool and the stunning view.
Our climate is sub-tropical and the area offers many holiday attractions, beaches, scuba diving, fishing, riding, bush walking, golf, tennis; craft markets, clubs and restaurants abound. Mt Warning National Park is only 20 mins drive away and the bright lights of the Gold Coast 35 mins away - This is also a good place to simply relax! We are happy to share our beautiful place and will do everything we can to make your stay memorable and enjoyable. No smoking in the house. Please phone ahead. Bookings essential.

Uki see Murwillumbah

Tell other travellers about your favourite B&Bs

Ulladulla

Guest House+Self-contained Accom.   NRMA ★★★★☆
Address: "Ulladulla Guest House", 39 Burrill Street, Ulladulla, 2539
Name: Andrew & Elizabeth Nowosud
Telephone: (02) 4455 1796
Beds: 7 King/Queen, 2 Double, 2 Single (9 bedrooms)
Bathroom: 9 Ensuite
Tariff: B&B (full) Double $90-$170, Single $80-$160, Credit Cards.
  Vouchers accepted Garden suite only, off peak midweek - surcharge $10.
Nearest Town: Ulladulla

Award winning Ulladulla Guest House is beautifully and conveniently located in the heart of the fishing village of Ulladulla, overlooking the picturesque harbour.
Originally a typically 1940's holiday cottage, it has been imaginatively extended and updated and now offers luxurious ensuite accommodation with spacious, well-equipped rooms having custom-designed furniture and original artwork. Executive suites include a marble bathroom with spa. Two self-contained units are also available.
Surrounded by lush sub-tropical gardens, the Guest House is perfectly suited to a relaxing holiday. After a leisurely gourmet breakfast, guests have the choice of lingering in the lounges surrounded by African artwork; ambling outside with a book to find a secluded nook; plunging into the heated pool or one of the spas; enjoying a sauna after a work out in the gym or exploring the many attractions of the South Coast, including bushwalking, diving, fishing, golfing and numerous other activities.

Uralla see Armidale

NEW SOUTH WALES

Urunga
Bed & Breakfast   NRMA ★★★☆
Address: 4 Morgo Street, Urunga, NSW 2455
Name: Pilot House
Telephone: (02) 6655 6090 **Fax**: (02) 66556090
Beds: 3 Queen, 1 Single, (4 bedrooms)
Bathroom: 1 Ensuite, 2 Private
Tariff: B&B (special), Double $110, Single $60, Dinner $25
Nearest Town: Coffs Harbour 20km

The Pilot House is ideally situated in the heart of Urunga, halfway between Sydney and Brisbane. It was built on a rise in 1868 to accommodate the pilot who assisted ships, laden with precious timbers, to navigate the entrance of the Bellinger River into the Pacific Ocean. Your hosts Erika and son Michael, who both have travelled worldwide, are looking forward to caring for you during your stay. Spectacular views from the verandah make breakfast a highlight and relaxing by the palm shaded pool a carefree and exhilarating experience. Within walking distance you can:-

- *enjoy a round of golf at the Urunga Golf course*
- *try your skill at the local bowling club*
- *catch a fish in the Bellinger River or in the sea*
- *stroll along the footbridge to the beach*

Within 25km radius you can visit:-
- *Coffs Harbour's lively seaport*
- *Bonville International Golf Course*
- *Bellingen - quaint, historical town*
- *Dorrigo Plateau with several national parks ideal for birdwatching - and bushwalks.*

Wagga Wagga
"Boutique" Guest House
Address: 102 Kincaid Street, Wagga Wagga, NSW 2650
Name: Crepe Myrtle
Telephone: (02) 69214 757
Fax: (02) 69214 757
Beds: 4 Queen, 1 Single (4 bedrooms)
Bathroom: 2 Guests share
Tariff: B&B (special) Double $95, Single $75, Sorry No children, Credit Cards (MC/BC/Visa/Amex). Vouchers accepted $15 surcharge
Nearest Town: In Wagga 1 1/2 km Post Office, 2 1/2 hours Canberra

This award winning guest house as featured on "Getaway" and rated four stars by the Sydney Morning Herald is a recently restored 1870's former hotel, nestled in the heart of Wagga Wagga. Just a short walk to the main street and Murrumbidgee River. It's perfect for that short break and offers colonial yet stylish luxury. Four bedrooms are furnished with forged iron queen beds, crisp cotton sheets, fluffy towelling robes and chocolates. It offers two bathrooms, library, formal lounge, breakfast / sitting room and a paved shady courtyard surrounded by cottage gardens. The gourmet breakfast is a highlight! Freshly squeezed orange juice, fruit platter and natural yoghurt followed by home baked muffins or scones, croissants, wholegrain breads - homemade jams / marmalades, cream cheese then espresso coffee or your choice of teas.
Kim an artist and John a chef and collector of Australian memorabilia will ensure a memorable stay! Upon arrival you are soon offered fresh coffee or tea and baked treats, log fires have already been lit and all only a few minutes walk to antique shops, restaurants and gardens. Sorry no facilities for children.

NEW SOUTH WALES

Wagga Wagga
Self-contained Bed & Breakfast
NRMA ★★★☆
Address: 46 Murray St, Wagga Wagga, NSW 2650
Name: Windsor Cottage Bed & Breakfast
Telephone: (069) 214451
Mobile: (014) 639423
Beds: 2 Double (2 bedrooms)
Bathroom: 1 Guests share
Tariff: B&B (special) Double $85, Single $70, Children welcome, Credit Cards (BC/MC/VISA). Vouchers accepted
Nearest Town: In central Wagga, 500 metres Wagga Base Hospital

Windsor Cottage, lovingly restored by Carole and Jeff, is centrally located, close to shops and restaurants. It offers the privacy of self-contained accommodation or total pampering by your hosts. The charm and comfort of its antique beds, Damask linen, electric blankets and tartan robes extend to the cosiness of the sitting room with its log fire. The spacious bathroom boasts a claw-foot bath and separate shower, plus an adjoining toilet and traditional 'outhouse'. A rustic farmhouse kitchen overlooks the cottage garden with shady paved area and off-street parking at the rear. As a Home Economist, Carole expertly presents, freshly squeezed orange juice, spiced fruit compote with natural yoghurt, home-baked muffins, Brioche buns, whole grain breads with homemade jams / marmalade. Finally enjoy Italian coffee or your choice of English teas. Alternatively, treat yourself to a cooked breakfast of Eggs Benedict. An Irish welcome awaits you with afternoon tea served on arrival.

Wagga Wagga
B&B Self-contained Accom.
Address: Hillary Street, North Wagga Wagga
Name: Wagga Wagga Country Cottages
Telephone: (02) 6921 1539
Beds: 1 King/Queen, 1 Double, 2 Single (2 bedrooms)
Bathroom: Private
Tariff: B&B (continental) Double $85, extra person $15. Credit Cards.
Nearest Town: Wagga Wagga, Junee

Wagga Wagga is approximately halfway between Sydney and Melbourne, so is a great stop-over place.
Our cottages are 4 minutes out of town with elevated rural views of the country side. If you like peace and quiet and the privacy of self-contained accommodation you will enjoy what we offer.

NEW SOUTH WALES

Wagga Wagga
Homestay
Address: Lagoonside Bed & Breakfast
1 Beckwith Street, Wagga Wagga 2650
Name: Lagoonside Bed and Breakfast
Telephone: (02) 6921 1308
Fax: (02) 6921 1332
Mobile: 0417 202 123
Email: idonald@wts.com.au
Beds: 1 Double, 2 Single
Bathroom: 1 Guest Share. Thick towelling robes.
Tariff: B&B (full or continental) Double $83, Single $63. Not suitable for children. Credit Cards: Bankcard, Mastercard, Visa. Vouchers accepted
Nearest Town: Wagga Wagga

Enjoy the lovingly restored 1890 Victorian home (recognized by the Heritage Act) overlooking the Wollundry lagoon with its peacefulness and abundant birdlife... Enjoy the central heating and log fire at breakfast to keep you snug in winter and the breezy evaporative cooling system for comfortable summer living... Enjoy the mixture of early Australian and European furniture... Enjoy the comfort of your host's lounge and sitting rooms... Enjoy the verandahs to catch the northern winter sun and to find the cooling summer breeze... Enjoy the tranquil garden setting to while away your waiting time with a book or your thoughts... Enjoy an easy level walk beside the lagoon and past interesting older homes to the centre of town where you will find restaurants, cinemas, theatres etc. Whatever you need for your stay in Wagga Wagga is available when you enjoy the hospitality of Maggi and Ian Donald. Newly listed .... awaiting rating.
Home Page: www.wagga.net.au/~idonald

Walcha
Homestay
Address: "Strathleigh",
Woolbrook, NSW 2354
Name: Anne & Alex Robson
Telephone: (02) 6777 5812
Fax: (02) 6777 5812
Beds: 1 Double, 2 Twin (3 bedrooms)
Bathroom: 1 Guests share
Tariff: B&B (full) Double $70, Single $50, Children catered for, Dinner $20pp. Vouchers accepted
Nearest Town: Walcha

Strathleigh is conveniently located just 6km off the Oxley Highway, halfway between Sydney and Brisbane, and 70km from Tamworth and Armidale.
We run cattle and sheep on 3000 acre property of undulating to hilly country. The McDonald River runs through the property, offering great trout fishing and lovely picnic spots. You may like to spend extra time observing or, hands-on with farm activities such as mustering or shearing in season.
We have a tennis court and some marvellous scenery for bushwalkers in kangaroo country.
Enjoy a pleasant trip on the XPT from Sydney to Walcha Road Station and return the next morning, or stay a few days.

NEW SOUTH WALES

Walcha - New England
Wilderness Retreat & Farmstay+SC Accom.
Address: "Cheyenne", Walcha 2354
Name: Sue & Burgh Blomfield
Telephone: (02) 67779 172 **Fax**: (02) 67779 117
Beds: 1 Double, 3 Single (3 bedrooms)
Bathroom: 1 Private
Tariff: B&B (full) Double $80, Single $50, Children negotiable. Dinner $25. Campervan facilities available. Extra meals and weekly rates available on application. Vouchers accepted
Nearest Town: Walcha 40km

"Cheyenne" Wilderness Retreat - perched at the top of a mountainous gorge at the edge of the Oxley Wild Rivers National Park. Situated midway between Sydney and Brisbane, "Cheyenne" provides you the chance to get away from it all. Peace and tranquillity are the most outstanding features of this delightful hideaway together with its breathtaking views. Complement this with a variety of bushwalks into the gorge and around the property; plentiful wildlife and superb photographic opportunities.

And ... no where else can you feed endangered rock wallabies outside your cottage most evenings.

Cheyenne is unique - not only is it a wilderness retreat but a Farmstay, being a working sheep and cattle property with plenty for children to do and see, including feeding barnyard animals, watching sheep dogs working, shearing demonstrations; milking the cow; and spotlighting nocturnal animals.

Your accommodation is a cosy self-contained 3 B/R cottage with modern facilities and the warmth of a wood heater. Simply enjoy it and relax.

Many homes have facilities for campervans.
The ideal camping spot with electricity, bathroom,
laundry and friendly hospitality.
Tell campervanners about this when you see them.

NEW SOUTH WALES

Walcha - New England
Wilderness Self-cont. Farmstay Retreat
Address: "Hole Creek", Walcha, NSW 2354
Name: Rob & Katrina Blomfield
Telephone: (02) 6777 9189 (after 6pm) **Fax**: (02) 6777 9188 **Mobile**: 019 650 039
Beds: 2 Queen, 8 Singles
Bathroom: 1 Ensuite, 1 Private
Tariff: B&B (continental) Double $100, Single $50, Children under 12 years $30, Dinner $30 (BYO); Self-cont. rates: $45pp, $25 children under 12 years, Extra meals & weekly rates available on application. All linen provided. Bookings essential.
Nearest Town: Walcha 33km (midway between Sydney & Brisbane)

Relax and enjoy the best of the country — rugged mountain ranges — the Australian bush — wildlife — stars — authentic farm life — wilderness — solitude. They're all part of your holiday when you stay at Bloomfields Crossing - your own secluded country homestead bordering the magnificent Macleay Gorges Wilderness on a 1600 ha (4000 acre) fine wool merino stud and cattle property. Our aim has been to provide everything you need for a perfect country holiday with your family and friends in complete comfort and seclusion including slow combustion fire, log fire, electric blankets, laundry facilities. There is a fully equipped country kitchen with dishwasher, microwave and outside BBQ. You can spread out and relax in one of the two living areas and sunroom or enjoy the scenery from the spacious verandah. You can also enjoy spectacular bush walks, farm activities and farm tours, bush picnics, tennis on the main homestead clay court, sailing or eel fishing. See one of the deepest and most spectacular cliffs in Australia - over 400 mtrs - offering breathtaking views into the gorge below. We look forward to sharing our beautiful property with you.

NEW SOUTH WALES

Walcha
Bed & Breakfast   NRMA ★★★☆
Address: PO Box 51, Walcha, 2354
Name: "Country Mood B&B"
Host: Louise Gill
Telephone: (02) 6777 2877
Fax: (02) 67772877   **Mobile**: (018) 247854
Beds: 1 Queen, 1 Double, 1 Single (1 bedroom)
Bathroom: 1 Private
Tariff: B&B (full) Double $70,
Single $50, Children $8, Dinner $15pp. Vouchers accepted
Nearest Town: Walcha - 5km: west of Walcha on Oxley Highway

Country Mood — Country Hospitality:
Relax in seclusion and enjoy unique part of rural Australia in tasteful guest quarters - nestled amongst the garden terraces on our cattle & sheep property, "Wilgar". Attractively located in the hills of Walcha, with breakfast served in our elevated sunroom (or verandah) overlooking the tree-tops! Direct access to garden and tennis court. Perfect stopover between Sydney (5 hrs) and Brisbane (6 hrs) and a scenic drive via Gloucester. Plenty to see and do nearby — gorges, Wilderness, National Parks, golf course adjacent, deer farm, trout fishing, birdwatching, historical cottage, sculpture park. See our clear star filled skies at night and may experience snow in Winter. Tea/coffee making, fridge, TV, music, iron, delicious dinner on request. Our pets welcome yours!
We're well travelled, both overseas and Australia and love meeting all visitors. I serve a hearty breakfast. Stay overnight or stay awhile - only 1 hour from Tamworth and 40 mins Armidale.

Walcha
B&B Homestay   NRMA ★★☆
Address: 23E Fitzroy Street
Walcha NSW 2354
Name: John Fenwicke
Telephone: (067) 772 713
Fax: (067) 772 892   **Mobile**: 0417 243 814
Beds: 1 Queen, 2 single (2 bedrooms)
Bathroom: 1 Family Share
Tariff: B&B (full) Double $70, Single $35,
Dinner $15, Children half price.
Credit Cards Vouchers accepted
Nearest Town: Walcha (in the middle of town)

You are invited to enjoy living in this historic Terrace Home. Its colourful history old world charm and delightful atmosphere where you are treated as friends this 110 year old home is right in town, and is kept warm and has electric blankets.
There is only one "Walcha" in the world (pronounced "Wolka" an aboriginal sound). Discovered by John Oxley in 1818 the area is on the top of the Great Dividing range. The mountain air is clear and pure, there are wonderful waterfalls, breathtaking views of the Gorges and lovely walks to see our native animals in their natural environment.
This little town has friendly people, restaurants, clubs and sporting clubs. It is a good shopping town, or you can enjoy the finest trout fishing streams in NSW. A most charming building, Fenwicke House is just over the Apsley river bridge travelling east in Fitzroy Street.

Wallabadah
Homestay/Farmstay/B&B
Address: "Gemmawalla"
Name: "Gemmawalla" B&B
Telephone: (067) 471319
Beds: 6 Single (3 bedrooms)
Bathroom: 1 Private, 1 Family share
Tariff: B&B (full) Double $70, Single $40. Dinner $20 pp. Vouchers accepted
Nearest Town: Quirindi

"Gemmawalla" may be found 13km south of Wallabadah just off the New England Highway and just 45 mins from Tamworth - Country Music Capital. In our large weatherboard homestead we offer 2 bedrooms with twin beds and one twin room with private sitting room, spacious living area, large verandahs set in an attractive garden. We operate a mixed farming enterprise breeding fine wool merino sheep, beef cattle, with some cropping.

Our guests may enjoy a 4 wheel drive tour of the property with a commentary on the farming activities, magnificent views and abundant kangaroos and other wildlife. Alternatively you may choose to sit on the verandah and relax in the sun or wander along the creek and enjoy a picnic or barbeque.

Your hosts Geoffrey and Margaret have lived on "Gemmawalla" for over 30 years and are happy to share their home and experiences with guests.

Wallabadah also see Tamworth
Wangi Wangi see Lake Maquarie

Wellington
Self-contained Accom, Homestay
Address: The Cottage, "Gowan Green", Baker's Swamp, 2820
Name: Howard & Lindy Harris
Telephone: (02) 6846 7209
Fax: (02) 6846 7209
Beds: 1 Queen, 4 Single (3 bedrooms)
Bathroom: 1 Private, separate toilet
Tariff: Cottage $60 double per day. Children and extra adults $10 per person. Linen included. Gourmet breakfast basket if required. B&B (full) Double $80, Single $60, Dinner $25. Vouchers accepted includes free linen.
Nearest Town: 35kms south of Wellington

We know you'll love it here - everybody has so far! Sample country living to the fullest.
You'll be nestled beside the Bell River - children's explorer country and an artist's delight. There's 1600 acres to discover. Visit the Dubbo Zoo, nearby Wellington Caves, Arboretum or go goldpanning and wine tasting. Join in farming activities, cycle in safety or just relax in the peaceful surrounds.
Your own cosy cottage provides all the comforts of home - electric blankets, fluffy doonas, gas heating or open fire (wood provided), air conditioning and washing machine. The pine kitchen is fully equipped and there is a gas BBQ in the garden. Overnighters welcome.
Directions: *"Mud map" available.*

NEW SOUTH WALES

Wellington
Homestay/Farmstay/SC Accom.   NRMA ★★★☆
Address: "Glen Mitchell", Wellington, 2820 NSW
Name: Kim & Scott McConochie
Telephone: (068) 452287 **Fax**: (068) 452650
Beds: 3 Double, 5 Single (4 bedrooms)
Bathroom: 1 Ensuite, 1 Family share, 1 extra
Tariff: B&B (full) Double $90, Single $60, Family rates available. Dinner $20pp.
Campervans welcome.   Vouchers accepted during school terms
Nearest Town: Wellington is 18km south of home.

A warm relaxed welcome awaits you at Kim & Scotts interesting and comfortable homestead. Extremely large with a mixture of old and new. Guests have independent access to their private accommodation, or sleepout with its own kitchenette and bathroom, greatly used by families.
All is set in a picturesque garden, full of delightful birds and also sports a tennis court, which has been accepted for the ABC's Open Garden Scheme in Oct 96 & 97.
The family is third generation, operating a mixed enterprise of wool, cattle, cropping and a prime lamb "Texel" stud set in 1993 being one of the first to Aust. Looking after these sheep are Marema Shepherd Dogs. There are the usual farm animals with children loving to collect the eggs.
Two days isn't enough to see and do all the activities available within our Wellington, Dubbo, Mudgee district, but come and take time out with us.
An Aussie Host member.

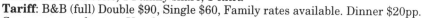

Private bathroom is for your use exclusively,
Guests share means you may be sharing with other guests,
Family share means you will be sharing with the family.

NEW SOUTH WALES

Wellington
Homestay
Address: 'Argyle',
Wellington, NSW 2820
Name: Argyle B&B Homestay
Telephone: (02) 6845 1770
Fax: (02) 6845 4092
Mobile: (019) 151 461
Beds: 1 Queen, 3 Single, (2 bedrooms)
Bathroom: 1 Ensuite, 1 Family share
Tariff: B&B (full), Double $75, Single $40, Dinner $20 per person, Children concession. Campervan facilities. Credit cards accepted. Vouchers accepted
Nearest Town: Wellington

Argyle is a comfortable country homestead on a 3000 acre family property. We offer our home for a tranquil stopover or as a base whilst visiting the many attractions in the area. Wellington boasts its unique Phosphate Mine, Caves, Burrendong Dam & Arboretum, Angora Rabbit Farm and Aboriginal Artefacts. Mount Arthur and its scenic bush walks is ten minutes away as is the 18 hole golf course on the picturesque Bell River. Argyle' is just 40 minutes drive from Western Plains Zoo and the city of Dubbo. We are situated on the road from Dubbo to Mudgee renowned for its good wines and wineries. Historic Gulgong is also in close proximity. You arrive at 'Argyle' after a comfortable 4 hour drive from Sydney or the central coast. Visitors are more than welcome to walk around our farm and take in the many aspects of country life. Three course dinners and country hospitality a specialty. **Directions**: *"Argyle" is situated 10 kilometres from Wellington on Campbells Lane left off the Wellington Mudgee Road.*

Wellington
Homestay B&B
Address: "Carinya Homestay",
111 Arthur Street, Wellington, NSW 2820
Name: Miceal & Helen O'Brien
Telephone: (02) 6845 4320/home
(02) 6845 1459/business
Fax: (02) 6845 3089
Mobile: (015) 459 794
Email: staywell@well-com.net.au.
Beds: 1 Queen, 1 Double, 5 Single, Cot available (3 bedrooms)
Bathroom: 1 Guests share
Tariff: B&B (full) Double $75, Single $65, Dinner $25, Children $15, Dinner $25. Vouchers accepted
Nearest Town: Wellington

Better service, better business.

"Carinya" is one of Wellington's finest Edwardian homes, surrounded by spacious gardens. Pool, tennis court, BBQ area and billiard table available. Easy to find on the southern approach to Wellington (from Orange) on the Mitchell Highway (opp. BP Service Station) but still so peaceful and private. Wellington has many fine atrractions: Lake Burrendong, Burrendong Arboretum, the Wellington Caves complex, and the Wellington Gateway Project.
Wellington's historic buildings are unique, numerous and very significant. You will find Wellington is close to Mudgee, Parkes, Geurie and Dubbo. Dinner extra and by arrangement. Parking and cot available. Children frequent adults welcome. Why not visit our **Home Page**: http://www.well-com.net.au/~staywell/

NEW SOUTH WALES

Wellington
Guest Homestead
Address: "Narroogal Park Guest Homestead", Narroogal Road, Wellington, NSW 2820
Telephone: (068) 467 223
Fax: (068) 467 224   **Mobile**: (015) 459 698
Beds: 3 Queen, 2 Double, 13 Single (9 bedrooms)
Bathroom: 3 Ensuite, 1 Guests share
Tariff: B&B (full) Double $120, Single $65, Dinner $20, Children $20. Credit cards.
Nearest Town: Wellington

Within 1 hour's drive of narroogal Park are day trips for fascinating places: famous Western Plains Zoo, Dubbo; Wellington Caves; Giant radio telescope, Parkes; Historic Gulgong; Wineries of surrounding area and Mudgee. Lake Burrendong 3 1/2 capacity of Sydney Harbour is only minutes away.
Step back in time to an era of relaxed country life at NARROOGAL PARK GUEST HOMESTEAD, 22kms south of Wellington, first established in the rich Bell River Valley in 1830.
Experience a holiday with old style luxury and service in the tranquil surroundings of this lovely property growing flowers for export and general grazing.
This historic 9 bedroom homestead with wide cool verandahs overlooks the swimming pool, tennis court and sweeping lawns. Roaring log fires on frosty nights. Magnificent avenues of century old pines and elms provide shady walks. Fish, bird watch and picnic by the placid Bell River. Horse and pony rides. Children, pets and horses welcome.

Wentworth Falls see Blue Mountains

White Cliffs
Underground B&B   NRMA ★★★☆
Address: PJ's Underground, Dugout 72, White Cliffs, 2836
Name: Joanne & Peter Pedler
Telephone: (08) 8091 6626
Fax: (08) 8091 6626
Beds: 5 Double, 7 Single (5 bedrooms)
Bathroom: 2 Guests share, 1 Family share
Tariff: B&B (continental) Double $70, Single $55, Children & Extra person $18, Dinner $20-$25, Campervans $20, Spa hire $10/$15. Full breakfast available.
Nearest Town: White Cliffs (255km from Broken Hill)

PJ's Underground is a unique B&B located underground in the pioneering opal mining town of White Cliffs, near Broken Hill.
Peter and Joanne welcome visitors to share their unique home, offering B&B in attractively renovated opal mines nestled under the 64 million year old roof of Turley's Hill.
Fossick for the elusive opal on the mining field (or even on our roof!). Borrow a good book from PJ's library, and rest in an outdoor oasis (a stark contrast to the surrounding countryside where the kangaroos & emus move through the saltbush and bare gibber plains.) Visit the Solar Power station, galleries and opal showrooms. Reflect on the day over a delicious dinner, and relaxing spa.
Come and enjoy the peace and tranquillity of the bush, experience the wonder of living UNDERGROUND and feel a little of the Pioneering Spirit of the Living Outback.

NEW SOUTH WALES

Wingen see Scone. Wingham see Taree

Wisemans Ferry
Homestay
Address: "Haze Valley",
167 Settlers Road,
Wisemans Ferry, NSW 2775
Name: Carol Larratt
Telephone: (02) 4566 4334
Fax: (02) 4566 4334 **Mobile**: (017) 829322
Beds: 4 Queen waterbeds (4 bedrooms)
Bathroom: 4 Ensuite
Tariff: B&B (full) Double $80, Single $60.
Dinner $25 by arrangement.
Children by arrangement. Vouchers accepted
Nearest Town: Wisemans Ferry. Just over an hour's drive from the north of Sydney.

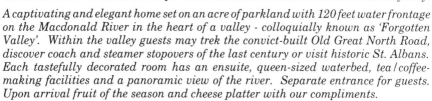

A captivating and elegant home set on an acre of parkland with 120 feet water frontage on the Macdonald River in the heart of a valley - colloquially known as 'Forgotten Valley'. Within the valley guests may trek the convict-built Old Great North Road, discover coach and steamer stopovers of the last century or visit historic St. Albans. Each tastefully decorated room has an ensuite, queen-sized waterbed, tea / coffee-making facilities and a panoramic view of the river. Separate entrance for guests. Upon arrival fruit of the season and cheese platter with our compliments.
BBQ, table tennis, and fishing gear to suit your leisure. boat hire, golf, lawn bowls or tennis available at the village or, if you prefer, bushwalking or fishing.
Group bookings minimum 2 couples for 2 night stay with dinner, bed and breakfast - $200 per couple. Ceramic painting and firing by arrangement as Haze Valley has its own kiln. Limited greenware / bisque and paints / brushes available at cost.
We look forward to greeting you and making your stay a happy and memorable one. Reservations required.

Wodonga see Albury.   Wollombi see Hunter Valley.

Wollongong - Figtree
Homestay/Bed & Breakfast
Address: "Wisteria Cottage",
75 Koloona Avenue, Figtree, NSW 2525
Name: Chris & Carolin Chapman
Telephone: (02) 4229 8958 **Fax**: (02) 4225 2110
Beds: 1 King or 2 Single (1 bedroom)
Bathroom: 1 Ensuite
Tariff: B&B (full) Double $85, Single $60, Dinner $24,
Credit Cards (MC/BC/VISA). Vouchers accepted $5 surcharge Public Holidays
Nearest Town: Wollongong 3km

Wisteria Cottage nestles at the foot of Mt Keira amid leafy trees and gardens attracting many native birds. It offers a delightful bedroom with ensuite facilities and guest entrance. A warm welcome awaits you, Chloe, the Cavalier King Charles spaniel will also make you very welcome.
The Illawarra offers many activities including fishing, bushwalking and bird watching. Beaches and Wollongong CBD are only 5 minutes away. A comfortable place to stop and break your journey travelling up or down the coast of NSW.

Wonboyn Lake see Eden. Woodford see Blue Mountains
Woodstock see Cowra

Wooli - Far North Coast
Homestay   NRMA ★★★☆
Address: 6 South Terrace, Wooli, NSW 2462
Name: Wooli Beachouse B&B
Telephone: (02) 664 97660 **Fax**: (02) 6649 7660
Beds: 1 King/Queen, 1 Double, 2 Single (3 bedrooms)
Bathroom: 2 Guests share
Tariff: B&B (full) Double $85, Single $65,
Credit Cards. Vouchers accepted
Nearest Town: Wooli - City Grafton

"High Quality Simplicity"

WOOLI BEACHOUSE

Right on the beach at "Wonderful Wooli" nestled snugly between the river and sea, you'll find Kel and Yvonne Kearns' charming "Wooli Beachouse Bed & Breakfast" deluxe and standard suites available.
There are magic views from your balcony watch frolicking dolphins at play or the thrill of sighting whales during the migrating season.
Honeymoons and special occasions are especially catered for - be pampered with a champagne breakfast, stroll along tranquil beach and enjoy the time together.
The amateur fisherman can choose between the best beach rock, estuary and deep sea fishing spots.
"High Quality Simplicity"

Woy Woy see Central Coast

Yamba - Angourie
Homestay B&B
Address: Angourie Point B&B
23 Pacific Street, Angourie NSW 2464
Name: Angouri Point B&B
Telephone: (02) 6646 1432
Beds: 2 Queen (2 bedrooms)
Bathroom: 1 Private, 1 Guest Share
Tariff: B&B (full) Double $70-$90, Single $50
Nearest Town: Yamba NSW 2464

Angourie Point Bed and Breakfast offers relaxed coastal living. Your host Jo Silvester will ensure that the traveller experiences all the charms of this special part of the world.
Take a walk along the unspoilt beaches which are famous for the excellent surfing waves and swim in the clear clean water. The fresh water pools at Angourie provide an added aquatic experience for the visitor. The Beachwood cafe, along with the famous lentil burgers of the Angourie store will fill the gastronomic needs of any traveller. Yuraygur National Park provides a wonderful coastal walk into Shelly Beach.
Comforts include two bedrooms with Queen size bed and quality soft furnishings, spa, bathroom, a spacious lounge area looking out to sub tropical garden. Non Smoking house.
Breakfast is served on the upstairs deck with stunning views of the Pacific Ocean.
For bookings and further information phone: 02-6646 1432 (home) or (02) 6646 3440 (business hours).

NEW SOUTH WALES

Yamba
Homestay
Address: Wynyabbie House,
Yamba Road, Palmers Island, NSW 2463
Name: Bev & Ian Wingad
Telephone: (02) 6646 0168
Mobile: (019) 456135
Beds: 2 Double, 1 Twin (3 bedrooms)
Bathroom: 1 Ensuite, 1 Guests share
Tariff: B&B (full) Double $90-$115, Single $60-$75,
Children $25, Dinner approx. $20. Credit Cards. Vouchers accepted
Nearest Town: Yamba and Maclean 10km, 50km north of Grafton

"Wynyabbie House" is a century old homestead set on 2 acres of superb gardens, right on the Clarence River, just 10 minutes from Yamba with its beautiful beaches, famous fishing and the Yuraygir National Park. The house has been lovingly restored and furnished with antiques (Bev's passion along with her cats, garden and golf), but all modern conveniences are available. A twin and a double room share the guest bathroom and there is also a deluxe room with ensuite and 2 bunks to accommodate a family.
Guests have the use of the salt water pool, tennis court and can fish off the jetty, relax in the gardens and use the guest lounge. A pasta restaurant is on the premises and breakfast is a very luxurious affair served on the verandah overlooking the river. Phone Bev or Ian for a brochure on their little piece of paradise.
Directions: 50km north of Grafton and 1 km towards Yamba off the Pacific Highway.

Yass
B&B Guest House
NRMA ★★★★☆
Address: "The Globe",
70 Rossi Street, Yass, NSW 2582
Name: Margaret & Ken Reidy
Telephone: (02) 6226 3680
Fax: (02) 6226 3680 **Mobile**: 018 632 492
Beds: 3 Queen, 1 Double, 1 Twin, (5 bedrooms)
Bathroom: 4 Ensuite, 1 Private
Tariff: Double $90, Single $65. Children week days only.
Credit Cards accepted.
Nearest Town: Canberra 55 mins away.

Margaret and Ken are proud owners of the wonderful old B&B The Globe. Together they have given The Globe a feeling of elegance and style. It accommodates 10 people all with ensuites except one which has a remarkably large private bathroom.
The rooms are all located upstairs and beautifully furnished complete with electric blankets, ducted heating and lovely fluffy towels! There is a large verandah overlooking historical buildings. Downstairs you will find a sitting room, library and billiard room for you to relax in.
The Globe is within walking distance of all towns amenities. Yass has an 18 hole golf course, bowling greens, walking tracks and close to cool climate vineyards. A lovely cottage garden complements the circa 1847 former hotel. Enjoy complimentary tea / coffee, cake and enjoy local port and chocolates by the log fire.

Yass also see Rye Park

Yass

Self-contained Accom.   NRMA ★★★
Address: 33 Comur Street, Yass, NSW 2582
Name: Woodhill's Apartments
Telephone: (02) 6226 3165 **Mobile**: 0419 016 138
Beds: 2 Queen, 1 Single (2 Bedrooms) (Extra single bed available if required)
Bathroom: 2 Private bathrooms
Tariff: B&B (continental) Double $85, Children $10, Full breakfast extra, Credit Cards.
  Vouchers accepted
Nearest Town: Yass

The old stairs that once led to a residence above "The Corner Store" now lead to the comfortable, beautifully appointed rooms of Woodhill's Apartments.
In each apartment the well-stocked kitchen provides a continental breakfast. A cooked breakfast may be ordered and delivered to your apartment, or served at "The Pampered Palate" - just a short stroll down Comur Street. Dinner may be ordered and delivered to your apartment. A variety of picnic hampers are available.
The living room is charmingly furnished. Television and gas heating ensure your comfort on the coldest nights.
The bedroom is pretty and spacious with a queen-sized bed, electric blanket and clock radio.
Yass, the hub of the fine wool producing Yass Plains for 150 years is now also famed for its wineries, beautiful countryside, galleries and craft. Yass Golf Club offers a friendly welcome with picturesque tree-lined fairways and first class facilities.

Yatte Yattah see Milton

Young

Guest House/B&B   NRMA ★★★★☆
Address: 100 Pitstone Road, Chinamans Dam, Young, NSW 2594
Name: Tilsawood Cottage
Telephone: (02) 6382 5183 **Fax**: (02) 6382 5183
Beds: 1 Queen, 2 Double, 2 Single (4 bedrooms)
Bathroom: 2 Ensuite, 1 Guests share
Tariff: B&B (full) Double $80-$90, Single $60-$70, Children discount, Dinner by request, Credit Cards. Vouchers accepted except Nov/Dec.
Nearest Town: Young - 4km south of Young

Tilsawood Cottage, near Chinamans Dam recreation reserve, offers the friendliness and hospitality you would expect from a country retreat. The unique Austrian style cedar cottage is furnished in antiques and old world charm yet facilities such as air conditioning and ensuites offer the comforts of modern day living. You will appreciate the homely atmosphere of the lounge room where a combustion fire will keep you warm in winter time. The comfortable bedrooms (some with balconies) all have heaters, electric blankets, clock radios, hairdryers, tea and coffee making facilities.
Hearty home-cooked breakfasts are served and dinner (by arrangement) features mainly German / European cuisine. A delightful cottage garden invites you to relax.
The busiest time of Young, culminating in the National Cherry Festival late November is traditionally cherry blossom time and harvest from mid September to late December. But the Gold Rush history, various other activities and attractions make Young a worthwhile year round destination.
Your hosts Gaby, Erwin and son Michael.   NMRA 3 & 1/2 star guest share rooms

Young also see Boorowa, Cootamundra

TIPS FOR EASIER B&B TRAVEL

★ **Ensuite and private bathroom** are for your use exclusively, **Guests share** bathroom means you may be sharing with other guests, **Family share** bathroom means you will be sharing with the family.

★ In the tariff section of each listing **'continental' breakfast** consists of fruit, cereal, toast, tea/coffee; **'full'** breakfast is the same with an additional cooked course; **'special'** breakfast has something special.

★ Do not try to travel too far in one day. Take time to enjoy the company of your hosts and other locals.

★ **Telephone ahead** to enquire about a B&B. It is a nuisance for you if you arrive to find the accommodation has been taken. And besides hosts need a little time to prepare.

★ The most suitable **time to arrive is late afternoon**, and to leave is before 10 in the morning.

★ **If you would like dinner** please give your host sufficient notice to prepare.

★ If you are unsure of anything ask your hosts about it. They will give you a direct answer.

★ Our B&Bs are mostly private homes. **Most do not accept credit cards.**

★ If you have made your reservations from overseas, check that your dates are correct. You might cross the dateline to come to Australia.

★ **Please let your hosts know if you have to cancel.** They will have spent time preparing for you.

★ Australian road signs are getting better, but your best directions come from asking a local.

★ Most listings show hosts accept vouchers. The only **vouchers accepted are Australian Bed & Breakfast Book vouchers.**

★ **Phone numbers throughout Australia are changing** to eight digits. For help to find your hosts' phone number phone Directory Assistance.

AUSTRALIAN CAPITAL TERRITORY

Canberra - Curtin
Homestay
Address: 126 Theodore Street, Curtin, ACT 2605
Name: Mollie & Tom Bialkowski
Telephone: (02) 6285 3956
Email: sap@clover.com.au
Beds: 1 Double, 1 Single (2 bedrooms)
Bathroom: 1 Ensuite, 1 Family share
Tariff: B&B (full) Double $60 first night, $50 thereafter, Single $30. Dinner $20 per person. Children $10. Vouchers accepted
Nearest Town: Woden Town Centre

We are two library orientated people who have travelled overseas and enjoy fellow travellers company. Tom is Polish, Mollie is English, both have been in Australia since children and love to give old fashioned hospitality.
We have a lovely house with a spa and deck and many birds come to our garden. Mollie is a story-teller and collects costumes and puppets to use in her stories. Tom is a bookseller and self-employed in Chinese herbal foods.
We are on two bus routes. One goes straight past Parliament House, the other to Civic and major town centres.
There is much to see in Canberra and your hosts will pick you up in the evening from bus, train or plane if desired. There are tea making facilities in both rooms and a small sitting room is available. Our Australiana book collection is quite comprehensive. Dinner can be arranged for weekends. No smoking by request. Pets by arrangements.

Canberra - Downer
Self Contained Accommodation
Address: "White Gums", 23 Padbury Place, Downer, Canberra ACT 2602
Name: Joanna & John
Telephone: (02) 6248 9368
Fax: (02) 6248 9368
Beds: 1 Double, 2 Single (2 bedrooms). Babies welcome (cot available)
Bathroom: 1 Ensuite
Tariff: B&B (full) Double $65-$75, Single $45-$55, Children $10-$25. Weekly discounts. Dinner by prior arrangement $15pp BYO. Vouchers accepted
Nearest Town: Canberra - 5km or 5 mins north of City.

Situated in a quiet cul-de-sac your B&B has its own entrance, garden patio and spacious sunny outlook.
Downer is a pleasant, leafy inner northern suburb only minutes from the city centre. Beautiful walks in the bush and family bikes available for the many bicycle trails.
Your self-contained unit has a bedroom with ensuite and living room / dining area with kitchenette. Sofa bed in living area. Electric blankets and under carpet heating make for cosy evenings. Accommodation includes full breakfast and tea & coffee making facilities. Dinner by prior arrangement.
We like meeting people and exchange ideas and view points. We invite you to dine with us or enjoy your privacy as you wish. Smoking outside. Pick up service may be arranged. Enjoy your stay.

AUSTRALIAN CAPITAL TERRITORY

Canberra - Farrer
Homestay
Address: "Tregilly"
(Canberra south - please phone first)
Name: Peter & Marie
Telephone: (02) 6286 4022
Mobile: (019) 129 727
Beds: 4 Single, 1 Queen,
1 Double sofabed (1 Private Suite
and 2 bedrooms)
Bathroom: 1 Ensuite, 1 Guests share
Tariff: B&B (full) Private suite $98 first night $88 thereafter, Twin and Queen $80 first night $70 thereafter, Single rates available. Vouchers accepted $10 surcharge on Suite
Nearest Town: Canberra (We are 12 minutes from Parliament House)

Tregilly features old brick, cathedral ceilings and pine. In a tranquil setting with sweeping Bush and City views in large native gardens backing onto Reserve, the accommodation is decorated in Laura Ashley style, with quality beds. Generous breakfast is served in our dining room (log fire in winter) or on the verandah. Cool off in our turquoise pool, stroll in the Bush spotting kangaroos, enjoy a leisurely game of croquet and be charmed by our abundant birdlife. Easy access for Canberra sightseeing, Art and Craft galleries, National Trust properties, sheep stations, tennis courts and golf courses. The lovely Brindabella Hills, spectacular Snowy Mountain snowfields and south coast beaches are great day visits. Restaurants closeby. Our hobbies are classic cars, golf, tennis, bushwalking and painting. Both ex Navy, together with "Holly" our Labrador, we enjoy welcoming people to our lovely environment. We also let a coastal cottage 2 hours from Canberra.

Canberra - Florey
Bed & Breakfast
Address: "The Pines", 37 Twelvetrees Cres,
Florey, ACT 2615
Name: Colleen Adair
Telephone: (02) 6259 1387
Mobile: 0416-259 138

THE PINES ATTIC

Beds: 2 Double, 1 Single (2 bedrooms) extra bed if needed.
(One room is wheelchair accessible).
Bathroom: 2 Ensuites (one ensuite is wheelchair accessible)
Tariff: B&B (continental) Double $85-$95, Single $65-$75, Children $20. Private attic with sitting room (ensuite under)/ Private room with courtyard and ensuite. Vouchers accepted Mon-Thurs only + $5-$10 surcharge.
Nearest Town: Belconnen (1.5 km) Canberra City (15 km)

The "Pines" offers cosy lodgings with complete privacy and comfort. Our guests will enjoy the tranquillity and charm of this lovely modern spacious home set on a secluded block sheltered by pines and surrounded by a delightful garden. (House and garden completely wheelchair accessible).
Your hosts Colleen and Adrian offer warm hospitality and friendly conversation and guidance on local attractions. The "Pines" is a 5 min walk and 2 min cycle to the picturesque Lake Ginnindera and 12 mins by car to Canberra City. (Bikes available) Dinner and entertainment packages are available for your special occasions. Your hosts will provide pre-dinner champagne, chauffeuring to and from restaurants, port on return. Varied choice of restaurants.
Looking forward to meeting you.

AUSTRALIAN CAPITAL TERRITORY

Canberra - Hall
Self-Contained Accommodation
Address: Please phone
Name: "Last Stop Ambledown Brook"
Telephone: (02) 6230 2280
Fax: (02) 6230 2280
Beds: 2 Double, 3 Single (3 bedrooms)
Bathroom: Bathroom: 2 ensuites
Tariff: B&B (full) Double $80, Single $40, Children under 14yrs $10, Dinner $25pp (BYO).
Nearest Town: Hall 10 minutes, Canberra 20 minutes

LAST STOP AMBLEDOWN BROOK
On our forty acres, just 20 minutes from town, we have renovated two carriages ..... a 1929 TRAM and a 1935 TRAIN. The tram has two bedrooms, sitting room and a bathroom. One bedroom has a double four poster and the other has two single shearer's beds. The sitting room has 1930's leadlight windows that allow views of the peaceful countryside and surrounding hills.
The train, an old corridor style, features a double bedroom, a bathroom with an original 1920's silver hand basin and an additional sitting room, with a sofabed, and views from every window.
A barbecue, tennis court and pool are available for guests. Within walking distance are three wineries. kangaroos are not infrequent visitors to our spring fed stream at the bottom of our land .... another pleasant stroll. We have featured in "Home Beautiful" and "Getaway".
A recent addition is a guest's dining room which overlooks the Brindabellas. By prior arrangement, a home cooked 3 course meal can be enjoyed in these surroundings.

Canberra - Hall
Farmstay
Address: "Arambie Homestead",
2 McCarthy Rd., via Hall 2618
Name: Arambie Homestead
Telephone: (02) 6230 2391
Mobile: (041) 630 239
Beds: 2 Double, 1 Single (3 bedrooms)
Bathroom: 1 Guests share
Tariff: B&B (full) Double $70, Single $60, Children negotiable, Dinner negotiable.
Nearest Town: Canberra

We are delighted to share our lovely home with its breathtaking views of the Brindabella Mountains and Murrambidgee River with you.
Come laze beside the swimming pool or take a 5 min stroll to the river and drop in a line. If you enjoy wine tasting then our local vineyards are 5 minutes by car. Wandering through the garden or over the 40 acre property with its abundance of bird and wildlife or just relaxing in front of a log fire. You will treasure the memories of your idyllic stay at Arambie Homestead.
Stables, dressage ring and paddocks available. Please enquire.

AUSTRALIAN CAPITAL TERRITORY

Canberra - Manuka
Homestay
Address: 14 Bremer Street
Griffith/Manuka, Canberra ACT 2603
Name: Sue Hall
Telephone: (02) 6295 3501 **Fax**: (02) 6295 3501 **Mobile**: (0414) 377 388
Beds: 2 Queen, 1 Single (3 Bedrooms)
Bathroom: 1 Guests Share
Tariff: B&B (full) Double $80, Single $50, Dinner $25. Not suitable for children.
Vouchers accepted
Nearest Town: Canberra

Sue and Pat Hall are ex cocoa planters from Papua New Guinea and run an art gallery from their home, located in popular Manuka which is in the hub of Canberra's top restaurants, coffee houses, boutique bars and fine shopping. A beautiful home with salt water pool, courtyard and sculptured gardens, interesting art exhibitions and only minutes walk to Parliament House, The High Court, The National Art Gallery and a host of other tourist spots.

Regular bus service is located right outside the front gate and it is not far from the interstate rail service (2 mins). A perfect location for that quiet get away or walk directly through parks to join the busy cafe scene at Manuka. Only 5 mins drive from CBD. Sue has spent many years working in the museums and tourist industries and will be pleased to help you get the most out of your visit to Canberra.

Canberra - Narrabundah
Homestay
Address: "Thisilldo", 34 Scott Street, Narrabundah, ACT 2604
Name: David & Romayne Ash
Telephone: (02) 6295 2671 **Fax**: (02) 6239 7773
Email: dash@effect.net.au
Beds: 1 Double (1 bedroom)
Bathroom: 1 Ensuite
Tariff: B&B (full) Double $65, Single $50. Dinner $25pp (carafe of wine per couple). No children.
Nearest Town: Canberra city centre 10 minutes

Bed & Breakfast as you would wish it to be. Large sunny room with ensuite overlooking a Floriade prize winning garden. The only sounds at night are courtesy of our resident frogs. David and Romayne are former "Poms" coming to Canberra from Sydney twelve years ago. They ran a well known English pub, the Boot & Flogger, for six years.

They will be pleased to show guests the sights of Canberra, which are, in the main, within a mere ten minutes drive. Reasonable rates can be arranged for such guided tours.

Smoke if you wish, but maybe not at dinner, as the food is too good! The size of the breakfast is only limited by your capacity and, if you desire, can be enjoyed in the garden.

Come and treat yourself to a small portion of old fashioned hospitality.
Try us!

AUSTRALIAN CAPITAL TERRITORY

Canberra - Narrabundah
Homestay
Address: Please phone
Name: John & Esther
Telephone: (02) 6295 2837 **Fax**: (02) 6295 6992 **Mobile**: (0419) 276 231
Email: je@acm.org
Beds: 2 Single incl 1 waterbed (1 bedroom)
Bathroom: 1 Ensuite
Tariff: B&B (full) Double $85, Single $65, Dinner $25pp by arrangement. Credit Cards (Visa/MC/BC/Amex/Diners)
   Vouchers accepted
Nearest Town: 6kms south of Canberra City Centre, 3km SE of Parliament House.

Our multi-award-winning house is in a quiet street in Upper Narrabundah, within 10 minutes of Canberra's major tourist attractions. We can meet you on arrival by plane / train / bus, and can offer advice about what to see and do in Canberra, and about local restaurants. There is an ACTION bus stop 130 metres from our front door.
We have appreciated the hospitality we have experienced at B&Bs in Australia, New Zealand, United States, Britain, Ireland and Europe , and we aim to treat our guests in a similar manner.
Esther is a history teacher and John is a semi-retired information technologist. Our interests include travel, history, genealogy, music, gardening and embroidery. We have a 13-year-old blind miniature poodle who likes to make visitors feel welcome (but, if necessary, we can tell her to keep her distance or put her outside). We prefer that you do not smoke indoors.

Multi-award-winning house, quiet street, 130 metres from ACTION bus stop. Can meet your transport on arrival.

AUSTRALIAN CAPITAL TERRITORY

Canberra - O'Connor
Homestay   NRMA ★★★☆
Address: "Pasmore Cottage",
O'Connor, ACT - Please phone
Name: Alan & Sue
Telephone: (02) 6247 4528
Fax: (02) 6247 4528
Beds: 1 Queen, 1 Double,
1 Single (2 bedrooms)
Bathroom: 1 Ensuite, 1 Private
Tariff: B&B (full) Double $75-$85, Single $65-$70, Children over 12 years $20, Dinner $20 (2 courses + wine). Credit Cards. Vouchers accepted
Nearest Town: Canberra City

Only 3kms from the city, Pasmore Cottage is situated in a quiet street in an easy to find location. Close to most tourist attractions, restaurants, both universities and Calvary Hospital. An attractive garden surrounds this carefully renovated and extended early Canberra cottage. Colourful parrots feed in the garden daily.
Complimentary afternoon tea is served under the Linden tree in summer or in the sunny courtyard or guests lounge in winter. Fresh flowers and chocolates compliment the tastefully decorated bedrooms. Guests are welcome to relax and read, enjoy music or TV in the lounge room. Tea, coffee and home-made biscuits are always available. Ducted heating ensures winter warmth.
A freshly prepared full or continental breakfast, including fruit, is served in the sunny dining room or courtyard. Home cooked dinner available by prior arrangement.
We use and enjoy the many attractions Canberra has to offer the visitor and are happy to assist with sightseeing itineraries.

Canberra - Queanbeyan
Homestay   NRMA ★★★★☆
Address: Benbullen Homestay,
RMB 2013, The Ridgeway,
Queanbeyan, NSW 2620
Name: Bill & Carolyn Baggett
Telephone: (02) 6297 6101
Fax: (02) 6297 6101
Beds: 3 Queen, 6 Single (5 bedrooms)
Bathroom: 2 Ensuite, 1 Private
Tariff: B&B (full) Double $90, Single $75, Children $10-$15. Credit Cards. Vouchers accepted $10 supplement luxury & family units only.
Nearest Town: 15 km east of Canberra, 4km east of Queanbeyan on Kings Highway

"Wow, what fabulous views of the ACT", are the first words guests say when seeing BENBULLEN's marvellous panorama, and things only get better from there. Our 4 1/2 star NRMA rating confirms that you are somewhere special.
Our home of 55 squares, on 4 acres of secluded land 15 kilometres form Canberra, has three widely separated units, with full facilities for complete privacy. The Luxury Suite with three rooms pampers you, children love their loft bedroom in the Family Suite and Gumnut Cottage, nestling under a nearby gum tree, is a private retreat for two. All units are air-conditioned, with fridge, TV, video, tea & coffee, hairdryer, cutlery and crockery. We pamper the inner person too, with a multi choice hot breakfast to start your day. A billiard room, videos for all, cubbyhouse and toys, swimming pool, tennis court, bushwalking and birdlife, all make your stay truly relaxing.
BENBULLEN HOMESTAY, makes visiting Canberra wonderful.

Canberra - Sutton (NSW)
Self-contained Farmstay
Address: "Goolabri Park", RMB 1591 Federal Highway, Sutton, NSW 2620
Name: Linda, Gordon & Brian Luton
Telephone: (06) 230 3294
Fax: (06) 230 3575
Email: goolabri@dynamite.com.au
Beds: 18 Double, 24 Single (3x2 bedrooms, 9x1 bedroom units)
Bathroom: 12 Ensuite
Tariff: 2 bedroom unit $140 for up to 5 people - sleeps up to 8 ($10 each extra person), 1 bedroom unit $100 for up to 2 - sleeps up to 4 ($10 each extra person); Breakfast extra - $10 cooked, $7 cold, Dinner à la carte. Discount offered for longer stay, Credit Cards.
Nearest Town: Canberra 17 km

Goolabri Park is a Thoroughbred Horse Stud set on nearly 150 hectares of picturesque, undulating country just 15 minutes from the centre of Canberra. In addition to the two stallions; broodmares and foals, we also run a small herd of beef cattle, some chickens, and other farm animals.
We also have a tennis court, billiard table, table tennis table, heated indoor pool, children's playground, fish and yabbies in the dams and golf course with watered greens.
Because we are situated so close to the ACT our guests can enjoy the many attractions of Canberra for part of the day and then return to the farm to relax for the rest of the afternoon and evening. There is plenty to keep the children occupied. Guests can be involved in the day to day running of the horse stud and farm or go bush walking around the property. There is a large population of kangaroos and abundant birdlife. The restaurant is open Friday & Saturday nights.

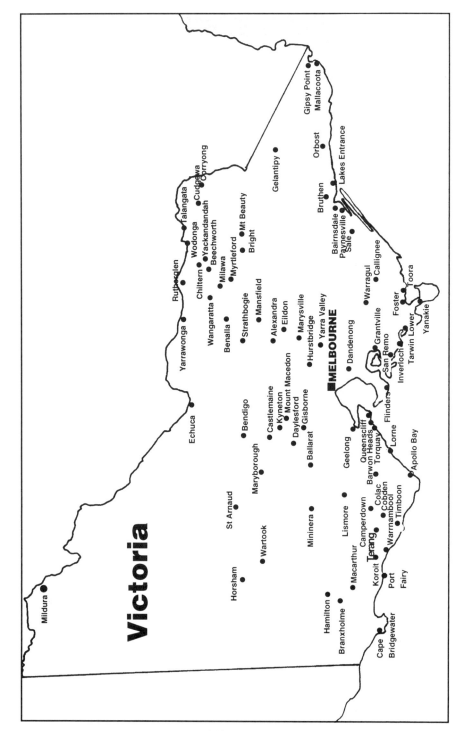

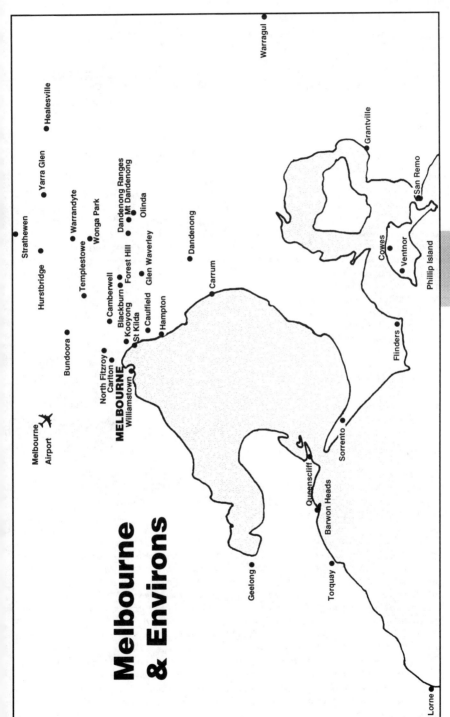

VICTORIA

Alexandra RACV ★★★☆
Farmstay with self-contained Accommodation
Address: "Idlewild Park", RMB 1150, Alexandra, 3714 Victoria.
Name: Elizabeth & Don Deelen
Telephone: (03) 5772 1178
Fax: (03) 5772 1178
Email: idlewild@discover-australia.com
Beds: 2 Queen, 3 Single, (3 bedrooms) **Bathroom**: 1 Ensuite, 1 Private
Tariff: B&B (full) Double $90-$120, Single $60, Children $30. Dinner $30. Vouchers accepted $20 surcharge on 1 night bookings only.
Nearest Town: Alexandra 5km

Whether it be an action packed family holiday or a peaceful weekend for two, then "Idlewild Park" perfect for you! This 2000 acre grazing property has it all! Just 130km from Melbourne, the Alexandra district offers an abundance of activities including biking, golf, horse-riding, fishing, water and snow skiing or bush-walking in the nearby tranquillity of Fraser National Park. The property carries cattle, sheep, horses and poultry. Perhaps you'd like to just spend a few days mingling with the animals, or take part in seasonal farm activities. The large comfortable homestead has colourful gardens, a tennis court and a magnificent view of Mount Cathedral. Guests have a private entrance, self catering facilities, air conditioning and fresh flowers.
Many native animals and birds surround the farm. Pick up service available from V-Line bus. Don and Elizabeth welcome you warmly on arrival with refreshments in their beautiful garden or in the large country kitchen.
Home Page: discover-australia.com/vic/idlewild

Apollo Bay - Great Ocean Road
Farmstay
Address: 925 Barham River Road, Apollo Bay, VIC 3233
Name: Arcady Homestead: Marcia and Ross
Telephone: (03) 52376493 **Fax**: (03) 52376493
Mobile: (041) 935 6828
Beds: 1 Queen, 2 Double, 3 Single, (4 bedrooms)
Bathroom: 1 Guests share
Tariff: B&B (full), Double $90, Single $45, Dinner $25 per person, Children half price. Vouchers accepted
Nearest Town: Apollo Bay

Set on sixty scenic acres, part farmland, part natural bush.
After sharing breakfast with our Kookaburras, explore the Otway Forest trails, visit tree-fern and glow-worm gullies and waterfalls, see some of the tallest trees in the world or visit Port Campbell National Park, which embraces some of Australia's most spectacular coastline. The fisherman has the choice of river fishing (Trout) 200 metres from the homestead or surf and sea fishing at Apollo Bay.
Swimming, surfing golf, horse-riding and of course, the region is a bush-walkers paradise. The valley abounds with bird-life, King Parrots, Gang-Gangs, Rosellas, Fairy Wrens, Yellow Robins, Silver Eyes, Bower Birds and, if you're lucky, glimpses of our shy Grey Goshawk, unique to the Otway Ranges.
Participate in the farm activities or just relax with a good book and a cool drink in the garden or simply drink in the vista of our valley. The choice is yours.
Our home has wood fires and spring water. Our beds are comfortable, our meals country-style, our atmosphere relaxed & friendly. So ring us now.
Smoke free home.

VICTORIA

Apollo Bay
Self-contained Accommodation
Address: 665 Barham River Road, Apollo Bay, Victoria 3233
Name: Carol & Frits Wilmink
Telephone: (03) 52 376 987
Beds: 1 Double, 3 Single (2 bedrooms)
Bathroom: 1 Private
Tariff: B&B (full) Double $95.
Each extra night $80. Extra person per night $30.
Vouchers accepted $10 surcharge - Monday to Thursday (inclusive)
Nearest Town: Apollo Bay, 7km

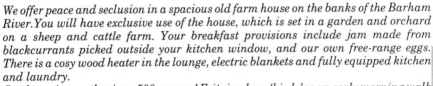

We offer peace and seclusion in a spacious old farm house on the banks of the Barham River. You will have exclusive use of the house, which is set in a garden and orchard on a sheep and cattle farm. Your breakfast provisions include jam made from blackcurrants picked outside your kitchen window, and our own free-range eggs. There is a cosy wood heater in the lounge, electric blankets and fully equipped kitchen and laundry.
Our home is over the river, 500m away! Frits is a keen 'birdo' so an early morning walk may be arranged, or a careful look at a 'Satins' bower.
Explore the Otway National Park, Great Ocean Road, or watch our fishing fleet offload crayfish in the harbour. We have rainforest, waterfalls, beaches, fishing, shell and historical museums, Saturday morning craft, food and plant market, excellent eating places, and a community which welcomes visitors!

Bairnsdale - Johnsonville
Farmstay
Address: "Meningie Homestead" Johnsons Road, Johnsonville, VIC 3902
Name: Judy & David Moresi
Telephone: (03) 5156 4362
(03) 5156 4361 **Fax**: (03) 5156 4362
Beds: 2 Double, 2 Single (3 bedrooms)
Bathroom: 3 Ensuite
Tariff: B&B (continental) Double $70, Single $45; Dinner $20 (3 course). Vouchers accepted
Nearest Town: Lakes Entrance (15km east)

We named our home "Meningie Homestead", Meningie being the aboriginal word for mud, which is what we built our house from. We live on a 20-acre property which runs down to the Tambo River renowned for its bream fishing. It's also a great spot for swimming and guests are most welcome to use our tennis court.
Our house is architecturally designed and takes full advantage of the great views of the nearby hills and surrounding countryside. The living areas are very spacious and the three guests' bedrooms are tastefully decorated and all have their own ensuites.
We have a very relaxed lifestyle offering real country hospitality and we are delighted to have guests eat with us.
From our property it's only a short drive to the local beaches and lakes, the State forests and the popular Buchan Caves.

Bairnsdale also see Paynesville

VICTORIA

Ballarat
Heritage Country House
Address: "Yuulong" RSDN 136, Scotsburn via Ballarat, Vic. 3352
Name: Margaret Barber
Telephone: (03) 5341 3726
Beds: 1 Queen, 1 Twin, 1 Single (3 bedrooms)
Bathroom: 1 Guests share
Tariff: B&B (continental) Double/Twin $98, Single $88, Dinner $30pp.
Campervans welcome, own bathroom + power.
Nearest Town: Buninyong 5km, Ballarat 15km on Midland Highway

"Yuulong" homestead is 15km south of Ballarat and 5km south of Buninyong on the Midland Highway. The brick house, built in 1889 is on the National Register of Historic homes and is classified by the National Trust and offers guests elegant and luxurious accommodation.

Being close to the large city of Ballarat it is ideally located for guests to visit its many attractions - Sovereign Hill, the Wildlife Park, Art Gallery, Lake Wendouree and the adjacent delightful botanical gardens etc, etc. Nearby Buninyong has an excellent golf course.

"Yuulong" - meaning "hilly country", a working stud cattle and stud sheep property, has a large terraced garden leading down to a lake where many species of bird life abound.

A silver service dinner by arrangement for guests, served in the elegant dining room with pre-dinner drinks and wine with meals.

Stay at "Yuulong" for visits to the National Wool Museum at Geelong and the famous nearby Werribee Park.

Gift Vouchers

Our B&B vouchers are for a double room for one night's B&B. They cost $89, and if you order one as a gift, we will include a free
Australian Bed & Breakfast Book
worth $16.95

Send your cheque to
Moonshine Press
59 Quirk Street
Dee Why
NSW 2099

VICTORIA

Ballarat
Self-contained Accommodation
Address: "Amber Cottage"
317 Doveton Street Sth, Ballarat, 3350
Name: Rosemary Barnett
Telephone: (03) 5332 6824
Fax: (03) 5332 6824
Beds: 1 Double, 4 Single (3 bedrooms)
Bathroom: 1 Guests share
Tariff: B&B (continental - basic supplies provided) $80 for 2 - $180 for 6 people.
Children welcome Vouchers accepted
Nearest Town: Ballarat central

Amber Cottage is a completely self-contained house, and although almost in the centre of Ballarat it is in a quiet street.
The cottage is a comfortable and tastefully furnished miner's cottage with all facilities for six people. Visitors may stay for one night or many nights in our famous town full of attractions.
All linen is provided and there are three bedrooms, lounge with TV, kitchen with all equipment, separate bath/shower and toilet and a laundry with washer and drier. Basic necessities are provided and visitors can have a leisurely visit unrestricted in any way.
Ballarat has the Begonia Festival in March, Jazz Festival at Easter and many historical and wildlife attractions. Visitors will need to ring Rosemary to have the cottage opened ready for them. There is an answering service at any time.

Ballarat
Homestay
Address: "Craig On Sturt", 1525 Sturt St, Ballarat, VIC 3350
Name: "Craig On Sturt" J & M Fox
Telephone: (03) 5333 3733
Beds: 2 Queen, 1 Twin (3 bedrooms)
Bathroom: 2 Ensuite, 1 Private with spa

Tariff: B&B (full) Double $100, Single $80, Dinner from $20. Credit Cards. Vouchers accepted $15 surcharge.
Nearest Town: Melbourne 113km, Wineries 1 hour, Grampians 1 1/2 hrs, West Coast 1 1/2 hrs.

"Craig on Sturt"
"Craig" built in 1930 has Antique decor and is situated on the loveliest part of tree lined Sturt St.
We are only a block from lovely Lake Wendouree and a short relaxing stroll to Ballarat's world renowned Begonias and Botanical Gardens.
Experience our relaxed atmosphere and on your arrival take time with us for some complimentary refreshments.
O' what a breakfast! It will keep you going all day and dinner can be provided by prior arrangement. If dining out, Courtesy transportation is available along with a coffee by the open fire on your return. No smoking please.
"There are no strangers here only friends who have never met"
Your hosts: John & Marlene Fox

VICTORIA

Ballarat - Mt Helen RACV ★★★☆
Homestay
Address: "Woodside", 120 Fisken Road, Mt Helen, Ballarat, Vic 3350
Name: Joan & David Goldsmith
Telephone: (03) 5341 3451
Email: dgold@netconnect.com.au
Beds: 1 Queen, 2 Single (2 bedrooms)
Bathroom: 2 Private
Tariff: B&B (full) Double $80, Single $50. Vouchers accepted
Nearest Town: Buninyong 2km; Ballarat 9km to the north.

'Woodside' is a charming country home situated in Mt Helen, one of Ballarat's prettiest suburbs and only ten minutes from the city centre and Sovereign Hill. Our comfortable house is furnished with antiques and spacious guest lounge has a cosy pot belly stove. Set in a large English-style garden, 'Woodside' is close to native forest with lovely views of the surrounding countryside. Crimson Rosellas, Black Cockatoos and superb Blue Wrens can be found in the garden and occasionally koalas climb one of the tall eucalyptus trees.
From our ten acre property, guests have easy access to numerous restaurants, botanical gardens and historic buildings in both Ballarat and Buninyong.
Our interests include reading, antiques, gardening, films and Royal tennis.
'Woodside is noted for its tranquillity, a place where you can relax and unwind. We offer you accommodation with lots of comfort, friendly service and hearty home-cooked breakfasts. A warm welcome awaits you.
No smoking inside please. **Directions**: *Please telephone*

Ballarat RACV ★★★★
Homestay
Address: "Al Hayatt", 800 Mair St., Ballarat, 3350 VIC
Name: M & R White
Telephone: (03) 5332 1396
Mobile: (015) 501363
Beds: 2 Queen, 2 Single or 1 Queen, 2 Single (2 bedrooms)
Bathroom: 1 Ensuite, 1 Private
Tariff: B&B (full) Double $90, Single $70, Children by arrangement. Vouchers accepted $10 Surcharge
Nearest Town: Ballarat - 900 metres west of GPO.

"Al Hayatt" is an Edwardian double storey home in the centre of Ballarat. Named after a hospital in Egypt where the original owner convalesced during the first World War. The original leadlighting subsequently depicts Egyptian themes. Antique furnishing enhance the gracious ambience and allow guests to experience the feeling of life in a different era.
A full silver service breakfast is served in the formal dining room - has open fire. Surrounding this comfortable, centrally heated building are a variety of mature trees and shrubs in a well-tended "old world" garden. One large bedroom has its own private sitting room adjacent and such a delight. Guests share another large lounge with TV. Walk to galleries, theatres, restaurants, beautiful Lake Wendouree and Botanic Gardens.
110km from Melbourne. Off street parking.
A very warm welcome is assured to all our guests with complimentary refreshments and homemade goodies on arrival.

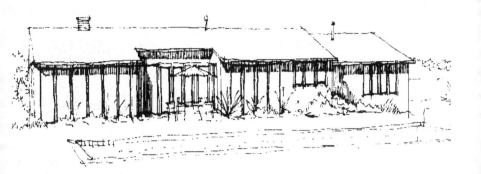

Ballarat - Buninyong
Homestay/Self-contained
Address: Barlfour B&B, PO Box 473, Buninyong 3357
Name: Merrin and Ed Davis
Telephone: (03) 5341 8039 **Fax**: (03) 5341 8494
Beds: 2 Queen (2 bedrooms)
Bathroom: 2 Ensuites
Tariff: B&B (full/special) Double $110, single $80. Self Contained: $150 one couple, $20 per extra person. Credit Cards: Bankcard, Mastercard, Visa.
Nearest Town: Buninyong

Only one hour twenty minutes and seven traffic lights after leaving the Melbourne Arts Centre car park, you can be relaxing in the luxurious accommodation at Balfour, set on a 40 acre property. From all windows of the two double ensuite bedrooms and large private sitting room with kitchen facilities, there are superb views across rolling fields to Mt Buninyoung.

Balfour is well situated for you to relax and enjoy our tranquillity, walk down bush tracks watching the birdlife or play golf at the nearby uncrowded courses. From here you are ten minutes to Sovereign Hill in Ballarat, or use us as a base to take day trips to the ship wreck coast, the Grampians or local and Avoca wineries.

Enjoy our traditional B&B hospitality and silver service breakfasts, or if you prefer, self contained occupancy guarantees exclusive use of the facilities with complete privacy and breakfast when you choose.

Continental breakfast consists of fruit, cereal, toast, tea/coffee.
Full breakfast is the same with a cooked course.
Special breakfast has something special.

VICTORIA

Ballarat
Self-contained Accommodation
Address: 702A Dana Street, Ballarat, VIC 3350
Name: "Roseneath" Pauline Martin
Telephone: (03) 5332 1512
Beds: 1 Double (1 bedroom)
Bathroom: 1 Private
Tariff: B&B (continental) Double $80, Single $65. Vouchers accepted
Nearest Town: Ballarat

"Roseneath" is a lovely Edwardian cottage situated only five minutes walk from the centre of Ballarat - a provincial city renowned for its historic buildings, gracious architecture and picturesque attractions (including Sovereign Hill and a wildlife park).
The self-contained unit allows you to come and go as you please. It includes your own sitting room, bedroom and bathroom. You are also welcome to rest in the adjoining private courtyard and garden. Efficient heating, electric blanket, tea and coffee making facilities and fridge allow you to relax and enjoy the romantic setting.
Art galleries, antique shops, restaurants and Ballarat's beautiful Lake Wendouree are all within easy walking distance.
Continental breakfast includes fresh coffee, fresh fruit, cereals, a variety of breads and homemade jams.
You will be warmly welcomed and your privacy respected.

Ballarat
Self-contained Accommodation
Address: 102 Somerville St., Buninyong, VIC 3357
Name: Glenn & Kerry Bishop - "Coach House"
Telephone: (03) 5341 3615 **Mobile**: 0419 522 623
Beds: 1 Double, 3 Single (1 bedroom)
Bathroom: 1 Ensuite
Tariff: B&B (full) Double $90, Single $45, Children $10 (once only).
Nearest Town: Ballarat

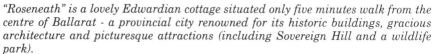

The Family Getaway
The Coach House situated in historic Buninyong, near Ballarat, offers a unique family experience.
Children are welcomed by age appropriate indoor and outdoor games, tree-lined and grassed playing areas, playground, television and video.
The beautiful Botanic Gardens, with natural spring, ducks, playground, fishing and picnic areas are within easy walking distance.
Adults will enjoy the panoramic rural views, spectacular sunsets from the private courtyard, and the ambience of the recreated Coach House.
Families can take advantage of our close proximity to Sovereign Hill and the many other Goldfield's attractions.
Combined with the efficient, modern convenience of gas heating, electric blankets, microwave and en suite. Linen, towels and generous breakfast basket provided.
We have 3 young sons and a Siamese cat.

VICTORIA

Ballarat
Homestay RACV ★★★★
Address: "Gardens House",
1511 Sturt Street, Ballarat, Vic 3350
Name: Jan & Malcolm Lee
Telephone: (03) 5331 4957
Fax: (03) 5331 8497
Beds: 2 Single (1 bedroom)
Bathroom: 1 Private
Tariff: B&B (full) Double $100, Single $75.
Nearest Town: Ballarat - 112km Melbourne.

Gardens House is the home of Jan and Malcolm Lee. We are delighted to share it with visitors to Ballarat. The house is 1920's two storey, set in an interesting garden. When you stay at Gardens House, there will be no other guests. Privacy and tranquillity are assured.
The guest bedroom is upstairs. It is bright and fresh, and faces out over the rear garden and parklands. The twin beds have electric blankets. The room has its own dressing room and private bathroom.
Our guests have exclusive use of an elegantly furnished sitting room with comfortable chairs, colour TV and an open fire. A full cooked breakfast is served in the dining room or conservatory which overlook the rear garden.
Gardens House is on Ballarat's tree-lined Sturt Street. It is only a few minutes walk to Lake Wendouree and the Botanical Gardens.
Guests are welcome to smoke outdoors.

Ballarat
Self-contained Cottage
Address: 3 Linaker Lane, Ballarat, 3350
Name: Julie Anne
Telephone: 1800 353 354 **Mobile**: (015) 512159
Email: beacham@tpgi.com.au
Beds: 2 Double, 1 Single (2 bedrooms)
Bathroom: 1 Private
Tariff: B&B Double $95, Single $60, Dinner N/A, Credit Cards, Weekend package $200. Breakfast hamper provided.
   Vouchers accepted

Lalor Cottage is a tiny miner's cottage looking our on the poppet head & mine at Sovereign Hill. The real thing, built in the 1850's still with its shingle roof hidden under the corrugated iron, and for most of last century home to the Chinese market-gardens who continued to live in the area after gold ran out.
Restored to give the feel of a worker's cottage complete with an extensive cottage garden - fruit trees, herbs and roses, a breakfast basket is provided.
The living room has an open fire, the bathroom is complete with claw-foot bath and the 2 bedrooms have brass & iron beds, hot-water bottles and lots of blankets.
Ballarat offers lots of opportunity to explore our golden past and with the opening of the new Eureka Exhibition an exciting new dimension will be added. Lalor Cottage is very well located in the centre of these attractions.

Barringo Valley see Mount Macedon

Barwon Heads

Self-contained Suite
Address: 37 Carr Street
Barwon Heads Victoria 3227
Name: River-tree Retreat
Telephone: (03) 5254 3030 **Fax**: (03) 5254 3044
Beds: 1 Queen (1 Bedroom)
Bathroom: 1 Private
Tariff: B&B (full) Double $95, Single $85.
Vouchers accepted ($15 surcharge)
Nearest Town: Ocean Grove (3km) Geelong (20km)

Come and stay with us in our seaside village where you can enjoy walks along long sandy ocean surf beaches, relax on the banks of the Barwon River, tour the delightful Bellarine Peninsula or begin your journey along the Great Ocean Road.

You will have a self contained suite (own entrance, TV, stovette, etc) that has been prepared with those little extras in mind that we hope will make your stay an enjoyable and memorable one. The decor tastefully complements the naturalness of the slate floors, brick walls and timber ceilings. You may choose to have a cooked breakfast delivered to your door, or a basket of ingredients to prepare your own light breakfast at your leisure.

We can assist you with detailed information about this part of Victoria and the bus from Geelong passes our front door. Overseas correspondence with IRC is welcomed. Non Smoking.

Directions: *Please phone for bookings and further details.*

Batesford see Geelong

Beechworth

B&B Gourmet   RACV ★★★★☆
Address: 34 Loch Street,
Beechworth,
Victoria 3747
Name: "Kinross"
Telephone: (03) 5728 2351
Fax: (03) 5728 3333
Beds: 2 King/Twin, 3 Double (5 bedrooms)
Bathroom: 5 Ensuite
Tariff: B&B (full) Double $148, Single $120. Dinner $42pp (4 course).
Credit Cards (VISA/BC/AMEX/MC/DC).
Nearest Town: Albury/Wodonga 39km N, Wangaratta 37km S.

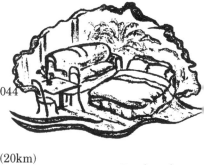

When did you last enjoy an open log fire in your bedroom? The cheerful, cosy ambience of a log fire is the style of Kinross.

Kinross in Beechworth, historic hub of the N.E. Victoria, is a colonial home restored with loving care. Kinross, with the elegance and tranquillity of an English country house, is a friendly intimate place. Just 10 guests. The fully serviced rooms (double or twin) are furnished with period pieces that Sotherbys would like to get their hands on. With open fires, doonas, electric blankets, comfy lounge chairs, stylish en-suites, T.V. and tea and coffee making facilities, enjoy the luxury of it all.

How could you refuse a full English breakfast, served on a white damask tablecloth. Dinner? Well, it's more like a dinner party than a restaurant. Meet your fellow guests and have a surprisingly inexpensive four course meal. Steve will make you feel pampered as you enjoy Anne's superb cooking.

VICTORIA

Beechworth RACV ★★★☆
Homestay
Address: "Golspie", 4 Malakoff Road, Beechworth, Victoria 3747
Name: Ken & Elaine Melville
Telephone: (03) 5728 2713
Fax: (03) 5728 2713
Beds: 1 Double, 2 Single (2 bedrooms)
Bathroom: 1 Private
Tariff: B&B (full) Double $70, Single $50, Dinner $30pp. Vouchers accepted
Nearest Town: 1km from the centre of Beechworth on the Wangaratta Road

Golspie near the gorge

On the outskirts of the historic town of Beechworth, Golspie offers comfort and personal hospitality in a tranquil setting, with views to the gorge and surrounding countryside. About 3 1/2 hours drive from Melbourne, Beechworth is located in the north-east of Victoria. It may be approached from either Wangaratta or Albury-Wodonga, which are both situated on the Hume Highway.

Golspie is a comfortable walking distance from the town centre and historic sites, and is well placed for those who enjoy bushwalking, wine tasting or trips to the nearby mountains and neighbouring townships.

Features include double or twin accommodation in a smoke-free environment, private sitting room, guests' bathroom, wood fire heating, electric blankets, tea-making facilities, traditional country breakfast including home-made bread and jams, and dinner by arrangement.

Contract Bridge players will be especially welcome, and may be assured of a couple to "make up a four".

Beechworth RACV ★★★★
Homestay
Address: Apple Tree Cottage, 16 Frederick St., Beechworth
Name: Apple Tree Cottage B&B
Telephone: (03) 5728 1044
Fax: (03) 5728 1044
Beds: 1 Queen (bedroom)
Bathroom: 1 Ensuite
Tariff: B&B (full) Double $75, Children up to 1 yr, Credit Cards. Vouchers accepted
Nearest Town: Beechworth 1.2km from P.O.

A cottage in the country situated at Beechworth in the scenic May-Day Hills.
IF you require a superbly comfortable undisturbed nights sleep, in a spacious room.
IF you enjoy the ambience of antique cedar furniture, fine china and lace.
IF you like to settle into a wing backed armchair and enjoy a book accompanied by good music, or simply sit in quiet comfort. A happy garden or a warm fire.
IF you enjoy wineries and gourmet food. History, we have been here since 1853, bush walks, golf.
IF you collect or simply love antiques.
IF you enjoy the very special beauty of this fine NE Country, especially our Bakery.
Then Apple Tree Cottage is just the place for you.
You will want to start the day with a splendid country breakfast of course. Pamper yourselves and stay at Apple Tree Cottage.

VICTORIA

Beechworth
Guest House
Address: 5 Dingle Road, Beechworth, 3747
Name: Beechworth House Bed & Breakfast
Telephone: (03) 5728 2817
Fax: (03) 5728 2737 **Mobile**: (015) 357849
Beds: 3 Queen (3 bedrooms)
Bathroom: 1 Ensuite, 1 Guests share
Tariff: B&B (full) Double $110, Dinner by request,
Credit Cards.
Nearest Town: Beechworth

Beechworth House
BED & BREAKFAST
& GALLERY

Beechworth House provides quality accommodation and service. It is a new house built in the early colonial style and full of the old world charm of yesteryear. There are two large rooms upstairs with a share bathroom. The downstairs room has private facilities and French doors that open into the garden. There is a large sitting room for guests use, furnished with books, magazines, tea & coffee making facilities and a television set. A cooked breakfast is served in the sunny formal dining room with starched linen and silver cutlery.

Beechworth House is set in a peaceful pastoral environment with views from all rooms. It is adjacent to the La Trobe University Beechworth Heritage Campus.

Beechworth is a historical goldmining town set in the beautiful Mayday Hills just off the Hume Freeway between Albury and Wangaratta. There are many festivals, markets, fine restaurants, art galleries, shops and historical sites to visit.

Benalla   RACV ★★★★ & ★★★☆
Farmstay + Inn House B & B
Address: Yarrawonga Rd, Benalla,
Nth East Vic.
Postal: RMB 1090, Goorambat, 3725
Name: Rhyllis Siggers & Family
Telephone: 61 (03) 5764 1273
Fax: 61 (03) 5764 1352
Beds: 2 King, 1 Double, 2 Single (3 bedrooms)
Bathroom: 1 Ensuite, 1 Guests share
Tariff: B&B (special) Double $95. Ensuite $110. Single $75. Children half price. Dinner 2 or 4 course available on request.
Nearest Town: Benalla 10 mins.

"Yaridni" is a 1500 acre parklike merino property, just North of Benalla, in North East Victoria, only 13 km off the Hume Freeway (Sydney-Melb) on Yarrawonga Rd. where you will immediately feel at home. Ideal stop-over Melb / Sydney.

Set on a rise overlooking the property, it has sunny front patio, large games room, warm friendly farm kitchen, formal dining room, lounge with open fire and beautiful views. We work and own "Yaridni" and run 4000 merinos and crop 500 acres.

We specialise in real Aussie hospitality, serve fine regional food and wine and take pleasure in making your stay a memorable one. Wildlife, especially kangaroos can be seen at dusk and it is a bird-lovers paradise. The stars and sunsets have to be seen to be believed. "Yaridni" is 2 1/2 hours Melbourne drive or by bus or train, 2 hours by Very Fast Train. 8 hours from Sydney, 5 hours from Canberra. Drive, or we will meet Sydney / Melb. train or bus at Benalla. Nearby are wineries, Winton Raceway, gliding, golf, historic towns. Watch our Border-collies round-up sheep or just relax after a great night's sleep.

Bendigo - Mandurang Valley
Homestay   RACV ★★★★
Address: 180 Mandurang Road, Mandurang, VIC 3539. Please phone
Name: Rupertswood Country Home
Telephone: (03) 5439 5532
Fax: (03) 5439 5532   **Mobile**: (0417) 393 086
Email: ruptwcl@net.con.net.au
Beds: 2 Double, 2 Single, (3 bedrooms)
Bathroom: 1 Ensuite, 1 Private
Tariff: B&B (full), Double $90 - $110, Single $70 - $80, Dinner $35. Children concession. Vouchers accepted $20 surcharge for weekend and public holidays
Nearest Town: Bendigo - 8 minutes city centre

Our spacious modern home overlooking the lovely Mandurang Valley provides a relaxing stay, yet is only 6km from all the attractions of historic central Bendigo.
HERITAGE SUITE: One double bedroom / ensuite with large sitting room and superb antique furnishings.
FEDERATIONS SUITE: One double and one twin bedroom, bathroom and large sitting billiard room. For complete privacy this suite is only offered to one party at a time.
Both suites feature log fires, ceiling fans, books, music, games etc. and restful bush and lake views. Stroll around our extensive gardens, bushwalk adjoining State Forest or visit nearby wineries, orchid farm and pottery. Kangaroos, birds, native flora and fauna abound. Flexible meal times, generous breakfasts including home baked muffins, breads and croissants are a feature. Dinner by arrangement. Chilren are welcome.

Bendigo   RACV ★★★★☆
Self-contained Accommodation
Address: 170 McCrae St, Bendigo
Name: Jubilee Villa
Telephone: (03) 5442 2920
Fax: (03) 5442 2580
Beds: 2 Double, 1 Single (2 bedrooms)
Bathroom: 1 Ensuite
Tariff: B&B (full) Double $100-$130, Single $80, Children $15. Smoking outside only. Vouchers accepted $25 surcharge Mon-Thurs
Nearest Town: Bendigo P.O. 500 metres

Jubilee Villa is situated in the heart of our historic golden city. Our home and adjacent renovated servants quarters were born in Bendigo's boom years and shares the city's rich history. We offer our guests Victorian splendour with all the comforts of today and total privacy in their spacious suite. A coach port links the guests suite to our home ensuring ease of service to provide our guests with scrumptious breakfast and the best of hospitality.
The separate quarters has its own entrance, off street parking and level access. Guests enjoy the luxury of an ensuite spa and intimate breakfast room.
An enormous aspen shades our large garden and provides a peaceful setting for a barbeque or just a quiet rest.
Just a step away are some of Bendigo's finest attractions including historic sites, galleries, the Chinese Museum and restaurants. Our position ensures you the full Bendigo experience in Four Star comfort.

VICTORIA

Bendigo RACV ★★★☆
Homestay/Farmstay+Self-contained Accommodation
Address: "Skye Glen Llama Farm", Clearing Ct,
Mandurang Valley, Bendigo VIC (Please phone)
Name: Heather & Rod MacLeod
Telephone: (03) 5439 3054 **Fax**: (03) 5441 5051
Mobile: (015) 349733
Beds: 2 Queen, 2 Single (2 bedrooms)
Bathroom: 1 Ensuite, 1 Private
Tariff: B&B (full) Double $75-$85, Single $55-$60,
Children welcome. Vouchers accepted
Nearest Town: Bendigo 8 km

Skye Glen Llama Farm offers the best of both worlds - a tranquil, rural retreat in picturesque Mandurang Valley - yet only minutes from Bendigo tourist attractions.
Nearby One Tree Hill Regional Park provides lovely wildflower walks, wildlife - close to historic winery, potteries and wildflower nurseries.
Our Chilean llamas have blended well with the Scottish theme that decorates the spacious bedrooms with ensuite and private bathroom, full equipped guest kitchen, library and games room with log fire and billiard table.
Wander through the heather gardens and orchard as you meet Roscoe and llama friends. Be as private as you wish with separate entrances and guest lounge room containing colour TV and video.
Enjoy your Scottish country breakfast by the open fire.
Skye Glen offers warm hospitality with a wee touch of Scotland.
"Ceud Mile Failthe" (A hundred thousand welcomes)

Bendigo RACV ★★★☆
Homestay Self-Contained Accommodation
Address: Whistle Inn B&B
213 Allingham Street
Kangaroo Flat, Vic 3555
Name: Ken and Marian Craze
Telephone: (03) 5447 8685 **Fax**: (03) 5447 8685 **Mobile**: 015 844 821
Beds: 2 Double, 4 Single (3 bedrooms)
Bathroom: 2 Ensuites
Tariff: B&B (full) Double $80, Single $45, Children welcome. Vouchers accepted
Nearest Town: Bendigo on Calder Highway

Located adjacent to historic Kangaroo Flat railway station on the Melbourne side of Bendigo. Five minutes from historic CBD.
Guests have a large bed sitting room with wood fire or cooling. This room has an ensuite with spa.
A separate room contains bunks and a well appointed kitchenette. An adjacent attractive outdoor area has a gas BBQ available.
The other suite is a centrally heated twin share with lounge and ensuite.
All of this is situated in a pleasant garden. Ideally situated close to the attractions of Bendigo.
Hosts welcome the opportunity to chat with guests and are most willing to assist with sightseeing planning. Children are most welcome.

VICTORIA

Bendigo
Self-contained Accom. **RACV ★★★★**
Address: 176 Williamson St., Bendigo
Name: "Gardena"
Telephone: (03) 5443 0551
Beds: 1 Queen (1 bedroom)
Bathroom: 1 Private
Tariff: B&B (continental) Double $90-$110.
Vouchers accepted $10 surcharge.
Accepted Monday to Thursday.
Nearest Town: Bendigo - centrally situated 1km from Shamrock Hotel.

Barbara and Peter would like to welcome you and let you experience the charm of their fully renovated federation style home with all the conveniences of modern living while keeping the feeling of the past. Gardena is furnished in beautiful antiques and you can enjoy a spa and watch TV or have a game of chess before retiring to a comfortable four poster brass bed with its satin sheets and crisp white linen. After a relaxing sleep-in take your time while enjoying your continental breakfast which is fully supplied in the kitchenette. Gardena has got cosy log fires and electric blankets for winter warmth while in summer there are fans for your comfort or perhaps a dip in the pool. We are just a short walk to central Bendigo with its many tourist attractions or take a short drive to discover wineries, gold ghost towns or antique shops and weekend markets.

Bendigo
Homestay
Address: Lot 8 Durston's Rd., Maiden Gully, VIC 3551
Name: "Benlee"
Telephone: (03) 5449 6510
Beds: 1 Queen (1 bedroom)
Bathroom: 1 Ensuite
Tariff: B&B (full) Double $65-$75 Vouchers accepted
Nearest Town: Bendigo

Benlee is situated 8km from the centre of Bendigo. Our rural retreat is set on 9 acres of natural bushland where guests can relax and appreciate the peace and tranquillity of the area.
We offer spacious, comfortable accommodation where you can enjoy your own private lounge room or join our family which includes two school age boys and a dog.
A hearty country style breakfast is served in either the dining room, the barbeque / pergola area, or on the front verandah overlooking the extensive garden and bushland.
We both have travelled extensively and enjoy sharing our interests with our guests.
A warm friendly welcome will greet you to our home, but being non smokers ourselves, we thank you for not smoking indoors.

Please help us provide the best hospitality in the world.
Fill in a comment form for every place you stay.

VICTORIA

Bendigo - Spring Gully   RACV ★★★☆
Homestay+Self-contained Accom.
Address: "PineTrees" Bed & Breakfast
on One Tree Hill, 6 Allott Court,
Spring Gully, Bendigo, 3550
Name: Leila & Harry
Telephone: (03) 5442 8801 **Fax**: (03) 5444 4575
Email: sam@bendigo.net.au
Beds: 1 Queen, 2 Single (2 bedrooms)
Bathroom: 1 Private, 1 Family share
Tariff: B&B (full) Double $75-$85, Single $55-$65, Children $15.
 Vouchers accepted

Pine Trees Bed & Breakfast (One Tree Hill)

Nearest Town: 4km south of Bendigo town centre - Spring Gully/Mandurang Rd.
PineTrees, where the city's edge meets the Iron-bark forest, One Tree Hill, Bendigo, Goldfield Centre of Victoria. Treat yourself! Be charmed by the atmosphere and creature comforts of the private queen bedroom suite, be pampered in the Long Drawing Room. Indulge in a Roman bath! Scrumptious breakfasts! No traffic noise! Enjoy the wide verandah ... Hop the back fence to bushland trails. BBQ in the courtyard ... Potteries, wineries nearby. Or choose the S.C. "Inn" a miniature country cottage. PineTrees, only 5 minutes drive to City Centre; tour the Central Deborah Mine, be enthralled by the Chinese Museum and grand buildings of the Gold Rush, experience the Talking Tram ... Explore shopping arcades, antique markets, galleries. Thrill at the recently uncovered terraced waterfalls ... Sample our great delis, pubs, restaurants. Come soon, be delighted by the true country elegance of PineTrees. We'd love to please you!

Bendigo
Self-contained Cottages RACV ★★★★☆
Address: 13 Anderson Street,
Bendigo, VIC 3550
Name: The Cottages Bendigo
Telephone: (03) 5441 5613
Fax: (03) 5444 4313
Beds: 2 Double (2 bedrooms)
Bathroom: 2 Ensuite
Tariff: B&B (full) Double $100-$125.
Nearest Town: Bendigo P.O. 900 metres

The Cottages Bendigo - is a most unusual Bed & Breakfast experience; with two Luxury Guest Cottages nestled in Chris & Mavis's beautiful cottage gardens. Named "Robin's Nest" and "Hyacinth Bouquet", these two fully self-contained cottages are furnished with antiques and cater exclusively for couples, providing a romantic retreat in a secret quiet location, only a short stroll to town centre. The property is steeped in history and is located adjacent to the site of the famous Greater Hustler Gold Mine.
Restaurants, art galleries, theatre and most sporting facilities within walking distance. We have established a reputation as a unique Australian B&B experience, and have featured in various magazines papers and on radio. Your hosts have travelled and lived on most continents, so appreciate the finer points of hospitality. We promise you a memorable stay, with the desire to return again and again - like so many of our guests. Picture yourselves enjoying a home cooked breakfast (served by your hosts), in the gardens or in the privacy of your own cottage.
Phone, fax or write for further details.

Birregurra see Lorne, and Colac

Branxholme see Hamilton

Bright RACV ★★★☆
Homestay
Address: "Yarrara Homestay" 3 Walkers Lane, Bright, VIC 3741
Name: Y. Whitecross
Telephone: (03) 5755 1850
Beds: 1 Queen, 2 Single (2 bedrooms)
Bathroom: 1 Ensuite, 1 Private
Tariff: B&B (continental) Double $60, Single $35. Vouchers accepted
Nearest Town: 1 1/2 km west of Bright

We offer a tranquil, secluded split-level home with 11-metre solar heated pool on 4 acres of garden and orchard. Situated high in the mountains, overlooking Bright, gateway to the Victorian Alps. The balcony view of the valley and mountains are only surpassed by the variety of trees that present four seasons of colour. Kangaroos, wombats, beautiful parrots, birds and other wildlife often roam the house surrounds. We offer two guest rooms – one queen and one twin, both with private bathrooms. A guest lounge and laundry facilities are available.
Don is a retired Primary School Principal, active in gardening and sport. Yvonne has interests in Art. A cat also lives with us.
Bright has beautiful walks, quaint tourist shops and restaurants. Snow in winter is less than one hour drive away, trout fishing, gold panning, bush walking venues are all around us. For senior people and overseas visitors we offer free, when available, a 4X drive along the ridge to view the High Country.
Hope to see you soon ... But please advise am or pm arrival.

Bridgewater Bay see Cape Bridgewater

Bright RACV ★★★★☆
Homestay
Address: 'Thorley Manor',
Morses Creek Road, Wandiligong, VIC 3744
Name: Alison & Jim Anton
Telephone: (03) 5755 1538
Fax: (03) 5750 1146 **Mobile**: (018) 573 506
Beds: 1 King, 1 Double, 2 Single, (2 bedrooms)
Bathroom: 1 Ensuite, 1 Private
Tariff: B&B (full), Double $95, Single $65,
Dinner $30, Children $30. Vouchers accepted
Nearest Town: Bright

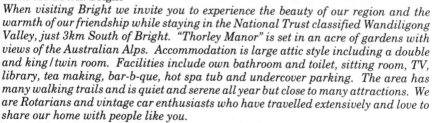

When visiting Bright we invite you to experience the beauty of our region and the warmth of our friendship while staying in the National Trust classified Wandiligong Valley, just 3km South of Bright. "Thorley Manor" is set in an acre of gardens with views of the Australian Alps. Accommodation is large attic style including a double and king / twin room. Facilities include own bathroom and toilet, sitting room, TV, library, tea making, bar-b-que, hot spa tub and undercover parking. The area has many walking trails and is quiet and serene all year but close to many attractions. We are Rotarians and vintage car enthusiasts who have travelled extensively and love to share our home with people like you.
Australian cuisine and folklore nights and package deals available. Dinner and picnic lunches provided with prior arrangement.

VICTORIA

Bright RACV ★★★☆
Homestay
Address: Germantown Lodge,
Tawonga Road, Bright VIC 3741
Name: Alan & Ruth Collis
Telephone: (03) 5755 2360
Beds: 1 King/Twin, 1 Twin (2 bedrooms)
Bathroom: 1 Guests share
Tariff: B&B (continental) Double $80,
Single $50, Dinner 2 course $15, 3 course $20.
Full breakfast $5 extra per head. Vouchers accepted
Nearest Town: 6km south-east of Bright

Our home is a large rustic log cabin with pine-lined interior, cathedral ceilings, large lounge-room and wide verandahs. The house is set on 14 acres in perhaps the most scenic area of Victoria. We are surrounded by hills and mountains and have a spectacular view of Mt Feathertop, Victoria's second highest mountain, snow-capped during winter and spring. Victoria's major snowfields (Mt Buffalo, Falls Creek, Mt Hotham) are nearby.
A maximum of 4 guests at a time ensures that you are treated as someone special. Dinner with your hosts available by arrangement.
We would be pleased to share the evenings with you in our lounge-room (log fire when cool). We may be able to suggest things to do and see while in Bright and help with your holiday planning.
We are old car enthusiasts (vehicles date from 1909 to 1961) and a tour of the town or district is offered in a 1920's Fiat.
Please phone for brochure.

Bright RACV ★★★☆
Homestay/Farmstay   aglta member
Address: "Buckland Valley B&B", Buckland Valley Road, Porepunkah, 3740
(Signposted from roundabout)
Name: Lisa Page & Bill Buckley
Telephone: (03) 5756 2656
Beds: 1 Queen, 2 Double (3 bedrooms)
Bathroom: 3 Ensuites
Tariff: B&B (continental) Double $85, Single $60. Dinner $30 for groups only.
Credit Cards. Vouchers accepted
Nearest Town: Bright

Buckland Valley B&B is a unique bush retreat you'll never forget, BUT still within 15 minutes drive from Bright. Set on 22 totally private acres at the foot of Mt Buffalo, surrounded by wild life with fresh water creek at your door. Plenty of bush walking, bird watching, fishing and general relaxation on the menu here.
Guests have their own lounge and dining area separate from hosts which boasts a huge riverstone open fire with the rustic feeling of yesteryear. Rooms have comfortable old world charm, electric blankets, private ensuites and down filled doona's. Other attractions include hang-gliding, horse riding, wineries, top restaurants, festivals, skiing, art galleries, water activities and much more. Our B and B is a smoke free ,adults only retreat. Packages available for groups and longer stays.

VICTORIA

Bright RACV ★★★★
Homestay

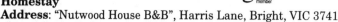

Address: "Nutwood House B&B", Harris Lane, Bright, VIC 3741
Name: David Bell
Telephone: (03) 5756 2084 **Fax**: (03) 5750 1771 **Mobile**: 015-039 424
Beds: 2 Double (2 bedrooms)
Bathroom: 2 Ensuites
Tariff: B&B (continental) Double $90, Single $60.
Nearest Town: Bright

Nestled at the foot of Mt Buffalo, Nutwood House is set on 11 private acres with superb mountain views. Internal decor is English country cottage style of yesteryear, complete with grandfather clock. A guest TV lounge leaves the main guest lounge free for a quiet fireside chat.
The area abounds with wildlife and offers many varied activities including horse riding, powered hang gliding, fishing, caving, skiing, abseiling, to name a few, plus lots of lovely walks.
A great natural waterfall-fed swimming hole in the Buckland river is only seconds away.
Facilities include: ensuites, spa room, two guest only lounge rooms, open fire, free tea / coffee & biscuits all day, hair dryers. Domestic pets catered for. Relaxation massage available. Our hospitality will bring you back year after year. Cooked breakfast on request.

Bruthen, East Gippsland
Bed & Breakfast

Address: Cnr. Main St & Omeo Hwy, Bruthen, 3885
Name: Bruthen Bed & Breakfast
Telephone: (03) 5157 5616
Beds: 1 Queen, 1 Double, 1 Single (2 bedrooms)
Bathroom: 1 Ensuite, 1 Private
Tariff: B&B (continental) Double $70-$90, Single $65-$70. Children welcome.
Credit Cards (BC/MC/VISA/Amex) Vouchers accepted Australian B&B
Nearest Town: Approximately 15 minutes drive from Nowa Nowa or Bairnsdale (approx 25 km).

In earlier times Bruthen was a busy port town. Steam ships navigated the Tambo River to Mossiface. Stockmen, bullockies and gold prospectors took refreshment and lodgings in the town. The coach stopped outside O'Keefe's Royal Mail Hotel, which is the present day Bruthen Bed and Breakfast.
Bruthen is located in the beautiful Tambo Valley, central to mountains, lakes, beaches, wineries, golf courses, Buchan Caves and much more.
Relax on the verandahs and enjoy tranquil rural scenery. If you are especially privileged, wild egrets will fly down and walk right up into the garden.
Picnic in the Main Street Gardens or at the Ramrod swimming hole. Thermoses filled. Post office, public telephone, shops and various amenities nearby. Linen, TV, tea and coffee facilities, lounges, heating, fans and tourist information provided. We do not allow pets or smoking in the rooms. Advance bookings appreciated.

Buninyong see Ballarat

VICTORIA

Callignee - Gippsland
Homestay/Bed & Breakfast   RACV ★★★☆
Address: "Callignee Getaway",
Callignee South Road, Callignee
North, Victoria 3844
Name: Rosemary Nevill & David Abbott
Telephone: (03) 5195 5457
Beds: 1 Double + sofa bed
(1 bedroom + sitting room)
Bathroom: 1 Private
Tariff: B&B (full) Double $85, Single $70, Dinner $20.
  Vouchers accepted
Nearest Town: 18km south of Traralgon (180km east of Melbourne)

Nestled in the Strzelecki Ranges in the heart of Gippsland, close to Traralgon, Tarra-Bulga National Park and the Grand Ridge Tourist Road, 'Callignee Getaway' is a five acre Land for Wildlife property. This picturesque hillside property offers guests panoramic views, rambling garden walks, abundant bird and animal life . Guest accommodation is a charming and relaxing private suite with a separate guest entrance and courtyard. Facilities include television, video, tourist information, fridge, barbecue and lots of little 'extras' to make your stay special. Car touring and bush walking opportunities abound which makes 'Callignee Getaway' an ideal base for exploring Central Gippsland - unique rainforest areas to the south, the Victorian Alps and historic goldmining town of Walhalla to the north, and the taste-tempting Gippsland gourmet Deli Trail. As one guest wrote "Surpassing all expectation, everything is perfect - great birding, food, surroundings and warmly welcoming hosts".

Camperdown - Lismore RACV ★★★☆
Rural Retreat
Address: "Kooraweera Homestead",
RMB 2235, Camperdown, 3260 Victoria
Name: J & D Deane
Telephone: (03) 5593 8235 **Fax**: (03) 5593 8235
Beds: 1 Queen, 2 Single (2 bedrooms)
Bathroom: 1 Ensuite, 1 Private
Tariff: B&B (special) Double $80, Single $50. Dinner $15-$30. (No facilities for children under 10). Accommodation plus all meals: Double $130, Single $90.
Vouchers accepted
Nearest Town: Camperdown

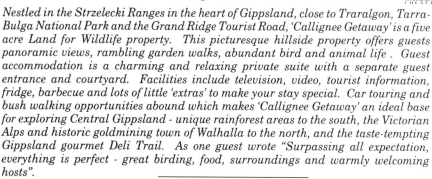

"Kooraweera" invites guests to enjoy being pampered in "Olde Worlde" charm and comfort. Our homestead is set amidst old fashioned gardens and lakes.
A western district sheep and cattle property that is central to many interesting areas - coastal national parks, craters, lakes, and historical parks of Ballarat and Warrnambool.
We offer personalized service with bedrooms that possess open fires and tea/coffee making facilities.
You can either join us for meals or have formal, serviced, candlelight dinners in the dining room. Meals are home cooked using farm produce, seasonal vegetables and preserves.
For guests who love activity, we offer tennis, boating, swimming, seasonal farm activities, walking, and bird observing. For guests who wish simply for peace and relaxation, there are many garden nooks that invite you to read or meditate and the sunsets over our lake can be breathtakingly beautiful.

Cape Bridgewater - Bridgewater Bay
Guest House   RACV ★★★☆
Address: "Sea View Lodge",
RMB 4370, Bridgewater Road, Cape Bridgewater, VIC 3306
Name: Phil & Sue Arnold
Telephone: (03) 5526 7276
Mobile: 0418 525 750
Beds: 2 King/Queen, 2 Double, 4 Single
(6 bedrooms) **Bathroom**: 6 Ensuite
Tariff: B&B (full) Double $75-$90, Single $55-$65, Children $20. Dinner $20.
Campervans welcome. Credit cards.   Vouchers accepted
Nearest Town: 20km west of Portland

Discover the secrets of the Discovery Coast at Sea View Lodge, on the beach at spectacular Bridgewater Bay - 20km from Portland. Peace, quiet and solitude. Enjoy the secluded beaches, rugged cliffs and spectacular coastal scenery of Cape Bridgewater. Grand finale of the Great Ocean Road.
New stone building, built on the lines of the original Sea View Hotel. Spacious rooms with ensuites and stunning ocean views. Cosy lounge, library and dining rooms. Tea and coffee making facilities available. The perfect getaway.
Scenic attractions - just a short walk or drive away - blowholes, petrified forest, seal colony, Bridgewater Lakes, secluded beaches, giant sand dunes, limestone caves, Discovery Bay.
Surrounded by National Parks - Mt. Richmond, Discovery Bay, Mt Eccles, Lower Glenelg, Cape Nelson, Bat's Ridges Fauna Reserve.
Laze away the hours or take part in local activities including fishing, surfing, walking, canoeing, caving, snorkelling, scuba, wineries, emu farm.
The Great South West Walk goes right past our front door.

Castlemaine   RACV ★★★★
Homestay
Address: "Wisteria House", 256 Barker Street,
Castlemaine, Victoria 3450
Name: Janene & Ian Thomson
Telephone: (03) 5470 6604 **Fax**: (03) 5472 1024
Email: wisteria@mail.netcon.net.au
Beds: 2 Queen, 1 Single (2 bedrooms)
Bathroom: 1 Ensuite, 1 Private
Tariff: B&B (full) Double $95-$105, Single $70-$75, Children by arrangement. Credit cards (Mastercard/Visa/Bankcard)‛. Vouchers accepted midweek by arrangement.
Nearest Town: Castlemaine

Castlemaine, in Victoria's historic goldfields region, features some of the finest examples of early colonial living in Australia. Staying with us lets you experience all this and much more. Sample fine food from local restaurants and coffee shops. Linger in art and craft galleries, museums and National Trust homes. Taste fine wines from renowned wineries. Discover the remains of frenetic goldfields camps.
Wisteria House, built in 1874, retains the ambience of that era, while modern amenities tastefully combine to provide quality accommodation. Guest accommodation is in-house or a self-contained suite (with full breakfast provided).
Heating, electric blankets and doonas for winter in all bedrooms. The lounge room with its open fire is an ideal place to relax, talk about what you have done, or to get to know new-found friends. And breakfast is terrific!
What others say.... "Wonderful hospitality. Opened a new world of B&B."
A beautifully presented establishment. Charming and attentive hosts."
Home Page: http://www.innhouse.com.au

Chiltern
Farmstay
Address: Lancashire Gap Rd, Chiltern
Name: "Forest View"
Telephone: (03) 5726 1337 **Mobile**: (0411) 117223
Beds: 1 Queen (1 bedroom)
Bathroom: 1 Ensuite
Tariff: B&B (full) Double $75, Single $50. Dinner $30 double. Vouchers accepted
Nearest Town: 3km from Chiltern off the Yackanandah Rd.

Chiltern is very conveniently located between Albury/Wodonga and Wangaratta on the Hume Highway (between Sydney and Melbourne). It is close to Beechworth, Yackananda and Rutherglen. The area is very interesting historically because of its association with gold.
"Forest View" is about 2km from the highway but just across the road from an extensive forest renowned for its wildlife and flowers. Our small farm includes emus as well as very quiet sheep and cattle. Our outside living area includes a pool and BBQ and welcomes smokers even though our house is a non-smoking area. A winery "Walkabout" in June and a Jazz Festival in November are just some of the other attractions in the area. The Murray River, Hume Weir and snow fields and other places of interest are all within a short distance.

Colac - Birregurra - Lorne
Homestay
Address: Please phone ahead.
Kirrewur Bed & Breakfast
Princes Highway
Warncoort Vic 3243
Name: Kath Walsh
Telephone: (03) 5233 6283
Mobile: 019 408 319
Beds: 1 Queen, 1 Double, 2 Single (3 bedrooms)
Bathroom: 1 Ensuite, 1 Private, 1 Guests Share
Tariff: B&B (full) Double $95-$110, Single $65-$75, Children $35. Vouchers accepted Mon-Thurs apart from Easter and Dec 25 - Jan 31.
Nearest Town: Colac 9km, Birregurra 10km, Lorne 50km.

Relax and enjoy country hospitality in historic Victorian home (c.1862). Central heating and open fires in the winter, where you can curl up with a book, or watch TV in the guest sitting room. A large north facing verandah provides a sunny retreat on warmer days to sit and take in lake and countryside views. For the energetic there is a tennis court and a practice fairway to try your golf shots. You will find the butlers pantry with tea and coffee making facilities stocked with home made biscuits and slices. Breakfast is served on fine china in formal dining room. A ten minute drive will take you to Lake Colac for fishing and boating, or local golf courses and bowling greens. Central to Otway National park, Great Ocean Road, Lorne, Apollo Bay and the Lakes and Crater Country near Red Rock and Camperdown.

Cowes–see Phillip Island

VICTORIA

Corryong - North East Victoria
Homestay
Address: 57 Donaldson St., Corryong, 3707
Name: Mother Hubbard Bed & Breakfast
Telephone: (060) 761570 **Fax**: (060) 761570
Beds: 2 Double (2 bedrooms) **Bathroom**: 1 Ensuite, 1 Guest Private
Tariff: B&B (continental) Ensuite Double $100, Single $80. Guest Private Double $80, single $60.
Nearest Town: Albury/Wodonga 122km

"Wannawong" Aboriginal for "place on the side of a hill", is a Federation style home built in 1916. This recently restored home is comfortably furnished. Two double rooms are available with tea and coffee making facilities in each room. A cozy family bathroom offers a double shower, which also makes an ideal enclosed "bubble bath" and spa. Breakfast may be served on the verandah, or just relax there and enjoy the peace of the mountains and the special visits of the wild parrots.
Corryong is 122 km to the East of Albury / Wodonga and is the centre of the "World", being almost halfway on the most scenic route between Sydney and Melbourne. Corryong is also a logical stop on extended routes from Gippsland, the NSW South Coast, Cooma, Canberra and Albury / Wodonga. The town is the last resting place of the "Man from Snowy River" and offers interesting town walks, drives to waterfalls and scenic views. There is immediate 4WD access to some of the most exciting and beautiful high country in south east Australia. Corryong is close to the snow in winter and cool, trout-laden mountain streams in the summer. In autumn and spring the streetscapes will rival those of any town.

Cudgewa - Upper Murray .RACV ★★★
Self-contained Accommodation
Address: "Elmstead",
Ashstead Park Lane, Cudgewa, VIC 3705
Name: Marja & Tony Jarvis
Telephone: (02) 6077 4324
Beds: 1 Queen, 1 Single (1 bedroom)
Bathroom: 1 Ensuite
Tariff: B&B (continental) Double $70, Single $45, Children under 12 $7. Vouchers accepted
Nearest Town: Corryong 12km, Albury/Wodonga is 129km west on the Murray Valley Highway.

We are a young family on a beef-property which has been in the family for four generations.
The newly renovated guest cottage provides a queen sized bed, single bed with trundle, wood-heater, fully equipped kitchenette and an en-suite.
It is situated in a picturesque garden amongst magnificent old elm trees with panoramic views over the Snowy Mountains. Cudgewa is nestled in the foothills of the Snowy Mountains. Tourist attractions include Burrowa-Pine Mountain National Park, Corryong with its Pioneer Museum and Jack Riley's grave (man from Snowy River). The snow-fields are just over an hour away via the world renowned Snowy Mountains Hydro Electric Scheme on the scenic Alpine Way. There are many good fishing streams in the area.
Preferably non-smokers
Home Page: http://www.travelaustralia.com.au/s/18949

VICTORIA

Dandenong Ranges - Kalorama
Elegant Bed & Breakfast RACV ★★★★☆
Address: Rosehill Lodge, Kalorama Terrace,
Kalorama, VIC 3766 (Car entrance)
(rear of)1280 Mt Dandenong Tourist Road, Kalorama
Name: Catherine & George Hill
Telephone: (03) 9761 8889
Fax: (03) 9761 8889 **Mobile**: 0411 826 874
Email: geh@ozmail.com.au
Beds: 1 King or 2 Single plus 1 Double with parlour. **Bathroom**: 2 Ensuite
Tariff: B&B (full) King $110, Double $95, Single $70,
Dinner from $20, Lunch picnic basket to order.
Nearest Town: Montrose/Mt Dandenong (Melbourne 34km)
Seeking a comfortable bed, charming rooms and separate guest dining room / lounge in a central delightful and quiet location directly on the Mount Dandenong Tourist Road in the beautiful Dandenong Ranges, where you can enjoy superb food of your choice and just rest, or visit the many local tourist attractions then Rosehill Lodge should be your choice With trained and sincere hosts who will warmly and sincerely welcome you to ensure a memorable stay, Rosehill Lodge is managed by Catherine Hill previous owner of Rosbar House and assisted by internationally known Culinary Olympic Gold Winning Chef and industry awarded Hospitality educator George Hill. Extended stays attract special rates. Cooked breakfast is inclusive, lunch and dinner if required will be dependent upon your chosen menu. Please note, in the interests of the majority of our guests we discourage smoking indoors.
Internet: Http. / /www / ozemail.com.au. / -geh
Home Page: http.//www.ozemail.com.au./-geh

Dandenong Ranges - Mt. Dandenong
Country House & Cottages RACV ★★★★☆
Address: 1411-1413 Mt. Dandenong Tourist Road,
Mt. Dandenong, VIC 3767
Name: Penrith Country House Retreat
Telephone: (03) 975 12391 & (03) 9751 2447
Fax: (03) 9751 2391 (03) 9751 2447
Beds: 6 Queen, (6 bedrooms)
Bathroom: 6 Ensuites
Tariff: B&B (full), Double $100-$210,
Single $95-$200. Children $25. Dinner by arrangement. Credit cards accepted.
Nearest Town: Mt. Dandenong. Olinda

"A different world" - The Ultimate Escape"
*Only one hour from Melbourne, Penrith is a peaceful, private, tranquil retreat, nestled in the heart of the Dandenong Ranges, overlooking the Great Dividing Range. Take time to relax, reflect upon and enjoy the pleasures of life as it was meant to be. Meander through 3 hectares of private 80 year old gardens, listed with the Australian Open Garden Scheme. This botanical wonderland of eucalypts, conifers, English and American oaks, elms, giant tree ferns, over 100 different varieties of rhododendrons and a spring fed stream meandering through the lower reaches of the garden forms a delightful setting for that romantic interlude or a re-appreciation of nature.
Be indulged in "olde worlde" luxurious, romantic spa-suites. Feast upon delicious gourmet meals by arrangement. Alternatively, pamper yourself in our private self contained Bavarian or hermit house cottages. All the attractions of the Dandenong Ranges are minutes away, with the Yarra Valley just a 30 minute drive.*

Dandenong Ranges - Mt Dandenong
Idyllic Homestay RACV ★★★★☆
Address: "Tavlock", Toorak Road, Mt Dandenong, Victoria 3767
Name: Peter & Linda Beaumont
Telephone: (03) 9751 2336 **Fax**: (03) 9751 2336 **Mobile**: (019) 413755
Beds: 2 Queen (2 bedrooms)
Bathroom: 2 Ensuite
Tariff: B&B (full) Double $100 - $125, Gourmet dinner by arrangement, Licensed Credit Cards.
Nearest Town: Olinda 48 km east of Melbourne

Set on nearly an acre of delightful gardens and nestled in one of Victorias most visited areas - is "Tavlock". Our home began his history at the turn of the century and now provides a welcome peace to weary travellers.
Our 2 spacious bedrooms with ensuites boast lots of fluffy towels, feather pillows, cozy quilts and all luxuries. Also, there is a separate lounge for guests with tea and coffee making facilities, CD, colour TV, books, magazines and games.
Enjoy the company of our resident kookaburras and rosellas whilst having a sumptuous breakfast on the verandah or on cold days breakfast is beside the fire in our country kitchen.
Peter and I have previously lived on Norfolk Island where "A big smile, warm welcome and lasting friendships" are legendary.

VICTORIA

Dandenong Ranges - Mt Dandenong
Luxury Bed & Breakfast RACV ★★★★
Address: 1434 Mt Dandenong Tourist Road, Mt Dandenong, Vic 3767
Name: Greg & Val
Telephone: (03) 9751 1064
Beds: 3 Queen (3 bedrooms)
Bathroom: 3 Ensuite
Tariff: B&B (full) Double $125-$225,
Single N/A, Children N/A, Dinner N/A; Credit Cards.
Nearest Town: 40km east of Melbourne

As our special guest at "Fern 'n' Chestnut" your choice of various luxury period style suites will impress. Our business has been built on our reputation as caring hosts. This combines well with the 'homely' feel of our rooms, to afford you that 'home away from home' experience.

Our suites are fully detailed and incorporate all the home comforts such as: real log fire in your own private lounge, large corner spa ensuite, brass or four poster beds, hot drinks trolley, chocolates, flowers, towels and gowns. For your entertainment we equip you with VCR, TV, CD player, books, magazines, games and of course plenty of fire wood!

We are situated in the heart of the famous Mount Dandenong mountain ranges. The area is renowned for the fresh air, forest walks, gardens, tea rooms, Puffing Billy railway and the William Ricketts sanctuary.

We know how demanding travelling is. We provide the ideal retreat for that special interlude during your busy holiday schedule!

Home Page: www.discover-australia.com/fc/

Gift Vouchers

Our B&B vouchers are for a double room for one night's B&B. They cost $89, and if you order one as a gift, we will include a free
Australian Bed & Breakfast Book
worth $16.95

Send your cheque to
Moonshine Press
59 Quirk Street
Dee Why
NSW 2099

VICTORIA

Dandenong Ranges -Olinda
Self-contained Accom.
Address: "Quiddity", Spencer Road, Olinda, 3788
Name: "Quiddity Cottage"
Telephone: (03) 9751 1077
Fax: (03) 9751 1939
Beds: 1 Queen (1 bedroom) **Bathroom**: 1 Private
Tariff: B&B (breakfast provisions) Mon-Thur $125 per night, Weekends: Fri & Sun $170, Sat & public holidays $210, Two consecutive nights: Fri & Sat or Sat & Sun $340, Sun & Mon $265, Three consecutive nights: Fri through Sun $475, Weekly $750. Children N/A, Credit Cards (VISA/MC/BC).
Nearest Town: Olinda

Panelled cathedral ceilings, log fire, French doors onto terraced verandahs, gourmet kitchen. Nestled into a garden, surrounded by bush, umbrella tree ferns, and towering mountain ash.
Quiddity Cottage is located on an 11 acre, "Land for Wildlife" property, in the heart of the Dandenongs. However, it is conveniently close to antique shops, galleries, charming restaurants and cafes, native forest bush walks, and heritage gardens. The Yarra Valley wineries are also within easy reach.
Quiddity Cottage is designed to use state-of-the-art environmental technology and has a Five Star energy rating from Energy Victoria. It is entirely constructed of recycled and plantation grown timbers.
Full breakfast supplies, fresh flowers, thoughtful extras. Generous packages are available for multiple night stays.

Dandenong Ranges -Olinda
Self-contained Cottage
Address: "Brambledene" Spencer Road, Olinda, Vic 3788
Name: "Brambledene Cottage"
Telephone: (03) 9751 1077
Fax: (03) 9751 1939
Beds: 1 Queen (1 bedroom)
Bathroom: 1 Private

Tariff: B&B (breakfast provisions) Mon-Thur $125 per night, Weekends: Fri & Sun $170, Sat & public holidays $210, Two consecutive nights: Fri & Sat or Sat & Sun $340, Sun & Mon $265, Three consecutive nights: Fri through Sun $475, Weekly $750. Children N/A, Credit Cards (VISA/MC/BC).
Nearest Town: 3.7km from Olinda Village, off Olinda-Monbulk Road.

Brambledene Cottage was established in the 1880's as part of a guest house which provided a stopover for the Cobb and Co Coach and later was visited by artists from the Heidelberg School inspired by the idyllic surroundings. This link with the past is echoed in the old world charm of this fully self-contained cottage set in 2 1/2 acres of heritage hills garden. The open fire in the bedroom and the cosiness of the cottage with its antique furnishings, create a feeling of traditional warmth reminiscent of a bygone age. The luxury of today is not forgotten with the provision of gas heating throughout, TV, video, CD/radio and a full equipped kitchen. Country breakfast ingredients are provided along with a picnic hamper on request. The galleries, antique shops, gardens, restaurants and wineries of the Dandenong Ranges are close by. Relax and indulge yourselves in this perfect retreat.

VICTORIA

Dandenong Ranges - Upwey
Homestay+Self-contained Accom. RACV ★★★★☆
Address: 6 Day Street, Upwey, 3158 Victoria
Name: Talanoa Bed & Breakfast
Telephone: (03) 9752 5407 **Fax**: (03) 9752 5457
Mobile: (019) 387 891
Email: talanoa@ozemail.com.au
Beds: 1 King, 2 Double, 2 Single (3 bedrooms)
Bathroom: 1 Guests share, 1 Private
Tariff: B&B (full) Double $110, Single $80, Children $30, (Use of both bedrooms for families $170), Dinner $30, Credit Cards (BC/VISA/MC).
Vouchers accepted Surcharge $10
Nearest Town: 4km west of Belgrave; 1km N/E off Burwood Highway at Upwey

Talanoa, (which means "talking amongst friends") is a place where you can stop and enjoy a moment, take in the view of the hills, breath the fresh mountain air, watch the wild birds and relax in the quietness of our home. Upstairs, you will find all comforts, with 2 beautifully furnished bedrooms, 1 double and 1 twin, being ideal for family stay, friends travelling together, or simply for couples who are looking for a quiet and relaxing time away. Our facilities include a lovely clean, modern bathroom, guest lounge with TV, video player, log fire, games, books and magazines, breakfast / dining area with fridge, microwave, and tea & coffee making facilities. Downstairs is a double bedroom with private bathroom. Being ideally located between the Mt Dandenong Tourist Road and Burwood Highway we are only minutes from the tourist highlights of the ranges like Puffing Billy, the many gardens, tea houses and restaurants. Come and join us, we know you will be comfortable.

Home Page: www.link.net.au/drt/pages/accom45/welcome.htm

Daylesford RACV ★★★☆
Farmstay
Address: RMB 2390, Franklinford, VIC 3461
Name: Joy & Eric Sartori
Telephone: (03) 5476 4207
Beds: 2 Double, 2 Single (2 bedrooms)
or 1 King/Twin, 1 Double (2 bedrooms)
Bathroom: 1 Private or Guest share
Tariff: B&B (full) Double $100, Dinner $20.
Nearest Town: 16 km north of Daylesford on Daylesford–Newstead Road

We are the fifth generation of the original settlers to farm this beautiful valley. Our comfortable home retains the large freestone kitchen warmed by a wood fire stove. It is surrounded by a cottage garden from where we obtain most of our fruit and vegetables which you may enjoy in your evening meal. We also make jams and preserves.

Two hundred yards from the homestead is the "Jim Crow", a magnificent trout stream where guests may try their luck with the rod, pan for gold, rubies and sapphires, or just walk along and enjoy while looking for platypus.

Our 400 acre property has a large bush area with nature trails, wildflowers and seventy resident kangaroos.

This is an historic gold area, the hillsides showing over 40 tunnels driven into the buried river beds. Much time may be spent inspecting the black smith, museum and relics of a past era. Close to the only world standard mineral water spa complex in Australia.

VICTORIA

Daylesford - Hepburn Springs
Guest House RACV ★★★☆
Address: Mooltan Guest House,
129 Main Rd. Hepburn Springs 3461
Name: Eddie Beacham
Telephone: (03) 5348 3555
Freecall 1800 353 354
Fax: (03) 5348 3555
Email: beacham@tpgi.com.au
Beds: 9 Double (3 with ensuite), 2 Twin (11 bedrooms)
Bathroom: 3 Ensuite, Guests share
Tariff: Weekend Package - 2 nights B&B (full) plus dinner 1 night $250/$320 per double, $170 per single. Midweek: B&B (full) Ensuite $95, Standard $75 per double, $50 per single. Dinner available (fully licensed), Children welcome. Credit cards. Vouchers accepted Sunday - Thursday.
Nearest Town: Daylesford - 3 km south

Built in 1924 and set on an acre of gardens and lawns, Mooltan has always been part of the tradition of "Taking the Waters" at Hepburn Springs which has brought visitors from all over the world to this unique part of Australia. The spa resort has always provided a range of hydrotherapy activities including mineral water baths. Now you can also try flotation tanks, massages, spa couches and saunas. We specialise in hearty English breakfasts. The bedrooms, featuring brass beds, are individually decorated and open onto broad verandahs. Two large lounge rooms offer a wide range of activities - books, music, games, TV. Tennis court. In Winter, open fires, in Summer, wide verandahs and a gazebo, and throughout the year the changing mood of the garden makes Mooltan a relaxing environment from which to explore an area rich in all aspects of Australia's culture - gold, waterfalls, kangaroos, bush, native birds and gardens. Directions: Take Hepburn Springs roa

Echuca RACV ★★★★☆
Bed & Breakfast
Address: 'Etan House',
11 Connelly Street, Echuca, VIC 3564
Name: Libby & Bill Gorman
Telephone: (0354) 807 477
Fax: (0354) 807 466
Mobile: (019) 439 429
Beds: 4 Double (4 bedrooms) **Bathroom**: 4 Ensuite
Tariff: B&B (full), Double $115-$140, Single $100. Children by arrangement. Vouchers accepted Surcharge $34 - Sun-Thurs only.

Nestled between two rivers in the historic port area of Echuca, the location of ETAN HOUSE, built in 1864, combines peace and tranquility with the convenience of a central location.
When you arrive at ETAN HOUSE, you step into history blended tastefully with modern comforts and the warmth of a friendly caring family atmosphere. Each of the 4 double rooms has superbly appointed ensuites with features such as original claw baths, marble topped vanities and gold taps. Guests have a private entrance along with guest lounge and dining rooms. Log fires throughout, electric blankets and hydronic heating ensure warmth and comfort in winter while ducted cooling and a 10 metre tiled swimming pool complete our year round appeal. Other features include lawn tennis court, a fully equipped guest kitchen, antiques throughout, cottage garden and a banquet breakfast featuring home made bread, freshly squeezed juice and eggs and bacon.

VICTORIA

Echuca RACV ★★★★☆
B&B+Self-contained Accom.
Address: "Murray House", 55 Francis Street, Echuca, Victoria 3564
Name: Len Keeper & Doug Hall
Telephone: (0354) 824 944 **Fax**: (0354) 806 432
Beds: In House: 1 King/Twin, 4 Queen (5 bedrooms) Cottage: 1 Queen, 2 Single (2 bedrooms)
Bathroom: In House: 5 Ensuite Cottage: Private
Tariff: B&B (continental plus) Double $150, Single $95.00. Cottage Tariff $100-$130. Children in cottage only. Credit cards. Vouchers accepted $56 Surcharge

A traditional bed and breakfast - "Victoria's finest; hosted by two legends of the industry". Once the architectural beauty of the surroundings, art works and furniture is absorbed, what most affects guests is Murray House's air of seclusion provided by its unusual array of public areas. Read a book in front of a flickering fire, watch a movie in the sitting room. Breakfast on Danish pastries, individual fruit platters, various toasted breads, preserves and fruit juices. Dine out in one of Echuca's wonderful restaurants and home to a turned down bed - heated or cooled rooms, depending on the weather. Cocktail hour is the favourite time of day when guests amble into the library to discuss their day's activities and shamelessly brag about their antique finds. Our greatest pleasure is to share our home.
Directions: Please telephone.
Home Page: http://www.innhouse.com.au/murray.html

Flinders see Mornington Penninsular

Eildon RACV ★★★☆
Homestay
Address: 'Maranatha' 208 Snobs Creek Rd, Eildon, 3713
Name: Maria & Frank Stow
Telephone: (03) 5774 2773 **Fax**: (03) 5774 2773
Beds: 2 Double, 2 Single (3 bedrooms)
Bathroom: 1 Guests share + extra toilet
Tariff: B&B (full) Double $80, Single $45, Children (primary school) $15. Dinner $15. Cot available. Vouchers accepted
Nearest Town: 6km west of Eildon, Goulburn Valley Highway

'Maranatha' is a secluded mudbrick home situated in over 100 acres of natural bush. Spectacular views of the Goulburn Valley can be enjoyed while breakfasting on the wide verandah.
Guests share their own sitting room. A well stocked library is available.
We offer real country-style hospitality, quality cuisine and tea or coffee is available at all times. Formal evening meals are available or perhaps try a bush meal around our blazing campfire.
Our guests can try their luck with a rod in nearby Lake Eildon or the Goulburn River; enjoy 18 holes at the scenic golf course less than 10 minutes away; drive to view the highest cataract waterfall in Victoria only 4km up Snobs Creek Road and then continue on for winter snow play; tramp through State Forest; climb to wonderful views of surrounding countryside or just relax in a hammock on the verandah.
We look forward to meeting you.

VICTORIA

Foster RACV ★★★★
Homestay. Hillcrest Farmhouse Bed & Breakfast
Address: RMB 2796 Ameys Track, Foster, Victoria 3960
(Postal) PO Box 267, Foster 3960
Name: Les and Rosemary Francis
Telephone: (03) 5682 2769
Fax: (03) 5682 2769
Beds: 1 King or Twin, 1 Double, (2 bedrooms)
Bathroom: 1 Ensuite, 1 Private
Tariff: B&B (full) Double from $80-$90, Single $50, Children 5-12yrs half price.
Dinner $25pp. Credit Cards. Vouchers accepted
Nearest Town: Foster 3kms

Hillcrest is an historic farmhouse (circa 1880) which we have restored to recapture the charm, warmth and friendly atmosphere of a traditional country home. In a peaceful setting on a hilltop it overlooks the surrounding farmland and the countryside towards Wilsons Promontory.
We are centrally located to the main scenic attractions of the Promontory Coast, the magnificent National Park of Wilsons Promontory, the unspoilt beach of Waratah Bay, the Strzelecki Ranges and the Fishing Ports. The area also offers a wide range of arts and crafts.
We offer comfortable country style guest rooms, a spacious guest lounge and dining room with open fire. A hearty breakfast is served and dinner is available by arrangement with country fare. RACV 4 Stars, VTOA accredited.
Directions: *2km up Ameys Track off the Sth Gippsland Highway, 400 metres east of the Foster Turnoff.*

Foster - South Gippsland - Wilson's Promontory
Homestay/Self-contained Accom. RACV ★★★★☆
Address: RMB 3216 Fish Creek/Foster Rd, Foster, VIC 3960
Name: Norman & Paddy Broberg
Telephone: (03) 5682 2953
Fax: (03) 5682 2953 **Mobile**: 014 013 529
Larkrise POTTERY & FARM
Beds: 1 King or 2 large single, 1 Queen (2 bedrooms)
Bathroom: 2 Ensuite
Tariff: B&B (full) Double $85-$100, Single $70-$80, Dinner by arrangement $25pp, Credit Cards.
Nearest Town: Foster 2.7 kms.

Larkrise Pottery and Farm overlooks Wilson's Promontory, and offers easy access to the national parks, fishing villages, and pristine beaches for which this area is renowned.
We offer high quality self-contained accommodation, including two guest bedrooms, each with ensuite, one bathroom being fully equipped for those in wheelchairs. There is flat undercover access from the carport, wide doors, and a spacious private conservatory/living area, with stunning views of the Prom. and the night sky. We provide a full country breakfast, featuring home-made and local produce. Additional features include cosy wood combustion heating, TV, radio/tape/CD player, electric blankets, microwave oven, toaster, tea and coffee making facilities, and much more. Relax and enjoy our peaceful and beautiful surroundings, watch the potter at work, or wander over the 40 acre property which includes cattle pasture-land, large dams, and approximately 20 acres of fern gully and blackwood forest, inhabited by many native birds and animals.

VICTORIA

Geelong - Batesford
Homestay
Address: "Lilydale House",
Dog Rocks Road, Batesford, VIC 3221
Name: Frances & George Belcher
Telephone: (03) 5276 1302 **Fax**: (03) 5276 1026 **Mobile**: (019) 955815
Beds: 2 Queen, 2 Single (3 bedrooms)
Bathroom: 1 Ensuite, 1 Private, 1 Family share
Tariff: B&B (full) Double $120, Single $80, Children under 14 $20 each. Dinner $30. Credit Cards (BC/MC/VISA). Vouchers accepted $35 surcharge
Nearest Town: 12km north-west of Geelong on the Midland Highway to Ballarat.

Lilydale House is a gracious homestead surrounded by 200 acres of bushland fronting the Moorabool River and looking across the picturesque valley to nearby wineries. Stroll to the river and search for koalas, kangaroos, echidnas and other wildlife frequently seen and observe the abundant birdlife. Enjoy the spacious guests sitting room with open log fire, stereo, TV and video, or in warmer weather sit outdoors or take a dip in the swimming pool. You are well placed to visit Ballarat (Sovereign Hill), Geelong (National Wool Museum), the Bellarine Peninsula, Great Ocean Road, and Melbourne is only 80km to the north-east.

Meals are served in the splendid dining room with dinner available by prior arrangement. Our home has 2 guest and 1 family share bathroom - we offer guests a private bathroom, so a third party arriving would use the family bathroom. We have 2 quiet dogs to add to the homely atmosphere.

Home Page: http://www.innhouse.com.au

Geelong RACV ★★★★
Homestay
Address: "Narrawong", 240 Hunts Rd.
Moriac, 3240
Name: Neil & Phyl Drew
Telephone: (03) 5266 1220
Fax: (03) 5266 1320 **Mobile**: (018) 321 899
Beds: 1 King & 2 Twins (2 bedrooms). Own entrances.
Bathroom: 1 Ensuite & 1 Private
Tariff: B&B (full) Double $95, Single $75, Dinner $25. Credit Cards (VISA/MC/BC)
Nearest Town: 19km west of Geelong, off the Princes Highway

"Narrawong" means "a place of many trees".
An old working cattle farm sets on 300 acres of gently undulating land on a quiet rural road. We are only 20 minutes from central Geelong, 1 hour 20 minutes from Melbourne, 50 minutes from Ballarat or 20 minutes from some of the most renowned surf beaches in Victoria plus the Great Ocean Road and the Otway Ranges. 10 minutes Deakin University.
Guests are offered a luxurious private guest bedroom with ensuite and either King size or twin beds overlooking a courtyard garden. Tennis court with lights, open fires, antique furniture, armfuls of fresh flowers and an atmosphere of great charm set in a beautiful large park-like garden.
Phyl has a very high standard of culinary arts and a full breakfast is included. Evening meal by prior arrangement. Smoking not permitted in the house.
Your hosts interests are gardening, classical music, reading, wine and food, travelling and embroidery. Please phone or fax ahead.

Geelong - Mt Moriac
Farmhouse Bed & Breakfast   RACV ★★★☆
Address: "Tema Dairyfarm", 75 Simmonds Road,
Mt Moriac, VIC 3240
Name: Terry & Marion Kosseck
Telephone: (03) 5266 2043 **Fax**: (03) 5266 2043
Mobile: (014) 676007
Beds: 1 Double, 3 Single (2 bedrooms)
Bathroom: 1 Guests share
Tariff: B&B (full) Double $75-$100, Single $55-$70, Children welcome POA - cots/ highchairs available, Dinner from $15 by arrangement, Credit Cards. Vouchers accepted excluding Christmas & Easter holidays
Nearest Town: 19km west of Geelong on Princes Hwy the A1 to Warrnambool. 16km north of the Great Ocean Road. 98km south west of Melbourne.

Enjoy warm country hospitality at TEMA, our working dairy farm, on top of the Barrabool Hills, in a quiet no through road, off the Princes Highway, close to the Great Ocean Road, Surfcoast Beaches, Otway Ranges, Geelong.
Guests are encouraged to feel at home and relax in our spacious Australian homestead with your own private entrance, lounge/dining room, TV/video, games, fridge, tea/ coffee, etc. Enjoy the birds and magnificent views on a farm walk or in the rose garden patio overlooking Mt Moriac.
Your farm-cooked breakfast includes homemade bread, jams and farm fresh eggs. Children and adults are most welcome to watch or join with farm activities - milking cows, feeding calves, lambs, chickens, dogs and the farm cat or try yabbying.
Tourist maps and information are available for local attractions, scenic flights, cruises, tours, wineries, gardens, Harley Davidson, camel and horse rides.

Gelantipy - East Gippsland
Farmstay+Self-contained Accom. RACV ★★★
Address: Karoonda Park, Gelantipy, Vic 3885
Name: Paul & Judi Sykes
Telephone: (03) 5155 0220 **Fax**: (03) 5155 0308
Beds: (3) Small Cottage: 1 Double, 6 Single (2 bedrooms, 1 bathroom) (6) Large Cottage: 1 Double, 8 Single (3 bedrooms, 1 bathroom) Motel: 1 Queen, 1 double 2 singles (2 brms) ensuite bathrooms
Bathroom:
Tariff: B&B (continental) Double $75, Single $40, Children $14, Dinner $18. Motel Units (continental) $80 Double, $45 Single. Credit Cards (BC/MC/VISA). Vouchers accepted
Nearest Town: Buchan (famous for limestone caves), Bairnsdale is the commercial centre.

Karoonda Park is located in the foothills of the Snowy Mountains 55km from the Victorian - NSW border. Home of the Karoonda Hereford Stud this operating farm runs sheep for fat lamb production. Horse riding lessons, hourly rides and longer tours available - booking necessary. Tennis court, swimming pool, climbing wall and recreation room. Close proximity to Snowy River and Alpine National Park. Self-contained cottage accommodation with the option of meals with host family or B&B. Close to Buchan Caves. Karoonda Park is situated on Gelantipy Road 112km from Bairnsdale 3875.

VICTORIA

Gipsy Point - Far East Gippsland
Guest House/S.C. Accom./Licensed Restaurant   RACV ★★★★
Address: Gipsy Point, Vic 3891
Name: Gipsy Point Lodge
Telephone: 1800 063 556 **Fax**: (03) 5158 8225
Beds: 3 Queen, 3 Double, 8 Single (8 bedrooms)
Bathroom: 8 Ensuite
Tariff: Dinner, B&B (full) $100 per person.
Children welcome (tertiary/secondary 80%,
primary/pre 60%). Credit Cards (VISA/BC/MC),
No pets. Vouchers accepted
excluding Christmas and Easter school holidays.
Nearest Town: Mallacoota

Gipsy Point Lodge is a small guest house at the head of Mallacoota Inlet. Surrounded by Croajingolong National Park and the waterway, the Lodge has a feeling of remoteness and tranquillity in a bushland setting.
The Lodge provides a comfortable home base for access to a remarkable diversity of environments - the forests, rivers, lakes and coastline. The area is unspoiled and famous for its beauty and serenity. The rivers and the Inlet are noted for fishing.
The Lodge has eight rooms and three self-contained cottages. Rooms are large, comfortable and en-suite with double or twin beds. Amenities include a licensed restaurant, guest lounge, billiards room, tennis court, a boat launching ramp and jetties, and motor boats for hire.
Activities include fishing, boating, surfing and swimming, bird and nature observation, photography, bushwalking, sightseeing, picnics and barbecues.
Special weeks are held for bird watchers and field naturalists.

Gisborne South
Farmstay
Address: RMB 10 Couangalt Road,
Gisborne Sth, 3437 Vic
Name: "Peechelba Park B&B" Mick & Betty Martin
Telephone: (0354) 283610 - Answering service
Fax: (0354) 283610 - phon **Mobile**: (015) 506435
Beds: 2 Double, 2 Single (3 bedrooms)
Bathroom: 1 Guests share
Tariff: B&B (full) Double $65, Single $45,
Children half price, Dinner $15pp,
Campervans facilities. Vouchers accepted
Nearest Town: 9km south of Gisborne just off Calder Highway
A friendly smile, a warm comfortable bed and plenty of good food await you at Peechelba Park Bed & Breakfast. Air-conditioned lounge, TV, video, cosy wood fire and complimentary tea/coffee. Your hosts, Mick and Betty Martin, retired to train harness race horses and breed Boer goats on this peaceful 40 acre property, which they share with native birds and kangaroos. Located 45km north of Melbourne and 300 metres off Calder Freeway. Within half hour of Mt Macedon's renowned gardens or the easily climbable, mysterious Hanging Rock (World class Mamelon volcanic formation) or Melbourne Zoo or craft town of Daylesford / Hepburn with spa and mineral springs. Adventurous one hour's drive to historical gold mining provincial cities of Ballarat and Bendigo. Wineries abound. We take pleasure in assisting you with tours to make your stay a happy and enjoyable one. Can meet at Sunbury, Melbourne railway stations or Melbourne airport.

Grampians see Mininera & Wartook

Grantville
Homestay/Traditional B&B
Address: Lot 1 Grantville-Glenalvie Road, Grantville, 3984
Name: Fran & Les
Telephone: (03) 5678 8384
Beds: 2 Double, 1 Twin (3 bedrooms)
Bathroom: 3 Ensuite
Tariff: B&B (full) Double from $90, Single from $65, Children not catered for, Dinner $20pp, Credit Cards (VISA/MC/BC).
Vouchers accepted $20 surcharge spa suite, $10 ensuite without spa.
Nearest Town: 23km north of Phillip Island, 400m off Bass Highway.

Nestled in five acres of natural Australian bush, 'Gumtips' offers a rural romantic retreat away from the stresses of everyday life. Sip a glass of your favourite wine in our candlelit spa ensuites or relax by our huge open fire. Enjoy a game of pool on our full size billiard table in the private guest lounge. Watch the rosellas and possums feed in their natural environment. Take a 15 minute trip to Sanremo to watch the pelicans feed, then visit Phillip Island with its world renown Koala Reserve and Penguin Parade. Take a leisurely drive to Coal Creek at Korumburra and the beautiful beaches of Inverloch and Wilsons Promontory or enjoy a game of golf at one of the beautiful courses of Lang Lang, Leongatha, Korumburra or Wonthaggi.
Come and meet our pet geese Salt and Pepper and our goat Ivory.

Hamilton - Branxholme
Farmstay+Self-contained Accom.
Address: "Inverary Homestead", Caroona Lane, Branxholme 3302
Name: Stuart & Margaret Dufty
Telephone: (03) 5578 6212 **Fax**: (03) 5578 6269
Mobile: (019) 139 952 **RACV** ★★★☆
Beds: Homestead: 1 Queen, 2 Double, 2 Single (3 bedrooms) S.C. Cottage: 1 Queen, 1 Twin, 1 Single, 1 Double (4 bedrooms)
Bathroom: Homestead: 1 Private, 1 Guests share S.C. Cottage: 1 Private
Tariff: B&B (full) Double $90-$110, Single $70-$85, Children POA. Dinner $30pp. S.C. Cottage from $90 or $400-$500 per week. Credit Cards (BC/MC/VISA). Vouchers accepted $20 surcharge. Not accepted Easter or Public Holiday weekends
Nearest Town: 23km south of Hamilton.

A warm friendly welcome awaits you at "Inverary" our two storey bluestone homestead, built 1867. "Inverary", is surrounded by an historic rambling garden with tree-canopied pathways. Enjoy afternoon tea under the Illawarra Flame Tree or inside by the fire, or stroll to see the wedge-tailed eagles. We live on a 680 Ha property and run 5000 merino sheep.
Stuart is a keen sailor and a fourth generation Australian farmer who enjoys taking visitors around the farm explaining our extensive treeplanting program. Both he and Margaret (an accredited local tour guide) will gladly help visitors with itineraries.
Stay in 2 charming guest rooms upstairs or an historic former Governess and School-room on the ground floor; the latter with open fireplace and ensuite bathroom. Dinner is countrystyle cooking using local ingredients served in the candle-lit dining room. We are central for day trips to the Grampians, Shipwreck Coast and a good overnight stay between Melbourne and Adelaide. We look forward to your visit. No smoking indoors. **Directions**: *Please phone.* **Home Page**: http://www.innhouse.com.au

VICTORIA

Hamilton - Branxholme
Historical Homestead RACV ★★★★
Address: Chrome Rd, Branxholme 3302
Name: Jeanie Sharp
Telephone: (03) 5578 6221
Fax: (03) 5578 6249 **Mobile**: 018 528 228
Beds: 3 Queen, 2 Single (4 bedrooms)
Bathroom: 1 Private, 1 Guest share
Tariff: B&B (full) Double $110-$130, Dinner $30pp.
Credit cards. Vouchers accepted Monday to Thursday.
Nearest Town: Hamilton

"Arrandoovong" was first settled in the early 1800's. The two storey bluestone homestead was built in the 1850's. The historic gardens are dominated by giant English oaks and a permanent stream which is shaded by poplars, elms and old pines, offering pleasant walks and relaxation.
Our property is 500 hectares and runs 5000 fine wool merino sheep and we have implemented an extensive native tree planting programme.
The spacious guests rooms, offering queen size beds, and guests bathrooms, are upstairs. You can spend time relaxing on the verandah or balcony, walking in the grounds or along the creek.
We are situated conveniently to the Grampians, Great Ocean Road, Portland, Port Fairy and wineries, while Hamilton offers a wonderful selection of historic and cultural interests, an ideal stopover Melbourne - Adelaide.
Your stay at "Arrandoovong" will be memorable, hospitable and something special. Jeanie and Bill look forward to your company.

Healesville see Yarra Valley
Hepburn Springs see Daylesford

Horsham RACV ★★★☆
Traditional Bed & Breakfast
Address: 25 Landy Street, Horsham, VIC 3400
Name: Garrett's Bed & Breakfast
Telephone: (03) 5382 3928 **Mobile**: (015) 337 576
Email: jgarrett@tpgi.com.au
Beds: 1 Queen, 2 Singles, (2 bedrooms)
Bathroom: 1 Guests share
Tariff: B&B (full) Double $85, Single $65, Dinner $25.
Nearest Town: In Horsham

Our home, Casa del Sol, is a block off the Wimmera River, and only a short walk from the Botanic Gardens, the tennis and croquet courts, the race track, and the main business area. Our two upstairs bedrooms have either single or double beds each, reading lamps, electric blankets, and clock-radios. Available also are a fridge, coffee and tea-making facilities and a variety of fresh, homemade biscuits. The lounge offers a piano, television, radio/stereo, magazines, games and books.
Our full breakfast menu caters for all appetites and, weather permitting, you can have breakfast in the BBQ area or around the pool. The lush gardens are different, and well worth a stroll. A fully operational blacksmith shop is also on the premises. Ample off-street parking is available.
We have a wide range of interests - from gardening and antiques to theatre, art and music.
We look forward to your visit. Please telephone.

VICTORIA

Inverloch RACV ★★★★☆
Homestay/Bed & Breakfast
Address: Hill Top House,
Lower Tarwin Rd., Inverloch, 3996
Name: Aileen & Bruce Mitchell
Telephone: (03) 5674 3514
Fax: (03) 5674 3 514
Mobile: 041 9575 038
Beds: 2 Queen (2 bedrooms) **Bathroom**: 2 Ensuite
Tariff: B&B (full) Double $95, Single $65, Dinner - Family + Gourmet - price on application, Credit Cards (BC/VISA/MC).
Nearest Town: 3km east of Inverloch
Come and share our spectacular ocean, inlet and rural views. Inverloch is situated on a lovely piece of coastline between Phillip Island and Wilson's Promontory.
Enjoy this seaside village with its quiet secluded beaches or drive in the green hills of South Gippsland visiting the wineries, cheese tastings, farms, parks and gardens.
Our home is landscaped on 2.5 acres overlooking Inverloch. We have two spacious queen and twin bed / sitting rooms with ensuites where you can rise at your leisure after a wonderful night's rest then relax over a generous home cooked buffet breakfast.
Gourmet and family dinners are available with home-grown produce and tasty Gippsland cheeses a speciality.
Guests are requested not to smoke indoors and our accommodation is unsuitable for children or pets.
We have both travelled widely and would like now to return the hospitality we received in many countries.
We are less than 2 hours from Melbourne by car and if arriving by bus you will be met in Inverloch (by prior arrangement).

Johnsonville see Bairnsdale
Kalorma see Dandenong Ranges

Koroit RACV ★★☆
Guest House
Address: Please telephone for directions
Name: The Olde Courthouse Inn
Telephone: (03) 5565 8346
Beds: 4 Double, 10 Single (8 bedrooms)
Bathroom: 3 Guest share
Tariff: B&B (full) Double $70-$75, Single $40;
Children POA. Dinner $18-$20. Credit Cards. Vouchers accepted

Nearest Town: Warrnambool 20 km, Port Fairy 20 km; 5km north of Princes Highway.
Built in 1901 as an hotel, The Olde Courthouse Inn has now been restored and converted into a small, intimate and comfortable Guest House providing quiet and restful accommodation ideal for singles, couples, families and small groups. It features olde worlde charm, simplicity and a homely atmosphere, all of which are conducive to a sense of relaxation and well-being.
Here guests are able to enjoy warm and friendly hospitality provided by hosts and two delightful dogs in a quiet historic country town from which there is easy access to many major tourist attractions within scenic south-west Victoria.
Facilities and services include single use, twin share or double bedrooms, electric blankets, conveniently placed bathrooms, guest's lounge with open fire and coloured television, pantry with refrigerator and tea and coffee making facilities, country style breakfasts in the dining room and off street parking.
An evening meal with emphasis on home cooking is available on prior arrangement.

VICTORIA

Kyneton
Country House - RACV ★★★★☆
Address: Kyneton Country House,
66 Jennings Street, Kyneton, VIC 3444
Name: Mary & Paul Reid
Telephone: (03) 5422 3556
Fax: (03) 5422 3556

Beds: 4 Queen, (4 bedrooms) **Bathroom**: 2 Ensuite, 1 Guests share
Tariff: B&B (special) Midweek: Double $100-$125, Single $75-$100, Children by arrangement. Dinner $40-$50. Special packages on weekends and public holidays. Credit Cards (Diners, Bankcard, Mastercard, Visa).
Nearest Town: Kyneton is 84km northwest of Melbourne.

Magnificent National Trust homestead (1862) in historic Kyneton. Built of handmade bricks for a miller, its gracious rooms are filled with antiques and watercolours. Visitors are treated as friends and spoiled with every comfort. Sunny verandahs open onto a colourful country garden. Inside are comfortable sitting rooms, a well-stocked library, a log fire, four charming bedrooms with delightful views and a choice of ensuite or shared bathrooms. This is a smoke-free home.
Mary's cooking, recommended in the "Good Food Guide", combines traditional country fare with original touches using fresh local produce.
Kyneton is a thriving market town amongst the peaceful villages and quiet country lanes of central Victoria. It is ideal for exploring Daylesford and Hepburn Springs, mysterious Hanging Rock, Mt Macedon's vineyards and gardens, and 19th century goldrush towns, Maldon and Castlemaine.
Paul and Mary are happy to share their knowledge of this picturesque area and its history.
Home Page: http://www.innhouse.com.au/kyneton.htm

Kyneton RACV ★★★★
Country House
Address: "Moorville",
1 Powlett Street, Kyneton, VIC 3444
Name: Fran & John Wigley
Telephone: (03) 5422 6466
Fax: (03) 5422 6466
Beds: 3 Double, 2 Single (4 bedrooms)
Bathroom: 2 Ensuite, 1 Guests share
Tariff: B&B (special) Double $100-$125, Single $70, Children POA. Dinner $35pp.
Nearest Town: In historic Kyneton, 84km from Melbourne.

At Moorville breakfast is served with a view, overlooking the Campaspe River and parkland near heritage listed Kyneton Botanic gardens. Home-made, and local produce, even eggs from Fran's fowls complement the fresh country style meals.
Built in 1902 the large Edwardian home offers spacious rooms and a warm, friendly welcome. Relax with a book on the veranda, play a leisurely game of petanque in the garden. For the more energetic have a game of tennis, or a swim in the indoor pool. The Kyneton area offers living history, local spa water, wineries, antiques, book shops and many galleries. There are wonderful tours to take around the town, see the many bluestone buildings, the nineteenth century street-scapes, take a stroll beside the river. There are 16 meetings at the pretty race course every year, and 4 golf courses within a short drive.
Easy disabled access. Smoke free home.
*RACV ****

VICTORIA

Lakes Entrance
Self-contained Accommodation
Address: 37 The Esplanade, Lakes Entrance, Vic 3909
Name: Lou's B & B
Telephone: (03) 5155 2732 **Fax**: (051) 552732 **Mobile**: (041) 8634 013
Beds: 2 Queen (2 bedrooms)
Bathroom: 2 Ensuite
Tariff: B&B (full) Double $80-$120, Single $60-$105. Credit Cards. Vouchers accepted same day restriction Dec/Jan & East week.
Nearest Town: Lakes Entrance - right in the centre of the town, by the lake.

We, who live and work in the Lakes District, are very proud of our part of Victoria, 60 miles of Lakes System, and 90 miles of vast unspoiled ocean beach, backed by the majestic mountain high country.
We offer our hospitality to you, the traveller, to enjoy - we want you to come here, to share our lifestyle in this magnificent corner of Victoria.
We will happily assist with arrangements for district sightseeing.
Lou's B & B - formerly "Dostine's" is, centrally situated, modern design, built and decorated with quality fittings only. We endeavour to have our guests feel totally comfortable in a quality atmosphere. Secure off-street parking is provided. Non-smokers only.
Hearty breakfasts including home-baked bread and jams, with menu to suit your taste and squeezed fruit juices, are served in our bright sunroom looking to the front lake. BBQ available. The locale has many and varied restaurants (10 mins walk).

Lakes Entrance RACV ★★★★
Self-contained Accommodation
Address: Broadlands, PO Box 497, Bairnsdale, VIC 3875
Name: Bayview Lodge
Telephone: (03) 5153 0476
Fax: (03) 5153 0476
Beds: 1 Double (+ extra bed in lounge), 2 Single (2 Bedrooms).
Bathroom: 1 Private.
Tariff: Double $110 per night. Children $15 per night.
Nearest Town: Bairnsdale

*Bayview Lodge is a luxury renovated 100 year old cottage that nestles right on the shores of Jowes Bay, part of the Great Gippsland Lake system. As such it commands spectacular views over the lake and our private farm land. As a fully self contained RACV**** cottage it offers an unforgettable opportunity to experience the atmosphere and privacy of Australia's earliest buildings. Luxurious bedding and some antique fittings give this lodge a very special glow. Complete quiet and privacy is assured with your hosts occupying detached buildings. Service aims to be friendly and first class. Just relax in our natural hot sulphur springs or catch a bream for tea off our private jetty. We have our own boat ramp, beach, golf course, and 4 acres of private gardens. From the front verandah you can watch the most magnificent sun sets across the lake. Bernardine and Brian invite you to share in the ongoing discovery of arguably the most romantic and magical lodge in Eastern Victoria.*

Some homes share the bathroom, others have bathrooms exclusively for guests
– they are indicated in the listing.

VICTORIA

Lakes Entrance RACV ★★★★☆
Boutique Bed & Breakfast
Address: 17 Clara Street (PO Box 750),
Lakes Entrance, Vic 3909
Name: Déja Vu B&B
Telephone: (03) 5155 4330
Fax: (03) 5155 3718 **Mobile**: (018) 351550
Beds: 3 King/Queen, 2 Single (4 bedrooms)
Bathroom: 4 Ensuite
Tariff: B&B (full) Executive or Studio suites:
Double from $125-$140, Single $90, Dinner on request, Mid-week (special)
packages, Credit Cards, No smoking.
Nearest Town: Lakes Entrance 2 km (2 mins by canoe)
"Déja Vu" Not Just B.B

Position - Picturesque Property, Peace - Privacy and Pamper are some of many reasons
making this premium B&B accommodation outstanding.
Déja Vu offers you luxurious comfort and splendid hospitality.
High on a narrow strip of land protruding from above the waters of the North Arm lake
proudly sits "Déja Vu" a modern 4 level accommodation - architectural innovative
design, capturing the waters below with ocean lake and wilderness views beyond the
township opposite.
Imagine watching from your (bed)room balcony the splendour of colours of the ever
changing skies just before the sun rises over the water. Or at the end of a peaceful day
- from your Spa watch the day fade into night while the moonlight creates a magic
mystical display of lights on the simmer of the water below assisted by the town lights
reflection dancing to the wake of the passing boats.
Home Page: http://www.inhouse.com.au/dejavu.htm

Lakes Entrance - East Gippsland
Bed & Breakfast - RACV ★★★★☆
Address: 1-9 Creighton Street,
Lakes Entrance, Victoria 3909
Name: Bruce & Maureen Livingstone
Telephone: (03) 5155 2699 **Fax**: (03) 5155 2559
Beds: 3 Double, 2 Single (4 bedrooms)
Bathroom: 4 Ensuite
Tariff: B&B (full) Double $120, Single $90.
Credit cards (MC/VISA/BC only). Vouchers accepted
$25 Surcharge Double, $10 Single.
Nearest Town: Lakes Entrance

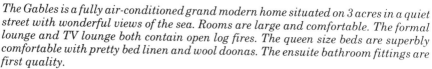

The Gables is a fully air-conditioned grand modern home situated on 3 acres in a quiet
street with wonderful views of the sea. Rooms are large and comfortable. The formal
lounge and TV lounge both contain open log fires. The queen size beds are superbly
comfortable with pretty bed linen and wool doonas. The ensuite bathroom fittings are
first quality.
A full breakfast is served in the sunroom overlooking the outdoor solar heated
swimming pool and spa. Watching the magpies, parrots and kookaburras take their
daily swim in the pool is a delightful floor show. Breakfast which includes homemade
local produce is served at a time to suit you.
Upstairs in a large playroom is the home gym and exercise equipment.
Dinners are not provided. There are many restaurants nearby, or buy prawns fresh
from fishing trawlers and bring back to eat, all facilities provided. The BBQ is also
available.

VICTORIA

Lismore see Camperdown
Lorne see Colac

Lorne, Otway Ranges RACV ★★★
Two self-contained Cabins
Address: 115 Division Road, Murroon via Deans Marsh, VIC 3242
Name: Pennyroyal Raspberry Farm
Telephone: (052) 363238 **Mobile**: (019) 330 284
Beds: 1 Double, 2 Single (2 bedrooms)
Bathroom: 2 Ensuite
Tariff: B&B (continental) Double $70&$85, Single $55, Cooked breakfast $8 per person.   Vouchers accepted
Nearest Town: Lorne/Colac/Deans Marsh 25 minutes
'Cabins for two' - smoke free Discover two distinct worlds in the renowned Otway Ranges: the spectacular Great Ocean Road, and hidden treasures of the Otways hinterland.
Ours is a working berry farm set on 20 secluded hectares, half bush, where we provide bed and breakfast for a limited number of guests.
Two cabins with ensuite bathroom and kitchen, each for two people. Attractively furnished, and featuring many personal touches, THE LODGE (double bed) and THE CABIN (twin or double bed), have verandahs overlooking the berry rows and sweeping valley views. There are many birds to delight you, and the rosellas will come in to feed. The continental breakfast includes compote of fruit from our orchard, newly baked bread and Dawn's preserves. A cooked breakfast is available for $8 per person. Dine at our 'local' pub and nearby restaurants, or please yourself in your own kitchen.

Lorne, Otway Ranges - Birregurra
Heritage Bed & Breakfast RACV ★★★★
Address: Elliminook Heritage Bed & Breakfast, Birregurra - Please phone ahead.
Name: Jill & Peter Falkiner
Telephone: (03) 5236 2080 **Fax**: (03) 5236 2423
Mobile: (018) 107021
Beds: 2 King/Queen, 1 Double, 2 Single (4 bedrooms)
Bathroom: 3 Ensuite, 1 Private with spa bath.
Tariff: B&B (full) Double $95-$140, Single $80, Children by arrangement, Dinner by arrangement. Credit cards (VISA/BC/MC/DC).
Nearest Town: Lorne 40km, Colac 20km

Elliminook, c1865, is a National Trust classified homestead set in a rambling garden at Birregurra on the Barwon River. The homestead is realisation of a dream of co-owner, interior designer Jill Falkiner, to renovate and restore an heritage home. The result as featured in Australian House and Garden and by other writers, is a superbly restored Victorian home with a beautiful blend of exposed timber, hand made bricks, warm ambient colours and antique furnishings.
Be pampered in romantic bedrooms with private or ensuite facilities, relax in the rose filled courtyard or in the glow of an open fireplace. Enjoy indulgent breakfasts in the formal dining room and welcoming hospitality to enjoy a unique accommodation experience.
From Elliminook you can explore the scenic Otway Ranges, The Great Ocean Road and Shipwreck Coast. Golf, tennis, lakes and historic gardens are within easy drive. Nearby restaurants provide fine cuisine.
We invite you to be our welcome guest.

VICTORIA

Lorne - Eastern View
Bed & Breakfast RACV ★★★★
Address: "Lorneview Bed & Breakfast",
677 Great Ocean Road, Eastern View.
(PO Box 323, Aireys Inlet, 3231)
Name: Nola & Kevin Symes
Telephone: (03) 5289 6430
Beds: 1 Queen (1 bedroom)
Bathroom: 1 Ensuite
Tariff: B&B (continental) Double $100-$120, Single $80-$100, Credit Cards.
Nearest Town: Lorne 14km, Aireys Inlet 6km

Our home is nestled amongst native bush just 300m from the Memorial Archway over the Great Ocean Road, and overlooks the ocean to Lorne and the Otway Ranges. We offer accommodation in a self-contained non-smoking room containing QS bed, ensuite, TV, wood and electric heating, air-conditioning, CD and tape player, tea and coffee facilities, refrigerator, iron and ironing board, crockery, cutlery, but no cooking facilities. A generous continental breakfast, including home-made muffins, is served in your room, on your own private verandah, or on the front balcony of our home overlooking the sea. Dinner is not available but there are many excellent restaurants within 5-10 minutes drive, and barbecue facilities are provided. A games room with billiard table is available for guests. Other activities include bird watching, beach and bush walking, golf, fishing, surfing and swimming. An excellent base for exploring the Otway Ranges and Great Ocean Road
Directions: *Please phone ahead.*

Macarthur see Port Fairy

Mallacoota RACV ★★★☆
Homestay
Address: Mareeba Lodge,
59 Mirrabooka Road, Mallacoota, VIC 3892
Name: Anne & Wally Studd
Telephone: (03) 51 580 378
Beds: 1 Double, 4 Single (3 Bedrooms)
Bathroom: 1 Guest share
Tariff: B&B (full) Double $60-$70, Single $45-$60; Dinner $20 (3 course), $18 (2 course). No Pets. No children under 12. Vouchers accepted
Nearest Town: 23 km south east of Genoa on the Princes Highway, 1-6 km northwest of Malacoota P.O. *Anne and Wally offer personalised service and invite you to holiday in a homely, comfortable, scenic location and become part of the resident family if you wish or a guest lounge is provided for use at your leisure, the choice is yours. We offer clean, quiet, comfortable, ground floor accommodation. Modern shared facilities, electric blankets, bed lamps. Comfortable lounge with TV, radio, heater, fan, tea and coffee making facilities, large fridge, freezer. There is a barbecue available. Rooms are serviced daily. Off street parking. By arrangement dinner and lunch are available. Meals are served in the air conditioned dining room with a view of the ocean, lake and Gabo Island. Mallacoota has a population of 1,200 residents and is a tranquil unspoiled area surrounded by a National Park with a lake system of 320 km of shore line picnic spots with barbecue facilities, bushwalking, beaches, swimming, sailing, golf, tennis, fishing, flora and fauna and restaurants. Local tours are available by arrangement. Those staying more than two nights will be taken on a guided tour of beaches and surrounding area FREE. Anne or Wally would be happy to discuss with you ways of making your stay enjoyable. A phone call is always welcome (best times early morning or evening).* R.A.C.V. Rating three & half star.

Mandurang Valley see Bendigo

Gift Vouchers

Our B&B vouchers are for a double room for one night's B&B. They cost $89, and if you order one as a gift, we will include a free ***Australian Bed & Breakfast Book*** worth $16.95.

Send your cheque to
*Moonshine Press
59 Quirk Street
Dee Why
NSW 2099*

Mansfield
Homestay & S/C Cedar Cottage
Address: Logan Lodge, 20-24 Logan Street, Mansfield 3722
Name: Paul and Elva Rush
Telephone: (03) 5775 2058
Fax: (03) 5775 2058
Beds: In house: 1 Double. In Cottage: 1 Double, 4 Single (sleeps up to 6) (Motel style)
Bathroom: House: Private bath and spa. Cottage: Private bathroom.
Tariff: House: B&B (continental) Double $90, single $50. Cottage: B&B (continental/ingredients for full if requested) Double $90. Dinner available.
Nearest Town: Mansfield

Mansfield - "Gem of the High Country". Experience our personalised country hospitality at "Logan Lodge" with home-made biscuits/cakes on arrival. We offer "best of both worlds" being situated in town at the end of a leafy street yet overlooking rural views. Access to shops, cinema and restaurants is a 10 minute stroll or treat yourself to our 3 course "Country Fare" dinner. We supply all bed linen and towels, our continental breakfast offering choices of cereals, yoghurts, fruits, muffins, crumpets, home-made jams and breads (included in tariff). Safe, off street car parking available, and automatic security lighting for night access. "Logan Lodge" is heated in winter with access to hot spa bath, and cool for summer with our solar heated swimming pool one metre from your door. Free use of Bar-B-Q and four channels of coloured TV. Horse riding, fly fishing, camel treks and helicopter flights can be arranged.

Mansfield
Traditional B&B
Address: Akoonah, Delatite Lane, Piries via Mansfield 3722
Name: Alan and Bronwen Searle
Telephone: (03) 5777 3441 **Fax**: (03) 5777 3442
Beds: 1 Queen, 3 Single (3 Bedrooms)
Bathroom: 1 Ensuite, 1 Guests Share
Tariff: B&B (full) Double $120, Single $60, Dinner $25 pp (by prior arrangement). Not suitable for children under 10 years of age. Credit Cards Accepted
Nearest Town: Mansfield 12 km.

Akoonah is a large, gracious home in a park like garden setting overlooking the Delatite River. Built to take advantage of magnificent views, the house is both heated and air-conditioned, and the rooms large and comfortable. Guests enjoy afternoon tea by a picture window with views of the river and Mt. Buller, or summer breakfasts on the terrace overlooking the pool. In winter there is coffee by a log fire and a drying room provided for skiers.

Only 10 minutes from Mansfield (restaurants, golf, tennis, markets) and Lake Eildon (water sports) and 20 minutes from Mt. Buller and Stirling (skiing), Akoonah is a wonderful base to explore this legendary area. Enjoy trout fishing in our Delatite and nearby Howqua Rivers, horse rides and camel treks, a noted local winery, and scenic flights by aircraft, helicopter or balloon. Akoonah has a private airstrip with hangar facilities.

Our guests will receive a warm welcome from hosts Alan and Bronwen, an enthusiastic one from Cassie, the blue heeler, and a quieter one from Katia, the family cat. Due to the proximity of the river, Akoonah is unsuitable for young children. We request no smoking in the house.

Directions: *Please phone for direction.*

Maryborough
Farmstay+
Self-contained Accom.
Address: "Eany Farm",
Talbot-Majorca Road, Majorca via Maryborough, VIC 3465
Name: Ivan & Norma Barrett
Telephone: (03) 5464 7267 **Mobile**: 015843649
Beds: 1 Queen, 2 Double, 5 Single (5 bedrooms)
Bathroom: 2 Guests share
Tariff: B&B (full) Double from $75, Single from $45, Children $10-$25, Dinner $15, Campervans $25. Vouchers accepted Mid-week, off peak. $10 surcharge peak time.
Nearest Town: Majorca 12km south-east of Maryborough. Maryborough 160km north/west of Melbourne.

Eany Farm offers great farm holidays or luxury overnight stays. Eany Farm is a small interesting property rich in self sufficiency and producing fruit, berries, vegetables, goats milk, eggs and beef. Sample the all organic produce, enjoy farm activities or be pampered with generous Aussie country hospitality.
In-House: Guests have 2 double and 1 twin bedrooms and 1 bathroom, use of large living area, open fire, billiard table and pianola. SC Cottage: 2 bedrooms, spacious living, wheelchair access.
Eany Farm in the gold fields district of Victoria is central to wineries, historic towns, reservoirs for fishing etc. State forests for bush walking, cycling, bird watching or horse riding, you may bring your own horse if you wish. Outdoor - playground, table tennis, barbecue, pony rides, tennis 1.5km.
RACV ★★★☆

Marysville - Narbethong
Self-contained Accommodation
Address: St Fillan,
723 Maroondah Hwy, Narbethong 3778
Name: Helen and Rex Goulding
Telephone: (0359) 637 126
Email: st.fillans@discoveraustralia.com.
Beds: 2 Queen (2 Bedrooms)
Bathroom: 2 Private
Tariff: B&B (full) Gardeners Cottage:
Double $140-$160. Maids Quarters:
Double $115-$135. Single $65-$75
Nearest Town: Marysville.
85km east from Melbourne on Maroondah Highway.

Accommodation is self contained in either the refurbished Maids Quarters (Cottage Style) or the recently restored Gardeners Cottage. Circa 1910. The Gardeners Cottage has a large open fire in the lounge and the bathroom has a double spa and shower. The Maids Quarters is centrally heated and has separate breakfast and sitting rooms. Both facilities have a colour TV and queen size beds.
St Fillan is close to the snow fields and to nearby attractions. Floodlit waterfalls, horse riding, golf and good restaurants. Late checkouts. Full breakfast included.
RACV ★★★★
Home Page: discover.australia.com/vic/st.fillan

VICTORIA

Melbourne RACV ★★★☆
Guest House
Address: 21 - 25 George Street,
East Melbourne, Victoria 3002
Name: Georgian Court Guest House
Telephone: (03) 9419 6353 **Fax**: (03) 9416 0895
Email: georgian@dataline.net.au
Beds: 18 Double, 10 Twin, 6 Single (32 bedrooms)
Bathroom: 18 Ensuite (New bathrooms including baths & spas), 10 Guests share
Tariff: B&B (continental) Double $69, Single $59, Children $10. Credit Cards. Vouchers accepted surcharge $20 ensuite bathroom
Nearest Town: Melbourne City

Georgian Court Guest House is conveniently situated in the inner city residential area of East Melbourne. Located on tree-lined George Street together with some of Melbourne's finest houses. Within walking distance to MCG, Tennis Centre, Olympic Park, city centre shops and restaurants.
Georgian Court offers inexpensive Bed & Breakfast accommodation with lots of comfort, charm and friendly service. Complimentary breakfast is served in the antique furnished dining room each morning.
The guest bedrooms have been recently redecorated and all have colour tv, tea and coffee making facilities, radio / clock / alarm. Most rooms have their own private bathroom (extra cost). Share bathrooms are beautifully decorated in marble and antique tiles.
Private off-street parking and laundry. Evening meals are also available.
RACV 3 1/2 Star
Winner of Certificate of Commendation 1993 Victorian Tourism Awards.
Home Page: http://www.wps.com.au/georgiancourt

Melbourne
Guest House
Address: 13-23 Hawke Street,
West Melbourne, Vic 3003
Name: Miami Motor Inn
Telephone: (03) 9329 8499 **Fax**: (03) 9328 1820
Beds: 15 Double, 40 Single, 30 Twin, 4 Triple
Bathroom: 23 Ensuite, 12 Guests share
Tariff: B&B (full) Double $52-$84,
Single $36-$70, Children negotiable,
Dinner $10. Credit Cards (VISA/MC/BC). Vouchers accepted
Nearest Town: We are very close to City Centre

The Miami is very conveniently located to the city and public transport. It is a short walk to Victoria Market and within easy reach to many of Melbourne's tourist attractions. Our reception is open each day from 7 AM until midnight and there is a night porter on duty for the rest of the night.
Our rooms range from standard economy consisting of a bed, small desk and chair, wash basin and ceiling to floor wardrobe to twenty three newly appointed ensuite rooms consisting of bed, shower, toilet, basin, colour TV and tea / coffee making facilities. All rooms are centrally heated.
Extra facilities include self service laundry and ironing room, pool table, hot and cold drink machines and a TV lounge, also at no extra charge ample off-street parking. Pay phones are available for local, interstate or international calls.
Our evening meals are served weekdays only and consist of a soup, selection of main course and dessert.

VICTORIA

Melbourne - Blackburn RACV ★★★☆
Self-contained Accommodation
Address: 7 Jeffery Street, Blackburn,
Victoria 3130
Name: Lyn & Chris Russell,
"Bethbiri Brook Blackburn B&B"
Telephone: (03) 9878 6142
Fax: (03) 9878 6600 **Mobile**: 0419 545452
Beds: 1 Queen, 1 Double (2bedrooms)
Bathroom: 1 Private ensuite
Tariff: B&B (Continental) Double $90, Single $80 (Inquire, weekly rates for serviced apartment), Extra Adult $20. Credit Cards: Amex, Visa, Mastercard, Bankcard. Vouchers accepted by arrangement.
Nearest Town: Melbourne city centre, 35 mins drive (15kms. East).

This charming self-contained cottage provides an attractive atmosphere as you relax in our beautiful half-acre rustic garden with stream running metres from your window. Bellbirds, kookaburras, and other wildlife are seen in this unique National Trust area. A short walk to bus and railway, and twenty minutes train journey to scenic Dandenong Ranges. Five minutes from major shopping complex, restaurants, theatres, swimming pool and sporting facilities. Airport bus services are close by. If you enjoy walking, we are 100 metres from 28-hectare Blackburn Lake Wildlife Sanctuary, a noted bushland park developed for the purpose of "preserving bushland and wildlife habitat of high scenic and educational value".
Guest accommodation has private entrance through covered sundeck. Cottage features main bedroom, separate lounge (2nd bedroom), ensuite, and fully equipped kitchen. Queen size bed (electric blanket), split-cycle air-conditioning / heating, TV in bedroom and lounge, refrigerator, stove, microwave and guest parking. Specialty handcrafts for sale.

Melbourne - Bundoora
Homestay
Address: 6 Amber Court, Bundoora, VIC 3083
Name: Cath and John Cantrill
Telephone: (03) 9467 1335 or 9386 5277
Beds: 2 Double, 1 Single, (3 bedrooms)
Bathroom: 1 Family share
Tariff: B&B (continental, full on request),
Double $50, Single $40, Dinner $15,
Children half price.
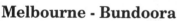
Nearest Town: 12 km N/E of city - Melways Map 19 J3

Bundoora is an attractive suburb and is situated east of the airport and north east from the city. Both can be reached by car in 20 minutes. We are well served by public transport. The tram stop is only minutes away and the ride to the city is an interesting 45 minutes. The bus service, which passes close to our front door, provides a regular and reliable link to the Watsonia Railway Station. The train journey to the city takes from 35-40 minutes.
Our home is a comfortable two-storey dwelling. Guests have their own bathroom which includes bath and shower.
Guests can choose to have their meals separately or with us. We have travelled extensively throughout the U.K., Europe, America, Asia and Scandinavian countries. The needs of the tourist are known and appreciated by us.
We are committed to offer warm and friendly hospitality.
Please write or telephone.

VICTORIA

Melbourne - Camberwell
Homestay   RACV ★★★★☆
Address: "Springfields",
4 Springfield Avenue, Camberwell,
3124 Victoria
Name: Robyn & Phillip Jordan
Telephone: (03) 9809 1681
Beds: 1 King, 2 Single (2 bedrooms)
Bathroom: 1 Guests share
Tariff: B&B (full) Double $90, Single $60, Children half price. Dinner $20. Vouchers accepted
Nearest Town: Camberwell is just 9km east of the city.

Welcome to "Springfields" - our attractive and spacious family home situated in a quiet tree-lined avenue in one of Melbourne's finest suburbs.
As well as the two guest bedrooms and adjoining bathroom, guests can enjoy the peace and privacy of their own lounge - or join us (professional couple and school age children) in our family room.
Two city tram routes and a city train (5 minutes walks) serve popular tourist and sporting attractions (Botanic Gardens, National Gallery, National Tennis Centre, MCG) and of course the city.
"Springfields" is a non-smoking homestay, where children are most welcome.
Having travelled widely as a family we appreciate the needs of travellers - a good nights sleep, fresh food and a chance to meet the locals. At "Springfields" we offer real Australian hospitality and friendliness. Our home is your home when you next visit Melbourne.
Same day bookings are <u>welcome, but advance bookings are recommended.</u>

Melbourne - Carlton
Bed & Breakfast
Address: "St. Elmo",
261 Amess St, North Carlton, 3054
Name: Eddie Beacham
Telephone: (03) 53483555 (Ask for Jodie)
Freecall 1800 353354 **Fax**: (03) 5348 3555
Mobile: (015) 512159
Email: beacham@tpgi.com.au
Beds: 1 King, 2 Double (3 bedrooms)
Bathroom: 1 Guests share
Tariff: B&B (continental) Double $80, Single $50, Children $20. Credit cards.   Vouchers accepted

St. Elmo is a classic Victoria double-fronted, double-storey terrace, only 4km from the heart of Melbourne. Built in 1904, it retains all its traditional features - open fireplaces, high ceilings, very large rooms, billiard room and library.
Furnished with antiques, each room is distinctive and all bedrooms have open fires. Located in a quiet leafy street, this house is an important part of the distinctive historic and architectural character of Carlton.
A choice of public transport - tram or bus has you in the centre of Melbourne in minutes, and we are walking distance to Lygon St and Brunswick St restaurants and shops and the Melbourne Zoo.
The house is reserved entirely for guests. A special breakfast is available each morning. During its history, St. Elmo has been a private hospital, and in the stable the site for the manufacture of the Rising Sun badges for the Diggers' slouch hats.

Melbourne - Carrum RACV ★★★☆
Bed & Breakfast
Address: 49 Valetta Street, Carrum, Victoria
Name: Brian McKenzie
Telephone: (03) 9772 1435
Beds: 1 Double, 2 Single (2 bedrooms)
Bathroom: Guests share
Tariff: B&B (full) Double $70, Single $40.   Vouchers accepted
Nearest Town: Carrum

I offer the amenities of a friendly Aussie home. This homely atmosphere includes two peaceful bedrooms which have electric blankets, colour TV. Home made bread for breakfast.
Tea & coffee available anytime. Aussie BBQ on request ($15 a head)
It is a pleasant 5 minute walk to the white sandy beaches of Port Phillip Bay and the Patterson River which has the National Water Sports Centre upstream. Carrum railway station is 4 minutes away.
Gateway to the tourist attractions of the Mornington Peninsula which includes wineries, ocean surf beaches, golf courses and beautiful rugged scenery.
A member of Victorian Bed & Breakfast Council.
A smoke free home.

Melbourne - Glen Waverley
Bed & Breakfast - RACV ★★★★☆
Address: Cameo House -
Phone for directions
Name: Jo & George Murray
Telephone: (03) 9562 1212
Fax: (03) 9560 4675 **Mobile**: (018) 999102
Email: http://www.inn house.com.au/
Beds: 3 Queen, 2 Single (3 bedrooms)
Bathroom: 3 Ensuite (1 spa bath)
Tariff: B&B (continental) Double $95-$130, Single $85-$90. Credit Cards (BC/MC/VISA/AMEX/DC).
Nearest Town: 20 km south east of Melbourne

Enjoy friendly hospitality with a touch of luxury in charming guest rooms at Cameo House - an appealing home in a quiet, wide, tree-lined street with easy access to Melbourne city centre, Phillip Island and the Dandenong Ranges. All amenities are closeby - airport bus will pick up and drop off; walk to Monash University.
Each guest room features air-conditioning and heating, with separate outside entrance, TV, microwave, easy chairs, tea and coffee making facilities, electric blankets. The little extra touches such as bedside lamps, fresh flowers, magazines, cream biscuits and Twinings teas contribute to an enjoyable stay complemented by a generous breakfast in the relaxed atmosphere of your own room. Cooked breakfast with brewed coffee optional extra.
A home away from home with comfort and privacy assured. Smoke-free. Certified Tourism Business.

VICTORIA

Melbourne - Caulfield RACV ★★★★
Bed & Breakfast Inn
Address: 30 Booran Rd, Caulfield, 3162
Name: Jacquie Little
Telephone: (03) 9572 3969 **Fax**: (03) 9571 5310
Mobile: 0412 300 315
Beds: 2 Queen, 1 Double (3 bedrooms)
Bathroom: 2 Ensuite, 1 Private
Tariff: B&B (full) King $135, Queen $130, Double Twin $110, Single $90. Valid Sun-Thurs. Children over 12. Dinner by arrangement. Credit cards (except Amex).
Nearest Town: Melbourne

Lord Lodge is located just 20 minutes from the beautiful city of Melbourne, thus making the property a perfect base from which to explore this fascinating and diverse city.
Situated on 1.8 acres and surrounded by 100 year old trees, the house is a superb example of early Victorian architecture, circa 1800, with soaring 15 foot ceilings, elaborate cornices, marble fireplaces and Baltic pines floorboards.
The 60 foot turret provides excellent views of the surrounding area.
There are 3 guest bedrooms, all are large and each has its own distinctive character, all have complimentary port, welcome fruit bowl, fresh flowers and your bed is turned down at night with a 'good night' chocolate.
Described by a guests as "an experience of good taste" Lord Lodge is a member property of "Australia and New Zealands Finest B&Bs and Rural Retreats" - you are assured of a warm friendly greeting and discreet, unobtrusive service.
Breakfast is served in the superb dining room and includes croissants, cereals, fresh fruit in season, juice, scrambled eggs with smoked salmon or flaked trout, bacon and eggs.
For those with a fascination for horses, Lord Lodge backs onto Caulfield Racetrack and forms part of a large racing stable. The barn on the property was built at the same time as the house and was used in the Pharlap movie - it is still in use today and houses some of the 22 thoroughbreds in training here.

Melbourne - Forest Hill
Homestay: Private Suites
Address: "Chanleigh", 21A Jackson St., Forest Hill, 3131
Name: Kathie & Robert Chan
Telephone: (03) 9877 4849
Beds: 2 Queen, Single on request (2 bedrooms)
Bathroom: 2 Ensuite + 1 Spa room
Tariff: B&B (continental) Double $70-$120, Single $55-$85. Credit Cards accepted.
Nearest Town: Forest Hill - (Nunawading/Blackburn)

Two minutes walk from the popular Forest Hill Chase with its excellent shopping, cinemas, fitness centre, international food court and convenient bus service, "Chanleigh" offers a quiet retreat in Gum-treed surroundings. The suites are accessed from private balconies graced with palm trees and various plants, and brightly coloured local parrots frequent the area adding charm and colour. The suites are tastefully decorated, and a private spa room may be accessed directly from the suites and used by guests for a moderate additional fee. Each fully serviced suite has a private ensuite, queen sized bed, and is equipped with colour TV, microwave oven, fridge and tea & toast making facilities. The use of a cot or single bed may be arranged for an additional fee. Robert and Kathie have welcomed guests from many countries and are happy to adjust their breakfast menu to suit international guests or special diets. Kathie's Master's degrees equip her to cope with language difficulties, so limited English is no problem. We offer nightly or short-term accommodation in a choice of price ranges, and are committed to making your stay comfortable, quiet and enjoyable. Melways map 62, B-2.

The standard of accommodation in
The Australian Bed and Breakfast Book ranges from homely to luxurious,
but you can always be sure of superior hospitality.

VICTORIA

Melbourne - Hampton
Homestay
Address: 19 Orlando Street,
Hampton, VIC 3188
Name: Hayton Peggy
Telephone: (03) 9521 9187
Beds: 1 Queen, 1 Single (1 bedroom)
Bathroom: 1 Guests share
Tariff: B&B (full) Double $100,
Single $55, Children under 12 half price
Dinner $20. Vouchers accepted
Nearest Town: 16km from Melbourne

My home is a fully renovated Edwardian cottage, furnished with antiques, and made comfortable with ducted heating and open fireplaces. It is situated in a quiet street very close to a good swimming beach, and within easy walking distance of shops and the station for quick transport to the city.

My family have now left home, so you may share my house with lovable Henrietta the dog, Sissie the cat and myself.

I enjoy cooking and will include home made bread and jams with your breakfast. If you wish I will prepare your dinner.

I have travelled extensively and enjoyed this kind of hospitality in other countries. Please write or phone and the best time is early morning or around dinner. I have an answering machine so leave your name and phone number and I will ring you back as soon as possible

Melbourne - Hurstbridge
Bed & Breakfast
762 Main Road
Hurstbridge VIC 3099
Name: Helen and Malcolm Sterry
Telephone: (03) 9718 2943
Beds: 2 Queen, 2 single (3 bedrooms)
Bathroom: 2 Ensuite, 1 Private
Tariff: B&B (full) Double $90, Single $70.
Children welcome by arrangement. Vouchers accepted
Nearest Town: Melbourne 25km

Settled in the Yarra Valley, 'Bluehaven' at Hurstbridge will officially open on 1 January, 1998.

Our bluestone, double storey home offers the best of both worlds - a new home with old style appeal. Beautifully decorated guest rooms each with their own ensuite / bathroom, large sitting room with colour TV, video and book library, games area and tea / coffee making facilities, or sit and have a quiet chat in the main lounge in front of the open fire. Undercover, security car parking is available with a complimentary afternoon tea offered on arrival.

'Bluehaven' is only a three minute walk from the Hurstbridge railway station allowing easy access to the centre of Melbourne. Visit the various local tourist attractions, Yarra Valley wineries, Kinglake & Warrandyte National parks, Montsalvat, antique shops, craft markets, historic goldfields and many restaurants and cafes which are only a short drive away.

We offer comfort and warm hospitality in a non-smoking environment. Children are welcome by arrangement.

VICTORIA

Melbourne - Kooyong
Homestay
Address: Carlisle Bed and Breakfast
400 Glenferrie Road
Kooyong 3144
Name: Anne Carlisle
Telephone: (03) 9822 4847 **Fax**: (03) 9822 6637 **Mobile**: 0419 878 909
Beds: 2 Queen, 2 Single (3 bedrooms)
Bathroom: 1 Ensuite, 1 Private
Tariff: B&B (full) Double $130-$150. Credit Cards: Visa, Mastercard, Bankcard
Nearest Town: Melbourne 7kms.

Carlisle is a gracious Federation house and garden offering luxurious bed and breakfast accommodation and gourmet, in-house catering for your private entertaining needs. The house, built in 1910, has tall, elegant windows which frame the well established English garden. the large, light filled lounge room, the entrance hallways, magnificent dining room and private gazebo are for the exclusive use of guests. Quality sound equipment, television and video, your own tea and coffee-making facilities, and a well stocked refrigerator are discreetly positioned for use by guests at any time. On colder evenings, open fires add to the ambience and your enjoyment. A writing desk with telephone, set in a quiet alcove, may be used for business or personal paperwork.

The centre of Melbourne is 7 kilometres away, and the MCG, Tennis Centre, Victorian Arts Centre, Casino and the riverside entertainment and restaurant complex at Southgate, are a short train or tram trip away.

Melbourne - North Fitzroy RACV ★★★★
Self-contained Accom.
Address: 41 Rae Street
(Cnr. York Street), North Fitzroy, Vic 3068
Name: Slattery's Nth Fitzroy B&B
Telephone: (03) 9489 1308
Beds: 1 Twin (1 bedroom)
Bathroom: 1 Private
Tariff: B&B (full) Double $90, Single $70.
Nearest Town: Melbourne (CBD - 2km)

"Slattery's" offers superior self-contained accommodation in Melbourne's first suburb, 2km from CBD. North Fitzroy is a stimulating, interesting, attractive (yet quiet) inner Melbourne neighbourhood. Air-conditioned, centrally-heated apartment comprises bedroom with twin beds, separate sitting room, bathroom, kitchenette and meals area. Guest's first floor accommodation is separate from that of your hosts. You have your own tea & coffee facility, toaster, microwave, fridge, colour TV, video, electric blankets and garage parking. There is a roof garden with city skyline views. You will be close to public transport, hospitals, churches, theatres, Edinburgh Gardens, the Royal Exhibition Buildings - within walking distance of many restaurants in Brunswick and Lygon Streets which offer eat-in, take-away or dial-deliver services. Breakfast is your choice of cold or cooked. Adults only. Smoke free. Member of Inn House B&B.

Melbourne - St Kilda West RACV ★★★☆
Homestay
Address: 57 Mary Street, St Kilda West, 3182
Name: "Victoria House" Marcia McKay
Telephone: (03) 9525 4512 **Fax**: (03) 9525 3024
Mobile: (014) 804989
Beds: 2 Queen, 1 Twin (2 bedrooms/1 Twin apartment & 1 Queen)
Bathroom: 1 Private, 1 Guests share plus 1 extra toilet & hand basin
Tariff: B&B (continental) Double $100-$110, Single $85-$95
Nearest Town: Melbourne 5 kms

Our lovely home is situated in a quiet tree lined street in cosmopolitan St Kilda with its many restaurants and shops to suit all tastes and prices.
We are within walking distance to the beach with its interesting old pier and Pavilion where penguins can often be seen. The Albert Park Golf Course is within walking distance as is the Grand Prix Race track. A highlight on Sunday is a walk to the Upper Esplanade Craft Market, and later to the Victoria Market with all its exciting wares. The light rail or tram will have you in the city in 15 minutes via lovely St Kilda Road and the Swanston Street Mall. Boat trips leave regularly to go out in the Bay or across to historical Williamstown. Off street parking. Washing and ironing facilities available.
Established 1989. Facsimile facilities available.

Tell other travellers about your favourite B&Bs

Melbourne - Strathewen
Farmstay
Address: 1090 Strathewen Rd,
Strathewen, Victoria 3099
Name: William & Joan Christophersen
Telephone: (03) 9714 8464
Fax: (03) 9714 8464 **Mobile**: (019) 185086
Email: christow@ocean.com.au
Beds: 1 Double, 2 Single or 2 Doubles
(2 bedrooms) in separate homestead.
Bathroom: 1 Private
Tariff: B&B (full) Double $100, Single $60, Children over three $25, Dinner by arrangement. Vouchers accepted Monday to Thursday.
Nearest Town: Hurstbridge 15km, Yarra Glen 18km, Eltham 23km

The quiet and beautiful Arthurs Creek Valley, with its orchards, vineyards and grazing properties, is the approach to "Strathewen Hills", a mixed farm of 100 acres. Life here is very relaxed. **SUGARLOAF COTTAGE** *on the property, has verandahs all round and is opposite Mt. Sugarloaf in the Kinglake National Park. Wombats and kangaroos are common here. Parrots, galahs and cockatoos visit, while our cattle graze with content. Bill and Joan have been involved in the wine industry for some years and offer specialised assistance with Yarra Valley visits. A small vineyard has been planted and a winery is planned for the future.*
There are a number of excellent country restaurants and hotels nearby, for meals. A highlight of Saturday mornings is a visit to St. Andrews open market, followed by old wares at Joan's 'Curiosity Shop' at Panton Hill. There are fast electric trains, Hurstbridge to Melbourne, nearby.

Melbourne - Templestowe RACV ★★★☆
Homestay/Bed & Breakfast
Address: "Kookaburra Corner",
19 Unwin Street, Templestowe, VIC 3106
Name: Elaine & David Dodds
Telephone: (03) 9846 3800
Fax: (03) 9846 3391
Beds: 1 King (or 2 Singles), 1 Double, (2 bedrooms)
Bathroom: 1 Guest share
Tariff: B&B (full) Double $75, Single $60. Vouchers accepted
Nearest Town: Melbourne

ENJOY THE BEST OF BOTH WORLDS. Uniquely situated only 20 minutes from the bustling centre of Melbourne with all its major attractions, yet nestled in the heart of the lovely Yarra Valley Parklands. Attractive, with modern facilities, the house has picturesque views of Westerfolds Park on the Yarra River. Enjoy a delicious cooked breakfast in our friendly Dining Room, or on the patio with the Rosellas, King Parrots and Cockatoos. Explore the City and surrounds; or visit nearby Wineries, Victoria's First Goldfield, craft markets, large shopping centres. Later eat at one of the excellent local restaurants.
A few minutes walk away is Westerfolds Park, walk or cycle along its extensive tracks, or sit in the sun beside the Yarra River.
The area will enchant you as it did the Heidelberg School of Impressionists who painted nearby - a photographer's paradise. Expect a warm welcome with homemade refreshments (plus other small surprises).
*Brochure available.***Directions**: *Just 20 minutes from heart of Melbourne, 30 minutes from Melbourne Airport.*

VICTORIA

Melbourne - Warrandyte
Homestay+Self-contained Accom.
Address: "Pound Cottage", 80 Pound Road, Warrandyte, Vic 3113
Name: Carol & Tony Hampson
Telephone: (03) 9844 2607 **Fax**: (03) 9844 2607
Email: ahampson@ozemail.com.au
Beds: 2 Double (2 bedrooms)
Bathroom: 1 Ensuite, 1 Private
Tariff: B&B (full) Double $60, Single $40. SC. Accom:
Double $65, Single $45. Vouchers accepted
Nearest Town: Warrandyte. 25km E. of Melbourne.
Melways Ref Map 23 A12.

Our comfortable home is a few minutes walk from State Park and the River Yarra, ideal for bush walking and wildlife. Explore Warrandyte's craft shops and galleries, enjoy excellent local cafes and restaurants. A Craft Market is held on the 1st Saturday each month.

Located 40 minutes drive from Melbourne and within easy reach of the Dandenongs and Yarra Valley, we can introduce you to many attractions and delightful places to visit.

Relax on our deck with the birds, wander in our interesting garden where you may see a koala!

Stay in house or be self contained. We have two friendly dogs and are smoke-free. Home made refreshments offered on arrival and country breakfasts served. We look forward to welcoming you.

Melbourne - Williamstown
Homestay
Address: 4 Nancy Court, Williamstown, VIC 3016
Name: Barbara Fleischer
Telephone: (03) 9397 6846
Beds: 1 Double, 2 Single (2 bedrooms)
Bathroom: 1 Guests share
Tariff: B&B (continental) Double $80, Single $45.
Vouchers accepted
Nearest Town: Williamstown -
Melbourne 15 mins by car, 25 mins by train

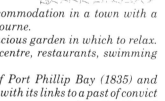

My home offers you comfortable, well appointed accommodation in a town with a unique charm of its own yet easily accessible to Melbourne.

Set in a quiet court, the house is sunny and has a spacious garden in which to relax. Centrally placed, it's an easy walk to the shopping centre, restaurants, swimming beach, yacht clubs, museums and public transport.

Williamstown is the oldest continuous settlement of Port Phillip Bay (1835) and visitors love the atmosphere of this old historic seaport with its links to a past of convict hulks and sailing ships. Picturesque views of Melbourne are seen from the Strand which follows the shoreline where black swans, pelicans and sea-birds feed.

A keen traveller I have enjoyed home-style hospitality in Australia and overseas. It's a great way to go!

Percolated coffee, or tea if you prefer, is served with your full or continental style breakfast.

Directions: *Please phone or write.*

VICTORIA

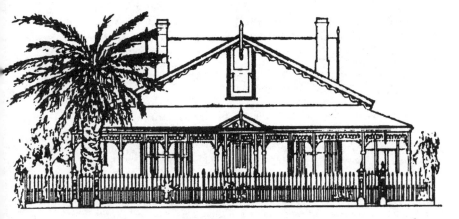

Melbourne - Williamstown RACV ★★★★☆
Bed & Breakfast
Address: "The Grange", 219 Osborne Street, Williamstown, VIC 3016
Name: Joan & Jock Williamson
Telephone: (03) 9397 6288 **Mobile**: (0412) 878 495
Email: thegrange@melbourne bed and breakfasts.8i.com
Beds: 2 Queen (2 bedroom)
Bathroom: 2 Ensuite
Tariff: B&B (full) Queen $130, Twin $145, Single $95. Special rates apply.
Nearest Town: Williamstown - Melbourne 20 mins by car, 30 mins by train, station 5 mins walk.

The Grange offers luxury accommodation in an elegant fully restored historic 'Victorian' home set in a quiet tree lined street unique to the historic seaport of Williamstown. The Grange is within easy walking distance of many of Williamstown's main attractions: shops, galleries, restaurants, Botanical Gardens, historic buildings, Nelson Place market, and the beach waterfront.

The Grange has an interesting history, commencing as a farm house circa 1870, and moved to its current location in 1905. Accommodation includes: private guest entrance, large bedroom, en-suite, dining and living rooms, central heating with open fires in winter months. Guest accommodation in the stunning restored Victorian portion of the house is separate from that used by our family. Not suitable for small children. No smoking indoors. Off-street car parking optional. Wedding packages available.

Enjoy the ambience, comfort and hospitality The Grange offers with the opportunity to explore the truly fascinating historic seaport of Williamstown.

Home Page: melbournebedandbreakfasts.8i.com/thegrange

Phone numbers throughout Australia are changing to 8 digits.
For help contact Directory Assistance.

VICTORIA

Melbourne - Wonga Park/Croydon RACV ★★★★☆
Farmstay, Self-contained Accommodation. With disabled access.
Address: 64-66 Brushy Park Road. Wonga Park 3115, Victoria
Name: Mal and Lois Yen
Telephone: (03) 9722 1393 **Fax**: (03) 9722 1316
Beds: 1 Queen, 1 Double (2 Bedrooms)
Bathroom: 2 Ensuite, 2 Private
Tariff: B&B (full) Double $95, Single $70. Credit Cards accepted.
Nearest Town: 6km Lilydale, 33km East of Melbourne

Friendly hospitality is offered at our fully self-contained home on a 24 acre hobby farm less than one hours drive from Melbourne. It is the gateway to the Yarra Valley with its famous wineries and is at the foothills of the Dandenongs.

We are within easy reach of good golf courses, restaurants, wineries, local craft markets at Warrandyte which also has nature trails around the Yarra River and State Park, and large shopping centres in Ringwood, Croydon and Lilydale. Less than 30 minutes away is Olinda on Mt Dandenong, famous for restaurants, rhododendrons and azaleas. Healesville Wildlife Sanctuary and the famous Puffing Billy in Belgrave are close by.

Malstead, which is 16 squares, offers you all normal home comforts including ensuites to both bedrooms, all linen and doonas, heating, TV and a fully equipped kitchen and laundry.

Have a morning dip or spa in our inground, solar heated salt pool.

Melbourne - Wonga Park/Croydon
Homestay   RACV ★★★★☆
Address: 33 Gatters Road, Wonga Park, 3115
Name: Onorina's Bed & Breakfast
Telephone: (03) 9722 1719
Beds: 2 Queen (2 bedrooms)
Bathroom: 2 Ensuite
Tariff: B&B (full) Double $95-$110, Single $75-$85.
Vouchers accepted $15-$25 surcharge
Nearest Town: Wonga Park - situated 8km Warrandyte, Melbourne 32km

ONORINA'S situated 40 minutes from Melbourne, 3km off Maroondah Highway in a tranquil semi-rural setting Wonga Park, gateway to the beautiful Yarra Valley. Close to the Dandenong Ranges, historic Warrandyte, and wonderful wineries of the region. Fine galleries, excellent restaurants and cafes, bush walking, horse riding, the natural beauty of the area has much to offer the traveller.

Our aim is to provide a warm welcoming atmosphere in tasteful, comfortable and tranquil surroundings. We offer two rooms with comfortable queen sized beds, wool doonas, electric blankets, private ensuites, one with spa bath. The guest's lounge contains fireplace, TV, music system, tea/coffee making facilities. A full hot breakfast with home made preserves is served in dining room or on the terrace overlooking the garden.

The Colella family, long time local orchardists, producing apples, pears and stone fruit welcome orchards walks on the family property.

Smoking permitted on the terrace. Please phone.

Milawa RACV ★★★☆
Homestay
Address: "Ercildoon", Snow Rd.,
Milawa via Wangaratta, Vic 3678
Name: Malcolm & Dorothy Gardner
Telephone: (03) 5727 3222 **Mobile**: (018) 574564
Beds: 3 Double, 1 Twin (4 bedrooms)
Bathroom: 1 Guest share
Tariff: B&B (full) Double $80, Single $50.
Nearest Town: Wangaratta

We live in this 1884 homestead built by our grandfather Colin Gardner - one of the first to settle in Milawa. The rooms are large, beds comfortable with an at-home atmosphere. A large lounge with an open fire, also a smaller private lounge with a TV, tea & coffee with biscuits freely available.
Walking distance from Brown Bros Winery - 2 minutes to Hotel Bistro, Coffee Lounge. 5 minutes King River. 5 minutes Friend's Restaurant. Only 16km to other restaurants. Many tourist towns and snow-fields nearby.
We will show you our private museum, the buggies, stables, blacksmith, shearing shed, just as they were 100 years ago in grandfather Colins era. Say hello to our buckskin stock horses.
We serve a good cooked breakfast with home-made bread. We both work out on the farm so it is advisable to ring in advance, but not essential. There is an airport at Brown Bros.

Mildura
Homestay, Bed & Breakfast
Address: Sturt Highway, Trentham Cliffs via Mildura.
PO Box 959, Mildura, 3502
Name: "Linsley House" Colin & Desley Rankin
Telephone: (03) 5024 8487
Beds: 2 Queen, 2 Single (3 bedrooms)
Bathroom: 2 Ensuites
Tariff: B&B (full) Double $75, Single $55, Credit Cards. Vouchers accepted
Nearest Town: Mildura

Our tranquil home is situated in a quiet rural setting, and has panoramic views of the garden and Murray River from the bedrooms. The large lounge/dining area includes: full kitchen facilities, TV, fridge, woodfire, air-conditioning and comfortable antiques.
Mildura is renown for its Oranges, Dried fruits, Wineries, Restaurants and Mediterranean weather.

VICTORIA

Mininera - Grampians District
Farmstay Bed & Breakfast RACV ★★★★
Address: Menenia Bed and Breakfast,
Mininera 3351
Telephone: (03) 5350 6536
Fax: (03) 5350 6591 **Mobile**: (019) 424 889
Beds: 1 King, 1 Double (2 Bedrooms)
Bathroom: 1 Ensuite, 1 Private
Tariff: B&B (full) Double $90-$105,
Single $80, Dinner $20, Children $20, Credit Cards:
Mastercard, Bankcard, Visa. Vouchers accepted $10-$25 surcharge
Nearest Town: Ararat

Escape and unwind.
At the end of our two kilometer driveway, Menenia offers you an intimate experience of fine food and quiet, relaxing surrounds. Delight in a memorable dinner if you choose and enjoy your leisurely breakfast in the traditional dining room.
Our 1881 bluestone homestead, stables, shearing shed and extensive English garden are hidden away in the Western district rural landscape. Menenia is centrally located on the Great Southern Touring Route between the mountains and vineyards of the Grampians, the gold history of Bullarat and the beauty Great Ocean Road. Escape to Menenia for a night, weekend or longer. German spoken.

Mornington Peninsula - Flinders/Cape Schanck
Bushland Retreat RACV ★★★★
Address: "Samburu",
Eastern Grey Rise, Flinders, Vic 3929
Name: Annabel & Jens Norlyng
Telephone: (03) 5989 0093
Fax: (03) 5989 0053
Beds: 2 Queen, 2 Single (2 bedrooms)
Bathroom: 2 Ensuite
Tariff: B&B (full) Double $120-$130,
Single $100, Dinner $30, Credit Cards (BC/MC/VISA).
Vouchers accepted $47 surcharge
Nearest Town: Flinders (20 km)

SAMBURU is a 50 acre property with more than half of its acreage devoted to wildlife conservation. Between Flinders and Cape Schanck with views to Bass Strait and adjacent to National Park, it is also not far from the wineries of Redhill.
Your comfortable guest wing accommodation with its own entrance is luxuriously furnished with antiques, and fine silver. Produce fresh from our own garden or local farms, free range eggs, fish from the local fisherman and meat dishes are cooked with an interesting aroma of fresh herbs. Open fires in winter, candlelit dinners, music and fine food compliment evenings of tranquillity and convivial hospitality. The floodlit dams are a stage for our visiting cabaret of kangaroos. Bush walks, farm walks and picnics can be arranged.
Your well-travelled hosts who have lived in Kenya, Nigeria, Indonesia and Europe offer friendly service. Hosts interests are bridge, golf, painting, wildlife and nature.
Directions: *Find Meakins Rd, turn into Gwenmarlin Rd, cross the bridge, up the gully, turn left into Eastern Grey Rise - "Samburu" is at the end. Beware jumping kangaroos.*

VICTORIA

Mornington Peninsula - Flinders RACV ★★★★☆
Bed & Breakfast
Address: Gwenmarlin House, Lot 11 Eastern Grey Rise, Flinders, Victoria
Name: Angela & Stephen Mackley
Telephone: (03) 5989 0085
Beds: 3 King (3 bedrooms)
Bathroom: 3 Ensuite
Tariff: B&B (full) Double from $140, Dinner by arrangement (Fully licensed). Children not catered for. Credit Cards.
Nearest Town: Flinders

Gwenmarlin House is a purpose built B&B set on 50 ares adjacent to Mornington Peninsula National Park. Accommodation is available for 3 couples offering luxurious king size beds and ensuites.
French doors in each of the beautifully appointed bedrooms lead to a private balcony offering magnificent views of National Park and Bass Strait. One of the many attractions is the prolific wildlife which can be seen from here including kangaroos which graze at dawn and dusk.
There is also a private guests lounge room with an open fire place and an endless supply of books.
You will be able to enjoy a full English breakfast in the dining room which has individual seating arrangements to guarantee guests privacy. Dinner is served by arrangement and there is also a weekend package available. Gwenmarlin House is fully licensed offering a variety of Australian wines. Rating 4 1/2 star.

Mornington Peninsula - Sorrento
Homestay RACV ★★★★
Address: 'Tamasha House', 699 Melbourne Road, Sorrento, VIC 3943. Melway P159 C11
Name: Naomi & Peter Nicholson
Telephone: (03) 5984 2413
Fax: (03) 5984 0452
Mobile: (019) 181686
Beds: 1 King, 1 Double, 2 Single (2 bedrooms)
Bathroom: 2 Ensuite

Tariff: B&B (full) Double $120, Single $90. Dinner from $30. Credit Cards (BC/MC/VISA/AMEX). Adults only. No pets. No smoking. Vouchers accepted $35 Surcharge
Nearest Town: Sorrento 1km, Melbourne 1 1/2 hours.

Renowned for its beautiful garden and fine food, Tamasha House is situated halfway between bay and ocean beaches and a short walk to both.
Guest rooms have their own private entrance from the garden. The rooms are decorated with a sea-side theme and feature paintings by local artists.
Afternoon tea is offered on arrival. Hosts, Naomi and Peter have been associated with the Mornington Peninsula for many years and can advise on the attractions of the area from personal experience. They can recommend places at which to eat or provide dinner if given notice. Breakfast is served in the dining-room and includes fresh juice, poached seasonal fruit, homemade bread and preserves as well as hot foods.
Historic Sorrento has a museum, galleries, dolphin swims, tennis, golf and beaches. It is close to National Parks, wineries and markets. Car ferry goes to Queenscliff.
Home Page: http://www.nepeanet.org.au/b_and_b/tamasha/

VICTORIA

Mount Beauty RACV ★★★☆
Bed & Breakfast
Address: 4 Stewarts Road,
Tawonga South, Vic 3698
Name: Braeview Bed & Breakfast
Telephone: (03) 5754 4746
Fax: (03) 5754 4746 **Mobile**: (018) 572834
Beds: 2 Queen, 1 Double, 2 Single (4 bedrooms)
Bathroom: 1 Ensuite with spa, 1 Guests share
Tariff: B&B (full) Double $98-$120, Single $50, Children over 12 welcome, Credit Cards (BC/MC/VISA).Vouchers accepted $18 surcharge
Nearest Town: Mt Beauty 1.5km
SPOIL YOURSELF YOU DESERVE IT.
Situated in the beautiful Kiewa Valley at the base of Mt Bogong in Victoria's High Country. Our Valley will revitalise you year round with its magnificent views, clean air and relaxed stress free lifestyle.
We offer warm summer days, cool nights, beautiful autumn colours, snow capped mountains and skiing.
Enjoy our complimentary picnic lunch while sampling the tastes of the many wineries. Explore the historic towns of Yackandandah and Beechworth. Catch a trout, play golf, go horse-riding, bushwalking, explore country markets or play with "Morse" our Staffy.
Braeview is a split level home in a quiet cul-de-sac 200 metres off the Kiewa Valley Highway and is smoke free.
The separate guest lounge room has a cosy wood heater, books, TV and stereo, outside spa. Our hearty country breakfast is served on the balcony with panoramic valley views.
A stay with us will put a smile on your face.

Mount Beauty
Bed & Breakfast + SC Accom.
Address: 40 Tawonga Crescent,
Mount Beauty, Vic 3699
Name: Jane's B&B
Telephone: (03) 5754 4036
Fax: (03) 5754 4036 **Mobile**: 0419876483
Beds: 2 Queen, 5 Single (3 bedrooms)
Bathroom: 1 Ensuite
Tariff: B&B (full) Double $100, Single $50.
Nearest Town: Bright

Ideally situated across the road from Mount Beauty Golf Course, looking over Mount Emu and the Bogong Ranges. Bus passes the house to Falls Creek.
Many other attractions: fishing, walking, horse riding, swimming, wineries and lovely picnic areas all around.
Accommodation:
1 Double Room: (bathroom opp. room)
1 Twin: (bathroom opp. room)
1 Twin (share bathroom if house is full)
1 Flat: with 1 Double and 1 Single bed (with shower bath).
Tariff: $50 per person
3 bedroomed holiday house also available on property. Sleeps up to 8. Tariff on application.

Mount Dandenong see Dandenong Ranges
Mount Moriac see Geelong

Mount Macedon - Barringo Valley
Homestay RACV ★★★☆
Address: "Mariah Vale",
92 Barringo Road, Mt Macedon, Vic 3441
Name: Phyllis & Ian Boyd
Telephone: (03) 5426 1281
Beds: 1 Double, 2 Single (2 bedrooms)
Bathroom: 1 Guests share
Tariff: B&B (full) Double $90, Single $55. Dinner $20-$30. Vouchers accepted
Nearest Town: 10mins (8km) from Gisborne and Mt. Macedon in Barringo Valley.

Our modern homestead in a garden setting with picturesque mountain and valley views, is situated on fifteen acres including natural bushland, overlooking a large lake with windmill and native water birds. Kangaroos and wallabies graze about the property, while koalas frequent nearby gums. Due to native planting, tiny birds twitter about the verandahs, while magpies, kookaburras and parrots feed from feeders in the garden and by the spectacular waterfall.
We offer our guests exclusive use of our lounge/dining area, overlooking garden and valley, with log fires or air conditioning, as the weather dictates.
Guests share a modern bathroom, and may choose the double or twin bedroom, each with its old-world charm. Coffee and tea making facilities, own entrances and undercover car parking are provided. No smoking please.
Breakfasts of homemade jams and fruits, cereals and wholemeal breads, or bacon with eggs from our free-range poultry, is included.
Hearty dinners or simple wholesome meals available by prior arrangement.
Home Page: macedonranges.com.au

Mount Macedon
Self-contained Accommodation
Address: 110 Glen Drouitt Road, Mt Macedon, 3441
Name: "Milindi"
Telephone: (0354) 262 209 **Mobile**: 041-958 1996
Beds: 1 Double (1 bedsitter)
Bathroom: 1 Ensuite
Tariff: B&B (continental) Double $75, Single $65.
Nearest Town: Gisborne 8km

Our cosy self-contained accommodation is nestled in the picturesque Barringo Valley, with views to the Macedon Ranges. Situated on ten acres, including a lake for that spot of fishing if you like fresh trout for dinner or cooked on the BBQ which is also available for our guests. Three acres of landscaped garden to get lost in with a picnic lunch alone or with the kids. Native birds are at the feeders and water birds frequent the lake. We have two small dogs that love that extra pat or two and chickens which provide fresh eggs for breakfast. We are not far from wineries, bush walks, Hanging Rock, wildlife park and horse trail rides. Our cosy bed sitter with 1 double bed and small sofa bed is ideal for that quick country getaway. Equipped kitchen, tiled bathroom, all linen supplied, TV, heating. Breakfast ingredients supplied.

VICTORIA

Mount Moniac see Geelong
Mudgegonga see Mytleford

Myrtleford - Mudgegonga
Farmstay
Address: "Orange Grove", RMB 2430, Blacks Flat Rd, Mudgegonga via Myrtleford, 3737 Victoria
Name: Mary Brewer
Telephone: (03) 5753 4513 **Fax**: (03) 5753 4540
Beds: 1 King/Queen, 1 Double, 3 Single (3 bedrooms)
Bathroom: 1 Private
Tariff: B&B (full) Double $80, Single $40, Children half price. Dinner $25. Vouchers accepted
Nearest Town: Myrtleford

Nestled in the quiet Mudgegonga Valley, our family has been farming "Orange Grove" for four generations and currently operates a beef cattle enterprise. The B&B is situated alongside the restored original 1880s pioneer homestead and provides comfortable modern accommodation in a traditional country atmosphere. The area is a bushwalkers' paradise surrounded by unspoiled hills which provide a home for some stunning and rare species of flora and fauna. For snow enthusiasts and skiers Mt Hotham, Mt Buffalo and Falls Creek are easily accessible. Water sports and fishing are available at nearby Lake Buffalo or the famous Hume Dam on the Murray River. The old goldfields of Mt Stanley, Yackandandah and Beechworth are a short drive away as are the wineries of Rutherglen and Milawa and the beautiful towns of Harrietville, Wandiligong and Mt Beauty. Whatever one enjoys in "getting-away" it can be done at "Orange Grove"

Myrtleford
Homestay   RACV ★★★★☆
Address: "Rosewhite House Rural Retreat", RMB2555, Carrolls Road, Rosewhite via Myrtleford
Name: Beverley & Noel Stone
Telephone: 1800 675 300 **Fax**: (03) 5753 5239
Beds: 1 King, 2 Queen (3 bedrooms)
Bathroom: 3 Ensuite
Tariff: B&B (full) Double $130, Single $95, Dinner $25/head, Credit Cards.
Nearest Town: Myrtleford

*Magnificent 'High Country' setting in beautiful Happy Valley just 12km from Myrtleford. We are central to all the north-east of Victoria has to offer. More than just a B&B, Rosewhite House Rural Retreat offers a variety of packages which include winery tours by courtesy car, fishing trips, horse riding, golf - you name it, we can arrange it! Each bedroom has its own private balcony overlooking the valley. Other features include a hot spa in its own gazebo, undercover parking, reverse-cycle air-conditioning in each room, complimentary guest laundry. All tariffs include a welcoming champagne and cheese platter supper. Fully licensed, we can provide evening meals with prior notice. Children by special arrangement only.
Call us on 1800 675 300 for a brochure.*

Narbethong see Marysville
Newhaven see Phillip Island

Olinda see Dandenong Ranges

Orbost
Homestay+B&B RACV ★★★☆
Address: "Riverview Rural Retreat",
15 Irvines Road, Orbost, Vic 3888
Name: Julie & Peter Young
Telephone: (03) 5154 2411 **Fax:** (03) 5154 1949
Beds: 1 Double, 2 Single (2 bedrooms)
Bathroom: 1 Guests share
Tariff: B&B (full) Double $80, Single $50, Children $20. Dinner $20. Credit Cards (VISA/MC/BC).
Nearest Town: Orbost 2km.
"Riverview" the easy to find country getaway.
Set in an elevated position overlooking the beautiful fertile Snowy River Valley, where majestic mahogany and graceful willow trees line the river banks. Picturesque Mount Raymond, beautiful golf links and wetlands with its birdlife are all clearly visible from the spacious verandahs of Riverview. Gardens with abundant native birds (daily fed) complete the peaceful environment. Guests are encouraged to feel at home, making full use of all modern conveniences this new home has to offer, with hearty home cooked country meals a real bonus. Also BBQ available. Regardless if guests choose to stay a while and take in all attractions Orbost and district have to offer, or stay just long enough for a restful break and sample of Aussie hospitality: hosts Julie and Peter will endeavour to see your stay is memorable, for your comfort is our concern.
Our brochure offers all information on directions and local attractions.

Otway Ranges see Lorne

Paynesville
Bed & Breakfast   RACV ★★★☆
Address: 39-41 Langford Parade, Paynesville, 3880 Victoria
Name: "The Crowes' Nest B&B", Hosts: John & Meaghan
Telephone: (03) 515 66699
Beds: 2 Queen, 2 Single (3 bedrooms)
Bathroom: 1 Guests share
Tariff: B&B (full) Double $90, Single $55. Children welcome.
Weekly rates, two-day packages. Credit Cards. Vouchers accepted
Nearest Town: Bairnsdale - 15 mins south on Paynesville Road.

A warm welcome awaits you at Paynesville's first B&B accommodation, on the beautiful Gippsland Lakes.
Delightfully renovated, and surrounded by a verandah and a large cottage garden, the house is only 400 metres from waterfrontage and all amenities (including overnight boat mooring and restaurants).
Read the papers, plan your day and enjoy a leisurely breakfast - after which, (to quote a favourite guest), "Ballast will not be a problem!".
The Lakes need little introduction whether your interests lie in boating, fishing, galleries, wineries, flora, fauna; or anything else found between the High Country and 90 miles of ocean beach!
Well-travelled, local hosts provide hospitality and atmosphere - plus many thoughtful extras, to ensure your stay will be the first of many.
Directions: 15 minutes from Bairnsdale. Follow "Ferry" signs to King St/Langford Pde corner, or B&B signpost on the Esplanade. As featured in "The Age", "Gourmet Traveller", "The Courier-Mail" and "Country Looks".
(An environmentally conscientious household).

VICTORIA

Paynesville
Bed & Breakfast RACV ★★★☆
Address: 1 Third Parade,
Raymond Island, Paynesville, Vic 3880
Name: Montague's Bed & Breakfast
Telephone: (03) 5156 7880
Fax: (03) 5156 7880
Mobile: (018) 100990
Beds: 1 King, 2 Queen (3 bedrooms)
Bathroom: 1 Guests share, 1 Family share
Tariff: B&B (full) Double $95, Single $65, Credit Cards. Vouchers accepted $15 on Double only
Nearest Town: Bairnsdale - 10 mins or 16km

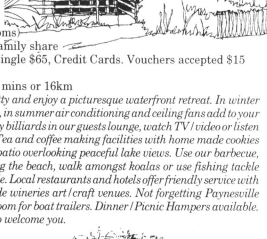

A short trip by ferry or sail to our jetty and enjoy a picturesque waterfront retreat. In winter warm your toes in front of our log fire, in summer air conditioning and ceiling fans add to your comfort. Relax in our indoor spa, play billiards in our guests lounge, watch TV / video or listen to music with a glass of local wine. Tea and coffee making facilities with home made cookies always available. Breakfast on the patio overlooking peaceful lake views. Use our barbecue, play golf or lawn bowls. Stroll along the beach, walk amongst koalas or use fishing tackle provided. Boats and cruises available. Local restaurants and hotels offer friendly service with great food Scenic drives may include wineries art / craft venues. Not forgetting Paynesville offers the best boating in Victoria! Room for boat trailers. Dinner / Picnic Hampers available. Our cat "Christie" would also like to welcome you.

Phillip Island - Cowes
Self-contained Accommodation
Address: 2 Roy Court, Cowes,
Victoria 3922
Name: Rothsaye on Lovers Walk
Telephone: (03) 5952 2057
Fax: (03) 5952 2057 **Mobile**: (015) 520 003
Email: rothsaye@discover-australia.com
Beds: 3 King un-zip to 6 Singles (3 cottages)
Bathroom: 3 Ensuite
Tariff: B&B (full) Double $90-$130, Single $80-$110. Dinner $35pp by arrangement. Credit cards (MC/BC/Visa). Tariffs seasonally adjusted.
Nearest Town: Cowes - 500 metres east of Post Office.

Directly on a superb secluded beach along floodlit lovers walk, award winning Rothsaye offers one of the most romantic and charming accommodations. The delightful private fully self contained cottages each feature antique furnishings, king-size beds, ensuites, kitchens (stocked for breakfast), laundries, lounge dining facilities, BBQ, patio and heaps more. Restaurants, shops, public transport and jetty are all within a 5-10 minutes leisurely stroll along lovers walk. With membership to Australia's finest B&B, Winner Hosted Accommodation Australia & Victoria Awards 1997 and named among Robinsons Top Ten in Victoria 1996 makes Rothsaye the perfect peaceful quality getaway. Alternatively the delightful new Abaleigh Cottage around the corner with spa bath has just opened and accommodates 2-6 people. All sporting facilities and island attractions, including the Penguin Parade are close by. Tariffs seasonally adjusted. **RACV ★★★★☆**
Home Page: discover-australia.com/finest/rothsaye

Phillip Island - Cowes
Homestay RACV ★★★☆
Address: 8 Miami Court,
Smiths Beach, RMB 5036 Cowes, 3922
Name: The Winnats
Telephone: (03) 5952 2273
Fax: (03) 5952 2273
Mobile: (191) 46497
Beds: 3 Double, 1 Single (4 bedrooms)
Bathroom: 2 Ensuite, 1 Family share
Tariff: B&B (full) Double $70 - $85, Single $65, Dinner from $20.
Nearest Town: Cowes

The Winnats or four winds is situated in a very quiet court with rural views close to two beautiful beaches on the south coast of Phillip Island. Wood fire adds to the warm friendly atmosphere. Large communal lounge, TV and dining area plus a small reading lounge.
Mary and Fred Lemmings are world travellers and welcome international visitors. The Winnats is central to all attractions, 10 mins drive to our famous Fairy penguins, nobbies and Grand Prix.
Mary and Fred would enjoy sharing their home. We are both Aussie Host trained. Dinner from $20, snacks from $6. Australian hospitality guaranteed including a great sense of humour.

Phillip Island - Cowes
Unique Private Hotel RACV ★★★★☆
Address: 7-9 Steele Street, Cowes,
Phillip Island, VIC 3922
Name: Castle Inn by the Sea
Telephone: (0359) 521 228 **Fax**: (0359) 523 926
Mobile: (015) 80 1962
Email: castle@nex.net.au
Beds: 3 Queen, 3 Single, (3 bedrooms)
Bathroom: 3 Ensuite
Tariff: B&B (full), Double $120 to $150 , Single $95,
(Weekend packages available) Dinner available, Children by arrangement.
Credit cards accepted.
Nearest Town: Cowes

A link with the early history of Phillip Island, "The Castle" is situated on Erewhon Point overlooking Cowes foreshore and nearby French Island. It is the perfect place for an overnight or indulgent holiday and every attention has been paid to ensure privacy with no intrusions to your peace. A well appointed club lounge and bar invites you to relax on arrival and comfortable and restful bedrooms are situated upstairs. All rooms have a well appointed bathroom and for a very romantic stay one of the rooms has its own spa and Moroccan inspired rooftop garden terrace. An intimate restaurant is situated downstairs where you may dine discreetly at candlelit tables.
Luncheons are available on request or pack a picnic lunch and potter round the island. Many packages available.
For booking: (0359) 521228
Home Page: urlhttp.//iscover-australia.com/finest/castle@phillip island

VICTORIA

Phillip Island - Cowes
Homestay   RACV ★★★★
Address: Cnr. Back Beach & Ventnor Rds,
Phillip Island, VIC 3922
Name: Peter & Kate Stephenson
Telephone: (03) 5956 8777 **Fax**: (03) 5956 8777
Mobile: (015) 828944
Beds: 3 Queen, 1 Single (3 bedrooms)
Bathroom: 2 Ensuite, 1 Private
Tariff: B&B (full) Double $100-$110, Single $75-$85, Children by arrangement, Dinner by arrangement. Credit card (BC). Vouchers accepted
Nearest Town: Cowes, Phillip Island

Penguin Hill Country House is situated on beautiful Phillip Island, Victoria. The house offers tranquil, charming and comfortable accommodation and is very close to the Penguin Parade.

Penguin Hill Country House offers three romantic bedrooms with private facilities, overlooking Bass Strait. We provide warm, traditional service and our main purpose is for you to have a wonderful stay.

Our guests eat at a large antique dining table with magnificent views. The antics of the sheep, geese and plentiful bird life are enjoyable and the large ships which sail along Bass Strait provide much interest.

We provide a delicious three course cooked country breakfast featuring local produce. Dinner is by arrangement only.

Linger by our log fire and feel yourself unwinding in winter, and enjoy our shady verandahs in summer.

Coffee and tea are available at all times and are included in all tariffs.

Phillip Island - Cowes
Farmstay   RACV ★★★★
Address: RMB 1165, Cowes, Victoria 3922
Name: Otira on Needle's Eye
Telephone: (03) 5956 8294 **Fax**: (03) 5956 8741
Mobile: (015) 568942
Beds: 2 Queen, 2 Single (3 bedrooms)
Bathroom: 2 Ensuite, 1 Private
Tariff: B&B (full) Double from $100, Single $70, Children $40, Dinner $25, Credit Cards (Visa/Mastercard/Bankcard).
Nearest Town: Cowes 6 km

"Otira on Needle's Eye" is situated in the picturesque countryside on Phillip Island, "Otira" homestead was built in the 1920's and has been charmingly renovated.

The 320 acre farm is used for breeding lambs and vealers, as well as the production of wool. Within close distance of Phillip Island's natural attractions (the famous Penguin Parade is only five minutes away), beaches, the village of Cowes and the Grand Prix circuit are all in close proximity.

A fully cooked breakfast made from fresh farm produce is served in the dining room. Dinner is available by prior arrangement. Complimentary tea and coffee available anytime.

Children are welcome to play on the tennis court, jump on the trampoline, feed the hens and pet lambs (seasonal) or run in the paddocks. Guests can sit under the shady verandah in summer or enjoy the open fire in winter.

Visa, Mastercard and Bankcard accepted.

Phillip Island - Cowes
Guest House   RACV ★★★★
Address: 37 Chapel St (cnr Steele St),
Cowes, Phillip Island, Victoria 3922
Name: Serena & Eric van Grondelle
Telephone: (03) 5952 3082 **Fax**: (03) 5952 3083
Beds: 2 Queen, 1 Double, 1 Single (3 bedrooms),
& 1 Double and 1 Double Bunk in self-contained unit ("The Mews")
Bathroom: 3 Ensuite
Tariff: B&B (full) Double $100 to $125, Single $75-$90, Children welcome, Dinner $30, Credit Cards (AMEX/MC/BC/DC/VISA).   Vouchers accepted $20 surcharge
Nearest Town: Cowes central

Situated in a rambling cottage garden in central Cowes and dating back to 1934, "Holmwood"s three charming rooms offer you period furniture and modern day comforts (ensuites, electric blankets etc.), with many personal touches to pamper you and make you feel special!
A traditional full breakfast is served at your leisure in the dining room, or you may prefer to enjoy it in the company of birds out on the front porch or decking. The guest lounge with open fire has big comfortable chairs, coffee/tea making facilities, TV, books, magazines and games.
Enjoy lunch or an intimate candlelit dinner at "Serena's", our adjoining small licensed restaurant.
A safe swimming beach is 150 metres down the road, and shops, restaurants, sport facilities and ferry terminal are within easy walking distance.
The Penguin Parade, Seal Rock, winery, nature walks are only a 10 minutes drive away. No smoking indoors please!

Phillip Island - Cowes
Self-contained Accommodation   RACV ★★★★
Address: "Nordic B&B", 31 Beach Street,
Cowes, Phillip Island, Vic 3922
Name: Ms Julie Ann Jamieson
Telephone: (0359) 521652
Mobile: (041) 9583453
Beds: 1 Queen, 2 Single (2 bedrooms)
Bathroom: 1 Private
Tariff: B&B (continental) Double $120,
Single $60, Children $15.
Nearest Town: Melbourne 137km.
Travel along Sth Gippsland Hwy and the Bass Hwy.

Nordic Bed & Breakfast is an elegant boutique fully self-contained upstairs apartment with Scandinavian decor situated on beautiful Phillip Island, famous for its fairy penguin parade. Nordic B&B is over the road from the Bay Beach - a haven for artists and only 3 minutes walk from Cowes. Visit restaurants, gift-shops, sporting facilities, churches and the dramatic ocean surf beaches. Nordic B&B offers peace, harmony, birds and banksias. Sleeps 4 and is ideal for families. It has a galley kitchen with fridge, microwave, stove, dishwasher and a well-stocked butler's pantry with breakfast provisions. Enjoy the tastefully decorated lounge/dining room, balcony, your own entrance and genuine Swedish lights to welcome you.
Visit the little fairy penguins at night and also the Grand Prix motor-cycle track. There is also safe off-street parking, or for adventure, catch the ferry from Stoney Point and walk to B&B.

VICTORIA

Phillip Island - Newhaven/San Remo
B&B/Guest House   RACV ★★★★☆
Address: Phillip Island Road, Newhaven,
VIC 3925,
(P.O. Box 223, San Remo 3925)
Name: "Banksia Park Estate" Norma Stack
Telephone: (03) 5956 7796 **Fax**: (03) 5956 6683
Mobile: (041) 989 1699

Banksia Park Estate

Beds: 3 Queen, 1 Triple, (4 bedrooms). Plus early settler's cottage - self contained.
Bathroom: 1 Ensuite/spa, 2 Ensuites, 1 Private, 1 Guests Share
Tariff: B&B (full) Double $110-$170, Single $50-$100, Dinner on request, Children over 12 years or by arrangement. Pets by arrangement, Credit cards (VISA/MC/BC).
Nearest Town: San Remo - 1 km

Banksia Park Estate is a modern homestead situated on 32 acres rural / bay views overlooking historic Churchill Island & Westernport Bay. It is just minutes away from Phillip Island attractions including the Grand Prix circuit, Penguin Parade and Koala Reserve. For those who enjoy fishing, swimming, surf and bay beaches, boating and wonderful nature walks, Banksia Park Estate is centrally located.
Our easy to find property (opp. Information Centre) boasts coastal wetlands with abundant bird life, walking tracks, solar salt water swimming pool, tennis court and farm animals. The friendly hosts are interstate and international travellers and welcome guests from all over the world.
Our clean and comfortable accommodation including hearty breakfasts plus large guest lounge with billiard table, wood fire, piano and licensed bar, provides you with the opportunity to relax and find your balance. All this together with magnificent gardens is the treasure you have been searching for. We have a Liquor Licence.

Phillip Island - Ventnor
Homestay - Traditional B&B   RACV ★★★★
Address: First Class B&B, Ventnor Road,
Ventnor, Phillip Island, VIC 3922
Name: Graeme Wells
Telephone: (03) 5956 8329 Free call 1800 632 301
Fax: (03) 5956 8373 **Mobile**: (018) 389 284
Email: gwells@iaccess.com.au
Beds: 1 Queen, 4 Double, 3 Single (5 Bedrooms)
Bathroom: 5 Ensuite
Tariff: B&B(full), Double $75-$100, Single $50, Dinner $20, Children $25, Campervan facilities. Credit cards. Vouchers accepted $20 surcharge at high seasons
Nearest Town: Cowes

Fine country accommodation with panoramic views of Western Port Bay and the Mornington Peninsula. A traditional Bed and Breakfast in a tranquil rural setting near to the Penguin Parade and Nobbies.
Each room offers comfort, ocean views, and private facilities. Your friendly hosts will delight you from our country kitchen while you enjoy our magic views. After a hearty breakfast you may ride our charming horse, or walk our wonderful beaches, visit the Wildlife or Koala parks, or relax at the winery, and at the end of the day eat at our table or at one of the many fine restaurants, or relax by a log fire, watch the sunset over the ocean or enjoy a game of pool.
Home Page: http://sunspot.sli.unimelb.edu.au/hotzpotz/phillipi/1stclass.htm

VICTORIA

Port Fairy
Homestay+Self-contained Accom.
Address: "Lough Cottage",
216 Griffith Street, Port Fairy Vic 3284
Name: Robert & Heather Towler
Telephone: (03) 5568 1583
Beds: 1 Double, 1 Single (2 bedrooms)
Bathroom: 1 Ensuite, 1 Guests share
Tariff: B&B (full) Double $70/$75, Single $45/$50. Dinner $20pp. Vouchers accepted
Nearest Town: Port Fairy

Lough Cottage is a late 19th century (c.1887) timber residence which has been sympathetically renovated and extended. Set in attractive cottage gardens, the house enjoys a rural outlook to the Moyne River and Belfast Lough, whilst the beautiful East Beach is 100 metres away at the rear.
Country style breakfasts are served in either the breakfast room, the dining room or the enclosed side verandah, all of which enjoy views of the garden. Tea or coffee making facilities are available for guests' use and evening meals can be provided by prior arrangement.
Our policy is to take only one couple at a time unless more than two come as a group. A warm welcome awaits guests at "Lough Cottage" as they explore the many pleasures of historic Port Fairy and the surrounding district.
A fully self-contained cottage is also available for bed & breakfast.

Port Fairy
Bed & Breakfast+Self-contained Accom. RACV ★★★☆
Address: "Boathouse on Moyne", 19 Gipps Street, Port Fairy, VIC 3284
Name: Denise & Gordon Harman
Telephone: (03) 5568 2608
Beds: 1 Queen, 2 Single (2 bedrooms)
Bathroom: 1 Ensuite, 1 Private
Tariff: B&B (special) Double from $85, Single $60, Cot $10, Credit Cards. Vouchers accepted
Nearest Town: Port Fairy

"The Boathouse on Moyne" is situated right on the historic Moyne River fishing port. If you wander out the front gate you are right on the jetty where the fishing trawlers bring in their catch. Being in the centre of the crayfish industry we offer the service of cooking your fresh cray for you. View the spectacle of Mutton Birds flying in to nest on Griffith Island. We are within easy walking distance of the shopping centre, main beach and restaurants. Make yourself at home in this recently renovated, self-contained apartment with guest lounge, TV, fridge and tea and coffee making facilities. We prepare generous breakfasts which include freshly-baked croissants, fresh fruit, juice and locally-made jams.
We are situated in a sheltered area on the site where the original residence formed shelter for a fishing boat, hence the name "The Boathouse on Moyne".

Australia is known as the friendliest country in the world
and our hosts will live up to that reputation.

Port Fairy
B&B+Self-contained Accommodation   RACV ★★★★
Address: "Kilkarlen", Survey Lane, Killarney, Vic 3282
Name: Richard & Carol Crawley
Telephone: (03) 5568 7258 **Fax**: (03) 5568 7258
Beds: 2 Double, 2 Single (3 bedrooms)
Bathroom: 1 Ensuite, 1 Private
Tariff: B&B (special) Double $80-$115, Single $80, Children $20. Credit Cards accepted.
Nearest Town: Port Fairy

For over 130 years Kilkarlen Homestead has looked out over the roaring Southern Ocean. In the morning all you'll hear are magpies and the sea. At Kilkarlen we provide you with the very best in overnight and family holiday accommodation. The fully equipped two-bedroom self-contained cottage is comfortably furnished in period style, yet offers every modern amenity, including luxury kitchen, lounge and bathroom, TV, video, laundry and BBQ.
You'll keep snug in winter by the redgum burning woodheater, while in summer relax by the french windows and enjoy the cool sea breeze. It's a pleasant stroll to the beach.
Breakfast is a gourmet hamper which includes fresh juice, home-made sourdough bread and organic Killarney strawberry jam, our own apple muffins - and the works with eggs if you prefer.
We also have a luxury bedsit flat overlooking the cottage garden.
Restaurants, shops and the other attractions of historic Port Fairy are just a few minutes drive away. And whale watching is a local attraction.
Close by are secluded beaches and the Tower Hill Nature Reserve. You could take a day trip to the Grampians or along the Great Ocean Road, or borrow our bicycles and explore locally.
Long stay rates available.
Directions: *Follow the signs from the Princes Highway or phone/fax Carol and Richard.*

Port Fairy - Macarthur
Country House RACV ★★★☆
Address: "Eumeralla", Burleigh Road, Macarthur (Please phone ahead)
Name: Adrian Jones & Sherrill Hanlon-Jones
Telephone: (03) 5576 1200 **Fax**: (03) 5576 1399
Beds: 3 Queen, 1 Double (4 bedrooms)
Bathroom: 2 Guests share
Tariff: B&B (full) Double $110-$130, Single $70, Dinner $25-$35, Credit Cards (VISA/MC/BC). Vouchers accepted $20 on $110 Room, $30 on $120 Room, $40 on $130 Room
Nearest Town: Macarthur 1km

Our grand historic homestead is built of stone and features generous rooms, high ceilings and wide verandahs which overlook a spacious established garden and farmland. Tranquil surroundings provide the ideal setting for a romantic and relaxing getaway. Within half an hour of The Great Ocean Road and Twelve Apostles, historic Port Fairy and Tower Hill nature reserve. The majestic Grampians Mountain Range, Hamilton with its renowned gallery and botanic gardens and local wineries are easily accessible from Eumeralla. Close by is Mt. Eccles National Park and lake Surprise with koalas and native birds.
Two guest sitting rooms, one with log fire; dinner is by arrangement and a full cooked breakfast is served on the verandah, in your room or the breakfast room. All rooms have pure wool doonas and blankets, electric blankets. Licensed and BYO, lunch hampers available, smoke free within the house. Not suitable for your children or pets.

Port Fairy
Guest House RACV ★★★★☆
Address: Kingsley Bed & Breakfast, 71 Cox Street, Port Fairy, Victoria 3284
Name: Peter Strickland & Angela Beagley
Telephone: (03) 5568 1269
Beds: 2 Queen (2 bedrooms) **Bathroom**: 1 Ensuite, 1 Private
Tariff: B&B (full) Double $85-$90, Single $55-$60. Credit Cards (Bankcard/Mastercard/Visa) Vouchers accepted
Nearest Town: In Port Fairy (500m west of Post Office)

Kingsley is a beautifully restored Federation house (c1913) located in the historic township of Port Fairy. Just a short walk from the town centre, beaches and River Moyne, Kingsley is the ideal place to stay and enjoy the town's natural and historic attractions.
We offer two individually decorated guest rooms, each with the comfort of queen-size beds, open fireplaces, ceiling fans and private bathroom facilities. The formal sitting room, with original Art Nouveau mantelpiece and pressed metal ceiling, is available for the exclusive use of our guests. Relax by fire in winter or take advantage of our shady verandah in summer. A leisurely breakfast is served in the dining room at a time to suit your plans for the day; tea and coffee making facilities are always available.
You can be sure of a warm welcome at Kingsley. Our two cats, are discretely kept away from guest areas, unless you are happy with their company.

VICTORIA

Port Fairy
Bed & Breakfast RACV ★★★★☆
Address: "Hickory House 1851",
4 Princes Street, Port Fairy, Vic 3284
Name: Rivka & David Waxman
Telephone: (03) 5568 2530
Beds: 2 Queen, 1 Single (2 bedrooms)
Bathroom: 2 Ensuite
Tariff: B&B (special) Double $100-$110,
Single $85, Children by arrangement,
Credit Cards (VISA/MC/BC).
Nearest Town: Hickory House 1851 is in
centre of Port Fairy near Council Chambers.

Hickory House situated in a quiet street in historic centre of Port Fairy began life as a Church of England school housing up to 250 pupils in its heyday. Now splendidly restored as the town's finest Georgian home, Hickory House offers discerning travellers superior B&B accommodation. Each spacious, delightfully decorated and charmingly furnished guest room has firm queen size bed with hand made quilt, ensuite and individually controlled heating. A special breakfast is served in the elegant dining room where guests enjoy Rivka's delicious home made croissants, breads, rolls and jams and the best coffee or tea in town.

Off street parking is available and guests are welcome to use the spacious sitting room and beautiful garden. Hickory House is centrally located near Port Fairy's several fine restaurants, shops, beaches and points of interest. A warm welcome is assured by your travelled and well-informed hosts.

Home Page: http://www.travelaustralia.com.au/s/13909

Queenscliff
Guest House RACV ★★★★
Address: Cnr The Esplanade &
Stevens Street, Queenscliff
Name: Maytone By The Sea
Telephone: (03) 5258 4059.
Freecall 1800 064 785 **Fax**: (03) 5258 4071
Beds: 8 King/Queen, 1 Twin (9 bedrooms)
Bathroom: 6 Ensuite, 2 Guests share
Tariff: B&B (full) Double $100 to $150, Single $70 to $130, Children under 6 $10, 7-14 $20. Dinner $25. Credit Cards (BC/MC/VISA). Vouchers accepted Monday to Thursday.
Nearest Town: Queenscliff

"Maytone By The Sea" Cnr The Esplanade and Stevens St Queenscliff.
Admire the breath-taking views through the Port Phillip Heads to Bass Strait from the wide verandahs and from the graceful bay windows of the upstairs lounge. Constructed in 1883, Maytone-By-The-Sea is a grand Italianate building and for many years was the officers' mess for the Queenscliff Fort. Now a graciously restored guest house, there are nine large bedrooms, most with ensuite and marble fireplaces, a well-appointed dining room, pleasant lounges and a sheltered formal garden. Hearty home-cooked breakfasts are part of the excellent country cuisine specialising in fresh local products. Situated right on the foreshore, guests can walk out the garden gate directly onto the beach and enjoy swimming or leisurely walks along the sand. Queenscliff has been described as "an open-air museum" but is a world apart, not a world away, being only ninety minutes from Melbourne, and also served by passenger and vehicular ferries. As well as mid-week stays, weekend packages are available and children are welcome.
Home Page: http://www.bol.com.au/maytone.html

Rosewhite see Myrtleford

Rutherglen
Homestay - Country Homestead RACV ★★★☆
Address: Lake Moodemere
Homestead Lakeside, Rutherglen, Vic 3685
Postal: PO Box 17, Rutherglen
Name: Peter & Helen Chambers
Telephone: (02) 6032 8650 **Fax**: (02) 6032 8118
Beds: 1 King, 2 Queen, 2 Single (3 bedrooms)
Bathroom: 1 Ensuite, 1 Guest share
Tariff: B&B (full) Double $100, With ensuite $120, Single $70 & $80, Children by arrangement. Dinner $45, Credit Cards (MC/BC/VISA).
Nearest Town: Rutherglen - 6km west of Murray Valley Highway.

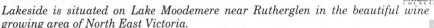

Lakeside is situated on Lake Moodemere near Rutherglen in the beautiful wine growing area of North East Victoria.
Guests stay in the spacious tastefully furnished Homestead. A choice of a double room with cosy early Australian decor and ensuite or there is a twin room and double room that share a bathroom.
Your hosts Peter and Helen Chambers belong to a wine growing family, and produce grapes on the property which also has sheep and crops. If you desire you will be taken on a guided tour of the farm. You can swim or take a two hour bush walk around the lake. A canoe is available and bird life abounds. Rutherglen offers a variety of eating houses to suit all tastes. Lakeside is only a few minutes from wineries, tennis and golf.

Rutherglen
Country Homestead RACV ★★★
Address: 'Greenmount', RSD 1350, Rutherglen, Vic. 3685
Name: Lorna & Bryan Cumming
Telephone: (02) 6026 7237
Beds: 2 Double, 2 Single (3 bedrooms)
Bathroom: 1 Ensuite, 1 Guests share
Tariff: B&B (full) Double $100, Single $50. Dinner $25 by arrangement.
Nearest Town: Rutherglen 16km west, Howlong 10km north, Murray River Crossing

Mixed farm
1860's homestead - furnished accordingly - adjacent to Morris Winery. Close proximity to Rutherglen, Albury, Wodonga, Howlong. Wineries, golf and bowling clubs. Historic towns of Chiltern, Beechworth and Yackandandah nearby. Restful accommodation. Home cooking. Inviting welcome awaits you.

One of the differences between staying at a hotel and a B&B
is that you don't hug the hotel staff when you leave.

Sale, Gippsland
Luxury Farmstay & Self Contained Heritage Accommodation
Address: "Kilmany Park", Settlement Road, Sale, Gippsland 3850 (Bookings essential)
Name: Kilmany Park Homestead and "The Cottage"
Telephone: (03) 5144 2222 **Fax**: (03) 5144 3937 **Mobile**: 0419 443 937
Beds: Homestead: 5 Queen, (1 pair Twins) (6 Bedrooms). Cottage: 1 Queen, 1 Double, 1 pair Twins, settee + trundle (3 Bedrooms)
Bathroom: Homestead: 1 Ensuite, 2 Private, 1 Guests Share. Cottage: 1 Private
Tariff: B&B (full) Homestead: Double $100, Single $90. Dinner by arrangement. Cottage: Double $80, Single $70, Extra person $25 each. Credit Cards accepted. Children in cottage only. Vouchers accepted ($20 surcharge for Homestead)
Nearest Town: Sale

Kilmany Park stands amid 700 acres of prime dairying land, just 5 minutes drive from Sale, in the heart of Gippsland. We offer 2 distinct choices in accommodation, being luxury Bed & Breakfast in the turn of the century heritage listed "Federation" mansion or self contained farm house accommodation in "The Cottage". A warm welcome awaits you from your hosts, Anne and Daryl, and they will be happy to assist with any arrangements while visiting Gippsland.

The homestead is listed with the National Trust, and has significant historical interest. The upstairs bedrooms are superbly decorated and offer a glimpse of the lifestyle of the "Squattocracy" of the 19th century. Downstairs, the grand drawing room with its National Trust listed art nouveau screen, is available for guests as is the full size billiard table, private dining room and cosy library / reading room. Kilmany Park is a non smoking household.

San Remo
Bed & Breakfast+Self-contained Accommodation
Address: 1 Ocean Grove, San Remo, VIC 3925 Please phone
Name: Beachside Cottage Miranda & Albert Sage
Telephone: (03) 5678 5622 **Fax**: (03) 5678 5595
Beds: The Cottage: 1 Queen, 1 Double, 2-3 Single (3 bedrooms). The Flat: 1 Queen bedroom/lounge. The Studio: 1 Queen, 1-2 Single, Family unit(2 bedrooms)
Bathroom: The Cottage: 3 Ensuite/The Flat: 1 Ensuite, kitchenette/The Studio: 1 Ensuite, kitchenette.
Tariff: Butler's Basket included in tariff.
The Cottage: Queen $90, Double $85, Single $45, Children (school age) $25, Dinner by arrangement $20, Weekly rate: stay seven nights pay for six. The Flat: B&B as Cottage, self catering $420 per week. The Studio: As Cottage and Flat, self-catering $420 per week double, $500 family.
Apply for rates for House parties. 10% reduction on all rates June to September inclusive. Credit Cards. Vouchers accepted $5 surcharge Queen October-May only.
Nearest Town: San Remo (in town)

Beachside Cottage is a charming home and studio set in a large, secluded and fascinating garden in a quiet foreshore location in the fishing village of San Remo. Accommodation is available on a Bed & Breakfast or self-catering basis and offers an ideal get-away with a sandy beach within metres. Beachside Cottage has a cosy wood fire, guest lounge, dining room, cooking facilities and guest laundry. Butler's basket breakfasts provided. San Remo is one and a half hours from Melbourne and is just two minutes across the bridge to Phillip Island with its many attractions, such as the Penguins, the Koalas and the Seals. Beachside Cottage is close to the Motor Cycle Grand Prix Circuit, and fishing, sailing, wind surfing, swimming and surf beaches, pelican feeding and rural and coastal walks. San Remo is serviced daily by motor coach from Melbourne.

Miranda and Albert assure you of a warm welcome and invite you to come and relax at Beachside Cottage. Stay a week and pay for six nights only. We are pleased to offer 10% discount on all rates from June to September inclusive.

Smiths Beach see Phillip Island

St. Arnaud
Homestay - Gourmet
Address: "Vyalla", 43 Alma Street, St. Arnaud, VIC 3478
Name: David Egan
Telephone: (03) 5495 2427
Beds: 3 Queen (3 bedrooms)
Bathroom: 2 Ensuite, 1 Private

Tariff: B&B (full) Double $80-$100, Single $60-$80. Dinner from $25. Credit cards. Vouchers accepted same day restriction Friday and Saturday.
Nearest Town: Ballarat 124km, Bendigo 100km, Horsham 107km

St. Arnaud and the surrounding areas have much to interest the visitor. Rich in history, the town is endowed with solid civic buildings, hotels and stores, famous for their cast iron work verandahs. Nearby, the bushland is a bird-lovers delight, with native animals and plants in abundance. The Pyrenees wineries are 30 minutes away, while the Grampians, Bendigo, and Ballarat, are each only about an hour's drive.
Vyalla, built in 1895, is a very comfortable, big Victorian home. Bedrooms are tastefully furnished, and the guest lounge with open fire place, games, and library, is sure to please. Meals at Vyalla are something to remember. Start the day with a full English breakfast, or choose from the range of tempting dishes on the Sunday brunch menu. Enjoy the delicacies included in your picnic hamper lunch, and return for a gourmet 3 course dinner. The highlight of the week is the 6 course silver service Saturday night dinner party.
Vyalla is a smoke free home, not suited to children Bankcard / Visa / Mastercard.

Strathbogie Ranges
Self-contained Cottage
RACV ★★★☆
Address: "Wondoomarook", RMB 5178 Kippings Rd, Strathbogie, Victoria 3666
Name: John & Lyn Sholl
Telephone: (03) 5790 5264 (Answering machine if not home)
Beds: 1 Queen, 1 Double, 2 Single (3 bedrooms)
Bathroom: 1 Private, 2nd toilet
Tariff: B&B (full self-prepare) Double $75, Single $35, Credit Cards (MC/VISA/BC). Vouchers accepted
Nearest Town: Strathbogie 8km; 25km from Euroa on the Hume Freeway

The luxury cottage is on the "Wondoomarook" wool-growing property in the heart of the world renowned Strathbogie superfine wool district, but only 2 hours drive from Melbourne. Breathtaking views of the ranges and Polly McQuinn's Resevoir. Natural wildlife abounds - kangaroos, wombats, koalas and, in the creeks, platypus.
Freshly laundered linen and towels are provided and beds are equipped with electric blankets. Chopped wood is provided for the slow combustion heater. A full self-prepare breakfast is provided while the modern kitchen is fully equipped. Radio / TV / CD / tape / video are available and the covered verandah has a gas barbeque. "Wondoomarook" is the perfect place to unwind, forget the stresses of city life and re-establish links with nature. Enquire about our fully catered weekend getaways for couples in association with the Tasty Affair Restaurant in Strathbogie.
Phone for bookings or brochure.

VICTORIA

Sorrento see Mornington Pennensula
Spring Gully see Bendigo

Tallangatta
Farmstay+Self-contained Accom.
Address: Please phone
Koetong Hotel for directions to "Gibberagee"
Name: Keith & Marilyn Bonser
Telephone: (02) 6072 7530
Beds: 1 Queen, 2 Double
Bathroom: 1 Guests share
Tariff: B&B (full) Double $80, Single $40,
Credit Cards. Vouchers accepted
Nearest Town: 30km east of Tallangatta on the Murray Valley Highway

"Gibberagee" is situated in a hidden valley surrounded by a state forest of Peppermint trees and Blue Gums. It is a stone, self-contained, two storey cottage lovingly fitted out entirely with local and recycled timber. It is completely self sufficient with solar power and set on a one hundred acre beef and lavender farm.
The owners Keith and Marilyn offer warm hospitality with a bottle of local wine for you to enjoy on your arrival, and the wood fire already burning in the heater in winter. A permanent creek at the bottom of the garden, adjacent bird life, animal life and just sheer tranquillity are features of Gibberagee. The local Koetong Hotel just four kilometres up the road is also owned by Keith and Marilyn and offers meals and country hospitality.
Directions: *Drive from Wodonga via Tallangatta to Koetong.*

Tarwin Lower - South Gippsland
Farmstay+Self-contained Accommodation   RACV ★★★☆
Address: "Barana Plains", Tarwin Lower (Farmstay), "Box Plains" (Self-contained)
Name: Anne Box
Telephone: (03) 5663 2244 **Fax**: (03) 5663 2390
Beds: 1 Double, 2 Single (2 bedrooms) **Bathroom**: 1 Guests share
Tariff: Farmstay - B&B (full) Double $90, Single $50, Children half price. Dinner $30. Credit cards. Self-contained - 1 Double, 3 Single with bathroom, fully equipped kitchen. Daily Double $80, $15 extra person. Linen and basket breakfast (continental) included. Phone (03) 5663 2244 Anne or (03) 5663 5281 Jan. Vouchers accepted
Nearest Town: Leongatha, Wonthaggi approx 40 kms.

Our colonial homestead nestles amongst the gum trees, in coastal south Gippsland, one hour from Phillip Island and Wilsons Promontory National Park. We farm 3,500 acres over three nearby properties, fattening bullocks. The area is rich in native wild life, and guests may like to see kangaroos in the wild, watch farm activities, play tennis, visit local craft shops, wineries or the state coal mine at Wonthaggi, or simply relax. Beautiful bay and surf beaches at Walkerville, and Venus Bay.
Having travelled myself, I am always interested in meeting folk from overseas.
I run Box Plains the cosy self contained cottage accommodation (built originally as Jackaroo Quarters) with my sister in law Jan. This is on one of the nearby properties, which is adjacent to a wetland reserve. A car is required if staying here. A disciplined dog is welcome at the cottage. Gopha our own dog is allowed in our part of the homestead.
Directions: *Please phone.*

VICTORIA

Terang
Homestay
Address: "Rosebank" Terang. Please phone.
Name: Judie and Denis Irving
Telephone: (03) 5592 1915 **Fax**: (03) 5592 2043
Beds: 1 Double, 3 Single (3 Bedrooms)
Bathroom: 1 Guests Share
Tariff: B&B (full) Double $100, Single $75,
Dinner $28 pp by arrangement.
Not suitable for children.
Vouchers accepted $20 surcharge
Nearest Town: Terang

Rosebank is situated in the Western District town of Terang, the heart of volcano country, between Camperdown and Warrnambool with easy access to the Great Ocean Road and the Grampians. Close to excellent golf course, bowling green, croquet lawn, tennis courts, swimming pool, racecourse and harness racing.
This gracious homestead built circa 1900 and serenely nestled in 3.5 acres of traditional English garden offers old fashioned service and comfort. Central heating (hydronic) combined with open fires provides a comfortable ambience in winter whilst the verandahs with garden views are a great setting for summer breakfasts under the watchful eye of Argus the peacock, Hamish the dog and Sasha the cat.
The garden has a park like quality with features including century old trees, formal rose garden, water garden etc. A relaxed atmosphere, delicious home cooking and friendly hosts await you at Rosebank.

Timboon
Farmstay + Self-contained Accommodation   RACV ★★★☆
Address: Inglenook Cottage, H Robilliards Road, Timboon, VIC 3268
Name: Carolyn Moore
Telephone: (03) 5598 3250
Fax: (03) 5598 3752
Beds: 1 Queen, 1 Double, 8 Single, (4 bedrooms)
Bathroom: 1 Ensuite, 1 Private
Tariff: B&B (full), Double $80.00, Single $50.00, Dinner $20.00. Children discount.
Credit cards accepted. Vouchers accepted
Nearest Town: Timboon

Enjoy a comfortable stay on a lovely 7 acre rural retreat, children will delight in meeting and feeding farmyard friends - cows, sheep, goats, donkey, pig, ducks, hens, geese, peacocks, dog and cats. Accommodation for 1 or 2 in a flat attached to the homestead, while a carload may stay in a separate 3 bedroom farmhouse. Linen supplied, warm beds with blankets, doonas, tea/coffee facilities, separate lounges. Menued cooked breakfasts served, a 3 course dinner of farm fresh produce is available, or try our house speciality - Indonesian cuisine. Prior booking essential. Timboon is off the Great Ocean Road and shopping town for the famous 12 Apostles on the shipwreck coast. Timboon offers golf, tennis, swimming, bush walking, bird watching, fishing, cheese factory, berry farm. Close to Port Campbell and Otways National parks, Camperdown and Warrnambool cities. Guests can be met at railway station. Local tours can be arranged. A warm welcome awaits you at Inglenook Cottage. Send for brochure with more information, now.
Directions: *Please Phone.*

Toora - South Gippsland
Guest House   RACV ★★★★
Address: RMB
1390 South Gippsland Hwy,
Toora 3962
Name: Miranda Farmhouse
& Cooks Garden
Telephone: (0356) 862557 **Fax**: (0356) 862 557 **Mobile**: 018 595 415
Beds: 2 Queen, 1 Double, 1 Single (3 bedrooms)
Bathroom: 3 Ensuite
Tariff: B&B (full) Double $90-$95, Single $60-$65, Dinner $30-$35, Credit Cards.
Nearest Town: Toora 2km

We are centrally located so our guests may visit Wilson's Promontory and Tarra Bulga National Park, a pristine rainforest with lyre birds, wombats, echidnas and wallabies. Our view of Wilson's Prom is spectacular. We offer a stylish guests only lounge room with roaring logfire, and our dining room features individual candlelit tables with fine china and glassware. Most of our Mediterranean style menu is sourced from local fresh ingredients and our extensive fruit herb and vegetable garden. The garden is organic and our philosophy is to produce the best of quiet hospitality, style comfort and lovely food whilst being environmentally friendly. We cater for vegetarians. Breakfast features seasonal fruit, free range eggs, homemade bread. Guests may enjoy a 2 night package with supper on the first night and dinner on the second or booking for single nights with dinner also available.

Torquay
Homestay   RACV ★★★☆
Address: 12 Casino Court, Torquay, Victoria 3228
Name: Just Junes B&B
Telephone: (03) 5261 3771
Beds: 1 Double, 2 Single (2 bedrooms)
Bathroom: 1 Private
Tariff: B&B (full) Double $75-$85, Single $60. Vouchers accepted March to November
Nearest Town: Geelong - 20km south of Geelong on Surf Coast Highway. Melbourne Airport 1 1/2 hours drive.

Just an hour from Melbourne, Torquay is the gateway to the Great Ocean Road. Enjoy a peaceful stay in a comfortable modern home, situated in a quiet court. The famous beaches of Torquay are only a few minutes away and the regions many attractions, including Surf Museum, Tiger Moth flights and wineries are all within easy reach. Local restaurants are many and varied - suiting the most discerning. Guests have undercover car parking and private access to their rooms. Private tours can be arranged. My main interests are travel, gardening and of course meeting people. Look forward to sharing some of your experiences over a welcoming drink. Children not catered for. Please phone for directions.

Upwey see Dandenong Ranges
Ventnor see Phillip Island

Gift Vouchers

Our B&B vouchers are for a double room for one night's B&B. They cost $89, and if you order one as a gift, we will include a free *Australian Bed & Breakfast Book* worth $16.95

Send your cheque to
Moonshine Press
59 Quirk Street
Dee Why
NSW 2099

Warragul - West Gippsland
Self-contained Acocmmodation and B&B
Address: 55 McDougal Rd, Neerim South 3831
Name: Blerick Mudbrick Cottage
Telephone: (0356) 281 507
Mobile: (015) 806 638
Email: blerick@wgcomp.com.au
Beds: 1 Queen, 2 Double (2 Bedrooms)
Bathroom: 1 Private
Tariff: B&B (full) Self-contianed: Double $80, $20 each extra person.
B&B (full) Double $95 Vouchers accepted

Experience a memorable get away in our cottage that will instantly charm you with its warmth and character, while providing all the modern facilities. Located just over one hour from Melbourne, it is set in the tranquil, dairy district of Neerim South, with beautiful views of the snow capped Mt. Baw Baw.
There are endless attractions in the immediate area: sampling gourmet food and wines, skiing, horse riding, 4WD tracks, troutfishing in alpine streams or enjoying nature walks and water falls in the nearby lush rain forests.
Return from your outing to enjoy the tranquil views from the verandah or relax inside roasting complimentary chestnuts in the cosy wood heater. Let the children feed the sheep or horses. The setting is ideal for the romantic couple, the family, or a group of friends. Guests are welcome to cater for themselves or a hearty breakfast of local produce will be provided. Colour TV, stereo, microwave, washing machine and dryer and linen are all provided. Well behaved dogs and children are welcome.

VICTORIA

Warrnambool
Homestay   RACV ★★★☆
Address: 'Wurroit Homestay',
RMB 9574, Goodwood Road,
Warrnambool, Victoria 3281
Name: Wendy & Peter McWhinney
Telephone: (03) 5569 1501
Fax: (03) 5569 1501
Beds: 4 Single (2 bedrooms)
Bathroom: 1 Private
Tariff: B&B (continental) Double $98, Single $49. Dinner by arrangement. Vouchers accepted $10 surcharge
Nearest Town: Warrnambool; 35 minutes north of Warrnambool midway between Woolsthorpe and Caramut.

Enjoy a traditional style Bed and Breakfast at 'WURROIT HOMESTAY' an historic pastoral homestead in the Western District. Set on a working Corriedale sheep property, the single-storey bluestone building was erected in c1872 for Robert Whitehead, son of a pioneer pastoralist, and still in the hands of descendants five generations later. Hosts Wendy and Peter are interested in meeting people and travel, and welcome guests to share the history of their home with them. Guests have full use of the spacious reception hall, sitting and dining rooms which look out to an English style garden, with rural vistas along Spring Creek. WURROIT is an ideal base for day trips to the coast; the Grampians National Park; and for the golf enthusiast, golf on top coastal courses. A taste of 'Australian Country' for the traveller from overseas. A friendly welcome from Wendy, Peter, and sheepdog Rosie is awaiting you.

Warrnambool
Bed & Breakfast
Address: 8/150 Merri Street, Warrnambool, 3280
Name: Guthrie Heights Bed & Breakfast
Telephone: (03) 5561 4950 **Fax**: (03) 5561 5331
Beds: 5 Queen, 2 Single (6 bedrooms)
Bathroom: 6 Ensuite
Tariff: B&B (full) Double $110 (city view), $125 (sea view), Single $85, Credit Cards.
Nearest Town: We are one block from Post Office.

There is nothing more relaxing than an early morning or late evening stroll along a sandy beach. Imagine waking up to beautiful sea views and old fashioned country hospitality in a glorious Georgian style terrace apartment.

At Guthrie Heights Bed & Breakfast you will be delighted with the facilities and attractions that will make your stay with us a special one. Guthrie Heights is centrally located in the coastal city of Warrnambool, 268km west of Melbourne and overlooks the main beach and breakwater, is just a short stroll to restaurants, shopping centre and major visitor attractions.
Facilities include generous suites equipped with ensuites, sitting area and your very own balcony with sea views.
You may spend time relaxing in your suite or enjoy the generous ground floor guest living area and kitchen. Our facilities provide privacy from hosts, a fully cooked breakfast and off street parking. Facilities are not suitable for children or pets and is a non smoking venue.

VICTORIA

Warrnambool
Homestay+Self-contained Accom. RACV ★★★★
Address: "Wollaston" B&B, 84 Wollaston Road,
Warrnambool, 3280
Name: Nan Dodds
Telephone: (03) 5562 2430 **Fax**: (03) 5562 2430
Mobile: (014) 499589
Beds: Homestead: 1 King, 1 Single Cottage: 1 Queen
Bathroom: Homestead: 1 Private Cottage: 1 Private
Tariff: B&B (full) Double from $90-$130,
Single $55-$95, No pets, No smoking.
Vouchers accepted $20 surcharge June/July/Aug weeknights.
Nearest Town: Warrnambool

Warm hospitality awaits you at Wollaston. Enjoy peace and tranquillity of the homestead (c. 1854) or private olde world cottage. Both overlook garden. Stroll through garden of old English trees to the Merri River. Open fires. Home baking included in full breakfast and on your arrival. All this and only 5 mins from CBD. Your host is a qualified masseuse. Relax with a massage and be pampered. Warrnambool has unlimited beauty with beaches, cliffs, sand-dunes, rivers, fishing, walks and whale watching in winter. Close to Tower Hill - a state game reserve and ancient volcanic area, Port Fairy, a historic fishing village and Koroit a piece of Ireland. A great starting point or finish to the Great Ocean Road and the famous 12 apostles, the Otways and the Grampians.
Homepage: http://www.standard.net.au/~garyradley/wollBnB.htm

Warrnambool
Homestay, Exclusive B&B RACV ★★★★☆
Address: Merton Manor
62 Ardlie Street
Warrnambool 3280
Name: Pamela and Ivan Beechey
Telephone: (03) 5562 0720
Fax: (03) 5562 0630 **Mobile**: 041-731 4364
Email: merton@ansonic.com.au
Beds: 1 King, 5 Queen, 2 single (6 bedrooms)
Bathroom: 6 Ensuites
Tariff: B&B (full) Queen $130, Single $95. Not suitable for children. Credit Cards. Vouchers accepted $15 surcharge single, $45 surcharge double
Nearest Town: WARRNAMBOOL

Relax in one of Provincial Victoria's finest Bed and Breakfasts located in the heart of Warrnambool and midway between Melbourne and Adelaide.

You are invited to experience the delights we wish to share when you stay in our magnificent Italienate Villa, built around 1880, and featuring our personal collection of antiques and art work.

We offer formal lounge, drawing, billiard and music rooms, all for your pleasure where you'll treasure the experience of living in a past era, and you'll be pampered with all the little extra's one expects with such opulence.

Along with open fires, and the modern comforts of today, including central heating, air conditioning and ensuites with double spas, you'll enjoy an unforgettable breakfast served in our Grand Dining Room.

Our home allows us to host a group of friends, couples or alternatively give total privacy to those requiring it. We guarantee a memorable stay.
Home Page: http://www.ansonic.com.au/merton

VICTORIA

Wartook - Grampians
Homestay   RACV ★★★★
Address: "Wartook Gardens", RMB 7372, Wartook , VIC 3401
Name: Royce & Jeanne Raleigh
Telephone: (03) 5383 6200 **Fax**: (03) 5383 6200
Email: wgardens@ozemail.com.au
Beds: 1 Queen, 2 Single (2 bedrooms)
Bathroom: 1 Ensuite, 1 Private
Tariff: B&B (full) Double $85&$95, Single $50, Children by arrangement, Dinner $30, Credit Cards.
Nearest Town: Hall's Gap (29km 30 mins), Horsham (48km, 30 mins)

'Wartook Gardens' is a comfortable country home on 70 acres in a magnificent 5 acres Australian Plant garden (approx 1000 species) with wonderful mountain views. Just 10 mins from the popular Zumsteins in the Grampians National Park - an all seasons destination. Close to waterfalls, lookouts, and lovely wildflower areas. Within easy access of wineries, Wimmera Lakes, Mt Arapiles and Little Desert National Park. Over 100 bird species recorded in the garden. Kangaroos and emus are constant visitors. Activities can include bushwalking, fishing, swimming, photography, drawing, sightseeing, picnics and BBQ's.
We offer one double room with ensuite, and one twin or double with private bathroom. Air conditioning, infloor heating, wood heater, ceiling fans, electric blankets, salt water pool, BBQ and under cover parking helps to make your stay very comfortable. We offer peace and quiet and friendly hospitality.
Please phone.

Wodonga
Bed & Breakfast
Address: "Braeside Bed & Breakfast", 3 Ardern Place, Wodonga, VIC 3690
Name: Coleen & Kevin Melbourne
Telephone: (02) 6024 4835 **Fax**: (02) 6056 3090 **Mobile**: (0418) 698 537
Beds: 1 Double, 2 King Single (2 bedrooms)
Bathroom: 2 Private
Tariff: B&B (continental) Double $80, Single $70, Children over 12yrs only,No pets. Credit Cards.
   Vouchers accepted $10 surcharge Double.
Nearest Town: Wodonga

Near the top of one of Wodonga's surrounding hillsides and 5 minutes from the centre of town, "Braeside" is set amongst an extensive garden of palms, ferns and gum trees. During the warmer weather, relax in the gardens or swim in the backyard pool. Spend a cool evening listening to music in front of the open fire in the lounge room or watch TV in the family room nestled in front of the second wood fire. The house is also centrally heated and the bedrooms are air-conditioned.
Coffee and tea making facilities are provided in rooms and a hearty continental breakfast (including muffins, croissants and freshly baked bread) is served either in the dining room or garden.
Wodonga is situated on the Hume Highway between Melbourne and Sydney. It is close to a popular winery area, a convenient distance from the snow and has numerous local activities.
Phone for directions.

Wilsons Promontory see Yanakie

VICTORIA

Yackandandah
**B&B +
Self-contained Accommodation**
Address: 9 Windham St,
Yackandandah, VIC 3749
Name: Serendipity B&B
& Possum's Nook Cottage
Telephone: (02) 6027 1881
Beds: 1 Double, 1 Twin. Cottage: 1 Double
Bathroom: 1 Guest share. Cottage: 1 Private
Tariff: B&B (full) Double $90, Single $48, Dinner $20pp, Cottage $80 Double.
Seniors cards catered for. Vouchers accepted $11 surcharge
Nearest Town: Beechworth - 20km south of Yackandandah

Set in an acre of lovely garden and surrounded by countryside this home has been built with mud bricks, bluestone, granite and bridge timbers giving it a special feel and appeal. Guests are accommodated in double and twin rooms with separate guest lounge and access to french Provence style patio and garden. A delicious cooked country style breakfast with freshly brewed coffee, home made jams and marmalades is provided. Picnic fare, lunches and dinner by prior arrangement. Within the grounds is a self contained cottage "Possum's Nook".
The small township of Yackandandah is just a 2 mins walk along a country lane. Nearby are; tennis courts, swimming pool, golf course. Walking tracks and bird life abound, and there is fishing in rivers and streams. The area is situated at the foothills of the Victorian Alps in a region steeped in goldmining history. A pleasant drive through beautiful valleys takes one to wineries and the historic townships of Beechworth (15 mins), Chiltern and Rutherglen.

Yackandandah
Self-contained Accommodation   RACV ★★★☆
Address: RMB 3180, Osbornes Flat Rd., Yackandandah,
3749 Victoria
Name: "Creek Haven Country Cottages"
Telephone: (02) 6027 1389 **Fax**: (02) 6027 1026
E-Mail Address: creekhav@albury.net.au
Beds: Country Cottage: 1 Queen, 2 Single   Miners Cottage:
2 Queen
Bathroom: 1 Private in each cottage
Tariff: B&B (special) Double $80, Single $60, Children $10.
Extra Adults $15. Vouchers accepted
Nearest Town: Yackandandah

Nestled in the foothills of the Victorian Alps near the historic town of Yackandandah is accommodation that offers peace, tranquillity and seclusion. Your hosts Ros and Graeme will have this quiet retreat just right for you ensuring you will have a memorable stay. The cottages have country style elegance with a touch of rustic. They are fully equipped enabling accommodation for two to six persons. Crisp linen, warm doonas and electric blankets are provided. The open living areas with an invitingly warm pot-belly stoves are furnished with comfortable lounges, chairs and television. A delicious country breakfast is supplied and fresh bread is delivered daily. Full kitchen facilities are included. A gas barbeques are situated in the beautiful cottage gardens. The creek, a short walk away complements the peace and privacy. Native birds, kangaroos, and bushland as well as trout in the creek will add to your pleasure.

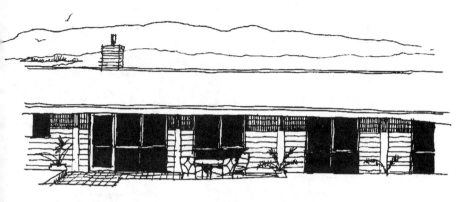

Yanakie - Wilsons Promontory
Guest House
Address: "Vereker House", Iluka Close (Foley Road), Yanakie, South Gippsland
Name: Vereker House
Telephone: (03) 5687 1431 **Fax**: (03) 5687 1431
Beds: 4 King/Queen, 4 Single (4 bedrooms)
Bathroom: 4 Ensuite
Tariff: B&B (full) Double $80-$100, Single $50-$70, Dinner $25, Credit Cards (VISA/MC/BC).
Nearest Town: Yanakie - Wilsons Promontory (3km)

Vereker House is easily located adjacent to Wilsons Promontory National Park, the southernmost park on the mainland of Australia. The house of traditional mud-brick construction has a rustic ambience and charm which will suit the discerning traveller. Panoramic views to mountains and sea are afforded from the house.
Local activities provide for boating, fishing, surfing, swimming, diving, walking, hiking. The area also provides for golf, horse riding and boat trips to offshore islands. Local wineries, pottery and craft shops are within easy reach and scenic day trips to Phillip Island may be undertaken comfortably.
Guest facilities include a well stocked library, lounge/dining room, log fire, stereo. Boat parking is provided at the house. A four course dinner is provided by arrangement.
Home Page: http://www.bol.com.au.verekerhouse/v.html

Tariffs are constant for this year. However some may have had to change slightly. Alway check.

VICTORIA

Yarra Valley - Yarra Glen
Self Contained Accommodation
Address: "Alcheringa"
2248 Melba Highway Dixons Creek Vic 3775
Name: Tanya and Rohan Scott
Telephone: (0359) 652 284
Beds: 1 Queen, 3 Singles (1 Bedroom)
Bathroom: 1 Private
Tariff: Double $100, each extra person $30. Family rate available. Discount for longer bookings. Breakfast basket can be arranged.
Nearest Town: Yarra Glen 10 km

If you need to unwind and relax, "Alcheringa" is the place for you. Our open-plan rustic cabin with sweeping verandah is situated high on the hill with majestic views over the Yarra Valley.
In winter relax in front of the open fire. Wake up in the morning and see the kangaroo's hopping along. We also have wombats and lyrebirds nestling on our 116 acre property which backs on to the Toolangi State Forest.
We are situated amongst 28 magnificent wineries. Other local attractions are hot air ballooning, trail rides, bush walks, fishing, golf and the Healesville Wildlife Sanctuary is nearby.

Yarra Valley - Healesville
Homestay
Address: 'Wide Horizons', Lot 27, Juliet Crescent, Healesville, 3777
Name: Corry & Peter Skilbeck
Telephone: (03) 59 624119
Fax: (03) 59 624571
Beds: 2 Queen, 2 Single (3 bedrooms)
Bathroom: 3 Ensuite
Tariff: B&B (full) Double $110-$120, Single $80. Dinner $30, Credit cards (BC/VISA/MC). Vouchers accepted surcharge $29, Not available Saturdays.
Nearest Town: Healesville

Designed and specifically built as a Bed & Breakfast retreat, our 4 1/2 star federation style home stands on a hilltop overlooking Healesville. Set on 1 1/2 acres amidst the trees 'Wide Horizons' has an atmosphere of peace and beauty often remarked on by guests. Three delightful bedrooms each have their own ensuite, individual air-conditioning, tea-making and most comfortable beds. An open fire, relaxing music and good food draw people to our guest lounge. Breakfast is a speciality with an extravagant buffet of home-cooked delicacies. Dinner is available by arrangement. Native birds frequent the garden and the Maroondah Dam, which is within walking distance. It's only a short drive to Healesville Sanctuary or the world class wineries, the galleries and the natural beauty of the Yarra Valley. 'Wide Horizons' caters for adults, has wheelchair access and is non-smoking. HHHHK
Directions: *Turn off Maroondah Hwy 2km East Healesville P.O. at Graceburn Ave. Follow B&B signs.*
Home Page: http://www.innhouse.com.au

VICTORIA

Yarra Valley - Healesville
Bed & Breakfast   RACV ★★★☆
Address: 'Brentwood',
506 Myers Creek Road,
Healesville, Vic 3777
Name: Pat & Gustaaf van Driel
Telephone: (03) 5962 5028
Fax: (03) 5962 4749 **Mobile**: (019) 411365
Beds: 2 Queen, 2 Single (3 bedrooms)
Bathroom: 3 Ensuite
Tariff: B&B (full) Double $95, Single $55,
Children by arrangement. Dinner $25/$35. Vouchers accepted No surcharge weekdays. $15 surcharge weekends.
Nearest Town: Healesville - 8km Post Office

Relax and enjoy our beautiful bush setting, and hospitality. "Brentwood" once a turn of the century Guest House, on 18 acres is surrounded by towering gums and ferny gullies and adjoins State Forest Reserve. Now modernised, it is a much loved family country home and offers comfortable ensuite Bed and Breakfast accommodation, separate entrances. Sit on the verandah and view of the many species of birds living in the garden and neighbouring bush. Wake to the call of the Lyrebird, breakfast with a Wallaby, relax to the sounds of the creek. Healesville is well known for its "Wild life" sanctuary, beautiful Picnic areas and fabulous Yarra Valley wineries.
We have lived in Europe, Kenya and Indonesia and have travelled extensively throughout Australia and overseas. We enjoy meeting people and will gladly help visitors with their itinerary and introduce guests to favourite beauty spots and local attractions.

Yarrawonga
Homestay
Address: RMB 4120,
Yarrawonga, VIC 3730
Name: Mrs Lorna Irvine
Telephone: (03) 5744 2541
Beds: 2 Single, (1 bedroom)
Bathroom: 1 Ensuite
Tariff: B&B (full), Double $60, Single $30
Nearest Town: Yarrawonga 7km west of town on Murray Valley Hwy.

The cosy country style bedroom has its own bathroom, a dining-lounge room with tea making facilities and wood-burning fire. There's a choice of breakfasts, and also supper.
The white house is set amongst trees on 5 1/2 ha of open country about 2 km from the Murray River. There are native birds in the bush garden, a small memorabilia museum, fishing and picnic spots on the sand bars of the river. Local excursions include Lake Mulwala, Rutherglen wineries, Cobram orchards and Linley Park Animal Farm.
Yarrawonga, in the centre of the Sun Country Area offers an art gallery, clock museum, river cruises as well as a golf course, bowling greens, many excellent restaurants and 3 licenced Clubs with poker machines.
Your host specializes in country cooking, is experienced in caring for people, likes art and craft work, collecting old wares, travelling and gardening.
Directions: *Please phone or write.*

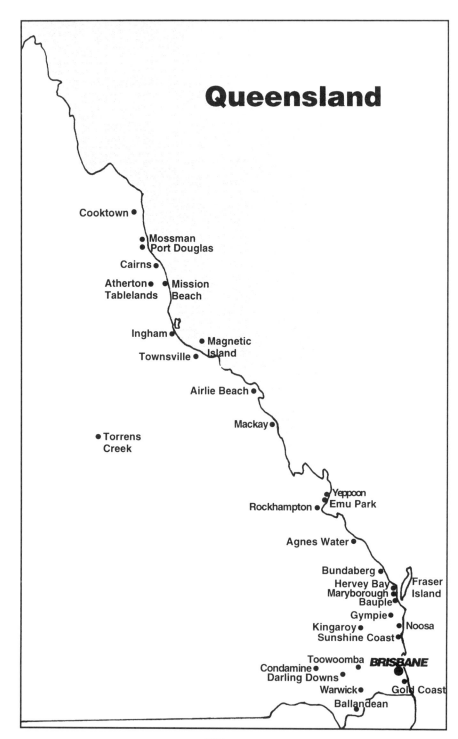

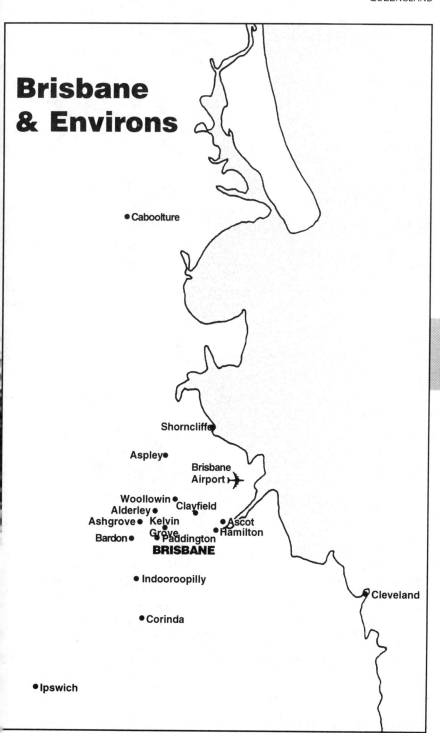

QUEENSLAND

Agnes Water - Town of 1770
Homestay RACQ ★★★★
Address: 2510 Round Hill Road,
Agnes Water, QLD 4677
Name: Hoban's Hideaway
(Bob & Helen Hoban)
Telephone: (07) 4974 9144
Fax: (07) 49749144
Beds: 3 Queen, 2 Single (3 bedrooms)
Bathroom: 3 Ensuite
Tariff: B&B (full) Double $88, Single $80.
Dinner $28. Credit Cards. We do not cater for children.
Nearest Town: Agnes Water. 4km from Agnes Water on right hand side of the road. Clearly sign posted.

WINNER
'93, '94, '95
TOURISM AWARDS

Hoban's Hideaway is a purpose built B&B with an Australian theme throughout. Nestled on 40 acres in amongst majestic gum trees, tropical palm trees, flowering shrubs with abundant birdlife and kangaroos. It is a base for exploring the nearby National Parks, enjoying a reef adventure, or a unique experience on an environmental tour. Hoban's has the best of both worlds, a tranquil bush setting and yet only 5 minutes from the beach where one can swim year round. The guest rooms are tastefully decorated with private facilities, guest lounge, dining room, outside eating/relaxing area called the 'Nook', large shady verandahs, swimming pool and BBQ facilities. Delicious country style breakfast and evening meal can be enjoyed on the 'Nook'.
Agnes Water is only a few kilometres from the picturesque Town of 1770, the birthplace of Queensland.
Hoban's Hideaway won Tourism Awards in 1993, 1994,1995 and 1996. Your stay will be a memorable one!

Airlie Beach - Whitsundays
Homestay+Self-contained Cabin
Address: PO Box 661, Airlie Beach, Qld 4802
Name: Lea & Peter Payne
Telephone: (07) 4946 1280
Fax: (07) 4946 1280 **Mobile**: 018-182 572
Beds: 2 Double, 2 Single (2 bedrooms)
Cabin: 1 Double
Bathroom: 1 Guests share
Tariff: B&B (continental) Double $55, Single $35, Children half price. Vouchers accepted
Nearest Town: Airlie Beach 14km, Proserpine 14km

We live in paradise in all year round sunshine. Our house 'Tibooburra' is on 5 acres with a swimming pool and BBQ, with superb views across the valley and Conway Ranges. There is also a guest lounge with a pool table, TV and complimentary tea and coffee. We are only minutes away from Airlie Beach and Shute Harbour, the jumping off point for the Whitsunday Islands and the Great Barrier Reef for snorkelling, diving and swimming. P.A.D.I. diving courses are available in Airlie Beach. Also sailing, bareboat charters, fishing, rainforest tours, bush walking, horse riding, tandem parachute jumping, bungy jumping, helicopter rides, sea planes, golf at Laguna Quays where the skins competition is held, also wildlife park (crocodiles, possums, snakes and more). Airlie Beach has many restaurants, coffee shops and tourist shops.
We are only ten minutes from Proserpine which is an old cane farming town.

Angourie Point see Yamba

QUEENSLAND

Atherton Tablelands - Evelyn Central
Rural Stay - S. C. Accommodation   RACQ ★★★
Address: Possum Valley,
Evelyn Central via Ravenshoe, Qld 4872
Name: Possum Valley Rainforest Cottages
Telephone: (070) 978177 **Fax**: (070) 978177
Email: possumvalley@bigpond.com
Beds: Each cottage: 2 Double, 2 Single (3 bedrooms)
Bathroom: Private
Tariff: 1-3 Days: Double $75, Single $60, Extra person $5; 4-7 Days: Double $60, Single $55, Extra person $5; Weekly Double $350, Single $300, Extra person $20. Children under 10 $2.50 per day. Breakfast continental, self serve $5 per person per day if required. Credit Cards (MC/BC/VISA).
Nearest Town: We are 31km south of Atherton.

Paul and Hilary will welcome you to our misty mountain retreat. At an altitude over 1000m and surrounded by rainforest, we are naturally air-conditioned and pleasantly cooler than the coast. We offer the peace and privacy of your own fully self-contained cottage (two available) separately located on our 156 acre property.

The three bedrooms cottages are timber panelled, attractively situated, and suitable for up to 6 persons each, with a BBQ and verandah for relaxing, a dam for swimming and rainforest walks. Wildlife abounds. Being 5km from the next house, we don't have mains electricity, but continuous limited power is provided by environmentally friendly hydro generator.

The area has many natural attractions including volcanic craters, lava tubes, waterfalls, rainforest, walking trails and beautiful scenic drives. We enjoy tranquillity that's hard to find in these hectic times, so come and share it with us.

Atherton Tablelands - Herberton
Homestay   RACQ ★★★★☆
Address: "Banyula"
Cnr Zingelmann Rd & Bishop Rd,
Wondecla via Herberton 4872
Name: Terry & Noelene Mays
Telephone: (07) 409 62668
Fax: (07) 4096 2668
Email: mnxv33@ozemail.com.au
Beds: 2 Queen (2 bedrooms) **Bathroom**: 1 Private
Tariff: B&B (full) Double $80, Single $60,
Dinner $25pp, Children not catered for. Credit Cards (BC/MC/VISA). One party booked at one time. Vouchers accepted
Nearest Town: Herberton 13km, Cairns 120km

Banyula, meaning "many trees", aptly describes this peaceful five acre bushland property. Native birds inhabit the area during the day and in the evenings small wallabies and possums come to feed near the house. At 900 metres above sea-level, our climate is cooler than the coast. The area is rich in history and easy access can be made to the regions diverse attractions including volcanic craters, waterfalls, world-heritage rainforests and steam trains. Being without children, we have travelled extensively around Australia, New Zealand and Europe and offer our guests the warm hospitality for which Australians are famous. The sunroom, family room, large verandahs, and undercover car parking are available for our visitors and home-cooked evening meals with wine can be arranged. In winter relax beside our wood fire. We are proud to be nationally accredited and members of "Australia and New Zealand's Finest B&B's and Rural Retreats". Please phone. **Home Page**: www.austbb.com.au

QUEENSLAND

Atherton Tablelands - Lake Barrine
Farmstay+Self-contained Accommodation & Bed & Breakfast
Address: "Topgate"
Boar Pocket Road, Yungaburra, Q.4872
Name: Topgate Farmstay Bed & Breakfast
Telephone: (07) 40953775
Fax: (07) 4095 3436 **Mobile**: (041) 902 9650
Email: Andre_Delfos@TopgateFarmstayBandB.com
Beds: 1 Queen, 4 Single (3 bedrooms)
Bathroom: 1 Private
Tariff: B&B (continental) Double $85, Children $10,
Cottage only, 6 persons $375 week, Campervans welcome. Breakfast is optional. Deduct $5/person.
Nearest Town: Yungaburra 15km W, Cairns 54km NE
Our Cattle Stud property is situated in the "lakes district" on the Atherton Tablelands, 900m (2700ft) above sea level. We breed Australian Droughtmaster cattle, and also Herding Border Collie and Kelpie dogs. Guests are welcome to participate in farming activities including training of the dogs. The property is on a ridge with spectacular views of the hills, rainforest and our two creeks and dams.
The cottage itself is modern and spacious. It comes with a fully equipped kitchen, microwave, colour TV, large automatic washing machine and linen. Native birds are to be seen in the surrounding bush. Aquatic life, including platypus, can be observed on the creeks and dams. Many attractions are close by. Energetic guests can go for walks, the rest can immerse themselves in the "peaceful, idyllic, pastoral lifestyle". Enjoy!
Ideal as a base to tour the Atherton Tablelands. Your hosts: Andre & Elizabeth Delfos.
Home Page: http://www.topgatefarmstaybandb.com/

Atherton Tablelands - Ravenshoe
Rural Bed & Breakfast
Address: PO Box 591,
Tully Falls Road
Ravenshoe, QLD 4872
Name: The Pond Cottage
Telephone: (07) 4097 7189
Fax: (07) 4097 7189
Beds: 1 Queen, 2 Single,
Double sofa bed (open plan)
Bathroom: 1 Private
Tariff: B&B (full) Double $75, Single $70, Children + $5, Dinner $20.
 Vouchers accepted
Nearest Town: Ravenshoe - 9km south off Kennedy Highway

If you're looking for a cool change away from coastal humidity, a stay at the Pond Cottage could be the answer. Situated 9km from Ravenshoe - at 3000 feet above sea level, Qld's highest town - the cottage overlooks a tree fern lined pond and is surrounded by plantation timber. The historic timber town is gateway to the gulf savanna and majestic waterfalls, volcanic hot springs, World War II campsites and the Undara lava tubes are within easy reach by conventional car. The cottage is fully self-contained and total privacy is assured by its location away from your hosts' home. Self cater or join your hosts for dinner. A delicious wholesome hamper breakfast is supplied on arrival for enjoyment at your leisure. Stay overnight or explore the rest of the Atherton Tablelands using the cottage as a base. See Anne's fabulous mouse collection, thought to be one of the largest in the world. No they don't bite!
Home Page: http://www.bnbnq.com.au/pondcottage

QUEENSLAND

Atherton Tableland - Yungaburra
SC. Accom. Secluded Cottage/Homestay B&B   RACQ ★★★★★
Address: "Bracken Ridge", Vance Close, Tinaroo Park, Qld 4872
Name: John & Myra Eggers
Telephone: (0740) 953421 **Fax**: (0740) 512636 **Mobile**: 0418 778959
Email: pynecottage@iig.com.au
Beds: 1 King, 2 Queen, 5 Single (4 bedrooms)
Bathroom: 3 Private, spa baths
Tariff: B&B (full) Double $100/$120, Single $70, Dinner $25. S/C Cottage $95
Vouchers accepted
Nearest Town: Yungaburra 15km, Cairns 65km

Tour the Far North while staying at our 'Home Beautiful' award winning Queenslander-Timber Pole Home, on rural acreage overlooking Lake Tinaroo. Close by are Tourist Destinations, Lake Barrine, Lake Eacham, waterfalls, rainforest walks, majestic curtain fig trees. Lake Tinaroo has facilities for fishing, swimming and all water sports. Two person canoe available to explore the lake for birdlife, platypus and catch redclaw. The charming Heritage village of Yungaburra has award winning restaurants, antique, art/craft shops. Play golf on the naturally air conditioned Tableland. Cairns and Barrier Reef trips only one hour away.
After your day touring, you will return with anticipation to your deluxe, private self-contained unit, tastefully furnished with heirlooms and antiques but with all mod cons (with 2 person spa bath) ensuring your comfort. Relax and have a pre dinner drink and watch the spectacular sunset over the lake. Enjoy cuisine from fresh local produce, tender Tableland beef, local seafood and freshwater redclaw crayfish (in season). Dinner by arrangement.
Bracken Ridge Cottage is secluded and set apart from our home. It is fully self contained, built on 4.5 acres of natural bushland and adjoins a rainforest walk to the lake. Private romantic experience for a couple or would suit family wanting a comfortable holiday. Large deck with undercover gas/wood barbecue which adapts to a cosy wood fire to have sundowners or enjoy the wonderful clear nights star gazing. We look forward to meeting you and to ensure your stay is enjoyable and memorable.
Home Page: http://www.bnbnq.com.au/brackenridge

QUEENSLAND

Ballandean
Homestay
Address: Ballandean Lodge
Rees Road, Ballandean, 4382
Name: Dietmar & Dorothy Gogolka
Telephone: (07) 4684 1320 **Fax**: (07) 4684 1340 **Mobile**: 0419 705 228
Beds: 1 Queen, 1 Double, 2 single (3 bedrooms)
Bathroom: 3 Ensuites
Tariff: B&B (full) Double $105-$120, Single $60-$75, Dinner $25, Children by arrangement. Credit Cards: Bankcard, Mastercard, Visa. Vouchers accepted Mid week only.
Nearest Town: Stanthorpe 20kms North

Come and share with us the peace and tranquillity of our recently restored turn of the century Queenslander. Our home nestles in between stone fruit orchards and grapevines of Queensland's temperate Granite Belt. Enjoy the privacy of your own comfortable room with ensuite. The views from the verandah are superb looking towards Sundown National Park. Sit and relax while watching the sunset.

Bird life abounds, take a walk through our newly formed gardens of five acres and pause to enjoy the quiet atmosphere amongst the native trees and bush rocks.

Just a short distance away are the beautiful National parks of Girraween and Bald Rock. For the four wheel drive enthusiast the Sundown National Park is easily accessible.

Also close by are the famous wineries of the region where visitors are made very welcome.

We are only a 2 1/2 to 3 hour drive from Brisbane and the Gold Coast and 40 minutes from Warwick. We are looking forward to making you welcome at Ballandean Lodge's smoke-free homestay.

Bauple see Maryborough

Brisbane
Bed & Breakfast
Address: 405 Upper Edward St, Brisbane, 4000
Name: Annies Shandon Inn
Telephone: (07) 3831 8684 **Fax**: (07) 3831 3073
Beds: 8 Double, 20 Single (19 bedrooms)
Bathroom: 4 Ensuite, 4 Guests share
Tariff: B&B (continental) Ensuite $50-$60, Double/Twin $50, Single $40, Extra person $10, Children $10, 4 car spaces.

Quaint, pretty with lovely period decor in blue and pink in the middle of the city, "Annies Shandon Inn" was started as a Bed & Breakfast by the present owners grandmother "Annie" 100 years ago. Pig skin deeds on wall are dated "Brisbane Colony of NSW 1857". A place of history popular with both local and overseas tourists. Restaurants and bus at door, also quite close to Wickham Tce specialists and the Sheraton Hotel and conference venue.

Managers on premises at all times.

Your hosts: Carmel and Mal.

Always have a phone card with you.
Most public phones do not take coins.

QUEENSLAND

Brisbane
Bed & Breakfast RACQ ★★★
Address: "Thornbury House",
1 Thornbury St,
Spring Hill, Brisbane, 4000
Name: Michelle Bugler
Telephone: (07) 3832 5985
Fax: (07) 3832 7255 **Mobile**: (015) 577 532
Beds: 5 Double, 6 Single (9 bedrooms)
Bathroom: 1 Ensuite, 3 Guests share
Tariff: B&B (continental plus) Ensuite $100, Double $90, Single $55, Dinner $15,
Credit Cards. No smoking in-doors. Vouchers accepted
Nearest Town: Brisbane City 1km GPO

Built as a merchant's house, Thornbury House is a charming early colonial residence (circa 1886). Situated in a quiet leafy street, it is within easy walking distance of the city or cosmopolitan Fortitude Valley. Recently refurbished, the house has a guests' sitting room and a delightful courtyard garden where breakfast is served among the greenery of palms honeysuckle and grapes. Here paw paws have planted themselves, lending a tropical element to the fresh fruit salad offered with cereal and yoghurt and home-baked delights. Tea and plunger coffee facilities are on hand for guests who also have use of a fridge, microwave and laundry. All rooms come complete with fine linen, bathrobes and colour televisions. Many fine restaurants, pubs and weekend markets are closeby as is the Brisbane River where a ferry ride to Southbank Parklands and the Cultural Centre is a must for any visitor to Brisbane. Airport shuttle bus stops at door.

Brisbane - Alderley
Homestay
Address: "Fernhaven",
5 Elgin Street, Alderley,
Brisbane, QLD 4051
Name: Joyce & Kevin Brooks
Telephone: (07) 3356 7762
Mobile: (015) 020035
Beds: 1 Double, 3 Single (3 bedrooms)
Bathroom: 1 Ensuite, 1 Family share
Tariff: B&B (full) Double $60, Single $35, Children negotiable. Dinner $15.
Campervans $20.   Vouchers accepted
Nearest Town: Brisbane city - north-west suburb 10 mins from city heart

"Fernhaven" is a spacious 1929 home in a quiet suburb among native trees where parrots feed and resident possums are often seen at night. It is ideally situated for motorists, with easy access to freeways north and south to the beaches or west to the ranges, yet only ten minutes from the city heart. Alternatively buses or half-hourly city trains are within walking distance as are several restaurants.
Ours is a non-smoking home but the deck and garden are welcome areas for a snack, drink or cigarette in warm sunshine or welcome shade.
We enjoy people, travel and nature, and pursue enthusiastically our hobbies of sewing / handcrafts and vintage cars. Kevin is easily persuaded to treat you to a tour in his '25 Buick or '29 Ford. We have travelled Australia extensively, are happy to make travel suggestions, and would love your company.
Directions: *Please write or phone.*

QUEENSLAND

Brisbane - Ascot
Homestay
Address: 11 Mayfield Street, Ascot, Brisbane, QLD 4007
Name: Eileen Jonsson
Telephone: (07) 3868 1948
Beds: 1 Queen (1 bedroom)
Bathroom: 1 Private
Tariff: B&B (continental) Double $75, Single $50
Nearest Town: Brisbane (Ascot approximately 10mins from city centre)

An elegant family residence built in Mediterranean style with adjacent inground pool set amidst tall palms and flowering shrubs. Entry to residence is via a private bitumen driveway. The bedroom overlooks the pool.
Your accommodation is within easy walking distance to Eagle Farm Racecourse. Racecourse Road offers the visitors an excellent variety of venues including coffee shops, gourmet restaurants, smart boutiques, unique giftware and other business outlets. A stroll down Racecourse Road brings you to Bretts Wharf famous for delicious cuisine. Next to the wharf are the Brisbane Rivercats which run from Hamilton past Dockside, CBD up to St Lucia and University. Your hostess is a music teacher with interests in arts and has also travelled extensively. Please phone your hostess Eileen 3868 1948.

Brisbane - Ascot
Homestay
Address: Cheshunt House, 259 Lancaster Rd., Ascot, Brisbane, Qld 4007
Name: Cheshunt House
Telephone: (07) 3268 4603
Mobile: (015) 764 500
Email: carolP@qimr.edu.au
Beds: 3 Double, 2 Single (4 bedrooms)
Bathroom: 2 Guests share
Tariff: B&B (full) Double $90-$100, Single $55, Credit Cards.
Nearest Town: Brisbane

Cheshunt House is a lovely old Queenslander with heaps of history. It has been lovingly restored and now welcomes visitors to come and enjoy a pleasant overnight (or longer) stay. Cheshunt House has 4 bedrooms decorated as in days gone by and features a marble open fireplace in the TV/lounge and wide verandahs. It is situated in the beautiful inner suburb of Ascot in Brisbane and so offers easy access to the city, airports, racecourses, north/south arterial road and the fashionable Racecourse Road.
Eagle Farm Racecourse is across the road, Doomben Racecourse is within walking distance and Albion Park Raceway is a short drive away. The airports, transit centre and central business district are all just seven kilometres away with bus, train and ferry services giving easy access to all. Our two dogs spend most of their days sleeping outdoors in the sun. Sorry we cannot accommodate children.
Smoking: Outdoor areas only.
Pick-up service: By prior arrangement.

Brisbane - Ashgrove
Homestay/Bed & Breakfast
Address: "Thistledown"
15 Kauri Road Ashgrove
Name: Bert and Eunice Leitch
Telephone: (07) 3366 6991
Fax: (07) 3366 6824   **Mobile**: 015-028 753
Email: pleitch@onaustralia.com.au
Beds: 1 Queen, 1 Twin, 1 single (3 bedrooms)
Bathroom: 1 Guests Share
Tariff: B&B (continental/full)
Double $80, Single $45.
Vouchers accepted with minimum of 2 nights stay.
Nearest Town: Brisbane City (5kms)

You are invited to experience the ambience of a stay in a stately Queensland home. Thisledown is located in Ashgrove, a leafy inner suburb of Brisbane. This lovingly restored "Queenslander" provides an ideal setting in which to experience the unique style and relaxed way of life so characteristic of this lovely sub tropical city. Enjoy the breezy open verandahs, charming leadlights and polished floors that are the hallmarks of the true 'Queenslander'. French doors opening from the ground floor lounge provide direct access to the covered terrace, gardens and swimming pool. In summer enjoy the experience of sleeping under a romantic mosquito net, swim in the enchanting pool day and night. Relax in winter by the cosy fireplace. Enjoy al fresco breakfast in the sun on the verandah in the tree tops summer or winter. Bert and Eunice are eager to share the pleasures of their home and their genuine Scottish hospitality with you.

Brisbane - Aspley
Homestay
Address: 199 Kirby Road, Aspley, 4034
Name: Patsy, Roger & Will Cloake
Telephone: (07) 3263 5940
Fax: (07) 3268 2661
Mobile: (018) 871217
Beds: 1 Queen, 1 Double (2 bedrooms)
Bathroom: 1 Guests share
Tariff: B&B (full) Double $70, Single $45, Children negotiable, Dinner $20/$25.
Nearest Town: Brisbane City - 20 mins by car; 30 mins by public transport.

You are very welcome to enjoy our hospitality and break bread with us. Accommodation is in our large, cavity-brick, architect-designed 1960's home surrounded by a very pleasant herb garden.
Your home away from home is a smoke-free environment with guests' area including an expansive lounge-dining room, library and north facing 12.5 metre pool.
Aspley is a suburb 9 miles north of Brisbane's centre. Our home is located close to shopping and dining facilities as well as several bus routes to both the city and Sunshine Coast attractions.
Our interests are heritage/environment and social issues, wine and food, gardening and entertaining. We have extensive knowledge of local and Australian history and geography plus a substantial Australiana library. We enjoy cooking local produce and look forward to discoursing widely with our guests.
Directions: *Please write or phone.*

QUEENSLAND

Brisbane - Bardon
Homestay
Address: Stuartholme Rd,
Bardon, Brisbane, Qld 4065
Name: Anne
Telephone: (07) 3369 8093
Fax: (07) 3369 8093
Beds: 1 Double, 2 Single (3 bedrooms)
Bathroom: 1 Guests share, 1 Single Room with shower.
Tariff: B&B (full) Double $60, Single $35, Dinner $15. Vouchers accepted
Nearest Town: Brisbane - 4km west of city

A warm welcome and generous hospitality awaits you. My home is low set in the front leading to a terrace with a variety of tropical plants, passion fruit and grape vines organically grown. Jacaranda trees surround the rear of my timber house which has city lights and tree top views from bedrooms. Steps lead to a landscaped garden hosting many birds. All rooms have ceiling fans and heaters. Bardon is a green inner city suburb close to Paddington with its antique markets and restaurants.
I have worked in England, Malaysia, Africa and Nauru, and visited North and Latin America, Europe, Middle East and Asia.
Travel advice on tourist destinations if required.
My interests include tennis, walking, theatre, art, music and antiques. Complimentary tour of Mount Coottha. Free pick-up from City Transit Centre. Laundry and garage facilities. Regular bus service leaves over the road to city and return - 5.30am to 11.00pm.
Directions: *Please phone.*

Brisbane - Bardon
Homestay
Address: "Maggies Place",
50 Lizzie Street, Bardon, QLD 4065
Name: Maggie
Telephone: (07) 3366 6647
Beds: 2 Double (2 bedrooms)
Bathroom: 1 Guests share, 1 Family share
Tariff: B&B (continental) Double $50, Single $35, Children welcome. Family/Weekly rates negotiable. Vouchers accepted
Nearest Town: 4.8 kms from Brisbane GPO. Adjacent suburbs - Paddington, Red Hill, Milton.

I live in my comfortable, spacious family home located in an old established inner-city suburb which backs onto Brisbane Forest Park, is two minutes from the nearest bus stop and is easily accessible within 10 minutes by car to the following attractions:
- Mount Coot-tha Scenic Lookout, Botanical Gardens and   Planetarium
- SouthBank Parklands (Swimming, Restaurants, Craft Markets, Entertainment etc)
- Cultural Centre (Art Gallery, Museum, Theatres)
- Brisbane Convention & Exhibition Centre
- Treasury Casino
- Central Business District
- Bronco's Rugby League Club (5 minute walk)
and for the adventurous and curious, scenic bush walks are only a 5 to 10 minute walk away through quiet surburban streets with many restored Queenslanders to view. Off street parking is available as is complimentary tea & coffee making facilities, fridge, micro-wave, T.V. and B.B.Q. I have a zest for living and believe life is like a sandwich - the more you add to it the better it becomes. A happy welcome awaits you from your hostess Maggie.

QUEENSLAND

Brisbane - Clayfield
Homestay
Address: "Torcross",
18 Victoria Street, Clayfield, QLD 4011
Name: Trish Barrkman
Telephone: (07) 3262 4801
Mobile: (019) 617584
Beds: 2 Double, 3 Single (5 bedrooms)
Bathroom: 1 Ensuite, 1 Family share
Tariff: B&B (continental) Double with ensuite $75, Double $66, Single $33, Children half price.
1Dinner $18. Vouchers accepted
Nearest Town: Brisbane - 5km from city.

I live in one of the older suburbs of Brisbane with Queensland style homes set on large blocks with beautiful gardens. A swimming pool and deck are enjoyed by guests and in winter a cosy fire burns for all to enjoy. Our home is a short walk (5 mins) to public transport train / bus, banks, Post Office, restaurants antique shops and much more. A walk along Kedron Brook is a nice spot to stroll, early morning or late afternoon. The train service takes 8 mins to the city, Sth Bank, Art Gallery and Museum also to Transit Centre where most tours leave from. The main North / South Highway is just 10 mins away and the airports are both close by ($10.00 taxi). I have travelled extensively myself and enjoy the contact with others, both from overseas and Australia. Sightseeing trips can be arranged and whenever possible a complimentary service to your next departure point is provided. Smoking area available. (The deck and garden welcomes you.) Baby sitting available. Dinner by arrangement.
Directions: *Please phone or write.*

Brisbane - Clayfield
Homestay
Address: "Wonga Villa",
194 Bonney Avenue, Clayfield, Qld 4011
Name: Rosalyn & John Whiteley
Telephone: (07) 3862 2183
Fax: (07) 3862 2183
Mobile: 0411551811
Email: whiteleyj@anta.gov.au
Beds: 3 Queen, 1 Double (4 bedrooms)
Bathroom: 2 Guests share
Tariff: B&B (full) Double from $90, Dinner $20, Credit Cards.
Vouchers accepted $10 surcharge
Nearest Town: 10 mins from Brisbane CBD

Picture yourself enjoying the warm and friendly atmosphere of a bygone era in a magnificent Queensland colonial residence. Located in one of Brisbane's most prestigious suburbs, Wonga Villa offers you peace and tranquillity, large airy rooms with soaring ceilings, beautiful antiques and the finest linen. Wide verandahs and tropical palms add to the serenity and graceful beauty of this elegant home. Stay a while and go shopping, take in a show, dine out or perhaps explore the Riverside Markets. Business travellers take a break from the fast lane, at Wonga Villa you'll unwind and rejuvenate ready for another busy day. Close to domestic and international airports, an easy walk to trains and buses, and a short cab fare to major shopping centres, restaurants and the City Heart, Wonga Villa offers you everything you need on your next visit to Brisbane.
Book today and experience Bed & Breakfast hospitality the way it was always meant to be.

QUEENSLAND

Brisbane – Corinda
Homestay
Address: 32 Balderstone Street, Corinda, Brisbane, QLD 4075
Name: Margaret Falk
Telephone: (07) 3379 3908
Beds: 1 Queen, 1 Double (2 bedrooms)
Bathroom: 1 Ensuite, 1 Family share
Tariff: B&B (continental) Double $55, Single $30, Children welcome.
Dinner $15 if required. Vouchers accepted
Nearest Town: Brisbane

Corinda is in the western suburbs of Brisbane, a very delightful area. There are many old homes with lovely gardens with many trees.
My home is in a quiet street, low set with a northeasterly aspect. A sun-room opens from the main bedroom, this is cool in summer and warm in winter. This bedroom has an ensuite.
I am a retired teacher and have travelled extensively. I enjoy company and would be very happy to assist with suggestions for places to visit. The Corinda railway station is but a few minutes walk - the service is very regular. It takes 20 minutes to the city. A continental breakfast will be provided but arrangements for a cooked breakfast could be made.
Please phone for further details.

Brisbane - Hamilton
Private Hotel
Address: 114 Kingsford Smith Drive, Hamilton, Brisbane 4007
Name: Barry & Heather Orchard
Telephone: (07) 3862 1317 or 1800 777 590 (within Australia)
Fax: (07) 3862 2658
Beds: 10 Double, 12 Twin, 4 Single (26 bedrooms)
Bathroom: 6 Guests share
Tariff: B&B (full) Double $43, Single $39, Credit Cards.
Nearest Town: Brisbane - 10 mins from the airport and the city centre

Kingsford Private Hotel is a three storey brick building with parking underneath which has been owned by the same family for eleven years and who now have decided to include free of charge a fully cooked breakfast served in a dining room overlooking the Brisbane River.
A free pick-up service is provided from the Brisbane Airport and the Transit Centre and with the city bus service at the door and the City Cat ferry service a short walk away, access to the city centre by road or river is very convenient.
All room have vanity basins with hot and cold water as well as their own television and refrigerator.
A fully equipped kitchen is available for guests' use at any time.
We provide twenty-four hour reception and to make bookings please write, phone or fax. Within Australia please make use of our 1800 freecall number.
Managers are on the premises at all times.

QUEENSLAND

Brisbane - Indooroopilly
Homestay
Address: 9 Stanley Street,
Indooroopilly, Brisbane, Qld 4068
Name: Peter Kafcaloudis
Telephone: (07) 3378 5643
Beds: 1 Double, 2 Single (2 bedrooms)
Bathroom: 1 Guests share
Tariff: B&B (full) Double $60,
Single $35. Dinner $15. Vouchers accepted
Nearest Town: 7km west of Brisbane city centre
My home is a modern house, surrounded by lush tropical plants, situated in a quiet area. The house has plenty of large windows to let in natural light and catch the cool breezes. The kitchen and meals area have views to the garden and courtyard, which leads to the salt water pool.
I have travelled extensively overseas and throughout Queensland and can help with any information you require or questions you have about different destinations in Queensland, to make your stay a pleasant and memorable holiday. A hot cooked breakfast is provided, coffee and tea are always on the boil. I can cook dinner for you or you can eat at the numerous restaurants which are nearby. Non-smokers preferred. Indooroopilly has a train and bus service and a large shopping complex all within easy walking distance from my house. I am 30 minutes by car from the airport and 10 minutes from the city centre.
Lone Pine Koala Sanctuary, Mt. Coot-Tha Botanical Gardens, and Planetarium are nearby and easily reached by bus.
Directions: Please phone.

Brisbane - Kelvin Grove
B&B, Guest House   RACQ
Address: Catherine House
151 Kelvin Grove Road
Kelvin Grove 4059 QLD
Name: Joy Harman
Telephone: (07) 3839 6988
Fax: (07) 3839 6988 **Mobile**: 041-9791 224
Beds: 4 Queen, 1 Double, 2 Single (5 bedrooms)
Bathroom: 1 Ensuite, 1 Private, 2 Guest Share
Tariff: B&B (full) Double $95, Single $50, Dinner $25, Children over 12 years $15. Credit Cards. Vegetarians catered for. Vouchers accepted
Nearest Town: Brisbane - 2km. (7 mins walk)
Catherine House is a beautiful two storey Victorian-style colonial home, circa 1881. It is located at the city fringe in Kelvin Grove, within walking distance of all the amenities of Brisbane: Wonderful outdoor restaurants, cinemas, theatres, the magnificent Cultural Centre, the Performing Arts Complex and Southbank with acres of beautiful parklands and craft markets.
The home is a large, warm and friendly residence, where you can relax and feel welcome. Your hostess Joy, with years of hospitality experience, is also a chef, so you can be assured of some "old-fashioned pampering" with wonderful food - perhaps taken on the back deck overlooking the tropical gardens and swimming pool.
There is a family sized room and four double bedrooms all with the comforts of home. Regretfully, Catherine House is unsuitable for small children.
Pick up service: available from Roma Street Transit Centre (bus coach and train) or Brisbane Airport.

QUEENSLAND

Brisbane - Paddington
**Bed & Breakfast &
Self-contained Accommodation**
Address: "Waverley",
5 Latrobe Terrace,
Paddington, QLD 4064
Name: Annette Henry
Telephone: (07) 3369 8973
Fax: (07) 3876 6655 **Mobile**: 0419 741 282
Beds: 2 King, 2 Queen, 4 Single (4 bedrooms) **Bathroom**: 4 Ensuite
Tariff: B&B (full) Double $85, Single $55. Weekly rate for Self-contained accommodation $350. Credit cards (Visa/MC/BC/DINERS/Amex) Vouchers accepted
Nearest Town: Brisbane city 2 1/2km to GPO, 1.25km to CBD.
*Paddington is an inner Brisbane suburb renowned for charming traditional Queenslander homes. It is a shopping / business area with cosmopolitan restaurants, street cafés, antiques, galleries, boutiques and more. Transport (bus) is 20 metres along Latrobe Terrace and rail within 1/2km. Taxis are always available and the city is within walking distance.
"Waverley" was built by H. Sheard in 1888. It is a large timber home on three levels in the Queensland colonial style. The house has been totally renovated and restored in 1995 and now has modern conveniences with old-fashioned charm. The top level has 2 Queen bedrooms with ensuite. All rooms have colour TV and reverse cycle air conditioning. The middle level contains two guest suites which have separate kitchen / dining areas and ensuites. They are self-contained with their own entrances. Guests are welcome to use all facilities but no smoking please, except outdoors. The lower level has a laundry, outdoor entertainment area and garden. The car park can accommodate three cars with ease. It is off street parking available from Cochrane St. You can be assured of a warm welcome for overnight and short term accommodation. Please telephone or write for bookings.*

Brisbane - Shorncliffe
Bed & Breakfast
Address: "Naracoopa", 99 Yundah St.,
Shorncliffe, Qld 4017
Name: David & Grace Cross
Telephone: (07) 3269 2334
 Mobile: (0412) 147456
Email: glc.lib2@mailbox.uq.edu.au
Beds: 2 Queen (2 bedrooms)
Bathroom: 2 Ensuite
Tariff: B&B (continental-weekdays/special-weekends) Double $80-$90, Single $60, Children half price. Vouchers accepted
Nearest Town: Brisbane 21 kms

*Experience gracious hospitality in historic bayside Queenslander, Naracoopa, which presents a casual elegance and charm, reminiscent of Shorncliffe, the original 'dress circle' of Brisbane. Naracoopa, lovingly restored by your hosts, has tastefully appointed bedrooms, individually decorated with antiques, fine linens, and private ensuites. Served on your private verandah is a sumptuous continental breakfast of home-made breads, jams, with tropical fruits. A luxurious Hot Springs outdoor spa beckons, and in winter, a crackling fire awaits.
Naracoopa is a short stroll to the bay, cliffs, pier, where you enjoy glorious sunsets along established walkways. Shorncliffe offers restaurants, golf, fishing, yacht club. One block walk to train whisks you into Brisbane in 30 minutes, and easy access to the Gateway Arterial, sees you off to the Coasts and Airport in no time.
Your hosts, David and Grace, Art teachers and Artists, along with our three teenage children, welcome you to our non-smoking home.* **Directions**: *Please phone or write for details.*

Brisbane - Wooloowin
Self Contained Accommodation
Address: 45 Lisson Grove
Wooloowin 4030, Brisbane, QLD
Name: Mornington House
Telephone: (07) 3262 6462 **Fax**: (07) 3862 2772
Beds: 1 Queen, 1 Double (2 bedrooms)
Bathroom: 1 Ensuite, 1 Private
Tariff: B&B (Continental) Double $90, Single $75. Credit Cards. Vouchers accepted
Nearest Town: Brisbane

Built in the 1880's as a town residence for a pastoral family, "Mornington" exemplifies the charm of its era. It is located on the edge of historic Clayfield and Albion, inner Brisbane suburbs dotted with picturesque Queenslanders, many dating from the colonial era. Huge trees, camphor laurels, Morton Bay figs and palms date from these times and add to the ambience of a bygone age.

Swim in a large salt water pool; barbecue near the fish pond and wander down to the local at Albion to select a bottle from their famous wine cellars, and browse through the discount stores at Lutwhyche. Wander into Queen Street by fast city-train and escape to country markets on weekends.

Buderim see Sunshine Coast
Burleigh Waters see Gold Coast

Bundaberg, Coral Isles
Homestay
Address: Jacaranda House,
328 Bourbong St/Cnr Kennedy,
Bundaberg, QLD 4670
Name: Herb and Shona Tayler
Telephone: (07) 4152 5858 + answerphone service
Fax: (07) 4152 5858
Beds: 2 Queen, 2 Single (3 bedrooms)
Bathroom: 1 Guests share + 2nd toilet
Tariff: B&B (full) Double $70, Single $60.
Nearest Town: 3-4 hrs north of Brisbane via Bruce Highway

JACARANDA HOUSE is an authentic early 1900's Queenslander. Nestled on half an acre of trees with a large saltwater pool, it is the ultimate relaxation.
YOUR HOSTS Herb and Shona, encourage guess to make use of the house, with reading, TV or music areas, day facilities with 24hr tea / coffee, fridge / snack making facilities, balcony, verandah and outdoor areas.
AT JACARANDA HOUSE your day starts with full cooked breakfast on the balcony, or in the kitchen, this includes Shona's homemade jams and muffins.
CLOSE to the CBD guests can enjoy the beauty of Bundaberg's historic buildings, a stroll by the river, beaches, islands / coral viewing, whale watching, the famous Turtle Rookery or one of the many Clubs and Restaurants.
SUBTROPICAL Bundaberg is a comfortable drive North from Brisbane or a great stopover when travelling South from Cairns.
COURTESY pick up available from Bus / Rail and Airport.

Bundaberg

Homestay   RACQ ★★★☆
Address: Whiston House
9 Elliott Heads Rd,
Bundaberg, QLD 4670
Name: Vic & Sharron Sumner
Telephone: (07) 4152 1447
Fax: (07) 4152 1447
Mobile: 0419 393 776
Beds: 3 Queen (3 Bedrooms)
Bathroom: 1 Ensuite, 1 Guest Share
Tariff: B&B (full) Double $70-$90.
Credit Cards: Mastercard, Visa, Bankcard
Nearest Town: Bundaberg 2kms

Whiston House is a beautiful high-set Queenslander, circa 1920, which has been restored to its original charm, set in one acre of tropical gardens. We have a lovely tropical shaded pool area to relax by. We offer a homely, casual atmosphere and guests have full use of the house with its spacious lounge room and shaded verandahs. Bundaberg is an easy 4 hour drive from Brisbane airport and we are only 2 kms from the centre of town which has many restaurants and many other attractions. Whiston House is close to renown Mon Repos Turtle Rookery and Lady Elliott and Lady Musgrave Islands which boast some of the best coral viewing and diving on the Great Barrier Reef. Whale watching is seasonally available from nearby Hervey Bay.

Caboolture

Bed & Breakfast House
Address: 166 King Street, Caboolture, QLD 4510
Name: Mary & Michael Lanigan
Telephone: (07) 5495 6289 **Fax**: (07) 5495 1727
Beds: 3 Double, (3 bedrooms)
Bathroom: 2 Ensuite, 1 Guests share
Tariff: B&B (full) Double $49, Single $39, Children POA, Dinner $15 (BYO),
Credit Cards.
  Vouchers accepted
Nearest Town: Caboolture 1km

Lanigans Bed & Breakfast House offers guests a relaxing friendly stopover. 15 mins drive to spectacular Glass House Mountain Ranges, or Bribie Island National Park with golden beaches.
Caboolture town is halfway between Brisbane and the Sunshine Coast on Hway No. 1 and we are 1km on the west side and easy to find. The house is fully air-conditioned with double beds in each room and security door locks, TV lounge and spacious dining room. A saltwater heated pool, a Hawaiian hot spa fully covered with romantic lighting and music to impress that special person, or soothe you for a great sleep. Your hosts Mary & Michael have years of experience in running a B&B in Ireland and then as now we promise to give our guests great value and good home cooking and a warm Irish welcome.

The standard of accommodation in
The Australian Bed and Breakfast Book ranges from homely to luxurious,
but you can always be sure of superior hospitality.

QUEENSLAND

Cairns
Guest House
Address: 461 Draper Street,
Cairns, QLD 4870
Name: Draper's City House
Telephone: (07) 517 352
Fax: (070) 517 352 **Mobile**: 018 744661
Email: info@bnbq.com.au
Beds: 3 Queen, 1 Double,1 Single,
2 Twin share, 1 triple (8 bedrooms)
Bathroom: 2 Guests share
Tariff: B&B (tropical), Double $65, Single $45,
Dinner $20. Credit cards accepted.   Vouchers accepted
Nearest Town: Cairns 2 kms

Draper's House is situated within easy walking distance to the city or 15 minutes bus ride to the heart of town. Our lovely old home was previously the parsonage for a church. High ceilings, old world charm, air cooled by the soft whirr of fans. Picture yourself in the lush tropical surrounds of your private resort with a saltwater pool. Sip "Sundowners" on the treetops deck watching the nightly migration of the flying foxes overhead. A thousand words can be summed up in "there's good, there's better, there's DRAPER'S". Tour pick up at the door. Airport shuttle bus direct to Draper's call. Now Marilyn or the cat. Accommodation and car hire package available.

Cairns
Homestay
Address: "The James Street Cottage",
25 James St., Cairns, QLD 4870
Name: Leanne & Brian
Telephone: (070) 519114
Fax: (070) 519114
Mobile: (0419) 778455
Beds: 2 Queen, 1 Single (3 bedrooms)
Bathroom: 1 Guests share,
1 Family share
Tariff: B&B (full) Double $65, Single $45,
Dinner from $20, Credit Cards.   Vouchers accepted
Nearest Town: Cairns - 3km north of city

Our 'Queenslander" has lots of charm. Just 3km from the city centre we offer a unique blend of tropical ambience with all the convenience of a city location. We are happy to pick you up from your arrival point and arrange further transfers and bookings as required.
Cairns CBD has excellent Duty Free Shopping, or simply enjoy the delights of our tropical city. Flecker Botanical Gardens and Centenary Lakes are within easy walking distance and we're happy to lend you our bikes and pack a tropical lunch.
Join us for a drink and share your days experiences, or simply relax in our garden retreat and have a dip in the pool.
We serve a generous Aussie breakfast and you're welcome to join us for an evening meal. We concentrate on serving fresh tasty tropical fare combined with gracious hospitality. Our cat "Mudge" will sleep peacefully through most of your stay.
Enjoy our city location with country style hospitality.

QUEENSLAND

Cairns ✓
Homestay/B&B
Address: "Lily Creek House",
Law Street, Cairns. Please phone
Name: Len & Sue
Telephone: (070) 516331
Fax: (070) 516331 **Mobile**: (018) 772998
Beds: 2 Queen (2 bedrooms)
Bathroom: 1 Ensuite, 1 Guests share
Tariff: B&B (tropical) Double $65, Single $35.
 Vouchers accepted
Nearest Town: Cairns City 3km

Overlooking Lily Creek, our traditional Queenslander is the perfect place to enjoy your holiday. We have travelled extensively, enjoy active lives and look forward to sharing our home, and local knowledge, with you.
Lily Creek House is only 3km from the domestic and international airports, and the city. There is a walking / bicycle path to the Botanical Gardens and into the city; Trinity Bay is a short walk away and features parklands and much birdlife. Tourist pick-ups and local buses are nearby, along with many excellent restaurants.
Our home is a tastefully renovated Queenslander. All rooms feature French doors and timber floors. One room has a / c and ensuite. The verandah and garden are ideal spots for relaxing.
We are happy to help with any queries regarding your forthcoming holiday, and pick-ups from transport can be arranged. Smoking - outside. Two dogs and a cat in residence.

Cairns
Homestay
Address: 82 Hannam Street, Westcourt, Cairns
Name: Cairns Homestay
Telephone: (070) 518859 **Fax**: (070) 518859
Beds: 1 King, 3 Double, 2 Single (6 bedrooms/Famiy room sleeps 4)
Bathroom: 2 Guests share
Tariff: B&B (continental) Double $65, Single $45, Children $15.
 Vouchers accepted
Nearest Town: Cairns centre 3kms

We have a large, two storey home, tastefully furnished with spacious fan cooled rooms. There is a large lounge / reading room with TV on each level with a well-equipped kitchen (guests cooking by arrangement) and bathroom / toilet. Laundry facilities available.
A large patio area beside our swimming pool is an ideal place to enjoy your breakfast. We are located in a leafy suburb of Cairns just 2 minutes from K Mart (60 shops and food stalls) and also the departure point for the bus service to Cairns Centre and Casino 3km and 12km to Airport. A pick-up / drop off point for tour buses is just around the corner. Best position in Cairns for a homestay. Two night minimum stay. Discounts for longer stays apply. Call us for further information, we would love to have you stay with us.

Please let your hosts know if you have to cancel.
They will have spent time preparing for you.

QUEENSLAND

Cairns - Brinsmead
Homestay
Address: Brinsmead, Cairns, Queensland - Please phone
Name: Lex & Jenny
Telephone: (070) 551639
Beds: 1 Queen, 2 Double (3 bedrooms)
Bathroom: 1 Ensuite, 1 Guests share
Tariff: B&B (continental) Double $65, Single $35. Vouchers accepted
Nearest Town: Cairns

We are situated in Brinsmead, a suburb 12km from the city of Cairns. Our home features 3 bedrooms, one queen air conditioned with ensuite, and two double share bathroom -a family and TV, sunroom with guest refrigerator including lounge dining room and bar area.
Continental breakfast is served in sun room or around the pool.
My wife and I are in the photography business and enjoy outdoor activities. We can organise interesting trips for you to explore in the area. Cairns is a modern cosmopolitan city, close to the Great Barrier Reef, small islands, rain forests and wilderness. The famous Kuranda Train and Sky Rail, is only a short distance away. Excellent bus service to city. Pick up service by arrangement. Please write or phone. Stay a week and have a free trip to Green Island on us. Thank you for choosing Jenny's Homestay.

Cairns - Clifton Beach
Homestay
Address: Clifton Beach, Cairns, Queensland
Name: Please phone
Telephone: (07) 4055 3739
Beds: 1 Queen, 2 Single (2 bedrooms)
Bathroom: 1 Guests share
Tariff: B&B (continental) Double $65 & $75. Vouchers accepted $5 surcharge on $75 room
Nearest Town: Cairns

A small tropical home at Clifton Beach 23km from Cairns City. Frequent bus service. Walk to the beach and village shops. Close to Palm Cove for Quicksilver Reef trips. Sky-Rail for the Gondola ride to the Rainforest Village of Kuranda and close by "Wild World" to see a variety of Australian animals, birds and reptiles.
My home has ceiling fans throughout and bedrooms have air conditioning.
Non smoking please.
Vouchers accepted, surcharge on $75 room $5.

Tell other travellers about your favourite B&Bs

Carrigan's Bed and Breakfast

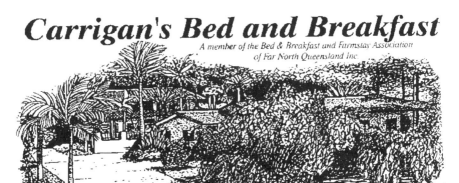

A member of the Bed & Breakfast and Farmstay Association of Far North Queensland Inc

Cairns - Earlville
B & B
Address: 9 Moowooga St., Earlville, Cairns, QLD 4870
Name: Carrigan's Bed & Breakfast
Telephone: (070) 332258 **Fax**: (070) 546203 **Mobile**: (014) 458554
Email: carrigan@tpgi.com.au
Beds: 1 Queen, 1 Double, 3 Single (3 bedrooms)
Bathroom: 2 Guests share
Tariff: B&B (full) Double $70, Single $45. Children POA. Vouchers accepted
Nearest Town: Cairns - 6km

Experience Bed & Breakfast with a difference! Set on 3/4 acre we offer you complete privacy with guest rooms totally separate from the main house but with your hosts nearby to look after your comfort, help you with your tours and extend true North Queensland hospitality.

Our guest rooms (1 Queen, 1 Twin and 1 Triple) are serviced by two guest share bathrooms. All rooms are air conditioned with private entrances which open onto a balcony overlooking the salt-water pool and surrounded by tall palm trees.

Your breakfast will be served beside the pool where you can soak up the atmosphere of the tropics amongst lush foliage and abundant birdlife.

The peace and serenity of the area in no way betrays the fact that you are only 6km south of Cairns city centre and just minutes from the largest shopping centre in town.

We are very close to Sizzler, K.F.C., McDonalds, a great fish & chip shop, several local restaurants, clubs, hotels and takeaways.

We offer a TV lounge/games room for your entertainment and in poolside area there is a fridge, microwave and 24hr tea & coffee making facilities.

For stays of 3 nights or more we offer complimentary airport, rail or bus station pick ups, by prior arrangement of course.

The attractions of the Cairns area are too numerous to mention. Surrounded by World Heritage rainforest and the beautiful tablelands on one side and the Great Barrier Reef and tropical islands on the other.

Come and visit us soon!

Cairns - Edge Hill
Homestay - B&B
Address: 48 Russell St., Edge Hill, 4870
Name: Norah and Bernie Hollis
Telephone: (07) 4032 4121 & 1800 802 566 **Fax**: (07) 4053 6557 **Mobile**: (0418) 770737
Beds: 3 Queen, 2 Single (3 bedrooms, all air conditioned)
Bathroom: 3 Ensuites
Tariff: B&B (full) Double $75-$95, Single $65. Dinner optional $20. Vouchers accepted
Nearest Town: 5km Cairns and 5km to Airport.

SIMPLY THE BEST: Come stay with Bernie & Norah in the comfort of your Queen sized, air conditioned room with private access. Just 5 minutes drive from Cairns International Airport and City Centre. Enjoy a beautiful 10 minute walk through lakes environmental parks and rain forest boardwalk to our stunning Botanical Gardens - a real plus for bird & plant enthusiasts.

Chat to Bernie about his many adventures in the rich far north, even watch his video "This Way to Cape York". Both Bernie and Norah are true locals and Norah can give you a few tips on painting as she is a local Folk Art teacher.

Plenty of tips on the many and varied day tours, with a full information board and booking service. Free pick-up from Airport or other arrival point. Enjoy the many wonderful restaurants and treats of the "Magic North". Breakfast is served by the pool, you may even want to throw a line in our creek and catch some fresh seafood.

We have full Council approval and insurance cover which will ensure your stay a happy and safe one. Come and be a part of our family, as one guest wrote "Thank you very much for welcoming us to your home as guests, we leave as friends" - Jenny Mitchell, Hampshire UK.

Let us spoil you and make your holiday one to remember.
Home Page: http://www.bnbnq.com.au/cairns bnb

Cairns - Edge Hill ✓
Homestay
Address: "Pyne Cottage", 7 Pyne Street, Edge Hill, Cairns
Name: Terry & Marilyn Foreman
Telephone: (07) 4053 7773 **Fax**: (07) 4051 2636 **Mobile**: (015) 141598
Email: pynecottage@iig.com.au
Beds: 1 Queen, 1 Double, 2 Singles (3 bedrooms) 1 detached unit
Bathroom: 2 Ensuite, 1 Private
Tariff: B&B (Special) Double $70-$75, Single $50. Vouchers accepted $5 surcharge
Nearest Town: Cairns City 5km South.

Share with us our homely lifestyle in residential greenery and within 3 minutes easy walking distance you can enjoy Cairns Botanical Gardens - restaurants - craft shop - old time dancing - tennis - Flying Doctor -public transport and our renowned Red and Blue Arrow Rainforest Mountain Tracks overlooking Cairns and the inlet, we are just five minutes from Cairns city and 3.5 kms from the airport. Reputably the best location, built in the very early 1940's by coach builder and former Mayor of Cairns, Richard Gelling, this historical dwelling languishes in the bosom of aged residential rainforest. Crafted in local timbers in an early Australian design featuring polished silver ash floors, high ceilings and wide enclosed verandahs and silky oak doors gives this home instant character together with our collection of antiques. Library, tea and coffee facilities available. Bedrooms have fans and air-conditioning.
Guests number is limited to 6 thus ensuring your privacy. A continental breakfast of croissant/toast, freshly squeezed orange juice or other, fresh tropical fruits, tea and coffee is included. We regret we don't have the room for children. No smoking inside - outside is fine. We would be happy to pick up from your arrival point by prior arrangement. Our interests are golf, gardening, local history, camping and football. Resident quiet and cuddly chihauau (Rocky)
We look forward to seeing you soon.

QUEENSLAND

Cairns - Edge Hill
Self contained accommodation
Address: 9 Bellevue Crescent, Edge Hill, Cairns, Qld 4870
Name: Lew & Dell Price
Telephone: (07) 4053 1761
Beds: 2 Single (1 bedroom)
Bathroom: 1 Ensuite
Tariff: B&B (special/tropical) Double $65, Single $35, Children $10, Dinner $15.
Vouchers accepted
Nearest Town: Cairns

Our Queensland style home is in a tropical setting overlooking Cairns and Trinity Inlet. The Cairns Botanical Gardens, Centenary Lakes and walking tracks are popular areas in this suburb - and the Visitors Centre at the Royal Flying Doctors Base is five minute walk away.
The guest unit is ensuite with a kitchenette (TV, fridge, microwave etc). It has a separate entrance and opens into a small private sitting area in the garden.
We have hosted many guests - sometimes as members of the Friendship Force and through Rotary.
Our interests include golf, bridge, arts, gardening and travel. Visitors arriving by public transport will be met. Assistance in a choice of day trips to the Barrier Reef, Daintree Rainforest and Kuranda and the Atherton Tablelands or any other attractions can be provided or personal tours arranged.
Directions: *Please phone (07) 4053 1761*

Cairns - Edmonton
Homestay
Address: Please phone or fax (answer machine available)
Name: Barbara
Telephone: (070) 554720
Fax: (070) 554720
Beds: 1 Queen, 1 Double, 4 Single (4 bedrooms)
Bathroom: 1 Guests share
Tariff: B&B (continental) Double $70, Single $45, Children half price, Campervans $20 (up to 4 people). Vouchers accepted
Nearest Town: 11km sth of cairns, 1 1/2km off Bruce Highway.

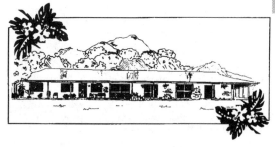

My modern ranch style home is situated against the backdrop of the Great Dividing Range, surrounded by Pummelo orchard and only 20 minutes drive sth of Cairns or 10 minutes walk to regular bus service; shops, economical bistro, fast food outlets, close by in historical Edmonton (5 minutes drive). You will enjoy relaxing by the pool soaking in the peace and quiet or unwinding on the verandahs watching cockatoos and lorikeets steal my fruit
Bedrooms are security screened with ceiling fans and large windows to catch evening breezes. Use of laundry (small fee), complimentary tea/coffee, microwave available; guest share television lounge. When not working my orchard I enjoy oil painting, golf and walking my friendly female boxer. I can organise car hire, Reef and rainforest, Sky Rail tours etc on your arrival. Looking forward to greeting you.

QUEENSLAND

Cairns - Freshwater
Homestay
Address: Please phone
Name: Anna Marie
Telephone: (0740) 55 1473
Beds: 1 Double, 2 Single (2 bedrooms)
Bathroom: 1 Family share
Tariff: B&B (continental) Double $60, Single $35.
Nearest Town: Cairns

My house is in a quiet garden suburb surrounded by trees and lots of native birds. I am close to public transport, ten kilometres from Cairns City Centre and five minutes from the airport. About one kilometre away is a pick-up centre for most of the popular tours, Kuranda - The Tablelands - The Great Barrier Reef and others. I have over the years entertained many overseas visitors and in turn have enjoyed the hospitality of others in many countries. It is great sharing experiences over a cool drink relaxing on the back deck after the days activities.
Directions: *Please phone. Pick up by arrangement.*

Cairns - Freshwater
Homestay
Address: Please phone
Name: Jock & Enid MacDonald
Telephone: (07) 4055 1198 **Fax**: (07) 4055 1198
Beds: 1 Queen, 1 Double, 2 Single (3 bedrooms)
Bathroom: 1 Ensuite, 1 Guests share
Tariff: B&B (continental) Double $65, Single $45, Children under 12 yrs half price. Dinner $15. Vouchers accepted
Nearest Town: Cairns (10 km)

We are in our 50's and have lived in remote areas of Queensland with many interesting experiences. We have a friendly Labrador-cross dog who lives outside the house.
Our B & B homestay is a modern ground level brick home set on 1 acre of tropical gardens in the foothills of the Rainforest Ranges surrounding Cairns. The house is elevated, overlooking sugar-cane fields and beautiful forested hills. We have a double bedroom with ensuite and private entrance connected to our home, and two bedrooms with guests bathroom in the house. Our swimming pool is surrounded with tropical palms and colourful shrubs for your private relaxation after visiting the tropical wonderland sights. Pick-ups for the Kuranda Train, Barrier Reef trips, and other tours 100 metres from the house. Local pubs and restaurants within walking distance. Bus transport to city 100 metres away. We look forward to sharing our relaxed north Queensland life-style with you, and ensuring you enjoy the sights of our beautiful area.

Phone numbers throughout Australia are changing to 8 digits.
For help contact Directory Assistance.

QUEENSLAND

Cairns - Freshwater
Homestay
Address: "Rafiki", 128 Petersen St, Freshwater, Cairns, 4870
Name: Bill & Agnes Beattie
Telephone: (07 4058 1146
Fax: (07) 4058 1146
Beds: 1 Double (TV), 3 Single (3 bedrooms)
Bathroom: 1 Guests share
Tariff: B&B (full) Double $65, Single $45, Dinner on request $20. Vouchers accepted
Nearest Town: Cairns

[IBBI]

Rafiki is the Swahili word for friend.
We have a beautiful, secluded, cool and quiet home surrounded by many rare and unusual palms and trees from all over the tropical world. Freshwater is a picturesque garden suburb 10km from the colourful cosmopolitan city of Cairns. Tour pick-up points, bus-stops, a pub and restaurant etc. all within easy walking distance.
Our impeccable bedrooms have ceiling fans; there is a guests refrigerator, iron and ironing board, washing machine and hair-drier etc. Breakfast and dinner are served on our "Rainforest" patio. Pick-ups arranged at your request from your arrival points in Cairns.
Whatever your interests - why not escape to "Rafiki"?!
Member of Independent Bed & Breakfast International.

Cairns - Freshwater
Homestay
Address: Please phone
Name: Gateway House
Telephone: (07) 4055 1914
Fax: (07) 4032 5291
Beds: 3 Double (2 bedrooms) Cot available
Bathroom: 1 Guests share
Tariff: B&B (continental) Double $65, Single $45, Children half price, Dinner $12. Vouchers accepted
Nearest Town: Cairns

Freshwater is a pretty suburb between canefields and the hills just ten minutes by car from the city of Cairns.
Suburban buses service the area with a bus stop at the bottom of our street. Nearby Freshwater Connection is a collection point for tours and we are happy to drive our guests there in the mornings, or they may walk. There are hotels, takeaways and restaurants in walking distance.
We are lifetime residents of the area and share our home with our dog and cat. The house has two wings with a central lounge and kitchen area. Our guests are very welcome to spend evenings with us or they may use the sitting room adjacent to their bedrooms. The large park behind the house and the tropical garden ensure that there are always numerous bird calls to start your day.
Special dietary needs can be catered for.

QUEENSLAND

Cairns - Kanimbla
Homestay
Address: "Woongaridge",
Lake Morris Road, Kanimbla (Please phone first)
Name: Mick & Sherryn Hannagan
Telephone: (070) 341784
Fax: (070) 342135
Beds: 1 Queen, 1 Double, 1 Single (2 bedrooms)
Bathroom: 1 Guests share
Tariff: B&B (full) Double $75-$85, Single $55,
Children age 5-12 $15, Dinner $20. Vouchers accepted
Nearest Town: Cairns 7km away

Set high on the hills amongst lush rainforest and overlooking the magnificent panoramic views of Cairns, Trinity Bay and surrounding mountains, you will find our uniquely beautiful home built extensively of rich grained local timbers with wide lazy verandahs and high ceilings, very welcoming and interesting. Enjoy abundant birdlife, rainforest walks, and bush setting, yet only 7km from the city scene. We offer sincere and generous hospitality in the true tradition of Bed & Breakfast with stylish luxury. Beautifully decorated guest rooms, one double and one family suite with private lounge and patio, saltwater pool, all with views of our tropical paradise an great photographic opportunities. Relax on the verandah and enjoy the scenery with freshly brewed coffee and home baked goodies or perhaps a glass of wine, and don't miss a delicious evening meal (by arrangement). One very lovable dog called "Hoots" will welcome you warmly with us.

Cairns - Kuranda
Farmstay+
Self-contained Accommodation
Address: Lot 4 Koah Rd, Kuranda,
MSI 1039 Kuranda, FNQ 4872
Name: Greg Taylor, "Koah B&B"
Telephone: (070) 937074
Fax: (070) 937074
Email: koah@ozemail.com.au
Beds: 2 Double, 2 Single (2 bedrooms)
Bathroom: 1 Ensuite, 1 Private
Tariff: B&B (continental) Cabin $85, Double $65, Single $45. Children under 15 half price. Dinner $12. Credit Cards. Vouchers accepted
Nearest Town: Cairns 35 mins

Comfortable country home on 10 acres 10 mins from the township in the Rainforest Kuranda and 30 mins from Cairns and Great Barrier Reef offering a fully self contained Cabin for family with balcony overlooking native bushland and large dam also in home accommodation of 2 double bedrooms with double opening doors onto verandah 1 guest bathroom (ensuite) fully insulated and screened with ceiling fans each bedroom can be fitted with single folding bed for children. Breakfast on home grown tropical fruits on verandah amongst native birds and wallabies, short distance from Kuranda where they have the Markets, Aboriginal Dancing, Butterfly Sanctuary, restaurants and Skyrail Cableway. Koah is renowned for its tropical fruits such as mangoes and lychees and its Barn dances where you can enjoy local hospitality. Suggested tours and hire cars arranged. Paraplegic and Quadraplegic Ass Members. **Home Page**: http:/www.ozemail.com.au/~sandsana/index.html

Cairns - Stratford
Superior Homestay RACQ ★★★☆
Address: "Lilybank", 75 Kamerunga Rd, Stratford, Cairns, 4870
Name: Mike & Pat Woolford
Telephone: (07) 4055 1123 **Fax**: (07) 4058 1990
Email: bbnetwork@internetnorth.com.au
Beds: 3 King/Queen, 2 Double, 4 Single (5 bedrooms)
Bathroom: 5 Ensuite (2 with full size bath)
Tariff: B&B (full) Double $65-$75, Single $45-$55, Children by arrangement.
Vouchers accepted
Nearest Town: Cairns - 8km from city centre.

"Lilybank" a spacious, traditional Queenslander home, featured on TV's 'Good Morning Australia' and a 1997 'Frommer's Favourite'.

For 35 years "Lilybank" was the home of the mayor of Cairns, renowned for his hospitality, which we are resuming by warmly welcoming you to our home.

Bedrooms are air-conditioned with private entrances, there is a swimming pool, off-street parking, guest's private verandahs and living room with TV, video, microwave, fridge, tea/coffee making and laundry facilities. A happy blend of privacy and hospitality.

Several excellent restaurants, hotel and takeaways are nearby, all within easy walking distance.

We've travelled widely, our children are adult and have left home and we have two friendly poodles and a talkative galah, all restricted to hosts' area.

Breakfast is served in our 'Garden Room' and includes home-grown tropical fruit, continental and/or your choice of cooked breakfast.

"Lilybank" is handy to tour 'pick-up' points and public bus. We provide a knowledgeable tour booking service to ensure you make the most from your holiday.

Home Page: http://www.ozemail.com.au/~gdaymate/qldacc2.htm

Tell other travellers about your favourite B&Bs

QUEENSLAND

Cairns - Trinity Beach
Homestay   RACQ ★★★☆
Address: 29 Moore St, Trinity Beach, 4879 QLD
Name: 'Beach House'
Telephone: (07) 4055 6304. From o'seas: 61-7-4055 6304 **Fax**: (07) 4055 6304
Beds: 1 Queen, 1 Twin (2 Bedrooms)
Bathroom: 1 Guests share
Tariff: B&B (special) Double $70, Single $45, Children over 5yrs -14yrs $15. Vouchers accepted
Nearest Town: Cairns 17 mins

Come stay with us a while in our tropical bungalow in Trinity Beach, situated on a hill overlooking the beach and ocean. Trinity Beach is located in the heart of all North Queensland's attractions which include the Reef and Daintree Rainforest, Kuranda, Skyrail, Aboriginal Cultural centre, Wildlife Parks and on the way to Port Douglas. Cairns City is a 20 minute bus ride away. We are only a stroll away from numerous restaurants and a hotel. The air conditioned guest rooms have pleasant outlooks and individual entrances. The guest share bathroom is shared by a maximum of four people. Breakfasts include Gina's special Jungle Juice, papayas, mangoes, lychee fruit (in season) and full cooked meals. Guests will be picked up by prior arrangement. We are true locals and can assist you with your sightseeing plans.

The standard of accommodation in
The Australian Bed and Breakfast Book ranges from homely to luxurious,
but you can always be sure of superior hospitality.

QUEENSLAND

Cairns - Trinity Beach
B&B + Self-contained Accom.
Address: "Absolute Beach Frontage", 6-10 Peacock Street, Trinity Beach, QLD 4879
Name: Kay & John Lane
Telephone: (07) 4055 6664 **Fax**: (07) 4055 6664 **Mobile**: (015) 230197
Beds: 1 King/Queen, 2 Double, 2 Single (4 bedrooms)
Bathroom: 1 Ensuite, 1 Private, 1 Guests share, 1 Family share
Tariff: B&B (tropical) Double $75-$85, Single $48. Dinner optional extra. Self contained apartment - price on application.
 Vouchers accepted $5 surcharge
Nearest Town: Cairns (15km north of city)

Kay, John and son Tim welcome you to their clean, spacious tropical absolute beach frontage home, with the warm blue ocean waters outside the front fence and rainforest canopy at the rear of the property. The privacy and peaceful environment in which the house is situated is truly paradise. Swim in the large magnificent salt water pool or walk a few steps through the front gate onto the golden sands and paddle in the warm, but refreshing ocean waters, or simply take a relaxing stroll on the beach and around the nearby scenic headland.

Local attractions, include several restaurants, sidewalk cafes, sailing, golf, bowls, windsurfing, scenic walks, aeroplane flights, parachuting and shopping at the village centre or at the major shopping complex some five minutes drive or by public transport. Excellent bus services into Cairns and pick-up points for daily coach tours is a short two minute level walk from our house. Son Tim, a recognised top windsurfer also sails catamarans and is willing to provide tuition on all watersport activities.

After a restful night sleep in harmony with the gentle sounds of cooling sea breezes and ocean lapping the foreshore, rise to a new day with a generous tropical style breakfast served either by the pool, on the elevated verandah, in the courtyard, or in a personal shady setting on the warm beach sands overlooking the early morning sparkling waters of the Pacific Ocean.

Tea and coffee making facilities always available and cookie jar full of Kay's favourite delicious homemade biscuits is a treat that all guests enjoy.

All rooms are air-conditioned and look onto the beach. Baskets of fruit and fresh flowers on your arrival help to make you feel at home.

The luxury self-contained air-conditioned unit, with a private entrance, overlooks the landscaped swimming pool and includes queen and twin rooms, modern kitchen, bathroom, laundry, private living room, and bar area. Television and video facilities included. Can accommodate up to five with reduced rates for three or more people.

Complimentary pick-up from the Cairns International and Domestic Airports. Advice, as required on tours, rent-a-cars, shopping and other great places to visit during your stay.

With total respect for your privacy, Kay and John are available and will do everything possible to make your stay an enjoyable and memorable experience.

Sound too good to be true - you be the judge, we know you will not be disappointed.

QUEENSLAND

Cairns - Whitfield
Homestay
Address: Please phone
Name: "Benbullen", Stan & Fay
Telephone: (070) 535 428
Fax: (070) 551 383
Mobile: 018 183 787
Beds: 2 Queen, 1 Double,
1 Single (3 bedrooms)
Bathroom: Guest share
Tariff: B&B (tropical) Queen $70, Double $65, Single $50. Vouchers accepted
Nearest Town: Cairns

We invite you to come and enjoy the hospitality of our lovely home "Benbullen" meaning our high quiet place.
Situated in the scenic hills of Cairns, surrounded by tropical gardens and lush rainforest slopes.
Awake in the morning to the sounds of parrots, kookaburras and native birds from your comfortable bed.
Come downstairs to a delightful breakfast by the sparkling pool and maybe enjoy a cool swim before embarking on your busy day of sightseeing or take a walk to the nearby Botanical Gardens or Lakes.
After a hectic day visiting our many attractions: Barrier Reef, Daintree Rainforest, Kuranda, join us for a cool beer on the verandah overlooking the lights of Cairns.
For those wishing to see Cairns' many sights and attractions, public transport is only 2 minutes walk with city and airport only 5 minutes by transport. Hire car and tour bookings available, also pick up from arrival points by prior arrangement.
Hoping to welcome you soon.

Cairns - Yorkeys Knob - Half Moon Bay
Homestay/Self contained accom.
Address: Buckley Street,
Yorkeys Knob
Name: Peter & Maggie
Telephone: (07) 4055 7224
Beds: 1 King, 2 Singles (2 bedroom)
Bathroom: 1 Private, 1 Guests share
Tariff: B&B (continental) Double $60 Single $45.
2 bedroom self contained flat $75 for two plus $15 per extra person. Vouchers accepted
Nearest Town: Cairns 17km

The house reflects a blend of Mediterranean and tropical architecture. Each room has ceiling fan, plenty of cupboard space and looks onto lush garden, large salt water pool and BBQ. You can relax by the pool or under large shade trees.
The house is situated 200 metres from Half Moon Bay with its beautiful sheltered white sandy beach; and miles of Coral Sea coast.
The Half Moon Bay licensed Boat Club (temporary membership available) has boat ramp, restaurant, all club facilities at reasonable prices. Golf, sailing, diving, fishing, reef, rainforest and tableland trips pick up near door. Excellent restaurants and cafe closeby.
We can lend you fishing gear and bicycles. Buses to Cairns or Port Douglas stop nearby. Permanent residents include two friendly dogs and a cat, restricted to owners studio area.
Pool area unsuitable for small children.

Cairns - Yorkey's Knob
Homestay+
Self-contained Accommodation
Address: 36 Janett St,
Yorkey's Knob, Cairns, Queensland 4878
Name: "Villa Gail"
Telephone: (070) 558178
Fax: (070) 558178 **Mobile**: (015) 161706
Beds: 2 Double, 3 Single (4 bedrooms)
Bathroom: Ensuite
Tariff: B&B (continental) Double $75, Single $55, Children half price.

Rooms fully self contained and air conditioned - "Villa Gail" on Millionaires Row was originally designed by my wife and I over 15 years ago to make the most of our unique elevated location at Yorkey's Knob. A cool Mediterranean-style, the house is set within lush tropical gardens overlooking the beach with magnificent views across the Coral Sea. From the delightful in-ground swimming pool spacious guest's verandah or your own large room, you can really relax and enjoy our tropical lifestyle. Your accommodation is fully self-contained with ensuite, fridge, TV, coffee-making facilities etc. A continental breakfast is provided. Villa Gail is only 15 minutes from Cairns - a colourful city with variety of shops, restaurants and entertainment. Closer to home is the picturesque Half Moon Bay Golf Course, Yacht Marina and Clubhouse, restaurants, village shops etc. Tours to the World Heritage Wet Tropics Rainforest, the Outback and the Great Barrier Reef all pick up from our door.

Capricorn Coast - Emu Park
Self-contained B&B
Address: "Sandcastles", 2 Sandy Lane, Zilzie, 4702
Name: Tony & Trish Francis
Telephone: (07) 4938 8232 **Fax**: (07) 4938 8313
Beds: 1 Queen, 2 Single (2 bedrooms)
Bathroom: 1 Private
Tariff: B&B (tropical) Double $60, Single $50, Children $15, Dinner $15 (by arrangement), Credit Cards (BC/MC/VISA).
 Vouchers accepted
Nearest Town: Emu Park 2km

Sandcastles is a modern home plus two bedroom self-contained unit situated 20 metres from the sands of Zilzie Beach on the beautiful Capricorn Coast, just 10 minutes to Rosslyn Harbour for the ferry to Great Keppel Island and boat trips to the Barrier Reef, 15 mins further to the night life of Yeppoon and then on to the tranquil rainforests of Byfield.
Guests enjoy wandering through our award winning tropical gardens, swimming in either the ocean or pool, long beach walks, fishing, kite flying, bicycling, boating or just relaxing!
Your tropical breakfast can be served poolside, in your room, or on your private verandah. Dinner can be provided or guests may prepare their own, or make use of the BBQ in the poolside cabana. Restaurants and shops are at nearby Emu Park, at Rosslyn Bay and Yeppoon.
We welcome guests for B&B or accommodation only.
Smoking outdoors only.

QUEENSLAND

Capricorn Coast - Emu Park
Self-contained Accommodation
Address: 24 Archer Street,
Emu Park, QLD 4702
Name: "Zebulon"
Telephone: (07) 4939 7184
Fax: (07) 49397 184
Beds: 2 Double, 2 Single (3 bedrooms)
Bathroom: 1 Ensuite, 1 Private
Tariff: From $300 per week for the house or $60 to $110 per night for the house.
Nearest Town: Yeppoon (19 km) and Rockhampton (44 km)

"Zebulon" is a restored 100 year old Queensland cottage nestled in its own beautiful tropical garden. It is a peaceful and secluded haven, with sea views from the large front verandah up in the tree tops. The house is traditionally furnished and fully equipped, including automatic washing machine, TV, video and CD stereo.
"Zebulon" is just a stone's throw from the beautiful beaches, shops and other amenities of this small friendly town. Monthly markets are a popular attraction and there is a good golf course.
The Capricorn Coast has an idyllic tropical climate with moderate summers and warm sunny winters. It offers much to do and see - from Great Keppel Island to the National Parks of Byfield. From good tourist attractions to walking, fishing and swimming. It's all here in this beautiful location in the nicest of ways.
Brochure and visitors guide available.
Great Keppel Island is approx 30 minutes by ferry.
Pse see the back of the listing form for their logo.

Capricorn Coast - Yeppoon
Bed & Breakfast
Address: 44 Todd Avenue, Yeppoon, 4703 QLD
Postal: PO Box 614, Yeppoon, 4703 QLD
Name: Rob & Angela Blatch
Telephone: (07) 4939 5719 **Fax**: (07) 4939 5577
Beds: 3 Queen, 2 Single (4 bedrooms)
Bathroom: 4 Ensuite
Tariff: B&B (continental) Double $75, Single $55.
Credit Cards.
   Vouchers accepted
Nearest Town: Yeppoon

Come and enjoy a night or more with us in our stylish beachside home. Tastefully decorated guest rooms, with much loved and interesting artwork throughout. Rooms are air-conditioned for your comfort. While Away has a guest lounge and separate TV room. Opposite our home is a great beach for walking, cycling, or fishing. Breakfast is tropical buffet style. Indulge in breads, cereals, fresh juices (Yeppoon is a major pineapple growing area), fruit salad, yoghurt, home baked muffins. Espresso coffee and quality teas provide a great start to your day. Yeppoon is 38km NE of Rockhampton. We can advise on many attractions incl. Keppel Islands, Great Barrier Reef and much more. We have travelled extensively and will make sure your stay with us is a memorable one. Our home is smoke free and not suitable for children.
To avoid disappointment please phone in advance.

QUEENSLAND

Cleveland
Homestay
Address: "Bay View", 96 Smith Street, Cleveland, QLD 4163
Name: Lothar & Ingrid Schaper
Telephone: (07) 3821 2475
Fax: (07) 3821 2475 **Mobile**: (0149) 678552
Beds: 1 Queen, 2 Single (2 bedrooms)
Bathroom: 1 Guests share
Tariff: B&B (full) Double $70, Single $35.
 Vouchers accepted
Nearest Town: Cleveland

Bay View house is situated on a hill in the township of Cleveland on beautiful Moreton Bay. Moreton Bay can offer something new every day of the year. Our house has a cosy atmosphere with a great balcony upstairs overlooking Moreton Bay, views to Moreton and Stradbroke Islands. Our pool invites you for a swim after a day of sightseeing. Tennis courts and sporting facilities are just around the corner. The township of Cleveland has lots to offer with beaches, Sunday Markets, ferries and water taxis to visit the islands, train and busses to Brisbane which is just 30km away. From the charming Harbour of Cleveland you can visit Moreton Bay, go Whale Watching in Aug, Sep, Oct or just sit in one of the coffees shops or hotels overlooking the water and enjoy the relaxed atmosphere. We are happy to pick you up from your arrival point and can help you in planning your days. Please phone for advance bookings, write or fax.

Clifton see Darling Downs

Condamine
Farmstay - Homestead
Address: Nelgai, Condamine, Queensland 4416
Name: David & Priscilla Mundell
Telephone: (07) 4627 7124
Fax: (07) 4627 7124
Beds: 6 Single (4 bedrooms)
Bathroom: 1 Ensuite, 1 Guests share
Tariff: B&B (full) With ensuite: $40pp, Guest share bathroom: $35pp, Children half price, Dinner $25. Full board with ensuite $110pp, Guest share bathroom $100pp. Campervans $20. Vouchers accepted
Nearest Town: Condamine 16km, Miles 47km

The Mundell family have been in the Condamine District for over a hundred years. Nelgai is a 4000 acre short-horn cattle and grain growing property with abundant wildlife on the Condamine River. Birdlife on the Arubial Lagoon often rivals that of anywhere in Australia.
Welcome to our comfortable "Georgian colonial style" homestead. Twin room with ensuite, twin and 2 single rooms with guest shared bathroom. Open fire in drawing room and woodstove in TV/kitchen. Plenty of country cooking using local and home grown produce. Sit on the verandah sipping a cool drink, watching the setting sun, wildlife coming to house dam and night skies. Those staying longer on full board tariff options are helping with daily and seasonal farm activities, bushwalking, fishing, seeking native flora and fauna, picnicking and boiling tea in the "fastest quart pot in the west". We look forward to meeting you.

QUEENSLAND

Darling Downs - Clifton
Farmstay   RACQ ★★★★
Address: 'Robsley', M.S.
29 Hogarth Road, Clifton, Queensland 4361
Name: Rob & Gillian Hogarth
Telephone: (076) 959139 **Fax**: (076) 959138
Mobile: (015) 656 082
Beds: 1 Double, 2 Twin (3 bedrooms)
Bathroom: 2 Guests share (Private if required)
Tariff: B&B (full) Double $75, Single $45, Children half price. Dinner $25. Full board: $120 per person per day. Vouchers accepted
Nearest Town: Toowoomba 57km - local towns Pittsworth, Clifton 30km

Robsley is part of the Hogarth's original land holding on the Darling Downs in southeast Queensland, taken up in 1867. Now owned by Rob & Gillian, Robsley consists of 2200 acres of attractive river country on which we run cattle and crop. Our house is large and comfortable, set in extensive gardens with a pool and tennis court. We have 3 bedrooms, 2 bathrooms for our guests, and like to offer our visitors a big welcome and taste of outback Australia. Only 2 1/2 hours drive from Brisbane, we are easily accessible for even the busiest scheduled traveller.
For those who wish to sample the Robsley hospitality for a day or a week, we have bed & breakfast or full board rates.
Our days are full of farm experiences, delicious food and happy company. One can be as relaxed or energetic as one wishes - the farm offers lots of activity, and the squatters chair on the verandah also beckons!
Some of our options: bushwalking, birdwatching, bush picnics, horseriding (experienced riders), golf, tennis, swimming, fishing. Native animals abound.
We are a member of the Queensland Host Farm Association.

Darling Downs - Killarney
Homestay+Farmstay
Address: "Oaklea" The Head via Killarney, 4373
Name: Rosemary & Neil Peterson
Telephone: (07) 4664 7161
Beds: 1 Double, 2 Single (2 Bedrooms)
Bathroom: 1 Guests share, 1 Family share
Tariff: B&B (full) Double $70, Single $45, Children under 15 half price, Dinner $15. AFBB Vouchers accepted
Nearest Town: Killarney 25km west, Boonah 52km east

Nestled in a picturesque valley at the Head of the Condamine River, "Oaklea" is surrounded by the mountains and National Parks of south-east Queensland's scenic rim. Birdlife and other native life abound. The air is clean and clear, and due to the high altitude the night sky is particularly beautiful. The atmosphere, needless to say, is peaceful and relaxing.
Enjoy mountain and rainforest walks, birdwatching, day trips to Queen Mary's Falls, Browns Falls, Moogerah Dam, or Warwick's historic attractions. Relax in the quiet peacefulness of our garden. "Oaklea" is part of a property which has been home to Peterson families for over 90 years. Originally dairying country it now produces beef cattle. Rosemary and Neil have lived and worked in both the city and country. We are two hours from Brisbane and the Gold Coast, and one hour from Warwick. We look forward to welcoming you.

Gift Vouchers

Our B&B vouchers are for a double room for one night's B&B. They cost $89, and if you order one as a gift, we will include a free *Australian Bed & Breakfast Book* worth $16.95.

Send your cheque to
Moonshine Press
59 Quirk Street
Dee Why
NSW 2099

Emu Park see Capricorn Coast
Eumundi see Sunshine Coast

Gold Coast - Burleigh Waters
Homestay+Self-contained Accommodation
Address: Please phone
Name: Captain Eric Wilson and Edith
Telephone: (07) 5576 0911
Beds: 1 Queen, 1 Sofa, 1 Divan (1 bedroom)
Bathroom: 1 Ensuite
Tariff: B&B (full) Double $70, Single $35, Dinner $10. Vouchers accepted
Nearest Town: Burleigh Heads 1km

Your holiday home is a large two-storey, modern, comfortable, brick residence, located in a quiet suburban street. Off-street parking available.
Midway between Coolangatta Airport and Surfers Paradise, it is walking distance to the beach and the Burleigh Heads National Park. You are only 15 min. drive from Jupiters Casino, Pacific Fair and Oasis Shopping Centres.
Your private & spacious quarters has a Queen size bed, a sofa bed, its own entrance, a single divan, a TV, bathroom ensuite and kitchenette leading out to a shaded courtyard by the solar heated swimming pool.
Make your own meals or enjoy breakfast served by the captain and his partner, Edith, who will help you plan your stay if you wish. Feel welcome and enjoy a good night's sleep at a smoke-free homestay. Free airport transport available.

QUEENSLAND

Gold Coast - Palm Beach
Self-contained B&B
Address: 1320 Gold Coast Highway, Palm Beach, QLD 4221
Name: Fatima and Mike Cizmic
Telephone: (07) 5535 3403 **Fax**: (07) 5535 3403 **Mobile**: (018) 177 722
Beds: 1 Queen (1 bedroom)
Bathroom: 1 Private
Tariff: B&B (continental), Double $30 - 2 nights minimum stay. Or $180 per week.

Located in the centre of Palm Beach only 10kms from Surfers Paradise, self contained ground floor flat.
Ocean views 50m from (patrolled) beaches for fishing or swimming and only a short walk to shops and public transport.
Private bathroom, queen size bed, light cooking facilities, laundry, TV and video, off street parking.
2 nights minimum stay $30 per night.
No smoking in the house.
Phone for directions and bookings.
Continental breakfast served.

Gold Coast - Parkwood
Homestay
Address: 13 Mansfield Court, Parkwood, 4214
Name: Aarundale Rest
Telephone: (07) 5571 6161
Fax: (07) 5571 6612
Beds: 2 Queen, 2 Single (3 bedrooms)
Bathroom: 1 Ensuite, 1 Guests share
Tariff: B&B (full) Double $75, Single $45, Dinner $20. No children.
Credit Cards: Mastercard, Bankard, Visa. Vouchers accepted
Nearest Town: City - Gold Coast

Aarundale Rest is an Elizabethan style home, set high on a hill in a quiet court, with views of the nearby Hinterland. Three attractive Guest Rooms are situated upstairs together with large lounge where guests may relax and enjoy tea / coffee, reading and television.
Breakfast is served downstairs in our dining room, where we enjoy sharing warm hospitality and enlightening guests on the many tourist facilities of the Gold Coast. Six minutes drive to the Broadwater, central to Movieworld, Seaworld, Dreamworld, Golf Courses, Bowling Greens and Australia Fair Shopping. Approximately 40 minutes drive to beautiful Mt Tambourine National Park. Travel by train from nearby Helensvale Station to Brisbane City.
Many weekend craft markets are available along the coast, and beaches cater for all ages with calm Broadwater or beautiful stretches of sand and surf.
Relax in the outdoor spa heated for year-round use. BBQ facilities are available.
Don't forget to book for the Indy.
Non smokers preferred - outdoor areas available.
Home Page: arunrest@ozemail.com.au

QUEENSLAND

Gold Coast Hinterland - Tamborine Mountain
Mountain Retreat - Homestay   RACQ ★★★★★
Address: 19-23 Witherby Crescent, Eagle Heights, Tamborine Mountain, 4271
Name: Carolyn & Michael
Telephone: (07) 5545 3595 **Fax**: (07) 5545 3322
Beds: Queen/King, Double/Twin, Single (4 bedrooms)
Bathroom: 4 Ensuite
Tariff: B&B (full) Double $110 - $157, Single $90 - $137. Extra single bed $60, Dinner BYO. Credit Cards. Vouchers accepted $40 surcharge. Vouchers not accepted Friday, Saturday and all Public Holidatys
Nearest Town: Nerang - proceed 14km north along Pacific Highway. Just past Movie World turn off to Tamborine Mountain.

Tamborine Mountain Bed and Breakfast
Relax and enjoy the uniqueness of our Bed and Breakfast while enjoying the peace and tranquillity of the Gold Coast hinterland and its rain forests.
At 485 meters (1600 ft) Tamborine Mountain Bed and Breakfast offers spectacular coastal views from Moreton to the Tweed.
By day, explore any of the nine national parks which meander around the mountain - two of which are within easy walking distance of Tamborine Mountain Bed and Breakfast. Visit country markets, browse through craft and antique shops, galleries and garden centres, watch colourful hang gliders or try the many eating places. Then, when the sun sets, marvel at the horizon sparkling with the night lights of the Gold Coast as you unwind by our cosy fire.
Connected by covered walkway, the detached reverse cycle air conditioned bedrooms (either double or twin share) have their own ensuite - with fresh, soft rain water!
Enjoy a healthy breakfast of toasted home-made bread, jams and other treats as you soak up the sun in our conservatory eating area or on the deck with its backdrop of ever-changing views.
Warning: You may have to share your breakfast with our natural wildlife!
Regrettably we do not have facilities for children under 11 years.

HomePage:www.pecan.com.au/ouraustralia/ogc/sites/tamborine_mountain_bed_&_breakfast.5199

QUEENSLAND

Gold Coast Hinterland - Nerang
Self contained Accommodation
Address: Villa Cornici
Nerang 4211, QLD
Name: Villa Cornici
Telephone: (02) 9328 6398/(07) 5596 0185
Mobile: 018-753 463
Email: cornici@ozemail.com.au
Beds: 1 Double, 1 Twin **Bathroom**: 1 Ensuite, 1 Private
Tariff: B&B (continental) $75 per person (adults only). Credit Cards accepted.
Nearest Town: Nerang 3 kms. Brisbane International airport 50 mins. Coolangatta Airport 35 mins. Gold Coast beaches easy acessy be car. Dream World and Movie World close by.

CORNICI

Villa Cornici is a fully self contained Mediterranean residence luxuriously appointed and decorated in the finest of taste featuring antiques and artwork. It has two double bedrooms each with its own bathroom, and is equipped with a designer kitchen with terrazzo bench tops, separate laundry facilities and fully furnished living areas and cable TV. From the terrace there are magnificent views to the hinterland and beyond. A lock up garage is available.
A tropical paradise in your very own sanctuary in the heart of the Gold Coast sub tropical climate with cool Summer breezes and warm Winter days.
A place to renew your spiritual values and unwind after the city pressures of business and stress. A basket of fresh tropical fruit awaits you for your healthy retreat, you will return home feeling refreshed and invigorated.
Nerang is located at the foothills of the hinterland and only 10 minutes by car to the Marina Mirage complex and famous Main Beach restaurants and side walk cafes. A chauffeur driven car can be arranged on request. . Non smokers only.

Gold Coast Hinterlands - Mt Tamborine
Bed and Breakfast/Self Contained
Address: "Woodleigh", 13 Munro Court,
(off Lahey Lookout Road), Mt Tamborine, QLD 4272
Name: Cynthia & Ian Portas
Telephone: (07) 5545 3121 **Fax**: (07) 5539 0886 **Mobile**: 0418 722016
Beds: 1 Queen, 2 Double
Bathroom: Each bedroom has own ensuite.
Tariff: B&B (full), Double $90, Single $65. 3 nights $240, Weekly $450. Long weekend $150 (Fri-Sat) or (Sat-Sun). Extra person $25 per night. Free laundry facilities, Credit cards accepted. Vouchers accepted $10 surcharge overnight or 2 nights minimum
Nearest Town: Canungra 7 km. Gold Coast 38 km.

Poised atop Mt Tamborine and set on 10 acres of lawn with 180 degree panoramic views of the Gold Coast, Canungra and Mt Warning, this new federation style homestead has its own swimming pool, outside wood BBQ and undercover gas BBQ available for guest use. Each unit has colour T.V., 24 hour movie channel / CNN News, microwave, refrigerator, tea and coffee facilities, lounge, dining table and ensuite. Breakfast is self catered from provisions provided which includes fruit, cereal, toast, bacon, eggs, etc.
Wake up at your leisure to the call of kookaburras and lorikeets. Listen for the call of a frog mouthed owl. Perhaps you will see a kangaroo hop by. You might like to feed Tory, the horse, who thinks he is Mr Ed. We would suggest you stay 2 or 3 days and use "Woodleigh" as a base. A 35 minute drive to Surfers Paradise, 50 minutes to Brisbane and entrance to Lamington National Park with all its scenic beauty, trail walks etc. The mountain also has many craft shops, quaint tea houses and the like. Comments from our Guest Book: "So peaceful so comfortable". "Next best thing to home". "Wonderful hospitality". "Absolutely beautiful". "What a pleasant surprise". "Peace personified". "The nicest place we've stayed".

Gympie
Farmstay
Address: 835 Tin Can Bay Rd, Gympie, QLD 4570
Name: Tip & Hazell Perry
Telephone: (07) 5483 3879
Beds: 1 Queen, 2 Single (2 bedrooms)
Bathroom: 1 Private
Tariff: B&B (full) Double $75, Single $40. Dinner $15-25. Campervans facilities available (1). Accommodation with all meals on request. Vouchers accepted
Nearest Town: Gympie 12km, Brisbane 170km south

Our home is on a forty-acre undulating property, with a creek and picturesque dams, 12km out of Gympie, on the main Rainbow Beach Road. Guest accommodation is separate, with its own sitting-room, bathroom and kitchenette. The bed is a romantic four-poster. There is an open fireplace and a piano in the sitting-room.
We offer a peaceful, quiet, relaxing, rural environment with charming walks and abundant bird life. Our fare includes organically home-grown vegetables, fruit, herbs, and home-made preserves. We love cooking; superb meals our speciality!
We run horses and cattle on the property, and raise our own pigs and poultry. There is swimming, surfing and fishing at Rainbow Beach; the ferry to Fraser Island is 70 minutes drive away. We can organise surf fishing trips with tackle etc. if required.

Hampton see Toowoomba (country)

Ask your hosts for tourist information.
They are your own personal travel agent and guide.

Hervey Bay
Bed & Breakfast & Self-contained Cottage   RACQ ★★★☆
Address: The Bay Bed & Breakfast, 180 Cypress Street, Urangen, Hervey Bay, QLD 4655
Name: Wolf Hennes
Telephone: (07) 4125 6919
Beds: 3 Queen, 2 Double, 5 Single, (8 bedrooms)
Bathroom: 1 Ensuite, 2 Guests share, 1 Family share
Tariff: B&B (full), De Luxe Room Double $80 (2 people only), Standard Room Double $60, Single $35. Special rates for longer stays. The Cottage: Sleeps 6-8, self-contained, without breakfast $20 per person per night, with breakfast $30 per person per night, (minimum 4 persons per night). Credit cards accepted.
Nearest Town: Hervey Bay 300 km north of Brisbane

Bay Bed & Breakfast is set in beautifully tropical gardens and offers single, double or family accommodation. With its own swimming pool it is central to both the beach and shops. Watersports, golf, tennis and many other attractions are easily accessible. Bookings for tours to nearby Fraser Island and whale watching can be arranged. The whale watching season goes from August to October.
Main house accommodation is on a B&B basis only with a delicious variety of home-cooked breakfasts available. The cottage can be used for family or other groups without breakfast. Special rates apply for longer stays. For example: Cottage $400 weekly for up to six people.
Free pick-up and transfers to Hervey Bay Airport, Bus Terminal and Hervey Bay Ferry.
Home Page: http://www.austr-ian-alien-contacts.com.au/bab/bay

Hervey Bay - River Heads
Bed & Breakfast   HBCC
Address: 709 River Heads Rd,
River Heads, 4655
Name: River Heads Bed & Breakfast
Telephone: (07) 4125 7247
Mobile: 041 7733 567
Beds: 1 Queen, 1 Double, 2 Single (3 bedrooms)
Bathroom: 1 Ensuite, 1 Guests share
Tariff: B&B (full) Ensuite $70, Share Double $65, Single $50, second night bookings less $5 Vouchers accepted
Nearest Town: Hervey Bay - 10 minuets drive

Situated on 2 1/2 acres with Million Dollar views, overlooking the Mary & Susan Rivers, where yachts are anchored. Our home is tastefully furnished for your comfort. You may like to enjoy your hearty breakfast on the verandah and watch tame kookaburras, magpies and various other birds that visit us morning and late afternoons (4pm). Hopefully see kangaroos drinking at the water hole, while you experience our magnificent sunsets. (Photographers delight!)
We are only a three minute drive to Barge, taking you to World Heritage listed Fraser Island, 4WD hire can be arranged.
Day bus tours pick up at door. Experience unforgettable Whale Watching - August - October at Hervey Bay.
Maybe just relax fishing at River Heads, or swim at sandy beaches in Hervey Bay. On Sundays you may pick up a bargain at the markets: Smoking on verandah.

Hervey Bay - Urangan
Bed & Breakfast
Address: 50 King Street,
Hervey Bay - Urangan, QLD 4655
Name: Hervey Bay "Oceanic Palms"
Telephone: (07) 4128 9562
Free call number 1800-358 442
Fax: (07) 4128 9562
Email: beach@austr-ian-alien-contacts.com.au
Beds: 2 Double, 4 Single (2 bedrooms)
Bathroom: 1 Ensuite, 1 Private
Tariff: B&B (continental) Double $65-$75, Single $55-$65, Children N/A, Credit Cards. Vouchers accepted
Nearest Town: Hervey Bay - 300km north of Brisbane

Superb position and accommodation. 2-min walk to sandy beach with pelicans, Urangan Pier (great fishing spot). Walk to shops, takeaways, restaurants, great seafood, many tourist attractions, pubs, pokies, great entertainment for all ages. Golf, tennis, bowling, all sports and watersports. We can advise and book all your Fraser Island tours, Great Barrier Reef, Whale Watching (Aug-Oct), Eco-tours, 4WD-hire, local / reef / deep sea fishing tours, diving lessons / tours. Relax in solar heated pool and spa in beautiful lush tropical gardens with mango, banana, citrus fruit trees, watch parrots, birds, flying foxes. Lovely outdoor setting, BBQ, large guest lounge (TV, VCR, fridge, tea / coffee) decorated with unique artefacts from Asmat / Kurawei from Irian Jaya. Eva & Walter (former crocodile hunter & explorer) welcome you for an interesting and memorable stay. Free pick up from airport, bus terminal, ferry. Sorry, no children. Non-smokers only. English, German and Indonesian spoken.
Home Page: http://www.austr-ian-alien-contacts.com.au/bab/beach

QUEENSLAND

Ingham
Homestay
Address: "Como Estate",
Como Road, Ingham, QLD 4850
Name: D & J Ganza
Telephone: (077) 772165
Fax: (077) 772335
Beds: 1 Queen, 2 Double,
1 Single (4 bedrooms)
Bathroom: 1 Guest share, 1 Family share
Tariff: B&B (full) Double $60, Single $35, Children half price. Dinner by arrangement. Campervans $20. Vouchers accepted
Nearest Town: Ingham. Townsville: 110km south.

Our home is situated on a sugarcane farm in the centre of the rich sugarcane growing area of the Herbert River District centred on Ingham.
Our area is noted for its excellent fishing, camping and sporting facilities in cluding two bowling clubs and an excellent golf course.
Should you wish to stay a few days to explore the attractions of our area a daily rate would be negotiable.
You may have family dinner with us or, if you prefer, only bed and break fast
Directions: *Please phone.*

Ipswich
Homestay
Address: "Villiers" Bed & Breakfast,
14 Cardew Street
East Ipswich, Queensland 4305
Name: Joyce Ramsay
Telephone: (07) 3281 7364
Mobile: (0412) 038 054
Beds: 1 Double, 2 Single (2 bedrooms)
Bathroom: 1 Guest Share
Tariff: B&B (full) Double $55-$60, single $30-$35, Children half price (under 2: free)
Nearest Town: Ipswich 2kms West

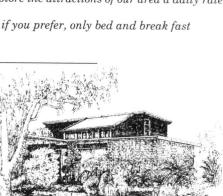

Quiet, charming homestay, cooked "Aussie" breakfast, guest bathroom, guest lounge with TV and tea & coffee making, or join your hosts for talk and TV after a pleasant day sightseeing and exploring. Two minute walk to electric rail, one stop from Ipswich CBD or train to Brisbane. Short walk to restaurants, club, antiques, park and river. Ipswich offers unique streetscapes, heritage buildings and trails, steam train rides, friendly relaxed atmosphere. Country beauty spots abound and our central location makes day tripping a breeze.
Things to do: hot air ballooning, weekend beginners and experienced horse trail rides through Australian bush, or see Australia's unique fauna (EMU's, Wallabies, Koalas). Gold and Sunshine coasts, Darling Downs and Moreton Bay Islands accessible by car or rail.
Brisbane Airport to my door by pre-booking the Ipswich Airport Express Bus. Top floor of house, quality linen, use washer/dryer.

Kilarney see Darling Downs

QUEENSLAND

Kingaroy - South-East Queensland
Farmstay
Address: MS 514, Kingaroy, QLD 4610
Name: Moira & Peter Curtain
Telephone: (07) 4164 4262 **Fax**: (07) 4164 4121
Beds: 4 Single (or 2 Single, 1 double on request)
(2 bedrooms)
Bathroom: 1 Guests share
Tariff: B&B Full accommodation with full board
Double $200, Single $100, Children $50. Horse Riding included. **OLD BOYNESIDE**
Nearest Town: 42 km south-west of Kingaroy on Bunya Highway. Homespun Holidays

Old Boyneside is a working property in one of the richest agricultural areas of Australia. It combines the breeding of cattle and horses with the cultivation of crops such as peanuts, beans and grain. The 2500 hectares include a wide range of terrain, soil type and vegetation, from black soil flats and undulating red volcanic loam to steep, forested mountain ranges where several kilometres of boundary are shared with the spectacular Bunya Mountains National Park. The countryside is ideally suited to a variety of pursuits, including bushwalking, bird-watching and Old Boyneside's specialist activity - horse riding.
The homestead is constructed of - and lined with - Australian hardwood, has a large open fire and a spacious guest wing comprising two bedrooms, private lounge, bathroom and sunroom.
Around the homestead, guests are welcome to savour the peace and quiet and to become acquainted with the resident birds and animals.

Kingaroy District
Farmstay+Self-contained Cottage
Address: Goodger Rd.
2.5km east of Kumbia
Name: Doug & Aileen Findlay
Telephone: (07) 4164 5507
Fax: (07) 4164 5507
Beds: 1 Double, 3 Single (2 bedrooms)
Bathroom: 1 Private
Tariff: $60 daily for cottage for family.
Meals extra if requested. Dinner $15.
Vouchers accepted
Nearest Town: Kumbia

"Surrey Park" is an attractive little cottage on a 1000 acre family property. We grow peanuts, sorghum, maize, soya beans and other crops. We have cattle and pigs so guests can participate in farm activities - milk a cow, feed the pigs, drive a tractor and there's horse riding too with billy tea and damper in the bush. The beautiful Bunya Mountains are only a 30 minutes drive away. Here you can feed the parrots, see other birds and animals and enjoy the many scenic walks through the rainforest.
Peace and beauty surrounds "Surrey Park". If you wish you can be independent and provide your own meals or you can enjoy meals at the homestead with us. Towels and linen provided and an open fire place assure winter warmth. We welcome children.
Directions: Please phone.

Lake Barrine see Atherton Tablelands

QUEENSLAND

Mackay
Homestay
Address: 10 James Street,
Mackay, 4740
Name: Heather Heggie
Telephone: (07) 4957 3348
Beds: 1 Double, 2 large Single
(2 bedrooms)
Bathroom: 1 Family share (1 person only)
Tariff: B&B (full) Double $40, Single $30,
Children half price; Dinner $15pp (3 course). Vouchers accepted
Nearest Town: Mackay

I live in an old Queenslander, ie high set house with verandahs on three sides. The house is in walking distance of city with theatre, bus terminal and convenience stores nearby. Mackay has many lovely beaches which are quite near, with a tropical rain forest in the mountains approximately one hour's drive away. There is a short drive to the Harbour - the base of many tourist boats which ply between the Great Barrier Reef, its islands and the mainland. Dinner is available by arrangement. There is room for your car under the house if necessary. The house has been a one family home for all its life of 83 years.

Mackay, Whitsunday District
Guest House - Farmstay   RACQ ★★★☆
Address: "Eagle Nest Farm"
Gormley's Road, Seaforth, 4741 Qld
(Please phone first)
Name: Anne & Helmut Kley
Telephone: (07) 4959 0552
Fax: (07) 4959 0552
Mobile: (018) 776668 ,0418 747 751
Email: hke@m130.aone.net.au
Beds: 6 Queen, 6 Single (6 bedrooms)
Bathroom: 6 Ensuite
Tariff: B&B (full) Double $59, Single $45.
Dinner by arrangement $15.   Vouchers accepted
Nearest Town: Mackay 40km

Eagle Nest Farm is an idyllic cattle farm of 250 acres (100 ha) set amidst tropical bushland with sea and island views. We are a German couple who migrated to Australia in 1990. Our luxurious homestead was built by ourselves, designed to host guests from all over the world.
You can go bushwalking or horse riding, enjoy the ocean views, swim in our pool or just relax in total tranquillity. It's only a 10 minutes drive to Cape Hillsborough National Park with its tame kangaroos, lovely beaches and fishing spots. Spend a day at Eungella National Park watching a platypus and discover Finch Hatton Gorge. We can also arrange for you tours to the magnificent Whitsunday Islands and the Great Barrier Reef. Or enjoy a day of fishing on our own boat!
Full breakfast, afternoon tea or coffee, good international meals. Try our home brewed beer or a glass of Australian wine with your dinner.
Campervans and pets welcome.
Winner of multiple Tourism Awards.

Magnetic Island
Homestay   RACQ ★★★
Address: "Marshall's Bed & Breakfast"
3 Endeavour Road, Arcadia Bay,
Magnetic Island, North Queensland 4819
Name: Paul & Stella Marshall
Telephone: (07) 4778 5112
Mobile: (015) 150665
Beds: 2 Queen, 1 Double, 4 Single (4 bedrooms)
Bathroom: 1 Guests share, 1 Family share
Tariff: B&B (continental) Double $50, Single $35, Children over 12yrs only - $15, Dinner from $10, Credit Cards.   Vouchers accepted
Nearest Town: Townsville

Magnetic Island is Australia's best kept secret. It is 8kms off the Queensland coast and is accessible by passenger or vehicular ferry.
The waters surrounding Magnetic Island are part of the Great Barrier Reef Marine Park, there are 24km of walking track in the island's National Park and 23 bays around its coastline.
Nestled in the most beautiful part of the island is "Marshall's", a spacious home designed for the tropics, with well appointed rooms, each with its own ceiling fan for those warm, balmy nights.
You can relax in the half acre of garden listening to the birds, stroll into the hills searching for koalas, or wander down to the beach to soak up the sun. It's like a small country town on an island. Take a day trip to the Reef or snorkel and dive our fringing reefs and wrecks. There's fishing, sailing and horseriding, or simply enjoy the warmth.
No smoking indoors

Maryborough
Homestay B&B
Address: 59 Woolgool Rd, Tinana,
Maryborough, 4650 QLD
Name: Trevor & Annette Stewart
Telephone: (071) 213 567
Fax: (071) 213 567
Beds: 2 Queen (2 bedrooms)
Bathroom: 1 Guests share
Tariff: B&B (full) Double $95, Single $75
, Dinner optional by arrangement $20. Vouchers accepted $10 surcharge
Nearest Town: Hervey Bay

Come and stay at Jacaranda Retreat and enjoy the tranquil surroundings of the fully landscaped gardens. This cavity brick modern Queensland home is set on a peaceful one acre lot and is only minutes to Maryborough City. Outdoor seating provided and an environmental park is just metres from the home where you can stroll and observe the flora and fauna. The home caters for all seasons and we have 2 comfortable, attractively furnished rooms for guests with separate guest bathroom. Our tariff includes a continental or cooked breakfast. Tea and coffee available throughout the day. Maryborough is situated 270km north of Brisbane and 30 minutes travel by car to Hervey Bay, gateway to Fraser Island. The days can be kept busy with sightseeing trips to the local historical attractions.
Our interests include meeting people, gardening, cycling, walking and listening to music. Family pet dog. Smoking outdoors.
Directions: *Please write or telephone.*

Maryborough - Bauple
Farmstay - B&B   RACQ ★★★★
Address: Strelitzia Park, Stottenville Rd, Bauple 4650
Name: Judith Kent
Telephone: (0741) 292 457 **Fax**: (0741) 292 457
Beds: 3 Queen (3 bedrooms)
Bathroom: 1 Guests share
Tariff: B&B (full) Double $85-$100, Single $50, Dinner $20, Credit Cards (VISA/MC/BC). Children not catered for.
Vouchers accepted $10 surcharge
Nearest Town: Maryborough 40km north on Bruce Hwy.

Strelitzia Park is a tropical fruit farm at Bauple which is approximately halfway between Gympie and Maryborough. The farm covers 50 acres of peaceful and pretty countryside, over 2000 tropical fruit trees of every imaginable type. Mangoes, Lychee, Longans, Macadamia nuts, Carambola, Jak fruit and a host more. Guests are encouraged to eat the fruit from the trees in season.
The central attraction is a huge dam fully stocked with Yellow Belly and Bass. Watch the sun go down as you cast your lure over the tranquil water. Your host will cook your catch if you choose.
The comfortable accommodation is in a guest wing separate from but attached to the main homestead - your meals are taken with your hosts Kev and Judith in the elegant main homestead surrounded by fine art lovingly collected over the years.
Coffee and tea making facilities are in the Guest Wing - always home cooked biscuits - a never ending supply.

Maryborough
Homestay
Address: "Eskdale House", 53 Pallas Street, Maryborough, Qld 4650
Name: Peter & Jacqui Holtorf
Telephone: (07) 4121 3153
Beds: 3 Double, 2 Single (4 bedrooms)
Bathroom: 1 Guests share, 1 Family share
Tariff: B&B (full) Double $95, Single $75, Credit Cards
Nearest Town: Maryborough - 250km north of Brisbane

National Trust listed "Eskdale House" c1864, reflects the elegance and charm of a bygone era. Features of this colonial Georgian building include: walls of sandstock bricks moulded in an onsite kiln, lime mortar from burnt coral, joinery including a staircase of local red cedar, a cellar and an underground water catchment tank. Originally the residence of Mayor James Dowzer and later, Federal Parliamentarian Edward Bernard Cresset Corser, your hosts Peter and Jacqui welcome you to share their large comfortable home.

The 4 spacious upstairs guest bedrooms have French doors opening onto a verandah which gives a delightful view of the 3/4 acre of trees and gardens. If you are lucky you might spot our geriatric cat, now too old to chase the abundant bird life.

"Eskdale House" is situated in a quiet suburb close to a large park, lagoon and golf course and is within walking distance of the CBD.
Courtesy pick up and transfers to airport or transit centre.
We regret we cannot cater for children and pets. No smoking indoors.

Maroochydore see Sunshine Coast
McPherson see Sunshine Coast Hinterland

QUEENSLAND

Mission Beach
Homestay+Self-contained Accom.
Address: 'Leslie Lodge'
5 Leslie Lane,
Mission Beach South, 4852
Name: Don Davis
Telephone: (07) 4068 8618
Fax: (07) 4068 8623
Beds: 1 Large Queen or 1 Twin (1 bedroom)
Bathroom: 1 Private
Tariff: B&B (full) Double $60, Single $30, Children using s/sofa $15; S.C. $250 wk, Overnight $75-$90.
Vouchers accepted
Nearest Town: 1 1/2 hrs south Cairns

Secure and private accommodation is offered in delightful property - manicured lawn and garden. Use of swimming pool and 4 mins stroll to delightful sandy beach opposite Dunk Island accessible by water taxi or ferry - rainforest walks and fishing.

Mission Beach South
Homestay+Self-contained Accom.
Address: 'Campbell Court'
1 Leslie Lane, cnr Campbell Tce,
Mission Beach South. 4852
Name: Linda Sellars
Telephone: (07) 4068 8695 (H.) & (07) 40 68 8311 (W.) **Fax**: (07) 4068 8623
Beds: 1 Queen, 1 Double, Single sofa (2 bedrooms)
Bathroom: 1 Ensuite, 1 Private
Tariff: B&B (continental) Double $60, Single $30, S.C. $250-$350, Overnight $75-$110. Vouchers accepted
Nearest Town: 1 1/2 hrs south Cairns

Superb accommodation of Queensland's Barrier Reef Coast opp. Dunk Island. Tropical rainforest tracks nearby. Great salt water pool in delightful setting. Handy all tours and attractions and only 4 min stroll to sandy beach and fishing.

Mt Tamborine see Gold Coast Hinterland

The standard of accommodation in
The Australian Bed and Breakfast Book
ranges from homely to luxurious,
but you can always be sure of superior hospitality.

Mossman - Newell Beach
Homestay
Address: "Side-The-Sea" B&B,
148 Marine Parade,
Newell Beach, 4873 QLD
Name: Margaret Cooper
Telephone: (07) 40981213
Fax: (07) 40983672
Beds: 1Queen, 1 Double (2 bedrooms)
Bathroom: 1 Ensuite
Tariff: B&B (special) Double $80,
Single $50.
Vouchers accepted
Nearest Town: Mossman 7km, Port Douglas 25km

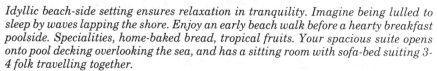

Idyllic beach-side setting ensures relaxation in tranquility. Imagine being lulled to sleep by waves lapping the shore. Enjoy an early beach walk before a hearty breakfast poolside. Specialities, home-baked bread, tropical fruits. Your spacious suite opens onto pool decking overlooking the sea, and has a sitting room with sofa-bed suiting 3-4 folk travelling together.
Centrally located for exploring Mossman Gorge, Daintree River with crocodile cruises and Cape Tribulation rainforest areas. Drive 20 minutes to Port Douglas tourist Mecca and cruise to the Barrier Reef for an unforgettable experience. Port restaurants feature local seafoods whilst various excellent restaurants / take-aways are closer. Golfing and bird-watching are nearby.
My involvement in Christian and community activities keep me busy and I enjoy cooking, sewing and hospitality. Having travelled extensively, I am committed to making your stay both comfortable and memorable. Be warned, folk generally stay longer than planned.
Home Page: http://www.cyberlink.com.au/bedbreakfast/sidethesea

Nerang see Gold Coast Hinterland
Newell Beach see Mossman
Noosa see Sunshine Coast
Noosa Valley see Sunshine Coast
Palm Beach see Gold Coast
Parkwood see Gold Coast Hinterland

Port Douglas
Homestay
Address: "Marae", Lot 1 Ponzo Rd., Shannonvale
Postal: PO Box 133, Port Douglas 4871
Name: Andy Morris
Telephone: (070) 984900 **Fax**: (070) 984099 **Mobile**: 015-967 557
Email: marae@internetnorth.com.au
Beds: 3 Double (3 bedrooms)
Bathroom: 2 Ensuite, 1 Private
Tariff: B&B (full) Double $80-$100: Double $80; Ensuite King $90; Ensuite Pool Room $100; Single $60. Dinner $25. Credit cards.
Nearest Town: Port Douglas is 15km south.

"Marae" a truly tropical house with every comfort - perched like an eagle over the Shannonvale and Cassowary Valleys - the Mossman Gorge casts the evening shadow - wild things fly and feed - the peace and privacy are absolute. By day the spectacular Coral Sea or the mystical gloom of the Rainforest. Sundowners on the deck to a chorus of green tree frogs and swallows feeding on the wing - a myriad of spectacular birds - bandicoots and goannas in the bush. Bird watchers can indulge their hobby while relaxing by the swimming pool.
At "Marae" guests missing their animal friends will be consoled by a pampered dog and an opinionated Sulphur Crested Cockatoo (watch your buttons).

Private bathroom is for your use exclusively,
Guests share means you may be sharing with other guests,
Family share means you will be sharing with the family.

Ravenshoe see Atherton Tablelands
River Heads see Hervey Bay

Rockhampton
**Homestay/
Bed and Breakfast   RACQ ★★★★**
Address: "Mamelon Lodge",
329 Hobler Avenue,
North Rockhampton, C.Q. 4701
Name: Bob & Joy McCartney
Telephone: (07) 4928 8484 **Mobile**: 014 896 805
Email: joy@intours.com.au
Beds: 1 Queen, 1 Double, 2 Single (2 bedrooms) **Bathroom**: 1 Ensuite, 1 Private
Tariff: B&B (full) Double $75, Single $50, Children 5yrs to 16yrs $15 (children under 5yrs not appropriate). Vouchers accepted
Nearest Town: Rockhampton - C. Q'land off Bruce Highway

Enjoy friendly genuine country hospitality in quiet city suburb, with spacious ground level accommodation, and lock-up garage. Luxury ensuited air-conditioned bedroom / retreat has all amenities, including an office desk and guests lounge, and opens out on to well-kept gardens.
Home made afternoon tea served on arrival, if desired. Cooked breakfast (incl. fresh tropical fruits) served on patio, with mountain and city views.
MAMELON LODGE B&B is centrally situated to many tourist attractions. Local attractions include Great Barrier Reef & Scenic Beaches; Koorana Crocodile Farm; Dreamtime Aboriginal Cultural Centre; Natural Limestone Caves; Heritage Walk; and famous Botanical Gardens & Zoo (free).
Your Hosts, Bob & Joy McCartney, warmly welcome you.
For Bookings, please phone or Email.
Courtesy pick-up available from bus / rail / airport.

Sunshine Coast - Buderim
Bed & Breakfast
Address: 33 Quiet Valley Cres, Buderim
Name: Mr & Mrs Judd
Telephone: (07) 5445 5419 **Fax**: (07) 5479 1313
Beds: 1 Double, 2 Single (2 bedrooms)
Bathroom: 2 Private/Guests share
Tariff: B&B (full) Double $70, Single $45. Special rates for extended stay and for small children. Vouchers accepted
Nearest Town: Buderim

Buderim is at the centre of the Sunshine Coast - a 40km stretch of beautiful sandy ocean beaches. The district offers a wide variety of activities.
Our new home is in a tranquil bushland setting beside a natural rain forest on Buderim Mountain. The Buderim Village is 2km away. It is a small village with Australia's original ginger factory, now a popular market. There are good restaurants, antique shops and several sporting venues such as bowls, croquet, tennis and golf. Rain forest walks are also here.
The beaches are approx 9km away. Handy to the new shopping and department store facilities. Close to the famous Glasshouse Mountains, the relocated Ginger Factory. Maleny / Montville panoramas and unique shopping.
Tours to famous Barrier Reef can be arranged through travel agents. Guests pick up from Maroochy Airport -15km. Brisbane Airport pick up by arrangement. City accessible by motorway in 1 1/4 hours.
TV, lounge, family room available to guests.
Conducted tours to local attractions by arrangement.

QUEENSLAND

Sunshine Coast - Maroochydore
Bed & Breakfast   RACQ
Address: 168 Mons School Road,
Buderim, QLD 4556
Name: Suncoast Bed & Breakfast
"on Buderim"
Telephone: (0754) 768423
Fax: (0754) 768423
Beds: 1 Queen, 2 Twin (2 bedrooms)
Bathroom: 1 Guests share
Tariff: B&B (continental) Double $85,
Single $65, Children not catered for. Credit Cards (VISA/BC/MC).
Vouchers accepted
Nearest Town: Buderim/Maroochydore 5km approx.
Suncoast B&B "on Buderim", genuine Swiss hospitality and council approved! Our property is carved out of an ancient sand stone cliff and surrounded by a botanical reserve. This tranquil setting assures a good night rest in our fully air-conditioned, modern bedrooms yet is only 15 minutes from the famous surf beaches of the Sunshine Coast and its capital, Maroochydore. We are the ideal base for day trips, be it the Hinterland, the Blackall Ranges, Noosa Everglades and eateries, the Mooloolaba Underwater World or the golden beaches. The peaceful garden setting may be inviting enough to laze the day away on our large, shady sundeck, or in the cool, elegant courtyard.
Information and help is given for local sightseeing, day excursions, travel hints and bookings. Years of experience in tourism and the hospitality industry will guarantee a memorable stay in our home. Alfred and Janet will look forward to your visit!

Sunshine Coast - Noosa
Bed & Breakfast, Self-contained Unit
Address: "Amaroo"
Noosa Lakes Bed & Breakfast
P O Box 78, Tewantin-Noosa, Qld 4565
Name: Sigrid & Otto
Telephone: (07) 5447 1263 (please phone/fax
first for availability and directions).
Fax: (07) 5449 8000 **Mobile**: (018) 714138
Email: noosabnb@ottel.com.au
Beds: 2 Queensize (2 bedrooms) S.C. Unit.
Kingsize with ensuite.
Bathroom: 1 Guests share, Separate toilet

Tariff: B&B (extended continental) Double $55, Single $35. S.C. Unit: $65 (incl. breakfast). Dinner & Afternoon tea by arrangement. Campervans $15 (2 persons). Special rates for extended stay.   Vouchers accepted
Nearest Town: Tewantin 7km, Noosa 10km, Airport 30km.
Before we immigrated from Germany we preferred B&B on our European trips. Now we like to share our cosy chalet-style home in peaceful bushland surroundings with like-minded overseas and domestic travellers. Our large 2 storey-house on a 10 acres property is situated 10km from Noosa on the Sunshine Coast (130km north of Brisbane) which we discovered after many trips around Australia. We instantly felt in love with cosmopolitan Noosa, the "St. Tropez" or "Carmel" of Australia; in our view the best and very special spot. Noosa has many great ocean beaches, national parks with rainforest, the world heritage-listed Fraser Island and a picturesque hinterland with arts and crafts markets. With our 16 years of local knowledge we can advise you and arrange trips to these places, Great Barrier Reef (150km north), etc. Join us for an afternoon tea and walk down to the lake for sunset, refresh in our natural pond or use our spa with sauna for a nominal fee.

Sunshine Coast - Noosa
Homestay
Address: PO Box 295, Noosaville, QLD 4566 (Please phone)
Name: Summer House Blue
Telephone: (07) 5442 4347 **Fax**: (07) 5442 4347
Beds: 1 Queen, 1 Twin, 1 King single (3 Bedrooms)
Bathroom: 1 Ensuite, 1 Guests share
Tariff: B&B (tropical) Double $70-$80, Single $45. Vouchers accepted
Nearest Town: Noosa Junction 3km

Summer House Blue is an attractive restored fisherman's cottage set in a quiet location one street back from Noosa River. Within walking distance of many restaurants and streetside cafes offering a variety of cuisines to suit all tastes and pockets.
A great sleep in comfortable beds followed by a Queensland breakfast of seasonal tropical fruits, breads and spreads. Then off to explore this "piece of paradise"..... stroll beside the river, hire a boat and go fishing (bait shop around the corner), cruise to the everglade's. A short drive takes you to Hastings Street, the mecca for 'foodies' and boutique shoppers. Walk around our compact National Park with its secluded beaches. Visit historic Eumundi and experience the famed Saturday markets. For day trips the adventurous 4WD tour to Fraser Island is a hit, as is the scenic tour of the Glasshouse Mountains and a 'craft crawl' of the hinterland towns of Maleny and Montville.
Directions: Please phone. For advance bookings phone/fax/write for a brochure.

Sunshine Coast - Noosa Valley
Bed & Breakfast
RACQ ★★★★
Address: 93 Duke Road, Noosa Valley, 4562
Name: Noosa Country House B&B
Telephone: (07) 5471 0121
Fax: (07) 5471 0121
Beds: 3 Queen (3 bedrooms)
Bathroom: 3 Ensuite
Tariff: B&B (full) Double $70-$120, Single $70-$90, Credit Cards. Vouchers accepted
Nearest Town: Noosa Heads 12km, Eumundi 6km

Noosa Country House is situated on twelve acres in the beautiful sub-tropical Noosa Valley, 10 minutes from Noosa Heads and Eumundi, and 90 minutes north of Brisbane. A federation style home, with verandahs all round, overlooks a large cottage garden and undulating farmland, studded with towering gums, a lagoon, and kangaroos in the back paddock.
A timber deck, which overlooks the valley, accommodates a large spa, heated in winter- cool in summer - a superb place to sip a glass of champagne and watch the many birds.
Bedrooms have beautiful linens, fresh fruit and flowers, home-made goodies, tea and coffee making facilities, refrigerator and country views. A delicious breakfast is served on your private verandah, or in the dining room. Around the corner is the Noosa Valley Country Club and picturesque golf course, restaurant, tennis and squash courts.
We offer personalised service, in a friendly atmosphere, setting your own schedule as you wish.
" Not just accommodation - an experience of true country hospitality."
Directions: 1km from Noosa-Eumundi Road.

QUEENSLAND

Sunshine Coast - Noosa Valley
Bed & Breakfast
Address: Noosa Valley Manor
115 Wust Road
Doonan 4562
Name: Liz and Peter McDonald
Telephone: (07) 5471 0088
Fax: (07) 5471 0066
Mobile: 015-034 053
Beds: 3 Queen, 2 Single (4 bedrooms) **Bathroom**: 4 Ensuites
Tariff: B&B (full) Double $85-$115, Dinner $25, Credit Cards. Vouchers accepted Mon-Thurs Only + $6.50 surcharge
Nearest Town: Noosa 15km

TRANQUILLITY AND COMFORT.
For a quiet weekend away or that special holiday or honeymoon, come to Noosa Valley Manor. Nestled in the scenic Noosa Valley and close to Noosa's famous beaches, Hastings Street restaurants and shops you can get away from it all and yet the things you want and need are close by.
For the traveller there is so much to see and do, from the beaches to golf courses to shopping and fine dining experiences. The temptations and treats of Noosa are all around for you to enjoy, the rainforest retreat and peace are also close at hand. Come and stay with your hosts, Liz and Peter soon, we look forward to catering for your special needs. Stay for a day or stay for a week, we are sure you will take something home to remember from our special piece of paradise.
See you soon at NOOSA VALLEY MANOR.

Sunshine Coast Hinterland - Eumundi
Bed & Breakfast
Address: 15 Eumundi Noosa Road,
Eumundi, QLD 4562
Name: Taylor's
Damn Fine Bed & Breakfast
Telephone: (07) 5442 8685
Fax: (07) 5442 8168
Beds: 3 Queen (3 bedrooms)
Bathroom: 3 Ensuites
Tariff: B&B (full), Double $85-$110
Nearest Town: Eumundi

Relax in the timeless charm of our surprisingly different old Queenslander (circa 1898) lovingly restored to provide even the best of modern comforts.
Expansive mountain views offer the perfect backdrop beyond the four acres of rolling private parkland which is bounded by the North Maroochy River. Laze away warm summer nights on wide verandahs by the pool with that special person and a good chilled wine. Likewise, cool winter nights provide the perfect excuse to snuggle up around the open fires and make you feel you could stay here forever. Just 400 meters away are the famous Eumundi Markets as well as fine restaurants and two lively pubs where the locals make you welcome.
If it's activities you seek you've come to the right place. Beautiful Noosa main beach is just 15 minutes away. Tennis, golf, fishing, boating, bushwalking, scenic drives and cosmopolitan shopping are also nearby. English and German spoken.

Sunshine Coast Hinterland - Mapleton
Homestay
Address: 97 Flaxton Drive, Mapleton, QLD 4560

Name: P.J. & J.R. McPherson
Telephone: (07) 5445 7678
Fax: (07) 5445 7653 **Email**: petermac@babe.net.au
Beds: Homestead; 3 Queen, 2 Single, (4 bedrooms) Cabin; 1 Queen 1 Single
Bathroom: Homestead; 2 Ensuite, 2 Private Cabin; 1 Ensuite
Tariff: B&B (full), Double $80, Single $60. Credit cards accepted
Nearest Town: Mapleton

Eden Lodge is located at the northern end of the Blackall Range one km from Mapleton village.
The Lodge is a modern colonial style, has four bedrooms; two of them have ensuites, TV, fridge and kettle whilst the other two have own bathrooms. Three have queen size beds and the other twin singles.
There is a fully self-contained studio in our garden which sleeps four.
Breakfast includes in-season fresh fruit, juice, cereals and a cooked meal if desired. There are excellent restaurants close to the Lodge where other meals are available. Guests use the main dining area for breakfast and have use of a comfortable lounge with TV and wood fires on chilly evenings.
There are many scenic attractions within minutes drive of the Lodge. National Park walks, art galleries, glass blowing, potteries and craft shops.
Smokers can use outside areas including the gazebo.
Please phone before arrival.

Tamborine Mountain see Gold Coast Hinterland

Toowoomba (country) - Hampton
Homestay   RACQ ★★★★
Address: Wilkes Rd., Hampton
Name: Valden House
Telephone: (07) 46979277
Fax: (07) 46393 273
Mobile: 0414 742 784
Beds: 2 Queen, 1 King/Twin (3 bedrooms)
Bathroom: 1 Ensuite, 1 Private, 1 Family share
Tariff: B&B (full) Double $70, Single $50, Dinner by arrangement, Credit Cards.
Nearest Town: Crows Nest 12km north Hampton, New England Highway

A pleasant drive through an avenue of trees will bring you to Hampton from Toowoomba (32km) where we offer friendly, country hospitality in our home situated in 'tall timber country'. Guests accommodation is on our second floor and includes a sitting room with TV and tea and coffee making facilities, although we welcome sharing of sunroom and lounges. Breakfast is served in our sunroom (with log fire in cooler weather) and includes fresh juices and home-baked bread. National Parks abound with comfortable walks for all ages. Antique shops, orchid nursery, golf courses, fishing, historical museums all just a short drive, with wineries further afield. You may choose to relax in the peace and quiet of our garden and bush surround whilst enjoying a Devonshire tea. Perhaps finishing the day with an evening meal at Queensland's oldest continuous licensed hotel.

QUEENSLAND

Toowoomba
Homestay RACQ ★★★★
Address: "Jacaranda Grove", 92 Tourist Road, Toowoomba, 4350
Name: Richard & Jan McIlwraith
Telephone: (07) 4635 8394
Fax: (07) 4635 8394 **Mobile**: 0419 660544
Beds: 1 King, 1 Queen (2 bedrooms)
Bathroom: 1 Ensuite, 1 Private
Tariff: B&B (special)King $130, Queen $105, Single $65. Children not catered for. Vouchers accepted $40 surcharge for King, $20 surcharge for Queen.
Nearest Town: 5 mins to Central Business District. 1 1/2 hrs to Brisbane. 2 hrs to gold Coast. 3hrs to Noosa

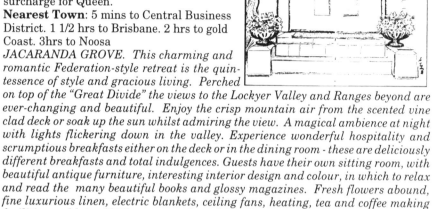

JACARANDA GROVE. This charming and romantic Federation-style retreat is the quintessence of style and gracious living. Perched on top of the "Great Divide" the views to the Lockyer Valley and Ranges beyond are ever-changing and beautiful. Enjoy the crisp mountain air from the scented vine clad deck or soak up the sun whilst admiring the view. A magical ambience at night with lights flickering down in the valley. Experience wonderful hospitality and scrumptious breakfasts either on the deck or in the dining room - these are deliciously different breakfasts and total indulgences. Guests have their own sitting room, with beautiful antique furniture, interesting interior design and colour, in which to relax and read the many beautiful books and glossy magazines. Fresh flowers abound, fine luxurious linen, electric blankets, ceiling fans, heating, tea and coffee making facilities and lots of little extra touches which discerning guests appreciate.
There is a "terracotta gallery" in our semi-formal garden which is very private and leafy and with numerous rare and scented plants and vines. The garden seats beside the weeping cherry beg guests to unwind whilst listening to the birds and admiring the terracotta urns, planters and pots etc.
Perhaps guests would like to experience our Indulgent Weekend package - feasting for two days and two nights - brunch on the deck; dinner in the Dining Room by candlelight. Bridal packages are also available. POA.
Our interests are many and varied and include tennis, golf, horse racing, the arts and crafts, travel, food and restaurants, gardening, antiques, architecture and design, Bridge, movies and current events.
There is lots to see and do in and around this beautiful garden city and with prior notice we can prepare a gourmet picnic basket full of wonderful delights whilst guests visit local and nearby attractions - abundant antique shops, extensive variety of restaurants and coffee shops, art galleries, Rim fire winery, gardens and parks (spectacular especially during the Carnival of Flowers last week in September), museums, National Trust buildings, country pubs, national parks, specialist nurseries, boutiques, Sunday markets, bird habitat, the Bunya Mountains (rainforest walks), golf courses or perhaps a personal tour of Toowoomba. Make this city your stop over to Noosa, to whale watching at Hervey Bay, Brisbane or the Gold Coast or west to the Outback.
We look forward to welcoming guests for an interesting and memorable stay.
Directions: Directions / Bookings. Please telephone giving 24 hours notice. Brochures available. Pick up service available. (Answering machine)

QUEENSLAND

Toowoomba
Homestay
Address: 12 Girrawheen Street,
Toowoomba, 4350 Qld
Name: Janey Westaway
Telephone: (076) 356931
Beds: 1 Queen, 2 Single (2 bedrooms)
Bathroom: 1 Ensuite, 1Family share
Tariff: B&B (continental) Ensuite $60,
Single $40, Children $20, Dinner 2 courses: $20pp,
3 courses: $25 pp. Campervans facilities.
Nearest Town: Toowoomba - 4km from CBD

Located 4km from CBD
This inviting homestay is in a cul-de-sac street with a parkland setting.
Wake up listening to the birds, inhale the fragrance of the garden and enjoy being amongst antique furniture.
Healthy, hearty meals and picnics available upon request.
Directions: *Please phone.*

Toowoomba
Bed & Breakfast Inn
Address: 135 Russell Street,
Toowoomba
Name: Maryann Andersen
Telephone: (07) 4639 2055
Fax: (07) 4632 0160
Beds: 4 King/Queen, 8 Double
(12 bedrooms)
Bathroom: 8 Ensuite, 4 Private

Tariff: B&B (full) Double $85-$160, Single $75-$160, Children $25, Dinner $35-$45, Credit Cards. Vouchers accepted Sun-Thurs for standard room only (without fireplace)
Nearest Town: 3 city blocks to Toowoomba CBD

In the heart of the garden city of Toowoomba, 90 minutes from Brisbane, is "Vacy Hall", a colonial mansion lovingly restored to provide rest and comfort to the discerning traveller.
Twelve bedrooms in this historic mansion provide you with a "Bed & Breakfast experience" that is reminiscent of the glory days of old Queensland's past. Indulge yourself in front of the open fires in winter or in the deep shade of the verandahs in summer.
All rooms have phones, tea and coffee making facilities, central heating or fireplaces and most open onto wide verandahs with surrounding gardens.
Breakfast and room service are available; dinner by arrangement. Vacy can be an ideal venue for small conference, seminars and meetings, or family reunions.
Vacy is located in a quiet convenient area of the city. A stay at Toowoomba's finest B&B is an experience you will always remember with pleasure.
Two night packages, mid-week and corporate rates available on request.

Tell other travellers about your favourite B&Bs

QUEENSLAND

Torrens Creek - North-west Qld, Outback
Farmstay
Address: "Cheltenham",
Torrens Creek, QLD 4816
Name: Jeff & Rayna Bucknell
Telephone: (077) 417249
Fax: (077) 417306
Beds: 1 Double, 2-4 Single (2-3 bedrooms)
Bathroom: 1 Guests share, 1 Family share
Tariff: B&B (full) Double $90, Single $60, Children half price. Dinner $20. Campervans $20.
Special rates for extended stay please enquire.
Nearest Town: Torrens Creek 30km, Hughenden 1 hour, Charters Towers 2 hours.

You can discover how early settlers lived by being our welcome guests on our 10,000 hectare working cattle station. Our homestead is an attractively renovated 1930s shearers' quarters, with 1990s comforts and a preserved sense of the past. We both love Australian history (Jeff's family pioneered the sheep and cattle grazing industry, and has worked the land since 1826; and Rayna is a former English and History teacher). We collect country artifacts and memorabilia which give our visitors insight to life "off the beaten track". We share our station with beef cattle, milking cows, pet sheep, horses, pigs, poultry and parrots. You can enjoy our famous country meals (vegetarians catered for) and appreciate our incredible wildlife - more than 150 species of birds, and kangaroos, echidnas, goannas and dingoes inhabit the property. We're close to several National Parks, and the historic towns of Hughenden, Charters Towers, Aramac and Longreach. Take the time to experience our lifestyle; it's active if you're seeking adventure, and tranquil enough for a perfect artists' retreat.

Townsville
Farmstay
Address: "Sapote Grove",
PO Box 5712, Mail Centre,
Townsville, QLD 4810
Name: Jill & John Weil
Telephone: (077) 780118
Fax: (077) 780118
Beds: 1 Double, 1 Single (2 bedrooms)
Bathroom: 1 Private
Tariff: B&B (special) Double $70, Single $40, Children half price. Dinner $20. Campervans $20. Vouchers accepted
Nearest Town: Townsville - 50 km (35 minutes drive)

"Sapote Grove" is a rare fruit farm and dairy goat stud using permaculture principles in the hills west of Townsville. We have a comfortable open-plan home with modern facilities set in quiet natural bush surroundings. The climate is pleasant most of the year except for occasional discomfort during the hot summer and wet season (January to March). Our orchards supply the fruit for your breakfast table. Our own jams and honey are served with breakfast. Dinner consists of a hot meal with desserts made from exotic fruits. Fruits available in season include white sapote, black sapote, jakfruit, papaw, and carambola. Ideal bird watching area. Aboriginal rock paintings nearby. (Turtle Rock - Dept of Environment site).
No smoking please.
Directions: *Please write or telephone. 24 hours notice preferred.*

Townsville
Bed & Breakfast Inn
Address: 32 Hale Street,
Townsville, QLD 4810
Name: Coral Lodge Bed & Breakfast Inn
Telephone: (07) 4771 5512
Fax: (07) 4771 5512 **Mobile**: (0419) 791588
Beds: 9 Double, 8 Single (10 bedrooms)
Bathroom: 2 Private, 2 Guests share
Tariff: B&B (continental) Double $48-$58, Single $38-$48, Children $7. Tariff review as per 1/4/98. Credit Cards (BC/MC/VISA).
Nearest Town: Townsville
Coral Lodge is a quaint Bed & Breakfast Inn, recently refurbished in Victoriana style. We offer stylish budget accommodation in a quiet street just 200 metres from the city centre of Townsville.
Eight pretty guest rooms (5 double / single, 3 twin), all have colour TV, mini fridge and airconditioning.
Ladies and gentlemen's bathrooms and a country style guest kitchen are tiled and decorated in heritage style.
A guest dining room and guest laundry are also available. Two self contained studio units each have double bed and double bunks, cooking facilities and private bathrooms.
Possums reside in our tropical gardens and enjoy being fed just after dark each evening.
Coral Lodge is a pleasant and convenient place to stay offering "budget with style" accommodation when you visit Townsville. Tour desk, parking and credit card facilities available.

Townsville
Historic Guest House
Address: 20 Cleveland Terrace, Townsville
Name: The Rocks Historic Guesthouse
Telephone: (07) 47715700
Fax: (07) 47715711 **Mobile**: 015166293
Email: therocks@ultra.net.au
Beds: 7 Double, 2 Single (8 bedrooms)
Bathroom: 1 Ensuite, 1 Guests share, 1 Family share
Tariff: B&B (continental) Double $88-$120, Single $78, Children $10 extra, Dinner $25, Credit Cards (BC/MC/VISA). Vouchers accepted same day restriction
Nearest Town: Townsville
Joe, Jennie and Sebastian live in one of Townsville's most loved buildings - The Rocks - newly restored to her Victorian grandeur, she exudes a charm and beauty to delight the senses. Guests can enjoy the individually decorated private bedrooms or refresh in either the ensuite, family share or guest bathroom with fixtures for people with disability. The Rocks boasts wide open verandahs, decked with planters chairs, overlooking Cleveland Bay and Magnetic Island, a billiard room, a spa, a Victorian drawing room with piano and grandfather clock and soon a moon watching observatory. Breakfast is served on a newly saved 14 seater farm table on collectable English China and silverware in the dining room / library, amongst eccentric collections.
In the evenings Sri Lanka cuisine is the norm and the atmosphere created by kerosene lamps and the smell of curry always inspires good conversations.
The Rocks central location makes for an easy leisurely walk to the beach, city heart, night life and restaurant area.

**Urangan see Hervey Bay. Wondecla see Atherton
Yepoon see Capricorn Coast. Yungaburra see Atherton**

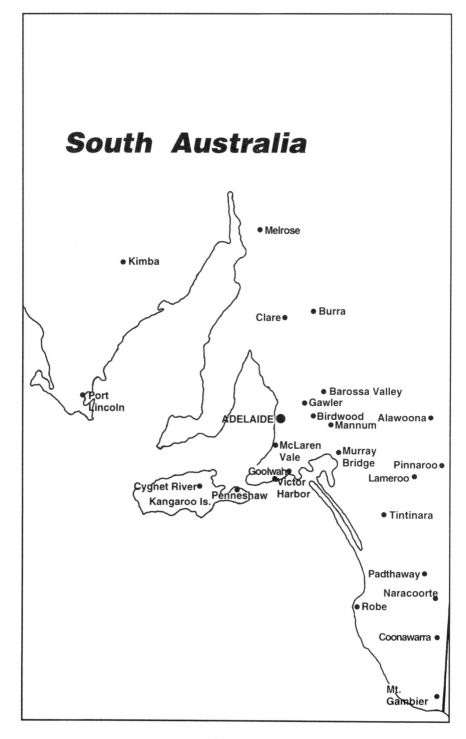

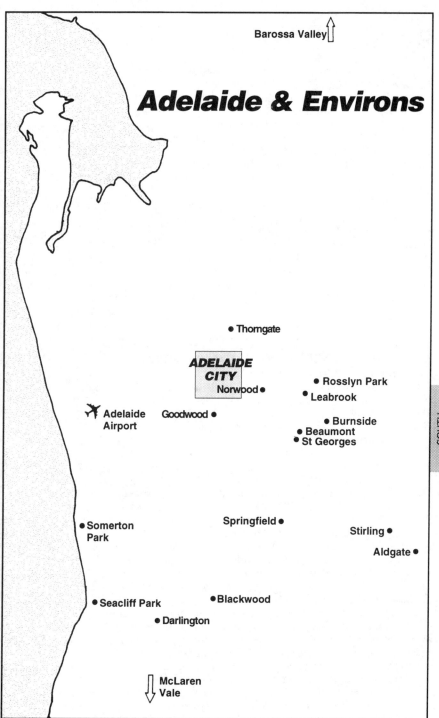

SOUTH AUSTRALIA

Adelaide
Self-contained Accommodation   RAA★★★☆
Address: 108 South Terrace, Adelaide, SA 5000
Name: The Old Terrace
Telephone: (08) 8364 5437 **Fax**: (08) 83646961
Mobile: 0416150655
Beds: 1 Double, 4 Single (3 bedrooms)
Bathroom: 1 Ensuite, 1 Private
Tariff: B&B (continental) Double $95, Extra person $35, Children $20. Discounts for stays of one week or longer. Credit Cards.Vouchers accepted $15 surcharge
Relax in the privacy of your own delightful two-storey terrace house, ideally situated in the heart of Adelaide, directly opposite Parklands and Rose Gardens. Only a short walk to the colourful Central Markets, theatres, Festival Centre, Casino, CBD and delectable restaurants. One of a row of historic houses built in 1880, we can accommodate a party of 2 to 6 guests (Sole use). Ideal for families and small groups. Consisting of 3 bedrooms, lounge, dining room, kitchen and 2 bathrooms and furnished with a charming blend of Asian, antique and provincial furniture including a unique carved and gilded Balinese marriage bed, private courtyard garden at rear. Facilities include laundry, washing machine and dryer, telephone, colour TV, modern kitchen with gas oven and microwave, quality linen. Airport bus service to door. Danish, French and German spoken. Colour brochure available. **Home Page**: http://wwwcyberlink.com.au/bedbreakfast/dd/terrace

Adelaide - Aldgate (Mt Lofty Ranges)
Boutique Private Inn   RAA ★★★★
Address: Cnr Kingsland & Strathalbyn Road, Aldgate, SA 5154
Name: Aldgate Village Inn Bed & Breakfast
Telephone: (08) 8370 8144 **Fax**: (08) 8339 4899
Beds: 4 Queen or 12 Single (4 bedrooms),
incl 1 apartment with kitchette fac.
Bathroom: 2 Ensuite (1 with luxury spa), 2 Private
Tariff: B&B Double $89-$185, Single $35,
Children $10, Dinner $15pp. Credit cards (VISA/MC/BC
Amex, Diners, Eptos). Vouchers accepted
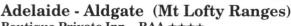
Nearest Town: Adelaide 20 mins
Aldgate is a small colonial village in a picturesque valley of orchards, vineyards, market gardens, small farms and lush eucalypt forest in th Mt Lofty Ranges which cradle the City of Adelaide. Uniquely situated a scenic 20 mins from the CBD yet retaining its bushland environment. A tourist's mecca surrounds, including the Barossa Valley and other major wineries, Cleland native flora and fauna conservation park, Warrawong Sanctuary, Botanical Gardens, Heysen Walking Trail, artists' studios, gourmet restaurants, Hahndorf, beaches, the River Murray, Aboriginal Cultural Centres and within day trips to Kangaroo Island. From Mt Lofty the views of the City and coastline are spectacular. The Village Inn, a heritage listed stone two storey building built in 1882 as a general store has been charmingly restored embracing the ambience of a bygone era with the welcoming freshness of modern amenities. Fresh flowers, folk art, crisp white linen, home cooked goodies, log fires in winter in every room and views of the surrounding wooded hills and village make it an idealistic base for your stay in S Aus. Although an intimate four roomed private Inn it is spacious. Families, couples, backpackers, every need is catered for. Privacy or friendly communal activity the choice is yours. There is even a very private spa apartment with a queen size four poster. Boutiques, markets, antiques, coffee shops, enhance the village atmosphere.

Nation Ridge Country Retreat

Adelaide - Aldgate
Boutique Inn   RAA ★★★★☆
Address: 11 Nation Ridge Road, Aldgate, SA 5154
Name: Arboury Manor
Telephone: (08) 8370 9119 **Fax**: (08) 8370 9484
Beds: 3 Queen (3 suites)
Bathroom: 3 Ensuite
Tariff: B&B (continental/buffet style) Double $95-$150, Midweek discount. All major credit cards. Room Facilities: Silver service dining. Each room is individually decorated, intimate and distinctive comprising of guest lounges, QS beds, ensuites, thick fluffy bathrobes, hair driers, direct dial STD/ISD, television, CD/cassette players, air-conditioners, fridges, tea/coffee, ironing facilities
Nearest Town: Adelaide-Aldgate

Discover our intimate hide-a-away, the perfect year round retreat. Indulge yourself in gourmet dining and gracious hospitality while relaxing in casual elegance. It's hard to imagine a nicer place in which to hide out, good book in hand with fireplaces blazing. Set in two acres of heaven with views second only to the exquisite indulgence of its designer suites overlooking the wooded valleys and vineyards below.
What makes it so special is that in every sense of the world you can enjoy its privileges, you become our personal house guest, arriving as a stranger, departing as a friend, yet the atmosphere remains professional and your every need is catered for.
Situated twenty minutes drive from Adelaide CBD and within easy driving distance of some of South Australia's most famous wineries, beaches and historic attractions. \
Home Page: arboury@bigpond.com

One of the differences between staying at a hotel and a B&B
is that you don't hug the hotel staff when you leave.

SOUTH AUSTRALIA

Adelaide - Beaumont
Homestay RAA 3 1/2 Stars   RAA ★★★☆
Address: 10 Bayview Crescent,
Beaumont, SA 5066
Name: Ella & Brian McLaren
Telephone: (08) 8379 3969
Fax: (08) 8364 4914
Beds: 1 Queen or Twin, 2 Single
(2 bedrooms) **Bathroom**: 1 Guest share
Tariff: B&B (full) Double $70, Single $40, Children - Pre-school $5, Up to 15yrs half price. Dinner $15. Credit Cards (BC/MC/VISA). Vouchers accepted
Nearest Town: Burnside 3 minutes, City of Adelaide Centre 15 minutes
"Hunterbury" nestles in the foothills of the beautiful Mt Lofty Ranges, close to the city. There are uninterrupted views of the city and the bay from Glenelg to Port Adelaide and beyond. Night views are spectacular from the guest balcony.
We are in our early retirement years with lots of hobbies and interests ... travel, sport, art. Historic Beaumont House is within walking distance of many other points of interest including Cleland, the Australian fauna park. Numerous hiking trails are also close by. Day and half day tours of the wine regions such as the Barossa Valley, Adelaide Hills, Fleurieu Peninsula and more can be arranged. Cooked breakfasts are included in the tariff. Other meals eg. snack, picnic baskets for those hills excursions are available and costed to suit your requirements. Guest living area has colour TV, books, fridge, toaster. Home made biscuits, tea and coffee making are available at all times. Heating in winter, airconditioning in summer. Concessions for families and extended stays. Pick up service - by arrangement.
Directions: *For bookings and directions - Please write, fax, or phone.*

Adelaide - Burnside
Self-contained Accommodation
Address: 542 Glynburn Road,
Burnside, SA 5066
Name: "Petts Wood Lodge"
Val & John Shave
Telephone: (08) 8331 9924
Fax: (08) 8332 5139
Mobile: (018) 829666
Beds: 1 Queen, 1 Double, 1 Single (2 bedrooms) **Bathroom**: 1 Ensuite, 1 Private
Tariff: B&B (continental) Double $85, Single $70, Children $15. Vouchers accepted $15 surcharge
Nearest Town: Adelaide 10 mins by car.
Petts Wood Lodge is a charming English Tudor style home with old world character nestled amidst a pretty cottage garden with a willow-lined stream.
Choice of 2 fully self-contained retreats adjoining main residence. Downstairs accommodation is beautifully furnished and decorated with every comfort of home. Leadlights and lace. Double bedroom and sofa bed in lounge for 3rd person. The Attic Suite features a romantic lacey 4-poster bed. Each has private outside entrance, BBQ area within wisteria covered walled garden. Relax under the willows and feed the ducks in the stream. Artists are welcome to use John's well equipped studio in the loft. Nearby are several restaurants, lovely parks, shopping, National Trust property - Beaumont House, swimming pool, tennis courts. (tennis racquets available), all within walking distance. Bus at the door for city shopping, theatres, Art Gallery, etc. Near Australian Wildlife Park, Waterfall Gully, walking trails. Ideally located for day trips to Kangaroo Island, Barossa Valley winery tours.

Adelaide - Blackwood
Ryokan (Japanese Style)
Address: 16 Brightview Avenue
Blackwood, SA 5051
Name: Allessandro Maandini's Ryokan
Telephone: (08) 8370 3507 **Fax**: (08) 8370 3507 **Mobile**: (0412) 178 026
Email: maandini@adam.com.au
Beds: 1 Queen, 1 Double, 2 Single (2 Bedrooms)
Bathroom: 2 Ensuites plus traditional Japanese steam bath. 1 ensuite sauna.
Tariff: B&B Double $150 per night. Very special backpackers rates available. Single rates negotiable. Children by arrangement. Campervans $20 per night. Dinner by prior arrangement. Credit Cards: all except Amex. Vouchers accepted two per night per double).
Nearest Town: Blackwood/Adelaide City 15 minutes

Allessandro Maandini's Ryokan is a Japanese style B&B! Whilst you don't have to sleep on the floor, you will enjoy the unique decor, not only of the Ryokan (pronounced DEE-'O'-KARM) but of the very unusual architecture of the house; not to mention the friendly host. Maandini is a comedy writer and designer. He will entertain you and gladly show you his unique collection of racing and vintage + classic cars. Rarely will you see another Formula two car awaiting restoration in a lounge room setting! Enjoy the open fire in this stunning Japanese inspired contemporary home amongst tall trees. Experience the city lights, nearby quality restaurants, golf courses, the wine country or adjacent Flora + Fauna Reserves. Alternatively just relax in the JAPANESE STEAM BATH.
In-house tours, Rolls Royce transfers / tours, rides in racing car or vintage car tours can be arranged. Fully catered gourmet meals (Japanese or European style) also available by prior arrangement.
Homepage: http://www.adam.com.au/~maandini/snakes.html.

SOUTH AUSTRALIA

Adelaide - Burnside/St Georges
Homestay+Self-contained Accommodation
Address: "Kirkendale",
16 Inverness Avenue, St. Georges, SA 5064
Name: Jenny & Steve Studer
Telephone: (08) 8338 2768
Fax: (08) 8338 2760 **Mobile**: 0412 102516
Email: kirken@merlin.net.au
Beds: 1 Double, 2 Single (1 suite/2 bedrooms)
Bathroom: 1 Private
Tariff: B&B (continental) Double $75-$90, Children $15, Dinner $15, Cooked breakfast at nominal extra cost. Credit Cards (VISA/BC/MC/AMEX/DC). Vouchers accepted
Nearest Town: 5km SE Adelaide, 10 mins city centre, 20 mins Airport.

Appealing "Country-style" 3 room suite, nestled in peaceful, leafy garden, sun-dappled patio, french doors, terracotta floors, rose garden. Fresh flowers, fruit basket, generous breakfasts, real coffee, books, magazines. Private entrance, quiet location.
Jenny and Steve are well travelled with many interests .... sports, the arts, history, gardening.
Restaurants, parks, shopping and bus nearby. Tours arranged.
What guests say.....
"What a break, I knew I would love it and I did! Beauty with peace and quiet".
"Absolutely perfect! We'll be sure to return".
"Beautiful setting and peaceful and tranquil - birds and nature - accommodation spotless and new - well done. Warm welcome and made to feel comfortable".
"Wonderful (as usual); this must be one of the nicest places to stay in Adelaide".
"Charming, comfortable, warm - friendly environment .... perfect! Thank you for making our stay in Adelaide a wonderful experience".
Home Page: http://www.cyberlink.com.au/bedbreakfast/kirkendale

Adelaide - Goodwood
Homestay
Address: 29 Albert St, Goodwood, SA 5034
Name: "Rose Villa" Doreen Petherick
Telephone: (08) 8271 2947
Beds: 1 King/Twin (1 bedroom)
Bathroom: 1 Ensuite
Tariff: B&B (full) Double $90-$95, Single $70. Vouchers accepted
Nearest Town: Adelaide 3km to GPO

'Rose Villa' is a charming elegantly furnished private suite (with own entrance) adjoining a sandstone Edwardian villa, built at the turn of the century. King size bed (can be altered into 2 singles), en-suite, RC air conditioning, TV, tea, coffee facilities, lounge-dining area overlooking garden. It is ideally situated in the historic suburb of Goodwood, within walking distance of trendy Hyde Park, with its flowers shops and boutiques, cafes and coffee shops - a great place for my guests to stroll. Famous Haigh's Chocolates outlet is closeby as are trams (to the bay) buses and trains to the city. Candlelit breakfast served in dining room or prepared al fresco in the garden.
My overseas trips have given me an appreciation of what is required in the hospitality industry.
'Rose Villa' is roses, romance and caring hospitality - It is Adelaide's Best Kept Secret. You are most welcome.
Directions: *Please phone or write.*

SOUTH AUSTRALIA

Adelaide - Leabrook
Homestay/B&B   RAA ★★★☆
Address: "Leabrook Lodge B&B",
314 Kensington Rd, Leabrook,
5068 South Australia
Name: Barbara Carter
Telephone: (08) 8331 7619
Fax: (08) 8364 4955
Email: barbara.carter@bigpond.com

Beds: 2 Double, 2 Single (4 bedrooms) **Bathroom**: 2 Ensuite, 2 Private
Tariff: B&B (full) Double $80-$90, Single $45-$75, Children by arrangement.
Dinner $20. Credit card. Vouchers accepted
Nearest Town: Adelaide 5km

Leabrook Lodge is ideally located in a prestigious suburb, surrounded by some of the best parks and gardens. The charming stone bungalow with warm period decor, provides guests with a restful atmosphere where they can relax and enjoy their stay. Depending of the weather, a full breakfast is served in the courtyard and no effort is spared to ensure the best is offered with regard to comfort and style.
Downtown Adelaide is 5km by bus or car and there is easy access to the Barossa, Southern Vales wineries, golf courses, beaches tennis etc.
Dinner and picnic baskets by arrangement - 200m to excellent restaurants. Free dinner on Wednesday night with family.
Because we have spent many years in Adelaide, and have travelled extensively, we are able to offer assistance to plan your day or to arrange any tours as required.
Reduced rates for winter. Bankcard, Visa and Mastercard accepted.
Home Page: www.users.bigpond.com/barbara.carter

Adelaide - Norwood
Homestay
Address: 101 Kensington Road,
Norwood, SA 5067
Name: "Laurel Villa"
Telephone: (08) 8332 7388 after hours please.
Fax: (08) 8431 5902
Beds: 1 Double, 4 Single (3 bedrooms)
Bathroom: 1 Guest share
Tariff: B&B (continental) Double $70, Single $45, Cooked breakfast available at nominal extra cost. Children over nine years of age. Vouchers accepted
Nearest Town: Norwood, Adelaide 3km

Laurel Villa is an early Victorian home, with thick bluestone walls, high ceilings, ceiling roses and chandeliers. Located in the historic Kensington-Norwood area (one of Adelaide's earliest settlements), many of the early buildings of the 1840s still exist. Surrounded by lovely homes and gardens, walks are both historically interesting and pleasant. Laurel Villa's two large twin-bedded and one double-bedded room have electric blankets and antique washstands with old-style jugs for making tea and coffee. Breakfast, served in the dining room before a log fire in winter, or on a sunny patio, may bring such surprises as home-made oatmeal or bran muffins, or "Apple Dutch Babies" (Laurel Villa's owner loves to spoil her guests!) She is well-acquainted with South Australia's unique attractions such as the Flinders Ranges and Kangaroo Island, and is a member of the National Trust and the local historical society.
The nearby Norwood Parade, one of Adelaide's most popular shopping areas with a distinct Continental flavour, boasts an assortment of good cafes and restaurants and colonial-style pubs offering "good tucker" at very reasonable prices.
Smoking is permitted in the garden.

SOUTH AUSTRALIA

Adelaide - Rosslyn Park
Homestay RAA ★★★★
Address: 17 Mary Penfold Drive,
Rosslyn Park, SA 5072
Name: Mary Penfold Panorama
Telephone: (08) 8332-6684
Fax: (08) 8332-6684
Mobile: (015) 392414
Beds: 2 Double, 2 Single (2 bedrooms)
Bathroom: 2 (for Guest only)
Tariff: B&B (continental) Double $90, Single $75, Children welcome. Dinner on request. Vouchers accepted
Nearest Town: Adelaide 6km

Welcome to one of Adelaide's exclusive suburbs, Rosslyn Park and enjoy staying next to the cradle of South Australia's wine industry - the original and famous Penfold's Vineyard established in 1884, only 6km from the city centre. You will experience the comfort of a modern, luxurious, two storey, air conditioned residence, with excellent views by day, but at night you can take in the broad, sweeping panorama of city lights, spread out across the Adelaide Plains beneath you - a lasting beautiful memory. You will appreciate the well appointed guest facilities including the indoor spa. Two large bedrooms are either double (Queen size beds) or twin. Colour TV, stereo, electronic organ and outdoor barbeque facilities are available for your use.

Nearby, a good selection of restaurants, Penfold and Stonyfell winerys, cafes and hotels all offering food at reasonable prices. Public transport within short walking distance. Car parking available on site. Your hosts, Bruce and Marian Jennings, a retired professional couple, who enjoy meeting people. Smoking: outdoors only. **Directions**: *Please telephone of fax for brochure with map. Discount available for longer stays.*

Adelaide - Seacliff Park
Homestay
Address: PO Box 319,
Brighton, SA 5048
Name: Ruth Humphrey & son Tim
Telephone: (08) 8298-6671
Fax: (08) 8298 6671
Beds: 1 Double, 2 Single (2 bedrooms)
Bathroom: 1 Guests share
Tariff: B&B (full) Double $54, Single $32;
Children & Dinner by arrangement. Vouchers accepted
Nearest Town: Brighton 2km, Adelaide 14 km

Ours is a quiet suburb on the slopes behind Seacliff quite near to the popular beaches of Brighton and Glenelg. There are good shopping complexes within a short drive and we are close to bus and train routes to the city.
This is also an excellent base for touring the Southern Vales (wineries and scenery) and Fleurieu Peninsula with its beautiful scenery and many points of interest.
We have a spacious home with a large pleasant garden. Our two guest bedrooms are upstairs, with guest bathroom and a guests' lounge area. There is cooling in summer and an open fire downstairs in winter. For everyone's well-being we do not allow smoking or pets in the house.
Having travelled widely ourselves, we feel that we can cater for the needs of visitors. Our many guests, both from Australia and overseas, have enjoyed their stay with us, and we look forward to welcoming them back as well as making new friends.
Directions: *Please write or phone.*

SOUTH AUSTRALIA

Adelaide - Somerton Park
Guest House RAA ★★★☆
Address: 19 King George Ave.,
Somerton Park, SA 5044
Name: John & Marilyn Forster
Telephone: (08) 8298-3393
Beds: 1 King-size or 2 Single
(1 bedroom)
Bathroom: 1 Ensuite
Tariff: B&B (full) Double $55,
Single $40. Vouchers accepted
Nearest Town: Glenelg 2.5 km north, Adelaide 12 km east

Our home is in a residential area 600 meters from the beautiful Somerton Beach. We are 2.5 kms south of Glenelg, a bustling seaside resort with Amusement Park, sports and entertainment areas, and "a mile" of shopping and dining along Jetty Road. A City bus passes the house and travels through Glenelg en route to Adelaide. A vintage tram runs from Glenelg to the heart of Adelaide. Use our bicycles if you would like to pedal along the Esplanade. Of course, a swim in the sea or a walk on the beach can be as invigorating or serene as you wish to make it!

Guests are accommodated in a lovely, new bedroom with a rear garden view, en suite bath, private entrance, colour TV and off-street parking. There is a choice of king-size, single, or twin beds. Warm, freshly baked bread is included in the breakfast. No smoking indoors please.

Adelaide - Springfield
Homestay RAA ★★★☆
Address: "Wharfedale",
Springfield, 5062 Please phone
Name: Romaine & Chris Dawson
Telephone: (08) 8379 1935
Mobile: 0419824402
Beds: 2 Queen, 1 Double
(3 bedrooms)
Bathroom: 1 Ensuite, 1 Private
Tariff: B&B (full) Suite $165,
Double $95, Single $75, Dinner $20. Vouchers accepted surcharge
Nearest Town: Adelaide 6km

Built to capture the best of sun and shade, Wharfedale House sits alongside gentle hills with spectacular views. Close to the city, it is perfect for relaxation or as a base to explore local wineries, heritage architecture, walking trails, parks and Kangaroo Island. Set among prominent homes linked to early colonial life, Wharfedale is built in Mediterranean style and surrounded by mature poplars and plane trees. Providing quality accommodation, comfort, privacy, you can choose to stay in the ground floor guest room - a queen bedroom with ensuite and lounge or you may stay in the first floor private suite which sleeps 4. This has queen bedroom, double bedroom, bathroom, huge sitting room (open fireplace, fridge & toaster) and balcony. R / C air-conditioning is available for all guests. Non smokers preferred. A cooked breakfast is inclusive in all tariffs.
We are keen walkers and offer ideas for day trips if needed.
Off street parking; use of laundry available.

SOUTH AUSTRALIA

Adelaide - Thorngate
Homestay
Address: 4 Carter St, Thorngate, 5082
Name: "Myoora" *Member of Bed & Breakfast South Australia Town and Country*
Telephone: (08) 8344 2599
Fax: (08) 8344 9575
Mobile: (041) 428 321
Beds: 3 Queen, 1 Double (4 bedrooms) **Bathroom**: 3 Ensuite, 1 Private
Tariff: B&B (full cooked) Double ensuite spa $190, Double ensuite $170, Double $150. Credit Cards.
Nearest Town: Adelaide City 3km

Connoisseurs of Australian architecture and 19th century history will delight in their representation at Myoora.
This 1892 Victorian homestead smack bang in the heart of Adelaide has been restored to offer guests an elegant and peaceful retreat.
Open fires, ensuite facilities, 2 private sitting rooms and even a traditional drawing room provide the grace of the era for your sojourn in either of the four guest rooms (two with spa baths), tastefully decorated with original paintings, antiques and Persian rugs, all in the traditional style.
The grace and charm is not only captured inside Myoora. Outside, shady trees decorate the acre of garden, with a heated swimming pool and spa awaiting or, for the more energetic, a grass tennis court beckons.
Only three kilometres from city, and minutes from cafes, shopping boutiques, and delightful parklands, this really is a luxurious place to recoup.

Adelaide Hills - Birdwood
Self-contained Accommodation RAA ★★★☆ *Member of Bed & Breakfast South Australia Town and Country*
Address: 38 Olivedale St., Birdwood, 5234
Name: Birdwood Bed & Breakfast
Telephone: (08) 8568 5444 **Fax**: (08) 8568 5444 **Mobile**: 015 360 285
Beds: 2 Double, 2 Single (3 bedrooms)
Bathroom: 1 Ensuite, 1 Private
Tariff: B&B (full) Double $80-$120, Children $15pp. Dinner $25pp, Credit cards.
   Vouchers accepted $30 surcharge Studio
Nearest Town: Birwood. 45 km NE Adelaide GPO

Two delightful private cottages; nestled in a secluded native gardens; a bird-watching haven. THE STUDIO: a quaint mud brick cottage, decorated with period furnishings, intimate dining beside a wood-fire. Romantic lace-canopy over bed, and hand embroidered linen. Ensuite spa and bubble bath. Chocolates, biscuits and port to savour. KOOKABURRA COTTAGE: Timber cottage, wood panelled country style decor. Two bedrooms, ideal for families and singles. Air-conditioned, electric heating and cosy electric blankets. Romantic master bedroom. Sample homemade preserves and country craft. Welcome treats and touring assistance.
Your hostess is an award-winning Australian wildlife artist whose private studio is open to guests. Each cottage displays her original pastel paintings, and Pam can advise guests on wildlife experiences in South Australia.
Birdwood's village atmosphere reflects its German heritage. Birdwood is centrally located between Hahndorf and Barossa Valley, 35km from Adelaide.
Home to the National Motor Museum, with wineries, galleries, restaurants, antique shops, and family attractions nearby. Bush walking and cycling.

SOUTH AUSTRALIA

Adelaide Hills - Stirling
Self-contained Accommodation RAA ★★★☆
Address: 6 Glenside Rd,
Crafers, SA 5152
Name: Nancy & Nigel Monteith
Telephone: (08) 8339 2266
Fax: (08) 8370 8292
Beds: 1 Queen, 2 Single
(2 bedrooms)
Bathroom: 1 Private
Tariff: B&B (Provision for full)
Double $100, Single $90, Children $15. Vouchers accepted $20 surcharge
Nearest Town: Stirling

Montesca Lodge offers superb accommodation in 1 double &1 twin bedroom and a spacious lounge overlooking the garden. Enjoy fresh flowers and fruit, TV, air-conditioned and electrically heated comfort.
Provisions for a country cooked breakfast are available in the sunny, well-equipped kitchen. Relax and stroll through the gardens, have a game of tennis on the all weather court or explore the town, wineries, crafts, restaurants and galleries of the Adelaide Hills. Day trips can be made exploring the FLEURIEU PENINSULA, VICTOR HARBOUR AND BAROSSA VALLEY, McLAREN VALE AND CLARE wine districts.
The garden has been open under the 'open garden' scheme and contains many oaks, elms and other trees over 100 years old. Camellias are a major feature of the several acres of garden and woodland.

Alawoona - near Riverland
Farmstay - RAA ★★★☆
Address: "Briaken Park",
Alawoona, South Australia 5333
Name: Ken & Juliette Griffiths
Telephone: (08) 8587 4326
Fax: (08) 8587 4366
Beds: 1 Double, 2 Single (2 bedrooms)
Bathroom: 1 Guests share,
1 Family share
Tariff: B&B (full) Double $70,
No facilities for children. Dinner $20.
Full Board $75 per person. Vouchers accepted
Nearest Town: Loxton 50km

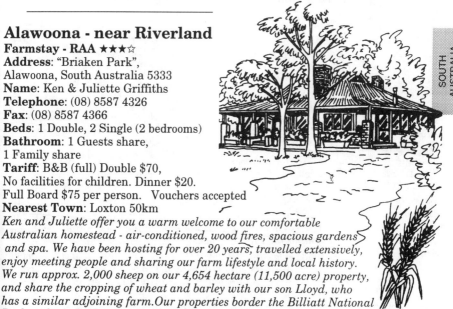

Ken and Juliette offer you a warm welcome to our comfortable Australian homestead - air-conditioned, wood fires, spacious gardens and spa. We have been hosting for over 20 years, travelled extensively, enjoy meeting people and sharing our farm lifestyle and local history.
We run approx. 2,000 sheep on our 4,654 hectare (11,500 acre) property, and share the cropping of wheat and barley with our son Lloyd, who has a similar adjoining farm. Our properties border the Billiatt National Park and we also host numerous kangaroos and emus.
Loxton in the beautiful Riverland wine and fruit growing area is only an easy drive of 50km. **Directions**: 240km east of Adelaide on Murray Bridge - Loxton Highway. Phone for directions.

SOUTH AUSTRALIA

Barossa Valley - Nuriootpa
Guest House   RAA ★★★☆
Address: "Karawatha Guest House",
Cnr Greenock & Stonewell Rds,
Nuriootpa, 5355
Name: Tony & Cheryle Pinkess
Telephone: (08) 8562 1746
Beds: 2 Queen, 1 Double, 5 Single
(4 bedrooms) 3 double sofa beds available
Bathroom: 3 Ensuite, 1 Private
Tariff: B&B (full) Double $70-$80, Single $45, Children $10-$15, Dinner $15, Campervans welcome. Vouchers accepted
Nearest Town: Nuriootpa, 3.5km.

- *"Friendly people, comfy beds and nice big breakfast"*
- *"Plenty of good food, good wine, good times - thanks for everything"*
- *"What more can I say, I had a great time being one of the family - I'll be back"*
- *"Like a good B&B in England - Plus!!"*

Just a few comments found in our treasured Visitor Book. "Karawatha" meaning "a place in the pines" boasts being the first B&B in the Barossa Valley is set on 5 acres consisting of almond orchard and incorporates our large two storey home. Our three private guest units are on the ground floor all with ensuites and private facilities. We have a pool which we encourage our guests to enjoy an Aussie BBQ. Enjoy exploring the famous wineries, restaurants, craft shops and the 'olde world' charm of the Barossa Valley. Karawatha is also centrally located for day trippers to visit Adelaide, the Riverland and the Clare Valley regions.
Halfway between Nuriootpa and Greenock. (3.5km from Nuriootpa).

Barossa Valley - Tanunda
Self-contained Accommodation
Address: Lawley Farm, **RAA ★★★★**
Krondorf Road, P.O. Box 103,
Tanunda S.A. 5352
Name: Sancha & Bruce Withers
Telephone: (08) 8563 2141
Fax: (08) 8563 2141
Mobile: 041 781 3567
Beds: 5 King/Queen, 1 Double,
1 Single (7 bedrooms) **Bathroom**: 6 Ensuite

Tariff: B&B (full) Double $120-$143, Single $90, Children $16-$25.
Nearest Town: Tanunda 5 km

Lawley Farm, in the centre of the Barossa, offers four star quality accommodation in an historic setting of great charm. There are six self-contained suites - two each in the original cottage and barn (circa 1850) and two in the unique "new cottage" with an atmosphere of history emanating the old stone and timbers from which it was built. Antique cottage furnishings combine with modern amenities to give a special sort of pleasure and relaxation. Facilities include games room, spa baths, romantic old cellar and 1.5 ha of orchard and native woodland where guests can enjoy a picnic or barbecue or just stroll and pick the fruit in season.
A country breakfast is provided in the farmhouse dining room or guests can prepare their own with provisions supplied.
The farm is ideally situated for enjoying the many attractions of the Barossa - wine tasting, good restaurants, galleries, museums, historic buildings, country walks, balloon flights - all within 10 km. **Directions**: *Please phone.*

SOUTH AUSTRALIA

Barossa Valley - Tanunda
Self-contained Accommodation   RAA ★★★★☆
Address: "Blickinstal Hillside B&B",
Rifle Range Rd, Tanunda, SA 5352
Name: John & Alicia Gerkens
Telephone: (08) 8563 2716
Fax: (08) 8563 2716
Beds: 5 Queen, 1 Double,
4 Single (6 bedrooms)
Bathroom: 6 Ensuite

Tariff: B&B (full) Double $98-$135, Single $98-$135, Children $30. Credit cards. Vouchers accepted $18-$51 surcharge.
Nearest Town: Tanunda 4km

Enjoy the best of both worlds from our tranquil hillside retreat; the peace and quiet of the country and the unique European heritage of the Barossa, with its great food and wine.
"Blickinstal" which means 'view into the valley' is set amidst rolling hills and vineyards just five minutes from historic Tanunda and its renowned restaurants, wineries, art and craft galleries, antique shops and rich heritage.
Our 100 acre property, nestled in the foothills, offers spectacular views over the Valley. The four modern, beautifully appointed bed-sitter units and two new split-level lodges, RAA rated 4 1/2 star, are fully self-contained, with homely, personal touches like fresh flowers, fruit, real coffee and our own farm fresh eggs. Enjoy the delights of the Region, explore the nearby Conservation Park, take scenic walks, or just relax and savour the panoramic views and magnificent sunsets. We look forward to making you welcome at Blickinstal!

Birdwood see Adelaide Hills

Burra
Self-contained Accommodation
Address: Truro Street, Burra, 5417
Name: Burra Heritage Cottages
-"Tivers Row"
Telephone: (08) 8892 2461
Fax: (08) 8892 2461
Beds: 7 Double, 2 Single (2 bedrooms per cottage)
Bathroom: 1 Private each cottage
Tariff: Per cottage B&B (full) Double $90-$120, Single $85, Children $25. Credit Cards. Vouchers accepted $15 surcharge.
Nearest Town: Burra

This row of six self contained cottages, built in 1856, is on the registers of the National Estate, State Heritage Items and the National Trust. Four four roomed cottages have been renovated to a high standard including underfloor heating in the new bathrooms. Accommodation includes a cosy wood fire in the parlour (wood supplied), beds with dunas and electric blankets and ingredients for a hearty country breakfast. Private cottage gardens. The cottages are situated in a semi rural environment on the edge of town with views over rolling hills and the Redruth Gaol, where Breaker Morant was filmed. Burra is Australia's premier historic copper mining town (1845) and the whole town has been proclaimed a State Heritage Area.
Cottage owners Maureen and Barry Wright have travelled Australia extensively, published a book of charts of the River Murray, and own Sara's Antique Shop in Burra.
We recommend visitors allow at least two days to explore.

Clare Valley - Sevenhill
Country House   RAA ★★★★☆
Address: College Road, Sevenhill via Clare, SA 5453
Name: Thorn Park Country House
Telephone: (08) 8843 4304 **Fax**: (08) 8843 4296 **Mobile**: 0412 411 152
Beds: 6 Double (6 bedrooms)
Bathroom: 6 Ensuite
Tariff: B&B (full) Double $260, Single $160. Dinner $45, Children $95. Credit Cards (BC, Visa, MC, AMEX, Diners).
Nearest Town: Clare 6 kms

In the heart of the Clare Valley lies Thorn Park Country House, a truly magnificent country home of traditional Australian style. Set in 60 acres of pastoral splendour it boasts tranquil vistas of undulating farmland studded with towering gums, grazing sheep and a dam; home to native ducks and other birdlife.
The homestead was built in the 1850's from stone quarried on the site and was extensively restored in recent years to its original magnificence. The tranquil gardens feature hawthorn, elms and roses; a surround to the homestead in the traditional manner.
The house spreads itself to include six bedrooms, each with its own ensuite, with accommodation for 12 guests. The reception areas include a spacious drawing room, intimate library and magnificent art collection.
David and Michael are devoted to memorable dining, with food prepared utilising fresh, local produce. Meals are accompanied by the truly magnificent wines of the Clare Valley region.
For enquiries and reservations: Telephone (08) 8843 4304 Fax (08) 8843 4296
Award Winner Logo

Always have a phone card with you.
Most public phones do not take coins.

SOUTH AUSTRALIA

Coonawarra - Naracoorte
Individual Farm Cottages   RAA ★★★☆
Address: Wongary Farm,
Concrete Bridge Rd. Joanna via Naracoorte.
Postal: Box 236 Naracoorte, SA 5271
Name: Robert & Diana Hooper
Telephone: (08) 8762 3038
 Fax: (08) 8762 3394
Mobile: (0418) 838213
Email: Wongary@rbm.com.au
Beds: 3 Queen, 1 Double, 8 Single,
(6 bedrooms)
Bathroom: Ensuite, Private, 1 Spa bath
Tariff: B&B (continental) Double $100-$110, Single $60, Children welcome. Dinner by arrangement. Credit cards. Pets welcome. Vouchers accepted $20 surcharge
Nearest Town: Midway Melbourne/Adelaide......at Joanna. 20 kms from Naracoorte
Individual, cosy, restored, Multi Award Winning, self contained cottages with private bathrooms featuring either a luxury, heated, 2-person spa or deep cast-iron bath. Linger over generous complimentary breakfast provisions with fresh farm eggs and quality plunger coffee. Wood fires, Queen sized beds, linen, electric blankets, air-conditioning, laundry, colour TV, antiques, books, games, lawn-tennis, pond, farm animals and relaxing BBQ patios are freely provided for your comfort and enjoyment.
Cottages accommodate two to eight guests and nestle amidst rolling fields and vineyards close to the famous World Heritage Naracoorte Caves or Coonawarra's winning wineries and superb regional restaurants **Home Page**: Wongary@rbm.com.au.

Cygnet River see Kangaroo Island

Gawler
Farmstay   RAA ★★★★
Address: Oxley Farm
Fairley Road Kangaroo Flat, Gawler 5118 SA
Name: Andrew & Rhonda Brooke
Telephone: (08) 8522 3703 **Fax**: (08) 8522 3703
Mobile: (041) 986 9957

Beds: 4 Queen, 12 Single (4 Bedrooms) **Bathroom**: 4 Ensuites
Tariff: B&B (full) Double $80, Single $60, Lunch and Dinner by arrangement. Children: 0-5 years free, 5-12 years $10, over 12 years $20. Credit Cards: Mastercard, Bankcard, Visa.
Nearest Town: Gawler

OXLEY FARM
Each room has reverse cycle air-conditioning, and solid colonial timber furniture, television and radio. Purified filtered water supplied as required. Each room has its own outdoor setting surrounded by palm trees. A fully cooked farm style breakfast included in tariff. Kennels are available, no smoking allowed in rooms.
Set in acres of native gums you can feed the baby farm animals, help with the daily goat milking, or just enjoy a pleasant walk around the farm. Relax in the spa or have a game of half court tennis. KANGAROO FLAT
Historic Gawler only 5 mins away (golf, swimming pool, pub, cafes, coffee shops) trotting (free entry for guests) and horse racing tracks. Famous Barossa Valley wineries only 25 mins away.
Roseworthy college agricultural interpretation centre only a few kilometres away.

SOUTH AUSTRALIA

Goolwa - The Coorong
Country House   RAA ★★★★☆   Member of Bed & Breakfast SOUTH AUSTRALIA TOWN AND COUNTRY
Address: Birks Harbour,
138A Liverpool Road, Goolwa, SA 5214
Name: Michael & Luise Andrewartha
Telephone: (08) 8555 5393   **Fax**: (08) 8555 5228   **Mobile**: 017 940715
Beds: 3 Queen (3 bedrooms)   **Bathroom**: 3 Ensuite
Tariff: B&B (full) Double $125 to $135,
Special packages available. Credit Cards
(VISA/MC/BC/AMEX/DINERS).Vouchers accepted $40 surcharge
Nearest Town: 1.7km Goolwa, 90km south of Adelaide on the Murray River.

Historic Goolwa lies on the Fleurieu Peninsula near the Murray Mouth. Birks Harbour can arrange access by water and air to the world renowned Coorong, a unique dramatic waterway, the home of ancient Aboriginal culture, hundreds of bird species and wildlife.

The private guest entrance lobby with its refreshment facilities leads to the three luxury air-conditioned bedrooms, with queen sized beds, electric blankets, TV and spacious ensuites.

The huge living room with its large open fireplace is a comfortable place to relax with a wide range of books, CDs, videos and historic local information.

The delicious breakfast features homemade jams and local produce.

The house is surrounded by mature trees, walled gardens and spacious land which leads down to the private marina providing tranquillity for outdoor relaxing.

There is ready access for river trips, fine restaurants, local wineries, historic railway and river history and wildlife.

Residential liquor license available featuring local wines.

Kangaroo Island - Cygnet River
Homestay   RAA 3 1/2 Star   RAA ★★★☆
Address: "Koala Lodge", Playford Highway,
Cygnet River, Kangaroo Island, SA 5223
Name: Ken & Gisèle Wright
Telephone: (08) 8553 9006   **Fax**: (08) 8553 9006
Beds: 2 Double, 3 Single (2 bedrooms)
Bathroom: 2 Ensuite
Tariff: B&B (continental) Double $85, Single $75,
Children $15. Credit cards. Vouchers accepted
Nearest Town: Kingscote (8 mins by car or 14km)

A koala or two to greet you, friendly hosts to welcome you; it happens at Koala Lodge! Surrounded by magnificent gum trees, abundant with birdlife and over a hundred fruit trees, Koala Lodge gives a peaceful, country atmosphere yet offers all the facilities of first class accommodation. Our two units are spotlessly clean and have been described by former guests as delightful, superb, tastefully decorated, home away from home etc. Each room provides everything for your comfort and privacy; own entrance, ensuite, R/C air-conditioning, colour TV, refrigerator, tea and toast facilities. A lovely continental breakfast is served to your room. Kangaroo Island offers Australian flora and fauna at its best, has many wonderful natural attractions to appreciate and is truly a bird watcher's paradise. Gisele speaks French fluently and we also operate Boomerang Rent-A-Car.

Everyone is very welcome at Koala Lodge and we will make sure your holiday is one you'll never forget.

SOUTH AUSTRALIA

Kangaroo Island - Penneshaw
Traditional Bed & Breakfast RAA 4 1/2 Star
Address: "Seaview Lodge, KI",
Willoughby Road, Penneshaw,
Kangaroo Island, SA 5222
Name: Neil & Sue Schultz
Telephone: (08) 8553 1132
Fax: (08) 8553 1183
Beds: 4 Queen, 2 Single (5 bedrooms)
Bathroom: 4 Ensuite, 1 Guests share
Tariff: B&B (full) Double $79-$110, Single $41, Children $27 (1-14yrs). Dinner $26 (Children half price). Credit cards. Vouchers accepted
Nearest Town: 1km west of Penneshaw on Willoughby Road.

This historic guest house built c1860 contains a total of fifteen rooms of which only five are used for guest's bedrooms. Three double rooms all have open fireplaces, original polished floors and all have ensuite.

Being situated only 1km from the Ferry Service, Seaview Lodge is an ideal base to discover the many pleasures of this beautiful island. We will make sure guests are properly catered for as we are fully licensed and provide evening meals with prior arrangement.

The cottage style gardens have an abundance of roses, daffodils and other older style cottage plants which attract Blue Wrens, Goldfinches, Honeyeaters etc. Simply sitting on the verandah with a drink or cup of tea or coffee is very relaxing.

Your hosts live on the premises and so will ensure guests enjoy old fashioned hospitality, together with the charm of this former guest house and its location will make guests' stay on Kangaroo Island a truly memorable one.

Lameroo
Farmstay RAA ★★★☆
Address: Meranwyney Host Farm and Wildlife Sanctuary, Box 51 Lameroo, South Australia 5302
Name: Kay & Doug Day
Telephone: (08) 8576 5215 **Fax**: (08) 8576 5215
Beds: 1 Double, 3 Single (3 bedrooms)
Bathroom: 1 Ensuite, 1 Private
Tariff: B&B (full) Double $90, Single $45, Children under 2 No charge, 2-14 half price. Dinner $18. Full accommodation $90 per person per day, includes all meals, guided farm tours and demonstrations. We only take one booking at a time. Vouchers accepted
Nearest Town: Lameroo *Meranwyney Host Farm offers a real farm holiday with traditional Australian country hospitality. Located between the Billiat and Ngarkat Conservation Parks in the unique Mallee region of eastern South Australia, Meranwyney is a 2,000 acre organic cereal and sheep farm, and a proclaimed wildlife sanctuary with 500 acres of heritage bushland. Hosts are middle aged with four grown children. Interests include people, books, theatre, music, education and travel. You will be the sole guests at Meranwyney and have a completely personalized holiday, enjoying genuine farm activities including sheep shearing, wool handling, machinery demonstrations, animal feeding, breadmaking, farm tours and guided bushwalks seeing native birds, animals, wildflowers and historic sites both European and Aboriginal all on Meranwyney. You have the use of all facilities in the air-conditioned homestead. All the meals are home cooked and mostly grown organically on the property. Meranwyney Host Farm is an Australian experience to treasure and remember.*

SOUTH AUSTRALIA

Mannum
Farmstay+Self-contained Accommodation   RAA ★★★
Address: Mannaroo Farm, East Front Rd, Mannum, S.A.   Postal: RSD 528.b Mannum 5238
Name: Bobbie & Ian Mann
Telephone: (08) 8569 1646 **Fax**: (08) 8569 1646
Beds: 2 Double, 2 Single (3 bedrooms)
Bathroom: 1 Private
Tariff: B&B (full) Double $85, Single $60, Children $10, Dinner $20.
Nearest Town: Mannum

Mannaroo Farm is a spacious homestead on a grain, sheep and cattle property of over 4,200 acres, situated 12 km from Mannum along scenic East Front Road.
The guests bedrooms and lounge have superb views of the River Murray and wetlands which abound with birdlife. A photographer and artists paradise! The guest suite includes own bathroom, lounge with open fire, many antiques, games room with large billiard table. Pedal or row boats are available. Farm tours include heritage scrub walk to mallee fowl nest and see fossils in the limestone cliffs. Attractions at Mannum, an historic river boat town, include the "Marion" paddle steamer, old wares and craft shops - also an attractive golf course.

McLaren Vale
Homestay+Self-contained Accommodation
Address: 56 Valley View Drive, McLaren Vale, SA 5171
Name: "McLaren Vale B&B Host: Bev Mitchell
Telephone: (08) 8323 9351 **Fax**: (08) 8323 9948 **Mobile**: (0418) 803379
Beds: (Trad.) 1 Queen, 1 Double, 1 Single (2 bedrooms) (Cottage) 1 Queen, 1 Double, 1 sofa bed (2 bedrooms)
Bathroom: (Trad.) 1 Guest share (Cottage) 1 Private
Tariff: (Trad.) B&B (full) Double $75, Single $50, Children negotiable. Cottage: B&B (full) Double $100, Min 2 nights. Children negotiable. Credit Cards (BC/VISA/MC/JCB). Vouchers accepted
Nearest Town: McLaren Vale 1km

McLaren Vale offers approximately 50 Boutique wineries, fascinating restaurants, plant nurseries, a chocolate factory, doll museum, antique and craft shops, also picnic areas, bush walks and beautiful beaches nearby. Enjoy a peaceful stay in traditional hosted accommodation, or the privacy of a two bedroom fully self-contained cottage - you share this with a host of Teddy Bears.
Both offer homemade bread, cake, biscuits, jams, fresh farm eggs, everything for a full cooked breakfast supplied in the cottage. Bev cooks for you at home. There are patchwork quilts, books, board games, TV and Video, CD player, BBQ and a picnic hamper is available. A pool table at home. The cottage is air-conditioned and there is a gas heater. Outdoor seating on the back patio. No smoking in the house or cottage. Inspection welcome. It pays to book. AA rated traditional 3 1/2 Star, Cottage 4 Star. WE SPOIL YOU!

Please help us provide the best hospitality in the world.
Fill in a comment form for every place you stay.

Melrose
Farmstay
Address: Box 17 Melrose, SA 5483
Name: Yvonne & Don Bishop
Telephone: (08) 8666 4209 or
(08) 8666 2152 **Fax**: (08) 8666 2155
Beds: 2 Double, 1 Single (3 bedrooms)
Bathroom: 1 Guests share
Tariff: B&B (full) Double $70, Single $50,
Children half price. Dinner $20. Campervans $20. Vouchers accepted
Nearest Town: Murray Town 15 km south of Melrose.

Travelling North, South, East or West. Looking for somewhere to stay? We invite you to visit Vondon Host Farm.
A stone homestead on a 6000 acre sheep and grain property, set in the Southern Flinders Ranges, close to major highways. We offer a unique stop over (or longer) experience with genuine friendly farm hospitality.
We are ideally situated for day trips with Mount Remarkable National Park minutes away. Melrose the oldest town in the Flinders Ranges is a great place to view old and historical buildings such as Jacka's Brewery, Old Couthouse Museum.
Our family has been in the area for 117 years and would be pleased to suggest places to visit. We look forward to sharing our lifestyle with you and to show you some of the working practices of a farming experience.
Directions: *Please phone. Brochure available on request.*
Home Page: dkbishop@bigpond.com

Mount Gambier
Hosted B&B
Address: "Berry Hill"
off Cafpirco Road, Mount Gambier
Name: David & Denise Bell
Telephone: (08) 8725 9912
Fax: (08) 8725 9912 **Mobile**: (018) 838242
Email: berryhill@seol.net.au
Beds: 1 Queen, 1 Double (2 bedrooms) **Bathroom**: 1 Ensuite, 1 Private
Tariff: B&B (full) Double $95-$100, Single $75, Dinner $25, Credit Cards. Vouchers accepted $20 surcharge. Not accepted during long weekend holidays (SA)
Nearest Town: Mount Gambier (5km west of Mount Gambier)

David and Denise welcome you to Berry Hill B&B as their guests, to relax in a spacious modern country home while enjoying the tranquil views of a rolling rural landscape over afternoon tea on arrival.
The B&B is situated on a berry farm. The 20 acres have been widely replanted with Australian native flora.
The house is nestled in an extensive garden which has a wide range of cottage and native plants ensuring a display of native birds.
Guests have their own entrance to a shared lounge with a log fire, where pre-dinner drinks are served.
Reverse cycle airconditioned rooms are tastefully decorated to ensure a restful stay.
Full cooked breakfast is available in the breakfast room giving guests an opportunity to sample some of the berry farm's delights.
All of this is available within a 5 minute drive of Mount Gambier. Dinner is available with prior notice.
Home Page: BerryHill.com.au

SOUTH AUSTRALIA

Mount Gambier
Homestay RAA ★★★☆
Address: Worrolong Road,
Mt Gambier, SA Postal:
PO Box 1309, Mt Gambier, 5290
Name: Worrolong Bed & Breakfast
Reet & Bernard Lindner
Telephone: (08) 8725 2256
Beds: 1 Queen, 1 Single (1 bedroom)
Bathroom: 1 Ensuite
Tariff: B&B (full) Double $80-$90, Single $70, Children $20, Dinner $20, Credit Cards.
Nearest Town: 10km east of Mt Gambier, on Worrolong Road, 500m from Glenelg Hwy.

Worrolong B&B is situated in a quiet and pleasant rural property of 95 acres adjacent to pine forests, just 10 minutes from Mount Gambier. Our spacious and comfortable unit has ensuite and two person spa bath, own entrance and undercover parking and barbecue area. We offer country hospitality and full cooked breakfast with your hosts or served to your room. Music is part of our life and we have a piano and electronic organ in our polished timber floor family room warmed by slow combustion wood heater. We have a smoke free home and resident colourpoint cat "Bronson".
Mount Gambier is known for its rich volcanic soil, Blue Lake, Limestone caves, freestone quarries, forestry, dairy farming and Crayfishing Industry at Port McDonnell. We are centrally located to historic Penola area where Blessed Mary McKillop lived and worked. The Coonawarra area is renowned for producing world class wines.

Murray Bridge
Homestay RAA ★★★☆
Address: Long Flat Rd,
Murray Bridge
Name: Mary & David Child
Telephone: (08) 8531 1153
Fax: (08) 8531 1649
Mobile: (015) 798 653
Beds: 1 King, 1 Double, 2 Single
(2 bedrooms) **Bathroom**: 1 Guests share
Tariff: B&B (full) Double $85, Single $75. Credit cards.   Vouchers accepted
Nearest Town: Murray Bridge

Childsdale Homestead is surrounded by a rambling verandah, which is perfect for reading or meditating in peace and solitude. And that about sets the scene for this charming country home, which was built in 1925.
Childsdale was restored in the early 1990's, and now provides two double bed-sitting rooms with guest toilet, bath / shower. Each room is tastefully decorated in country heritage theme and the open fireplace provides warmth and character.
Your tariff includes a huge, delicious breakfast, cooked in the bright, spacious kitchen (including home-made breads and jams) with a two course evening meal also on offer if required.
A stroll around the glorious garden often brings you face to face with the locals - peacocks, ducks and kangaroo going about their everyday business.
So leave the pressures of the city behind - Childsdale makes the perfect escape for a riverside break.

Naracoorte see Coonawarra

SOUTH AUSTRALIA

Naracoorte
Self-contained Accommodation
Address: 192 Smith Street, Naracoorte
Postal: PO Box 450, Naracoorte 5271
Name: Naracoorte Cottages
Telephone: (08) 8762 2906
Fax: (08) 8762 3851
Mobile: (018) 810 645
Beds: 2 Queen, 5 Single (4 bedrooms)
Bathroom: 2 Private
Tariff: B&B (full) Double $95, Single $75, Children under 18 yrs $20, Credit Cards. Vouchers accepted
Nearest Town: Naracoorte

Naracoorte features the World Heritage listed Naracoorte Caves, with beautiful limestone formations, rich deposits of fossilised extinct animals and the unique Bat Cave Teleview Centre. Nearby Bool Lagoon is a huge wetland of international importance where hundreds of bird species can be viewed. Also experience our museums, wine and red gum countryside.
Welcome to Naracoorte Cottages' handsome 1910 villa, in the heart of town, walking distance to shops, supermarkets, hotels etc. While cosy for a couple, it's spacious enough for two families or several couples. Four bedrooms. Sitting room with slow combustion heater, air conditioning, sofas, chairs, footstools, TV, video player and magazines.
Large country kitchen with recycled Baltic pine table and eight Federation chairs, air conditioning, full-sized refrigerator and stove, crockery, cutlery and glassware. Laundry with washing machine, iron, etc. Sunroom with cane chairs, doll's house and rocking chair. Enclosed garden with trees, lawn, gas barbecue and children's play equipment.

Naracoorte RAA ★★★☆
Guest House and Cottage
Address: 30 McLay Street, Naracoorte, SA 5271
Name: Dartmoor Homestead - Jane Frost
Telephone: (08) 8762 0487
Fax: (08) 8762 0481 **Mobile**: (018) 600930
Email: dartmoor@rbm.com.au
Beds: 3 Queen, 6 Single (3 bedrooms & cottage)
Bathroom: 1 1/2 Guests share, 1 Family share
Tariff: B&B (full) Double $115, Single $85, Cottage $85 (double). Dinner $20-$35, Credit cards. Vouchers accepted $20 surcharge for guesthouse
Nearest Town: Naracoorte 1km, Adelaide 330km, Melbourne 440km

Member of
SOUTH AUSTRALIA
Bed & Breakfast
TOWN AND COUNTRY

Since opening in December 1994 I have discovered that my guests have a way of saying it all when they stay here. The guest book is unanimous. Great beds, great breakfasts and great hospitality. What more can I say? It's what B&B's are all about. My guests come from all walks of life and they really do enjoy the experience of staying in this gracious, historical, heritage listed homestead. They love the decor and appreciate the attention to detail. Some like to chat, some like their privacy. A warm welcome awaits you so you feel at home straight away. Naracoorte is the perfect base for visiting the world famous wineries of Coonawarra and Koppamurra, World Heritage fossil caves, important wetlands, beautiful bush walks and tours, golf and scenic flights as well as museums and galleries. Eco, Cultural and Gourmet Tourism abounds here.
Directions: Down McInnes Ave near the Shell SS on Adelaide/Bordertown Road.

SOUTH AUSTRALIA

Padthaway
Homestay+Self-contained Cottage
Member of South Australia Bed & Breakfast Town and Country
Address: "Russell's Camp", PMB 39, Naracoorte, 5271 SA
Name: Annie Moorhouse
Telephone: (08) 8757 3061 **Fax**: (08) 8757 3060
Beds: In House: 2 King (2 bedrooms) SC Cottage: 1 King, 2 Single or Queen, 2 divans in sitting room (sleeps 6)
Bathroom: In House:1 Private, Cottage: 1 Private
Tariff: B&B (continental) Double $120, Single $60. SC Cottage: $80 for 2 people, $15 everyone after, Simple continental breakfast on request, Children welcome.
Nearest Town: Padthaway

Russell's Camp a quality year round experience is a rural property of 325 attractive, undulating hectares. It is situated near the renowned wine producing area of Padthaway., 2 1/2 hours driving time from Adelaide and 5 1/2 hours from Melbourne. It is central to Naracoorte, Bordertown, Keith and Kingston. An hours drive from Coonawarra, another famous wine region, the historic Penola with some very good restaurants and the quaint popular seaside town of Robe. These locations make an excellent day trip from Russell's Camp. Russell's Camp has two accommodation venues. The main homestead surrounded by a wonderful garden with lovely views of the surrounding countryside, a swimming pool and a tennis court. It has a private area for guests, consisting of an entrance morning room with a fridge, tea and coffee making facilities, two bedrooms, a bathroom and a comfortable sitting room ideal for one or two couples. A continental silver service breakfast is served in the main dining room or outdoors overlooking the garden. The cottage nestled amongst mallee (eucalyptus diversafolia) yaccas (xanthorrhoea) a short distance from the homestead is bright, comfortable and self contained. The cottage sleeps six and has a barbecue and outdoor furniture making this an excellent stop over or holiday spot for a family.The garden is accredited with Australias Open Garden Scheme with many native species such as banksia, correa, hakea, callistemon etc.

Pinnaroo
Farmstay RAA ★★★☆
Address: "Alcheringa", Pinnaroo, SA 5304
Name: Sonia and Trevor Wurfel
Telephone: (08) 8576 6171
Fax: (08) 8576 6171
Beds: 2 Double, 3 Single (3 bedrooms)
Bathroom: 1 Private
(We only take one group at a time).
Tariff: B&B (full) Double $70, Single $50. Dinner $15-$25. Full Board Adults $85. Children $40 (5-14 yrs).
Vouchers accepted
Nearest Town: Pinnaroo 25km

Enjoy extensive views of the surrounding country side from the spacious homestead. "Alcheringa" which adjoins Ngarkat Conservation Park, runs 3000 cashmere goats and 1000 merinos in addition to grain-growing. Hosts with wide interests, including travel and teaching, extend country hospitality - fine cuisine, relaxed hours on the vine-covered verandah or by a mallee stump fire, farm activities if you wish, including animal feeding, working sheepdog demonstrations and an insight into the Australian cashmere industry. Full board stays include informative 4WD tours into the mallee wilderness, bush BBQ with billy tea, emus, mallee hens, 'desert' wildflowers, dusk kangaroo photo safari. And in the evenings, superb sunsets followed by clear, starry skies. Private airstrip. A small detour on the shortest Sydney/Adelaide route, Alcheringa has been happily hosting guests since 1985.
Directions: *Please phone.*

SOUTH AUSTRALIA

Penneshaw see Kangaroo Island

Port Lincoln
Homestay   RAA ★★★☆
Address: "Swanmore", 12 Adelphi Tce, Port Lincoln, SA 5606
Postal: P.O. Box 1630, Port Lincoln, SA 5606
Name: Eric & Hazel Russell
Telephone: (08) 8682 2776 **Fax**: (08) 8683 3660
Email: swanmore@terra.net.au
Beds: 1 King, 2 Queen, 2 Single . King Size Double plus divan in Balcony Suite: Private Ensuite. Queen Sized Double plus divan in self contained flat on ground floor. Max 8 people. Bathroom: Private. Queen sized Double "In-House" adjacent to flat. Bathroom: Private.
Bathroom: 3 Private
Tariff: B&B (continental) Double $80, Single $70. Additional person $10. Vouchers accepted
Nearest Town: Port Lincoln (population 14,000) is located on Alternative Route 1,660km from Adelaide and 350km south of Port Augusta. Frequent air services from Adelaide (40 minute flight).

Hazel and Eric offer three different types of accommodation to suit guests' varying needs, all have space for relaxed living. Extensive balconies provide room for entertaining and vast scenic views over Port Lincoln's waterways and National Park. We are adjacent to Lincoln Cove Marina which offers a recreational swimming/leisure centre, tavern, boat trips to tuna farms and diving/fishing charter. Swanmore is on the waterfront and borders on an extensive walking trail. Picturesque Coffin Bay is only 40 mins by car.
Guests are offered total privacy to relax but may choose to join their hosts over breakfast, coffee, or a BBQ as they wish. A snooker table is available, colour TV is provided in all suites and a VCR. Non-smokers are preferred.
Directions: *Our illustrated brochure with map mailed on request. We will collect and return guests from and to the airport if required (10kms).*

SOUTH AUSTRALIA

Robe
Self-contained Accommodation
Address: 'The Criterion Cottage',
Bagot Street, Robe, SA 5276
Name: Mary McInerney
Telephone: (08) 8768 2137
Fax: (08) 8768 2137
Beds: 1 Double, 2 Single (2 bedrooms)
Bathroom: 1 Private
Tariff: B&B (full) Double $110 - $140, Extra person $20 each Vouchers accepted $56 surcharge: one night for two people. $28 surcharge two or more nights.
Nearest Town: Robe

The small settlers cottage, built in 1856, has been beautifully restored and extended. It has a sitting-room with log fire and small twin bedroom. A spacious sunroom / courtyard joins the sitting-room with the dining area and modern kitchen. A loft bedroom has a balcony overlooking the bay. Bathroom, laundry and undercover parking complete this delightful cottage.

Firewood, gas heating and plenty of hot water are provided, as are sheets, electric blankets, towels, radio-cassette, books and magazines. Ample food for a full breakfast is supplied.

The cottage is in the centre of the old township which has excellent shops and restaurants and safe swimming within two minutes walk. A cray fishing fleet operates throughout the summer months from the harbour, a secure haven for all pleasure craft. A golf course and tennis courts are nearby. There are also wonderful wild ocean beaches and National Parks. The winter climate is the mildest in the south-east. Commendation for conservation Royal Australian Institute of Architects Awards 1992.

Sevenhill see Clare Valley
Stirling see Adelaide Hills
Tanunda see Barossa Valley

Gift Vouchers

Our B&B vouchers are for a double room for one night's B&B. They cost $89, and if you order one as a gift, we will include a free
Australian Bed & Breakfast Book
worth $16.95

Send your cheque to
Moonshine Press
59 Quirk Street
Dee Why
NSW 2099

SOUTH AUSTRALIA

Tintinara RAA ★★★☆
Self-contained Cottage/House
Address: Dukes Highway -
Please phone. Postal:
PO Box 193, Tintinara, SA 5266
Name: "O'Deas B&B"
Prin Twelftree & Kathie Bridge
Telephone: (08) 8575 8023
(08) 8756 5018
Fax: (08) 8756 5018
Beds: 1 Queen, 2 Single (2 bedrooms)
Bathroom: 1 Private
Tariff: B&B (full) Double $85, Single $65,
Children $25, Campervans $20 per night, laundry, power,
toilet. Vouchers accepted $8 surcharge
Nearest Town: Tintinara 3km west, Bordertown 80km east, Adelaide 200km west.

Located on a sheep / cattle grazing property, O'Dea's was once the homestead of early graziers. A wide return verandah gives summer shade or winter sun and is one of the unique features as well as the rare window / doors leading from the bedrooms. Interior decor brimming with refreshing touches is smart and imaginative. O'Dea's is exclusively yours, with a lovely, relaxed ambience - offering; open log fires, crisp cotton linen, bathrobes, doonas, electric blankets, deep country bathtub, television, fully-equipped kitchen, and a laundry. Provisions for a full country breakfast can be enjoyed at your leisure. Tintinara, surrounded by ten national / conservation parks, has a picturesque golf course, is on route to Adelaide and Melbourne and the attractions and wineries of the S.E. of South Australia. It has an airfield and a daily coach service. Stay at O'Dea's and you'll experience "an Australiana Oasis!". Booking preferred. Children welcome. Smoke-free.

Victor Harbor
Homestay/Bed & Breakfast
Address: "Annie's House",
26 Sturt Street, Victor Harbor, SA 5211
Name: Annie & Dick Windsor
Telephone: (08) 8552 6092
Fax: (08) 8552 6092
Mobile: 0414239916
Beds: 1 King, 2 Single (2 bedrooms)
Bathroom: 1 Private
Tariff: B&B (full) Double $90, Single $75, Children $45. Vouchers accepted $5 surcharge
Nearest Town: Central in Victor Harbor, Adelaide 80km

Annie's House, a delightful circa 1923 stone fronted, solid brick Californian bungalow is centrally located in Victor Harbor within easy walking distance of the beach, town centre and local entertainment. Guest facilities include a Kingsize-four poster bed, tea and coffee making, private bathroom, exclusive use of sitting / dining room, open wood fires in guest rooms, television and radio / CD. Breakfast is served in the dining room. It is preferred that guests do not smoke in the house.
Victor Harbor is an historic whaling town which is rich in heritage and culture dating back to the 1800's including its famous Horse Drawn Tram to Granite Island and Coastal Steam Train. Victor Harbor can be a base for visiting nearby Kangaroo Island, River Murray Mouth and regional wineries.
Hosts Annie and Dick Windsor have lived and travelled overseas and are always delighted to welcome other travellers.

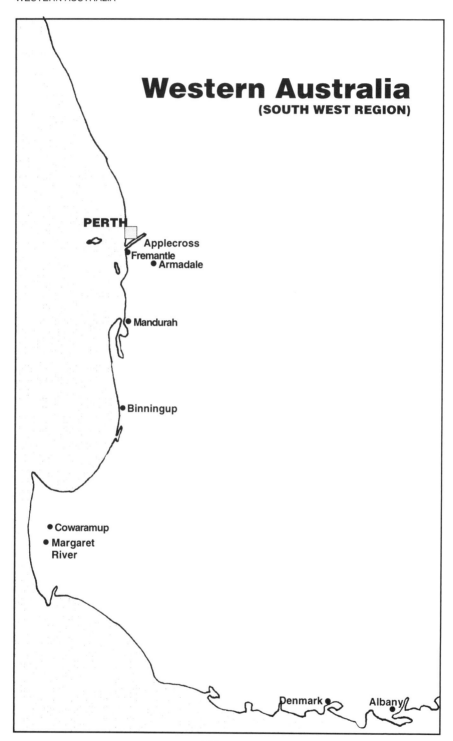

Albany
Homestay
Address: "Clarence House",
110 Hare Street, Albany, WA 6330
Name: John & Beth Berriege
Telephone: (08) 9841 5409
Fax: (08) 9841 5409 **Mobile**: 014 084253
Email: clarence@albanyis.com.au
Beds: 2 Queen (2 bedrooms)
Bathroom: 2 Ensuite
Tariff: B&B (special) Double $75-$85, Single $70-$80, Credit Cards (BC/MC/VISA). Vouchers accepted but not Xmas holidays nor Easter.
Nearest Town: Albany centre, 2 kms

Close to town, golf links and beaches Clarence House is the perfect place for those who desire five star luxury yet the warmth and friendliness of a home environment.
Situated high on the side of Mount Clarence guests can enjoy spectacular views over lake, beach and distant mountains while lying in bed, breakfasting on the balcony or enjoying the comfort of the cosy lounge. Whales can be seen in the winter months.
Both rooms are tastefully decorated in Laura Ashley style and have heating, electric blankets, TV, refrigerator, tea and coffee making facilities and comfortable chairs for relaxing. One room has scenic windows and sliding door onto the covered balcony. The other has a separate library and French doors opening into a cottage garden allowing guests their private entrance.
Breakfasts are our specialty, catering for all taste with an expansive menu including fresh baked bread and homemade jams. Indulge yourself!
Home Page: http://worf.albanyis.com.au/~clarence/

Albany
Bed & Breakfast
Address: "Greystone Bed & Breakfast"
161-163 Serpentine Road, Albany 6330
Name: Jan & Roy
Telephone: (098) 422 651
Fax: (098) 423 374 **Mobile**: (015) 993 917
Beds: 1 Queen, 1 Single (2 Bedrooms)
Bathroom: 1 Guests Share
Tariff: B&B (continental) Double $120, Single $60. Vouchers accepted $26 surcharge for May, June, July, August.
Nearest Town: Albany 1/2 km

GREYSTONE is an elegant comfortable home built of granite stone and blends beautifully with large camellias, a heritage listed honey locust tree making the gardens and lawns a romantic cool and quiet place to enjoy, along with weeping birch, mulberry poplars and oak. The large granite rocks, granite pond and large drifts of agapanthus create a handsome effect. Situated 400 kilometres South of Perth in the heart of Wine growing country, sightseeing and walks to thoroughly enjoy. Enjoy the freedom of hosts small farming property, great walks, cattle and many kangaroos, and company of hosts' Jack Russell 7 yr old dog.
Restaurants and historical interests within walking distance all in the central area. Complimentary afternoon teas, a no smoking house, sorry we do not cater for children. Airport pick up / return by arrangement.

WESTERN AUSTRALIA

Armadale
Homestay   RACWA ★★★★☆
Address: Elizabethan Village,
25 Canns Road, Bedfordale, WA
Name: "Anne Hathaway's Cottage"
Cheryl Gillmore
Telephone: (08) 9497 3942
Fax: (08) 9497 2247 **Mobile**: 0419949313
Email: cometpl@ozemail.com.au
Beds: 1 King/Queen, 2 Double, 2 Single (3 bedrooms)
Bathroom: 2 Ensuite, 1 Private
Tariff: B&B (full) Double $90-$130, Single $65-$75, Children $20, Credit Cards (BC/MC/VISA).Vouchers accepted $20 surcharge
Nearest Town: Armadale - situated in Elizabethan Village, 2km out of Armadale

*Visitors to WA are intrigued and delighted to find an authentic replica of the home of Shakespeare's wife Anne Hathaway, tucked away, 30km south of Perth in the picturesque Bedfordale hills, operating as a unique B&B. Indulgent, yet affordable, Anne Hathaway's Cottage is a 16th century reproduction farmhouse, complete with thatched roof, offering four and a half star, delightfully decorated, silver service accommodation with private facilities. AussieHost accredited, a choice of continental or full breakfast is offered, with flexible check in and check out times. Next door is the Elizabethan Village Pub, providing a range of award winning beers, brewed in a replica of Stratford's White Swan Inn. Counter meals are served either in the bar or in delightful alfresco areas, or a-la-carte is available in the cosy Cobwebs Restaurant. Armadale is the gateway to the south west, Margaret River, Bunbury, Albany regions.
Sorry - No smoking inside.*

Binningup
Self-contained Accommodation
Address: "Meiklejohns",
18 Doubleview Terrace,
Binningup, WA 6233
Name: Mike & Jan
Telephone: (08) 9720 1043
Beds: 1 Queen (1 bedroom)
Bathroom: 1 Private
Tariff: B&B (continental) Double $80. Vouchers accepted $10 surcharge
Nearest Town: Bunbury

*Binningup is a pretty, unspoiled beach resort 30km north of Bunbury and a pleasant two hour drive from Perth. It is well situated to explore the South West region of the State.
Our hilltop home overlooks the Indian Ocean and a public golf course. The views from the top storey guest unit are quite spectacular.
The guest accommodation is completely private, with a separate entrance. The air conditioned private apartment comprising a sitting room cum kitchen, double bedroom and separate bathroom, is tastefully decorated and comfortably furnished. The kitchen has tea/coffee making facilities, microwave, toaster and fridge. Breakfast provisions are provided and a gas barbecue is available for guests.
The queen size bed has an electric blanket, feather doonas and plump pillows. The sofa bed in the sitting room will accommodate an extra person.
We provide newspapers, books, magazines, games and colour television.
No smoking please. Unsuitable for children.*

Denmark
Homestead Bed & Breakfast

Shakespeare's Neuplace
HOMESTEAD BED & BREAKFAST

Address: Cnr Sth Coast Highway & Morley Road, NR Denmark.
Name: 'Shakespeare's Neuplace' Bill & Sandra Shakespeare
Telephone: (08) 9845 2111
Fax: (08) 9845 2111
Beds: 2 Queen (2 Bedrooms)
Bathroom: 1 Guests Share Ensuite
Tariff: B&B (full) Double $65, Single $40, Dinner $20. Not suitable for children.
Nearest Town: Denmark 17 km, Albany 35 km.

Shakespeare's Neuplace Homestead Bed & Breakfast is ideally located between Denmark and Albany on the south coast of Western Australia, a magnificent environment for those seeking a wonderful break.
Enjoy the warm friendliness of our on farm easy going country care. Sleep relaxed in clean salt tinged air, and wake up to bird calls and a luscious full breakfast.
Walk to Wilson's Inlet and watch the myriad of birds or see a woodturner at work. Fish or swim on pristine south coastal beaches. Visit a multitude of tourist attractions from our central location. Paint nature or perhaps watch the farmer at work with our beef cattle.
Your own private entry through a sunny courtyard, leads to spacious and elegantly furnished bedrooms with TV, electric blankets, heaters and adjoining en suite.
For your use we also offer a delightful sitting room with tea / snack making facilities, fridge, microwave, TV and <u>meals setting.</u>

Denmark
Bed & Breakfast   RAC ★★★☆

Address: 62 Bracknell Crescent, Denmark, WA 6333
Name: "Gumnuts B&B" Michael & 'Tricia Farrer
Telephone: (08) 9848 1344
Fax: (08) 9848 1900
Beds: 2 King, 1 Queen (3 bedrooms)
Bathroom: 1 Private, 1 Guests share
Tariff: B&B (full) Double $70, Single $35, Children N/A, Dinner $20, Credit Cards. Vouchers accepted
Nearest Town: Denmark - 4km west off Ocean Beach Road

Michael & 'Tricia invite you to join them and enjoy the quiet life on Weedon Hill among karri and marri trees. Sit and watch the birdlife from the balcony or take a walk along the Wilson Inlet. In winter relax in front of the fire with a good book.
We offer guests quality accommodation and our well appointed bedrooms have everything you could wish for, the guest lounge is equipped with tea and coffee making facilities.
Michael offers guests a walk before breakfast to work up an appetite!
Gumnuts is situated 4km from Denmark which is midway between Albany and the unique treetop walk in the Valley of the Giants so makes an ideal base from which to explore the lower south-west of WA. Guests can spend a day visiting the local wineries, potteries or swimming at William Bay.
Gumnuts is a non-smoking home.

WESTERN AUSTRALIA

Fremantle
Guest House　RAC ★★★☆
Address: 20/22 Ord Street,
Fremantle, WA 6160
Name: "Fothergills of Fremantle"
Telephone: (09) 335 6784
Fax: (09) 430 7789
Beds: 6 Queen, 5 Double/sofa beds,
2 Single (6 bedrooms)
Bathroom: 2 Ensuite, 1 Guests share
Tariff: B&B (full)　Room rates $95-$170,　Children $10.　Credit cards.　Vouchers accepted Surcharges:　$15 Std Rooms, $50 Garden ensuite, $80 Victorian spa room
Nearest Town: Fremantle

Welcome to "Fothergills" circa 1892, a lovely old unique limestone pair of semi's surrounded by grand residences and set in charming gardens.
Our home has commanding ocean and harbour views and is a 5 minute walk to town and all the wonderful old buildings, museums, the famous prison (now a fabulous heritage site - a MUST to view), fantastic restaurants and cappuccino strip famous for 'Freo'.
At No. 20 we offer 4 large beautifully furnished bedrooms, with share bathroom, and guest TV lounge, 2 lovely ensuites, one with large spa bath, each with their own TV. All rooms have bar fridges, tea & coffee facilities, comfy sofas, writing desks, bathrobes and hair driers.
The delightful breakfast room is in the adjoining No. 22 where Bob and June Anderson reside. A traditional cooked breakfast is complimented with fresh fruit and cereal, pots of tea and plungers of 'real' coffee. Non smoking.

Fremantle
Homestay
Address: 3 Munro Street, East Fremantle, West Australia 6158
Name: Val & Ron Pyman
Telephone: (08) 9339-4496
Beds: 2 Single (1 bedroom)
Bathroom: 1 Family share
Tariff: B&B (continental) Double $60, Single $35.　Vouchers accepted
Nearest Town: Fremantle 4 km

There are only 16 homes in our lovely quiet suburban street. By just strolling to the end of it, you are rewarded with a panoramic view of Fremantle Harbour, Swan River, Indian Ocean, especially magnificent at sunset!
We are within walking distance to excellent restaurants, yacht clubs, sporting fields and Rottnest Island ferries.
A few minutes away is Fremantle, with its museums, cafes, food, art, craft markets, fisherman's harbour, wonderful, cosmopolitan atmosphere. Fast reliable rail service to Perth, bus is one block away, either to Perth or Fremantle.
We have travelled overseas and Australia wide. Enjoy meeting people, and sharing our unique Aussie way of life.
We have a pool, patio where smoking is permitted, TV room, pianola, use of fridge. No pets allowed.
Tea and coffee making at all times.
The bathroom you may have to share is large.
We enjoy a very busy lifestyle. Ron is a Rotarian and you can be assured of a very warm welcome.

WESTERN AUSTRALIA

Fremantle
Bed & Breakfast   RAC ★★★★
Address: 6 Fothergill St, Fremantle, WA 6160
Name: Danum House
Telephone: (08) 9336 3735
Fax: (08) 9335 3414
Beds: 2 Queen, 1 Single (3 bedrooms)
Bathroom: 1 Ensuite, 2 Private
Tariff: B&B (full) Ensuite $100, Double $90, Single $75. Credit cards: Visa, Mastercard, Bankcard. Vouchers accepted
Nearest Town: Fremantle - 500 metres

Danum House is a lovely Federation home situated a short stroll from the heart of Fremantle which is a vibrant cosmopolitan port city, situated 17km from Perth. Our accommodation offers elegantly furnished bedrooms, one ensuite and two with own facilities, and the comfortable sitting room has TV and VCR. These facilities have earned Danum House a 4 star RAC rating. Fremantle offers many tourist attractions including the famous markets, prison museum, galleries and historic buildings. Local restaurants offer an amazing choice of international foods which must be sampled by all visitors to Western Australia. Excellent public transport to Perth and Rottnest Island makes Fremantle an ideal base for your West Australian holiday. Your hosts, Christine and Geoff, are well travelled, enjoy bush walking, sport, music and reading and look forward to making your stay a pleasant and relaxing one in a smoke free environment.

Fremantle
Bed & Breakfast
Address: 79 South Street, South Fremantle, WA 6162
Name: "Moonrakers"
Telephone: (08) 9336-2266
Fax: (08) 9336-2204
Mobile: (015) 384319
Beds: 1 Queen, 2 Double, 1 Twin (4 bedrooms)
Bathroom: 1 Ensuite, 1 Guests share
Tariff: B&B (full) Double $115-$140, Single $95, Credit Cards.
Nearest Town: Fremantle 1km

Warm and welcoming, "Moonrakers" means magical memories; the fragrant English cottage garden, the wide verandahs fringed with iron lace with views of the Indian Ocean, the heated swimming pool set in a secluded palm garden and the shady gazebo are all places in which to relax and unwind.
"Moonrakers", built in 1898 and lovingly restored by your host has high ornate ceilings, working fireplaces and polished floor boards. It is lavishly furnished with antiques and collectables and offers either a twin bedded room or two double rooms, one with a four-poster bed. The shared bathroom with its lead-light windows and deep claw-foot bath is simply luxurious. Also available is the pool-side garden cottage with its own ensuite, sitting area, air-conditioner, television and fridge. All rooms have clock radios, tea and coffee facilities, towelling robes, hair-dryer and individual toiletries.
"Moonrakers" is located just 1km from the centre of Fremantle with its numerous places of interests and open-air cafes.
You will be welcomed to this non-smoking home by your host Sally Gordon, a friendly Afghan Hound and Birman cat. Unsuitable for children.

WESTERN AUSTRALIA

Fremantle
Bed and Breakfast
Address: 15 John St., N. Fremantle
Name: Dawn Davies
Telephone: (08) 9336 2209
Fax: (08) 9336 2209
Beds: 1 Queen, 2 Double,
2 Single (4 bedrooms)
Bathroom: 2 Ensuite, 1 Guests share
Tariff: B&B (full) Low season: Double $60-$100, Single $40-$80. High season: Double $80-$120, Single $60-$100, Dinner $20, Credit Cards.
Nearest Town: Fremantle

The house is right on the River in North Fremantle. A Jetty for fishing and an Oval next door for joggers. We also have a swimming pool. Bedroom 1 has a large spa and a private balcony overlooking the pool and river and large Oval Bed. Bedrooms 2 has a 4 poster bed, ensuite and access to pool and beach. Bedroom 3 Double share facilities also overlooks pool and beach. Bedroom 4 2 Single beds overlooks Oval and beach share facilities. There is plenty of off street parking. BBQ near pool and TV room for guests. Use of kitchen. Breakfast served near pool in summer or near pot belly in winter. Easy walking distance to public transport and 5 mins by car to the heart of Fremantle, and of course a Very Warm Welcome.

Fremantle
**Bed & Breakfast/
Self-contained Accom.**
RAC ★★★★
Address: 74 Solomon Street,
Fremantle, WA, 6160
Name: "Westerley Bed & Breakfast"
Ian & Gillian Nicholas
Telephone: (08) 9430 4458
Fax: (08) 9430 4458
Mobile: 0419 834 306
Email: nichwest@opera.iinet.net.au
Beds: 2 Queen, 2 additional Singles (as required) (2 bedrooms)
Bathroom: 2 Ensuite
Tariff: B&B (full) Double $85, Single $70; Studio: Double $120, Single $100; Studio only (self-catering): Double $95, Single $80. Additional person $15. 10% discount for more than 3 days. Credit Cards (BC/VISA/MC). Vouchers accepted
Nearest Town: Fremantle

Westerley is a comfortable, spacious limestone and iron house, with high ornate ceilings and polished floorboards. Built in the 1880's, Westerley's character reflects Fremantle's varied history. We are a short walk to the centre of the city with its many diverse restaurants, the "cappuccino strip", the old Fremantle Prison, the markets, and the many other fine old buildings associated with Fremantle's seafaring tradition.
Within the old house itself, there is an elegant double bedroom, with ensuite, together with the use of the formal sitting room complete with TV, piano, CD player and an open fireplace.
The Studio opens onto the garden and pond area. It is self-contained, with ensuite, air-conditioned with overhead fans, and has its own entrance. It is equipped with a TV, refrigerator and microwave; indeed, all the facilities that a couple, or small family, might require to make their stay in Fremantle a memorable event.
Children welcome. Pets considered. Non-smoking.

Fremantle
Bed & Breakfast
Address: 82 Marine Tce,
Fremantle, 6160
Name: KILKELLY's Bed $ Breakfast
Telephone: (08) 9336 1744
Fax: (08) 9336 1571
Email: kilkelly@mail.wt.com.au
Beds: 2 Queen, 3 King Single (3 bedrooms)
Bathroom: 2 Guests share & spa
Tariff: B&B (continental) Double $95-$105, Single $75-$95, Children over 12yrs, Credit Cards.
Nearest Town: Fremantle

Kilkelly's 2 storey heritage home (circa 1883) offers first class quality Bed & Breakfast accommodation and personalised local hospitality to business and holiday travellers. Situated on Marine Terrace across from Fishing Boat Harbour and close to all Fremantle's major tourist attractions, the Esplanade Hotel and park, cafes / restaurants, cinemas, train / bus station and the central business district.
A deluxe continental breakfast is offered with complimentary leaf teas and ground coffee available at any time. Children under 12yrs are not catered for and we offer a non-smoking environment in the home. Guests are welcomed into the private courtyard garden.
Consider Kilkelly's for upmarket accommodation downtown - you won't be disappointed.
By reservation only.

Mandurah (Central)
Bed & Breakfast
RAC ★★★☆
Address: Albatross House
Bed & Breakfast
26 Hall Street,
Mandurah 6210
Name: Albatross House
Telephone: (08) 9581 5597
Beds: 2 Queen, 2 (king size) Single beds. (3 Bedrooms)
Bathroom: 2 Guests Share
Tariff: B&B (full) Double $90, Single $45. Suitable for children over 15 years of age. Vouchers accepted $10 surcharge
Nearest Town: Mandurah (we are central city of Mandurah) 1.5 km from Post Office Central.

Enjoy the personal breakfast service in the guest dining room or the cozy atmosphere of the lounge where tea and coffee is always on hand. Separate guest wing.
Take a leisurely walk to the estuary foreshore, the beach and the central shopping precinct or dine at one of the many quality restaurants.
Mandurah is only one hour's driving time from Perth with kilometres of sandy beaches (SEE THE SUN SET IN THE WEST!). The calm waters of the Peel Inlet and the Harvey Estuary makes it one of the largest inland waterways in Australia. With its protected wetlands, it is one of the state's most important bird watching regions as well as the largest breeding grounds of pelicans in WA. Explore the inlet and rivers with one of the local cruise operators or hire a boat. WE HAVE CANOES FOR HIRE. Play golf, catch crabs or visit the many other attractions in the area.

WESTERN AUSTRALIA

Margaret River
Farmstay
Address: 'Valley Views Bed & Breakfast",
Jindong Treeton Road,
Margaret River, WA 6285
Name: Jan and Barry Walsh
Telephone: (08) 9757 4573
Fax: (08) 9757 8181
Beds: 2 Queen, 2 Single, (3 bedrooms)
Bathroom: 1 Guests share
Tariff: B&B (full), Double $75, Single $55. Vouchers accepted $5 surcharge on long weekends and school holidays.
Nearest Town: Margaret River 17 km. Cowaramup 15 km, Busselton 38 km

We welcome you into our large spacious, colonial home set on 100 acres of picturesque farmland. The farm is surrounded by State forest on two sides in which wildlife abounds. We have a 13 year old daughter at home and four sons occasionally. We run a flock of fine wool merinos, horses, a friendly sheepdog and a small vineyard.

Relax and enjoy a peaceful environment with good country hospitality. Our location provides a convenient base to explore the Cape region with its many wineries, galleries, caves and beautiful beaches, horse riding nearby.

The bedrooms are large with adjacent bathroom and toilet facilities. Guests can enjoy a beautifully furnished sitting room with a cosy log fire. There is a bar area with a fridge, tea making facilities, TV, video and stereo unit. Wide verandahs surround the home.

Meals are available on request or try some of Margaret River's varied eateries. School age children only, smoking outside.

Margaret River
Bed and Breakfast Cottage   RAC ★★★★
Address: Willow Wood cottages
RMB 207, Rosa Brook Road,
Margaret River, WA 6285
Name: Jill and Ray Hinde
Telephone: (08) 9757 5080
Fax: (08) 97575 083/008
Beds: 1 Queen (1 bedroom)
Bathroom: 1 Private
Tariff: B&B (Special) Double $120-$140, Single $90-$100, Dinner by prior arrangement.
Nearest Town: Margaret River, 9 kms

Willow Wood Cottage

Willow Wood, situated on 30 acres, was formerly part of an old dairy property settled in the 1920's. The weatherboard cottage is located in the original orchard and represents the group settlement architecture featuring an exclusive use of timber, including jarrah dado panelling. Old twenties furniture and complementing linen have all been carefully chosen to capture atmosphere and character. A slow combustion wood fire surrounded by an old jarrah chimney piece provides winter warmth.

Facilities include tea / coffee making, refrigerator, tele / video, radio / cassette, all linen, crockery, cutlery, glasses, iron, board. Breakfast is served to either the cottage dining table or its verandah which provides beautiful views of the rolling country side. The Margaret River region is renowned for its boutique wineries, gourmet food, magnificent coastline, caves and majestic jarrah and karri forests.

We would like you to share our little piece of history with us and invite you to participate in our hospitality. (Smoke free establishment - No pets)

WESTERN AUSTRALIA

Margaret River
Guest House
Address: Cnr Walciffe & Devon, Margaret River
Name: Kangaridge Guesthouse
Telephone: (08) 9757 3939
Fax: (08) 9757 3939
Beds: 4 Queen, 2 Single (4 bedrooms)
Bathroom: 4 Ensuite
Tariff: B&B (continental) Double $99, Single $90, Credit Cards.
Nearest Town: 24 km from Margaret River

Unique 4 Star luxury accommodation set on 8 acres near Margaret River township, overlooking forest and prolific birdlife. Features indoor heated therapy pool and spa by the log fire. Only 4 suites so no crowds. All rooms queen sized with own ensuites, private decks, TV, video and tea making. Feather doonas and crisp white linen. Newly built (opened '96). Australiana style homestead with rambling decks all around.

Price is all inclusive with buffet continental breakfast, pitch & putt golf and mountain bikes. We offer a 10% discount card to local wineries restaurants craft centres and golf clubs. Close to town beaches, wineries, and kangaroo colony.
Adjacent to 30km of off the road cycleway.
Tariff from $99 per 2 people all inclusive, extra person $35 p/n. Cooked breakfast $5 per person.

Margaret River - Cowaramup
Guest House   RAC ★★★☆
Address: "The Noble Grape",
Lot 18 Bussell Hwy, Cowaramup 6284
Name: Louise & Chris Stokes
Telephone: (08) 9755 5538
Fax: (08) 9755 5538
Beds: 6 Queen, 1 Double, 4 Single (6 bedrooms)
Bathroom: 6 Ensuite
Tariff: B&B (continental) Double $75-$90, Single $55-$60, Children $20. Dinner $25. Credit Cards. Vouchers accepted May 1 - Dec 23 only.
Nearest Town: 10km to Margaret River

The Noble Grape is a charming guesthouse named for its famous neighbours, the wineries of the Margaret River region. From here, not only the vineyards but the world-class surf beaches of Australia's south west are all minutes away.
This colonial-style country house, with its antiques and lovely English cottage gardens, is actually just eight years old. It offers everything you'd find in a modern motel, except the chilly welcome. Louise and Chris Stokes make a stay at The Noble Grape feel like visiting old friends.
Breakfasts are special in the sunny dining room overlooking the garden. Watch native birds enjoy the flower beds while you enjoy some of Chris' freshly baked muffins. The Noble Grape is the very definition of serenity.
Six spacious rooms, each with ensuite and verandah, TV, radio, fridge, tea/coffee facilities, heating, ceiling fan. Catering for families and people with disabilities.

WESTERN AUSTRALIA

Perth - Airport
Bed & Breakfast Homestay   RAC ★★★☆

Address: Airport B&B, 103 Central Ave., Redcliffe, WA 6104
Name: Wendy & Jamie Brindle
Telephone: (08) 9478 2923   **Fax**: (08) 9478 2770
Email: brindle@wantree.com.au
Beds: 3 Double, 2 Single (4 bedrooms)
Bathroom: 1 Ensuite, 1 Guests share
Tariff: B&B (continental) Double (ensuite) $75, (share bathroom) $60, Single $40, Dinner $8.50, Children $20, Credit Cards.
Vouchers accepted
Nearest Town: Perth (8kms)

Airport Bed & Breakfast is conveniently situated 5 minutes from the International & Domestic airports with airport transfers available. Perth City is only ten minutes drive away and 5 minutes walk to public transport. Private charter tours with your hosts as guides are available. Light evening meals, at a cost of $8.50, are also available by prior arrangement.

Relax in home-style comfort in our spacious home which offers a guest lounge - TV - dining room, one double bedroom with en suite, two double and one twin with share bathroom, all with tea & coffee making facilities. Enjoy a hearty Continental breakfast to start your day and, to finish it, unwind with a relaxing drink on our patio where you can also enjoy a BBQ. Enjoy an evening stroll to the river or lunch at a local winery followed by an afternoon browsing the antique shops of historic Guildford. No pets or in-house smoking.

Perth - Applecross
Bed & Breakfast and Self-contained Accommodation   RAC ★★★★

Address: (Please phone)
Name: Maureen -
"Applecross B&B by the River"
Telephone: (08) 9364 7742
Beds: 1 Double, 1 Queen (2 bedrooms)
Bathroom: 1 Private
Tariff: B&B (full) Double $80, Single $45, Children $20. Vouchers accepted
Nearest Town: Perth - 7 kms

Hi There!
The SWAN RIVER is at our doorstep and we are looking towards the CITY OF PERTH which is only 8 minutes away. FREMANTLE is 15 minutes travelling and the bus stops are close. CYCLE WAYS are along our foreshore and we have BIKES if you feel energetic. The POOL area is also right outside your own private dining / lounge TV room. Here you may choose to have breakfast or in the summer evenings watch the sunset over KINGS PARK with your favourite drink! You have your own fridge and microwave.
Full hearty breakfast and tea / coffee making facilities available at all times. Close to FOOD STORES (one 24 hour service) RESTAURANTS, CHEMIST & LIBRARY, etc. Finding words to describe the panoramic views from every pretty room is not easy. Perhaps we can be excused for taking from our renowned Australian poet "BANJO" PATERSONS work "Clancy of the Overflow" and say it is indeed "A Vision Splendid." You'll love it!
Your Home Host - Maureen (Reg. Tour Guide)
Member R.A.C. of W.A. **** Rating

WESTERN AUSTRALIA

Perth - Applecross
B&B plus Self-contained cottage   RAC ★★★☆
Address: 7 Forbes Road, Applecross
(Please Phone)
Name: Lesley. Perth Bed and Breakfast
Telephone: (08) 9364 4498
Fax: (08) 9316 2840
Beds: 1 Queen, 1 Double (2 bedrooms)
Bathroom: 1 Private
Tariff: B&B (full) Double $75, Single $45, Children welcome. Credit Cards. Vouchers accepted
Nearest Town: Perty City - 7 kms.

Welcome to our home in Applecross. Jacaranda tree-lined streets, riverside walkways, up-market shopping and yachtclub luncheons are only a few of the temptations of this lovely suburb. Numerous, quality restaurants and eating houses, banks, post office, a news agency and most facilities are within two minutes walk. The bus runs by - Perth is the next stop, only seven minutes away!
The Casino, Zoo, Kings Park, Swan River ferries and Garden City shopping precinct are all close by, making ours one of the best locations in Perth.
Guest rooms comprise two delightful double bedrooms, each with its own breakfast setting, lounge / dining with TV, fridge and microwave, bathroom and laundry. The new self-contained Garden Cottage incorporates a sleeping loft and extra garden dining; is air conditioned, and fully furnished and equipped for up to four.

Perth - Hills
B&B Guest House   RAC ★★★★
Address: 86 Williams Street,
Gooseberry Hill, WA 6076
Name: Rosebridge House
Telephone: (08) 9293 1741
Fax: (08) 9257 2778
Beds: 3 Queen, 2 Single (4 bedrooms)
Bathroom: 4 Ensuite
Tariff: B&B (full) Double $90-$120, Single $65-$95.
Nearest Town: Kalamunda - 20km east of Perth

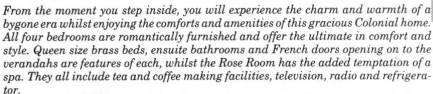

From the moment you step inside, you will experience the charm and warmth of a bygone era whilst enjoying the comforts and amenities of this gracious Colonial home. All four bedrooms are romantically furnished and offer the ultimate in comfort and style. Queen size brass beds, ensuite bathrooms and French doors opening on to the verandahs are features of each, whilst the Rose Room has the added temptation of a spa. They all include tea and coffee making facilities, television, radio and refrigerator.
Located just 30 minutes from Perth and 15 minutes from the Airport, Rosebridge House is conveniently situated on the edge of Gooseberry Hill National Park with its picturesque bush walks, especially in the wildflower season. It is a short stroll from the village of Kalamunda and its vast array of restaurants ranging from fine dining to casual cafes and coffee lounges. Local attractions include vineyards, orchards, Lesmurdie Falls, galleries, antique and curio shops.
Your hosts, Rosemary and Peter Bridgement, extend a warm welcome and look forward to the opportunity of entertaining you in their home.

WESTERN AUSTRALIA

Perth - Kalamunda
Kalamunda Bed & Breakfast RAC ★★★
Address: "Whistlepipe Cottage"
195 Orange Valley Road
Kalamunda, WA 6076
Name: Jean M Holbrook
Telephone: (08) 9291 9872
Beds: 2 Double, 3 Single (3 bedrooms)
Bathroom: 1 Ensuite, 1 Guest Share
Tariff: B&B (full) Double $80, Single $40, Dinner $15-$20, Childre (2-12 years) half price. Vouchers accepted (for use of double guest bathroom)
Nearest Town: Kalamunda 2kms. Perth 22 kms.

"Whistlepipe Cottage" is situated in picturesque Orange Valley in historical Kalamunda - originally a timber settlement in the late 1880's and later developing into an attractive hills suburb as part of the Darling Ranges.
I offer guests a comfortable stay in a stylish stone home, with log fire, healthy home cooking, and a friendly, relaxed atmosphere - all in a beautiful garden setting next to native bush area.
Be awakened by the kookaburras, and walk down Whistlepipe Gully, enjoy the waterfalls and wild flowers in Spring, or visit the local wineries, orchards, art and craft galleries or golf courses - the choices are many and varied.......
Your hostess has a background in agriculture and the humanities, and has hosted guests from many countries. With mainly home-grown vegetables, fruit and eggs, and the aroma of fresh home-baked bread to add to your enjoyment, your stay is sure to be a pleasant experience.

Perth - Kallaroo
Self-contained Accom.
Address: 29 Oleander Way,
Kallaroo
Name: "Springfield Cottage"
Telephone: (08) 9401 8149
Fax: (08) 9307 2347 **Mobile**: 0418941116
Beds: 1 Queen, 2 Single (2 bedrooms)
Bathroom: 1 Private
Tariff: B&B (continental) Double $95, Single $75, Children $25.
 Vouchers accepted $10 surcharge P/N, 3 night minimum.
Nearest Town: Perth 20km

You will love staying at Springfield Cottage, it has a lovely feeling of by-gone days set in an old world cottage garden. Large lounge, with wood fire, 2 bedrooms, country kitchen and dining, polished wood floor, front verandah, a large gum tree and BBQ in back garden. Sleeps 4-5 people. There are many places to enjoy nearby - Underwater World - including dolphins. Ferry to Rottnest Island, Whitford City shopping centre, theatres, restaurants, golf ($90-$100 inc. clubs) at world class Joondalup.
Excellent public transport to Perth and Fremantle.
Continental breakfast supplies included in tariff.
Weekly rates on application. Smokers use the verandah.

Phone numbers throughout Australia are changing to 8 digits.
For help contact Directory Assistance.

Perth - Kallaroo

Homestay   RAC ★★★☆
Address: Whitfords-By-the-Sea
25 Nautilus Way
Kallaroo, WA 6025
Name: Whitfords-By-the-Sea
Telephone: (08) 9401 8149
Fax: (08) 9307 2347
Mobile: 0418 941 116
Beds: 1 Queen, 4 Single (3 bedrooms)
Bathroom: 1 Guests Share
Tariff: B&B (full) Double $80, Single $40, Dinner $15.
Vouchers accepted
Nearest Town: Perth (21km)

A warm friendly welcome from Judy and Tim.
Sea views from guests lounge, TV, fridge, microwave oven, beverage facilities, selection of Australian literature and Aboriginal artefacts to browse through. 3 bedrooms tastefully furnished with comfort in mind. Stroll in our cottage garden or watch the sunset over the Indian Ocean sipping on your favourite Australian wine; visit the dolphins at Sorrento Quay; BBQ with friendly kangaroos; Pinnacle day tours; whale watching; Rottnest ferries; diving courses; car hire; bush walks or golf at famous Joondalup can all be booked here.
Excellent public transport to Perth and Fremantle. Weekend markets, shops and restaurants nearby. Country breakfast included.

Perth - Mt Lawley

Bed & Breakfast
Address: 92 Alma Road,
Mt Lawley, WA 6050
Name: Robin's Innercity
Bed & Breakfast
Telephone: (08) 9227 6482
Beds: 1 Double, 1 Single, (2 bedrooms)
Bathroom: 1 Family share, 2 Toilets.
Tariff: B&B (full), Double $65, Single $40.
Vouchers accepted
Nearest Town: City of Perth 1.5 kms

Mt Lawley is a lovely innercity suburb, close to Hyde Park and Northbridge, our cafe and nightlife district. Nearby are galleries and museums, a shopping centre and buses are a short walk away.
Our modern Federation style home, in a quiet street, has a delightful ambience and offers a double or single bedroom with all the facilities to make your stay a very comfortable one. There is central heating, a spacious bathroom, private guest toilet, laundry facilities, tea and coffee always available.
A full continental breakfast is served and there is a spacious lounge area from which double french doors lead to a relaxing patio and garden.
Our home is non-smoking and two poodles reside here.
Do come and visit and share our hospitality!

WESTERN AUSTRALIA

Perth - Mt Pleasant
Self-contained Accom.+B&B
Address: 25 A/B Raymond Street,
Mt Pleasant, WA 6153
Name: Anne Stewart
Telephone: (08) 9364 2995
Mobile: (041) 9916360
Beds: 6 Queen, 3 Single
(8 bedrooms/4 units)
Bathroom: 1 Ensuite, 3 Private
Tariff: B&B (continental) Double $75,
Single $55, Children $10, Dinner $20.
Nearest Town: Perth

For you we have a choice of 4 two bedroom self-contained units or B&B. The first unit has a traditional flavour with jarrah polished floor boards throughout and laced French doors with antique furniture. The main bedroom has an ensuite and a queen sized bed with French doors leading out onto a patio with BBQ. Other rooms, lounge, dining, fully equipped kitchen. Unit 2 is modern, tiled throughout in terra-cotta tiles with a salmon coloured walls and soft pastel colours in the 2 bedrooms. Units come equipped with dishwashers, microwaves, TVs & video, private laundries and telephone. Units 3 & 4 are again different. In all units I provide a continental breakfast and the newspaper is delivered daily. Local transport is 5 minutes walk away and the City of Perth 10 minutes drive away. Restaurants and shops are within walking distance and the Swan River for a walk, 10 minutes.

Perth - Scarborough
Holiday Units
Address: West Coast Highway, Scarborough
Name: Brighton-On-Sea
Telephone: (08) 9401 8149 **Fax**: (08) 9307 2347
Beds: Each units has: 1 Queen, 3 Single (2 bedrooms)
Bathroom: 2 Private
Tariff: B&B (continental) Double $75 (Weekly $490), Single $60, Children $15.
  Vouchers accepted 3 night min.
Nearest Town: Perth

Scarborough is Perth's most popular beach. These ideally situated apartments are in the heart of Scarborough, 2 minutes stroll to the seaside promenade beach, coffee shops, restaurants, food hall, weekend market, and a variety of night life, excellent public transport to Perth and Fremantle.
Ten minutes from Sorrento Quay, Underwater World includes dolphins in the open, Rottnest ferries, golf at Hammersley.
Each apartment is fully self contained and furnished with your comfort in mind, linen, microwave oven, iron, TV etc. Laundry facilities and open parking on premises. Cot available. Continental breakfast provisions for 3 days included in tariff. Weekly rates $490. Sleeps 4/5 people.

Can't contact your host? Phone Directory Assistance.

If you have enjoyed B&B in Australia

How about B&B in New Zealand

*To order
The New Zealand B&B Book
send AU$16.95 or the equivalent
in your currency to*

*Moonshine Press
59 Quirk Street
Dee Why, NSW 2099
Australia*

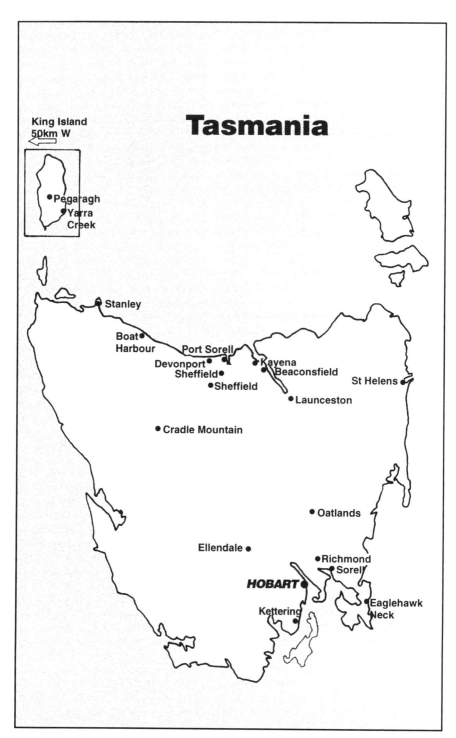

Beaconsfield
Guest House   RACT ★★★★
Address: 638 Greens Beach Road,
Yorktown via Beaconsfield, Tas 7270
Name: Peggy & Tom Mills
Telephone: (03) 6383 4647
Fax: (03) 6383 4647 **Mobile**: (015) 879519
Beds: 1 Queen, 2 Single (2 bedrooms)
Bathroom: 2 Ensuite
Tariff: B&B (full) Double $90, Single $70,
Children $25, Dinner $18-$25,
Credit Cards (VISA/MC/BC).
Vouchers accepted
Nearest Town: Beaconsfield 6km

Our property is a modern brick-timber, non smoking all ground level. Set on 3 acres of natural bushland on the banks of the scenic Tamar River. The garden is a mix of natives and traditional plants, lovely in spring with the daffodils and wattle trees. Easy access to magnificent beaches, wineries, national park and historic sites. Yorktown is the site of the third oldest permanent settlement in Australia.
We welcome our guests with home baked afternoon tea, then invite them to relax in the lounge or in the garden to watch the birds or the black swans on the river or maybe see a potoroo come to his daily feed.
We spoil our guests with little extras in the bedrooms like chocolates, fruit, flowers and spring water etc.
We are happy to provide dinner by prior arrangement including vegetarian meals.
Come and experience true Tasmanian hospitality and a warm welcome.

Boat Harbour, NW Coast
Self-contained Accommodation   RACT ★★★★
Address: 17266 Bass Highway, Boat Harbour 7321
Name: Ruth & Glenn Deans
Telephone: (03) 6445 1041
Fax: (03) 6445 1556
Beds: 6 Queen, 4 Single (8 bedrooms)
5 cottages comprising 2x1 bedroom
plus 3x2 bedroom.
Bathroom: 5 Ensuite with spa.
Tariff: B&B (full) Double $124, Single $100,
Children $15, Credit Cards.
Nearest Town: Wynyard

Soak in your own double spa, then snuggle up in front of the blazing fire with the one you love. Killynaught Spa Cottages are recently built in heritage style. Our romantic cottages are crammed with antiques and enchanting memorabilia. Beds are luxurious Queen size, including Miss Maude's half-tester, Aunt Aggie's 4-poster or Hannah's lacy brass and iron. Delicious wholesome country breakfast provisions are included and each cottage has its own private laundry.
Killynaught is set amidst rich farmland overlooking Bass Strait, a few minutes drive from magnificent Boat Harbour Beach with its choice of quality restaurants, or if you prefer to stay 'at home' order our gourmet fireside dinner platter.
Close to Rocky Cape National Park and a 35 minute coastal drive to historic Stanley, Killynaught Spa Cottages provide a perfect comfortable base from which to explore Tasmania's picturesque North West coast. Phone for our fantastic Winter rates.

TASMANIA

Cradle Mountain
Guest House
Address: 978 Staverton Rd., via Sheffield, TAS 7306
Name: Cradle Vista
Telephone: (03) 6491 1930
Fax: (03) 6491 1930
Beds: 2 Double, 2 Single (3 bedrooms)
Bathroom: 2 Ensuite, 1 Private
Tariff: B&B (continental) Double $105, Single $105. Dinner $25. Credit cards. Vouchers accepted $20 surcharge
Nearest Town: Sheffield

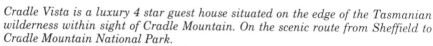

Cradle Vista is a luxury 4 star guest house situated on the edge of the Tasmanian wilderness within sight of Cradle Mountain. On the scenic route from Sheffield to Cradle Mountain National Park.
Nestled under the Triple Peaks of Mount Roland, Van Dyke and Claude, surrounded by beautiful cold climate gardens, with panoramic views from all windows taking in Bass Strait to Cradle Mountain.
After a day exploring Tasmania's wilderness, relax in comfort while waiting for a delicious three course meal (wines and pre-dinner drinks available.) to be served to you in the dining room, or if the weather is cool, snuggle up in front of the open fire sipping glue wine while discussing the days events with the other guests.
You can be assured of a warm welcome from your host, Ingrid, who also speaks fluent German and is fast gaining a reputation for her excellent hospitality.

Eaglehawk Neck
Homestay   RACT ★★★★
Address: "Osprey Lodge Beachfront B&B", 14 Osprey Road, Eaglehawk Neck
Name: Diane & Bill Melville
Telephone: (03) 6250 3629
Fax: (03) 6250 3031
Home Page: www.view.com.au/osprey
Beds: 2 Queen, 1 Single (2 bedrooms)
Bathroom: 2 Ensuite
Tariff: B&B (full) Double $85-$95, Single $65-$70, Dinner on request at booking, Credit Cards (VISA/MC/BC/AMEX). Vouchers accepted
Nearest Town: Eaglehawk Neck - 75km SE Hobart on A9.

We would love to share our home with you. It is in a garden setting right on a secluded beach. Built of western red cedar, it has a guest wing with two delightful spacious bedrooms, each with ensuite and a balcony overlooking beautiful Pirates Bay. In our large comfortable living area you can relax and gaze at the view, read, listen to music, or stroll on the beach. Across Pirates Bay are the Devils Kitchen and Tasman Arch and it is only fifteen minutes drive to the original convict settlement of Port Arthur. Nearby there are numerous walking tracks, with majestic coastal scenery both above and under water, and the chance to experience some of the world's best temperate water diving as well as deep-sea fishing, seal watching, horse riding, golf and sea kayaking. There are restaurants with local fare and we provide evening meals if you pre-book.

Ellendale

Self-contained Cottages RACT ★★★★
Address: Hopfield Cottages, Ellendale, Tas 7140
Name: Anne & John Trigg
Telephone: (03) 6288 1223
Fax: (03) 6288 1207 **Mobile**: 014-901 588
Beds: 3 Queen, 1 Double, 6 Single
(1, 2 and 3 bedrooms - separate cottages)
Bathroom: 1 Private each cottage
Tariff: B&B (full breakfast provisions provided)
Double $90-$100, Single $80, Children $16.
Credit cards: Bankcard, Mastercard, Visa.
Vouchers accepted same day restriction January and Easter,
Surcharge $15 except June, July & August.
Nearest Town: Ellendale - 80km Hobart

Nestled in the foothills of the famous Mt Field National Park you will find our delightfully restored Cosy Country Cottages. The cottages are a perfect blend of old and new, featuring lovely country furnishings tasteful modern conveniences and comfortable beds. Well equipped laundry facilities are available free of charge to guests. The extent and quality of facilities have earned Hopfield Cottages a four star rating with the RACT.
One cottage caters for two people only and would have to be one of the most romantic spots in the state. The other two cottages are very quaint and cosy and cater for up to six people. The cottages really are something special.
Ellendale is on the direct route for Lake Pedder / Mt Field National Park and the West Coast. Your hosts have special interests in trout fishing, woodturning and have written a comprehensive book on the district's heritage buildings.

Hobart

Guest House B&B RACT ★★★★
Address: 24 Gregory St., Sandy Bay, Hobart, TAS
Name: Merre Be's Colonial Accommodation
Telephone: (03) 6224 2900
Fax: (03) 6224 2911 **Mobile**: (015) 870 221
Beds: 1 King, 4 Queen, 5 Double,
2 Single (6 bedrooms)
Bathroom: 5 Ensuite, 1 Private
Tariff: B&B (full) Double $110, Single $85,
Children $15, Credit Cards. Vouchers accepted
Nearest Town: Hobart 1 1/2 km

MERRE BE'S COLONIAL ACCOMMODATION 1884
Be welcomed to an atmosphere of harmony and warmth, amid colonial unique treasures, sleep on very comfortable beds in luxurious spacious rooms, sing under hot strong showers, then enjoy gourmet breakfasts with home made bread and fresh plunger coffee or tea in our sunny dining room.
This lovely old grand, serene Victorian Cottage started life as a family home in 1884. One hundred years later in 1994 it was transformed to an elegant accommodation house catering for discerning guests. Merre Be's is one of only five residential homes in a quiet boutique street in the heart of the leafy bayside suburb of Sandy Bay. Easy walking to historic Battery Point, University, Hobart and Salamala Place, Yacht Club, Casino, a beautiful yacht filled deep water harbour, and 50 metres to shops, banks, taxi rank and bus stop makes this a superior location. Off street parking, all ground floor accommodation, direct dial telephones, electric blankets, guest lounge, sunny dining room

TASMANIA

Hobart - Battery Point
Colonial Guest House   RACT ★★★★
Address: 32 Mona St, Battery Pt, TAS 7004
Postal Address: PO Box 90, Battery Pt, TAS 7004
Name: Colville Cottage
Telephone: (03) 6223 6968
Fax: (03) 6224 0500
Beds: 6 Double (6 bedrooms)
Bathroom: All rooms ensuite.
Tariff: B&B (full) Double $105,
Single $88. (includes full cooked breakfast).
Credit cards: Visa, Mastercard, Bankcard.
Nearest Town: Hobart

Built in 1877 and surrounded by a rambling old-world garden, Colville Cottage is set in the heart of historic Battery Point.
Antique furniture and rugs, stained glass windows and verandah lacework call up the gracious living of last century while modern facilities combine to provide every comfort.
An appetising breakfast prepares you for the day ahead, and friendly personal attention by your hosts Louise Gerathy and Carl Hankey awaits when you 'come home' to Colville Cottage.
Your hosts live 'on site' and the home is centrally heated. Smoke free house. RACT ★★★★

Hobart - Battery Point
Guest House Bed & Breakfast
Address: Battery Point Guest House,
'Mandalay' (1878), 7 McGregor Street,
Battery Point, TAS 7004
Name: J Gordon
Telephone: (0362) 242 111
Fax: (002) 243 648 **Mobile**: (0418) 124 102
Email: gordonjb@ozemail.com.au
Home Page: http://www.tasmall.com.au/mandalay
Beds: 8 Double, 4 Single (5 bedrooms - "Mandalay"),
 2 self contained units
Bathroom: 6 Ensuite, 1 Private
Tariff: B&B (full), Double $95-$120,
Single $75-$95, Children $25, RMS "Titanic" Empire Suite $150, Casa Blanca $140.
Credit cards accepted.
Nearest Town: Hobart P.O. only 1 km away

* Best Location - Nestled above and overlooking Hobart's historic waterfront. You are only a few minutes walk from shops, galleries and restaurants.
* Traditionally appointed, with modern conveniences the spacious, sunny accommodation includes: * Lovely queen size Beds with ensuite facilities, * Off Street parking, * Non smoking house.
"Casa Blanca" - The Battery Point Cottage situated nearby. A lovingly restored 1840s cottage with accommodation for families up to six with two bedrooms, a kitchen, loungeroom, bathroom and private courtyard.
RMS "TITANIC" - The "Empire Suite" is a faithful replica of a First Class State Room on the RMS Titanic. You can lounge on the deck chairs, play deck games ..... and sink into the comfort of the "Empire Suite" in the evening.
"Mandalay" - Join guests by the fire in the comfortable lounge at night, or enjoy a beautiful English breakfast in the sunny dining room, in the morning.
Experience truly traditional Tasmanian Hospitality.

TASMANIA

Hobart - Battery Point
Waterfront Guest House RACT ★★★★☆
Address: 8 Clarke Ave., Battery Point,
Hobart, Tasmania 7004
Name: Jarem Waterfront Guest House
Telephone: (03) 6223 8216
Fax: (03) 6224 8443 **Mobile**: (018) 970411
Beds: 2 Queen, 1 King/Twin (3 bedrooms)
Bathroom: 3 Ensuite
Tariff: B&B (full) Double $95-$120, Single $80, Credit Cards.
Nearest Town: Hobart

Battery Point's only waterfront accommodation.
When we describe our location as "waterfront" we mean just that - in fact we overlook the Sydney-Hobart Yacht Race finish-line.
The Derwent River forms a stunning panorama with its pleasure craft and shipping, and beyond stretches Hobart's eastern shore.
Jarem offers fresh comfortable, rather stylish, centrally heated rooms, each with ensuite bathroom, hair dryer, direct dial telephones, colour television, guest dining and lounge rooms with spectacular water views. Guests enjoy our delicious breakfast menu, varied daily.
We are just a short stroll from the City's shops, restaurants, art galleries and renowned Salamanca Markets.
The narrow winding streets of Battery Point offer fascinating insights into Australia's colonial history. Smoke free house.

Hobart - Lindisfarne
Heritage Bed & Breakfast RACT ★★★★
Address: "Orana House", 20 Lowelly Road,
Lindisfarne, TAS 7015
Name: Claire and Brian Marshall
Telephone: (03) 6243 0404
Free Call: 1800 622 598
Fax: (03) 6243 9017
Beds: 2 Queen, 4 Double,
4 Single, (6 bedrooms)
Bathroom: 6 Ensuite
Tariff: B&B (full), Double $75-$95, Single $60,
Children $18. Credit Cards: Visa/Bankcard/Mastercard.
Vouchers accepted No surcharge
Nearest Town: Hobart (5mins)

ORANA HOUSE

Orana is a fine example of classic Australian Federation architecture. It was built in 1909 and is recorded by the National Trust.
Only 5 minutes from the centre of Hobart, the many attractions of the city are easily accessible. Nestled into Lindisfarne Bay on the beautiful River Derwent, Orana is set in extensive gardens and has off-street parking. Peace and quiet is a definite feature.
The verandahs are a lovely place to relax and enjoy the superb view with a cuppa and cake.
All rooms have been painstakingly restored and decorated in character with genuine antique furniture. Each room has its own en-suite.
Electric heating and electric blankets ensure a cosy night even in the middle of winter.
Enjoy a night by the log fire in the guest lounge which will return you to the era of your great grandparents.
Claire and Brian Marshall have a warm welcome just for you.

TASMANIA

Hobart - Rosny
Homestay+Self-contained Accommodation
Address: 11 Hesket Court,
Rosny, TAS 7018
Name: Kevin & Fay Hamilton
Telephone: (03) 6244 2458
Beds: 1 Double + rumpus room
Bathroom: 1 Private
Tariff: B&B (full) Double $70, Single $40,
Children half price. Vouchers accepted
Nearest Town: Hobart (7 mins by car)

Our home is in the suburb of Rosny, just 6km from the city (about 7 minutes by car). Please phone if there is any difficulty in locating the address. Rosny is on the eastern shore of the Derwent River and our home is situated in an elevated position in a quiet cul-de-sac commanding a panoramic view over the river, city and Tasman Bridge.
The guests' accommodation is self-contained on the lower level, containing a double bedroom with own bathroom and separate toilet. There is an adjoining large rumpus room with a single bed available for an extra adult or child, fridge, TV etc. Off street car parking is available. Closeby facilities include a public golf course, swimming centre, tennis and lawn bowls clubs together with scenic walkways along the river foreshore or to historic Bellerive village.
There are no resident children or pets to spoil a quiet stay with us.

Kayena - Launceston
Two Suites   RACT ★★★★☆
Address: Tamar River Retreat, RSD 123 Kayena Rd.,
Kayena, Tasmania 7270
Name: Anne & Jack McInerney
Telephone: (03) 6394 7500 **Fax**: (03) 6394 7600
Beds: 2 Queen
Bathroom: 2 Ensuite (one with large spa)
Tariff: B&B (full) Double $60-$96,
Single $60-$70 (seasonal prices), Children $10-$15 (fold up bed).
Dinner $25pp. Credit cards (Visa/BC/MC). Vouchers accepted
Nearest Town: Launceston 40km, Beaconsfield 15km, Exeter 20km, Georgetown 30km.

Better service, better business.

Our home is tucked away on four acres of waterfront land with breathtaking views. There is a BBQ area and heated spa to complement the comfortable rooms. Wood fires heat the house and games available.
We are ideally situated for day trips to many wineries, Georgetown (Australia's oldest town), Low Head, Tamar Valley, Launceston and all it offers, Cataract Gorge, Ben Lomond, Grindelwald, Lavender Farm, Asbestos Range National Park, Cradle Mountain, Green's Beach, Bridport, Scottsdale, Badger Head, Great Lake, Lake Barrington. We have lots of day trips worked out for you.
Our water has plentiful fish and we supply gear. We are members of Holiday Retreats.
Directions: *A 8 (Launceston to Georgetown) take B 73 to cross Batman Bridge, go 1km and turn right at C 724 to Rowella, go 3km and turn right into Kayena Rd, go a further 1km. OR A 7 (Launceston to Beauty Point Highway) take B 73 after Exeter, go to C 724 and turn left to Rowella, then as above.*

Tell other travellers about your favourite B&Bs

TASMANIA

Kettering
Self-contained Cottages
Address: "Herons Rise Vineyard", Saddle Road, Kettering, 7155
Name: Gerry & Sue White
Telephone: (03) 6267 4339
Fax: (03) 6267 4245
Beds: 2 Cottages: one cottage with 2 bedrooms, one cottage with 1 bedroom.
Bathroom: Both cottages with private bathrooms.
Tariff: B&B (full) Double $90-$100, Single $80-$90, Children $20, Dinner $20-$25.   Vouchers accepted
Nearest Town: 38kms south of Hobart.

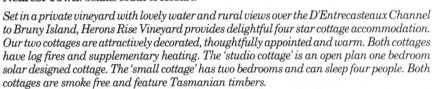

Set in a private vineyard with lovely water and rural views over the D'Entrecasteaux Channel to Bruny Island, Herons Rise Vineyard provides delightful four star cottage accommodation. Our two cottages are attractively decorated, thoughtfully appointed and warm. Both cottages have log fires and supplementary heating. The 'studio cottage' is an open plan one bedroom solar designed cottage. The 'small cottage' has two bedrooms and can sleep four people. Both cottages are smoke free and feature Tasmanian timbers.
A feature of staying at Herons Rise Vineyard is enjoying a bottle of wine from the vineyard and savouring a country style gourmet dinner featuring local ingredients.
Kettering is a good centre to explore the beautiful D'Entrecasteaux Channel region, Bruny Island, the Huon Valley, Hartz National Park and to visit Hobart. The area is noted for quality foods and wine, crafts and the superb water way with stunning scenery. We'll gladly advise about the rich variety of activities and things to do in the area. Do ask about our special rates for longer stays.

King Island - Yarra Creek
Homestay on Host Farm   RACT ★★★☆
Address: RSD 49 Yarra Creek, King Island, Tas 7256
Name: Graeme & Margaret Batey
Telephone: (03) 6461 1276
Beds: 1 Queen, 1 Double, 1 Single (2 bedrooms)
Bathroom: 1 Private
Tariff: B&B (full) Double $75, Single $65, Children negotiable, Dinner $20.
Hire car $65/day.
Vouchers accepted
Nearest Town: Grassy 15km

Enter our world, relax yourself with good food, clean sea air in country surroundings with the magic of an island holiday.
Enjoy the old fashioned values and the sense of belonging at our friendly host farm.
We your hosts offer you homestead accommodation on a picturesque beef farm at Yarra Creek. Our garden is home to many species of birds, and the natural fern gullies on the farm abound in native flora and fauna.
Experience the grandeur of Yarra Creek Gorge, situated on the boundary of our farm and the thrill of achievement on this gorge walk. Enjoy the unique scenery and observe the natural habitat of its fauna, including penguin peeping.
A hire car is available for guests to further explore King Island. We are involved in the local Field Naturalists Club and the Bird Observers Club of Australia.
Dinner is available on request.
Smoke free house, and brochure available.
Accredited member ITOT.

TASMANIA

King Island - Pegarah
Farmstay   RACT ★★★
Address: 1080 Grassy Road, Pegarah,
King Island 7256
Name: Pegarah Host Farm
Telephone: (03) 6461 1248 after 5pm
Beds: 2 Double, 2 Single (2 bedrooms)
Bathroom: 1 Ensuite, 1 Private
Tariff: B&B (continental) Double $60, Single $50,
Children $20. Dinner $10. Vouchers accepted
Nearest Town: Currie

Pegarah Host Farm
Situated 10km east of Currie on Grassy Rd, our guest house offers family accommodation consisting of a two room suite with private facilities.
This is on a 600 acre beef cattle property which carries around 500 head of stock mostly Angus, Herefords and Angus Hereford cross.
Native birds and animals are in abundance on the grassland and in the generous stands of bush which comprise of ti-tree, gum and blackwood. Island wildlife consists of wallaby, pheasant, quail, wild turkey and peacock to name a few.
Why King Island? Scenic, historic, compact, uncrowded, unhurried and unspoilt.
Nestled at the north west tip of Tasmania, King Island offers a wide variety of scenery such as long deserted beaches, rain forest, rural acres, coastal heathland and wild craggy shorelines. So why not stay on a farm?

Launceston
Homestay & Self-contained accommodation
Address: (Mail) 4 St Andrews Street, West Launceston, TAS 7250.
(Holiday House) 19 Neika Avenue, West Launceston, TAS 7250
Name: Clarke Holiday House
Telephone: (03) 6334 2237
Beds: Flat: 1 Double, 2 Single, (2 bedrooms).
Homestay: 1 Double, (1 bedroom)
Bathroom: Flat: 1 Private. Homestay: 1 Family share
Tariff: B&B(continental), Double $40, Single $30.
Flat from $60. Children in flat only. Vouchers accepted
Nearest Town: Launceston

Our home is in West Launceston, 10 minutes walk to the town centre, built of brick in 1960, has a private sunny position, with view overlooking Launceston. We offer clean, quiet, comfortable, ground floor accommodation, with modern shared facilities. A smoke free house, wood and OP heating. We have many books and a piano. Our interests, walking, snow skiing, fishing, motor bike and four wheel driving, reading, sewing, woodwork, gardening, music, dancing. Walking distance to Cataract Gorge chairlifts, fishing, lawn bowls, Penny Royal Gun Powder Mills Complex and food markets. Close to Country Club Casino and Veledrome. For bookings and directions please phone.

The standard of accommodation in
The Australian Bed and Breakfast Book ranges from homely to luxurious,
but you can always be sure of superior hospitality.

Launceston
Guest House RACT ★★★★
Address: 32 Brisbane Street,
Launceston, TAS 7250
Name: The Maldon
Telephone: (03) 6331 3211
Fax: (03) 6334 4641
Beds: 9 Double, 11 Single, (12 bedrooms)
Bathroom: 12 Ensuite
Tariff: B&B (continental), Double $80-$90,
Single $70, Children under 12 years $10.
Credit cards accepted.
Nearest Town: Launceston

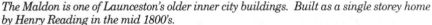

The Maldon is one of Launceston's older inner city buildings. Built as a single storey home by Henry Reading in the mid 1800's.
Dr James Pardey purchased the home in 1896 and added the 2nd floor in 1898. He used the building as his home and surgery until 1933.
The Maldon has been a B&B home since the mid 1900's, whilst retaining its Victorian charm and character with antique stained and ruby glass, wall panelling, ornate plaster work and fireplaces.
All rooms are in the original building which has been tastefully upgraded and all have ensuites, ISD phone, refrigerator, T.V., crockery, cutlery, some with microwave ovens. Ample off street parking.
2 minutes walk to shops, parks, restaurants.
Privately owned for friendly personal attention.

Launceston
Luxury Guest House RACT ★★★★
Address: 41 West Tamar Road,
Launceston, TAS 7250
Name: The Turret House
Telephone: (03) 6334 7033
Fax: (03) 6331 6091
Home Page: http://www.vision.net.au/~chalmers/warm welcome/turret
Beds: 2 Queen, 1 Twin (3 bedrooms)
Bathroom: 3 Ensuite
Tariff: B&B (full) Double $95, Single $65,
Children by negotiation, Credit Cards.
Vouchers accepted
Nearest Town: Launceston 1.5 km

David and Maureen will welcome you to The Turret House, which is a charming house of yesteryear, with many unusual features. Guests can climb the box stair to the turret to view Launceston. We have a large garden which is our love and David is landscaping it back to its former glory.
Set yourself up for the day with a full breakfast served in our elegant dining room, then visit the famous Cataract Gorge which is a 5 minute walk. We are ideally situated for touring the lovely Tamar Valley and wineries.
Each bedroom has an ensuite, ducted heating, TV, fridge, tea and coffee facilities, homemade cakes to enjoy, fruit, flowers and hand made soap. You are welcome to relax in the comfortable lounge and join us for a chat and port before retiring.
We are a smoke free house. Airport 20 minutes drive. Please phone for bookings and directions.

TASMANIA

Launceston also see Kayena

Oatlands & Hobart
Self-contained Colonial Cottages
Address: Waverley Cottages, Oatlands, Tasmania 7120 (please phone)
Name: Lynne Agnew
Telephone: (03) 6254 1264
Fax: (03) 6254 1527 **Mobile**: (018) 125 049
Beds: 8 self-contained cottages
Bathroom: Private

Waverley Cottage
COLONIAL ACCOMMODATION

Tariff: Oatlands: B&B (full) Double $120 (B&B 2 persons), each additional person $20 per day. Hobart: B&B (full) Double $140 (B&B 2 persons), each additional person $25 per day. 10% reduction if staying in both Hobart & Oatlands Cottages. Credit Cards.

The Waverley Cottage Collection of Colonial Accommodation offer family living in a colonial atmosphere and are classified by the National Trust. In the Waverley Cottage Collection are "Waverley Cottage" and "Croft" on our farm at Oatlands, in the heart of Tasmania. "Amelia" and "Forget-me-not" are in the village of Oatlands.

We also offer accommodation in Hobart in The Warwick Cottages (1854). They are situated 1km from the GPO in Old Hobart Town and conjoined convict brick cottages. "Annies Room" and "Pandora's Box" although identical in architecture and amenities both have their own special charm and character. Both cottages sleep four with a double room in the attic and two single beds downstairs.

Memory Lane Cottages (1890) are in the heart of Hobart. "Granny's Attic" and "Grandpa's Den" are the most recent restorations. They are a quaint pair of convict brick cottages separated by a carriage way.

The eight cottages have an aura of history, tranquillity and warmth. They have been restored to their original style and are furnished throughout with colonial pieces. Breakfast is supplied. All 8 cottages completely self-contained.

Port Sorell
Homestay RACT ★★★★
Address: "Newcroft", Port Sorell, Tasmania 7307
Name: Thea & Stuart Anderson
Telephone: (03) 6428 6835
Beds: 1 Queen, 2 Single (2 bedrooms)
Bathroom: 1 Private
Tariff: B&B (continental) Double $60, Single $40, Children 4-16 years $15. Dinner $15.
Vouchers accepted
Nearest Town: Devonport 19km

We have recently retired and built our home with the comfort and privacy of homestay (Bed and Breakfast) guests in mind. "Newcroft" is in a beautiful setting high among natural Tasmanian bushland with sweeping views of the Rubicon Estuary, Bass Strait and the Asbestos Ranges. The Asbestos Range National Park is a short drive away where you can experience kangaroos, wallabies, wombats, birds and water fowl in their natural habitat (especially at dusk). Electric BBQs are available at the National Park, or you can dine with us or at one of the restaurants nearby. "Newcroft" is 19km from Devonport and 12km from the airport on Tasmania's beautiful NW Coast. Lovely swimming beaches, walking tracks, bowls and golf courses are close by. We have tourist information available and are happy to advise you on the many interesting day trips you can take from "Newcroft". Dinner by prior arrangement. Wild life including wallabies may often be seen feeding in our garden.
Directions: *Please phone*

TASMANIA

Richmond
Farmstay+Colonial Accommodation   RACT ★★★☆
Address: Morville House", Prossers Road,
Richmond, Richmond, Tasmania 7025
Name: Richmond Country Bed and Breakfast
Telephone: (03) 6260 4238
Fax: (03) 6260 4423
Beds: 1 Double, 2 Single (2 bedrooms)
Bathroom: 1 Private
Tariff: B&B (continental) Double $70,
Single $45, Children $15. Vouchers accepted
Nearest Town: 5km NE of Richmond, 30 min drive NE of Hobart.

Robyn, Neville and our two sons look forward to sharing our fine old National Trust classified homestead (1870) with you. We live on a 40ha irrigation farm growing seed crops, peas, barley and wool. We are situated in the scenic Coal River Valley and have wonderful views of the valley and Mt Wellington.
The homestead has an old world ambience. The guest rooms consist of two adjoining bedrooms and a private bathroom. Our guests enjoy log fires and breakfast in the kitchen as well as our peaceful location and beautiful garden.
Richmond is one of Australia's best preserved old villages with the oldest bridge, school house and catholic church, good meals are available here too. We are conveniently located for trips to the East Coast, Port Arthur, Hobart, the Midlands and to the airport.
Directions: *Please phone.*

Richmond
B&B Colonial Accommodation
Address: Campania House, Campania
Name: Paddy Pearl
Telephone: (03) 6260 4281
Fax: (03) 6260 4493
Home Page: http://gindit.cowleys.
com.au/clients/camhouse.htm
Beds: 4 Double, 3 Single,
1 Suite (double, single and baby's cot in 2nd room)
(6 bedrooms)
Bathroom: 4 Guests share
Tariff: B&B (full) Double $105, Single $70,
Children half price. Dinner $20/$25. Credit cards. Vouchers accepted
Nearest Town: Richmond 7 mins. 1/2 hours to Hobart.

"CAMPANIA HOUSE"

The construction of Campania House was begun in 1813 by George Weston Gunning shortly after his arrival in Van Diemen's land in 1810. In 1813 he was granted 44 acres of the Coal River, one of the boundaries of Campania House, used in warm weather for swimming. Gunning prospered in all his enterprises and the Governor-in-Chief, Lachlan Macquarie breakfasted at Mr Gunnings on 22 June, 1821 stating in his account of the journey that "Mr Gunning had a new garden and other improvements".
Campania House is listed on the National Estate Register, offers colonial accommodation on three storeys, bed and country breakfast in oak panelled kitchen or paved courtyard, heating and log fires in every room, elegant drawing room and large garden with views of the verdant Coal River valley.
Campania is 7km from equally historic Richmond and half an hour from Hobart. Come and be restored.
Paddy Pearl, Campania House, Tasmania

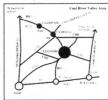

Shearwater

Guest House + Self-contained Accom. RACT ★★★☆
Address: "Castagni", Lot 5 Arthur Street, Shearwater, Tasmania 7307
Name: David & Rosemary Rabbetts
Telephone: (03) 6428 7389 **Mobile**: 019979478
Beds: 1 Double, 2 Single (2 bedrooms)
Bathroom: 1 Ensuite, 1 Family share
Tariff: B&B (full) Double $65, Single $35, Dinner $15. Vouchers accepted
Nearest Town: Devonport is approx 20km west on the Bass Hwy.

Tranquil bush retreat situated only minutes from the most beautiful sandy beaches. Abundant bird life and native fauna completes this pleasant 2.5 hectare property. Convenient to the Devonport Airport and the Spirit of Tasmania ferry terminus. Centrally located for Cradle Mountain National Park, Launceston, Stanley and the Nut, Lake Barrington scenic rowing centre, Sheffield Town of Murals, Mole Creek Caves and Wild Life Park and local excellent golf courses.
Enjoy all the comforts of a relaxed lifestyle in an Italian style farmhouse with warm and friendly hospitality.
A hearty English breakfast, served in your own private lounge overlooking natural bush and with tantalising glimpses of the sea.
Dinner available upon request.
All rooms have colour TV, tea making facilities and electric blankets.
We have two spoilt German Shepards, also on the property is a self-contained cottage with 1 double and 1 single bedroom. Tariff $45 per night.

Sheffield

GLENCOE FARM
circa 1890

Guest House
Address: Sheffield Main Rd., Barrington, Tasmania 7306
Name: Jim & Trish Shipley
Telephone: (03) 6492 3267
Fax: (03) 6492 3267 **Mobile**: (014) 827116
Beds: 1 Queen, 2 Double, 3 Single (4 bedrooms)
Bathroom: 4 Ensuite
Tariff: B&B (full) Double $92, Single $55, Children $25. Dinner O/A. Credit cards. Vouchers accepted
Nearest Town: 8km north Sheffield

Glencoe Farm was originally built as a dairy property to federation style in 1890, over recent years it has been renovated and restored. Each of its four bedrooms features an individual ensuite, guests enjoy the comfort of warm comfortable lounge and dining room with warm fires in winter and cool high rooms in summer. Full cooked breakfasts are included in the tariff with gourmet dinners extra to order.
The house stands in 23 of its original acres and supports pet farm animals including a friendly pig, Phillipa, sheep, goats, chickens and cattle. Ideal centre to stay for a few days while you explore Cradle Mountain Park, Kentish country, Sheffield town of murals, fishing in many rivers and lakes including world famous Barrington, see Tasmania's mid North Coast. Only 25 minutes from Devonport's "Spirit of Tasmania" and Airport.
Jim and Trish Shipley - Glencoe Farm Guest House - (03) 64923267.

Sheffield

Guest House RACT ★★★★
Address: "Atherfield Country Accommodation",
241 Jeffries Road, Sheffield, 7306 Tasmania
Name: Margaret Everett
Telephone: (03) 6491 1996 **Fax**: (03) 6491 1996
Beds: 1 Queen, 1 King or twin (2 bedrooms)
Bathroom: 2 Ensuite
Tariff: B&B (full) Double $98-$104, Single $80,
Children 5-16 $52, Dinner $25, All credit cards.
Vouchers accepted $18-$23 surcharge
Nearest Town: Sheffield 7km from PO
Directions: *"Atherfield" Jeffries Road, Sheffield is located 7km from Sheffield and is the first turning left off Spring Street, the Main Road to Cradle Mountain. C136.*

Passive solar, peaceful smoke free home set on 8 acres with small orchard, vegetable and flower gardens. The rear of the house is walled in glass with extensive mountain, valley and river views. The front faces Paradise Valley, Mount Roland and the Great Western Tiers.
Guests are accommodated in two luxuriously appointed bedrooms one double, one twin both with adjoining ensuites or two doubles as required. Tea making facilities are available in the guest dining room. Evening meals by prior arrangement. The guest lounge is equipped with radio and coloured television / video. A games room is available with billiard table and dart board. Local attractions include Sheffield town of Murals with golf and bowls clubs, Lake Barrington, International Rowing Course, Mount Roland, Mole Creek, King Solomon and Marakoopa Caves, Cradle Mountain National Park.

Sorell

Guest House & Fine Dining Restaurant
Address: "Blue Bell Inn", 26 Sommerville St,
Sorell, TAS 7172
Name: Blue Bell Inn
Telephone: (002) 652804 **Fax**: (002) 652804
Beds: 3 Double, 2 Single (4 bedrooms)
Bathroom: 2 Guests share
Tariff: B&B (full) Double $65, Single $45,
Children 3-12 $15. Dinner A La Carte. Credit cards.
Vouchers accepted
Nearest Town: Sorell - 100 metres to P.O.

The Blue Bell Inn is one of Tasmania's early inns built in 1829 of convict sandstone and fully restored to its original role of providing fine food and warm hospitality to travellers. The Blue Bell was the centre of Sorell's social scene last century. Today it's a comfortable place for travellers from all over the world.
Having travelled for years and now with a young family we look forward to travellers coming to us and sharing their experiences. We have an eclectic appreciation of art, music and food and we're only too pleased to cater to national culinary preferences, eg. bacon and eggs and God Save the Queen, pancakes and maple syrup, low cholesterol and high fibre, rice and miso soup, Edam and rye, croissants and café au lait etc. and that's just breakfast.
We're centrally located only 8 minutes from Hobart Airport; makes a great base.

St. Helens
Guest House/Self-contained Accom. RACT ★★★★☆
Address: "Warrawee", Kirwans Beach,
Tasman H'way, St. Helens, Tasmania 7216
Name: E & B Lawson
Telephone: (03) 6376 1987 **Fax**: (03) 6376 1012
Mobile: 041 932 4105
Beds: 4 Queen, 1 Double, 2 Single (6 bedrooms)
Warrawee Cottage: S.C. 1 Double,
2 Single + 4 bunk beds (3 bedrooms) Bathroom: 1 Private
Bathroom: 6 Ensuite
Tariff: B&B (full) Double $92-$126, Single $50, Children not under 5 in the Guest House. Dinner B.A. winter only. S.C. Cottage Double $60, $10-$15 extra adults person, $5 child under 10. Linen extra, Trained pets allowed in the SC Cottage. Credit Cards (BC/MC/VISA/American Express). Vouchers accepted. Cottage RACT ★★★☆
Nearest Town: St. Helens - 3km south of P.O.

First established in 1907, Warrawee is an elegant, quiet, comfortable, smoke free home set on 7 acres overlooking scenic Georges Bay. All the main bedrooms and guest lounge have bay views and open onto the spacious verandah. Cooked or continental breakfast with home made preserves is offered in the formal dining room.
Warrawee Cottage is a 3 bedroom self-contained colonial weatherboard home on our property and also has bay views. It is ideal for families.
An ideal base for exploring the North-East, St. Helens has fine coastal beach reserves suitable for scuba diving, surfing and fishing. Nearby is the St. Columba Falls, a rainforest walk and Chinese Cemetery at Weldborough.
Historic Derby, Mt William National Park and the Eddystone Lighthouse are all within easy reach. We are a member of Heritage B & B. Smoke free indoors.

Stanley
Homestay+Farmstay RACT ★★★☆
Address: "Myrtle Brook",
Forest, TAS 7330
Name: Hazel Langridge
Telephone: (03) 6458 3174
Beds: 1 Queen, 2 Single (2 bedrooms)
Bathroom: 1 Private, 1 Family share
Tariff: B&B (full) Double $75, Single $50,
Dinner $18, Children under 14 $15. Campervans welcome.
Nearest Town: Stanley 9km north of Bass Highway

"Myrtle Brook" is a delightful mellow brick 'home from home' where the ambience is delightful and the silence can be heard. It is set in spacious lawns through which runs Myrtle Creek. Organic tomatoes are grown commercially in large greenhouses - giving them the old fashioned taste. Farm animals are tame and can be handled. Children are especially welcome and have room to explore. A log fire gives cosy warmth in winter in a unique fireplace of local slate with a feature wall.
Experiences in the area include - historic Stanley (10mins), Rocky Cape NP the Wild West Coast, rain forests and rich farm lands.
Myrtle Brook is 300m off the Bass Highway at Wiltshire.

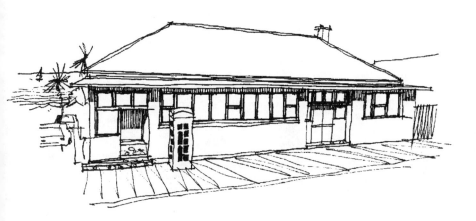

Stanley
Guest House
Address: "Philately House", 11-13 Church Street, Stanley, TAS 7331
Name: Elisabeth Ryan
Telephone: (03) 6458 1109 **Fax**: (03) 6458 1109
Beds: 1 Queen, 1 Single (2 bedrooms)
Bathroom: 1 Private
Tariff: B&B (continental) Double $90, Single $75, Children $15. Vouchers accepted April to November
Nearest Town: Stanley

In the heart of Australia's tidiest town, nestled at the base of the famous Nut overlooking panoramic views of Sawyer Bay, lies this quaint bed and breakfast establishment.
Philately House was first opened in 1898 as the official Post Office, Telephone Exchange, Telegram Office and a residence, in the newly established fishing village of Stanley.
Now, 100 years on, the establishment is a Bed & Breakfast with a fully operational Post Office.
This newly opened establishment has been renovated to bring the 1900's back to life with all the comforts of today.
Philately House comfortably accommodates up to 3 adults. In the charm of your lamp-lit room you can relax and enjoy a quiet night in front of your open log fire. Then retire to your Blackwood Queen size bed for a comfortable nights sleep.
Philately House also has kitchen and laundry facilities for your use and convenience.
Once you stay here you will be reluctant to step back into the 1990's.

Telephone ahead to enquire about a B&B.
It is a nuisance for you if you simply arrive
to find someone already staying there.
And besides hosts need a litle time to prepare.

Index

A

Aberdeen 165
Adaminaby 18, 19
Adelaide 392, 400
Adelaide Hills 400
Adelaide River 13
Adelong 19, 20
Agnes Water 332
Airlie Beach 332
Alawoona 401
Albany 417
Albury 21, 22
Alderley 337
Aldgate 392
Alexandra 242
Alice Springs 13
Alstonville 31
Angourie 229
Anna Bay 155
Annandale 171
Apollo Bay 242, 243
Applecross 426
Arcadia 172
Armadale 418
Armidale 23, 30
Ascot 338
Ashgrove 339
Aspley 339
Atherton Tableland 335
Atherton Tablelands 333
Avalon 177
Avalon Beach 172
Avoca Beach 80
Avoca Beach North 80

B

Bairnsdale 243
Balgowlah 173
Ballandean 336
Ballarat 244, 249
Ballina 31, 33
Balmain 174
Balmoral 175
Bangalow 75
Bardon 340
Barossa Valley 402, 403
Barringo Valley 303
Barrington Tops 108
Barrington Tops Area 99
Barwon Heads 250
Batemans Bay 34, 35
Batesford 272
Bathurst 36, 42
Battery Point 436
Bauple 376
Beaconsfield 433

Beaumont 394
Beechworth 250, 252
Beecroft 175
Bega 42, 44
Bega Valley 78
Bellingen 44, 45
Ben Lomond 106
Benalla 252
Bendigo 253, 256
Berambing 54
Bermagui 210
Berrima District 166
Berry 46, 52
Biddon 105
Bilgola Plateau 176
Binningup 418
Birdwood 400
Birregurra 262, 281
Blackburn 287
Blackheath 53, 55
Blackwood 395
Blayney 53
Blue Mountains 53, 66
Boat Harbour 433
Bodalla 67
Bolong 145
Bombala 67, 68
Boorowa 68, 69
Bowral 167
Braidwood 70
Branxholme 275, 276
Bridgewater Bay 261
Bright 257, 259
Brinsmead 349
Brisbane 336, 345
Brooklana 89
Bruthen 259
Buderim 381
Bundaberg 345, 346
Bundoora 286
Bungendore 71
Buninyong 247
Burleigh Waters 365
Burnside 394, 396
Burra 403
Burraneer Peninsula 177
Burrawang 168
Byron Bay 72, 75
Byron Hinterland 75, 78

C

Caboolture 346
Cairns 347, 361
Callala Bay 145
Callignee 260
Camberwell 288
Cambewarra Mtn 127
Camperdown 260
Canberra 234, 239
Candelo 78
Cape Bridgewater 261
Cape Schanck 300
Capricorn Coast 362

Capricorn Coast - 361
Careel Bay 177
Caringbah 178
Carlton 179, 288
Carrum 289
Cassilis (Hunter Valley) 131
Castle Hill 179
Castlemaine 261
Caulfield 290
Centennial Park 180
Central Coast 80, 84
Central Tilba 136, 138
Cessnock 118
Chiltern 262
Clare Valley 404
Clarence 57
Clayfield 341
Cleveland 363
Clifton 364
Clovelly 181
Clunes 76
Cobargo 84
Coffs Harbour 85
Coffs harbour 89
Colac 262
Collaroy Beach 182
Come-by-Chance 90
Condamine 363
Coolangatta 52
Cooma 90, 93
Coonamble 93
Coonawarra 405
Cootamundra 94
Copmanhurst 110
Coral Isles 345
Coramba 87
Corinda 342
Corryong 263
Cowaramup 425
Cowes 306, 309
Cowra 95
Cradle Mountain 434
Cronulla 182
Crookwell 96
Croydon 298
Cudgewa 263
Cygnet River 406

D

Dandenong Ranges 264, 268
Darling Downs 364
Darwin 14
Daylesford 268, 269
Delungra 123
Denhams Beach 35
Denmark 419
Dorrigo 97
Double Bay 183, 184
Drummoyne 184
Dubbo 98
Dungog 99
Dural 186

449

INDEX

E

Eaglehawk Neck 434
Earlville 350
East End 143
East Gippsland 259, 273, 280
Eastern View 282
Echuca 269, 270
Eden 100, 101
Edge Hill 351, 353
Edmonton 353
Eildon 270
Ellendale 435
Emerald Beach 88
Emmaville 107
Emu Park 361, 362
Erina 81
Eumundi 384
Evelyn Central 333

F

Far East Gippsland 274
Farrer 234
Faulconbridge 58
Figtree 228
Flinders 300, 301
Florey 234
Forbes 102
Forest Hill 291
Forster 103, 104
Foster 271
Fremantle 420, 423
Freshwater 354

G

Galston 185
Gawler 405
Geelong 272, 273
Gelantipy 273
Gilgandra 105
Gippsland 260, 316
Gipsy Point 274
Gisborne South 274
Glebe 186, 188
Glen Innes 106, 107
Glen Waverley 289
Glenorie 189
Gloucester 108, 109
Gold Coast 365, 368
Gold Coast Hinterland 367
Goodwood 396
Goolwa 406
Goulburn 168, 169
Grafton 109, 112
Grampians 325
Grampians District 300
Grantville 275
Great Ocean Road 242
Greenwich 190
Greenwich Heights 189
Grenfell 113
Gunning 114, 115

Guyra 115, 116
Gympie 369

H

Half Moon Bay 360
Hall 235
Hallidays Point 116
Hamilton 275, 276, 342
Hampton 292, 385
Hawks Nest 211
Healesville 328, 329
Hepburn Springs 269
Herberton 333
Hervey Bay 370, 371
Hills 427
Hobart 435, 436, 438
HorshamRACV 276
Howes Valley 117
Hunter Valley 118, 121
Hurstbridge 292
Huskisson 124

I

Indooroopilly 343
Ingham 372
Inverell 26, 122
Inverloch 277
Ipswich 372

J

Jamberoo 124
Jervis Bay 124, 144
Jindabyne 125
Jindabyne East 126
Johnsonville 243

K

Kalamunda 428
Kalorama 264
Kangaroo Island 406, 407
Kangaroo Valley 47, 52, 126
Kanimbla 356
Katoomba 58
Kayena 438
Kelvin Grove 343
Kempsey 127
Kendall 128
Kettering 439
Killarney 364
King Island 439
Kingaroy 373
Kooyong 293
Koroit 277
Kulnura 81
Kuranda 356
Kurnell 191
Kurrajong Heights 59
Kyneton 278

L

Lake Barrine 334
Lake Cathie 128
Lake Macquarie 129, 142
Lakes Entrance 279, 280
Lameroo 407
Lane Cove 191
Launceston 438, 440, 442
Lawson 60
Leabrook 397
Leichhardt 192
Lemon Tree Passage 156
Lennox Head 130
Leura 61
Lighthouse Beach 154
Lindisfarne 437
Lismore 260
Lorne 262, 281, 282
Lower Hunter Valley 160

M

Macarthur 313
Mackay 374
Maclean 130
Magnetic Island 375
Malabar Heights 193
Mallacoota 282
Mandurah 423
Mandurang Valley 253
Manly 193, 195
Mannum 408
Mansfield 283, 284
Manuka 236
Mapleton 385
Margaret River 424, 425
Maroochydore 382
Maryborough 285, 375, 376, 377
Marysville 285
McLaren Vale 408
Medlow Bath 63
Melbourne 286, 298
Melrose 409
Mendooran 131
Merewether 143
Merriwa 131
Merrygoen 131
Milawa 299
Mildura 299
Millthorpe 132
Milton 132, 133
Mininera 300
Mission Beach 378
Mona Vale 195
Monaro District 90-91
Moree 133
Morisset 129
Mornington Peninsula 300, 301
Moruya 35, 134
Moss Vale 169
Mossman 196, 379
Mount Beauty 302

INDEX

Mount Gambier 409, 410
Mount Macedon 303
Mount Panorama 38, 41
Mt Dandenong 264, 265
Mt Helen 246
Mt Lawley 429
Mt Moriac 273
Mt Pleasant 430
Mt Tamborine 368
Mt Warning 135
Mudgee 134
Mudgegonga 304
Mulbring 118
Murray Bridge 410
Murwillumbah 135
Myall Lakes 156
Myrtleford 304

N

Nambucca Heads 136
Naracoorte 405, 411
Narbethong 285
Narooma 136, 139
Narrabri 140
Narrabundah 236, 237
Narrandera 141
Nelligen 34
Nelson Bay 157
Nerang 368
New England 24, 221
New England Tablelands 106
Newcastle 142, 143
Newell Beach 379
Newhaven 310
Newport 196
Newport Island 153
Newtown 197
Nimmitabel 67
Noosa 382
Noosa Valley 383
North Fitzroy 294
Norwood 397
Nowendoc 144
Nowra 145
Nundle 146
Nuriootpa 402

O

Oatlands 442
Oberon 147
O'Connell 42
O'Connor 238
Olinda 161, 267
Orange 147, 151
Orbost 305
Otway Ranges 281
Ourimbah 82

P

Pacific Palms 104
Paddington 197, 198, 344
Padthaway 412
Palm Beach 198, 199, 366
Pambula 152
Parkville 164
Parkwood 366
Parramatta 200
Paynesville 305, 306
Pegarah 440
Penneshaw 407
Perth 426, 430
Petersham 199
Phegans Bay 83
Phillip Island 306, 310
Pinnaroo 412
Pokolbin 119
Port Douglas 380
Port Fairy 311, 314
Port Lincoln 413
Port Macquarie 152, 154
Port Sorell 442
Port Stephens 155, 160
Potato Point 67
Potts Point 201
Pymble 202

Q

Queanbeyan 238
Queenscliff 314
Quirindi 161

R

Ravenshoe 334
Richmond 443
River Heads 371
Robe 414
Rock Forest 39
Rockhampton 381
Rose Bay 203
Rosny 438
Rosslyn Park 398
Rutherglen 315
Rye Park 162
Rylstone 161

S

Salamander Bay 158, 159
Sale 316
San Remo 310, 317
Scarborough 430
Scone 163, 165
Seacliff Park 398
Sevenhill 404
Shearwater 444
Sheffield 444
Shipley Plateau 64
Shoalhaven 48
Shorncliffe 344
Singleton 120
Snowy Mountains 18, 19
Somerton Park 399
Sorell 445
Sorrento 301
South Gippsland 271, 319, 321
South West Rocks 165, 166
Southern Highlands 166, 170
Southern Tablelands 70, 208
Spring Gully 256
Springfield 399
St Georges 396
St Kilda West 294
St. Arnaud 318
St. Helens 446
Stanley 447
Stirling 401
Stratford 357
Strathbogie Ranges 318
Strathewen 295
Sunny Corner 171
Sunshine Coast 381, 385
Sunshine Coast Hinterland 384
Surry Hills 202
Sutton (NSW) 239
Sutton Forest 170
Sydney 171, 205

T

Tallangatta 319
Tamborine Mountain 367
Tamworth 206, 208
Tanunda 402, 403
Taralga 208
Taree 209
Tarwin Lower 319
Tathra 210
Tea Gardens 211
Templestowe 295
Tenterfield 212
Terang 320
Termeil 213
Terrigal Beach 83
The Coorong 406
Thorngate 400
Tilba 139
Tilba Tilba 137, 139
Timboon 320
Tintinara 415
Toora 321
Toowoomba 385, 387
Torquay 321
Torrens Creek 388
Townsville 388, 389
Trinity Beach 358, 359
Tumut 214, 216
Tweed Heads Hinterland 216

U

Uki 135
Ulladulla 217
Ultimo 204
Upper Murray 263
Upwey 268
Uralla 29
Urangan 371

INDEX

Urunga 218

V

Ventnor 310
Victor Harbor 415
Vincentia 144

W

Wagga Wagga 218, 220
Walcha 220, 223
Wallabadah 206, 224
Wanda Beach 158
Wangi Wangi 129
Warragul 322
Warrandyte 296
Warrnambool 323, 324
Wartook 325
Wellington 224, 227
Wentworth Falls 65
West Gippsland 322
White Cliffs 227
Whitfield 360
Whitsunday District 374
Whitsundays 332
Williamstown 296, 297
Wilsons Promontory 327
Wilson's Promontory 271

Wingen 164
Wingham 209
Wisemans Ferry 228
Wodonga 22, 325
Wollombi 121
Wollongong 228
Wonboyn Lake 100
Wonga Park 298
Woodford 66
Wooli 229
Woollahra 205
Wooloowin 345
Woy Woy 84

Y

Yamba 229, 230
Yanakie 327
Yarra Creek 439
Yarra Glen 328
Yarra Valley 328, 329
Yarrawonga 329
Yass 162, 230, 231
Yatte Yattah 133
Yeppoon 362
Yorkeys Knob 360
Young 69, 94, 231
Yungaburra 335

A WEEKS FREE B&B

FILL IN A COMMENT FORM AND YOU CAN BE IN THE DRAW FOR A WEEKS FREE B&B FOR TWO

- At each B&B you will find a comment form and an addressed envelope. Simply fill in a comment form and return it to us, and you will be in the draw for **a weeks free B&B**.

- Every comment form you send in will increase your chances of winning the **weeks free B&B**, so complete a form for each place you stay.

- We suggest you save your comment forms in one envelope, and send them in together at the end of your trip.

- If a B&B is temporarily out of comment forms you can complete one at the next one you visit.

- Each person staying can complete a comment form – a couple can complete two separate forms.

- Entries will be drawn on 21 December 1998 and the winner will be notified by mail immediately. Entries to the U.S. address below must be received by 30 October 1998.

The Prize
- The prizewinner will be given vouchers entitling them and a partner to 7 nights B&B at any B&B accepting vouchers in *The Australian Bed and Breakfast Book*.

- The stays can be any time in 1999. They need not be consecutive.

      Mail to: Pelican Publishing Company, Inc.
                 P.O. Box 3110
                 Gretna, LA 70054-3110
                 USA

ORDER FORM

The New Zealand Bed and Breakfast Book and *The Australian Bed and Breakfast Book* are attractive and interesting guides that give details of homes and private hotels where you can be sure of feeling at home immediately. In the United States they are available at better bookstores or can be ordered directly from Pelican.

_____ New Zealand Bed and Breakfast Book @ $17.95

_____ Australian Bed and Breakfast Book @ $15.95

Subtotal _____

*Shipping and Handling _____

**Sales Tax _____

Total enclosed _____

Visa/MasterCard card number: _____

exp. date: _____ signature: _____

*Add $2.50 postage and handling, plus 50 cents for each additional book ordered.
**Jefferson Parish residents add 8.75% sales tax, all other Louisiana residents add 4% sales tax. Prices subject to change without notice.

Name _____

Address _____

City, State, Zip _____

OVERSEAS ORDERS:

_____ New Zealand Bed and Breakfast Book $18.95 US funds

_____ Australian Bed and Breakfast Book $18.95 US funds

Total enclosed _____

Visa/MasterCard card number: _____

exp. date: _____ signature: _____

All payments must be made in International Money orders or charged to Visa or MasterCard. Payment for overseas orders includes airmail postage. *Prices subject to change without notice.*

To: **PELICAN PUBLISHING COMPANY**
P.O. Box 3110
Gretna, LA 70054

Name _____

Address _____

City, State, Zip _____